'A Church as it Should be'

*The Cambridge Camden Society
and its influence*

'The Round Church, Cambridge'. Watercolour of the interior by H. B. Harraden, showing the stone altar installed in 1843. It was removed in 1845 after a fierce controversy which rocked the foundations of the Cambridge Camden Society and led to its move away from its Cambridge power base. To the north of the altar is a stone credence, also removed. Richard Bankes Harraden (1778–1862) was a topographical artist who collaborated with his father, also Richard, on *Cantabrigia Depicta* (1811). He was a member of the Royal Society of British Artists, 1824–49 and exhibited there on various occasions (*English Heritage Photo Library*).

'A CHURCH AS IT SHOULD BE'

THE CAMBRIDGE CAMDEN SOCIETY
AND ITS INFLUENCE

Edited by

CHRISTOPHER WEBSTER
& JOHN ELLIOTT

SHAUN TYAS
STAMFORD
2000

Published in 2000 by

SHAUN TYAS
(an imprint of 'Paul Watkins')
18 Adelaide Street
Stamford
Lincolnshire
PE9 2EN

ISBN

1 900289 35 0

Printed and bound in the United Kingdom by the Alden Group, Oxford

CONTENTS

Dedicated by the editors
to the next generation.
James, Sophie, Alice,
Emily, Shaun,
Clare, Brent
& Faye

ACKNOWLEDGEMENT

Publication of this book was assisted by a generous grant from the Paul Mellon Centre.

NOTES ON CONTRIBUTORS

SIMON BRADLEY studied the early-nineteenth-century Gothic Revival at the Courtauld Institute, University of London. He is now Assistant Editor at *The Buildings of England, Ireland, Scotland and Wales* (Penguin Books).

GEOFF BRANDWOOD is a specialist in Victorian and Edwardian churches, has lectured and published widely on church architecture, including a biography of Temple Moore. He is a Main Committee member of the Victorian Society, and is in charge of the Society's events programme.

CHRIS BROOKS is Reader in Victorian Culture at the University of Exeter and is National Chair of the Victorian Society. He has written widely on Victorian culture, architecture and literature; his *The Gothic Revival* and *The Albert Memorial*, which he has co-authored, both appeared recently.

DALE DISHON is currently at work on a doctoral thesis in architectural history, focusing on the 1862 Exhibition building. She has written on Ruskinian influences on the work of G. E. Street for *Ecclesiology Today*.

JOHN ELLIOTT is a freelance architectural historian who specialises in the nineteenth century. He teaches at the Universities of London and Reading, is editor of *Ecclesiology Today*, is a council member of Ecclesiological Society and has published a number of items on the period.

HILARY J. GRAINGER is an Associate Dean of the School of Art & Design at Staffordshire University. For her PhD, she studied the work of Sir Ernest George and his partners, one of the leading late-Victorian architectural practices.

CHRIS MIELE is an architectural historian who worked for English Heritage from 1991 to 1998 and has now joined Alan Baxter & Associates, Consulting Engineers. He has published widely on the history of conservation and has edited a collection of essays on William Morris for the *Studies in British Art* series, published by the Paul Mellon Centre in London.

RODERICK O'DONNELL, a sometime Scholar and Bye-Fellow of Magdalene College Cambridge, is an authority on A. W. and E. W. Pugin; since 1982 he has been an Inspector at English Heritage.

ROS REID studied the work of George Wightwick. She now lectures and writes on architectural history.

JOHN SANDERS is a partner in the practice of Simpson & Brown architects, Edinburgh. He is engaged in research for a PhD at the Mackintosh School of Architecture, Glasgow, studying the late Gothic Revival in Scotland.

GAVIN STAMP is a lecturer at the Mackintosh School of Architecture, Glasgow School of Art, and is Chairman of the Alexander Thompson Society.

CHRISTOPHER STELL, O.B.E., is a consultant and former member of the staff of the Royal Commission on the Historical Monuments of England, founder member and former Honorary Secretary and Editor of the Chapels Society, and a Trustee of the Historic Chapels Trust. He is the author of *An Inventory of Nonconformist Chapels and Meeting-houses*, to be completed in four volumes.

CHRISTOPHER WEBSTER is an architectural historian in the Division of Historical & Critical Studies at Staffordshire University. He is a member of the Council of the Ecclesiological Society and has published a number of works on aspects of late-Georgian architecture.

DONALD WEBSTER is a music critic and writer on music – especially that associated with the church – following a lengthy career as a lecturer in Higher Education, organist, choirmaster, composer and conductor.

FOREWORD

It is now over 160 years since the founding of the Cambridge Camden Society, and 130 years since the publication of the last issue of *The Ecclesiologist*. However, the impact made by both on the shaping of the church in Victorian England is still readily discernible in the legacy of churches throughout the land built or altered in the period up to the beginning of the twentieth century, and, for all the considerable changes of the last hundred years, in much of the character of public worship found in the Anglican Church.

The role and influence of the Cambridge Camden Society and its successors during the Victorian era have attracted much interest over the years. Basil Clarke's assessment of Victorian ecclesiology and *The Ecclesiologist*, contained in his 1938 book *Church builders of the Nineteenth Century: A study of the Gothic Revival in England* and James White's *The Cambridge Movement: The Ecclesiologists and The Gothic Revival* of 1962 remain authoritative sources, complemented by a number of subsequent, valuable contributions such as those made by Peter Anson in his *Fashions in Church Furnishings* of 1960, and Dr Gilbert Cope in his *Ecclesiology then and now: A few more Words to Church Builders* of 1963. However, it is only with the publication of this present volume, that we have available a wholly comprehensive and coherent series of studies into the Society and its influences and one written from the ideal viewpoint of the closing years of the twentieth century.

Christopher Webster and John Elliott have brought together in this one volume a remarkable series of valuable studies of the Society and its influence contributed by a distinguished group of historians. The publication of these studies has grown out of the highly successful one-day conference on Victorian churchmanship and the Cambridge Camden Society organised by the present Ecclesiological Society at St Alban's Church and Centre, Holborn, London, in October 1997.

Since its founding in 1879, the Ecclesiological Society (or the St Paul's Ecclesiological Society, as it was known between 1879 and 1937) has sought consistently to foster, encourage and sustain the study of the arts, architecture and liturgy of the Christian Church; to work for the preservation of select churches threatened by demolition or insensitive alteration; and to promote seemly church architecture. Today, with a membership of almost 800, the

FOREWORD

Society is not only concerned to stimulate informed discussion about current ecclesiological issues, drawing upon contemporary theological, liturgical, cultural, intellectual and art-historical insights and movements that are shaping so much of the role and life of the Church. It is also keen to support those initiatives which will assist in a clearer and deeper understanding and appreciation of those factors that shaped the nineteenth-century Church, and which still provides the setting for so much Anglican worship today. With such a knowledge we should be able to secure the conservation of the churches of the period more effectively and consider their re-ordering and development to meet the legitimate liturgical and other needs of today more intelligently and sensitively.

The editors are to be commended for drawing together this series of papers covering one of the most extraordinary periods in the life of the Church in England and the unrivalled role of one body of individuals in shaping so much of the story. Whilst today we may properly question the nineteenth-century ecclesiologists' aim to recover an idealised vision of the pre-Reformation Church in England and their views on its ecclesiology (in the sense of the structure and operation of the Church), we rightly celebrate their creative achievements.

Paul Velluet, RIBA
Chairman of the Council of the Ecclesiological Society

PREFACE

In the closing years of the second millennium, in a society overwhelmingly made up of those whose only visit to a church is for a wedding or a funeral, there remains a remarkably consistent idea of what an Anglican church should look like, and how its clergy should dress and conduct themselves. That this ideal would have been instantly recognised by a group of pious Cambridge undergraduates more than a century and a half ago is even more remarkable. A commitment to Gothic architecture – whether medieval or a convincing copy – and a long chancel; stained glass; a cross on the altar table; a surpliced vicar intoning the prayers are just some of the items we now accept as quintessentially Anglican but which for the Camdenians represented innovation. Indeed, by the middle of Victoria's reign the buildings and services of the Church of England had changed significantly from their equivalents when she came to the throne, and if the change cannot be wholly credited to the Cambridge Camden Society, as the organisation would have wished us to think, it had indisputably been a major influence.

Perhaps inevitably, the Society's radical agenda was accompanied by controversy. George Gilbert Scott, the most prolific Victorian church architect, admitted that before his acquaintance with the Society and its publications, 'no idea of ecclesiastical arrangements or ritual propriety had crossed his mind',[1] yet at about the same time, R. D. Chantrell, who had an extensive ecclesiastical practice in Leeds, described *The Ecclesiologist* as 'a mischievous tissue of imbecility and fanaticism'.[2] The clergy too were by no means united in welcoming Camdenian innovations; despite the Society's impressive list of members which, by 1843, included two archbishops and sixteen bishops, there were many other among the clergy who were profoundly worried by what they perceived as the Society's intention to move Anglicanism in a Catholic direction. The controversy that surrounded the introduction of the stone altar at the Round Church in Cambridge illustrates the point.[3] Similarly, numerous congregations were deeply suspicious of, and hostile to, anything that they deemed to be a 'popish invention'. Yet change there certainly was: not only were almost all new

[1]   G. G. Scott, *Personal and Professional Recollections* (London, 1879), p. 86.
[2]   Quoted by B. F. L. Clarke, *Church Building in the Nineteenth Century* (Newton Abbot, 1969), p. 100.
[3]   Discussed fully in chapter 12.

churches built to these revised requirements but existing ones were modified or replaced to such an extent that only a tiny minority of Anglican churches have survived in their pre-Camdenian state, complete with galleries, a triple-decker pulpit and other Georgian accoutrements.

G. Kitson Clarke's statement that 'the nineteenth century was a very religious century'[4] is likely to strike us as simplistic, but it was indisputably a period of prolific church building and a level of church attendance that may seem well-nigh incredible in this age of agnosticism and indifference.[5] Much of the church building may, of course, be accounted for simply in terms of the rapid increase in population rather than as evidence of greater religious observation and piety. However, it is also clear that the Church of England – as an institution – underwent significant change during the century, as did the way the clergy saw their role in society. There were equally momentous developments to the buildings in which services were conducted. Occupying almost precisely the middle third of that century, and seeing itself as in the vanguard of the change, was the Cambridge Camden Society.

This book seeks to question the certitude of the Society's self-supported proclamation by examining the scope and extent of its role in the development of architecture and worship in the Victorian period, but also by placing its undoubted achievements in the broader context of the wide-ranging debates that are central to an understanding of religion in the reign.

It is now almost forty years since J. F. White's *The Cambridge Movement* first appeared and the editors of this volume were drawn to the project in part from a belief that a reassessment of the material was overdue, especially that concerning the Society's architectural influence. White was writing at a time when the products of the Victorian age were largely dismissed if not denigrated, and when the academic study of the period was still in its infancy. His book should not be neglected by those interested in the subject, but it is clearly the product of its time and of its author's professional background.[6] White had little recently published material on which he could draw when preparing his book and he made no pretence at expertise in architectural

[4]   G. Kitson Clarke, *The English Inheritance* (London, 1950), p. 11.
[5]   In 1801 the population of England and Wales was just 8.9 million and 535,000 members of the Church of England received communion on Easter Sunday, while by 1900, the population had increased to 32.5 million (an increase of 365%) with 1.9 million of them attending a communion service (an increase of 356%). This shows a slight decrease in the proportion of the population attending the Anglican church, but a huge numerical increase in attendance. It is largely in the second half of the twentieth century that a real decline has taken place: the Easter Day communicants in 1982 being just 1.468 million from a population of about 49.6 million. See A. H. Halsley (ed.), *British Social Trends Since 1900* (Basingstoke, 1988), for further details.
[6]   He was the Associate Professor of Preaching and Worship at the Perkins School of Theology in the Southern Methodist University, Dallas.

history. Handicapped by the absence of other studies which could have helped him to contextualise his subject, it seems he had little alternative that to concentrate on the material that had been published by the Society itself. Thus, somewhat inevitably, his account is dominated by the Society's own distinctly biased view of mid-nineteenth-century Anglicanism and, significantly, almost exclusively on its own assessment of the need for change and of its own role in bringing about that change.

In contrast, the present volume seeks to present a more considered view of the Society's wider influence, capitalising on the greatly expanded range of material now available on Victorian architecture, worship, music and society.[7]

Initially, this book grew out of a conference held in 1997. However, only a minority of the chapters here are by conference speakers and it has been the editors' intention that, rather than the book being, in effect, the conference proceedings or a loose collection of essays on a common theme, it should present a comprehensive coverage of the Society, its key members, its aims and influence, capitalising on the extensive range of expertise which the contributors have brought to the project. While the different viewpoints and interpretations of the contributors have been carefully orchestrated, editorial interference on questions of style have been kept to a minimum.

The editors are grateful to all the contributors for their enthusiasm and commitment to the project. They are especially grateful to Geoff Brandwood who has not only contributed two chapters and the mammoth, and hugely valuable, list of members, but in addition has advised on a number of points. For assistance in various ways, the editors also wish to thank Dr. Neil Bingham, Jo Hookes, Simon Lindley, Canon Paul Ferguson, Rev. Christopher Cornwell and the numerous librarians and archivists who aided the contributors.

[7] For instance, in recent years we have seen the publication of C. Brooks & A. Saint (eds), *The Victorian Church* (Manchester, 1995); J. S. Curl, *Victorian Churches* (London, 1995); P. B. Nockles, *The Oxford Movement in Context* (1991); and D. Adelmann, *The Contribution of the Cambridge Camden Society to the Revival of Anglican Worship, 1839–62* (Aldershot, 1997).

'Absolutely Wretched': Camdenian Attitudes to the Late Georgian Church

CHRISTOPHER WEBSTER

In 1838, only a matter of months before the founding of the Cambridge Camden Society – hereafter referred to as the Society – plans were prepared for building the little chapel at Pool in West Yorkshire. Late-nineteenth-century alterations have obliterated its original form, but its internal layout was almost identical to the surviving interior of St Stephen, Robin Hood's Bay, North Yorkshire (plate 1).[1] In 1849 Butterfield began All Saints, Margaret Street, London (plates 2 and 30) and the differences are startling. In some respects, the comparison may seem irrational and many of the differences between the churches in Pool and Margaret Street are easily explained: one is a small church built in an isolated part of the country, the other is in central London; one was built on a very limited budget, the other almost regardless of expense. But beyond these obvious dissimilarities, it seems clear that something much more fundamental must have happened in the eleven years which separates them. The way in which the later building was conceived and was intended to function does not simply represent a logical and evolutionary development of thinking over the course of half a generation, but appears rather to suggest a radical new way of conceiving a church. Although a sudden cataclysm is no longer a fashionable historiographical explanation for identified change, All Saints seems to imply that nothing short of a revolution in the form of Anglican worship had taken place.

In seeking to change opinions within the Church of England to the extent that a comparison of these two churches would lead one to conclude was achieved, the leading members of the Society prosecuted their cause with determination, zeal and absolute conviction. J. M. Neale, one of the Society's

---

[1] The principal difference between the churches at Pool and Robin Hood's Bay is that the former did not have a gallery or chancel. Pool was designed by R. D. Chantrell of Leeds and its arrangement is now known only through one of Chantrell's drawings (ICBS, File 2028, Lambeth Palace Library) It is likely that the plan was heavily influenced by the parishioners or incumbent since it is unlike Chantrell's other churches of this period. The church at Robin Hood's Bay was built in 1821. The name of its architect is not known.

founders and most active members, referred to 'the dogmatic spirit' which he considered 'to be the life and soul of *The Ecclesiologist* and of the CCS.'[2] Few would disagree, especially those unfortunate enough to be the recipients of the Society's frequent and vitriolic attacks. Indeed, an abiding feature of the Society's published material is its single-mindedness, or put less charitably, its arrogance.

Whether one agrees with the Society's objectives or not, few could fail to admire the extent of their achievements or the speed with which they were brought about. That 'the Victorian caricature of the Georgian Church of England as a lax and corpulent institution, consisting only of toadying place-hunters and squires rattling fire irons to stop an over-long sermon lives on even today'[3] is a mark of the Society's pervasive propaganda. Within a generation, Anglican churches and the worship within them, were indeed undergoing a far-reaching process of transformation and *The Ecclesiologist* could claim with a good deal of justifiable pride in its last edition in 1868 'we have the satisfaction of retiring from the field as victors.'[4] Not only were almost all new churches built according to their principles, but Georgian interiors and Georgian re-orderings of older churches were systematically replaced by ones that followed Camdenian principles.[5]

In analysing the tactics which the Society employed so successfully, it is instructive to see their campaign as having two distinct fronts: they promoted an agenda of those innovations they sought to introduce but equally important – especially in the early stages of the movement – in order to ensure the desired reception for those innovations, they devoted a significant amount of energy to undermining what we might term late-Georgian attitudes to churches and worship. It is important to remember that in the 1840s these attitudes were still comfortably accepted by the vast majority of

[2] Neale writing to Webb in 1846, quoted in D. Adelman, *The Contribution of the Cambridge Ecclesiologists to the Revival of Anglican Choral Worship 1839–62* (Aldershot, 1997), p. 25.

[3] Thomas Cocke writing in *The Georgian Group Newsletter*, September 1998, p. 5.

[4] *Ecclesiologist*, 29 (1868), pp. 315–6.

[5] J. M. Crook, *The Dilemma of Style* (London, 1987), p. 63, gives the following figures: 'By 1854 a quarter of all parish churches had been restored; by 1873 one third. Between 1830 and 1860, fifteen hundred new churches were built in England, as against only two thousand between the Reformation and 1830.' However, it is Geoff Brandwood's view that the figures for restorations exaggerate the extent of activity. His work on Leicestershire and Rutland show that even by 1860, 80% of churches remained unrestored. A similar pattern was replicated in various other counties including Cambridge, Devon, Durham, Essex, Lincolnshire and Suffolk. (G. K. Brandwood, 'Anglican Churches before the Restorers: a Study of Leicestershire and Rutland' in *Archaeological Journal* 147 (1987), pp. 383–408.) Significantly, when *The Ecclesiologist* ceased publication, the majority of churches were still untouched by the Society's initiatives.

Anglicans. Later chapters in this book will examine the physical and liturgical achievements of the Society *via,* for instance, the new churches of Butterfield or Carpenter. This chapter, however, will consider the Society's pronouncements about the Anglicanism it had inherited, the values and achievements of which had to be thoroughly discredited to allow the Society to operate in an arena unfettered by conservative attitudes to change. In this crusade – for 'crusade' it certainly was – there could be no grey areas. For the Society, the late Georgian church – whether we consider its buildings, its worship or its attitudes – was simply contemptible. Descriptions such as 'wretched'[6] or, for more extreme cases, 'absolutely wretched,'[7] abound in Camdenian literature. Reflecting these attitudes, the Vicar of Whitby, the Rev. William Keane, described his parish church in 1863 as 'now perhaps the most depraved sacred building in the kingdom...'[8] (plate 3) and a little earlier, the prolific architectural writer J. H. Parker, a Society member, condemned Samuel Pepys Cockerell's remarkable circular classical church in Banbury of the 1790s: 'such a building may have been well-enough adapted for the exhibition of gladiators or wild beasts in ancient Rome, but it is totally unfit for a Christian church'.[9]

It is a mark of the Society's influence that relatively little visual evidence of Georgian internal arrangements survive. Indeed, the unsuspecting might well assume that Anglican churches had *always* followed Camdenian principles. In seeking to demonstrate the extent of the changes the Society brought about, and as a means of establishing the architectural and liturgical context in which the Society developed, we need to address the question: what was the physical form of the Anglican churches which the Victorian age inherited; what did a typical late-Georgian church look like? There is no single example that adequately answers this question, but, for the sake of convenience, we can identify a number of different categories of buildings which together made up the corpus of Anglican churches when Victoria came to the throne.[10]

Firstly, there were the pre-Georgian churches – usually mediaeval – most of which had been 'Georgianized' to some extent. Georgianization often involved the introduction of galleries to increase accommodation, privately owned box pews – or 'pues' as the Society dismissively termed them – to

6   The Cambridge Camden Society, *Church Enlargement and Church Arrangement* (Cambridge, 1843), p. 7.
7   *Ecclesiologist,* 11 (1850), p. 134.
8   Quoted in A. White, *The Buildings of Georgian Whitby* (Keele, 1995), pp. 38–39.
9   Quoted in B. F. L. Clarke, *The Building of the Eighteenth-Century Church* (London, 1963), p. 230.
10   The writer acknowledges that these four subdivisions are not intended to be seen as definitive. For a more detailed analysis of the arrangements of pre-Victorian churches see N. Yates, *Buildings, Faith and Worship* (Oxford, 1991).

generate income and a 'three-decker' pulpit from which the service would be conducted and which would be sited where it would allow the parson and clerk maximum prominence, even if it meant placing it where it blocked the congregation's view of the altar. St Mary, Whitby, is a spectacular surviving example of a Georgian interior, showing vividly the extent of the churchwardens' ingenuity in achieving the maximum accommodation. Access to most of the galleries is from external staircases so that the minimum of ground floor sittings would be lost. The patron's pew is fitted within the chancel arch, largely obscuring sight lines from the nave to the altar. It was precisely this sort of pragmatic solution to the problem of limited church accommodation that the Society attacked most vociferously. Georgian patterns of worship often resulted in the more-or-less abandonment of the chancel since the focus was now on the pulpit and desk, and the Communion Service was celebrated only rarely, usually four times per year.

The 'old' Leeds Parish Church, demolished in 1837, illustrates this point well. It was a large structure, of cruciform plan, built mainly in the fourteenth and fifteenth centuries. Following a series of internal alterations and repewings carried out in the eighteenth century, by the early nineteenth century in effect a 'preaching box' had been created in the nave.[11] Here the pulpit was surrounded by box pews and galleries on all four sides, including one across the chancel arch containing an immense organ, forming a division between nave and chancel. In the seriously over-crowded nave, Morning and Evening Prayer were conducted. Conversely, the vast chancel – a space almost equal in area to the nave – was bare and abandoned, except for use during the latter part of the infrequently celebrated Communion Service.

Secondly, there were Georgian churches built before the Church Building Act of 1818 which were rectangular in plan but with a shallow 'chancel' and where the pulpit was placed at the east end, either in front of, or more usually, to the side of the altar. They followed a pattern popularised by Wren, who, in 1712, recommended his church of St James, Piccadilly, as 'beautiful and convenient, and as such, the cheapest of any form I could invent', contrasting it to the, 'Romanist ... larger churches [where] it is enough if they [the congregation] hear the Murmer of the Mass, and see the Elevation of the Host.'[12] The majority of Georgian churches belong to this group. Joseph Gwilt's St Margaret, Lewisham, designed in 1813, is typical.[13] The layout of the interior shows clearly the difference between the more

---

[11] T. Friedman, *Church Architecture in Leeds, 1700–1799, Publications of the Thoresby Society*, second series, 7 (Leeds, 1997), pp. 10–36.

[12] 'Letter of Sir Chr. Wren Upon the Building of National Churches', reprinted in *Wren Society*, 9 (1932), p. 17.

[13] The interior is illustrated in G. Worsley, *Architectural Drawings of the Regency Period* (London, 1991), p. 122.

prestigious rented pews towards the front of the church, and the free benches at the rear, a common arrangement for the period.

Thirdly, there were those churches built in the Georgian period which, internally, adopted a number of alternative arrangements to that above. For instance, there were those like Robin Hood's Bay which were rectangular in plan but with the pulpit attached to the north or south wall and with pews and galleries arranged to focus on it, rather than on the altar. In addition, there were a number of more innovative Neo-classical plans, for instance, ovals like David Stephenson's All Saints, Newcastle upon Tyne (1786–9), circles like George Steuart's St Chad, Shrewsbury (1789–92),[14] and Greek crosses like James Spiller's St John, Hackney, London (1792–7), but these were relatively rare.[15]

Fourthly, there were the churches which resulted from the 1818 Church Building Act. They form by far the largest group of churches erected during the 1820s and '30s and since they represented widely accepted models for new churches, they too had to be thoroughly discredited in the drive towards the type of church which the Society sought to promote. R. D. Chantrell's St Stephen's, Kirkstall, near Leeds (1827–9), is a typical example (plates 4 and 5). Almost all the churches in this group contained a large rectangular 'body' and a shallow chancel. Ground floor seats would usually face the altar, but those in side galleries would face north or south.[16]

While the constituents of these four groups differ from each other in several respects, they have a number of features in common: the form of the pulpit, the box pews, galleries and the limited importance of chancel and altar. While some of the post-mediaeval examples are best described as being stylistically 'Gothic', the Gothic details are generally slight and unconvincing. Where budgets were severely restricted, as at Christ Church, Cobridge, Stoke-on-Trent (1838–40), designed by L. G. Hales, a local brass-founder, the result could be especially mean and dreary (plate 6), but even where the budget was much more generous and the architect more eminent, as at St Mary, Haggerston, London (1826–27), designed by John Nash, the result was unlikely to have much in common with the mediaeval churches the Society admired (plate 7).

So we move to the next issue: what precisely did the Society find wanting in these late Georgian churches? For Neale, many did not even qualify for the title 'church' at all; they were referred to dismissively as

[14] T. Friedman, 'The Golden Age of Church Architecture in Shropshire', *Shropshire History and Archaeology,* 71 (1996), pp. 93–101. It is Friedman's conclusion that here the idea of a circular church was essentially the architect's rather than the church wardens'.

[15] See D. Stillman, *English Neo-classical Architecture,* II (London, 1988), chapter 11.

[16] The work of the Church Building Commission is discussed in M. H. Port, *Six Hundred New Churches* (London, 1961).

'preaching rooms or meeting houses'. Only if there was a nave and chancel that were 'well defined and separate'[17] could the noun 'church' be applied at all. But while the Society was damning in its criticism of Georgian churches,[18] its concerns went well beyond purely architectural matters; the churches were merely the physical setting for a form of service the Society found unacceptable, one that looked to a post-Reformation, Calvinist tradition. Furthermore, that these buildings and this form of service was comfortably accepted was, in part, a reflection of the Church of England's sense of worldly self-satisfaction that the Society felt compelled to denounce. In short, they attacked the Church of England on three fronts: for its architecture; for the form and conduct of its services; for its lack of spirituality and piety. Yet such a separation is potentially misleading since for the Society these three facets of Anglicanism's shortcomings were interlinked: only if services followed fully the rubrics of the Prayer Book would the internal arrangements of pre-Reformation churches have any validity, and only if both clergy and laity became more pious would the church as an institution be receptive to the spirituality that had been lost since the Reformation. The root cause of the problem was no mystery: Anglicanism had lost sight of the Catholic tradition from which it had been born. It seemed clear to the Society that rather than treasuring mediaeval churches and ritual for the links which they provided with Anglicanism's Catholic roots, the Georgians had done almost everything they could to disguise that tradition. Indeed, so far away from its roots had Anglicanism moved that it hardly dare mention them for fear of the highly emotive and often mindless charge of 'Popery' from its evangelical and low-church constituencies.[19]

The Society's condemnation of Georgian Anglicanism was indeed comprehensive, but in the context of this study, it is instructive to identify a number of key issues which were the focus of sustained criticism by writers in *The Ecclesiologist*. A primary concern which drew together architectural, liturgical and spiritual areas of criticism related to the Georgians' emphasis of pulpit rather than altar.

---

[17] The Cambridge Camden Society, *A Few Words to Church Builders* (Cambridge, 1841), p. 5.

[18] J. M. Neale and B. Webb, *The Symbolism of Churches and Church Ornament: a Translation of the First Book of the Rationale Divinorum Officiorum of William Durandus* (Leeds, 1843), p. cxxvii refers to 'the *ne plus ultra* of wretchedness, the Georgian Style.'

[19] *Petition of the Inhabitants of East Farleigh to the Archbishop of Canterbury respecting the alleged Popery of their vicar, Henry Wilberforce*, 1844, concludes 'Our minds are deliberately and firmly made up to resist, by all legitimate means, the introduction of any modified system of Popery in our parish.' Quoted in N. Yates, *Kent and the Oxford Movement* (Gloucester, 1983), pp. 37–41.

One of the great abuses of modern times is the monstrous size and untoward position of the pulpit. It, with the reading pue and clerk's desk, are in most modern churches placed immediately before the Holy Altar, for the purpose, it would seem, of hiding it as much as possible from the congregation. How symbolical is this of an age, which puts preaching in the place of praying! If prayer were the same as preaching, such a position would be more natural: but as the prayers are not offered to the people, but to GOD, our Church instructs us far otherwise.[20]

With such practices widespread, it is hardly surprising that the chancels of mediaeval churches were neglected, and in newer churches, they were reduced to the absolute minimum in area in the interests of economy and since they were not needed liturgically. There were additional concerns about 'church furniture', especially box pews and galleries. The Society devoted much energy to the removal of pews not only because they were wasteful of space,[21] but were without pre-Reformation precedent. Most significantly, as rented space, they represented an unacceptable 'private' domain within the house of God. It was widely acknowledged that their introduction had generated valuable funds for the upkeep of churches and the paying of clergy stipends but, for the Society, the evils they represented more than outweighed any economic benefits: they were socially divisive and encouraged smugness and self-satisfaction.[22] The potential for personal comfort and unseemly behaviour was a further cause for concern. Neale quotes the example of Tong Church: 'The Squire has built a pew in the Chancel; when the Commandments are begun, a servant regularly enters at the Chancel door with the luncheon tray!'[23] Such activities may well have been exceptional, but many pews were fitted with tables and comfortable chairs, and stoves for individual pews were not unheard of.[24] Such evils were compounded since the excessive space they consumed restricted the number of free seats available for the poor; in some parishes the poor were totally excluded because there was no room for them, for instance in Rochdale, Lancs, in 1819.[25] Much of this criticism was equally applicable to galleries but in addition they made the interiors of churches cramped and dark. 'GALLERIES UNDER ANY CIRCUMSTANCES ARE TOTALLY INADMISSIBLE. The greater part are, of course, nothing but raised platforms of pues: and all that has been written about pues is doubly strong against these.'[26]

[20] *Church Enlargement...*, *op. cit.*, p. 22.
[21] *Ibid.* p. 4.
[22] *Ibid.* Yates sees their removal as one of the Society's four principal aims. (*Buildings, Faith and Worship, op. cit.*, p. 134.)
[23] Quoted in J. White, *The Cambridge Movement* (Cambridge, 1962), p. 4.
[24] White quotes the example of Exton Church in Rutland. *Ibid.*, p. 7.
[25] F. Beckwith, 'Thomas Taylor, Regency Architect, Leeds', *Publications of the Thoresby Society*, monograph 1 (Leeds, 1947), p. 7.
[26] *Church Enlargement...*, *op. cit.*, p. 6.

Although the almost universal acceptance of Gothic as the most appropriate style for churches clearly pre-dates the Society's inception, there remained much scope for stylistic pronouncements in the pages of *The Ecclesiologist*. Such comments focused on two areas: Classicism was wholly inappropriate for churches and, secondly, it was not enough for a church to be nominally Gothic but its plan, silhouette, details and decorations needed to be 'correct'. While it is true that few new churches of the 1830s were Classical, there were large numbers in this style from earlier in the late-Georgian period (plate 8). They were particularly prevalent in the prosperous suburbs of major towns and cities – especially in the affluent parts of London – or in fashionable resorts like Bath and Brighton. They were thus the places of worship for a large proportion of the influential upper- and middle-classes, the support of whom the Society was especially anxious to win. Elsewhere there were numerous pre-Reformation churches that had, in varying degrees been Classicized by the introduction of, for instance, Tuscan columns to support the gallery, a tower rebuilt in the Palladian style or a Baroque pulpit and tester. Few churches were without Neo-classical monuments.[27] 'Gothick is the only Christian architecture...' claimed *The Ecclesiologist* while Classicism was invariably dismissed as 'pagan'.[28]

After 1839, establishing Gothic as 'the only Christian architecture' was largely uncontentious, but the battle for the acceptance of 'true' Gothic with all its Catholic symbolism and pre-Reformation details proved more difficult. Nevertheless, victory on this front was an integral part of the Society's agenda. Like Pugin, they were intent on pushing popular taste beyond an interest in Gothic merely for its picturesque qualities. The majority of churches erected in the 1820s and '30s might well have been designated as 'Gothic' but they were unmistakeably 'modern' in appearance and, except for the most basic features, quite different from the '...greatest glory which Christian architecture ... attained ... in the early part of the Decorated Style...'[29]

The Society sought to replace the thin veneer of Gothic found so often in the Commissioners' churches of the 1820s and '30s with churches modelled on 'the glorious architecture of the fourteenth century.'[30] This involved much more than archaeological accuracy for its own sake: the Society sought to re-introduce symbolism in the design of churches and also those features which were essential if one of the Society's key objectives was to be achieved: the restoration, 'so far as it was consistent with Prayer Book doctrine, [of] the

[27] For criticism of monuments see *ibid*, p. 29.
[28] *Ecclesiologist*, 2 (1842), p. 5.
[29] The Cambridge Camden Society, *A Few Words to Church Builders* (Cambridge, 1844), p. 6.
[30] *Ibid.*

ceremonial of the pre-Reformation Church.'[31] The desire to build churches that followed mediaeval precedent was thus not simply an aspect of Romantic antiquarianism, but an issue of central importance if liturgical reforms were to be achieved. This radical approach to the design of churches proposed, for instance, a clear separation of chancel and nave. This was to 'recognise an emblem of the Holy Catholick Church; as this consists of two parts, the Church Militant and the Church Triumphant,' the former being represented by the nave and the latter by the chancel.[32] Ideally, a church should contain a nave and an aisle at each side since 'thus we gain another important symbolism for our ground plan, the doctrine of the MOST HOLY AND UNDIVIDED TRINITY, as set forth in three parallel divisions which meet us as we enter the church at the west.'[33] In addition, the re-introduction to the chancel of several smaller features, such as sedilias, aumbryes and tables of prothesis[34] was fundamental for the accurate revival of a pre-Reformation Catholic ritual, especially at the Communion Service. For the Society, the Georgian architectural legacy was not just visually sterile but, more importantly, comprised churches where, in most cases, it was impossible for services to be conducted with appropriate decency and in accordance with the rubrics of the *Book of Common Prayer*.

However, the Society claimed the roots of the malaise in Georgian Anglicanism went beyond its architecture and worship. A change was needed in what we might term its attitudes. Neale and Webb gave more details of this in their book *The Symbolism of Churches and Church Ornaments*, published in 1845:

> Let us look at a Protestant place of worship. It is choked up and concealed by surrounding shops and houses, for religion, now-a-days, must give way to business and pleasure: it stands North and South, for all idea of fellow-feeling with the Church Catholic is looked on as mere trifling, or worse: the front which faces the High Street is of stone, because the uniformity of the street so required it: or, (which is more likely) of stucco, which answers as well, and is cheaper: the sides, however, are of brick, because no one can see them: there is at the entrance a large vestibule, to allow people to stand while their carriages are being called up, and to enter into conversation on the news of the day, or the merits of the preacher: it also serves the purpose of making the church warmer, and contains the doors and staircases to the galleries. On entering, the pulpit occupies the central position, and towards it every seat is directed: for preaching is the great object of the Christian ministry: galleries run all round the building, because hearing is the great object of a Christian congregation: the Altar stands under the organ gallery, as being of no use, except once a month:

[31] Yates, *op. cit.*, p. 134.
[32] *A Few Words to Church Builders*, *op. cit.*, p. 5.
[33] *Ibid.*, p. 7.
[34] *Ibid.*, pp. 11–12.

there are a few free seats in out-of-the-way places, where no one could hear, and no pues would be hired, and therefore no money is lost by making the places free: and whether the few poor people who occupy them can hear or not, what matters it? The Font, a cast-iron vase on a marble pillar, stands within the Altar rails; because it there takes up no room: the reading pue is under the pulpit, and faces the congregation; because the prayers are to be read to them and not addressed to GOD. Look at this place on Sunday, or Thursday Evening. Carriages crash up through the cast-iron gates, and, amidst the wrangling and oaths of rival coachmen, deposit their loads at the portico: people come, dressed out in the full fashion of the day, to occupy their luxurious pue, to lay their smelling-bottles and prayer books on its desk, and reclining on its soft cushions, to confess themselves – if they are in time – miserable sinners: to see the poor and infirm standing in the narrow passages, and close their pue doors against them, lest themselves should be contaminated, or their cushions spoilt, at the same time beseeching GOD to give their fellow-creatures the comfort which they refuse to bestow: the Royal Arms occupy a conspicuous position, for it is a chapel of the ESTABLISHMENT: there are neat cast-iron pillars to hold up the galleries, and still neater pillars in the galleries to hold up the roof; thereby typifying that the whole existence of the building depends on the good-will of the congregation: the roof is flat, with an elegant cornice, and serves principally to support a gas-lighted chandelier: and the administration of this chapel is carried on by clerk, organist, beadle, and certain bonnetless pue-openers.

We need not point out how strongly all this symbolizes the spiritual pride, the luxury, the self-sufficiency, the bigotry of the congregations of too many A PUE-RENTED EPISCOPAL CHAPEL.[35]

The passage actually says little about architectural style but much about the absence of piety. There is an insidious attack on the Georgians' worldliness, on their complacency and on their lack of spirituality. It focuses on an attitude to church-going and, implicitly, on the church as an institution, in which the form of the building is just one of the endemic faults.

There is ample evidence that the fundamentals of Georgian Anglicanism were indeed ripe for reform. Critics could point to the widespread practice of absentee clergy : in 1810 no less than 47% of Anglican clergy did not reside or do duty in their parish.[36] There was enormous inequality of clergy stipends: in the early part of the nineteenth century, the Archbishop of Canterbury received £27,000 a year while there were thousands of parochial benefices worth less than £150, many of which did not include a house.[37]

[35] *The Symbolism of Churches...*, *op. cit.*, pp. cxxviii–cxxix.
[36] C. Brooks, 'Building the Rural Church : Money, Power and the Country Parish' in C. Brooks and A. Saint (eds), *The Victorian Church* (Manchester, 1995), p. 55.
[37] S. C. Carpenter, *Church and People, 1789–1889* (London, 1937), p. 56. See also J. Wade, *The Extraordinary Black Book*, 1st edn (1820–3); reprinted (Shannon, Ireland, 1971). This important radical text contains almost 100 pages of supposed

Nepotism was rife: 'Bishop Spark of Ely, not content with his own stipend of £8,000, appointed two sons and a son-in-law to benefices worth £12,000 a year between them.'[38] The close ties between State and Church were a further cause for concern. That the Church failed to push for political reform in the 1820s and early '30s caused much resentment and even riots in some places, and political interference in the administration of the church – for instance the suppression of the ten Irish bishoprics in 1833 – was equally unacceptable elsewhere. On a local level, compulsory church rates caused much resentment. It was tempting for critics to look back on the Georgian clergy as essentially an extension of upper-class polite society in which the squire and vicar formed an alliance not only to provide mutual support on the round of local social engagements but together they represented secular authority in the parish, for instance, as Justices of the Peace or as the administrators of street cleaning initiatives.[39] In countless cases it seems that spiritual leadership took second place to worldly affairs.[40] That the church was ultimately subject to secular control *via* Parliament – rather than divine inspiration – was confirmed by the Royal coat of arms hanging in every church.

The secular nature of late Georgian Anglicanism is underlined by the motives which lay behind the setting up of the Commission to administer the 1818 Church Building Act, the organisation responsible for financing the majority of new churches built in the 1820s and '30s. Some writers have suggested that Parliament's primary concern was not in providing spiritual nourishment but one of state control to check the spread of political agitation, religious dissent and Catholicism.[41] Not only were the initiatives to build these churches far removed from the Camdenian concept of personal piety and charity but in some cases, the recipients of these new churches were openly hostile to their construction and saw them as impositions and an unwanted responsibility.[42]

For the Society, many of the shortcomings of the Commissioners' churches resulted from the Commission's conscious avoidance of any explicit

---

abuses of power and privilege by the clergy.

[38]   *Ibid.*, p. 57.

[39]   C. Brooks and A. Saint (eds), *op. cit.*, pp. 51–77.

[40]   N. Yates, *The Oxford Movement and Anglican Ritualism* (London, 1983), p. 38.

[41]   For instance: B. F. L. Clarke, *Church Builders of the Nineteenth Century* (Newton Abbot, 1969), pp. 20–21; M. H. Port, *Six Hundred New Churches* (London, 1961), pp. 1–20.

[42]   For instance: in Leeds two of the three churches paid for entirely from the first Parliamentary grant stood empty and unconsecrated for around six months because the local Anglicans refused to pay for the cost of 'enclosing' the sites, i.e. erecting a wall and railings – almost their sole financial commitment to the new buildings – and the Archbishop refused to consecrate them until the 'enclosing' was completed. (*Leeds Intelligencer*, 4 August 1825; 29 September 1825; 19 January 1826; 9 March 1826.)

reference to pre-Reformation models. Although the vast majority of their churches incorporated Gothic motifs, in almost all cases their churches were essentially Georgian preaching boxes in mediaeval dress. The Commissioners' rules and correspondence make it clear that they had little concern with stylistic niceties but were primarily concerned with more basic considerations: durability and cost. Seeking durability, they devoted much time to questions about the thickness of roof trusses and under-floor ventilation to preclude damp. On the question of cost, they used the vulgar calculation of cost per sitting. Thus a church costing £10,000 and providing 2,000 seats at £5 per sitting, was more desirable than one costing £9,000 but providing only 1,500 sittings at £6 each.

The hand-written book of Rules and Regulations includes in Rule 10: 'That the Commissioners do not build ... any church or chapel ... but on such a plan as they deem most expedient for affording fit and proper accommodation for the greatest number of persons at the least expense'.[43] Later on they resolve 'that as great economy in the construction of all churches and chapels to be built under the Act be observed as will be consistent [with rule 10].'[44] There is no passionate debate about the rival merits of first or second pointed, or whether pinnacles should be cusped or plain. Indeed, research in the Commission's archives reveals almost no reference to a desirability for Gothic. Their requirements could reasonably be satisfied with a Classical design, and often were. Furthermore, since the three 'attached' architects to the Office of Works who acted as architectural advisors to the Commissioners – Soane, Nash and Smirke – were all Classicists by training and inclination, and prior to 1818 had not built a single new church between them, the architectural mediocrity of the Commissioners' Gothic churches could have been anticipated.[45] The triumvirate between them eventually built twelve churches for the Commissioners, but generally the leading architects of the day declined to be involved with church building. It was left instead to the 'second tier' of the profession to make the best of the limited guidance offered by either the Commission or its advisors. R. D. Chantrell, working in Leeds, is typical of those who developed large and successful ecclesiastical practices in the 1820s and '30s.[46] He initially believed that the 1818 Act was 'a firm opportunity for restoring the best examples of Greece and Rome ...' but perceived Leeds and its neighbourhood had

---

[43] The Church Building Commission, *Rules and Regulations, etc,* p. 14 (hand-written, 1818). Unclassified papers in the archives of the Church Commissioners, London.

[44] *Ibid.,* Resolutions, no. 5, p. 17.

[45] ' ...neither administrators nor architects, clergy nor laymen possessed any passionate conviction about what they were doing.' J. Summerson, quoted in M. Port, *op. cit.,* p. xi.

[46] See C. Webster, *R. D. Chantrell, His Life and Work in Leeds 1818–1847, Publications of the Thoresby Society,* second series, 2 (Leeds, 1992).

CHRISTOPHER WEBSTER

'submitted to the county mania for plain Gothic works'.[47] Recognising the prevailing taste – and no doubt the potential financial rewards – he quickly acquainted himself with this unfamiliar style, working, as he later admitted, 'without system – merely adapting features to masses, to which I could give no just proportion.' He went on to explain that he and the other architects employed to design Gothic churches

> though generally well grounded in Greek and Roman architecture, found themselves called upon to construct works utterly at variance with Greek and Roman principles; and having no time to study or collect data, whereon to compose works in this (to them) new style, they were required at once to erect buildings equally at variance with its principles, in which the greatest number of sittings could be crowded into the smallest area, and adapt the fragments of the various mediaeval styles to their utilitarian masses.[48]

It is hardly surprising that the Commissioners' churches frequently brought forth derisory comments from the Society. In fact, barely had the paint dried before the criticism started.[49]

The very existence of organised religion, let alone any move towards the revival of a more Catholic ritual, had been compromised by the widespread acceptance of Enlightenment thinking in which philosophers sought rational explanation in place of Christian dogma, and had the effect of weakening the case of those who sought a liturgy of ritual, spirituality, conviction or visual splendour.[50] Some believed a more secular society was desirable in which 'the State, morals and education should be independent of religion',[51] in effect marginalising the influence of Christianity. Advocates of Utilitarianism sought to develop a system of morality quite independent of religious teaching.[52] While Enlightenment philosophy was the preserve of an intellectual minority, knowledge of the basic aims of the French Revolution was much more universal. The enthusiastic support that it received in England was further valuable ammunition for those wishing to question the whole basis of religious authority.

That the church was held in such low esteem that it became the butt of humour for large sections of the population in the eighteenth and early nineteenth centuries is clearly illustrated by the proliferation of satirical

[47] Chantrell writing to John Soane, 6 January 1821. Sir John Soane's Museum, Private Correspondence, xv, A, 32.
[48] *Builder*, v (1847), p. 300.
[49] Numerous critical accounts of Commissioners' churches appeared in the *Gentleman's Magazine* in the 1820s. See K. Clark, *The Gothic Revival* (London, 1975), p. 98.
[50] For instance: T. Paine, *The Age of Reason* (London, 1793).
[51] J. S. Curl, *Victorian Churches* (London, 1995), p. 45.
[52] See J. J. C. Smart and B. Williams, *Utilitarianism: For and Against* (Cambridge, 1973).

13

prints. Furthermore, they provide a useful insight into contemporary critical attitudes to Georgian Anglicanism. For instance, in the fifth plate in Hogarth's 'The Rake's Progress' series of 1735 (plate 9), the narrative concerns the rake's wedding. Not only is the whole service clearly a meaningless formality devoid of any spiritual significance, the details, too, are revealing : the board on which the Creed had been printed is so rotten that only 'I believe...' is still legible, pointing not only to neglect of the fabric but, perhaps more significantly, to a liberalism in which Anglicans need have no specific beliefs. The poor box is covered with a large spider's web, suggesting an arachnoid habitation in that part of the church least likely to be disturbed by humans! An inscription on the balcony states the church was 'beautified' in 1725, i.e. only ten years before the print was published; either the churchwardens had misappropriated the funds, or the work was badly done and the fabric quickly deteriorated.[53] As we move into the early nineteenth century, we find Rowlandson pursuing similar themes of disinterested worshippers, irreligious behaviour by the clergy, clerks or beadles, and neglected or mutilated mediaeval churches.

Even more outrageous was the growth in anti-religious erotic literature and illustrated material that 'achieved an unprecedented popularity' in the eighteenth century.[54] It points to both real, if exaggerated, improprieties committed by the clergy and, perhaps more significantly, to the low esteem in which they were held by much of the population. However, in fairness to Anglicanism, it should be stated that the market for anti-religious erotica was not confined to England.[55]

In the Society's comprehensive criticism of Georgian Anglicanism, the principal culprits were easily identified: the clergy who should have set a more appropriate lead; Parliament for its constant interference in religious affairs; the congregations for implicitly sanctioning the church's 'decline'. There was, however, a fourth group whose activities and attitudes needed reform for the Society's objectives to be met in full: the architectural profession. There is ample evidence that in the generation immediately before the inception of the Society, there were numerous calls for ecclesiastical building and restoration to be the domain of the clergy rather than the profession.[56] Given this well rehearsed proposal, it is perhaps surprising that the Society did not continue the campaign. However, it seems clear that it recognised the essential role of the profession and was more concerned to modify its attitudes and make them more sympathetic to the Society's wider aims. Yates sees the Oxford Movement as giving to the clergy 'a new concept of their role in society, one

[53]   J. Burke and C. Caldwell, *Hogarth: the Complete Engravings* (London, 1968), unpaginated.

[54]   P. Wagner, *Eros Revived* (London, 1990), p. 47.

[55]   *Ibid.*, pp. 72–86. The writer is grateful to Ruth Brompton for this material.

[56]   See also Chapter 2 of this book.

which was not primarily social or quasi-political but one which was profoundly and pre-eminently spiritual ... This new concept of priestly vocation...'[57] was the precise parallel to the new breed of church architect the Society sought to encourage. 'A Catholick architect must be a Catholick in heart.'[58] Simple architectural knowledge was not enough. 'In truth, architecture has become too much a profession: it is made the means of gaining a livelihood, and is viewed as a path to honourable distinction, instead of being the study of the devout ecclesiastick, who matures his noble conceptions with the advantage of that profound meditation only attainable in the contemplative life; who, without thought of recompense or fame, has no end in view but the raising a temple, worthy of its high end, and emblematical of the faith which is to be maintained within its walls.'[59]

While not claiming that 'none but monks ought to design churches',[60] Neale and Webb nevertheless protested 'against the merely business-like spirit of the modern profession' and demanded from it 'a more devoted and directly religious habit of mind. We surely ought to look at least for church-membership from one who ventures to design a church.'[61] They felt it was unreasonable to expect a church architect not to undertake a secular commission but 'we can never believe that the man who engages to design union-houses, or prisons, or assembly rooms, and gives the dregs of his time to church-building; is likely to produce a good church, or, in short can expect to be filled from above with the Spirit of Wisdom.'[62] The church architect must 'make great sacrifices', must 'forego all lucrative undertakings' if they involve the compromise of 'those principles which he believes necessary for every good building.' In church building he must not 'pander to the whims and comfort of a Church-committee' by suiting his design to any type of ritualism requested, especially if it involves 'defil[ing] a building meant for GOD's worship with pues and galleries and prayer-pulpits and commodious vestries.' Lastly, he must not even attempt to master all the styles of pointed architecture, let alone the various Classical ones and those of China, Egypt or Switzerland.[63] In short, according to *The Ecclesiologist*, the ideal architect is pictured 'pondering deeply over his duty to do his utmost for the service of God's holy religion and obtaining by devout exercises of mind a semi-inspiration ... The beautiful effect of every building is attributed to the architects' religious calling and lives'.[64]

[57] N. Yates, *The Oxford Movement, op. cit.*, p. 38.
[58] J. M. Neale and B. Webb, *op. cit.*, p. xx.
[59] *Ibid.*, p. xxi.
[60] *Ibid.*
[61] *Ibid.*, p. xxii.
[62] *Ibid.*, p. xxiii.
[63] *Ibid.*
[64] *Ecclesiologist*, 4 (1845), p. 279, quoted in N. Pevsner, *Some Architectural Writers of*

Perhaps such a change in the profession was desirable. In the first half of the nineteenth century there were few architects who specialised in ecclesiastical work and fewer still who were untainted by the unprofessional conduct endemic in the 'profession', exemplified by Dickens' Pecksniff. George Gilbert Scott recalled that in the 1820s when his uncle tried to find an architect – who should be 'a religious man' – to whom he could be articled, he was told 'there is scarcely a religious architect in London.'[65] The provinces were no better. William Bradley of Halifax, who undertook ecclesiastical commissions in the early nineteenth century, was described as 'not a man to be depended on – very idle [and] not fit to be an architect.'[66] In Leeds, John Clark, who designed a number of churches in the 1830s and '40s, confessed that 'architects' estimates are everywhere vilified as things in which no confidence can be placed; and what wonder that it should be so.'[67]

In its wide-ranging attack on the Georgian church, the Society sought to promote their aims not by claiming personal taste or arbitrary preference but by systematically undermining the aspirations and assumptions of all those who, up to this point, had been content not to consider that there were alternatives to Georgian Anglicanism. In doing this, Neale and Webb adopted a set of values which they promoted using a language which effectively precluded counter argument; a true Christian must surely support their manifesto since anyone not offering explicit agreement was, by that very act, laying their own Christian commitment open to question. Scott put it succinctly: 'One thing, however, never changed, the intolerance shown by them for all freedom of thought on the part of other men ... every one who differed from them was a heretic, or an old-fashioned simpleton.'[68] That Anglicanism changed dramatically in the middle of the nineteenth century and that the Society was a fundamental part of that change are beyond question. Whether the Society single-handedly brought about the change is much less certain. Members of the Society would have liked us to have thought of it having done so but in its pronouncement about the Georgian period was it attempting to re-write history? One of the Society's undoubted

---

the Nineteenth Century (Oxford, 1972), p. 127.

[65] G. G. Scott, Personal and Professional Recollections (London, 1879); new edn, ed. G. Stamp (Stamford, 1995), p. 53.

[66] Quoted in H. Colvin, A Biographical Dictionary of British Architects, 1600–1840 (New Haven and London, 1995), p. 152.

[67] Leeds Intelligencer, 26 February 1848 quoted in C. Webster, 'The Architectural Profession in Leeds, 1800–50' in Architectural History, 38 (1995), p. 185.

[68] G. G. Scott, op. cit., p. 206. In this respect, writers of the Society's publication continued a philosophy already established by Pugin. It is most clearly expressed in his True Principles of Pointed or Christian Architecture. Although it was not published until 1841, many of its key ideas grew out of a series of lectures Pugin delivered between 1837 and 1839. See also H. W. Kruft, A History of Architectural Theory (London, 1994), pp. 327–330.

successes was in the way it discredited the Anglicanism it inherited. In seeking to promote its desired innovations, it was careful to avoid any inference that these 'innovations' were the results of what might be thought of as the natural process of evolution, as a more mature development from Georgian Anglicanism. Rather, the Society sought to establish itself as the saviour of Anglicanism by continually focusing on its previous shortcomings and implying that they illustrated that it had become misguided and was in fundamental decay. In short, the Society sought to claim implicitly that it, working almost unaided, had rescued Anglicanism. However, in making such a claim, many earlier initiatives to bring about liturgical, spiritual or architectural change were conveniently overlooked, including some as far back as the eighteenth century. There is clear evidence that much that the Society sought to achieve was already developing, and in some cases, was firmly established long before the Society's inception.

Firstly, we can see that the serious study of the ecclesiastical architecture of the Middle Ages had a sound base by 1840. It is true that publications devoted to Gothic buildings had lagged behind those concerned with Greek and Roman architecture in terms of both quality and quantity, but volumes on the churches of the middle ages – and especially the cathedrals – were by no means negligible. The late eighteenth and early nineteenth centuries in fact witnessed the publication of numerous works by such authors as James Essex, John Carter, James Hall, Thomas Kerrick, John Britton, Thomas Rickman and Robert Willis – all of which followed scholarly archaeological principles, and many of them contained numerous sumptuous illustrations. Furthermore, we can see that while some of these works were essentially academic papers aimed at a limited and very specialised readership, for instance those which appeared in the pages of *Archaeologia*, others were much more populist in intent, for instance Britton's *Architectural Antiquities of Great Britain*, which appeared in five volumes between 1807 and 1826 or his *Cathedral Antiquities of England*, which appeared in 14 volumes between 1814 and 1835.[69]

The focus of individual books varies: some were interested in construction, e.g. of vaulting, some in the origins of Gothic, and others in developing an appropriate nomenclature, but all were essentially works of architectural history. None of them had any explicit agenda of using the past to inform the design of contemporary churches, although such a link was easily made by readers of these books, and in their own designs by those authors in this list who were also architects, for instance, Rickman. We may, therefore, wish to make a distinction between these earlier writers studying the past as an academic discipline and members of the Society studying the

[69] For modern assessments of all these books see D. Watkin, *The Rise of Architectural History* (London, 1983), pp. 53-67.

past as a means of influencing contemporary church design. But that aside, it would clearly be a grave mistake to assume that before *c*.1840 English churches and cathedrals of the middle ages were both little valued and little studied. Indeed, it was precisely because so much had already been published on mediaeval architecture that the Society was able to devote the bulk of its publications to the more contentious issues of liturgy, restorations, and the design of new churches. Yet even these 'crusading' objectives of the Society were not entirely novel; Pugin demonstrably precedes it.[70] On a range of issues, it seems clear that it is he who sets the agenda which the ecclesiologists pursue whether, for instance, it was in condemning the Classical orientation of contemporary English architecture and architectural education,[71] a loathing for the Mechanics' Institute as a means of training for the craftsman of church furnishing,[72] or the passionate emphasis on 'truth' in architecture.[73]

Secondly, it is clear that the Society's concerns for liturgical innovations were not unprecedented: the Church of England 'had begun its own very considerable rethinking of its liturgical outlook at least a generation before the launching of the Oxford Movement.'[74] The subject is covered thoroughly by Nigel Yates who devotes a whole chapter to 'A Return to Liturgical Orthodoxy', and in which he discusses a range of church plans, mainly from the period 1800–1840.[75] He concludes that, 'contrary to popular belief, significant developments had taken place during the two or three decades before the Oxford Movement in the ordering of church interiors which fore-shadowed a number of essential principles of ecclesiology. Foremost among these was the pre-eminence to be given to the altar, the relationship of altar and pulpit and the breaking up of the traditional composition of pulpit, reading-desk and clerk's desk.'[76]

Thirdly, while it is easy to criticise some churches of the 1820s and '30s for their cheap or unconvincing use of Gothic ornament or for the necessity of including galleries to maximise accommodation, there were a number of accomplished Gothic churches erected before *c*.1840. Rickman immediately comes to mind. His St John, Oulton in West Yorkshire (1827–9) was described in 1831 as 'one of the most chaste and elegant churches of pointed

---

[70]   See Crook, *op. cit.*, chapter 2; Pevsner, *op. cit.*, chapter XIII.

[71]   A. W. N. Pugin, *True Principles of Pointed or Christian Architecture* (London, 1841), pp. 29–30.

[72]   *Ibid.*, p. 33.

[73]   Pugin invokes or implies the essentialness of 'truth' extensively; usually, one suspects, when he could find no more rational justification for a particular pronouncement.

[74]   N. Yates, *Buildings, Faith and Worship, op. cit.*, p. 4.

[75]   *Ibid.*, chapter 6.

[76]   *Ibid.*, p. 115.

architecture to be met with in the Kingdom'[77] The Society would, no doubt, have found elements of it to criticise but it has a long chancel, steps which lead up to it, a vaulted rather than flat ceiling and the vestry in the form of a miniature chapter house. Rickman's scholarly but unexecuted designs for replacing the late seventeenth-century brick casing on St Mary, Birmingham (1820) is equally creditable.[78] James Savage, at St Luke, Chelsea (1820–4), produced a rare example of a post-mediaeval church with stone vaulting supported by flying buttresses.[79]

Many of the more peripheral church architects of the 1820s and '30s can be seen to have made serious studies of surviving mediaeval churches and incorporated elements of their archaeological studies in their designs for new churches. Two such examples are John Shaw's St Dunstan-in-the-West, London, begun in 1831 which 'borrows' the c.1400 lantern of All Saints, Pavement, in York or R. D. Chantrell's St Peter, Morley, West Yorkshire (1828–30) which uses elements of Ripon Minster's thirteenth-century west towers in its tower.

There were also precedents for the Society's desire that new churches should capture the effect and atmosphere of ancient ones. Interest in this theme in late-Georgian publications is by no means rare. For instance, T. D. Whitaker, writing in 1812, complained about the church in Arncliff, North Yorkshire:

> lately ... rebuilt with all the attention to economy and all the neglect both of modern elegance and ancient form, which characterises the religious edifices of the present day. If the disposition of our ancient churches cannot be adhered to, if modern art can no longer imitate the solemn effect produced by clustered columns and pointed arches, by the dignified separation of family chantries, the long perspective of a choir, and the rich tracery of its ramified window; surely the genius of an establishment calls for something in its most frugal erections more imposing than bare walls and unbroken surfaces, something at least which may inform a stranger at his entrance that he is not putting his head into a conventicle. Even the rubric requires that chancels shall remain as they have done in times past.

The writer proceeds to complain of the

> puerile affectation of what is called Gothicism, while it really consists in nothing more than piked sash-windows, which every other feature of the place belies. This, as it costs little, and makes one step to meet ancient prejudice, is perpetually attempted in the most frugal ecclesiastical works.[80]

[77] Quoted in N. Pevsner, *The Buildings of England: Yorkshire: West Riding* (Harmondsworth, 1974), p. 387.

[78] Rickman's drawings are illustrated in G. Worsley, *op. cit.*, p. 111.

[79] Illustrated and described in T. H. Shepherd and J. Elmes, *Metropolitan Improvements* (London, 1827), pp. 164–5.

[80] T. D. Whitaker, *The History and Antiquities of the Deanery of Craven*, 3rd edn (Leeds and London, 1878); new edn (Manchester and Skipton, 1973), pp. 580–3.

Similarly, the Society's opposition to large pews and unsightly, ramshackle galleries was not unprecedented. The following example is just one of many to be found among late-Georgian faculties. In 1789, the parishioners of Anston church in Yorkshire petitioned for a faculty to regularise the pews and remove the 'old loft' because it 'obstruct's ye Light of two Windows from ye Pulpit and the body of ye Church and contains Sittings for only six Persons and is so low that People who sit under it can't stand upright in their Pews.'[81]

Despite the 'preaching box' nature of the majority of the Commissioners' churches, the Commissioners themselves were not indifferent to liturgical decency. The 'Orders in Council' which defined the Commission's responsibilities included: 'That in every building to be erected under the authority of the Board, the character be preserved both externally and internally of an Ecclesiastical Edifice for Divine Worship according to the Rites of the United Church of England and Ireland'. In practice, the Commissioners stipulated that the pews should face the altar and that the altar should not be obscured by a tall, centrally placed pulpit.[82] Pulpit and reading desk were required to be separated and placed at either side of the chancel opening,[83] although not infrequently, this principle was ignored and three-decker pulpits continued to be used. Pew rents were an important element in the ongoing revenue income for the new churches, but even so, the Commission was keen to curb the worst of excesses of large and ostentatious private pews. But only if there were liturgical changes could deep chancels become justifiable and in the late-Georgian period there was still resistance to anything that even hinted at Catholicism; in some places there was positive hatred. When Christ Church in Skipton was opened in 1839, a writer in the radical *Leeds Mercury* used the headline 'Popery in an Anglican church' as a prelude to a lengthy diatribe which focused on the length of the chancel, the four steps that led up to the altar and the inclusion of a lectern.[84] This remarkable church was designed by Chantrell in 1836[85] and its advanced design further leads us to question the extent of the Society's innovations (plate 10). Churches with internal arrangements which met the approbation of the Society could only be built in large numbers if there was a conscious shift of Anglicanism in a more Catholic direction. In this respect, the Roman

---

The text comes from the second edition of 1812. The writer is very grateful to Dr Peter Leach for bringing this example to his notice. Further examples can be found in chapter 2.

[81] Borthwick Institute, York, D/C FAC 1789/2b. The writer is very grateful to Dr Terry Friedman for bringing this example to his notice.

[82] M. Port, *op. cit.*, pp. 62–3.

[83] *Ibid.*

[84] *Leeds Mercury*, 18 January 1840.

[85] C. Webster, *R. D. Chantrell, Architect...*, *op. cit.*, pp. 102–3 and plates 17(a) and 17(b).

Catholic Relief Act of 1829 (10 George IV, c. 7) was fundamental in helping to remove some of the endemic hostility to Catholics that had existed for generations,[86] and where hostility remained, at least Catholics and those with Catholic sympathies had the renewed confidence and security which the Act afforded, to face their critics. Furthermore, it was the Oxford Movement rather than the Society which first stressed the importance of the Catholic tradition as a fundamental part of Anglicanism.[87] The supremacy of the High Church wing over the Low Church evangelicals was another prerequisite for the Society's success. Here the seeds of victory may be traced to the unresolved debate that had raged in the Church of England since the Reformation. For two hundred years, the various factions had almost taken turns in dominating the Anglican hierarchy; there was nothing inherently novel in a swing towards High Church doctrines.[88]

So, are we to conclude, as the Society would have liked us to do, that it alone rescued Anglicanism from the spiritual torpor and architectural sterility of the late Georgian church, or did they simply capitalise on a series of mature, though disparate, initiatives, all of which have origins that can be traced to the late-Georgian period?

The writer is grateful to Dr Geoff Brandwood and Dr Terry Friedman for assistance and advice in the preparation of this chapter.

[86] Although Chadwick points out that 'Most Englishmen, Welshmen and Scotsmen were indifferent or hostile to the act.' He suggests political expediency over the problems of Ireland was a major factor in parliament's passing of the act. O. Chadwick, *The Victorian Church* (London, 1966), pp. 7–24.

[87] *Ibid.*, p. 170.

[88] The complexities of the pre-Victorian High Church tradition are examined in O. Chadwick, *The Mind of the Oxford Movement* (London, 1960), pp. 14–30.

The Roots of Ecclesiology
Late Hanoverian Attitudes to Medieval Churches

SIMON BRADLEY

James White's history of the Cambridge Camden Society, published in 1962, is entitled *The Cambridge Movement*. The implied parallel is of course with the Oxford Movement, generally considered to have started with John Keble's sermon on 'National Apostasy' in 1833; the further implication is that the Cambridge Ecclesiologists were as revolutionary in their effects on the Church of England.

However, such revolutions do not happen without preconditions; and the chief precondition for Ecclesiology was the widespread appeal which Gothic architecture already enjoyed, not merely as a secular taste, but as what was considered the one supremely Christian style.[1] To recover some idea of this appeal one must listen not only to antiquaries and architectural critics, but also to the voices of clergy and committed churchmen, promoted in bishops' and (especially) archdeacons' Charges, and voiced in a dozen multifarious periodicals. One must remember, too, that parish churches were conceived of at once as buildings for everyday use, and as manifestations of the 'Visible Church' on earth. Only thus does the climate of opinion which the Cambridge enthusiasts turned to their advantage become explicable.

First the myth must be addressed that the Gothic style was hardly thought of in religious terms before the late 1830s. The myth was undoubtedly encouraged by the indifference of the Commissioners for New Churches and the Incorporated Church Building Society to matters of architectural style.[2] At best, the choice of Gothic has usually been attributed to a lukewarm, half-conscious Associationism, ridiculed in 1843 by the younger Pugin: Gothic was thought 'Melancholy, and therefore fit for religious buildings!!!'.[3] But this was both to misrepresent and underestimate the contemporary power of the Gothic style.

[1]   For the secular interpretation of pre-Victorian Neo-Gothic taste see Kenneth Clark, *The Gothic Revival* (London, 1928, and later edns).
[2]   See M. H. Port, *Six Hundred New Churches* (London, 1961), p. 60, and G. L. Carr, *The Commissioners' Churches of London, 1818–37*, unpublished Ph. D. thesis, University of Michigan (1976), pp. 92–8.
[3]   *An Apology for the Revival of Christian Architecture* (London, 1843), p. 2.

One can distinguish several themes in the paeans of praise for Gothic. The most basic was the unreflecting recognition of pointed arch and pinnacle as reassuring denominational badges, which confirmed Anglican continuity with the medieval church. More sophisticated observers analyzed more closely the merits of Gothic for new churches and its particular beauties in old ones. The connection between Gothic architecture and profound religious feeling was already a convention of Associationist aesthetics by the late eighteenth century. Thus in 1793 the metaphysician Dr Frank Sayers contrasted the Greek temple with the 'impressive solemnities of devotion' evoked by a Gothic church.[4] Even those who denigrated Gothic on grounds of taste, such as the radical philosopher William Godwin or the critic Richard Payne Knight, commonly admitted its imaginative and devotional appeal.[5] As the Catholic priest Thomas Gabb ('Philo-Technon') wrote in the *Gentleman's Magazine* in 1802, only 'prepossession and cherished habits', not absolute beauty, weighed in favour of Gothic.[6] But such religious prepossessions were of course exactly what was wanted, given the Church of England's renewed sense of mission after 1818. Universalizing their own predilections, the Anglican admirers of Gothic anticipated that its revival could harness these associations, increasing the pastoral effectiveness of new buildings and bolstering loyalty to the old.

This connection with received religious ideas and denominational allegiances, however hard for a modern viewer to share, was nevertheless an essential part both of the motivation for the churches' construction and of their contemporary visual appeal. The very first communication the *Gentleman's Magazine* printed in connection with the New Churches scheme considered Gothic 'peculiarly calculated to excite sentiments of devotion ... whether ... merely from association of ideas, or from some other cause'.[7] The paramount Associationist philosopher Archibald Alison, writing in the *Edinburgh Review* in 1823, found that in a Gothic church, 'feelings of religion rush unbidden into the mind'.[8] John Britton in 1828 thought Gothic 'recognised both by the literate and illiterate, by the peasant and by the prince ... Can we hesitate, therefore, in ... preferring it ... in all our new churches?'[9]

4 F. Sayers, *Disquisitions Metaphysical and Literary* (London, 1793), pp. 27–8.
5 Godwin, *Life of Geoffrey Chaucer* (London, 1803), I p. 229; Payne Knight, *An Analytical Inquiry into the Principles of Taste* (London, 1805), pp. 162–75. On the latter see Andrew Ballantyne, *Architecture, Landscape and Liberty: Richard Payne Knight and the Picturesque* (Cambridge, 1997), pp. 240–5.
6 *The Gentleman's Magazine*, First Series, 72 (1802), pp. 117–8; identified in James M. Kuist (ed.), *The Nichols File of the Gentleman's Magazine* (Wisconsin, 1982).
7 *The Gentleman's Magazine*, First Series, 88/ii (1818), p. 507.
8 *Edinburgh Review*, 38 (1823), p. 136; identified in the *Wellesley Index to Victorian Periodicals* (Toronto, 1972-).
9 John Britton & A. C. Pugin, *The Public Buildings of London* (London, 1825–8), II p. 207.

Perhaps the best analysis of this associative power was given by Joseph Woods' *Letters of an Architect*, published in 1828 but written up to twelve years earlier. Since mankind found it difficult to shake off worldly thoughts, a church should have 'a decidedly different appearance from a common dwelling-house', to 'break the associations with the everyday employments of life, and gradually to form new associations with the objects of religion;' the Gothic style, 'already connected in our imagination with the duties of religion', was therefore fitter than any other.[10] The antiquarian architect John Chessell Buckler considered indeed that even the most indifferent Neo-Gothic church was 'assuredly more solemn than the gay models of Greece and Rome'; while the *London Magazine* remarked in 1829 that the much-admired tower of James Savage's St Luke, Chelsea (1820–4) 'produces its effect upon the popular mind, while the porticoes and cupolas of the Grecian school are passed by unheeded or despised' (plate 11).[11] Such arguments help explain why new classical churches were almost unknown by the mid 1830s, some time before the Camdenian onslaught began. Indeed, only the vernacular tradition of Georgian classicism, and the overwhelmingly classical training of the architectural profession, can explain why the absolute triumph of the various neo-medieval styles came no sooner.

The appeal of Gothic was thought to go beyond mere habit, however strong; its religious aura, to be experienced inside the church rather than out, was commonly analyzed also in terms of religious or sensory psychology. This approach owed much in particular to Edmund Burke's famous *Philosophical Enquiry into the Origins of Our Ideas of the Sublime and Beautiful* of 1757, for Burke's psychological starting points of terror and desire were situated within a religious argument from design, which linked sublimity with Divinity.[12] The sublime phenomena he listed included the dark, apparently infinite receding views in English cathedral aisles, and in the 1790s enthusiasts for Gothic architecture such as J. C. Murphy and John Milner made much of this point.[13]

Moreover, a loose but secure connection between Gothic and a religious mood may be traced back well into the seventeenth century, to John Milton's *Il Penseroso* (1632):

[10] Woods, *Letters of an Architect, from France, Italy and Greece* (London, 1828), I, pp. 10–11. Woods' letters, written in 1816–18, were emended in 1825–6.

[11] Buckler, *Views of the Cathedral Churches of England and Wales* (London, 1822), preface; *London Magazine*, Third Series, 2 (1829), p. 201.

[12] Ed. James T. Boulton (London, 1958), pp. 52, 63–9.

[13] Burke, *op. cit.*, pp. 75, 81; Murphy, *Plans ... of the Church of Batalha* (London, 1795) p. 1; Milner, *A Dissertation on the Modern Style of Altering Ancient Cathedrals* (London, 1798), pp. 49–50.

SIMON BRADLEY

But let my due feet never fail
To walk the studious cloisters pale,
And love the high embowr'd Roof,
With antick pillars massy proof,
And storied windows richly dight
Casting a dim religious light.[14]

Part of the heritage of every educated person, this passage became the greatest single cliché of writing on Gothic, particularly the last couplet or simply the phrase 'dim religious light', frequently used regardless of the absence of stained glass. From the 1790s it appears in whole or part in works by authors as diverse as John Milner and his fellow antiquaries John Carter, John Britton and Edward John Carlos; the architects Edmund Aikin and Samuel Beazley; topographical writers such as E. W. Brayley, George Todd and Thomas Smith; even in the anonymous *Aunt Elinor's Lectures on Architecture* (1843).[15] It crops up in periodicals ranging from the *Quarterly Review* to the *Gazetteer of Fashion*, from the *British Magazine* and *Blackwood's Edinburgh Magazine* to the *Civil Engineer and Architect's Journal*.[16] Ackermann's *Repository* for 1811 even ventured the extraordinary opinion that Gothic was 'but faintly relished before Milton wrote his beautiful lines on the subject'.[17] Furthermore, Milton was a model Protestant poet, author of the national religious epic *Paradise Lost*, and his appreciation of Gothic as authentically 'religious' helped dissociate it from medieval Catholicism.[18] Two explicit instances may be given. The *Quarterly Review* cited *Il Penseroso* in defence of Gothic against W. R. Hamilton, whose intemperate pamphlets on the Houses of Parliament competition stigmatised it as the style of priestcraft and superstition.[19] The same defence was mounted in Charles Anderson's *Ancient Models* (1840),

[14] *Poetical Works*, ed. Helen Darbishire (London, 1952–5), II, p. 146, ll. 155–60.
[15] Milner, *History ... of Winchester* (Winchester, 1798), II, p. 118; Carter, *Gentleman's Magazine*, First Series, 69 (1799), p. 668; Britton, *The History and Antiquities of the Cathedral Church of Salisbury* (London, 1814), p. 76; Carlos, *Gentleman's Magazine*, First Series, 102/ii (1832), p. 301; Aikin and Beazley in *Essays of the London Architectural Society* (London, 1808) pp. 19, 21; Brayley, *The History and Antiquities of the Abbey Church of St Peter Westminster* (London, 1818–23, with J. P. Neale), I, p. 17, II, p. 36; Todd, *A New Description of York* (York, 1830) p. 35; Smith, *A Topographical Account ... of Marylebone* (London, 1833), p. 105; *Aunt Elinor's Lectures on Architecture* (London, 1843), p. 122.
[16] *Quarterly Review*, 6 (1811), p. 63; *Gazetteer of Fashion* (1822–3), 3, pp. 65–6; *British Magazine*, 23 (1825), p. 50; *Blackwood's Edinburgh Magazine*, 29 (1831), p. 222; *Civil Engineer and Architect's Journal*, 4 (1841), p. 26.
[17] *The Repository of Arts, Commerce, Manufactures, Fashions and Politics*, First Series, 6 (1811), p. 318.
[18] See Duncan Griffin, 'Milton's Literary Influence', in Dennis Danielson (ed.), *The Cambridge Companion to Milton* (Cambridge, 1989), pp. 243–5.
[19] *Quarterly Review*, 58 (1837), pp. 68–9; W. R. Hamilton, *Letters ... to the Earl of Elgin on the New Houses of Parliament* (London, 1836–7).

albeit in the assumption that public taste, already committed to Gothic, needed only to be educated towards its greater appreciation.[20] The accusation that Gothic was 'superstitious' could also be countered by pointing to the pagan origins of classicism; Mary Anne Schimmelpenninck, apparently the only English female author to engage with architectural aesthetics during the period, found indeed that the attractive but Godless display of Grecian architecture concealed a 'blank and dreary void', but that Gothic, being Christian, created deep and complex beauties within its frame of 'vast and venerable simplicity'.[21]

Various attempts were made to analyze and particularise the religious appeal of Gothic, the greatest emphasis being placed on its verticalism as a mark of its heavenly aspiration. Milner's introduction to the much reprinted *Essays on Gothic Architecture* (1800) found that gables, tapering pinnacles and 'aspiring' pointed arches magnified the apparent height of Gothic buildings in a way denied to those in other styles.[22] A new generation of critics inherited the axiom (which indeed became common to several European cultures); for example, William Whewell, born in 1794, found the '*Idea*, or internal principle' of Gothic 'vertical, aspiring, intimate'.[23] Even Wordsworth saw the Gothic cathedral as

> ... with living aisles
> Instinct – to rouse the heart and lead the will
> By a bright ladder to the world above.[24]

Such naïve instances of verticalism as George Smith's needle-spired St Michael and All Angels, Blackheath, Kent (1828–30), however unacceptable by archaeological standards, reflect this conception of Gothic, it being generally agreed that its vertical character made it the pre-eminent style for steeples (plate 12).[25] The principle of verticalism now seems commonplace, perhaps, but it is worth remembering by contrast how little the eighteenth-century Gothic of William Kent and the Walpole circle departed from essentially classical proportions.

[20]   Charles Anderson, *Ancient Models* (London, 1840), pp. 41–2.
[21]   *Thoughts on the Classification of Beauty and Deformity* (London, 1815), pp. 315–16.
[22]   In J. Taylor (ed.), *Essays on Gothic Architecture* (London, 1800), pp. xvi–xviii.
[23]   *Architectural Notes on German Churches* (London, 1830), p. 4; see Paul Frankl, *The Gothic: literary sources and interpretations through eight centuries* (Princeton, 1960), pp. 447–90.
[24]   William Wordsworth, 'Ecclesiastical Sonnets' (1822), Part 3 No. XLII, ll. 9–10, in *Poetical Works*, ed. T. Hutchinson & E. de Selincourt (Oxford, 1904), p. 451.
[25]   See e.g. James Dallaway, *Anecdotes of the Arts in England* (London, 1800), pp. 104–5; E. J. Carlos, *Gentleman's Magazine*, First Series, 90/ii (1820), p. 127; *Magazine of Fine Arts* (1821), p. 134; *The Library of the Fine Arts*, 3 (1832), pp. 214–15.

Certain assumptions stand out within this attempt to evoke the Gothic 'mood' for pastoral ends, however complicated its relationship was with Neo-Gothic architecture in practice. Above all, continuity was already assumed between past and present, so that the religious impulses of the medieval worshipper and his modern counterpart, educated or not, were thought to respond to architectural stimuli in the same way. This assumption was itself no doubt reassuring at a time of rapid change and recent pastoral decline, suggesting as it did that ancestral wisdom was the key to present difficulties. As an anonymous pamphleteer of 1818 put it,

> our munificent ECCLESIASTICAL WORTHIES OF OLD ... have taught us that the aspirations of a religious soul may be excited and exalted by the grandeur of the temple in which they are indulged.[26]

A publication as Whiggish and sceptical as the *London Magazine*, citing Burke and Milton in an account of Westminster Abbey in 1821, found Gothic at once timelessly religious and religionizing:

> Wherever there is perception and sensation, an eye to see, and a capacity to feel, there is knowledge enough for Gothic architecture ... That North window alone, with its rich tracery, and delicate mullions ... has made more converts and upborne more trembling faiths, than all the volumes of Bellarmine put together...[27]

The saturation of the Church of England with such medievalism was even endorsed by the Primate himself. In 1832, when reform of Cathedral establishments was in the air, Archbishop Howley expounded the purpose of the Cathedral service to his diocesan clergy, assembled at Canterbury. It served, he said,

> to exalt the honour of God ... assisted by the effect of an architecture as far above ordinary buildings in style and dimensions, as the simple greatness of nature is beyond the works of art...[28]

Even the extreme Evangelical *Christian Observer*, jeering that cathedrals were 'formerly wholesale purgatory shops', would not countenance harming their buildings.[29] Moreover, if the Primate himself was ready to evoke the religious power of Gothic in a published document, then it is necessary to qualify Owen Chadwick's remark that by the early 1830s 'no-one knew what Cathedrals were for'; though Howley's appeal may have sounded defensive, it

[26] Anon., *A Letter ... upon the Society for Promoting the Enlargement and Building of Churches and Chapels* (London, 1818), p. 12.

[27] *London Magazine*, 4 (1821), p. 651; see Walter Graham, *English Literary Periodicals* (New York, 1930), p. 280.

[28] [William Howley], *A Charge delivered at the Primary Visitation in August and September 1832 by William, Lord Archbishop of Canterbury* (London, 1832), pp. 20–1; (the titles of similar publications are hereafter abbreviated to *Charge...*).

[29] *Christian Observer*, 33 (1833), p. 44.

had become something like official doctrine that the greater Gothic church at least had a unique place in national religious life by virtue of its architecture alone.[30]

The Church of England's appreciation of medieval church architecture, in its original and revived forms, was in itself no guarantee of archaeological rectitude, however. To the complacent eye, a plain brick lancet, a thin plaster vault or an ornamental feature quoted from a cathedral might suffice on a new church to signify the historical strength of the Anglican Communion and to evoke the same religious connotations which a real medieval building inspired. Above all, the admiration of greater, vaulted churches helps explain the costly preference for false rib-vaults, anathema alike to the Ecclesiologists and to the younger Pugin, in so many new churches of the 1820s and 1830s. It needed further exhortation by such architectural enthusiasts before it was accepted that a smaller church need not imitate a greater one. Such critics wrote so confidently and even intemperately because they understood not how little, but rather how much, community of feeling there was between them and their intended public, clerical and lay, whom they sought to alert to the finer beauties of Gothic when knowledgably and consistently deployed on simpler parish-type churches. The Camdenians have thus very appropriately been characterised as a 'reform movement', for they sought more to refine than to confound existing attitudes and tastes.[31] Their immediate successes are explicable only when it is understood how far general taste had already travelled.

It may be, also, that the triumph of archaeological Neo-Gothic in the Church of England had more to do with keeping its buildings visually distinct from the Nonconformists' than is commonly assumed. Something of the kind is suggested by the *British Critic* for 1840, in which the Tractarian churchman Thomas Mozley described the alarming experience of mistaking the new Methodist chapel at Newbury, Berkshire (1836–7), with its turreted and buttressed ashlar façade and lancet windows, for an Anglican chapel of ease (plate 13). Archaeological accuracy, he considered, would confound such sailing under false colours:

> Dissenters will copy the modern cheap church, but ... they will not copy lofty clerestories, long and ungalleried aisles, churches twice as high as they are wide, and four times as long, elaborately worked altars, carved oak ceilings, and such proprieties.[32]

---

[30] O. Chadwick, *The Victorian Church* (London, 3rd edn, 1971), I, p. 140.

[31] G. Germann, *The Gothic Revival in Europe and Britain* (London, 1972), p. 99.

[32] *British Critic*, Fourth Series, 28 (1840), pp. 478–9. Mozley was then rector of Cholderton in Wiltshire. On his authorship see his *Reminiscences* (London, 1882), II, p. 224.

SIMON BRADLEY

The desire thus to signify that a new church was Anglican should not be underestimated in explaining the success of Cambridge Ecclesiology, once Nonconformity too began to discover the religious appeal of Gothic.

Ecclesiology can also be interpreted in sociological terms, as a feature of parochial life and organization. Its precondition was what recent historians have presented as a process of professionalization, in parallel with that of the emergent secular professions.[33] Clerical corporate feeling, always encouraged by the 'clerical family' in which sons followed fathers into orders, was greatly augmented by the rising social standing of new entrants to the late Hanoverian Church. They were attracted partly by the rise in clerical incomes during the French Wars, especially those of lesser parochial livings; put simply, benefices were levelled up rather than levelled down.[34] The beneficed clergy of the first part of the nineteenth century had the self-confidence that only increased wealth can bring. Meanwhile many quietly withdrew from certain traditional, often unpaid roles, such as teaching, political organization or Poor Law administration, to concentrate on more purely 'religious' pastoral care.[35] This implied no decline in status; the clergy remained, in Owen Chadwick's description, 'learned, well-connected, socially acceptable, influential as magistrates are influential'.[36] Provincial clerical associations such as debating clubs and libraries helped meanwhile to foster a shared culture even in more isolated rural parishes.[37] Contemporaries were conscious of the changes; the Venerable Thomas Thorp of Trinity College, Cambridge, wrote in 1842:

the relinquishing of unseemly and unsuitable occupations ... the gradual approach to more uniformity and propriety of clerical manners and costume ... have become very much characteristic of the English Church.[38]

Thorp was of course also the first president of the Cambridge Camden Society; and, although it was open to laymen, the Society clearly had in its origins some affinities with such clerical associations, serving to keep interested parish clergy in touch with the fount of authority at Cambridge.[39] Indeed, theological differences apart, the most vigorous movements within the early nineteenth-century Church – the High Church alliance known as the

[33] See Alan D. Gilbert, *Religion and Society in Industrial England* (London, 1976), and Peter Virgin, *The Church in an Age of Negligence* (Cambridge, 1989).
[34] Diana McClatchey, *Oxfordshire Clergy 1777–1869* (Oxford, 1960), pp. 25–8.
[35] Anthony Russell, *The Clerical Profession* (London, 1980), pp. 38–41.
[36] Chadwick, *The Victorian Church*, I, p. 34.
[37] For examples see *Christian Remembrancer*, 7 (1825), pp. 649–52; Rev. W. Dealtry, *A Charge Delivered in ... 1834, at the Visitation in Hants* (London, 1835), pp. vi–viii.
[38] Thomas Thorp, *Charges Delivered at the Visitation of the Archdeaconry of Bristol* (Bristol, 1842–3), 1842, p. 31.
[39] Cambridge Camden Society, *Report* (1840), p. 9.

29

Hackney Phalanx, Evangelicalism, the Oxford Movement – all shared this sense of the special character and distinctive purpose of the clergy.[40]

Clerical self-confidence and self-consciousness had dramatic implications for parish life. The tightening control exercised by the clergy led to the decline of such communal lay bodies as the old church bands – one thinks of the old-fashioned Mellstock Quire in Thomas Hardy's *Under the Greenwood Tree* (1872) – and the eclipse of the once-important parish clerk.[41] It also transformed clerical attitudes to church buildings. By pre-Reformation tradition, the parish, through its elected churchwardens, looked after the nave, the incumbent or patron the chancel. The question of how well churches were maintained divides into two: how far they were kept sound, neat and tidy; and how well repairs respected or enhanced the architecture and fittings. In rural parishes at least, churchwardens were of themselves unlikely to pay much attention to the latter, especially if the incumbent was himself indifferent to architectural preservation. By contrast, the incumbent was on his part increasingly likely to oppose repairs or embellishments by his churchwardens which seemed to him destructive or tasteless.

For a cross-section of early nineteenth-century views on church maintenance, however, one must look above parochial level to concentrate on the archdeacons, whose attitudes and exhortations are often preserved in their Charges. These were initially delivered in person, like sermons or episcopal Charges, to the clergy of one of the sixty-two English and Welsh archdeaconries, assembled in a suitable church, often in their churchwardens' company; many were subsequently published or privately printed. Even by the refined standards of ecclesiastical history they are obscure documents; nonetheless, of more than 150 archdeacons who served between 1810 and 1843, the British Library holds printed Charges by forty; others survive reprinted in whole or part in contemporary periodicals.

The archdeacons were a varied body. A few held office *in commendam* with the bishopric, as in several Welsh sees.[42] Others held the dignity as a brief step on the ladder: the great church-builder Charles James Blomfield was archdeacon of Chester in 1822, bishop there in 1824, and bishop of London in 1828. Age at appointment likewise varied greatly: Blomfield was thirty-six, but William Barrow was seventy-six when made archdeacon of Nottingham in 1830.[43] Their Charges are no less miscellaneous. Topical or doctrinal questions naturally predominate over routine church maintenance or restoration, but enough asides, postscripts or appendices on the latter preclude

[40]   Virgin, *op. cit.*, p. 23; Russell, *op. cit.*, p. 38.
[41]   James Obelkevitch, *Religion and Rural Society: South Lindsey 1825–1875* (Oxford, 1976), pp. 147–9.
[42]   The bishopric and archdeaconry of St Asaph were held together, the bishopric of Bangor with the archdeaconries of Bangor and Anglesea.
[43]   *Dictionary of National Biography.*

the inference that they were merely the hobbyhorse of a few antiquarian eccentrics. Altogether, twenty-four archdeacons made recommendations on the subject, in Charges published between 1796 and the early 1840s. Furthermore, some archdeacons known to have promoted church restoration are silent on the subject in their Charges, most notably Robert Hurrell Froude of Totnes (father of the more famous Hurrell Froude), who encouraged medievalizing restorations of Devon churches from as early as the 1820s.[44]

Of our twenty-four, only two ran against the grain of Gothic antiquarianism. The first, Gilbert Heathcote, archdeacon of Winchester 1819–29, displayed well-meaning ignorance rather than active hostility. He found village churches (unlike cathedrals) 'too homely and unadorned' to excite devotional feelings, so recommended 'stability and neatness' in repair: fresh paint on wooden spires, doors and fittings; new battlements and pinnacles for parapets of unspecified design; smart new slate roofs instead of stone; and false ceilings to counter draughts.[45] If Heathcote recognised aesthetic values after a fashion, no such concession was made by the dreadful Edward Bather, archdeacon of Salop-in-Lichfield 1828–47; he denounced expenditure on 'useless decorations' and 'matters of mere taste', limiting positive recommendations to extra galleries to increase church-room cheaply.[46] Four further archdeacons – of Bangor, Derby, Nottingham, and Oxford – between 1817 and 1833 enjoined minimal preventative maintenance: generally, proper ventilation and the removal from against church walls of accumulated earth; otherwise they made no architectural observations.[47] Likewise, the visitation records of 1845–8 of Henry Kaye Bonney, archdeacon of Bedford 1821–45 and of Lincoln 1845–62, never step beyond routines of drainage, ventilation and so forth into the realms of aesthetics or archaeology.[48]

This leaves eighteen archdeacons – almost half those published – who expressed definite antiquarian sympathies: the 'soft' enjoining respectful piety towards the ancient fabric, the 'hard' stipulating restoration principles and techniques in detail. The 'soft' party includes Archdeacon Law of Rochester, who requested that ancient churches 'ought religiously to be preserved'

[44] *Archaeologia*, 17 (1814), pp. 128–37; Rev. G. Oliver & J. P. Jones, *The Ecclesiastical Antiquities of Devon* (Exeter, 1828), p. x; Piers Brendon, *Hurrell Froude and the Oxford Movement* (London, 1974), pp. 19–23.
[45] Gilbert Heathcote, *Charge...* (Winchester, 1820), pp. 11–12, 29, 31.
[46] Edward Bather, *Charge...* (London, 1830), pp. 11, 35.
[47] H. W. Majendie, bishop and archdeacon of Bangor 1809–30, *Charge...* (Bangor, 1817), pp. 23–4; Samuel Butler, archdeacon of Derby 1822–36 and bishop of Lichfield 1836–9, *Charge...* (London, 1826), pp. 11–12; George Wilkins, archdeacon of Nottingham 1832–65, *Charge...* (London, 1832), p. 31; Charles Carr Clerke, archdeacon of Oxford 1830–77, *Charge...* (London, 1833), p. 19.
[48] *Bonney's Church Notes*, ed. N. S. Harding (London, 1937).

(1820), and Archdeacons Headlam of Richmond and Hoare of Winchester, who formulaically acknowledged the 'pious zeal' and 'sacred fabrics' of our ancestors (1833, 1837).[49] More specific recommendations begin as early as 1796, with Joseph Plymley, archdeacon of Salop-in-Hereford.[50] He considered the very art of church-building lost: 'slight and airy' modern structures could not even exclude noise, still less inspire the 'pious contemplation' of a Gothic interior. Medieval walls therefore should not be compromised by enlarging or rearranging windows; new windows would anyway appear 'mean and discordant', since the knowledge of 'how to proportion them to the body of the church, and to each other' was lost. A dark church could be lightened by reinstating blocked lights and by copying exactly those existing, as well as by whitewashing and ceiling the interior. These last would soon be frowned upon, but otherwise Plymley set the tone for many later Charges. Particularly common were echoes of his politic insistence that careful restoration worked out more cheaply than rash rebuilding or the false economy of neglect: a powerful mixture of the practical and the aesthetic which the Cambridge men were to repeat in their time.

Plymley's kindred spirits in the 1800s included the well connected George Owen Cambridge F.S.A., archdeacon of Middlesex, and an important figure in the Hackney Phalanx.[51] His Charge of 1806 stressed that reverence to 'THE TEMPLE OF THE LIVING GOD' extended to its medieval features; alterations imperilled its 'original design and beauty', and risked structural damage and costly reconstruction.[52] His Charge of 1808 urged that medieval windows and weak points in the rubble walls should be repaired only by knowledgeable and experienced masons 'with the same materials and a similar plan'.[53] Another Fellow of the Society of Antiquaries of London was Charles Goddard, archdeacon of Lincoln 1817–44, whose first Charge cautioned against ignorant damage to tracery or carved stonework.[54] He later struggled to prevent the churchwardens of Bexley, his own parish, from installing a 'disforming and disfiguring' north gallery, setting out his case in a published letter in 1829.[55] The row was prefigured in his Charge of the previous year,

[49]   John Law, archdeacon of Rochester 1767–1827, *Charge...* (1820), p. 6; John Headlam, archdeacon of Richmond 1826–1854, *Charge...* (Richmond, 1833), pp. 10, 21; Charles James Hoare, archdeacon of Winchester 1829–47, of Surrey 1847–65, *Charge...* (Winchester, 1837), p. 12.

[50]   Joseph Plymley (after 1804 Joseph Corbett), archdeacon of Salop in Hereford 1789–1825, *Charge...* (Shrewsbury, 1796), pp. 11–19.

[51]   See P. B. Nockles, *Continuity and Change in Anglican High Churchmanship in Britain, 1792–1850*, unpublished D. Phil. thesis, University of Oxford (1982), p. xxxi.

[52]   George Owen Cambridge, *Charge...* (London, 1806), pp. 11–14.

[53]   George Owen Cambridge, *Charge...* (London, 1808), pp. 6–11, 17–19.

[54]   Charles Goddard, *Charge...* (London, 1818), pp. 46–7.

[55]   Charles Goddard, *A Letter from the Vicar of Bexley to the Churchwardens of that*

which attacked churchwardens' 'disposition to disfigure and destroy, at the expense of symmetry and proportion', in vain efforts to commemorate their year in office by alteration or embellishment; 'the staying hand of the clergy' should protect 'the religious feeling which attaches to these buildings'.[56] Compare Francis Wrangham, archdeacon of Cleveland and the East Riding, 1821: if his churchwardens could 'preserve or ... introduce, *under the superintendence of able Surveyors*, the venerable architecture of our forefathers, instead of incongruously jumbling together the styles of different ages', they would both save money in the long term and make their churches 'infinitely the more appropriate to the solemn worship of God': a typical combination of practicality and antiquarianism.[57] Such examples can be greatly multiplied from amongst the eleven remaining archdeacons in the sample. Since many of these men were born well back in the eighteenth century, they must have been responding to a broader shift in opinion. in other words, church restoration was not the special cause of a rising younger generation.[58]

The ground was thus prepared, locally at least, for the Ecclesiologists' little books of *Hints*. The difference is of course in the books' archaeological sophistication and stringent attention to detail. One can observe their effect on the society's president Thomas Thorp, who held the archdeaconry of Bristol jointly with his Cambridge fellowship. His Charge of 1837 referred already to the 'reform in architectural taste', which he hoped would preserve his churches' 'simple dignity, chaste proportions, and purity of style ... so conducive to vital piety'.[59] By 1842 he moved strikingly from the general to the specific, his Charge of that year being almost entirely devoted to the Cambridge orthodoxy on pews and chancels; it appended a list of the Ecclesiologists' publications, and urged that no churchwarden should act without consulting the incumbent and an architect endorsed by one of the university architectural societies.[60] Other Charges of the 1840s, however, indicate that this wholesale promotion of ecclesiology was exceptional. Edward Bigge, archdeacon of the newly formed district of Lindisfarne, devoted his entire Charge of 1843 to church architecture and restoration, but defended the institution of pews; Julius Hare, Archdeacon of Lewes, in 1840 denounced pews and insisted on scrupulously accurate repairs of medieval work, but evoked Gothic as an 'organic growth' of 'wondrous pervading harmony', a sign of his background in the speculative, Romantic culture of the 1820s at Cambridge: a wholly different tributary to the Neo-Gothic

Parish (London, 1829), pp. 29–30.

[56] Charles Goddard, *Charge...* (London, 1828), p. 40.

[57] Francis Wrangham, *Charge...* (York, 1821), p. 12.

[58] For dates of birth see J. Foster (ed.), *Alumni Oxonienses* (1891–2), and J. & J. A. Venn (eds), *Alumni Cantabrigienses* (1922), passim.

[59] Thomas Thorp, *Charge...* (London, 1837), p. 41.

[60] *Op. cit.* [see note 38, above], pp. 39–41.

stream.[61] All in all, then, there is no shortage of evidence that the bandwagon of medievalizing church restoration was rolling at a reasonable speed long before the Ecclesiologists jumped into the driver's seat and began cracking the whip.

The long gestation of Ecclesiological attitudes is clearer still from antiquarian writings proper. These anticipate again and again the sardonic tone of much early Ecclesiological prose, a tone naturally out of place in an archdeacon's address to clergy and churchwardens. The efforts of churchwardens and parish craftsmen to maintain or beautify their churches were particularly vilified.[62] The most forceful attack was an anonymous satirical booklet of 1825, entitled *Hints to Some Churchwardens, with a few Illustrations, Relative to the Repair and Improvement of Parish Churches*. It offered to expound the 'many splendid, curious and convenient ideas' of those churchwardens who had 'attained perfection as planners and architects'.[63] Too expensive for the average churchwarden, the book rather parodied in miniature the contemporary 'Cottage Book', in which architects published designs for small rural houses in coloured plates with flanking text.[64] ('Hints' also incidentally anticipates the Camdenians' genteelly titled *A Few Hints for the Practical Study of Ecclesiastical Antiquities* (1839), though such pamphlets by contrast exploited the new, cheaper print culture of fast typesetting and wood-pulp paper.) The plates show a variety of ways to spoil a medieval church, accompanied by unfalteringly deadpan texts:

> If the church is of stone, let the porch be of brick, the roof slated, and the entrance to it of the improved Gothic called modern ... placed so as to stop up what might be called a useless window ... An ancient Saxon entrance [should] ... be carefully bricked up, and perhaps plastered, so as to conceal as much as possible of the zigzag ornament...[65]

Other plates show windows blocked in contrasting material, battlements enlivened with red-painted vases, candlesticks and pineapples, and so forth.[66] The final plate illustrates a monstrous iron stovepipe bursting through a traceried window head to terminate above the chancel gable in a T-shape vaguely reminiscent of a cross: ironically recommended for '*effect, beauty* and *boldness*' and for the 'sublime' associations of a cloud of smoke

---

[61] Bigge, *Charge...* (Newcastle upon Tyne, 1843); Hare, *Charges...* (Cambridge, 1856), I, 1840 charge, p. 12, and memoir of Hare (by F. D. Maurice: *D.N.B.*), pp. xvii–xviii.

[62] See e.g. Dallaway, *op. cit.* [see note 25, above], p. 33; John Britton, *The Architectural Antiquities of Great Britain*, I (London, 1807), unpaginated, and also his *The Beauties of England and Wales*, XV/ii (London, 1814), p. 714.

[63] Anon., *Hints to some Churchwardens* (London, 1825), p. 5.

[64] Cf. e.g. Nicholas Carlisle, *Hints on Rural Residences* (London, 1825).

[65] *Hints* (1825), p. 8 and Plate I.

[66] *Ibid.*, Plates II, III, IV.

over the altar (plate 14).[67]

The intended audience appreciated the joke: the antiquarian-minded *Gentleman's Magazine* and the more strictly theological *Christian Remembrancer* and *Quarterly Theological Review* gave favourable notices, the latter expounding the book's 'lessons' over several poker-faced pages.[68] The High Church *British Critic* enjoyed the digs at the 'great and grave annual magistracy' of 'village Vitruvii and parochial Palladios'.[69] Architectural authors of the 1830s – W. H. Leeds, E. J. Carlos, the Rev. James Raine of Durham – harked back to it when they encountered architectural barbarities.[70] More importantly, the initial reception of the book shows how far its ideas had already entered the Anglican mainstream.

To enthusiasts for medieval architecture, the solution was simple: the clergy should take control of church and furnishings themselves. Such interventionism was possible since the incumbent traditionally had the right to supervise any repairs the vestry initiated or paid for.[71] This assumption marks several of the clerical handbooks, the proliferation of which from the late eighteenth century is another symptom of professionalization. The *Medicina Clerica* (1821) was full of suggestions for improving porch, pews and pulpit, while the *Parochial Letters* (1829) insisted that the incumbent should learn the rudiments of Gothic and of church maintenance, and should prevent 'uncouth' inscriptions on tombstones and monuments by composing them himself.[72] The *British Critic* for 1826 proposed a similar but more strictly archaeological activism, lamenting that

> between the proverbial parsimony of a vestry, the manoeuvring contrivances of churchwardens to serve their own ends, and the lamentable ignorance of country builders, the damage done in a greater or less degree to all our parochial churches seems almost irreparable.

The author urged his clerical readership to defend their churches from vestries which had lost the understanding of how to care for them, starting with proper drainage and ventilation, provisions requiring no expertise.[73] Meanwhile, the *Notes on Cambridgeshire Churches* (1827), published

[67] *Ibid.*, p. 30 and Plate XII.
[68] *Gentleman's Magazine*, First Series, 95/i (1825), p. 626; *Christian Remembrancer*, 7 (1825), p. 264; *Quarterly Theological Review*, 3 (1826), pp. 163–6.
[69] *British Critic*, Second Series, 23 (1825), pp. 640–1.
[70] *Fraser's Magazine*, 4 (1831), p. 292 (the *Wellesley Index* identifies Leeds' authorship); *Gentleman's Magazine*, First Series, 102/i (1832), p. 503; Raine, *A Brief Account of Durham Cathedral* (Newcastle upon Tyne, 1833), p. 135.
[71] See e.g. John Napleton D.D., *Advice to a Minister of the Gospel* (Hereford, 1801), pp. 45–6.
[72] Anon., *Medicina Clerica* (London, 1821), pp. 9, 32–3; Anon., *Parochial Letters* (London, 1829), pp. 61–70, 56.
[73] *British Critic*, Third Series, 2 (1826), pp. 388–9.

anonymously by George Richard Boissier of Magdalene College, attacked the archdeaconry for failing to back the clergy in church maintenance disputes with slothful or parsimonious vestries, and for laxity in allowing such rustic horrors as red brick infill and white-painted window frames.[74] That his book had some influence on a younger generation may be inferred from the honorary membership which the Cambridge Camden Society granted him at its foundation.[75]

To point out that the Ecclesiologists' church restoration campaign of the 1840s drew on the efforts and opinions of earlier generations of antiquaries is not to deny the novelty of their rigorous archaeology or liturgical attitudes; but their debt to tradition is irrefutable. Consider the *Few Words to Churchwardens, Suited to Country Parishes* (1841), largely written by J. M. Neale. Here once again are the familiar warnings against dampness, poor ventilation and the accumulation of earth, and the insistence that new work follow what it replaced in form, material and quality.[76] The prevailing mistrust of the churchwarden's ability is betrayed in the suggestion that any difficult cases be referred to the Ecclesiologists for advice.[77] Indeed, the *Gentleman's Magazine's* recommendation of the pamphlet contained no suggestion that it was more than a handy, cheap restatement of familiar arguments.[78]

This is to omit, of course, the Society's peculiar animus against 'pues'; and here, it might be thought, the Camdenians were preaching a new gospel. Once again, however, they prove to have drawn without acknowledgment on their forebears' efforts. The Camdenian case against pews combined antiquarian, aesthetic, practical, and theological or moral arguments: they wasted space; they appropriated church-room to a wealthy, subscribing minority, often leaving inadequate space for the poor; they made kneeling difficult, and (in 'square' pews) uniform eastward kneeling impossible; they commonly looked gaudy or ramshackle; they recalled theatres or lecture rooms; they emphasised social distinctions that should be set aside in the House of God.[79] Open, eastward-facing wooden benches were superior in every way.[80] The case was elaborated in Neale's pamphlet *A History of Pews* (1841), which argued that pews were an innovation of the Reformers, and

---

[74]   [George Richard Boissier], *Notes on Cambridgeshire Churches* (London, 1827), pp. 9–16.

[75]   Cambridge Camden Society, *Report* (1840), p. 25.

[76]   J. M. Neale, *Few Words to Churchwardens, Suited to Country Parishes* (London, 1841), pp. 6–9.

[77]   *Ibid.*, pp. 8–9.

[78]   *Gentleman's Magazine*, Second Series, 16 (1841), pp. 60–1.

[79]   Cambridge Camden Society, *A Few Words ... Country Parishes* (London, 1841), pp. 11–12; Cambridge Camden Society, *A Few Words to Churchwardens, Suited to Town and Manufacturing Parishes* (London, 1841), pp. 6–8.

[80]   *A Few Words ... Country Parishes* (1841), p. 6.

SIMON BRADLEY

(more practically) that even the tightest packed pews accommodated 20 per cent fewer worshippers than the same area of benches.[81] Such entertaining squibs as F. E. Paget's satirical tale *Milford Malvoisin, or, Pews and Pewholders* (1842) advanced similar arguments.

Such a concerted campaign had not been seen before, and James White assumed that it originated with the Society.[82] The shortcomings of pews and galleries certainly figured less frequently in Charges and clerical handbooks than stipulations on church maintenance. However, periodicals and antiquarian or architectural publications once more allowed greater latitude for criticism.

The first recorded complaint against pews seems to be that by the architect James Gibbs in 1728, on the purely aesthetic grounds that pews, like galleries, 'clog up and spoil' the 'right proportion' of church interiors.[83] Later in the century the architect James Essex, a more conscientious Goth than Gibbs, found pews such as those of St Sepulchre, Cambridge 'no ornament to any church', analogous there to the piecemeal alterations which had compromised its exterior.[84] The pews were indeed deliberately omitted when the church was illustrated for Britton's *Architectural Antiquities* in 1807 (plate 15).[85] This and many similar omissions are instructive: as church interiors became sought-after subjects for reproduction, their pews increasingly irked both artists and the amateurs who formed their market, whose expectations were shaped in turn by the reproductions they saw.[86] The more important the church, the more likely that ramshackle pewing would be denounced. In 1803 E. W. Brayley criticized the seventeenth-century pews in Exeter Cathedral nave, and John Britton lamented in 1826 that 'repeated denunciations' had not procured their removal.[87] Major churches scarcely better off included Cirencester and Bath Abbey.[88]

[81] J. M. Neale, *A History of Pews* (London, 1841), pp. 19, 59; later editions, in 1842–3, were styled *A History of Pues*.
[82] White, *The Cambridge Movement* (Cambridge, 1962), p. 106.
[83] James Gibbs, *A Book of Architecture* (London, 1728), p. viii; see Terry Friedman, *James Gibbs* (Yale, 1984), pp. 76–8, 331.
[84] James Essex, 'Observations on the Origins and Antiquity of Round Churches', *Archaeologia*, 6 (1782), pp. 176–7.
[85] Britton, *The Architectural Antiquities of Great Britain*, I (London, 1807), unpaginated.
[86] Cf. the 'empty' churches in e.g. Plate V of the Society of Antiquaries' *Some Account of the Abbey Church of Bath* (London, 1798), drawn by John Carter, and in W. Taylor, *Annals of St Mary Overie* (London, 1833), p. 45.
[87] Brayley, *Beauties of England and Wales*, 4 (London, 1803), p. 65; Britton, *The History and Antiquities of the Cathedral Church of Exeter* (London, 1826), p. 101.
[88] J. P. Neale, *Views of the most Interesting Collegiate and Parochial Churches of Great Britain* (London, 1824), I, Cirencester p. 2; Britton, *The History and Antiquities of the Abbey Church of Bath* (London, 1825), p. 64.

37

The Camdenians' aesthetic objection to pews, especially the high-backed, non-oriented variety, was thus more than a century old. What is more surprising is that their theological and pastoral arguments, even their preference for open benches (rather than uniform, low-backed pews), may also be traced back many years. The *Gentleman's Magazine* raised the subject as far back as 1801. Hostile asides by John Carter, its resident Neo-Goth, emboldened a correspondent to denounce pews as not merely unsightly but 'a flagrant insult, in a religious view, committed by a few individuals on the parishioners at large'; since all should meet equally before God, 'common benches' alone were needed, as in foreign churches, and in overcrowded churches it was 'as preposterous as ... cruel' that space for eight or ten should be arrogated for 'the occasional use of two or three'.[89] The correspondence that followed ranged from wholehearted endorsement, through suggested compromises such as opening up unoccupied private pews, to a virulently reactionary tirade against the 'revolutionary' implications of uniform seating.[90] Such suspicions notwithstanding, pews on the old model were increasingly attacked in print; for example, the *Orthodox Churchman's Magazine* in 1807 recorded with satisfaction the uniform, oriented repewing of Stepney church, in place of the high-sided 'sleeping pews' and quadrangular 'conversation pews' there before.[91]

The obvious justification for pews, in the broadest sense of enclosed rented seating, was their financial value to the Church; but in the face of accusations of simony this took pragmatism too far. Instead, pews were commonly defended as a means of fostering loyalty to one's weekly place in the parish church, an argument still current in the 1840s.[92] But for most reflective clergy the improved appearance, increased capacity and reduced social divisiveness of a reseated church made pews a necessary evil at best. A few senior clerics took up the battle: Archdeacon Goddard of Lincoln hoped that the New Churches Act of 1818 would provide also for the forfeiture of unattended pews for free parochial use; in 1821 the newly appointed Bishop Mant of Killaloe, an associate of the Hackney Phalanx, urged on his Irish clergy eastward-facing benches with space for kneeling; Archdeacon Oldershaw of Norwich in 1828 even dared to hope for copies of the 'old venerable benches' of the middle ages, also in eastward-facing rows.[93] Some

---

[89]   *Gentleman's Magazine*, First Series, 71 (1801), pp. 31, 117, 718. On Carter see J. Mordaunt Crook, *John Carter and the Mind of the Gothic Revival* (London, 1995).

[90]   *Gentleman's Magazine*, First Series, 71 (1801), pp. 782–3, 811–12, 902–3, 1097–8, 1102, 1177.

[91]   *Orthodox Churchman's Magazine*, 12 (1807), pp. 20–1.

[92]   See e.g. Rev. J. L. Petit, *Remarks on Church Architecture* (London, 1841), II, p. 140; Bigge (1843), pp. 16–18; Edward Scobell, *A Few Thoughts on Church Subjects* (London, 1843), pp. 55–6.

[93]   Charles Goddard, *Charge...* (1818) pp. 52–4; Richard Mant, *Charge...* (Belfast,

attacks on pews were without antiquarian or aesthetic content: the eminently practical *Medicina Clerica* found that they facilitated talking, sleeping and failing to kneel without detection during the service.[94] Moreover, the Evangelical party was just as offended by the sight of locked, empty pews in churches where others stood in the aisles.[95]

By the 1820s jibes at pews were therefore common from all sides, in all kinds of literature. The architect P. F. Robinson, deploring such 'huge packing boxes', made much of the more accommodating Neo-Gothic stalls he had introduced to Mickleham church in Surrey (plate 16).[96] Even Wordsworth recalled in 1827 the humble but inspiring faith of the peasantry of his youth, coming to 'lowly bench or sculptured stall': pews and piety plainly went less well together.[97] The younger Pugin's efforts in the early 1830s to influence the reseating of St Thomas's church in Salisbury in favour of benches showed more precocity of behaviour than originality of ideas.[98] Meanwhile, the researches of the Rev. W. S. Gilly, Vicar of Norham in Northumberland, into the ancient Waldensian Protestant church in Savoy, revealed that it had long used free, open seats and benches rather than pews, which Gilly too disliked.[99] The *British Critic* seized eagerly on this alternative Protestant tradition as another weapon in the moral armoury against the pew system.[100]

All in all, the Ecclesiologists seem to have brought little more than their own vehemence and energy in pamphleteering to the pew question. The less noisy Oxford Society certainly kept pace with its sister: a monograph of 1840 recommended as models the fifteenth-century benches of Great Haseley church, Warwickshire, and its Reports for 1840 and 1841 made clear its hostility to galleries and pews.[101] The Camdenians' *History of Pews* righteously proclaimed that 'from the first moment of our existence ... we have denounced them [pews] as eyesores and heartsores'; but even this phrase seems to have been taken from the Charge of Archdeacon Hare of 1840, which urged the replacement of pews, 'eyesores and heartsores', with benches

1821), Edward Berens, *A Memoir of the Life of Bishop Mant* (London, 1849), pp. 30, 58; John Oldershaw, *Charge...* (Norwich, 1828), pp. 6–7.

[94] Anon., *Medicina Clerica* (London, 1829), pp. 32–3.

[95] Ian Bradley, *The Call to Seriousness: the Evangelical Impact on the Victorians* (London, 1976), p. 64.

[96] P. F. Robinson, *Illustrations of Mickleham Church, Surrey* (London, 1824), pp. 17–18.

[97] Wordsworth, *Poetical Works* (1904), p. 256, sonnet 'Decay of Piety', l. 7.

[98] Benjamin Ferrey, *Recollections of A. W. N. Pugin* (London, 1861), p. 100; a date c.1833 seems indicated.

[99] W. S. Gilly, *Waldensian Researches* (London, 1831), pp. 366–7.

[100] *British Critic*, Fourth Series, 13 (1833), p. 189.

[101] T. W. Weare, *Some Remarks upon the Church of Great Haseley, Warwickshire* (Oxford, 1840), pp. 21–2; Oxford Society, *Report* (1840), p. 14; *Report* (1841), p. 19.

provided with backs.[102] In 1840 also Thomas Mozley attacked as 'old-fashioned' the taste for pew-packed church interiors.[103] Indeed, when the Incorporated Church Building Society revised its regulations in 1842 to stipulate benches rather than pews, it followed remonstrances from half a dozen local church building societies, rather than the exclusive complaints of the Cambridge Ecclesiologists: all in turn the culmination of a sporadic campaign decades long.[104] Nor was the transformation rapid thereafter; barely half of parish churches appear to have lost their pews by c.1860.[105] All in all, then, the 1840s were an episode in a process of slow change in church seating, not a period of sudden transformation.

The great splash Cambridge Ecclesiology made in the 1840s also owed much to its fulfilment of a longstanding hope, now largely forgotten, that architectural education might spread amongst the clergy, even that church restoration might dispense with architects altogether. It was widely believed well into the mid-century that the great cathedrals had been designed by the clergy themselves, and architects' efforts to restore medieval churches were meanwhile found wanting almost as often as churchwardens'.[106] The hope that the clergy might learn to direct repairs to their own churches was foreshadowed in Thomas Rickman's famous *An Attempt to Discriminate the Styles of English Architecture* (1817).[107] Rickman was of course trying to widen his book's appeal, and in itself this is scarcely evidence of clerical interest in the subject. Within a decade, however, formal clerical instruction in medieval architecture was being widely recommended. The *Quarterly Theological Review*, inspired by Britton's volumes on the English cathedrals, regretted its absence from the clerical curriculum, especially since the 'multifarious avocations' of professional architects prevented them paying close attention to the subject.[108] In 1828 an obscure Hampshire magazine called *The Crypt*, a quirky but otherwise characteristic production of provincial clerical-antiquarian culture, suggested lectures and examinations on church architecture at Oxford and Cambridge, with Chairs in church maintenance and restoration.[109] In the same year John Britton suggested that routine instruction in the arts at the public schools and universities would have

[102]   *A History of Pews* (London, 1841), p. 4; Hare (1856), I, 1840 *Charge...*, p. 12.
[103]   *British Critic*, Fourth Series, 28 (1840), p. 476; see above, n. 32.
[104]   T. V. Parry, *The Incorporated Church Building Society 1818–1851*, unpublished M. Litt. thesis, University of Oxford (1984), pp. 95–8, 160.
[105]   See e. g. G. K. Brandwood on Leicestershire and Rutland, *Archaeological Journal*, 144 (1987), p. 392.
[106]   See Andrew Saint, *The Image of The Architect* (London, 1983), pp. 19–50.
[107]   Thomas Rickman, *op. cit.* (London, 1817), p. iii.
[108]   *Quarterly Theological Review*, 3 (1826), p. 147.
[109]   *The Crypt*, 2 (Ringwood, 1828), p. 248; 3, p. 172; vol. 2 makes the interesting assertion that the superiority of Cambridge over Oxford in such knowledge had 'often been observed'.

prevented the Commissioners for New Churches from being so lamentably ignorant architecturally.[110] It may not be too fanciful to connect these hopes with M. H. Bloxam's *The Principles of Gothic Architecture Elucidated by Question and Answer* (1829), which was deliberately couched as a catechism as the most effective means of imparting detailed information.[111] Bloxam's family background was ecclesiastical-cum-educational: his father, Dr Richard Rouse Bloxam, was headmaster of Rugby School, and his younger brother J. R. Bloxam, later an important figure in Newman's circle, was in orders at Magdalen College, Oxford.[112] So it may well be that his book was designed for formal instruction at school or university, and from its large sales and numerous later editions it must certainly have reached many who could not have afforded expensive folios on the subject.[113]

Nonetheless the care and study of churches was not taken up, despite the modernization of the curriculum at both Oxford and Cambridge in the 1830s. Oxford made a modest beginning in the early 1830s, in the shape of papers on the evolution of Gothic read by the young Hurrell Froude to the Ashmolean Society, but these seem to have inspired no immediate imitations.[114] The *Foreign Quarterly Review* in 1838 still lamented the absence of professors of 'Christian Archaeology' who might prepare the clergy to confound churchwardens and provincial builders.[115] A correspondent to the *Gentleman's Magazine* in 1839 went further: ordinands should be taught 'competent knowledge of the principles of ecclesiastical architecture', and each diocese should appoint a specialist architect to repair or enlarge churches, parsonages and schools.[116] In 1840 Archdeacon Hare of Lewes recommended in his Charge both architectural instruction for the clergy and the establishment of a system of diocesan architectural committees with clerical and lay professional membership.[117] By this date the younger Pugin's installation as a lecturer in 'ecclesiastical antiquities' at Oscott College could

---

110 Britton & Pugin, *op. cit.* [see note 9, above] (1825–8), II, pp. xii–xiii.

111 M. H. Bloxam, *The Principles of Gothic Architecture Elucidated by Question and Answer* (1829), p. 3; cf. the children's *Pinnock's Catechism of Architecture* (6th edn, London, 1822).

112 S. L. Ollard, 'The Oxford Architectural and Historical Society and the Oxford Movement', *Oxeniensa*, 5 (1940), pp. 146–160.

113 H. T. Kirby, 'Some Notes on Bloxam's Principles', *Architectural Review*, 103 (1948), pp. 27–8.

114 Published in the *British Magazine* in 1832–3 (vol. 1, pp. 546–52, 2, pp. 14–20, 3, pp. 22–8), and in Froude's *Remains* (London, 1838), II, pp. 337–68.

115 *Foreign Quarterly Review*, 22 (1838), p. 27; by the archaeologist Harry Longueville Jones (*Wellesley Index*).

116 *Gentleman's Magazine*, Second Series, 11 (1839), p. 259. The latter practice of course became widespread from the 1840s.

117 Hare, *op. cit.* [see notes 61 or 102, above], I, 1840 *Charge*, p. 20.

be pointed out as a model to the Anglican universities.[118] Pugin's teaching was certainly closer to what Anglican enthusiasts had in mind than the architectural courses instituted in 1841–2 by the new University College and King's College in London, which were wholly secular and practical in character; even the Anglican King's College appointed only a 'Professor of Construction' (the engineer-architect William Hosking), though this title later changed to 'Professor of the Principles and Practice of Architecture'.[119]

The hearty welcome given to the Oxford and Cambridge architectural societies thus drew on hopes that they might supply this long-felt want of direction. The architectural journalist W. H. Leeds greeted the Oxford Society as a 'good augury' for public taste; the *Civil Engineer and Architect's Journal* echoed him more than once, admitting in 1840 that 'it is to the clergy that we must look for the preservation of old edifices, and for the observance of good taste in the erection of new ones': a remarkably deferential statement for a lay professional magazine.[120] The *Art Union*, no less latitudinarian in character, declared that clerical instruction in Gothic was so urgently needed that both university societies deserved 'all the attention and assistance in our power to bestow'.[121] The antiquarian barrister J. H. Markland addressed his book on the reform of church monument design to the Oxford Society in the same year, in earnest of his belief that it was the best conduit for his ideas to those who could best put them into effect.[122] Even as the Cambridge Camden Society began firing off pamphlets and the first diocesan architectural societies began to take shape, the hope was expressed in some quarters that the university societies, admirable in themselves, were merely transitional phenomena before the university authorities at last adopted the subject.[123] Moreover, the early campaigns of the Ecclesiologists to reform new church architecture coincided in the late 1830s with the dismay of professional architects at the declining expenditure on the average church, and the dwindling opportunities it offered for architectural ambition. The *Civil Engineer and Architect's Journal* began its first number of the 1840s with this lament:

[118] See George Pace, 'Alfred Bartholomew: a Pioneer of Functional Gothic', *Architectural Review*, 92 (1942), pp. 99–102.

[119] Colvin, *Biographical Dictionary*.

[120] Leeds in *The Travellers' Club House*, by Charles Barry (London, 1839), pp. 8–9; *Civil Engineer and Architect's Journal*, 2 (1839), pp. iii, 226, 3 (1840), p. 132, 4 (1841), pp. 338–9.

[121] *Art Union*, 2 (1840), p. 40.

[122] J. H. Markland, *Remarks on the Sepulchral Memorials of Past and Present Times* (London, 1840), p. 5.

[123] E.g. by W. B. Sarsfield Taylor, *The Origin, Progress, and Present Condition of the Fine Arts in Great Britain and Ireland* (London, 1841), I, p. xviii.

Why does the Church appeal so powerfully to the beautiful monuments built by our ancestors ... if she herself thinks it beneath her to keep up the dignity of the estate she has inherited? Oh! how eloquently can her ministers dwell on the solemn thoughts inspired by the long-drawn aisles of our ancient cathedrals ...! But when it comes to the expenditure of the vast sums under their control, how totally do they neglect their favoured dogmas ... Empirics are employed, the men who can do the dirty work cheapest; nothing is allowed for architecture, nothing for the decorative arts...[124]

At this historical moment it was no longer enough just to choose Gothic to appear committed to religious architecture.

This huge capital of goodwill and expectation helps to explain the university societies' explosive numerical growth, and the volume of publications that even the less celebrated Oxford Society attained. Had the two indeed been merged into official university schools, it is likely that the Camdenians' combative extremism would never have reached such heights that many of their former friends inside and outside the ministry deserted them.[125] The *Civil Engineer and Architect's Journal*, so enthusiastic in 1840, was by 1842–3 already disgusted by the dogmatism and assumption of infallibility amongst many in the university and diocesan architectural societies alike; and it greeted the Camdenians' partial dissolution in 1845 over the Round Church restoration controversy with the satisfaction proper to the downfall of 'a *clique* of overgrown schoolboys'.[126]

The Ecclesiological 'boom' of the 1840s was thus long in preparation. It drew on a solid tradition of mostly uncontentious antiquarian concern for the buildings in the care of the clergy; indeed, antiquaries and clergy of the period often showed a truer respect for the whole range of ancient styles than was common in the brasher pronouncements of the 1840s, backed though they often were by so much greater archaeological knowledge. The parish clergy, urged on in many cases by their superiors, were more disposed to care for their church buildings since conceptions of their proper 'professional' roles were being transformed. Their financial security and high social standing further strengthened their hand against their churchwardens, and to some extent also against the emerging architectural profession, which in turn had yet to prove itself where Gothic church architecture was concerned. Even in the absence of any heartfelt concern for ancient churches as holy places or 'works of art', they remained symbolic of the Establishment's status as the national Church; once that status was restricted and redefined after the late 1820s, the Church became increasingly anxious to reconstitute these claims on

---

[124] *Civil Engineer and Architect's Journal*, 3 (1840), p. 1.
[125] See White, *The Cambridge Movement*, pp. 183ff.
[126] *Civil Engineer and Architect's Journal*, 5 (1842), pp. 399–408; 6 (1843), p. 51; 8 (1845), p. 71. For the Round Church controversy see Elliot Rose in *Victorian Studies*, 10 (1966), pp. 119–44.

the basis of a renewed emphasis on its ancient inheritance. The accusations of 'Popery' hurled at the Ecclesiologists in the 1840s showed how delicate this task was to be.

'Fond of Church Architecture' – the Establishment of the Society and a Short History of its Membership

GEOFFREY K. BRANDWOOD

Towards the end of 1839 John Mason Neale wrote some prophetic words in his diary about the new-born Cambridge Camden Society. 'If I am not very much mistaken,' he noted, 'that Society will tend to produce effects of which at present we have a very faint idea.'[1] In a short time, probably even shorter than Neale could have imagined, the prediction came true as the CCS achieved an influence of which undergraduate pressure groups can usually only dream. It had the good fortune to be founded by the right people, in the right place, at the right time. A combination of circumstances fuelled the success of the young Society. On a practical level, for example, there was easier travel to enable people to see the monuments they loved, and there were improvements and lower costs in publishing and postage. Crucially, the Society caught a mood of the time. The intellectual ground in which the Cambridge message would flourish had already been carefully and abundantly sown both in terms of churchmanship and a widespread interest in church architecture. The former is best demonstrated by the Oxford Movement with its emphasis on the 'sacramental, sacerdotal and Catholic',[2] and which so much appealed to the young men of the CCS. The fascination with antiquities and church architecture was deeply rooted as can be seen from Simon Bradley's work in chapter 2, and the CCS represented a rallying point which many would rush to. It is no coincidence that a similar, if less pugnacious society, was begun in Oxford at much the same time and local architectural societies were about to spring up in various counties. But, above all, the Society had gifted leaders who combined passion with effectiveness.

This is not the place to attempt a full-scale history of the Society as that has already been ably undertaken by James White in his 1962 book, and, more recently, Dale Adelmann has made an important contribution in discussing

---

[1] Lambeth Palace Library, MS 3107 (hereafter Neale, Diary), 26 Nov. 1839. I am most grateful to Chris Miele for drawing my attention to this diary. What occasioned Neale's comment was a threat to the fledgling Society from J. O. Halliwell (see below, p. 49).

[2] This phrase is from C. Brooks, 'Building the Rural Church', in *The Victorian Church*, ed. C. Brooks and A. Saint (Manchester, 1995), p. 65.

the early years of the Society and its role in promoting choral music.[3] Here the objective is to offer a detailed account of the beginnings of the Society using the results of fresh research, and to try and explain why it took so firm a root. The second part of the chapter examines the size and nature of the membership, drawing on material published in the Appendix.

As is well-known, the prime movers in founding the Society were two undergraduates, Benjamin Webb and J. M. Neale who enlisted the help of their tutor Archdeacon Thomas Thorp in their endeavours. Webb (1819–85) came from a comfortably-off London home – his father owned a wheelwright's business in Doctor's Commons – and he attended St Paul's School. As his diary and a memoir by his son make clear, he moved gradually away from an Evangelical position to take a serious interest in the 'higher' manifestations of Anglicanism before going up to Cambridge.[4] At the age of seventeen he 'Read *Oxford Tracts* for first time, and liked them much'.[5] In January 1838 he went 'to Mr Mortimer's Chapel in Gray's Inn Road, where [there] was a choral service & ornamented altar.'[6] Immediately before his first term at Cambridge in 1838 he 'Began to attend frequent services at S. Paul's, and to observe fasts.'[7] His interest in church architecture may have been kindled at this moment too when he made the acquaintance of the London antiquary, E. J. Carlos, and visited many City churches with him.[8] During his first vacation Webb saw much of Carlos ('whose talk very Romanizing') and later Carlos would become one of the first honorary members of the CCS.[9] Webb's circle of school friends included S. N. Stokes and G. R. Kingdon who would join him at Cambridge and who would play their part in the CCS. Two other Old Paulians known to Webb and who would become active in the CCS were already at Cambridge — A. S. Eddis and E. G. Griffith. It was from the latter that Webb took advice about studying under Thomas Thorp, Archdeacon of Bristol, Rector of Kemerton (Glos), and tutor at Trinity. Webb seems not to have met Thorp until he arrived in Cambridge but immediately 'found him charming.'[10]

3   J. F. White, *The Cambridge Movement: the Ecclesiologists and the Gothic Revival* (Cambridge, 1962); D. Adelmann, *The Contribution of the Cambridge Ecclesiologists to the Revival of Anglican Choral Worship 1832–62* (Aldershot, 1997).

4   Bodleian Library MS.Eng.misc.e.406 (hereafter 'Webb, Diary'); C. C. J. Webb, 'Benjamin Webb', *Church Quarterly Review* 75 (1913), pp. 332–4.

5   Webb, Diary, 16 Nov. 1837.

6   Webb, Diary, 28 Jan. 1838. He presumably liked what he experienced since he went again in March but 'Could not get into [it] for the Crowd.'

7   Webb, Diary, 18 Sep. 1838. Fasting is something he continued at Cambridge, sometimes making himself faint and ill as a result.

8   Webb, Diary, 18 Sep. 1838.

9   Webb, Diary, 12 Jan. 1839. Carlos appears with nine others in the first list of honorary members in 1840.

10   Webb, Diary, 12 Oct. 1838.

Apart from old friends, Webb made new ones and his diary entries in late 1838/early 1839 mention many who became early CCS members.[11] Among them was Neale (1818–66) who was to be Webb's neighbour at rooms in Bishop's Hostel, and the pair formed a deep personal friendship.[12] Neale also came from London but had an awesomely rigid family background – 'very Evangelical & very stiff', Webb called it, evidently basing his judgement on personal experience![13] His grandfather was a successful china manufacturer and his father a clergyman who died when Neale was only five. Mrs Neale moved John and his sisters to Shepperton where he was educated first by the local rector before being sent to boarding schools. In 1836 he went to Cambridge to prepare for University entrance under Dr James Challis, Plumian Professor of Astronomy, winning a scholarship and entering Trinity in the Michaelmas term. Adelmann convincingly suggests Neale's 'Evangelical upbringing wrought in him a seriousness, zeal and certitude about his religious convictions that was a permanent and unshakeable aspect of his very character.'[14] Both he and Webb were terrifically hard workers and their characters complemented one another. Adelmann quotes Neale's biographer, Eleanor Towle, when she said Webb was:

> a man of great critical ability, an iron will, and, together with a comprehensive grasp of great subjects, surprising patience in working out details. In many ways the friends were fitted to supplement each other. Neale's impetuosity was restrained by Webb's calmer judgment, and his rash conclusions corrected by the relentless force of logic.[15]

There is, of course, no inevitability that the CCS would be created where it was, when it was, and by whom it was. Admittedly Neale and E. J. Boyce had spent some of the long vacation of 1837 visiting churches.[16] They were then joined by others but that is just the sort of thing Romantically-inclined, antiquity-pursuing young men would do in the 1830s. There is no evidence of the fire and the passion that so characterised the CCS until the

---

[11] They include E. T. Codd, C. Colson, P. Freeman, H. Goodwin, G. T. P. Hough, E. R. Neville-Rolfe ('saw a good deal of him' – Diary 4 Feb. 1839), L. Poynder.

[12] One hesitates to quote his exact words – 'The intimacy with Neale became very intimate indeed' (Diary 10 May 1839) – for fear of late twentieth-century prurient misinterpretation but they are important in understanding the close bond between the two, their joint service to the CCS, and the way they produced so much work together.

[13] Webb, Diary, 9 Jan. 1841.

[14] Adelmann, op. cit., p. 12.

[15] Adelmann, op. cit., pp. 14–15 quoting Towle, *John Mason Neale D.D.: a Memoir* (1906), p. 33. Adelmann comments 'However romanticized this characterisation sounds, it would appear to be quite accurate', a view the present writer certainly supports.

[16] E. J. Boyce, *Memorial of the Cambridge Camden Society, Instituted May, 1839, and the Ecclesiological (late Cambridge Camden) Society, May, 1846* (London, 1888), p. 8.

spring of 1839. It was not until April of that year that Webb read Rickman, and it was February 1842 before he seems to have studied Pugin's *Contrasts*.[17] In fact, events might have taken a very different course. By March 1839 Webb and a number of the people who would create the CCS had a different project in mind. This was to found 'a High Church Club'. Neale joined the group and on 15 March the first meeting took place. The name of the group, the 'Ecclesialogical Society' [*sic*], was borrowed from the *British Critic* (according to Webb, who underlined the 'a'). A month later Webb read the first paper to the society on the Apostolic Fathers and it was agreed he would prepare another, as would Neale and Harvey Goodwin.

At the same time Webb 'Bought Chants and Incense' in London and a few days later was taking a trip out from Cambridge 'with [Charles] Colson to Cherry Hinton: and first critically examined the architecture' (it was the same day as he read Rickman). On 30 April, having been up at Cambridge for six months, he went to the Round Church in Cambridge for the *first* time (again with Colson) – even though this remarkable Norman church lies only 300 yards from the entrance to Trinity. Webb had by now been making models of fonts and it was when he showed these to Neale on 6 May that the latter confessed himself to be 'fond of Church Architecture'.[18] Events now began to gather pace for the next day 'Neale & [Webb] made plans for an architectural Society' and Neale introduced Webb to another player in the CCS story, E. J. Boyce. The following day Boyce, Colson and Mesac Thomas said they would join. Then, on 9 May Neale gave a small wine party for six others at which the 'Cambridge Camden Society' was born.[19] On this heady day Neale was made President and Webb Secretary and Treasurer. A 'Church Scheme' was drafted and sent off to the printers. Two days later Neale, Webb and Colson were off at Teversham church, examining the late 14th-century brass of William de Fulbourne which they brought back and mounted.

Meantime, the Ecclesialogical Society continued and there is no reason to suppose that the young enthusiasts had any particularly grand notions in

[17]   Webb, Diary, 13 Apr. 1839, 14 Feb. 1842. Interestingly it was Pugin who seems to have initiated dialogue with the CCS in late 1841 (Webb, Diary, 30 Nov. 1841).

[18]   Webb, Diary, 6 May 1839.

[19]   The others there were Thomas, Lewthwaite, Lingham, Boyce, Colson and Webb. On 11 May Charles, Codd, Howson and F. and W. Randolph joined. On 16 May Cole was elected (Webb, Diary, 9, 11, 16 May 1839). Details of these people appears in the Appendix. Oddly, not all of them are noted as founders in Boyce's *Memorial*. Boyce's records or memory may have been at fault but nonetheless I have followed his *Memorial* in the Appendix in indicating the founders. Boyce forms an interesting case. Despite his close involvement with the founding of the Society, he soon disappeared from the centre of things and was no longer a member in 1846. Like the Rev. G. R. Boissier, the Cambridge ecclesiological pioneer, before him, perhaps Boyce became immersed (or submerged) in his parochial responsibilities.

mind for their architectural club. But then a critical event took place. A week or so after the CCS was set up, J. O. Halliwell of Jesus College (later a great Shakespearian scholar) proposed to found a rival society to be called the Fullerian, after Thomas Fuller (1608–61), the seventeenth-century divine and historian of Cambridge University. Nearly half a century later, Boyce in his *Memorial of the Cambridge Camden Society* claimed that the opposition stemmed from 'the black-balling of one or two men who had been proposed for membership.'[20] No other reason for Halliwell's action is known but, although Boyce's statements sometimes need taking with a little caution, his explanation seems entirely plausible. At any rate, the resistance seems to have galvanised the proto-ecclesiologists into action and they determined upon a grander society that would see off the opposition. So, along went Neale, Webb and Boyce one late May evening to see their tutor, Thomas Thorp, carrying the brass of William de Fulbourne with them.[21] According to Boyce this was after 10 o'clock in the evening and 'They entreated him to come to the rescue, and they did not leave him until he had promised to call forthwith a Public Meeting.' Webb's version, written in his diary just after the event, is that the three of them went along to Thorp to ask him to be their President and that, far from being harassed into acceptance, 'he joyfully assented.'

No truly 'Public Meeting' seems to have taken place before the end of May, and Boyce presumably recollected an event in Neale's rooms where the CCS committee met and 'over 30 [were] present'.[22] The next day Webb led a large party brass rubbing in Trinity College chapel. Before the summer vacation various other meetings and discussions took place, the church scheme was revised, and adjustments made to the committee but it seems unlikely that the CCS could be thought of as a well-organised, fighting machine until the autumn of 1839. These foundations were laid after everyone returned to Cambridge from the Summer vacation. Webb noted the first 'general meeting of CCS' in Thorp's rooms in his diary entry for 20 October and more meetings and discussions followed on. The committee was organised and it was determined that the Chairman should be W. N. Griffin until Neale had taken his degree.[23] The object of the Society was stated quite simply, according to its 1839 'laws', as 'the study of Gothic Architecture, and of Ecclesiastical Antiquities, and the restoration of mutilated Architectural remains'.[24] It attached great store to winning distinguished persons to its ranks

[20] Boyce, *Memorial*, p. 9.
[21] The date is not absolutely clear. Webb's Diary records the meeting in an entry dated 20 May.
[22] Webb, Diary, 24 May 1839.
[23] Webb, Diary, 29 Oct. 1839.
[24] Boyce, *Memorial*, p. 35. This was broadened in the new laws of 1846 which encapsulated the widened aims of the Society: 'to promote the study of Christian Art and Antiquities, more especially in whatever relates to the architecture,

and one of the first moves was the election of Professor Whewell as a vice-president. He was followed later by the eminent Professor Robert Willis. In courting prominent figures within the University, it is quite likely that Thorp may have played his part as a more mature figure who was part of the University establishment. The Society was *now* ready to go public and on 9 November the first such public meeting took place at the Philosophical Rooms. Papers were read on Adel church, Yorkshire by W. H. Lewthwaite and on St Peter, Cambridge by J. J. Smith. Although there was subsequent abortive discussion on the name, it was at this meeting that the title of the Cambridge Camden Society was fixed – it being thought particularly appropriate since this was the anniversary of the great antiquary's death.[25]

The scene was now set for the rise of the CCS, and the Ecclesialogical Society was a casualty. It was dissolved in December and, although there were proposals for 'a new & more select & practical Society', it never got off the ground and a final meeting was held in March 1840 to divide up the group's books.[26] The activists in the CCS had quite enough on their plates. Neale and Webb put tremendous energy into the Society and Webb was soon 'Thoroughly overwhelmed with CCS work', a complaint he would reiterate again and again. The atmosphere in which they operated must have been immensely stimulating to these able young men in a hurry. The Society faced opposition and controversy, particularly over 'Romanising', which kept it on its mettle. Halliwell's threat to the original CCS had already forged it into a stronger instrument. Then, suddenly, even he came round and joined. But this was ever so briefly since he resigned a month later after an acrimonious dispute. This seems to have stemmed from criticism by Thorp after Halliwell's paper to the CCS on the Round Church. He penned 'an offensive letter to Thorp' and described the Society as 'puerile'.[27]

---

arrangement and decoration, of churches; the recognition of correct principles and taste in the erection of new churches; and the restoration of ancient ecclesiastical remains.' (*Ecclesiologist*, 5 (1846), 256).

[25]   Webb, Diary, 9 Nov. 1839. There was one other attempt to change the name. Strangely it came from none other than Thorp who advocated a change to Ecclesialogical 'and as a vignette to all our engravings to have the head of Spelman with his work *De reparandis Ecclesiis*' (Neale Diary, 24 Nov. 1839). This was Sir Henry Spelman (1564?–1623), the historian and antiquary, who had been at Trinity. Webb recorded this too and seemed to imply that both the Spelman and Ecclesialogical names were intended (Webb, Diary, 24 Nov. 1839).

[26]   Webb, Diary, 3, 9 Dec. 1839, 11 Mar. 1841.

[27]   The paper 'On the Church of the Holy Sepulchre, Cambridge' was one of four read on 23 Nov. 1839. Halliwell also attacked the CCS in the *Cambridge Chronicle* but was himself 'cut up' in the *Gentleman's Magazine* (Webb, Diary, 27 Nov, 2 Dec. 1839). The 'puerile' epithet (actually spelled 'peurile') is quoted in Neale, Diary, 26 Nov. 1839.

Nonetheless it flourished. By mid-December 1839 it boasted 118 members (as opposed to 107 in the Oxford equivalent)[28] and was clearly aiming as high and as wide as possible.[29] It was beginning to engage in the practical business of restoration as described by Chris Miele in Chapter 12 and was receiving praise from the *Gentleman's Magazine*.[30] The volume of work was such that an assistant secretary, a Mr Canham, was employed to help the three hon. secretaries, Webb, Colson and E. T. Codd.[31] Also it was actively developing a very prestigious base of supporters. Neale noted in December 1839 that the Bishops of Gloucester & Bristol (Thorp's diocesan), Nova Scotia, and Ely had joined the cause. By the time of the publication of the first Society *Report* in July 1840, it had acquired the Archbishop of Canterbury and the Cambridge University Chancellor for patrons, five bishops, three masters of colleges and the Dean of Peterborough for vice-patrons.[32] The distinguished honorary members it lined up in the first year included the sculptor Sir Francis Chantrey, the antiquary E. J. Carlos, Sir S. R. Maitland (Librarian to the Archbishop of Canterbury), and, significantly, a number of architects since the Society needed to work with this profession just as much as the clergy.[33] Pugin was certainly considered but, in an unusual display of discretion, the Society rejected him; as Neale confided to his diary, 'we are already too much accused of Popery to render so violent a man a desirable Honorary Member.'[34]

The genius of the CCS lay in providing something for anybody with the faintest interest in churches. It had much to offer – meetings to go to, learned papers to hear, visits to local churches, a stream of publications to read, and the knowledge that members were part of a pioneering organisation

---

[28] Neale, Diary, 10 Dec. 1839.

[29] Membership costs, from January 1841, stood at 10s. entry fee and 10s. a term for ten terms. Members could 'compound for all future subscriptions, by one payment of Five Guineas' (notice at the back of the 1840 *Report*). The latter was a good deal and this explains why just over half the members are indicated as life members at the end of the 1840s.

[30] It 'speaks lauditorily of the CCS' (Webb, Diary, 4 Jan. 1840). See also note 27.

[31] Webb, Diary, 24 Feb. 1840. On 25 Jan. 1841 Webb describes him as 'an employé of CCS'.

[32] The following year the title 'vice-patrons' was dropped in favour of patrons, although the two 'patrons' in 1840 still headed the list but reverentially slightly separated from the others. The Archbishop gave his assent to patronage in May 1840 (Webb, Diary, 26 May 1840).

[33] The architects were George Basevi junior, C. R. Cockerell, Thomas Rickman and Anthony Salvin. Interestingly, that important Gothic pioneer, L. N. Cottingham, was never an honorary or an ordinary member. The Rev. G. R. Boissier, a pioneer of ecclesiology, and Sir Thomas Phillipps, 'the greatest bibliomaniac of the day' (Neale, Diary, 21 Nov. 1839) were also honorary members.

[34] 5 Dec. 1839.

helping to improve the Established Church. In the first five months of 1840, six meetings were held at which thirteen papers were given on subjects ranging from bells, crypts, brasses, the Society's church schemes, to individual churches or groups of churches. These gatherings were also opportunities to examine drawings and other gifts to the Society, to comment on designs for new churches and restorations, and to hear about the progress of the Society generally. For the energetic, 'Camden Field Days' were organised to churches in and around Cambridgeshire (the one that Webb joined to Huntingdonshire in November 1840 did not get him back home till 11.30 p.m.). There was also a constant round of correspondence as the CCS became a focal point for those who carried out church work in the 'correct' manner. But the greatest achievement of the CCS was a prodigious publication record. If the meetings and occasional days out were aimed at the Cambridge membership, it was the printed word that really disseminated the Society's message. 1839 saw the Church Schemes (issued free to members, 6s. 6d. a hundred to non-members) which showed church visitors what to look for and record. The Society came to believe that in these 'our great and original strength may be considered to lie.'[35] Visitors were further aided by *A Few Hints on the Practical Study of Ecclesiastical Antiquities for the Use of the Cambridge Camden Society* (attributed to Neale and J. F. Russell). By the time the first *Report* was published in 1840 the *Hints*, priced at 1s. 6d., were in a second edition and the first two parts of *Illustrations of Monumental Brasses* were available at prices varying from 3s. to subscribing members to 5s. for non-subscribing non-members.

1841 was an *annus mirabilis* for the Society. Not only did a record number of members join (see figure 1) but there was an abundant and diverse programme of publication. The first part of *Transactions* came out at 5s. 6d., offering the better-off and serious-minded the papers which had been read to the Society in 1839–41. Again for the studious there was Webb's *An Argument for the Greek Origin of the Monogram IHS* which, 'considering the nature of the subject ... has had a very good sale,' it was reported next year.[36] For anyone considering getting rid of box-pews, a reading of Neale's *History of Pews* would provide ample persuasion.[37] At the end of the year the Society's polemical journal, *The Ecclesiologist*, was born to keep the growing numbers of non-Cambridge members in touch with the Society's activities, although it

[35] *Report* (1841), p. 35, by which time they had reached the seventh edition and the number of particulars increased from the original 58 to 260. The Oxford Architectural Society had been sent 1,000 copies of the seventh edition.

[36] *Report* (1842), p. 22; 300 had been sold by the end of July 1841 according to Webb (Diary, 30 Jul. 1841).

[37] It went into second and third editions with a supplement in 1842 and 1843 and the spelling changed to 'pues'.

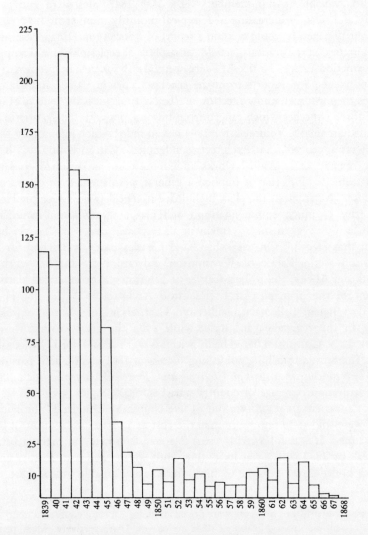

Figure 1: Numbers joining the Society annually, showing the much active period, with its peak in 1841, and the dramatic fall-off after 1845. The information is presented graphically, partly because this shows so clearly the contrast in the two phases which appear, and partly to avoid the spurious accuracy inherent in giving precise numbers. Whilst exact membership numbers at can be stated at certain points in time (as presented in the table in this article), it is not possible to be so precise about every individual's joining date. For example, I have taken the 1839 total as the 118 given in Neale's diary entry of 10 Dec., but a few (like J. O. Halliwell) may have joined and left before this, and a few may have joined in the last three weeks of the year. In 1846-7 it is not always possible to say which of the two years saw certain members' elections (in this case I have split the numbers equally between the two years). If any fine tuning was possible it would make no appreciable difference to the broad picture.

was also available to non-members.[38] By May 1842 sales were said to be 'rapidly and steadily increasing'.[39] A typical monthly number in 1842 ran to about thirty pages. It would contain a report of a Society meeting, criticism of new churches or restorations, articles on aspects of ecclesiology, and snippets of information under 'Notices'. There were also book reviews, letters from correspondents, and reports from the sister societies in Exeter and Oxford. Perhaps the most well-known feature of *The Ecclesiologist* is its reviews of new and restored churches which ranged from fulsome praise to the excoriation of benighted architects. Volume 3 for 1844 has an index which infamously listed 'Architects approved' and 'Architects condemned'. Categorisation was based on the reviews of individual works and it must not be assumed, as James White seems to do,[40] that it implied a general, permanent state of grace or otherwise. Nonetheless, the elect included Butterfield (whose Coalpit Heath 'is worthy of much commendation') and Carpenter (whose Birmingham church 'is a very great improvement in all respects upon what has yet been seen in that place').[41] On the other hand Charles Barry was slated for his restoration at the Palace of Westminster, Edward Blore for his work at Westminster Abbey, and Robert Carver of Taunton was pronounced 'entirely ignorant of the principles of Ecclesiastical Architecture.'[42] Equally H. E. Kennedy's 'Italian' bellcote at Llanllechyd, Caernarvonshire, 'comes of [his] ... dealing in the revived-pagan' style, while even the great Gothic Revival pioneer, L. N. Cottingam, fared badly with his work at Hereford Cathedral.[43]

The most astonishing publishing success of 1841 was the first part of *A Few Words to Churchwardens on Churches and Church Ornaments* which aimed at the saturation coverage of country parishes. 5,000 copies were sold in six weeks – sufficient to reach two out of five churches in England.[44] Individual copies were sold at 3d., no more than the cost of a better quality pint of beer at the time.[45] It was followed by part 2 aimed at 'town and manufacturing parishes'. By 1842 part 1 was in its thirteenth edition and part 2 in its sixth, while a boiled-down version of both tracts was available 'on a sheet, for

---

[38] The journal was not included in the membership fees. There were twelve parts a year; the first fifteen numbers were priced at 4d. (or 8d. for a double number) and then went up from November 1842 to 6d. or 1s. respectively. Most people probably took out a subscription – 5s. a year – payable to T. Stevenson, the Cambridge publisher.

[39] *Report* (1842), p. 23.

[40] White, *op. cit.* [note 3], pp. 124–5.

[41] *Ecclesiologist* 3 (1844), p. 113. The other architects in the 'approved' category were J. M. Allen, J. M. Derick, B. Ferrey, J. P. Harrison, J. Hayward, C. Kirk and E. Sharpe.

[42] *Ibid.*, pp. 44, 99, 158.

[43] *Ibid.*, pp. 86, 113.

[44] *Report* (1841), p.85.

[45] Bulk supplies could be had at 5s. for 25, 10s. for 80, or 10s. for 100.

distribution, or suspension in Vestry-rooms.' There was no escape for workmen either since the Society brought out a sheet proffering advice to those engaged on restoring a church and another to those who happened to be building one. No doubt many an earnest incumbent thrust these sheets into the hands of builders in an attempt to secure the kind of reverential behaviour and sense of sacred purpose that was fondly thought to have been in the minds of medieval masons. Thus the Society catered for a readership from the university professor to the journeyman builder. The stream of publications was kept up until the Society moved from Cambridge and this success reflects the fact that it was supplying avid readers with what they wanted – again proof that the intellectual climate was ripe for the work of the Society.

A key, early influence of the Society was in its successful export of ecclesiology beyond British shores. If ecclesiology could be turned into a science at home, then it was natural to believe that its laws could apply equally abroad. Of course, allowance had to be made for local conditions – climate, materials, labour and so on – but it seemed perfectly reasonable to sit in Cambridge and work out what needed to be done. The very first article in *The Ecclesiologist*, after the opening 'Address' explains the Society's role in advising on church design in New Zealand. In 1845 Benjamin Webb read and published an important paper 'On pointed Architecture as adapted to Tropical Climates'[46] and in 1847 *The Ecclesiologist* published the first of a long-running series of articles on church architecture in the colonies. Practical assistance was given to ensure that correct models were used; for instance, the designs of St John the Baptist, Cookham Dean, Berks, went off to Tasmania and those of St Paul, Brighton, to the United States.

The Society was mounting a kind of military campaign. As such it needed a high degree of practical organisation. We have seen how the Society took on paid secretarial help in the form of Mr Canham, while to get its message out to the wider world it relied on a sophisticated distribution system. At the back of the 1840 *Report* is a list of 37 agents covering the British Isles from whom publications might be obtained. By 1841 there were 36 and the list was headed by three publishers – T. Stevenson in Cambridge, J. G. F. & J. Rivington in London, and the famous Oxford publisher, J. H. Parker. These three firms were the joint publishers of *The Ecclesiologist* (printer Metcalfe & Palmer of Cambridge) and they evidently handled the main distribution of material. In 1846 there were 84 agents plus those in London and Cambridge who could supply Society literature. When publishing tailed off markedly from 1846, the great period of Camdenian proselytising was over and the initiative was being taken over by the new county-based societies, as Chris Miele comments (see chapter 12). But by then the Society had done such a successful job that no-one could have an excuse

---

[46]   In the Society's *Transactions* 3 (1845), pp. 199–218.

for having missed the Camdenian message.[47]

The Size of the Society and its Changing Structure

Anyone who was connected with the Church of England and its church-building activities and who failed to notice the CCS must have led a very isolated existence. Awareness was unavoidable but the reactions varied greatly. In *The Times* readers could find praise for *A Few Words to Churchwardens* while the *Gentleman's Magazine* and the *British Critic* also gave the CCS support. Within two years of its creation the Society had the patronage of the two primates of England and Ireland and twelve other bishops. Boyce proudly calculated that in 1843 the number of bishops had risen to sixteen, and that there were 31 peers and M.P.s, seven deans and diocesan chancellors and 21 archdeacons and rural deans.[48] Not all of these luminaries liked what they found but controversy is the stuff of which publicity is made. By 1842 the Evangelical Bishop of Winchester, Charles Sumner, had withdrawn his patronage and preached against the CCS.[49] He was followed by others, notably Henry Philpotts of Exeter in 1844 whose high-profile secession during the height of the Exeter Diocese surplice controversy was plastered over practically every newspaper in the country. On a more positive and practical level, in 1842 the Society successfully petitioned the Incorporated Church Building Society to amend its *Suggestions and Instructions* to would-be church-builders and restorers. Furthermore, although the Camdenian presence was naturally strong around Cambridge, it was well spread over the country as the mapping of incumbent members of the Society in figure 2 shows (overleaf).

As with any successful pressure group, the influence of the CCS was out of all proportion to its numerical size. At no time did the membership exceed 1,000. The Society was not shy of showing itself in a favourable light but the largest membership it was ever able to claim was on 13 February 1845 when Webb announced to the 41st meeting that 'the Society numbered nearer 900 than 800 members'.[50] The table on p. 58 records the size of the Society's

[47] An inventory of Society publications is given in White, *op. cit.*, pp. 237–42.
[48] Boyce, *op. cit.*, p. 10.
[49] Webb, Diary, 6 Mar. 1842.
[50] Webb's statement is perfectly trustworthy. Given that there are known to have been 796 members in mid-1844 and that *The Ecclesiologist* lists 84 people joining between the 1844 list and up to and including 13 Feb. 1845, this gives a maximum of 878 (given that the Bishops of Exeter and Lincoln had resigned). This figure would be reduced somewhat by an unknown but fairly small number of deaths and resignations (most resignations did not occur until later in 1845; in all 121 seceded that year). By comparison, this was one third more than the venerable Society of Antiquaries. This body had 656 members in 1845 according to its printed membership list. In 1840 it had 694. The subsequent fall was due to efforts to weed out fellows who failed to pay their subscriptions.

Figure 2: A Camdenian geography in 1845. The map shows the location of incumbents who were members of the CCS in that year. Curates have not been included since they would be less able to exercise practical influence on church building and arrangements. There is, not surprisingly, a cluster around Cambridge, and also London where it is explained by the concentration of population and churches, and the greater opportunities for advanced churchmanship. The dotted area in south central England represents the Diocese of Oxford where Cambridge men were less likely to gain livings than their Oxford counterparts. There is a complete lack of Camdenian incumbents in Wales, largely because Welshmen gravitated to Oxford rather than Cambridge.

membership at the various points when it can be accurately gauged. It is fortunate that printed membership lists were issued with some regularity and that most, though not quite all, new members were listed in the pages of *The Ecclesiologist* after it began publication in late 1841.

Numbers of members in the Cambridge Camden and Ecclesiological Societies

Date	Patrons	Hon. members	Others	Total	Source
[Early] May 1839				8*	*Report* (1840), 13
'Founders'				39#	Boyce, *Memorial*, 39–40
Dec. 1839				118	*Ibid.;* Neale, Diary, 10 Dec. 1839
Mid-1840	12	10	169	191	*Report* (1840)
End 1840	13	13	*c.*223	*c.*249	*Ibid.,* supplement
Mid-1841	20	14	262	296	*Report* (1841)
Mid-1842	22	13	453	488	*Report* (1842)
Mid-1843	25	15	640	680	*Report* (1843)
Mid-1844	28	14	754	796	*Report* (1844)
13.2.1845				>850	*See* fn. 50
Mid-1846	13	12	667	692	*Report* (1845–6)
Mid-1849	13	14	586	612	*Report* (1848–9)
Mid-1853	12	15	540	567	*Report* (1853–4)
Late 1856	17	15	475	507	*Report* (1854–6)
Mid-1863	29	19	370	418	*Report* (1863–4)

The *Reports* may be found at the British Library (class mark Ac. 5625/18, lacking 1853–4), Cambridge University Library (Cam.c.500.9–10, lacking 1854–6 and 1863–4), and Lambeth Palace Library (1841–3 only under H5194). Boyce's *Memorial* is available in all these libraries.

NOTES:

* Or 7 if one counts those who attended Neale's wine-party mentioned in Webb's diary entry for 9 May.

This is calculated from the first membership list totalling 118 names which asterisks 'those who joined the C.C.S. *immediately* upon its institution, at the Meeting in May, 1839.' White, *op. cit.,* 41 adds the number up one short, at 38. This first membership list is now only known in its reprinted form in Boyce's *Memorial*; Neale obviously totted up the total for his diary entry on 10 Dec.

The rather pedantic use of the 'c.' is because, for ordinary members, the supplement to the 1840 *Report* lists 54 members elected in the Michaelmas term. Since five members appearing in the main 1840 list do not reappear in the one for 1841, it is possible some of them may have left the Society before the end of 1840.

James White, *op. cit.,* 242 lists *Reports* for 1857, 1858 and 1859. They may well contain printed membership lists for these years. Unfortunately, I have not traced copies.

From the outset accusations against the CCS of Romanising tendencies were legion and, judged from an Evangelical perspective in the 1840s, this was perfectly justified. Its liturgical position and the detail of the related controversies are explored in more depth by the present writer in Chapter 4. Matters reached a climax following the Round Church controversy, the attacks from the prominent Evangelical Francis Close of Cheltenham, and the withdrawal of the patronage of the Bishops of Exeter and Lincoln. The Committee went so far as to suggest the dissolution of the Society, although whether this was really what it wished is debatable. The ensuing ballot of members produced 271 votes against dissolution and 109 in favour. Everything came to a head at the stormy Sixth Anniversary Meeting on 8 May 1845 which ensured that the Society would carry on. The result was that it moved its base from Cambridge to London and, being still run by the same people, was outwardly little changed.[51] Admittedly the name of the Society was altered to the 'Ecclesiological late Cambridge Camden Society', some 121 members seceded and, for a time *The Ecclesiologist* was produced (officially) independently of the Society, but the causes to be fought remained much the same.

But in terms of its membership structure the Society became a very different body after 1845. As figure 3 shows, it was dominated by Cambridge men until 1845 whereas afterwards new recruits from Oxford were the more numerous. But most dramatic was the fall-off in numbers of people joining as shown in plate 17. From 1847 fewer than 20 people joined each year and often the number was a miserable half dozen or so. The Society also saw a major transformation in its patronage. The young CCS had gone to great lengths to secure episcopal patrons but by the middle of 1846 all the English bishops had withdrawn, shrewdly distancing themselves from the controversial group. For nearly ten years afterwards the Society had only Scottish, Welsh and overseas bishops as episcopal patrons.[52] A final significant change was that the profession of the later recruits was vastly different from the CCS years. In its early days the Society appealed particularly to the clergy (or those who later joined the Church). In the 1839–45 period under 5% of the members were architects or artists; during the remaining years of the Society almost one third (76 people) of all new recruits fell into these categories. Although its numbers dwindled and the passion of the early years had mellowed, the Society was still considered significant by architects and ecclesiastical artists. They regularly brought along drawings to meetings and the attendance lists at Anniversary Meetings include some of the greatest names in the Gothic Revival. Among those gathered for the 23rd such meeting, which coincided

51 Committee members who provided continuity from 1844 to 1846 were Webb and F. A. Paley (as secretaries), A. J. B. Hope (elevated from the committee to Chairman in 1845), P. Freeman and H. Goodwin (appointed auditors in 1845, formerly Chairman and Treasurer respectively), F. W. Witts and J. S. Forbes. The new faces on the 1845–6 committee were all old stagers in the Society, notably Neale who became an hon. secretary.
52 See Appendix. Also Lord Lyndhurst, High Steward of Cambridge University, remained a loyal patron.

with the International Exhibition, were Barraud, Burges, Ferrey, Lavers, Prichard, Scott, Skidmore, Slater, Street, S. S. and W. M. Teulon, White and M. D. Wyatt.

Figure 3: The educational origins of Society members up to 1845 and after. The columns record total numbers in the two periods and the dominance of Cambridge graduates in the earlier period (and within it the dominance of men from Trinity and St John's).

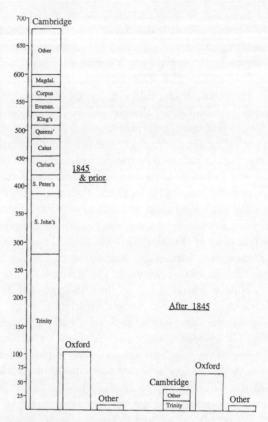

The Later Years

1845 closed one chapter in the Society's history. It had been in existence for six eventful and successful years, but there were many more years of life left as it continued with Neale and Webb as secretaries and with A. J. B. Hope as the vigorous chairman. Hope's contribution to the Society is discussed in detail by Chris Brooks in Chapter 6. He became President in 1859 in succession to Archdeacon Thorp and at the same time Neale stood down as joint honorary secretary leaving Webb to carry on alone. From 1859 the Rev. William Scott of Christ Church, Hoxton, took over as chairman. 'In its old age, the Society continued to function smoothly though quietly,' noted James White.[53] Publications were much fewer in number in the 1850s. There was the second series of *Instrumenta Ecclesiastica* in 1856 and the Society gave its 'sanction' to

[53] White, *op. cit.*, p. 221.

Neale and Helmore's *Hymnal Noted* but the main publishing outlet was *The Ecclesiologist*. In the 1850s it dealt with an ever wider variety of subjects and paid particular attention to music. In the '60s the sole publication apart from *The Ecclesiologist*, was the *Report* for 1864. Committee meetings continued to be held regularly and the chief burden of business was the examination of architects' designs. There was also a musical sub-committee until 1862. For the general membership, it seems that, apart from the publications, the only opportunity to engage with the Society was the annual anniversary meetings. Here they could hear about its fortunes and the state of a huge range of ecclesiological matters. The last real triumph was the Medieval Court it organised for the vast 1862 International Exhibition, having taken over the mantle Pugin had worn in 1851 for the Great Exhibition. William Burges and William Slater were charged with the arrangements and they packed a vast array of ecclesiological art into the fifty foot square area – work by Street, Burges, Teulon, White, Preedy, Skidmore, Earp and others for whom the glorious achievements of a long-lost age were still the appropriate mode of expression in industrialised Victorian England.[54]

Although the depth and range of items in *The Ecclesiologist* maintained a good standard and the committee felt able 'to record the general prosperity of the Society' at the 21st anniversary meeting in 1860, by this time the Society was in decline. By 1864 its membership had halved from the peak in 1845, and, as discussed earlier, recruitment was negligible.[55] By 1868 the condition was terminal. Webb was still shouldering most of the workload after nearly thirty years and no doubt felt his energies might be better channelled into his highly successful ministry at St Andrew, Wells Street. Hence *The Ecclesiologist* (no doubt in the voice of Webb) spoke of 'the growing pre-occupations of those whose pens have for so long chiefly kept it alive.'[56] The journal therefore ceased publication with its 139th number in December 1868. Putting on a brave face, it declared 'we do not say that the Ecclesiological Society is to be dissolved'. Yet without *The Ecclesiologist* all life ebbed out of the Society. However, a great many of the former members were still alive. As they thought about the Anglican Church in their elderly years, they could (and probably did) say they had been part of a Society that had made an extraordinary contribution to transforming the entire appearance of churches and the worship that took place within them.

Acknowledgements:
I am most grateful to Rosemary Hill, Chris Miele, and Teresa Sladen for reading the draft of the chapter and making many helpful suggestions for its improvement.

---

[54] For details see *Ecclesiologist* 23 (1862), pp. 34, 73–5, 168–72, 204.
[55] This led to a situation whereby life members became a gradually increasing proportion of the total, rising from 48% in 1848 to 52% by 1864.
[56] *Ecclesiologist* 29 (1868), p. 315

'Mummeries of a Popish Character' – the Camdenians and Early Victorian Worship

GEOFFREY K. BRANDWOOD

In 1850, looking back over the previous decade, ecclesiologists could take justifiable pride in their achievements. Interest in their subject had grown by leaps and bounds and they could be especially pleased that so many features of their programme had become, in so short a time, a generally-accepted part of Anglican church building or restoration schemes. But, beyond the physical transformation, such changes were signs of important shifts in attitudes to, and methods of, conducting worship. Change, however, was not the monopoly of Tractarians and Camdenians since the Evangelical movement had been encouraging greater devotion for decades. In fact, contrary to the oft-promoted view of decay and neglect, the Evangelical Bishop of Worcester, Henry Pepys, noted as follows in a charge of 1844:

> In reviewing the history of our church since the Reformation it is hardly possible to note a time when its prosperity and usefulness was more remarkable than the period immediately preceding the publication of the *Oxford Tracts*. An increased degree of zeal, a more entire devotion to their sacred functions, was manifest among the clergy.[1]

It was this Evangelical advance that must have been in the mind of Tractarian-to-be, John Keble, when he remarked in 1828 on 'the amazing rate at which Puritanism seems to be getting on all over the kingdom.'[2] But by about 1840 the initiative had been wrested by a new breed of men under the spell of the Oxford Movement and who included the dynamic leaders of the CCS. This chapter begins by looking at some aspects of the way early nineteenth-century churches were used. It moves on to examine the forces

[1]   A charge to ordinands quoted in *The Times*, 25 Dec. 1844. The bishop, who went on to stress the great harmony within the Church in this earlier time may have been gilding his particular lily somewhat for his own purposes. The end of 1844 was a time of great strife in the Church over innovations, notably the introduction of the weekly offertory and preaching in the surplice, with which he had no sympathy.

[2]   Quoted in H. E. Hopkins, *Charles Simeon of Cambridge* (London, 1977), p. 117. There is a nice irony in Keble's use of the derogatory 'Puritanism' since the Tractarians would soon be branded with the opposite polarity.

behind the new trends, where the CCS stood in the process, and what changes were introduced. It concentrates on the early Victorian years, roughly up to 1850 (which also include the heyday of the CCS) and the storm over 'Papal Aggression'. Judged at a century-and-a-half's remove, and, indeed, against widespread custom and practice in the late nineteenth century, the changes in the 1840s were astonishingly modest in themselves, but they stirred up furious opposition and deep-seated passions. In inflaming these the CCS certainly played its part.

Using the Pre-Ecclesiological Church

The awful spiritual state of the late Georgian Church and the shocking condition of its buildings are to a large extent, an early Victorian construct, fostered by many groups and individuals – not least by Pugin and the ecclesiologists. Although there were undoubtedly plenty of cases of abysmal neglect which could be held up as icons of profanity, modern research has tended to show that the majority of late Georgian churches were probably kept in what we might regard as a reasonable state of repair.[3] They were mostly weather-tight and the internal arrangements worked in terms of the needs and customs of the day. However, the young activists of around 1840 felt otherwise and did an immensely good job in selling their message. As for the services themselves, 'it would appear,' to quote Nigel Yates, 'that most Anglican services were conducted with decency but little outward ceremonial.'[4] 'Plain, simple, and impressive' is how one opponent of change described the services he was used to.[5] 'Lack of devotional spirit' and 'idleness and apathy' are words that occurred to men of the new school[6] (see plates 17 & 18).

Much is known about the physical arrangements of pre-Victorian churches from old plans, drawings, photographs and quite a number of surviving examples. Rather less is clear about the services that took place within them, but there is enough to show how they offended the serious 'new

---

[3] My own work on Leicestershire supports this for the period 1790–1840. Some 10 to 15% of churches might be described as being in 'bad' condition (requiring substantial repairs), and half as being in 'good' condition (needing no or very minor work): full details are published in *Archaeol. J.* 144 (1987), pp. 384–91.

[4] W. N. Yates, *Buildings, Faith and Worship, the Liturgical Arrangement of Anglican Churches 1600–1900* (Oxford, 1991), p. 63.

[5] So said 'Amicus Ecclesiae' in a letter to *The Times*, 20 Nov. 1844 and noted that such a description could be applied to three out of four of the Kensington churches or chapels. At the fourth, Holy Trinity, Brompton, 'the congregation have inflicted on them ... mummeries of a Popish character'.

[6] First phrase is taken from C. J. Abbey & J. H. Overton's *The English Church in the Eighteenth Century* (2nd ed. London, 1887), p. 450, a work which did not have much good to say about Georgian worship. The second comes from *Ecclesiologist* 13 (1852), p. 53.

men' – the Tractarians and Camdenians – of the 1830s and '40s. First, attention to celebrating holy communion fell far short of the new Victorian ideal. About three-quarters of parishes had quarterly celebrations (or less) – in other words, barely meeting the thrice-a-year minimum enjoined upon each parishioner by the Prayer Book.[7] More regular celebrations usually only took place in the larger centres of population. Ecclesiological caricatures often show the communion table piled up with sundry clutter in desecration of its holy purpose. The focus of worship on most Sundays lay, therefore, not in the sanctuary, but at the three-decker pulpit. This had first been devised in the early seventeenth century, had become standard in the eighteenth and early nineteenth centuries, with the last ones being installed in the early 1840s. On non-Communion days the minister conducted the whole service from the reading desk (the middle tier) except when he ascended the top stage, or pulpit proper, for the sermon. The usual tradition was to preach in the black gown rather than the surplice, although there were places where the surplice was used. The lowest stage was occupied by the parish clerk who played an important role in the services. Before the Reformation he was in minor orders and acted as assistant to the priest but, in the nineteenth century, the clerk was a paid lay person who was appointed in a variety of ways. This might be by the minister, via hereditary office, or, in some places a pauper might be chosen in order to relieve the parish of his maintenance. Sometimes a gentleman might become the parish clerk and then appoint a deputy in his stead. The clerk had a number of duties. He led the responses, announced notices and briefs, read over the psalm before it was sung and also undertook menial jobs round the church. Perhaps few aspects of the early nineteenth-century Church are riper for re-evaluation than the role of the much-maligned clerk, held up as illiterate, musically incompetent, and too self-important. His office was often a casualty when change was brought in. At St John, Torquay, after the Rev. W. G. Parks Smith began to advance the conduct of services in 1844 'the reading desk was pulled down, a "lectern" substituted, the clerk dismissed, and a corps of clergymen appointed in his stead'.[8] Sedilia were provided for them and they divided the prayers and readings between themselves.

Services were long with morning prayer usually being something in excess of an hour and a half, and the afternoon or evening service rather less. Preaching and catechizing took up about 45 minutes during both services,[9] though there are stories of popular preachers being encouraged by their

[7]   Of which Easter was an obligatory occasion. The other times were taken to be Christmas and Whitsun, and many churches also held a communion service on a Sunday close to Michaelmas.

[8]   R. J. E. Boggis, *History of St John's, Torquay* (Torquay, 1930), p. 66.

[9]   Yates, *op. cit.*, p. 63. Benjamin Webb's first sermon took 37 minutes (Bodleian Library, MS. Eng. misc.e.406, entry for 5 Jan. 1843).

congregations to draw out the length of the proceedings by extended sermonising. 'Enthusiasm', however, was certainly not expected. It was commonly associated with those on either side of the Anglican *via media,* the Methodists and Roman Catholics, both devoted to irrational enthusiasm rather than the good sense and good order of the Established Church.[10] This antipathy to 'enthusiasm' has been held up to explain how the late eighteenth-century Anglican sermon developed with high moral, rather than theological tone, because 'these moralities were in great measure the recoil from Methodist extravagances.'[11]

The Prayer Book directs that members of the congregation play their proper part in the prayers, psalms and responses to the versicles. How far they did so is shown by an interesting sermon by the Rev. W. J. E. Bennett, a key figure in the new approach to worship in the late 1830s and '40s (and whose advanced methods led to serious controversy).[12] 'How few of the congregation repeat the *Amen,*' he laments. Only the clerk answers. After the minister says 'O Lord, open thou our lips,' what sense is there in the reply 'And our mouth shall shew forth thy praise' if no mouth is opened to record that praise! How widely Bennett's strictures could justly be applied, we shall probably never know. But, his appeal is symptomatic of the desire for greater devotion in worship and the strict following of the rubrics among those with Tractarian and ecclesiological leanings.

The standard of musical accomplishment was an easy target for the critics, especially where there were 'choir bands'. These were composed of groups of singers plus a variety of instrumentalists, the combination of which depended on the musical skills and availability of instruments in the community (but which invariably included a bass instrument, i.e. a serpent, a bass or 'cello).[13] Much fun has been poked at the choir bands and no doubt their standard varied as much as did their composition. Some relied on the widely-used collections of metrical psalms and service settings by Sternhold and Hopkins or Tate and Brady whose catchy popularisations of scriptural passages were objectionable to serious-minded Victorian clergymen.[14] But some parishes had quite ambitious repertoires of music and undertook the singing of anthems, settings of the *Magnificat, Te Deum, Nunc Dimittis,* other passages of scripture, and occasionally a few hymns. The musicians most

[10] This linkage of reaction to Methodists and Roman Catholics was suggested to me by Dr Thomas Cocke whose words I use.

[11] Abbey & Overton, *op. cit.,* p. 465.

[12] *A Sermon on the Neglect and Apathy of the Public in the Psalmody and Responses in the Church Services* (3rd ed., London, 1841).

[13] The useful term 'choir band' comes from Mr Stephen J. Weston who has researched this field and to whom I am indebted for a discussion.

[14] This reaction was not new. Their 'miserable, scandalous doggerel' was condemned by John Wesley (quoted in Hopkins, *op. cit.,* p. 40).

frequently occupied a western gallery.[15] In churches where there was no western gallery, they often stood up at the west end. During the performance of music, the congregation would stand up and turn round towards the musicians, hence the expression 'turn to face the music'. This practice gives greater meaning to box pews where seats are arranged round three or four sides. There seems to be no evidence for instruments supporting church singing before the 1740s and they appear to have been in decline in favour of organs well before the impact of ecclesiology.[16] In Leicestershire in 1832, 23 out of 191 churches (12%) had organs,[17] while, for Staffordshire, it is said that an extraordinary 49 out of 116 churches (42%) had them in the 1830s.[18] Under ecclesiological and Tractarian influence the days of the choir bands were numbered.

The Engines of Change

Despite the idea promoted in early Victorian times, the approach to services during the previous generation was neither always soporific nor unevolving. The contribution by vigorous Evangelicals in improving the standard of worship can be easily overlooked and they did much to breathe greater earnestness into religious life. The Evangelical approach stressed the importance of preaching while minimising the ceremonial aspects of worship. It fiercely opposed any Romanising tendencies and thus rejected what were to become identifying doctrines of Tractarians – baptismal regeneration, the real presence and eucharistic sacrifice. It was over these beliefs and the outward signs that went with them that the controversies of the 1840s took place, and in which the Camdenians were intimately involved (or implicated as their opponents might have said). But common cause was joined between Evangelicals and Tractarians over efforts to increase the number of services, especially communion. John Wesley had been keen to increase the frequency

[15] Or, perhaps, when one existed they were placed in an eastern gallery across the chancel arch.

[16] I have no definitive explanation for this. It may suggest that the choir band tradition was a good deal less vigorous than a reading of Thomas Hardy might suggest. The last choir band I am aware of disappeared from Hardy country in 1895 (F. W. Galpin, 'Notes on the Old Church Bands and Village Choirs of the Past,' *Proc. Dorset Natural History & Antiquarian Field Club* 26 (1905), 173). The question needs to be asked (but I am unable to answer it) whether choir bands were prevalent all over the country or whether they had regional concentrations. Orchestras as such did, however, find occasional favour in Anglo-Catholic worship, e.g. at All Saints, Babbacombe, Devon where there was no organ till 1894, after which a small orchestra augmented the organ until 1910. Anon., *All Saints Church, Babbacombe* (n.d.).

[17] Figures from the 1832 Visitation returns, Leics. Record Office 245'50/1–5.

[18] Yates, *op. cit.*, p. 64 quoting D. B. Robinson (ed.), *Visitations of the Archdeaconry of Stafford 1829–1841* (London, 1980), pp. xx–xxi.

of its observance and his Oxford Methodists bound themselves to receive it weekly.[19]

For Newman in 1828, the Evangelicals represented one of the two main parties of the Church, the other being the 'Orthodox'. The latter covered wide ranges of churchmanship for which labels are neither precise nor constant through time and included those said to be 'High Church'. This term 'appears to have been coined by Richard Baxter in the 1650s but only gained common currency in political and theological discourse in the 1690s and 1700s and ... for Whig pamphleteers, the label was a pejorative synonym for "Tory".'[20] P. B. Nockles describes a pre-Tractarian High Churchman as upholding some form of doctrine of apostolic succession, believing in the supremacy of Holy Scripture, valuing the writings of the early Fathers, supporting in a qualified way the primacy of dogma and emphasising the doctrine of sacramental grace both in the eucharist and in baptism. 'He tended to cultivate a practical spirituality based on good works nourished by sacramental grace and exemplified in acts of self-denial and charity ... He upheld the importance of a religious establishment but insisted also on the duty of the state as a divinely-ordained rather than merely secular entity, to protect and promote the interests of the church.'[21] The High Church party had a good deal of vigour in it during the generation preceding the Tractarians, for example, in a loose collection of individuals known as the 'Hackney Phalanx' (whose lay leader, Joshua Watson, was an early member of the CCS).

Just as Pugin and the ecclesiologists emerged from backgrounds prepared by others, so the success of the Oxford Movement can be seen as capitalising on existing High Churchmanship and capturing a mood of the time. Its leaders, like the Camdenians, were keen to emphasise their movement's achievements and underplay what others had done, but nonetheless Oxford profoundly shifted a whole section of church life in this country after 1833. Acceptance of the movement's principles carried with it a new cast of mind from which would follow a reappraisal of the way in which services would be viewed and, hence, churches arranged.

The day that John Keble preached the assize sermon before the University of Oxford – 14 July 1833 – came to be recognised by Newman (and hence the world at large) as the formal beginning of the Oxford Movement. Keble's subject was 'National Apostasy', triggered by the Whig Government's plans to reduce the number of Irish bishoprics in the interests of administrative efficiency and financial common sense. This was only a small part of the changes brought in by this reforming Government, but to

[19]   A. Russell, *The Clerical Profession* (London, 1980), p.102.
[20]   P. B. Nockles, *The Oxford Movement in Context; Anglican High Churchmanship, 1760–1857* (Cambridge, 1994), p. 27.
[21]   *Ibid.*, p. 26.

Tractarians-to-be it touched a raw nerve. To Keble and the Oxford men, the Church here on earth was very far from being just another public body (of which Establishment was a rather uncomfortable reminder) but was a truly divine institution. Its bishops traced their authority back to the Apostles themselves through the principle of apostolic succession, and, so, on ordination, each priest was touched by the spirit of the early Church in a direct way and became a very special member of society, dispensing the sacraments and teaching the word of God. From all this stemmed a high regard for the reverential conduct of worship in a suitable setting. Liturgical change in itself, like Gothic architecture, was neither an objective of nor a great interest to the leaders of the movement, though it was to follow almost as a natural outcome. Rigid observance of the canons and the rubrics of the Book of Common Prayer was one such result and was to have some bizarre consequences. From the very beginning there were Tractarian clergy who became enthusiastic, paid-up members of the CCS. In the late '30s a number of so-minded clergymen were starting to examine critically the way worship was conducted and their number grew in the '40s as further candidates were ordained, men influenced by the Tracts from Oxford or the doctrines of ecclesiology from Cambridge – and, quite likely, both. By the middle of the '40s a journalist estimated that there were over 500 'Newmanite' clergy at large and, he added ominously, 'they have the care of parishes.'[22] That would comprise something like one in thirty of the clergy as a whole, but their activism more than made up for their numerical inferiority. G. W. Herring's list of 958 Tractarian clergy reveals 104 (including curates) who can be safely said to have held parish appointments in 1845 but this is likely to be a considerable understatement of the reality.[23]

The Society's Position

The question now arises as to what stance the CCS took on the issue of liturgical arrangements and ceremonial, and it immediately comes up against two difficulties. First, it has to be asked whether there was any consensus

---

[22] J. S. Reed, *Glorious Battle: the Cultural Politics of Victorian Anglo-Catholicism* (Nashville and London, 1996), p. 29 quoting 'A provincial', *The Helston Case: Twelve Letters on the Rubric and Ritual Innovations. Reprinted from* The Standard (n.d., c.1844).

[23] G. W. Herring, 'Tractarianism to Ritualism: a Study of Some Aspects of Tractarianism outside Oxford, from the Time of Newman's Conversion in 1845, until the First Ritual Commission in 1867' (Oxford, Ph.D. thesis, 1984), vol. 2. The problem with this immensely valuable list is that it was not drawn up with a view to the sort of analysis attempted here and in many cases Herring states when a clergyman arrived but often not when he moved on; hence, for an entry like 'curate ABCtown 1842, incumbent XYZtown 1850' one cannot automatically assume the man was still curate at ABCtown in 1845. Clergymen sometimes had intermediate posts in, say, schools, universities or even in the Church abroad.

among the members themselves who, by 1845, numbered between 800 and 900.[24] Second, from the outset, the official position of the Society on any matters beyond the study of antiquities, architecture and the more basic arrangements for churches was that it did not have one. As the 'Address' at the start of the first volume of *The Ecclesiologist* noted, the intended appeal of the new journal was 'to all connected with or in any way engaged in church-building, or in the study of ecclesiastical architecture and antiquities' – no mention of the theory and conduct of worship. 'It is earnestly hoped,' it added with a sense of foreboding, 'that the motive of this little publication, liable as it is to misconstruction, will not be mistaken.' But, as James White crisply points out, 'the Society had a very distinct theological position.'[25]

For the purposes of this chapter, that 'distinct theological position' is taken to be the one adopted by the leaders of the Society, who very much dominated its activities – Neale and Webb, Thorp, some of the more prominent committee members like F. A. Paley, J. F Russell, and, later, Beresford Hope. Everything points to their having embraced the spirit of the Oxford Movement, and therefore the label 'Tractarian' can reasonably be applied to them. The founders clearly made a great effort to recruit far beyond the town of Cambridge, evidently contacting *alumni* whom they thought might be interested in being elected. The list in the appendix reveals nearly 450 names of people who joined before the end of 1841. A not insignificant number were men who had already left Cambridge, including nearly one in four who already held clerical appointments. Of these just over one in ten had such positions as far back as 1830, and nearly one in seven in 1835. Many early members must have thought they were joining little more than a specialist antiquarian society, created to focus the widespread interest in ecclesiastical antiquities that had burgeoned over the past half century. Such a society would naturally take an interest in church building and restoration and, indeed, many such local bodies shortly came into existence, the first being the Exeter Diocesan Architectural Society in 1841. Liturgical change and the promotion of Tractarianism would have been far from most people's minds. Into such a group, for example, fall two Bedfordshire clergymen who joined the CCS at the same time (8 Nov. 1841) and who probably knew one another. The squarson, the Rev. & Hon. H. C. Cust of Cockayne Hatley, restored his neglected church during the 1820s, filling it with an extraordinary display of woodwork ejected from Belgian churches, and commissioning stained glass from Thomas Willement about 1830. It was probably for these attractions that J. M. Neale visited Cust and his church twice in 1839–40 – 'the church is magnificent beyond description', he recorded.[26] The Rev.

---

24   *Ecclesiologist*, 4 (1845), p. 72.
25   J. F. White, *The Cambridge Movement: the Ecclesiologists and the Gothic Revival* (Cambridge, 1962), p. 131.
26   Neale's diary for 1838–40 (Lambeth Palace MSS 3107, fols 81v–83r, 101v.–103v).

William Airy came to Keysoe in 1836 and, during his long incumbency, devoted himself to antiquarian pursuits, contributing several learned papers to the local Antiquarian and Archaeological Society (established 1847) and one to the CCS itself on the font in Keysoe church. Airy did make efforts to improve his chancel in the 1840s but neither he nor Cust are known to have made liturgical changes.[27] Their position was no doubt similar to that of others whose interests were antiquarian rather than Tractarian, though unfortunately there is no means of quantifying the numbers. Significantly after the crisis of 1845 when the Society stood accused of being actuated by 'esoteric principles', it was older men, with M.A.s or of higher standing, that formed the largest part of the resignations.[28]

Many older clerical members of the fledgling Society were probably High Churchmen of the pre-Tractarian school, though a great deal more work is needed to determine how far this is so. One such prominent figure who joined early in 1842 and who was a great hero for ecclesiologists was the Rev. W. F. Hook, vicar of Leeds, who had famously just rebuilt and refurnished his church and who used a surpliced choir. Then there was Henry Philpotts, Bishop of Exeter (joined Dec. 1841). Philpotts, who detested Evangelicanism, was the most sympathetic of all the bishops towards the Tractarians but certainly was not one himself as his high-profile resignation from the CCS showed when he felt it had overstepped the bounds of the doctrinally acceptable. Another famous figure was Gladstone, later the most religious of Victorian Prime Ministers, who joined (also Dec. 1841) along with his son-in-law, Sir Stephen Glynne, M.P., the prolific compiler of church notes. Another old-style High Churchman to whom the Society appealed was Henry Bayley (joined Nov. 1841), Archdeacon of Stowe from 1826–44. As rector of West Meon with Privett in Hampshire, he repaired the church at Privett and built a new one at West Meon. From the same circle, an early member was the Rev. J. D. Watson, curate, rector at Guilsborough, Northants between 1835 and 1864. Two members of the important pre-Tractarian grouping, the Hackney Phalanx, were members, the Ven. W. R Lyall (joined Nov. 1843), Archdeacon of Maidstone, editor of the High Church *British Critic*, and who was to become Dean of Canterbury from 1845 to 1857, and Joshua Watson (joined before Nov. 1841). Watson, a layman, was the leading figure in the Phalanx, and was Treasurer of the S.P.C.K, active in the S.P.G., co-founder of the National Society (in 1811), a founder of the

---

27   I am much indebted to Chris Pickford for information on these and other Bedfordshire Camdenians.

28   The words 'esoteric principles' are taken from a letter by Professor Samuel Lee to Archdeacon Thorp *after* the sixth anniversary meeting at which the debate of the future of the society took place (quoted by White, p. 152). I use them because they sum up the way many felt about the society. The breakdown of those seceding from the society is in *Ecclesiologist*, 4 (1845), p. 217.

Church Building Society in 1817 and the Additional Curates Society in 1837 – all bodies with High Church, but not Tractarian, leanings.[29]

There was no lack of Tractarian members and the list in the appendix asterisks 101 of the 958 clergy whom G. W. Herring has identified as belonging to this school.[30] Leaving aside the leaders of the Society, the following is a selection, taken in alphabetical order (their titles are given as Rev. only if they were ordained at the time of joining the Society):

Henry Williams Baker (not listed by Herring) was the promoter and compiler of that most successful of Victorian hymn-books, *Ancient and Modern*, first published in 1861. He also edited other hymn-books, a devotional manual and composed a number of well-known hymns, most notably 'The king of love my shepherd is' (paraphrasing psalm 23), and 'Lord, thy Word abideth'.

Charles Beanlands, was at first curate at St Paul, Brighton, then in charge at St Michael & All Angels in the same town. Both churches were built by the Tractarian Henry Wagner to designs by architects (Carpenter and Bodley) who were members of the Ecclesiological Society.

The Rev. Walter Blunt was curate at Helston, Cornwall where he was involved in a well-publicised controversy over preaching in the surplice and other 'innovations'.

The Rev. William Butler (joined Nov. 1842). On moving to Wantage, he founded a famous sisterhood there in 1850 and ended his career as Dean of Lincoln.

T. Pelham Dale became one of the four priests imprisoned for illegal ritualistic practices under the workings of the Public Worship Regulation Act of 1874.

Sir John Harington was churchwarden at St Barnabas, Pimlico and a close friend and supporter of the Rev. W. J. E. Bennett.

The Rev. Thomas Helmore. The role of music in worship increasingly interested Camdenians, and it is not surprising to find Helmore, Precentor of St Mark's College, Chelsea, and of the Motett Choir, joining in 1849. He played a major part in the re-establishment of the choral tradition in Anglican church worship.

The Rev. John Keble. It has already been mentioned that the leaders of the Oxford Movement had little active concern or involvement with ecclesiological objectives and it is therefore interesting to find Keble joining the CCS as an ordinary member in November 1843. This may have been

[29] The figures in this paragraph have largely been identified through P. B. Nockles, *op. cit.,* pp. 14ff.

[30] Herring, *op. cit.*

GEOFFREY K. BRANDWOOD

under the stimulus of the patron of his living at Hursley in Hampshire, *Sir William Heathcote*, who had, himself, joined the Society six months before.

The Rev. C. F. Lowder. One of the great figures among ritualistic clergy working in slum areas was Fr Charles Lowder. As a curate at St George's-in-the-East, he joined the Society in 1852. In 1866 he went as priest to the new church of St Peter, London Docks, where he combined advanced liturgical practice with active social commitment in this area of grinding poverty, until his death in 1880.

The Rev. J. W. H. Molyneux (joined before mid-1840), was, as perpetual curate of Sudbury, Suffolk, from 1855, the second 'most notorious man in the county for his Puseyism [after the Rev. George Drury]. ... His forthright teaching from the pulpit about the Holy Eucharist, the Real Presence..., and the sacrificial nature of the Priesthood brought about a storm of abuse.'[31] He also made ritual innovations but was willing to discontinue any that were declared illegal.

George Nugée (joined 1843) became one of the curates at the advanced St Paul, Knightsbridge under the Rev. W. J. E. Bennett and went on to found a nursing sisterhood at Wymering, Hampshire. He was at St Paul's at the same time as *the Rev. James Skinner* was senior curate at the daughter church of St Barnabas, Pimlico (from which Bennett was forced to resign in 1850).

The Rev. W. Upton Richards joined the CCS in 1845 or '46 when he was minister at Margaret Chapel. He then became the first vicar of All Saints, Margaret Street in 1849, where his advanced ceremonial proved too much for Beresford Hope and his wife. The Hopes suspected what 'looks very like a secret burning of incense' in 1850 and the quarrel with Richards rumbled on through the 1850s.[32]

The Rev. Edward Stuart joined in 1846 or '47 and was first vicar at the important Tractarian church of St Mary Magdalene, Munster Square from 1852 .

A. D. Wagner, who joined in Nov. 1842, followed in his father's footsteps as a great patron of church-building in Brighton where he was responsible for encouraging the use of advanced ceremonial.

[31]   Quoted by R. Tricker in *Anglicans on High, a Selection of Suffolk Churches and Suffolk People who have been Part of the Catholic Revival in the Church of England* (privately printed, Ipswich, 1988), p. 31.
[32]   H. W. & I. Law, *The Book of the Beresford Hopes* (London, 1925), pp. 170–5. In 1854 Alexander Beresford Hope shifted his allegiance for a while to St Mary Magdalene, Munster Square and St Andrew, Wells St, and continued to complain about Richards.

Returning now to the question of the Society's official position, its leaders were wise in trying to limit their publicly-declared interests largely to physical fabrics. The storms that greeted Hurrell Froude's *Remains* (1838–9), revealing the extreme inclinations of a member of the Oxford Movement, and Newman's Tract 90 (1841) on the catholicity of the Thirty-nine articles, showed how disastrous doctrinal controversy would have been to the new Society. But, sure enough, it was not long before the CCS *was* being assailed by critics as having a distinct agenda that led, dangerously, in a Romanising direction. As early as 3 November 1839, Neale's diary records how the Evangelical Dean of Trinity, William Carus, 'had been speaking strongly against the Camden on the score of Oxfordism.'[33] It is therefore not surprising that a month later, on 5 December, he noted how it had been decided *not* to invite the Society's most obvious recruit to join it – 'Pugin as a Roman Catholic was rejected perhaps prudently. We are already too much accused of Popery to render so violent a man an Honorary Member.'

The publication of the translation of Durandus in 1843 and *Hierurgia Anglicana* between 1843 and 1848 were sufficient to convince anyone of what was in the minds of the leaders of the CCS, if they had not already noticed. Interestingly and significantly, neither publication was brought out under the banner of the CCS. The Durandus translation by Neale and Webb took readers into the arcane world of religious symbolism. It was entitled *The Symbolism of Churches and Church Ornaments: a Translation of the First Book of the* Rationale Divinorum Officiorum, which had been written by Durandus, the late thirteenth-century Bishop of Mende.[34] The work was 'dedicated to the Cambridge Camden Society by two of its Founders'. These founders' introduction, half as long as the work they were dusting down, took what many might have regarded as an unhealthy, Romanising interest in such matters as the emblems of the Passion, roods and the fact that 'Catholic ritual is indeed symbolical from first to last.'[35] There is no overt advocacy of change but where the authors' hearts lay is clear in a statement such as –

> The symbolisms which Protestantism introduced were few and easily understood .... After the Rebellion, but still more after the Revolution, those faint traces of symbolism died away onto that *ne plus ultra* of wretchedness, the Georgian style.

Hierurgia Anglicana was 'edited by members of the Ecclesiological, Late Cambridge Camden Society' (apparently under the general editorship of the Rev. J. F. Russell, perpetual curate of Enfield).[36] The work was highly

---

[33]   Neale's diary in Lambeth Palace Library MS 3107, entry for 3 Nov. 1839.
[34]   The publishers in London and Cambridge, Rivingtons and Stevenson respectively, also were publishers of *The Ecclesiologist*. The Leeds publisher was T. W. Green.
[35]   p. liii.
[36]   Russell is identified by Vernon Staley in his 1902, greatly-enlarged edition of the

scholarly, producing evidence for the survival after the Reformation of crucifixes, vestments, incense, stone altars, the use of wafer bread and so on. It was obvious that the authors regarded such things as desirable and worthy of reintroduction if they had the chance, and that depended on whether the admired, old traditions were still sanctioned by the Church. The difficulty lay in knowing what was and what was not so sanctioned. The CCS very soon came face to face with this problem over the installation of the stone altar as part of the restoration of the Round Church in Cambridge (*see* chapter 12). What, on the surface, seemed like a simple attempt to introduce a dignified furnishing for which there were Anglican precedents, turned into a *cause célèbre* in which the altar, redolent of the concept of Eucharistic sacrifice, was declared illegal and the CCS publicly tarred with Popish intentions. It was only the first of many such cases that erupted from time to time during the rest of the nineteenth century.

The tale of opposition to the Society and its aims has been told by Elliot Rose[37] and James White,[38] and came to a head in 1844 with the Round Church crisis, the tussle with that Evangelical scourge, the Rev. Francis Close of Cheltenham in 1844, and the ensuing problems for the Society during 1845. Close's arguments may have been overstated and his facts sometimes incorrect but he captured the mood of the time and its deep-seated fear of 'Popery'. It was Close who produced the few memorable words in this unedifying exchange when he thundered:

> Romanism is taught *Analytically* at Oxford, it is taught *Artistically* at Cambridge – that is inculcated theoretically, in tracts at one University, and it is *sculpted, painted* and *graven* at the other ... in a word, ... the 'Ecclesiologist' of Cambridge is identical in doctrine with the Oxford *Tracts for the Times*.

Despite the probably disparate leanings of the individual members, the verdict on whether the Society as a whole stood as a brother alongside the Tractarians must surely be one of 'proven' (plate 19). The first issue of *The Ecclesiologist* in November 1841 contains several clear pieces of evidence. The very first article after the introductory address deals with the efforts the first Bishop of New Zealand would make to provide churches on his arrival in this, the youngest of England's colonies. There would be *daily* services from the day of his arrival and there were to be 'altars' (rather than communion tables). The next article deals with the restoration of the Round Church in Cambridge. Its dedication is given as 'S. Sepulchre'. 'S.', as opposed to 'St' was used as a party badge by those of advanced High Church persuasion. Then, after the business-like report of the twenty-first CCS meeting, comes a

Hierurgia.
37 E. Rose, 'The Stone Table in the Round Church and the Crisis of the Cambridge Camden Society,' *Victorian Studies* 10 (1966), pp. 119–44.
38 White, *op. cit.*, pp. 131–44.

discussion of how new churches should be built. Particular praise was given to a small church that is seemly despite being built on a tight budget. This 'most church-like of modern churches' was none other than Littlemore, Newman's chapel outside Oxford. The curate there, J. R. Bloxam, had provoked what was perhaps the first Evangelical attack on innovative arrangements, modest as they would seem later. They induced 'indescribable horror' in Peter Maurice, the Evangelical chaplain of All Souls' and New Colleges in 1837.[39] In the same month that the first *Ecclesiologist* appeared, Newman retired to make his home at Littlemore. 'Rumours about Littlemore were already rife. It was said to be planned as a college for teaching Newman's version of popery.'[40] Indeed, the previous year he had bought nine or ten acres of land on which to establish a monastic community. *The Ecclesiologist's* enthusiasm for Littlemore would not have been lost on staunch Protestants.

The Ecclesiologist was primarily intended for members of the Society, who, whatever their other differences may have been, sympathised with the cause of church building and restoration and for most of whom cautiously-advanced language would not be offensive. *A Few Words to Church Builders*, also published in 1841, was designed to spread the word outside the Society and was rather more temperate in its use of words. Nevertheless, it, too, clearly advocated some of the more advanced features of the day. The Society's use of 'S.' for 'saint' reappears and there is considerable interest in saints in terms of dedications and in imagery. The anonymous writer (in fact J. M. Neale) is careful to recommend only those saints 'commemorated in our own Calendar; not as undervaluing others, the Blessed Saints and Martyrs of the Most High, but in order that we may not give occasion to be accused of Romanism.' Other imagery sanctioned in the post-Reformation church, and probably not widely seen by Georgian church-goers, is favoured – crosses of various kinds, instruments of the Crucifixion, the pelican in its piety and so on. Then there is the preference for the term 'altar' instead of 'table', the advocacy of reredoses, sedilia, aumbries, credences and rood screens. In paragraph 53 there is the insistence on two altar candlesticks as 'commanded by the first rubric in the Prayer Book' [i.e. the Ornaments Rubric].

---

[39] P. Maurice, *The Popery of Oxford Confronted, Disavowed and Repudiated* (London, 1837), pp. 53–4. His 'horror' was aroused by 'a plain naked cross, either of stone or a good imitation of it, rising up and projecting out of the wall, from the centre of the table of communion ... I could not divest my mind of that fond delusion of the man of sin, who openly bows down before the image of the cross, and worships the painted wood or the cold stone. ... [In the east window I found] one pane of glass, like a drop of blood, polluting the whole, and upon this I found the representation of an ornamental cross, or crosslet. .... I take this ... to be the distinguishing emblem of the Second Person in the Trinity.' He goes on to object to the stone 'table' and credence table.

[40] O. Chadwick, *The Victorian Church*, 1 (3rd. ed., London, 1971), p. 193.

Change in the 1840s

The question that needs to be explored is, what tangible changes in worship were promoted and took place in early Victorian England, and to what extent was the Society involved in the process? It has been suggested already that when individuals were identified with the Oxford Movement this brought certain things in its train. It affected the way clergymen saw themselves and how they thought they should perform worship which, in turn produced definite views about the setting in which it was to take place. But Tractarians did not necessarily become ecclesiologists and, by the same token, as we have seen, ecclesiologists were by no means all Tractarians – hence the dissent in the ranks during the crisis of 1845 and the departure of 15% of the membership along with the best episcopal friend the ecclesiologists should have had – Bishop Henry Philpotts of Exeter. Furthermore, as research for this chapter has demonstrated to the present writer, there is no comprehensive body of evidence, along with documented dates, to enable a definitive picture to be painted of all the changes that did start at this time, and which formed a platform for what was to follow.[41] The discussion will therefore proceed along the following lines. First, we will say something of the practices of the two men who were the driving force behind the CCS, J. M. Neale and Benjamin Webb, and who might be regarded (and might have wished to be regarded) as role models. Then specific changes in the practice of worship will be examined, drawing on examples provided by Camdenian clergy whenever possible. The section that follows will review how the frequency of services altered.

Benjamin Webb, who began his career as curate to Archdeacon Thorp at Kemerton in 1843, was, in the words of his son, Clement, 'a man of conspicuous moderation'.[42] The younger Webb records him 'soon ... preaching "*in surplice*" and giving "Charles Smith the clerk some Gregorian [chant]s to practice with."[43] He is also known to have been an enthusiastic supporter of the eastward position,[44] but he never adopted eucharistic vestments. This was on the grounds of 'Christian charity, expediency, and prudence', as he told the Ritual Commission of 1867, rather than any dislike of them. In other words, he carefully avoided contentious items which could give offence and provoke controversy. So his services at St Andrew, Wells Street, where he was vicar from 1862, involved 'elaborate musical Eucharists without vestments or incense, and without insistence on fasting communion'.[45]

---

41 The best summary account is S. L. Ollard's *A Short History of the Oxford Movement* (2nd ed., Oxford, 1932), pp.113–44. It was first published in 1915.

42 C. C. J. Webb, 'Benjamin Webb', *Church Quarterly Review* 75 (1913), p. 330.

43 *Ibid.*, p. 339.

44 *Dictionary of National Biography* entry for Webb.

45 Webb, *op. cit.*, p. 346.

J. M. Neale, however, was in constant dispute with authority. He never held a parochial appointment and so was freer to pursue his liturgical ideals. At the end of 1842 he accepted a curacy at St Nicholas, Guildford but his reputation as a leader of the CCS went before him.[46] The Evangelical Bishop of Winchester, Charles Sumner, was quite familiar with the inclinations of the CCS and was 'doubtful as to the expediency of admitting one if its originators into his diocese'.[47] He therefore refused to license Neale. After a period of ill health and the consequent winter visits to Madeira, Neale was appointed in 1846 by Earl de la Warr (a fellow Camdenian) as Warden of Sackville College at East Grinstead. Fortunately for Neale, this was outside the jurisdiction of Bishop Gilbert of Chichester who, nonetheless, took a keen interest in Neale's activities there and, within a year, inhibited him from officiating in the diocese. On arrival, Neale had introduced what a local vicar derided as 'gew-gaw Popish chapel ornaments, and a fine belfry of bells, which annoy me from morning till night.'[48] Others complained about Neale's 'fancy papistical mountebankism'. There was a twelve-foot high 'Great Rood' in the chapel and the screen proclaimed Popery by its inscription 'Pray for the founders'.[49] Neale, independent both in means and of his bishop, never compromised. After he started the sisterhood of St Margaret at East Grinstead in 1855, he introduced what were surely the most extreme practices in any Anglican place of worship at the time. The oratory there was opened in 1856 and almost from the beginning the sacrament was reserved on the altar and the distinctly Roman Catholic rites of exposition and benediction were practised. From the start Neale wore a chasuble and by 1858 had installed Stations of the Cross. He used his extraordinary wealth of scholarship to produce service books for the oratory drawing on Roman, French and other continental office books. There was auricular confession, daily communion, incense, four vases of flowers on the altar. Then, immediately after the Consecration, the *Tantum ergo*. In the morning service the rite of the Adoration of the Cross was taken from a Roman Catholic source; in the afternoon the sisters made the Stations of the Cross. Widespread rumour surrounded Neale and, as E. S. Reed notes

> the low point was probably reached in 1851, when a dead woman's relatives and a mob carried off her coffin to prevent her being buried by Neale, as she had requested, stopping at an inn to open the coffin to make sure her body

[46] E. A. Towle, *John Mason Neale D.D., a Memoir* (London, 1906), pp. 54–5.
[47] *Ibid.*, pp. 55–6.
[48] Reed, *op. cit.*, p. 54. The following particulars are from the same source.
[49] Neale noted in his diary that, just as it was being installed on 17 Dec. 1846, 'in walked a Protestant clergyman. His disgust rendered him speechless for some time. Then he burst forth'. The event inspired Neale to verse: 'It would have moved a Christian's bowels | To hear the doubts he stated; | But the carpenters did | As they were bid, | And worked the whilst he prated.' (!)

was in it. When a mob of about 150 later tried to burn Neale's house down, Bishop Gilbert urged him to leave the diocese, but he refused.

But this has carried the story on beyond the 1840s to which we must return. One of the things that greatly interested the leaders of the ecclesiological movement was to make changes in the *sound* of the church services and the subject of music is explored in more depth in Chapter 15. Intoning parts of the service became a common practice and singing, both by the congregation and, where one existed, a choir, became more prevalent. Intoning was an early development and one of the things commonly complained of by those who sought to object to the new trends. A clergyman who had some singing ability might intone the opening sentences, the exhortation, absolution, prayers and the blessing.[50] In 1840 the rector of Devizes (since 1833), the Rev. E. J. Phipps, was summoned before his bishop to account for his liturgical embellishments of which intoning was one.[51] At St Mary, Penzance the whole service was intoned by a CCS member, the Rev. E. Shuttleworth, in 1843.[52] In Ipswich the first church to be influenced by the Oxford Movement was St Mary-le-Tower and here the vicar from 1838, the Rev. W. N. Steedger, intoned parts of the service.[53] Intoning was the first of a string of complaints made against the Rev. H. W. Wilberforce of East Farleigh, Kent in 1844.[54] The petitioners also berated their vicar for removing 'the singers ... from their accustomed place in the gallery into the chancel, as in Popish times.' Chants for the psalms, either Gregorian or Anglican, were used in advanced parishes and were approved by ecclesiologists. Chants and the choral tradition in general were greatly promoted by the work of the College of St Mark, Chelsea with which the Society associated itself.

One of the best-known aspects of change in the Victorian Church was the development of hymn singing. Hymns were uncommon before the beginning of the nineteenth-century and, like other innovations, were initially encouraged by Evangelicals. The initiative soon passed to the High Church and to men such as the Camdenian and the strongly Tractarian Rev. William Dodsworth of Margaret Chapel. He published *A Selection of Psalms, to which are added Hymns Chiefly Ancient* in 1837 for use in the chapel, but the key ecclesiological contribution to English hymnody was the work of John Mason Neale. His enthusiasm took time to develop and in 1840, perhaps suspicious of their Evangelical overtones, he had declared his 'general dislike of hymns'.

---

[50] This list is from N. Temperley, *The Music of the English Parish Church*, 1 (Cambridge, 1979), pp. 294–5.

[51] Tricker, *op. cit.*, p. 31.

[52] *Ecclesiologist*, 3 (1844), p. 2.

[53] *Ibid.*, p. 17.

[54] The petition to Archbishop Howley and the subsequent correspondence are reproduced in N. Yates, *Kent and the Oxford Movement* (Gloucester, 1983), pp. 37–51.

As he became aware of Tractarian translations of ancient hymns, his interest grew. His most important contribution was *The Hymnal Noted*, issued in two parts (in 1851 and 1854), with the support of the Ecclesiological Society behind it. Neale translated and edited the hymns and Helmore transcribed the melodies. But the book that swept all before it was *Hymns Ancient and Modern* which first appeared in 1861. It was compiled by Sir H. W. Baker, the Tractarian vicar of Monkland, Herefordshire and an early CCS member. Baker himself wrote several well-known hymns such as 'The king of love my shepherd is', and 'Lord, thy word abideth'. The great appeal of *Ancient and Modern* was that, as the title implies, it had an excellent blend of ancient, medieval and modern examples. A supplement was added in 1868. The first of several new editions came out in 1875 and it remains in wide use to this day.

The surpliced choir is commonly associated with the development of Tractarian worship and by the end of the century was commonplace. By 1869 one in five of London churches had them and this had increased to just over half (52.6%) in 1882,[55] though it may be expected that the figure for the rest of the country would have been rather less. The Rev. W. F. Hook of Leeds, that outstanding pre-Tractarian High Churchman, is often credited with the innovation. However, it seems even he was following in a strong local tradition as Temperley quotes evidence to show that, as far back as 1815, the then vicar, the Rev. Richard Fawcett, had employed a professional band of singers and three years later installed a surpliced choir of men and boys. Another case that apparently precedes Hook's is use of a surpliced choir at St James, Ryde in 1839 by the Rev. R. W. Sibthorp.[56] The rise of surpliced choirs has yet to be adequately charted but they seem to have been a considerable rarity in the 1840s.[57] When such choirs were established they were, of course, the death knell for the old choir bands. The latter also fell victim on the arrival of an organ, although, when *The Ecclesiologist* devoted an article to 'this stupendous instrument' and its positioning in 1843, the writer did not go so far as to suggest it was a necessity.[58]

Hymn-singing was generally welcomed by all wings of the Church but the same cannot be said for other changes in the 1840s. These were associated

---

[55] Quoted by Temperley, p. 279.

[56] Ollard, *op. cit.*, p. 123.

[57] The choir at St Paul , Knightsbridge was surpliced in 1846 (Ollard, p.128).

[58] Article dated Sept. 1843 published in vol. 3 (1844), pp. 1–5. The recommended position for an organ in parish churches was 'at the west end, either of the Nave or either Aisle, and *on the ground* [its emphasis]. Then, the singers being rightly placed in the Chancel, it will not drown the voices nor make them dependent on itself.' Chris Miele points out to me that it is an open question whether the Camdenians may be said to have wanted organs: some serious ecclesiologists like G. E. Street liked plainsong and mistrusted the congregational associations of organ music. He adds that, ironically, Neale, who was to become the leading Victorian hymnologist was, in the early '40s, against organs.

with a deep desire among many clergymen to perform the services in strict accordance with the rubrics of the Book of Common Prayer but, unfortunately, one person's viewpoint was not necessarily shared by all. Any practices which were unfamiliar to most churchgoers were liable to suspicion and opposition. In the middle of the decade, the Press was full of Popish interpretations of what could be experienced at various churches throughout the land. At Penzance, under the Camdenian, the Rev. Edward Shuttleworth we have 'ceremonies which have been introduced, render[ing the service] a close copy of the Roman Catholic mode of worship.'[59] The Rev. H. Coddington, another Camdenian, was responsible for the 'performance of Papistical practices' at Ware, Herts while at Holy Trinity, Brompton the congregation were treated to 'mummeries of a Popish character'.[60] Opponents of the 'innovations' openly declared that the practices were, in themselves, fairly trivial but their importance lay in the fact that they were symbols of the new, advanced churchmanship and the perceived Romish intent that went with it.

Among the features adopted by the new High Churchmen were turning to the east during prayers and the Creed, along with bowing to the altar and at the name of Jesus. Such activity took place at Ware, as it did at East Farleigh, Kent under the Rev. H. W. Wilberforce. Another case is at St John, Torquay where, in 1844 the Rev. W. G. Parks Smith began to introduce more advanced ceremonial and thus initiated parochial discord. A hostile account given in *The Times* (1 Feb. 1845) of proceedings there refers to three clergymen – called 'the celebrans, the epistler, and the gospeler' – who divided the reading of the prayers, lessons and epistle, with part of the prayers being read with the clergy turning their backs to the congregation.[61] Smith, for his part, was said to have prostrated himself at the altar rails at the start of the service (which probably meant kneeling for private prayer). Such bowing and turning to the east is probably the sort of practice the critics had in mind. Ironically, turning to face east during the Creed, which became a feature of new High Anglicanism, was not in fact a Roman practice.

One of the liturgical changes favoured by clergy of advanced persuasion was the eastward position at the prayer of consecration at holy communion, whereby the celebrant stood at the centre of the west side of the table with his back to the congregation as had been the practice in the medieval times. By the nineteenth century, however, the customary position was on the north, short side of the table, and facing south, thus following what was believed to be the intent of the Book of Common Prayer. The advantage of this in Protestant terms was that the celebrant's acts would be fully visible so there could be no real or imagined superstitious goings-on. It is

[59]   *The Times*, 18 Jan. 1845.
[60]   *Ibid.*, 27 Jan. 1845, 20 Nov. 1844, respectively.
[61]   1 Feb. 1845.

significant that the reference to 'the priest standing at the north side of the Table' comes in the rubrics at the *beginning* of the communion service. Unfortunately, by the time the priest gets to the prayer of consecration, he receives no new instruction about his proper position other than the loosely worded direction, 'standing before the Table ... he shall say the Prayer of Consecration'. What may have been obvious to churchmen in 1552 and 1662 was far from crystal clear to their early Victorian counterparts. Inventive attempts were made to reinterpret this as meaning that the celebrant should stand at the north end of the long side of the table and face east. Such a practice seems to have originated at Oxford in the 1830s and was adopted by Newman at St Mary's and at Littlemore.[62] *The Ecclesiologist* sought to clarify the point in 1851 – obviously in favour of the eastward position – by quoting a carefully-reasoned opinion by counsel on the matter.[63] Benjamin Webb, as mentioned already, was a strong advocate of the revival of this pre-Reformation practice, but from what date he and others introduced it remains somewhat obscure. Interestingly, it is curiously absent from the documented controversies in the middle of the 1840s and may have emerged a little later. It was, however, practised by the Rev. W. J. E. Bennett at St Barnabas, Pimlico from 1845.[64] The Court of Arches ruled against the eastward position at communion in 1870 but twenty years later Archbishop Benson pronounced in its favour. Despite its dubious legal status, the eastward position gained ground steadily. In 1882 it was adopted in 13.9% of churches in England and Wales (29.9% in London) and in 1903 by 40.1% of all English and Welsh churches.[65] Some clergymen who adopted the eastward position early on might also be expected to favour a stone altar as being redolent of ancient usage and associated with the concept of eucharistic sacrifice. Stone altars had been installed in various Anglican churches without deep, Popish motives being ascribed to them, thirty-one being said to exist in 1844.[66] However, the Round Church case brought the issue into the open and party lines were adopted.[67]

   As 1844 turned into 1845 it was preaching in the surplice and the taking of a weekly offertory that most inflamed passions within the Church of England. In 1842 Bishop Philpotts of Exeter had exhorted the Rev. Edward

[62]   Ollard, *op. cit.*, pp. 116–17.
[63]   12 (1851), pp. 94–6. The opinion was given by J. Addams and Edward Badeley of Doctors' Commons (one was an ecclesiastical, the other a common lawyer).
[64]   Ollard, *op. cit.*, p. 128.
[65]   Yates, *Buildings, Faith and Worship*, p. 144.
[66]   According to affidavits used in the Faulkner *v.* Litchfield case.
[67]   The ruling of the Court of Arches in 1845 was actually not against a stone altar *per se*, but against an immovable structure. Nonetheless, stone altars got a bad press and their party associations meant they appeared but rarely and always in High Church circumstances (e.g. Woodlands St Mary, Berks in 1852).

Shuttleworth of Penzance, whom we have already met, always to preach in the surplice at the morning service and so 'the surplice was for the first time in Cornwall worn whilst preaching.'[68] In the same year Bishop Blomfield of London gave his approval of the practice. Then, on 19 November 1844, following complaints about the innovating Camdenian, the Rev. Walter Blunt, curate of Helston, Philpotts laid down the requirements for his clergy.[69] The 'law, beyond all question which can now arise,' he stated, 'requires that the surplice be always used in the sermon, which is part of the communion service.' This was clear-cut according to the letter of Church law but he went on to extend the usage to all other services when a sermon was delivered, not out of any partisan motives but simply so 'that there be no longer any "diversity"' on the matter. Although the surplice was generally used in the Diocese of Durham where Philpotts had spent much of his early career,[70] and apparently elsewhere,[71] it was regarded as a party badge of men like Shuttleworth and Blunt and vigorous protests from meetings all over the diocese descended on Philpotts. The objectors were strongly supported by *The Times* which had moved from a position of mild support for Tractarianism to one of hostility by the end of 1844.[72] The vehemence of the protests was inflamed by the opportunity it gave Whigs and radicals to attack Philpotts and his espousal of robust Toryism. Furthermore Philpotts' agreement to Pusey's preaching two sermons at Ilfracombe in June 1843 (at a time when he was suspended from preaching at Oxford University) had given the bishop's opponents a Tractarian stick with which to beat him. The strength of feeling was such that Philpotts withdrew his order about the surplice on 23 December, telling his clergy to continue as they had previously done.[73] (see plate 20). This left at least one clergyman in a quandary. The Rev. Richard Ellicombe of Alphington, near Exeter, had previously preached in the surplice without anyone thinking anything of it but now his parishioners appealed for him to give it up. He initially agreed but on thinking about the literal meaning of Philpotts's words retracted fearing anger from the parishioners on one side and 'dread of the Bishop's disapprobation' on the other.[74] No such

68 *The Times,* 18 Jan. 1845.
69 His letter to his clergy is printed in *The Times,* 3 Dec. 1844.
70 As he pointed out in his letter (*ibid.*).
71 The Rev. W. J. E. Bennett said it was used in many counties: *The Principles of the Book of Common Prayer Considered* (London, 1845), pp. 342–3. Although Bennett was a partisan of innovation, there must surely be some truth in his statement. A further piece of evidence for the use of the surplice in northern pulpits comes in a statement in 1753 by the Archdeacon of Northumberland, Thomas Sharp that '"the use of the surplice by all Preachers in their pulpits" [is] quite decent but the clergy are not bound by it' (J. W. Legg, *English Church Life from the Restoration to the Tractarian Movement* (London, 1914), p. 377).
72 Chadwick, *op. cit.,* pp. 201–2.
73 In 1845 the Bishop of London also withdrew the approval he had given in 1842.

worries afflicted the young Rev. Francis Courtenay of St Sidwell's, Exeter who had found the surplice in use when he arrived, and who persisted with it after Philpotts's climb-down in the face of the widespread opposition. Thus he provoked the first ritual disturbances of the nineteenth century on two successive Sundays in January much to the alarm of the city authorities. On the second Sunday, the evening sermon was preached by the Rev. Dr Coleridge who thought fit to take as his text Isaiah 22.2 – 'Thou art full of stirs – a tumultuous city'(!) Tumultuous indeed was the crowd of 700 to 800 who followed Courtenay home, 'groaning and hissing and hooting'.[75] After this unseemly affair Courtenay wisely gave up the surplice in the pulpit. How widespread was the same reaction throughout England is at present an open question. Certainly at Ware, under Coddington, the surplice was still in use in the pulpit at the end of January 1845[76] and, despite the early setback in Exeter diocese, it gradually became a normal feature of the sermon. By 1872 it was found in 38.9% of London and London suburban churches and 72.5% of them ten years later.[77] Now it is almost universal in the Anglican pulpit (plate 21).

A parallel dispute in 1844–5 was the weekly collection, yet again something that later became standard practice. Its promoters were the same men who favoured the surplice in preaching. The main battleground for the latter was the diocese of Exeter but the weekly collection seems to have been fought for over a rather wider area. Not merely was it an unwanted innovation for many of the laity, it also touched their pockets. Authority for a collection is clearly given in the Book of Common Prayer, but only at the offertory during holy communion, which means that in most parishes, before the 1840s it could not have been practised more than four times a year if the rubric was followed. There was also some ambiguity as to the purposes for which it was intended. Some held that 'the Alms for the Poor' and the 'pious and charitable uses' referred to in the Prayer Book meant worthy causes within the parish alone, an interpretation which was almost certainly in the minds of men in 1662 but was not so relevant to the world's greatest industrial nation served by railways and the penny post. Coddington's weekly collection at Ware caused his parishioners offence.[78] So did that by another Camdenian, Rev. Samuel Walker of St Columb Major in Cornwall. 'Instead of confining the offertory to the Sundays and other holy days on which the

---

[74] *The Times*, 22 Jan. 1845. I have not traced the outcome of poor Ellicombe's dilemma. He wrote, 'I am so perplexed as to the most peaceable course to adopt as to the surplice!'

[75] *Ibid.*

[76] *The Times*, 27 Jan. 1845.

[77] Temperley, *op. cit*, p. 279, quoting figures from Charles Mackeson's surveys in London. Victorian London was more liturgically advanced than most parts of England, and lower figures should be expected elsewhere.

[78] *The Times*, 27 Jan. 1845.

Lord's Supper is celebrated,' it was reported of Walker, 'he has introduced it every on [*sic*] Sunday throughout the year and has applied portions of the money, so collected from pew to pew, to extra-parochial purposes'.[79] However, this was but one of a catalogue of complaints which also included wearing a surplice in the pulpit and the fact 'that he has introduced the sacring bell and *Ter Sanctus* before the communion service, contrary to the usual form of worship'. For the epicentre of discontent about the weekly offertory and for which there is a very full record, one has to turn to the village of Hurst in Berkshire. The story can be traced so well because one of the aggrieved parishioners was John Walter, the main proprietor of *The Times*, who made sure the proceedings were fully reported in his great newspaper. The perpetual curate, the Rev. A. A. Cameron, had the admirable intention of giving the money from the first and fifth Sundays to the sick and needy in the parish, with the proceeds from other Sundays going to such bodies as the Royal Berkshire Hospital, the Incorporated Church Building Society, the Additional Curates Society or the Society for the Propagation of the Gospel in Foreign Parts. Attacks on the weekly offertory here and elsewhere were variously made on the basis of its being an innovation and that it was an additional 'tax' on parishioners, while the better off claimed they were contributing to good causes anyway. In the interests of parochial peace, Cameron and many other clergymen suspended the practice, and bishops, like Henry Pepys of Worcester, warned that their clergy should proceed with sensitivity and with the consent of their flocks. The weekly offertory gradually re-emerged but seems not to have been as common as the use of the surplice in the pulpit. By 1869 a weekly collection was taken in 18.2% of churches in London and its suburbs. The percentage grew rapidly to 30.4% in 1872, 45% in 1875 and 56.1% in 1882.[80]

Another cause of discontent which arose from rubrical exactitude was the reading of the prayer for the Church Militant. This long prayer occurs in the communion service in the Prayer Book and is linked to two, rather contradictory rubrics. The one which precedes the prayer directs that it shall be said 'when there is a Communion', while one at the end of that service implies that this 'general Prayer' is to be part of services on non-communion days and other holy days. According to the Bishop of Worcester's Charge to ordinands in 1844 which endeavoured to keep them from falling into the pit of discord that innovation could bring, the reading of the prayer 'had been almost universally discontinued in our parochial churches'.[81] The bishop could hardly speak out against using the prayer but clearly did nothing to encourage it. He noted that its abandonment was in part due to the fact that it

[79]   *The Times*, 1 Mar. 1845, quoting from the *West Briton*.
[80]   As note 70.
[81]   He added that it had been discontinued in many cathedrals too. His Charge is printed in *The Times*, 25 Dec. 1844.

lengthened the service which was 'distressing to those who are in advanced years'.[82] Such niceties were not in the minds of Camdenians like Henry Coddington of Ware or Walter Blunt of Helston as they sought to follow a rigid observance of the rubrics. Once again, what began as an innovation (or, rather, rediscovery of a lost usage) by advanced churchman became common practice in time. Unfortunately I am unaware of any statistics to provide quantitative support.

Another popular feature of advanced worship was to have two candles on the altar. There was plenty of long-established precedent, especially in cathedrals and colleges but they were still a focus of Evangelical protest. They appeared, for example, as early as 1837 at Littlemore under J. R. Bloxam, being copied from the ones already in use at Magdalen College. The altar arrangement from Littlemore, complete 'with books and candlesticks was much admired, and it was copied exactly by Frederick Oakeley at the Margaret Chapel in London in 1839.'[83] A friend of Bloxam's was the Rev. Bernard Smith of Leadenham, Lincs, and he introduced not only altar lights, but also an altar cross, processional crucifix, and a stone altar in 1842.[84] The Rev. W. J. E. Bennett, who used altar candles, was emphatic that the long history of usage actually meant they were 'commanded' by the Church.[85] They are in fact specifically ordered by the royal injunctions of 1547. There was no legal challenge for a while and it was ruled in 1855 that they were allowable provided they were simply for lighting, and not ceremonial use. This remained the case until 1890 when they were allowed for purely ceremonial purposes by Archbishop Benson in his judgement of that year.

A further tradition that became popular, and which began as a Tractarian innovation, probably in the late 1830s, was the use of an altar cross and altar flowers. They were the focus of an unseemly incident in 1847 at St John, Torquay. Here, W. G. Parks Smith, chose to adorn the altar on Easter Day with a wooden cross, two feet high, decorated with flowers and evergreens and, on either side, a small glass flower vase.[86] Bishop Philpotts, who worshipped at the church, attempted to remove the vases at the

82 He also argued 'that the disuse of this prayer is of itself a proof that the surplice was not usually worn in the pulpit. Had it been so there would have been no difficulty in the minister returning from the pulpit to the communion-table, and reading the prayer ... It was because he wore a gown, and not a surplice, that this practice was found inconvenient, and therefore was discontinued.'

83 Ollard, op. cit., p. 119, quoting a letter from Oakeley to Bloxam. Ollard also quotes A. P. de Lisle (p. 124), who on a visit to Bloxam, found three parish churches in the neighbourhood of Oxford 'fitted up in a very Catholic way, with large candelabra in front of the altars and great wax tapers, besides two candlesticks on the altars themselves, and the cross and flowers, etc.'

84 Ollard, op. cit., p. 123.

85 The Principles of the Book of Common Prayer considered (London, 1842), p. 335.

86 Details from Boggis, op. cit., pp. 71–6.

offertory, to signify his disapproval. What he did not know was that they were attached to the altar by pieces of string for the sake of security. He pushed one vase behind the altar spilling the water and leaving the vase hanging in mid-air (he wisely left the other one alone). He informed Smith that his adornments were illegal and a Court of Inquiry was set up to examine the affair and which was, in effect, the trial of a minister for a ritualistic practice. This was held on 11 May when the Chancellor, the Archdeacon of Totnes, and three other clergymen heard about other innovations 'such as turning to the east during part of the service and the use of alms-bags instead of dishes, and also the dividing of the service of Morning Prayer between two ministers, all of which the Bishop disapproved.'[87] Judgement, based on the interpretation of the Ornaments Rubric, was delivered on 28 May against Smith who was admonished by his bishop not to reoffend. The altar cross was considered not allowable under Archbishop Grindal's enquiry of 1576 which asked 'Whether crosses, and such other relics and monuments of superstition, be utterly defaced, broken and destroyed.' Philpotts' comments about the cross are important as revealing the gulf between old High Churchmanship and the caste of mind of Tractarian-inspired clergy, interested as they were in the concepts of the real presence and eucharistic sacrifice:

> The outward, the material cross,' the bishop noted, 'is peculiarly unfitted to be placed in contact with the sacramental symbols. Instead of exciting the mind to due contemplation of the triumphant issue of our Lord's sufferings, it tends to chain it down to the sufferings themselves.

Crosses on altars, were not considered legal until 1857 and then it was stipulated that they must not be affixed (or appear to be affixed) to the table or retable.[88] Flower vases on the altar were given legality in 1870 by a Court of Arches ruling.[89]

Two marks of very extreme, new-style High Churchmanship were the use of eucharistic vestments and incense at an early date. S. L. Ollard links the revival of Eucharistic vestments to the publication of William Palmer's *Origines Liturgicae* of 1832 in which he argues the alb, chasuble and stole were ordered to be worn by the Prayer Book.[90] Eucharistic vestments are said to have been first worn in modern times at Wilmcote, Warwickshire in 1849.[91] Neale, in the vanguard as usual, wore a chasuble at East Grinstead in 1850,

---

[87]   *Ibid.*, p. 73.
[88]   Liddell & Horne *v.* Westerton/Liddell *v.* Beal.
[89]   In the *Elphinstone* v. *Purchas* case.
[90]   Ollard, *op. cit.*, p. 124.
[91]   *Ibid.*, p. 124. *The Oxford Dictionary of the Christian Church* (Oxford, 1997), 570, gives the date as 1845 but I have preferred to use that given by the earlier source. Herring, *op. cit.*, p. 90, says a few clergy wore chasubles and burned incense after 1845, but does not name examples, so his statement must be treated with much caution.

and vestments were used at St Thomas, Harlow, Essex, in 1852.[92] W. J. E. Bennett had vestments ready for use in 1850 but, in view of the increasing opposition to his practices at St Barnabas, Pimlico, he prudently decided to delay their use.[93] The red chasuble was first worn by the Rev. T. Chamberlain at St Thomas, Oxford, on Whitsunday 1854.[94] It is claimed there were other scattered attempts to employ full eucharistic vesture about 1850[95] but they must have been few and far between until well into the second half of the nineteenth century. When the remarkable Father Lowder set up the mission that became St Peter, London Docks in 1856, he wore vestments from the very outset and their usage has continued to this day. Two years later they were introduced at the mother church of St George-in-the-East, by the Rev. Bryan King, and were among the features targeted in the infamous riots in 1859–60.[96] Mackeson's invaluable survey of London churches shows that vestments were used in only 2.4% in 1869 and not rising above 5% by 1882.[97] The use of incense was exceptionally rare before the surge in ritualism in the late 1860s, although the Rev. Edward Stuart (joined the Society 1846–7) did venture to use it from 1854 (though vestments were delayed till Easter 1864).[98] This may have been its first modern use in an Anglican church, though there is a slight possibility that incense had been used at the Margaret Chapel under Upton Richards.[99] It was not until some time in the 1860s that the liturgically adventurous W. J. E. Bennett adopted it at Frome.[100]

Auricular, private or sacramental confession, the final 'innovation' to be considered here, aroused great passions and was seen by critics as both a Romanising advance, and as an offensive intrusion into family life, attacking

[92] *Ibid.*

[93] Day, *op. cit.*, pp. 8–9.

[94] Ollard, *op. cit.*, p. 124.

[95] G. W. E. Russell, *Saint Alban the Martyr, Holborn: a History of Fifty Years* (London, 1913), p. 295.

[96] Chadwick, *op. cit.*, pp. 498–9. P. Anson, *Fashions in Church Furnishings* (1965), p. 78 is evidently wrong in saying that the first use of vestments in a London church was by the Rev. Edward Stuart at St Mary Magdalene, Munster Square, in 1864.

[97] Temperley, *op. cit.*, p. 279. The figures for 1872 are 3.3.%, 4.6% in 1875 and in 1878 and in 1882 4.1%.

[98] Ollard, *op. cit.*, p. 129, quoting the Royal Commission on Ecclesiastical Discipline.

[99] H. W. & I. Law, *op. cit.*, pp. 170–1 tell how Alexander and Mildred Beresford Hope suspected Richards of the 'secret burning of incense' in 1850 but nothing was proved and they may well have been mistaken.

[100] Day, *op. cit.*, p. 17. Mackeson's London survey shows incense use in 1.4% of churches in 1869, 1.0% in 1872, 2.2% in 1875, 1.6% in 1878, 1.1% in 1882. Given the minute number of vestment- and incense-using churches, the dip after 1875 cannot be thought significant unless the examples and reasons are discovered and explained.

husband/wife and parent/child relationships. Then there was the secrecy that inevitably surrounded the process and dark fears as to what took place at confession. Women, many felt, were especially vulnerable and the case at St Saviour, Leeds in 1850, when a deacon was charged with asking indelicate questions of a married woman at confession, epitomised the prurient fears about what went on. Auricular confession was associated in many people's minds with the new sisterhoods and brotherhoods that sprang up in the '40s and which, themselves, were the object of anti-Tractarian suspicions.[101] These strands all came together for J. M. Neale in 1855 when he heard the confession of Emily Scobell, a young woman from Brighton, and was bitterly attacked by her outraged, Evangelical clergyman-father. Yet listening to troubled consciences was something with which many Evangelical ministers were familiar. Indeed, one of the exhortations in the Communion Service directs that 'no man should come to the Holy Communion, but ... with a quiet conscience' and, if he does not have one, he may turn to a 'learned Minister ... and open his grief ... and receive the benefit of absolution'. But the first *regular*, sacramental confession practised by Tractarian clergymen was, apparently, by Pusey, from 1838. Keble, too, was an advocate of confession at Hursley, as was Manning before his conversion to Rome. Such confession was condemned by Bishop Blomfield in 1842. Exactly how widespread it was in early Victorian England we shall probably never know, but it certainly took place in some of the more advanced churches and, by 1850, was more prevalent than, say, the use of eucharistic vestments or incense. It is highly likely that some of the more advanced Camdenian clergy practised auricular confession at an early stage – Keble, Manning and the Rev. W. J. Butler certainly did[102] – and, later, a declaration in 1873 in favour of the practice, signed by twenty-nine clergymen included the names of nine who appear in the list of Camdenians in the appendix.[103]

Frequency of Services

The Book of Common Prayer optimistically directs that morning and evening prayer are 'daily to be said and used throughout the year.' Nigel Yates notes efforts by late eighteenth-century bishops and archdeacons to encourage more

[101]   Walter Walsh's (in)famous, virulent book *The Secret History of the Oxford Movement* (4th ed. 1898) devotes much ink to uncovering the evils of the practice.

[102]   Walsh, p. 91, quotes Butler writing to Manning about confession at Wantage and airing the problem of husbands objecting to their wives entering the confessional. He gives the date as 29 Aug. 1840 but this must surely be a misprint for 1850 since Butler did not go to Wantage until 1846.

[103]   The declaration is printed at the back of T. T. Carter, *The Doctrine of Confession in the Church of England* (2nd. ed. 1885), pp. 301–2. The nine are A. R. Ashwell, W. J. Butler, J. C. Chambers, J. L. Galton, F. C. Grey, F.H. Murray, J. Skinner, G. C. White and G. Williams.

frequent services but the clergy usually replied that, although this was desirable, the laity failed to respond by attending.[104] Rubrical correctness could only be expected in cathedrals. Sunday was the day for church-going and people could expect one or more services within reasonable access. At rural churches there might only be one service (known as single duty). Yates quotes figures to show that in Norfolk three-quarters of churches had only single duty, whereas in the diocese of York, the number was rather less, with just over half the churches so served.[105] But, by the time the CCS was founded, there were already signs of change. In the diocese of Oxford, Yates adds, the number of churches with single duty was seventy-five in 1825 but fell to thirth-four in 1838 and continued to fall with only nine in 1866. Advanced clergymen in urban parishes attempted more ambitious things. At Bennett's St Paul, Knightsbridge, there were upwards of five services on Sunday and a choir, decently robed, to participate in them.[106] When the Rev. G. A. Denison (later Archdeacon of Taunton and famously prosecuted in the '50s for teaching the doctrine of the Real Presence), arrived at his parish of East Brent, Somerset, in 1845 he quickly introduced daily matins and evensong.[107] Similarly the Rev. W. J. Butler introduced daily services at Wantage shortly after his arrival in 1846 and they proved extremely popular, attracting anywhere between twenty-seven and a remarkable hundred one day in July 1860.[108] The most zealous clergy adjusted the times of the services to gain the greatest attendance, laying on early services with the aim of attracting working people. Daily services, however, remained the exception rather than the rule. In 1850 out of 600 or so London churches only fifty-six had daily services and by 1870 the number of metropolitan churches with such services was only 132.[109] They were, without doubt, signs of the new, advanced churchmanship which was a good deal more prevalent in London than in most areas of England.

It is widely known that few pre-Victorian parish churches had communion celebrations more than four times a year and that the frequency increased in Victorian times. But as with daily services, there are signs that more frequent celebrations were coming in even before Tractarian ideals were established, which perhaps supports the claims of the Bishop of Worcester, quoted at the start of this chapter, in relation to greater devotion immediately before the birth of Tractarianism. In Leicestershire, for example, where early Tractarian influence was decidedly lacking, there was an apparent significant shift in the pattern of observance in the period from 1832 to 1842 at churches

[104] Yates, *op. cit.*, p. 62.
[105] Yates, *op. cit.*, p. 57.
[106] G. T. Day, *William James Early Bennett, 1804–1886* (Frome, 1986), p. 7.
[107] G. A. Denison, *Notes on my life, 1805–78* (Oxford & London, 1878), p. 96.
[108] Herring, *op. cit.*, pp. 102–3.
[109] Reed, *op. cit.*, p. 68.

for which usable data exists:[110]

	% of churches	
	1832	1842
Up to and including 3 times a year	10	10
4 times a year	78	64
5–11 times a year	7	18
12 or more times a year	5	8

By the 1860s monthly celebrations had probably become the norm over many or most parts of England. Anthony Russell quotes figures for the diocese of Salisbury which show that by 1855 monthly celebration was common and a dozen years later it was usual:[111]

Out of 556 churches:	1855	1867
Monthly	181	292
Weekly	5	10

Russell also shows how in Oxfordshire there was a shift from quarterly to monthly between 1838 and 1866:[112]

	No. of churches	
	1838	1866
4 times a year	'Most'	10
5–11 times a year	17	21
Monthly	9	'Most'
3-weekly or fortnightly	–	20
Weekly	–	12
Daily	–	1

The daily case – Cowley – was exceptional, and this frequency was only found in the most ardent Tractarian parishes. It had been instituted by the extreme High-Church Rev. George Rundle Prynne at St Peter, Plymouth, but specifically as a response to the cholera epidemic of 1850. The same reason had led to daily celebrations at St Saviour, Leeds, the church founded by Pusey. However, apparently without such a cause, shortly after moving to Frome in 1852, Bennett not only increased the number of all services in general but also included a 7.00 a.m daily communion.[113] To ensure that early-rising working people had no excuse for not communicating, he even

110 Taken from Archdeacons' Visitations (Leics Record Office 245'50/1–5, /8, /9). The figures are converted to percentages for comparison purposes; usable data exists for 194 churches in 1832 and 245 in 1842.
111 A. Russell, *The Clerical Profession* (London, 1980), pp. 106.
112 *Ibid.*, pp. 103, 106. The figures presented here summarise those given by Russell in order to make a straight comparison between 1838 and 1866. He makes no mention of a greater frequency in 1838 so I have presumed there were no instances. Other information about Plymouth, Leeds, London Docks and Newland also comes from Russell.
113 W. N. Yates, '"Bells and Smells": London, Brighton and South Coast Religion Reconsidered', *Southern History* 5 (1983), p. 130.

had an occasional 5.15 a.m. celebration. Two Society members in the vanguard of liturgical advance, Fr Lowder and the Rev. James Skinner, both introduced daily celebrations at their respective churches of St Peter, London Docks, and Newland, Worcs., in the late 1860s.[114]

Opposition and Support

Neale's practices were, even by turn-of-the-century Anglo-Catholic standards, extreme and the fierce reaction is hardly surprising. Other innovating clergymen were much more moderate, and the early Victorian changes now seem wholly unexceptional, so the strength of the opposition they engendered needs some explaining. Of course, any change in any institution always has its detractors, but when that institution happened to be the Church of England, by law established, born in turmoil and bloodshed, and with a history of three centuries, then emotions naturally ran high. At the level of the typical parish (whatever that may mean) reforming clergy could expect to meet a wall of suspicion and resistance. Even in the supposedly more open, broad-minded late twentieth century, parochial discord is still often triggered by outwardly minor issues, and deep feelings are stirred by the externals of worship. In addition to all this, a number of factors conspired to produce a charged atmosphere as the Tracts were published and the CCS began its crusade. 1832, with its threats for the very overthrow of Church and State, was still a vivid memory, and fears of radical uprisings and revolution lingered long in the minds of those who had charge of the country's governance, industry and institutions. As this immediate danger passed, the Established Church found itself subjected to enforced change at the hands of the Grey and Melbourne Governments. Reform of the Irish bishoprics had triggered Newman's famous sermon of 1833, the Ecclesiastical Commissioners had been set up in 1835 to reform Church revenues, tithes were commuted in 1836 and the Pluralities Act of 1838 did much to eradicate absenteeism. Dissenters were still making advances at the expense of the Church of England although a greatly increased amount of Anglican church-building in the 1830s was doing something to resist this particular tide. However, the thing that struck most fear into the hearts and minds of those who resisted the new trend of change was no longer the threat of Nonconformity but its opposite – 'Popery'.

For staunch Protestants with an ingrained revulsion towards Rome, Catholic Emancipation in 1829 was another worrying advance for the Vatican and it made both friends and foes of the Church of England look at the national Church with a heightened awareness of its real or imagined shortcomings. The next quarter of a century was characterised by a constant

---

[114] Information, again, from Russell. Lowder's celebrations were at 5.45 a.m. and 8.00 a.m. Skinner celebrated seven times a year when he came to Newland in 1861, increasing to daily in 1867. In his memoirs (*op. cit.*, p. 96), Archdeacon Denison recorded that he introduced daily celebrations at East Brent in 1874.

GEOFFREY K. BRANDWOOD

fear of Roman Catholic progress and signs of it were read into minutiae as we
have seen. Such religious tribalism may now seem absurd but the late
twentieth-century history of Northern Ireland provides us perhaps with some
insight into how English Protestants, perceiving themselves under pressure,
felt and acted between 1830 and the early '50s. The CCS, although it
vociferously declared its Anglican credentials, was accused of promoting
Popery. Matters came to a head in 1844 with the Round Church crisis, attacks
from the Rev. Francis Close, and the resignations of the Bishops of Exeter and
Lincoln. Henry Philpotts of Exeter detailed his reasoning. In a letter dated 26
December 1844, which was reprinted in the Devon press and then in *The
Times*, he wrote:

> So little do I sympathise with any Papalizing party in the Church, that a few
> weeks ago I withdrew my name from the list of members of a society to
> which ... I had considered it an Honour to belong ... on discovering that its
> seal exhibited the Virgin Mary crowned, with the infant Saviour in her arms,
> and attended by two saints. ... This I deemed to be, at the least, a most
> injurious insult to the feeling of Protestants.[115]

The fact that the seal was designed by a Roman Catholic, 'that great master of
Christian device, Mr. A. W. Pugin' as *The Ecclesiologist* described him,
probably did not help.[116] Hitherto Philpotts had shown considerable
toleration towards Tractarian sympathisers. At this moment, however, he was
in the midst of the unseemly surplice controversy, and resignation from a
Society about whose aims he was now nervous, must have seemed a good way
of putting some distance between himself and what was seen as High Church
extremism. 1845 was the year of crisis for the CCS and attacks on the
advanced views of its leaders came from within the ranks. At the famous sixth
anniversary meeting at which the future of the society was debated, its suspect
inclinations were openly raised by Samuel Lee, Professor of Hebrew, and
Adam Sedgwick, Professor of Geology, both of them in holy orders. The
result of the deliberations and the reorganisation of the society was that 121
members (15%) seceded, and the Society moved its base from Cambridge to
London, leaving the leaders to pursue their brand of churchmanship as before.

---

[115] The letter was addressed to H. March Phillipps and read at a meeting in Torquay.
It was printed in *Woolmer's Exeter Gazette* whence it was taken for national
circulation in *The Times*, 30 Dec. 1844. From here it was taken up by other
papers. When reprinting the extract above, the vehemently Protestant *Lancaster
Gazette* (4 Jan. 1845) added its own gloss on those who resist innovations.
Referring specifically to people's opposition to preaching in the surplice, it said
'They resist because the wearing of the surplice, by authority, will be a triumph
to a party in the Church whose avowed object is to revive obsolete and
superstitious practices.'

[116] *Ecclesiologist*, 3 (1844), p. 185.

92

For the workings of Popish accusations at parish level and how they were dealt with, it is instructive to look at the well-documented Kentish case of East Farleigh which has already been touched upon and which was given a measure of national publicity by staunch Protestants. Readers of the *Lancaster Gazette* learned about the 'mummeries at East Farleigh' by the 'ultra-tractarian' H. W. Wilberforce in a transcript of the petition sent to Archbishop Howley by some of the aggrieved parishioners.[117] The Archdeacon of Maidstone, W. R. Lyall (a Camdenian), and, like his Archbishop, an old-style High Churchman, looked into the charges. Far from siding with the petitioners, he found their evidence flawed and, in part, simply untrue. His measured response injected a note of calm and common sense into the heated air of East Farleigh. Nigel Yates, in reproducing the documents comments: 'The strong support given to Henry Wilberforce by his archdeacon is very typical of the defence of the early Tractarians by the old-fashioned "high churchmen".'[118] He goes on to show how similar support was given by Archbishop Howley himself when he was drawn into the fray, and that the accusations were stirred up by a churchwarden, G. Kennard, as a result of personal grudges.

To give another, and slightly later, example of episcopal support for an ultra-High clergyman, we can return yet again to Bishop Philpotts.[119] The Rev. G. R. Prynne who came to St Peter, Plymouth in 1848, upset his opponents by his working with Priscilla Lydia Sellon's sisterhood, the Society of the Most Holy Trinity, established in Devonport the same year. In 1852 he was hauled up before Philpotts on allegations that he had compelled orphans in the sisters' care to attend confession and that he had asked 'corrupting questions'. It soon became evident that key witnesses were perjuring themselves, and Philpotts, who had defended the principle of confession in his Charge of 1851 (but discouraged 'the general habit'), exonerated Prynne. He remarked 'I acquit him even of indiscretion, and I pray God that every clergyman in my diocese may do his duty as well as Mr Prynne has done his.' The East Farleigh and Plymouth cases show how personality clashes could cause strife and how innovating clergy needed to proceed with sensitivity and restraint if they expected to avoid it.

It is probably true (though no statistics are available to support it) that it was easier to introduce new forms of worship at a new urban church rather than an existing one with old-style traditions. The Rev. Edward Stuart was fortunate when he went as minister at St Mary Magdalene, Munster Square when it opened in 1852 since there was no established tradition to inhibit advanced practices. From the first he used the eastward position, altar lights and a surpliced choir. Furthermore the situation was probably easier in

---

[117] *Lancaster Gazette*, 23 March 1844.
[118] Yates, *Kent...*, p. 41.
[119] The following is taken from Reed, *op. cit.*, p. 48.

London as there were a great many churches for people to chose from. There were opportunities for diversity in worship and throughout the nineteenth-century London was in advance of the rest of the country in terms of its modes of worship, not least at the Ecclesiological Society's model church of All Saints, Margaret Street under the Rev. Upton Richards. In country parishes, on the other hand, the prudent clergyman would introduce change gradually, often preceded by a gentle course of instruction so that his motives might not be misinterpreted.[120] A simple example is the desirability of kneeling when praying which was meant to follow when open benches replaced box pews. To establish a fully choral service with the consent of the parish, competently performed and with the choir in surplices, might take years to achieve. But very zealous clergy, like Bennett at Frome and Carter at Wantage, who acted with sensitivity and who showed their deep commitment to their parishes could sometimes bring about a very rapid transformation. Quite clearly implacable opposition to ceremonial and doctrinal change on the part of Anglicans was neither inevitable nor everlasting. The course of the rest of the nineteenth century clearly shows that. In the second half of the century worship in the Church of England moved bodily 'upwards'. What was 'high' in 1850 would be thought quite moderate in 1900. What was practised at the more advanced Anglo-Catholic churches in 1900 would have been not just inadmissable, but inconceivable in 1850.

1850 and Beyond

The development of ceremonial in the Anglican church is sometimes seen in Whiggish terms as some kind of inevitable, inexorable process. Furthermore it tends to be dominated by colourful cases, often set within atypical buildings. Elaborate ceremonial and the introduction of Continental practices only really came in after the late 1850s. They appeared with a new generation of young clergymen who spearheaded what came to be called 'ritualism', a term rarely used in the 1840s. A few of the those who joined the CCS during its glory days in the '40s can be said to be part of this phase, such as T. Pelham Dale, Upton Richards and A. D. Wagner, but younger key figures like Alexander MacKonochie or John Purchas mostly by-passed the Society in the '50s and '60s. Fr Lowder was a rare exception, joining in 1852. Others, like Fr R. W. R. Dolling, became active after the Society had faded away. G. W. Herring identifies the defining moment of change to ritualism as the publication of Purchas's *Directorium Anglicanum* in 1858.[121] He argues that ritualism was *not* an inevitable consequence of the Oxford Movement (and one would add, by implication, the Cambridge one too). This might be so but the debate is somewhat sterile in that ritualism, and the 'highering' of worship

---

[120]   Herring, *op. cit.*, p. 89.
[121]   *Op. cit.*, pp. 284–6.

generally, *did* build upon the existence of Tractarian and ecclesiological foundations, and we have no way of rerunning history to know whether something similar would have arisen without them. Given Victorian Romantic propensities, it is hard to conceive of the Victorian Church maintaining the plain dignity (if such it was) of the Georgian one.

The fierce opposition aroused by the changes in the '40s might have brought them to a stop, just as the Society nearly came to grief. 1845 was the key year. Certainly many clergy retrenched for a while, and, for its part, the Society had to reinvent itself, but the forces set in motion at Oxford and Cambridge were too strong to be halted. Earlier in this chapter much space was devoted to the disputes over the offertory and the surplice and, in particular, the diocese of Exeter. But, 250 miles away and at exactly the same time, the Tractarian and Camdenian Henry Alford was restoring his Leicestershire church of Wymeswold under Pugin and did not, so far as we know, attract any accusations of Popery. On the contrary, when the church reopened in 1846 with three days of rejoicing and services, various worthies and the correspondents in the local press were beside themselves with praise – no fears about Romanising or suspicious practices.[122] Leicestershire, around the Charnwood Forest area, was the scene of important efforts by Roman Catholics to expand their activities and, in 1848, the vicar of Whitwick actually thought that far from being a mark of Romanising, 'The restoration of [his] Church ... seems to present one efficient mode of defence' against four Catholic priests who had come to live in the parish.[123] As time went on there was less and less association of church restoration *per se* with Popery. Indeed, the Bishop of Peterborough was so convinced of its virtues that in his Visitation at Leicester in 1867, he reasoned with stupendous optimism that it induced more frequent attendance at church, more fervour in worship, etc., etc., more love of Christ, and, hence, 'more souls made over to salvation'.[124] Another sign of moderating attitudes was when, in 1850, the 'Rev. Francis Courtenay, once mobbed for wearing a surplice in the pulpit ... received a presentation to mark the "gratitude and esteem" of St Sidwell's.'[125]

[122]   *Leicester J.* 24 Apr. 1846.
[123]   Note in the appeal for funds in *Leicester J.* 6 Dec. 1850. Whitwick is very close to Mount St Bernard, founded in 1835 and the first abbey to be built in England since the Reformation. The driving force was Ambrose Lisle March Phillipps. Rosemary Hill tells me of a letter from Phillipps to John Bloxam (of Littlemore fame) stating that, of the 3,000 people in Whitwick, 'not more than 250 individuals are members of the Anglican church'. No doubt they were mostly like the 800 Osgathorpe parishioners that Phillipps also mentions, largely 'dissenters, Baptists and Ranters', rather than Catholics(!)
[124]   *Leicester J.*, 11 Oct. 1867, supplement.
[125]   *Exeter Flying Post*, 4 Apr. 1850, quoted in R. Newton, *Victorian Exeter* (Leicester, 1968), p.103; I am grateful to Chris Brooks for this reference.

1850, however, did produce a great furore arising from the re-establishment of the Roman Catholic hierarchy. Advanced clergymen came under attack once more, most notoriously in Lord John Russell's letter to the Bishop of Durham in November 1850. His words reflected the view that had been formed within Queen Victoria's mind, namely, that Church and State were less threatened by Rome than the insidious activities within the Church of England itself. Alighting upon the advanced practices of his day, Russell wrote, 'What then, is the danger to be apprehended from a foreign prince of no great power, compared to the danger within the gates from the unworthy sons of the Church of England herself?'[126] This formed a rallying-point for those opposed to change. St Barnabas, Pimlico, became the focus of protest and the disturbances, accompanied by condemnation from Bishop Blomfield, forced W. J. E. Bennett to resign (which was tragically ironic since Russell was a parishioner of the mother church, St Paul, Knightsbridge, where, according to Bennett, the innovations had not troubled him until the outcry of 1850).[127] Bennett moved to Frome and continued to worship with advanced ceremonial *but* with the support and, indeed, devotion of his parishioners. Advanced churchmanship, of which Bennett and Courtenay are but two high-profile representatives, survived the storms of 1850–1, just as church restoration, and the complex messages it represented, went on from strength to strength. The cases of the restorations at Wymeswold and Whitwick and of what happened to Bennett (post-1850) and Courtenay show that there *could* be popular support for such schemes and such men. Their story was repeated all over the country in less exciting circumstances, as the work of the Tractarians and the ecclesiologists bore fruit.

A key event in the 1850s was a legal judgment in 1857 which gave mild support for advanced churchmen, supporting as it did, a free-standing altar cross, credence table, (non-ceremonial) altar lights, and a cross on a chancel screen.[128] Next came the publication of the Rev. John Purchas's famous *Directorium Anglicanum* in 1858 on the liturgical side, and the completion of All Saints, Margaret Street, in 1859 on the architectural. In the '60s ceremonial and church-building and restoration burgeoned as never before.

---

[126] Chadwick, *op. cit.*, pp. 296–7.

[127] Bennett stated his case that Russell had been a happy parishioner hitherto and that the troubles at St Paul's were occasioned by the publication of the letter in *A First Letter to the Right Honourable Lord John Russell, M.P., on the Present Persecution of a Certain Portion of the English Church* (London, 1850). Unfortunately there is not space here to examine the complex question of whether Bennett's troubles were self-inflicted intransigence, the result of the bigotry of others, the product of hypocrisy by Russell (or, indeed, all of these things).

[128] The judicial committee of the Privy Council deciding on Liddell *v.* Westerton and Liddell *v.* Beal.

Architectural excess was toned down from about 1870, and there were attempts to do the same for liturgical practice through opposition to ritualism and the setting up of a Royal Commission on Ritual in 1867. The end result of the latter process was the well-intentioned but, as history was to prove, fatally misjudged Public Worship Regulation Act of 1874. The four clergymen (including Pelham Dale) who went to prison as a result of its workings were the martyrs for their ceremonial cause and the widespread sympathy for them demonstrated the folly of legislating for the externals of worship in this way. By the 1890s Anglo-Catholic clergy were able to conduct services with a freedom and in splendid architectural settings undreamed-of by the founders of the Oxford Movement and the Cambridge Camden Society in the heady days around 1840.

Acknowledgements:
I am deeply grateful to Thomas Cocke, Rosemary Hill, Chris Miele and Teresa Sladen for reading the draft text of this chapter and making important suggestions to improve it. I am also grateful to John Bailey, Chris Brooks and John Elliott for help in various ways.

'...blink [him] by silence'? The Cambridge Camden Society and A. W. N. Pugin.

RODERICK O'DONNELL

The Catholic convert A. W. N. Pugin (1812-1852) was one of the central figures of the Gothic Revival, as well as the most influential church architect of the period but subscribers to *The Ecclesiologist* (1841-1868) would have had little inkling of this.[1] It was his assertive Roman Catholicism which put them off, *The Builder* calling him somewhat tongue-in-cheek the 'virtual pope or chief pontiff' of the Gothic Revival.[2] Yet Pugin was one of the first Catholics to make contact with Oxford Movement personalities such as the Revd J. R. Bloxam of Magdalen College Oxford and he remained personally sympathetic to aspects of the Anglican Communion. However, as early as December 1839 Neale and Webb preferred the Quaker Rickman to the Catholic Pugin: '[we] determined today on inviting Rickman to join.' Pugin as a Roman Catholic was rejected – perhaps prudently: 'we are already too much accused of popery to render so violent a man a desirable Honorary Member'.[3] The Society as constituted in 1839 confined ordinary membership to 'members of the University of Cambridge', at that time still an exclusively Anglican and highly-clericalised body; both Neale and Webb were to become Anglican clergy. Although the membership expanded rapidly, and even included a Yorkshire Catholic gentleman, in 1846 the Society decided to expel members who became Catholic converts: 'their connexion would cease *ipso facto* upon publick profession of Romanism'.[4]

Yet the Society's founder members, notably Webb, who was one of the two honorary secretaries, sought out Pugin, and met him twice in Cambridge

---

[1]   R. O'Donnell, 'Pugin as a Church-Architect' in P. Atterbury and C. Wainwright (eds), *Pugin, a Gothic Passion* (New Haven and London, 1994), pp. 62-89.

[2]   *Builder,* 1 (1843), pp. 98-100.

[3]   J. M. Neale, *Diary*, Lambeth Palace Library, MS 3107, 5 Dec 1839 (information from Geoff Brandwood).

[4]   *Ecclesiologist,* 6 (1846), p. 5, referring to S. N. Stokes (see below, note 100). The ordinary membership 'being in communion with the Church of England' was redefined after 1846 'being omitted in the case of foreigners, being members of Catholic Churches': J. F. White, *The Cambridge Movement* (Cambridge 1962), quotations pp. 228-9, pp. 225-70.

as well as three times in London. Anglican commentators did not help the relationship by predicting that Pugin was about to rejoin the Church of England. Overall the Society as it represented the Anglican Gothic Revival (as opposed to Pugin's few individual Anglican patrons), was a hindrance rather than a help to him, and, as we shall see, it plagiarised his ideas while publicly berating him. Society members visited his buildings, read and exploited his teachings to such an extent that as Phoebe Stanton has observed 'Pugin [who] had earlier independently reached every conclusion to which the ecclesiologists were laying claim, had, in fact given [them] every opportunity to pick his ideas to pieces'.[5] There is a clear parallel between this attitude and Ruskin's notorious denunciations of Pugin.[6] By the time the Society's publications appeared in 1841, Pugin had already established certain principles particularly applicable to church architecture which *The Ecclesiologist* was to follow. The first might be called 'confessionalism' or 'denominationalism', the second 'integrism', the third 'liturgical antiquarianism', all of which were broadly Romantic attitudes. The fourth was 'rationalism' and the fifth 'reality', both part of the wider architectural debate of the period. The first three were particularly applicable to the vocation of church architect, the last two had much wider implications. By 1843 certain hostile commentators, such as W. H. Leeds and George Wightwick amongst architectural critics and later J. H. Newman among Catholic converts, were to dub this particularly totalitarian form of Revivalism as 'Puginism'.[7] Pugin was therefore seen to lead a whole architectural school or movement.

A central principle of *Contrasts* was that only a 'good' – or as it were a Catholic – man could produce good or Catholic architecture; 'correct' churches could not be designed by Protestants or Dissenters, no matter how good their credentials as antiquarians: Rickman the tabulator of Gothic styles was after all a Unitarian or Quaker. In 1838 Pugin attacked the Catholic Pro-Cathedral in London as 'the work of a protestant architect'[8] who by definition was therefore 'totally ignorant of any canonical regulation';[9] Pugin

---

5   P. Stanton, *The Gothic Revival and American Church Architecture: An episode in taste 1840–1856* (Baltimore, 1968), pp. 19–20; see also J. F. White, *op. cit.*, pp. 14, 76–7, 87, 117, 31, 179–180; N. Pevsner, *Some Architectural Writers of the Nineteenth Century* (Oxford, 1972), pp. 103–8; S. Muthesuis, *High Victorian Movement in Architecture (1850–1870)* (1972), pp. 1–2, 14–18; D. Watkin, *The Rise of Architectural History* (London, 1988), pp. 69–71.

6   John Ruskin, *Stones of Venice*, I (1851), pp. 371–3; for his jesuitical claim to have merely glanced at *Contrasts* see his *Modern Painters* (1856), III, p. 347; M. Belcher *A. W. N. Pugin: an Annotated Critical Bibliography* (1987), pp. 283–4, 301–2, 417, 442.

7   M. Belcher, *op. cit*, p. 214.

8   A. W. N. Pugin, 'Lectures on Ecclesiastical Architecture. Lecture the Second', in *Catholic Magazine*, n.s. vol II (June 1838), pp. 321–7.

9   A. W. N. Pugin, 'The Present State of Ecclesiastical Architecture in England.

would have been even crosser to know that he worked under the direction of a committee of 'Catholic gentlemen.'[10] Pugin's propaganda was intended to dismiss local Protestant architects from Catholic patronage; Rickman was still being commissioned to build Catholic churches in the West Midlands. The Society's encouragement of only High Church Anglican architects exactly mirrors the introduction by Pugin of a 'confessional' qualification into architectural practice, as Neale and Webb were to put it in their edition of Durandus, 'A Catholick architect must be Catholick in heart' and 'we ought to look for at least church-membership from one who ventures to design a church',[11] a point which was to be used against Pugin.

Pugin's 'integrism' read across from confessionalism to that of the choice of style: architects already in practice must (if they were to continue with church architecture) conform to his propagation of 'not a style ... but a principle'.[12] Thus, the well-established Catholic church architect J. J. Scoles was to be condemned in 'Present State' for designing 'the most original combination of modern deformities that has been erected for some time past for the sacred purposes of a Catholic church on the all front principles of the Dissenters a modern or pagan form of church'. The offending building was in the Neo-Norman style and had the plan of a Counter-Reformation church.[13] By contrast M. E. Hadfield was approved, 'for many earlier edifices by this architect were serious departures from the true Christian style, but what errors of judgement he may formerly have committed he now comes forward as a reviver of the true old school.'[14] This ranking of architects was to be followed in the 'approved' and 'condemned' lists of *The Ecclesiologist*.

Pugin, beginning dramatically with the consecration of Oscott College chapel in 1838, was to impose liturgical antiquarianism on the public worship of the Catholic Church in England. He published his own buildings in the Catholic press, while ostensibly reviewing the work of others, describing his own St Mary, Uttoxeter, Staffordshire (1839–40) (plate 22) as 'the first

Article the First', from *Dublin Review*, 20 (May 1841), pp. 301–48; (1843 edition), p. 49.

10 R. O'Donnell, 'The Interior of St Mary Moorfields', in *The Georgian Group Journal*, vol. VII, 1997, pp. 71–4.

11 J. M. Neale and B. Webb (trans), Bishop William Durandus, *The Symbolism of Churches and Church Ornaments: a Translation of the First Book of the Rationale Divinorum Officinorium*, with an introductory essay, notes, and illustrations by J. M. Neale and B. Webb of Trinity College (Leeds, 1843), pp. xx, xxii.

12 A. W. N. Pugin, *An Apology for Revival of Christian Architecture in England* (1843), p. 44.

13 A. W. N. Pugin, 'The Present State ... Article the Second', from the *Dublin Review*, no 23, February 1842; 'New Catholic Church at Islington' (1843), pp. 114–117, plates 15–16.

14 *Ibid*., 'St Bede's Masboro,' pp. 112–4, plate 14. Pugin had not as yet met Hadfield, whose name appears as 'Hatfield'.

Catholic structure erected in strict accordance with the rules of ancient ecclesiastical architecture since the pretended Reformation'.[15] The Society attempted to do the same for the Church of England, explicitly through *The Ecclesiologist* and implicitly in Neale and Webb's translation of Bishop William Durandus *The symbolism of Churches and Church Ornaments: a translation of the first book of the Rationale Divinorum Officinorium* (of 1843).[16] This antiquarianism concerned not only the plan but the furnishing and ritual use of churches. Pugin laid down what was required: a distinct nave and chancel, separated by a rood screen. He described this in the last two paragraphs of the first edition of *Contrasts* (1836), in much greater detail in 'Present State' and with singular beauty in the chromolithography plates of the *Glossary of Ecclesiastical Ornament* (1844). Both Pugin and the Society were involved in a relentless search for 'authority' and what was 'correct'

On the basis of this apparently shared liturgical antiquarianism, Pugin and Catholics such as Ambrose Phillipps and even Wiseman had an almost millenarian expectation that the Church of England was about to submit to the Pope. Even a single visit to a Pugin church and attendance at a liturgy could lead to a conversion, as with the sixteen-year old St George Jackson Mivart.[17] But instead it was to be through the Society that certain Anglicans found in this antiquarianism the increasingly comfortable belief that they were the true heirs of the pre-Reformation Church, thus avoiding the question of historical authority which so obsessed Newman. This move from an Oxford Tractarianism – properly so-called – to a Cambridge inspired Ritualism, accommodated a more *à la carte* religion. Here, ultimately, the Society was more successful than Pugin, whose precise liturgical views were to be challenged after 1848 in the Rood Screen Controversy. It was an Oxford Movement clergyman convert to Catholicism, J. M. Capes, the editor of *The Rambler*, who wrote 'we have been shocked by Mr Pugin's sympathy with the Anglican heresy. We have ever regarded Puginism as identical with Puseyism'.[18]

[15] A. W. N. Pugin, 'Chancel of St Marie's, Uttoxeter' in *London & Dublin Orthodox Journal*, vol IX, (20 July 1839), pp. 33–6. M. Belcher, *op. cit.*, pp. 41–42. For Oscott College Chapel, see R O'Donnell, 'Pugin at Oscott' in Judith Champ (ed.), *The Oscottian*, 150th anniversary issue (1988), pp. 45–66.

[16] *The Symbolism of Churches, op. cit.* Pugin was critical of Anglican ritual antiquarianism, see 'Present State', *op. cit.*, pp. 20, 131–143, concluding 'either the Common Prayer or the ancient models must be abandoned' (p. 143), but he is more sympothetic in *An Apology, op. cit.*, pp. 25–31; see also J. M. White, *op. cit.*, pp. 133–4, and A. Symondson, 'Theology, Worship and the Late Victorian Church', in C. Brooks and A. Saint (eds), *The Victorian Church* (Manchester, 1995), pp. 194–222.

[17] St George Jackson Mivart (1827–1900) was received into the Roman Catholic church after a tour of Pugin's churches which culminated in High Mass at St Chad's, Birmingham.

Pugin popularised a certain element of French-derived Gothic structural rationalism, largely in his *True Principles of Pointed or Christian Architecture* (1841), particularly in the claim 'it is in *pointed architecture* alone *that these great principles have been carried out*'.[19] As we shall see, Neale and Webb were to react to the 'mere' rationalism or functionalism of Pugin, claiming to add to his inadequate teachings in their translation of Durandus. More to English taste, because it was intimately bound up with English views on the Picturesque, was Pugin's architectural 'reality', perhaps his most decisive break with the Romantic world.[20] Pugin reacted very strongly against the decorators' and tradesmen's tricks of the Regency building and furniture-making world,[21] and the Society was to spread this gospel with the slogan 'let every material be real'.[22] Pugin also valued 'apparent legibility' in architecture, so that 'the external and internal appearance of an edifice should be illustrative of, and in accordance with, the purpose for which it is destined'.[23] There were also shared ideas on architectural propriety. It was against all these criteria that the first new church reviewed by *The Ecclesiologist* was to be 'condemned'.

Webb visited Pugin's incomplete St George's Cathedral, Southwark, in August 1841.[24] It prompted him to write to Pugin. The latter subsequently referred to 'a curious letter from a Cambridge clergyman coming to see me. He has the good spirit but is evidently yet much in the dark. I trust to enlighten him.'[25] He explained to Bloxam, 'the Camden men have been carrying on most gloriously lately. I have had some very interesting correspondence with their chairman.'[26] Pugin invited Webb and another

[18] J. M. Capes [?], *The Rambler*, 8 (1851), 'Churches versus "Rooms"', pp. 41–6, quotation taken from pp. 45–6. This was prompted by Pugin's *Earnest Address on the Establishment of the Hierarchy* (London, 1851), and Pugin's announcement in *The Tablet*, March 1851, p. 149, of his pamphlet *New View on Old Subject: the English Schism Impartially Considered*. See below, note 123.

[19] A. W. N. Pugin, *True Principles of Pointed or Christian Architecture* (London, 1841), quotation p. 1; see also pp. 1–22 (see note 45). For the best recent discussion of its genesis and influence see A. Saint, 'The Fate of Pugin's True Principles' in P. Atterbury and C. Wainwright (eds), *op. cit.*, pp. 272–82.

[20] S. Muthesius, *op. cit.*, pp. 1–2, 14–18; A. Saint, 'Pugin's Architecture in Context', in P. Atterbutry (ed.), *Pugin, Master of the Gothic Revival* (New Haven and London, 1995), pp. 78–101.

[21] A. W. N. Pugin, *True Principles*, *op. cit.*, pp. 22–38, 47–50.

[22] The Cambridge Camden Society, *A Few Words to Church Builders* (Cambridge, 1841), p. 5.

[23] A. W. N. Pugin, *True Principles*, *op. cit.*, pp. 35–6.

[24] B. Webb, *Diary* 1 August 1841, Oxford University, Bodleian Library, MS. Eng. Misc. 3.406. The writer is grateful to Geoff Brandwood for this information.

[25] P. Stanton, *Pugin* (London, 1971), p. 127. No date or addressee is given. B. Webb, *op. cit.*, 30 November 1841 includes, 'Pugin began a correspondence'.

committee member to visit him in London and Webb wrote to thank him.[27] In 1842 Webb wrote to Hardman with 'the enclosed letter from Mr Pugin [as] my excuse for writing to you' asking whether Hardman could 'supply ecclesiastical ornaments to persons not of your communion.'[28]

In 1842 Pugin made a return visit to Cambridge where he was guest of the 'Camden men' for two days. Another visit in 1843 coincided with Pugin's trip in connection with his new church in Cambridge, on which, as we shall see, *The Ecclesiologist* made no comment.

The Cambridge Camden Society has been described as 'the most influential undergraduate society of all time'.[29] The first edition of its journal, *The Ecclesiologist*, of November 1841, included a damning review of St Paul, Cambridge, a Commissioners' church then being constructed by the architect Ambrose Poynter, under the title 'New Churches'. Here *The Ecclesiologist* followed Pugin's *Contrasts*, the latter containing graphic plates of 'Contrasted Altar Screens', 'Contrasted Parochial Churches', 'Contrasted Royal Chapels', 'Contrasted Chapels',[30] as well as its attack on the Commissioners churches,[31] and a chapter 'On the Present Degraded State of Ecclesiastical Building'.[32] The second edition (1841) with its 'Contrasted Altars' showed a denuded medieval sanctuary crying out for restoration 'the effect of the destructive Protestant principles – a faithful picture of Protestant desecration and neglect'.[33]

Pugin's influence can also be seen in the tests against which the new church was seen to fail, the ethical standard of 'truth' being taken largely from *True Principles*. Criticism of decorators' gimmicks and of the Regency building world's 'imitations [of] stucco and paint and composition and graining not out of place in the theatre or ball-room' are owed almost directly

[26] Pugin to Bloxam, 19 December 1841, quoted in M. Belcher, *op. cit.*, p. 293.
[27] B. Webb, *op. cit.*, 28 December 1841,'Haskoll & I to Pugin's at Chelsea', and 29 December, 'I wrote to Pugin'.
[28] Webb to Hardman, undated letter, probably c.1842. The request referred to St Nicholas, Kemerton, later restored by R. C. Carpenter, of which Webb was curate and Archdeacon Thorp the patron. Earlier, in 1841, the Rev. Bernard Smith, an Oxford graduate, vicar of Leadenham, Lincolnshire, since 1839, wrote to Hardman asking if he could call to inspect church plate while passing through Birmingham on the way to Oxford. Smith to Hardman & Co, 15 March 1841. (City of Birmingham Museums and Library, Hardman Archives, Letters, 1841–97.)
[29] D. Watkin, *op. cit.*, p. 70; J. M. White, *op. cit.*; P. Stanton, *op. cit.*, pp.11–29.
[30] A. W. N. Pugin, *Contrasts; or A Parallel between the Noble Edifices of the Fourteenth and Fifteenth Centuries and Similar Buildings of the Present Day* (London, 1836), plates 4–7.
[31] A. W. N. Pugin, *Contrasts, op. cit.*, pp. 49–50.
[32] *Ibid.*, pp. 35–50.
[33] *Ibid.* (1841 edition), pp. 14–15; see also B. Webb, *op. cit.*, 14 February 1842, 'read Pugin's Contrasts'.

to Pugin, as is the conclusion, 'in GOD's house everything should be *real*'.[34] To Pugin as well as to the Society everything about St Paul's was wrong: the materials 'very red brick indeed, "relieved" by nice little white quoins "black bricks" intended, we presume, for a pied variety of Great St Mary's, the stone tracery meagre in detail, the brick piers and arches plastered to imitate stone; the roof ceiled in with applied wood principals'. But even more damning than these architectural 'lies' was the inadequate ritual plan and liturgical arrangement: the church was 'all gallery' with 'no chancel whatever'.[35] Finally the church failed a new stylistic test by using Perpendicular, now seen as 'debased', as against the model, firstly seen in Pugin's St Oswald, Old Swann, Liverpool (1841), of the English Decorated fourteenth-century country parish church, 'the first published example of the very parish style the ecclesiologists were proposing to call their own',[36] and illustrated extensively in the 'Present State' articles published in May 1841 and February 1842.

The pugnacious tone of *The Ecclesiologist* followed that of Pugin's own publications, in particular his ridiculing of contemporary London Catholic chapels in 1838: 'there is [St Mary] Moorfields like a theatre, with its proscenium and boxes ... Warwick Street a concert room ... Lincoln's Inn Fields, dark and grated, like a chapel for convicts ... St John's Wood ... savours too much of the nineteenth century',[37] and the 1839 attack on contemporary architects such as Charles Day whose St Francis Xavier, Hereford (1837–8), in the Greek Revival style, was condemned as 'a modern erection in the very worst style.'[38]

Pugin acknowledged the Society in the 1841 edition of *Contrasts* 'I cannot refrain from paying a just tribute to the Cambridge Camden Society, who have already done much, and are still going on admirably in the good cause.'[39] He even reprinted the original version of *The Ecclesiologist's* attack on St Paul's in his second 'Present State' article in February 1842, dismissing the milder form as reissued as the work of 'milk and water men'.[40] He quoted extensively

34 *Ecclesiologist*, 1 (1842), p. 11.
35 Quoted in A. W. N. Pugin, 'Present State', *op. cit.*, pp. 88–91.
36 P. Stanton, *Gothic Revival, op. cit.*, p. 22, cites a pamphlet on the church as yet not located by M. Belcher, *op. cit.;* H. R. Hitchcock, *Early Victorian Architecture in Britain*, (New Haven, 1954), 1, pp. 69–75; J. M. White, *op. cit.*, pp. 14, 76–7, 87, 117; A. W. N. Pugin, 'The Present State ... Article the First', *op. cit.*, particularly Plate VI (St Oswald, Liverpool) and Plates I, IV, XII, XVI (St Giles, Cheadle).
37 A. W. N. Pugin, 'Lectures on Ecclesiastical Architecture. Lecture the second', in *The Catholic Magazine, op. cit.*, pp. 321–37.
38 *Orthodox Journal*, ix (August 1839), pp. 129–32; A. W. N. Pugin, *Contrasts, op. cit.*, pp. 55–56.
39 A. W. N. Pugin, *Contrasts* (1841 edition), *op. cit.*, p. 75.
40 A. W. N. Pugin, 'Present State', *op. cit.* (1843 pagination), p. 91. The 'milk-and-water' revised text was issued in *Ecclesiologist*, 1 (1841–2), pp. 9–12. Pugin's original text appeared in 'Art[icle] III–1, 'A few Words to Churchwardens nos 1

from the Society's pamphlet *A Few Words to Church Builders,* which he greeted as 'the first distinct publication which has issued from the present Establishment, in which ecclesiastical architecture is viewed in its true light the remarks are so excellent and fully illustrate the principles of church architecture.'[41]

Pugin complimented the Society in comparing 'the practical good ... [of] their unpretentious publications [with] the united exertions of antiquarians of half a century ago',[42] and tantalisingly went on to use his own church in Cambridge to illustrate the points made in *A Few Words.* The Society was seen by Pugin as a useful engine in overthrowing the Georgian church-building system and as what he characterised as 'the Trade',[43] recommending that the warning '"Beware the Camden" be hung up *in terrorem* in every church-competing architect's office, to deter the present wretched system'.[44] In this Pugin and the Society were united, as well as in banishing the classical style, establishing the distinct vocation of church design and separating it from other architectural activity – as well as its strict denominational demarcation – and reforming liturgical practice.

The Society was strongly influenced by Pugin's central principle of the 'real' or 'reality' in architecture, particularly from *True Principles.* 'That there should be no feature not necessary for convenience, construction or propriety, that all ornament should consist of the enrichment of the essential construction of the building, the smallest details should have a meaning and a purpose, construction should vary with the material employed' and finally 'it is in pointed architecture alone that these great principles have been carried out'.[45] The penultimate of these was to be adumbrated under the Society's watchword 'Let every material employed be real'.[46] It is the aesthetic change represented by Pugin's 'reality' which is reflected by architects such as G. G. Scott at St Giles, Camberwell, and even more so by direct imitators – not to

and 2 [etc.]' in *Dublin Review*, xxiii, February 1842, pp. 88–90. It was reissued with Article 1 [etc.] as *The Present State, op. cit.,* pp. 80–123. See also J. M. White, *op. cit.,* pp. 117–120.

[41]   A. W. N. Pugin, *Present State, II* (1843 ed), *op. cit.,* pp. 61–2, the full text, pp. 61–8; J. M. White, *op. cit.,* pp. 113–5. Pugin failed to produce a vade-me-cum for the use of his own churches, in contrast to many publications of the Society; not until the 1850s did Catholics have the highly practical (and anti-Puginian) G. J. Wigley (trans), *St Charles Borromeo's 'Instructions on Ecclesiastical Buildings'* (1857).

[42]   A. W. N. Pugin in *Present State, op. cit.* (1843 pagination), p. 56. His St Andrew's Cambridge church is referred to pp. 63–4.

[43]   A. W. N. Pugin, *Contrasts, op. cit.,* plate [3] 'church competition dedicated without permission to the Trade'.

[44]   A. W. N. Pugin, *Present State, op. cit.* (1843 pagination), p. 91.

[45]   A. W. N. Pugin, *True Principles, op. cit.,* p. 1; J. M. White, *op. cit.,* pp. 179–80. See note 19.

[46]   *A Few words to Church Builders, op. cit.,* p. 5.

say plagiarists – of Pugin such as the Anglican R. C. Carpenter or the Catholic C. F. Hansom. However, for psychological, sectarian and tactical reasons, the Society did not dare acknowledge Pugin's authorship of these ideas. In a sense, the whole search for a preferred architect and later a model church by *The Ecclesiologist* was an attempt to distance itself from him: 'Pugin's sole fault, one feels, is that he was a Roman Catholic, otherwise he might have been accorded the favour granted to Butterfield.'[47]

The Society's relationship with Pugin has been characterised as personally friendly but officially cautious;[48] while the early years of *The Ecclesiologist* ignored his buildings, there was a favourable review of his *Glossary of Ecclesiastical Ornament* (1844),[49] a notice of one of his Anglican restorations in 1844,[50] and another in 1845.[51]

In March 1844 Pugin designed the seal of the Society and sent it to Webb;[52] it was therefore already in use when it was published in September 1844 in *The Ecclesiologist* (plate 23). Clearly 'designing their seal for them gratis',[53] was a high mark of friendship, described as 'from the able hand of that great master of Christian device, Mr A. W. Pugin'.[54] However, its overtly Catholicising iconography – a seated Virgin and Child flanked by St George and St Etheldreda, with St Luke (the patron of painters) and St John the Evangelist – elicited a predictably hostile reaction and some resignations.[55] That the Society was prepared to be associated with it at all is, perhaps, surprising. The figures are laid out in elaborate flat pattern niches inspired by

[47]   J. M. White, *op. cit.*, pp. 179–80.
[48]   D. Simpson, 'Art & Religion in the work of A. W. Pugin', unpublished Keele University PhD thesis (1973); J. M. White, *op. cit.*, gives an unsympathetic view of Pugin, pp. 95, 133, 179–80; but P. Stanton, *Pugin, op. cit.*, pp. 127–8, 138, 146, 173, and M. Belcher, *op. cit.*, pp. 241–2; 297–8, give a sympathetic one.
[49]   *Ecclesiologist*, 3 (1845), pp. 141–144. 'That ornament is not antagonistic but the servant of utility, not the destruction but the embellishment of use, is the grand principle which Mr Pugin has amply demonstrated in his former works', pp. 141–2. Pugin's use of colour and his exposition of historic vestments were especially appreciated.
[50]   *Ecclesiologist*, 3 (1845), p. 151, on St Nicholas Peper Harrow, Surrey. See also *The Tablet*, 28 September 1844, p. 611, quoting from *The Record* where Pugin was described as 'a papist'.
[51]   *Ecclesiologist*, 4 (1845), pp. 43, 194, 286–7 (reference from Geoff Brandwood) on St Mary, Wymeswold, Leicestershire. Pugin was named in the first two entries only. The patron was the Rev. Henry Alford, who had tutored John Morris before he went up to Cambridge in 1845, where as Paley's pupil, he became a Catholic: see below, note 99.
[52]   Webb's journal quoted in M. Belcher, *op. cit.*, p. 233.
[53]   Pugin to Bloxam, quoted in M. Belcher, *op. cit.*, p. 242.
[54]   *Ecclesiologist*, 3 (1845), pp. 184–5; otherwise the review merely explained the iconography of the seal.
[55]   M. Belcher, *op. cit.*, p. 233. See Chapter 4.

medieval brasses. The edges of the vesica form are filled out with a ruined church on one side and a spired church on the other, and beneath, the Round Church at Cambridge as restored by Salvin, a reference to the Society's *cause célebre*. The date 1839 given is that of the foundation of the Society.

There had been talk of opening a 'mission', as the initial Catholic presence was known, in Cambridge since 1838.[56] Beforehand, the nearest Catholic mass to be heard near Cambridge was at the private chapel of the Huddlestone family at Sawston Hall. Although at least twelve Catholics were reckoned to have matriculated as members of the University,[57] the proposed church was hardly for them nor for the townsfolk of Cambridge, but for the Irish, who had first arrived in East Anglia as migrant seasonal labourers. An Irish priest, Fr Bernard Shanley, arrived in February 1841. He described his flock as 'the followers of St Patrick', Cambridge as 'the strongest fort of our enemies' camp' and noted the difficulty of buying a site which 'we could not get for love or money from the pious inhabitants of Cambridge and it is not difficult to divine the cause – University influence'.[58] However, with the support of his bishop, Dr Wearing, and only one English Catholic, a site was bought almost opposite St Paul's church in the 'New Town'.[59]

Fr Shanley is reputed to have walked from Cambridge to London begging for the church. His 'subscribers' included four Catholic members of the University: the undergraduate Henry Munster[60] and the two noted earlier Catholic converts, Kenelm Digby[61] and Ambrose Phillipps,[62] all three of

[56] Pugin may perhaps have discussed a Cambridge church with the chaplain at Sawston Hall as early as in 1839. A. W. N. Pugin, *Diary,* 22 April 1839, quoted in A. Wedgwood *A. W. N. Pugin and the Pugin Family, Catalogue of the Architectural Drawings in the Victoria and Albert Museum* (1985), pp. 42, 82.

[57] Although some colleges, notably Trinity, allowed Catholics to matriculate, they could not take degrees until 1856, or hold fellowships until 1871; the Catholic bishops themselves attempted to forbid attendance at Oxford and Cambridge from 1867 to 1895.

[58] Bernard Shanley, *The Tablet,* 1 July 1843, p. 406. He was ordained at the Irish College in Paris, appears only in the *Catholic Directory,* 1844, as a priest at Coldham Hall, Suffolk.

[59] Bishop Wearing's appeal: *London and Dublin Orthodox Journal,* xiv, 19 March 1842, pp. 177–8. The 'one English Catholic [was] Mr Orpwood': *The Tablet,* 1 July 1843, p. 406 and the only recognisable Protestant contributor was the Marquess of Bristol.

[60] Henry Munster (1823–1894) matriculated 1841 but did not proceed to BA until 1858, two years after the Cambridge University Act: J. A. Venn, *Alumni Cantabrigienses,* II, 4, 408.

[61] Kenelm Digby (1797–1880) converted in 1825 continued in residence for 15 years, *ibid.,* II, 2, 299.

[62] Ambrose Phillipps (1808–1878), later Phillipps de Lisle, Pugin's friend and patron since 1837 was converted as a schoolboy. He matriculated in 1826, but took no degree because of ill-health, *ibid.,* II, 2, 274.

whom were members of Trinity College; the fourth was Thomas N. Reddington, whose mother had earlier made her chaplain's Mass available to Cambridge residents.[63] Playing his Irish card, Fr Shanley even got a contribution from Daniel O'Connell MP, 'the Liberator', as he was known, who had secured Catholic Emancipation in 1829, and whom he described as 'the greatest man in the world and the Queen's best friend in the British Empire'.[64]

While *The Ecclesiologist* ignored the church, University men fascinated by the religious implications of the Gothic Revival certainly visited it, including later converts to Catholicism such as T. E. Bridgett of Trinity, who described it as 'a very small building in an obscure street in the suburbs ... we had some difficulty in finding it'. Rather than architecture, it was the 'answers that Paddy gave'[65] to certain religious questions which impressed him. They might also have bought Pugin's drawing 'Design for the new Catholic Church of St Andrew Cambridge' engraved by T. T. Bury which was published in March 1842 and showed the projected church in plan, internal elevation three-quarter-elevation, with visiting figures in academic dress (Plate 24).[66] However such anticipated interest from 'gownsmen' had to be balanced by that of hostile 'townsmen'. On November 5 1841, threatening crowds gathered at this 'little entrenchment' defended by the Irish, the superintendent of Police and the town Watch Committee. Fr Shanley wrote later of 'astonished hundreds that witnessed our unhappy position' who 'now the danger is over ... make long speeches and a great noise about their sincere attachment to the ancient faith etc, but [who] at the hour of danger were in their happy homes and comfortable beds [but] I do not stand in the need of such feather-bed soldiers', a reference perhaps to the Camden men.[67]

The small church was built rapidly and opened in December 1842 when anti-Catholic tracts were distributed in the Market Place.[68] As late as 1863, a

63   Thomas N. Redington (1816–1862), later Sir Thomas, MP for Dundalk Co. Louth. *ibid.*, II, 5, 264. He was admitted as Fellow Commoner at Christ's, 1832.

64   *The Tablet*, 1 July 1843, p. 406.

65   C. Ryder, *Life of Thomas Edward Bridgett, Priest of the Congregation of the Most Holy Redeemer with characteristics from his writings* (London, 1906), p. 12. Bridgett (Trinity, 1847–1850) probably with John Morris (Trinity, 1845), the pupil of Paley at St. John's, who converted at Easter 1846 and then left Cambridge; see note 51, above.

66   'Design for the new Catholic Church of St. Andrew Cambridge' signed 'A. W. Pugin archit.' and 'T. T. Bury lith', copy at Central Library, Cambridge, M. Andr. J 40 650. It is crudely repoduced in the *London and Dublin Orthodox Journal*, xiv, 19 March 1842, pp. 177–8.

67   *The Tablet*, 1 July 1843, p. 406. There is no report in the *Cambridge Chronicle* or *Cambridge Independent Press* in their editions of 6 and 13 November 1841.

68   *Cambridge Chronicle,* 10 December 1842. P. Stanton, *Pugin, op. cit.,* p. 198, gives drawings 1840 and estimates 1841. This does not accord with the internal history

full-scale riot at the church lead to the arrest and even the imprisonment of two undergraduates.[69] At the opening, the Tory *Cambridge Chronicle* gave an 'account evidently from one connected with the place – probably that of the Priest himself: we give without alteration and of course are not responsible for its phraseology'.[70] It was consecrated in a two-hour ceremony on St George's Day 1843, followed by High Mass sung by Bishop Wareing 'the plain chant being used'. There was a sermon by the future Cardinal Wiseman, and a *Te Deum*. Later a dinner was held at the University Arms. The day's events were all reported in the Whig *Cambridge Independent Press*.[71]

By this time Fr Shanley, whose strident tones of Irish religious nationalism were perhaps off-putting, had been replaced by Thomas Quinlivan,[72] another Irishman who, however, saw himself more under the patronage of Huddlestons as well as having a possible charge for Catholic undergraduates. His successor, Canon Christopher Scott,[73] saw the obscure site of the church as a drawback for proselytism in the University. He was lucky enough to be given the present church of Our Lady & the English Martyrs designed by the architects Dunn & Hansom and built 1885–1890. As one of the most prominent Victorian buildings in Cambridge, it was the butt of much donnish humour.

As a friend of Bishop Wareing and known to other 'subscribers' listed by Fr Shanley, Pugin was the obvious choice as architect for the new church of St Andrew. By 1842, he had not only many controversial publications but also over thirty Catholic churches to his credit, including the future Catholic cathedral at Birmingham. The first references to Cambridge in Pugin's *Diary* are on 21 July 1841: 'Left London for Cambridge' and on 22 July 'Cambridge

---

of the mission; however, the rapid progress made in 1842 suggests that the attack was on the foundations rather than a mere site.

[69]   *The Tablet*, 1863, p. 301: 'Disgraceful riot by University men in a Roman Catholic chapel' and *Cambridge Independent Press*, 9 May 1863.

[70]   *Cambridge Chronicle*, 10 December 1842.

[71]   *The Tablet*, 7 January 1843, p. 7; 25 March, pp. 181–2; *Cambridge Independent Press*, 29 April 1843.

[72]   Thomas Quinlivan (1816–1885) born Co. Clare, Ireland, ordained for the Eastern District appointed at Cambridge July 1843, remained there until retiring in 1883. He began the Catholic school in 1843. Henry Woolfrey, in religion Dom Norbert (1819–1872) born Lulworth, Dorset, ordained a Cistercian priest at Melleraie, France 1823, returned to Dorset 1831, appears under Cambridge in *Catholic Directory*, 1843, only. Left for Australia 1846 where he died: George Oliver, *Collections towards the History of the Catholic Religion in Cornwall (etc)* (London, 1857), pp. 440–1.

[73]   Monsignor Christopher Scott (1838–1922) born in Cambridge. He was a convert and studied at Oscott and English College, Rome, ordained in 1862 for Northampton diocese, died *en post* in Cambridge 1922. M. N. L. Couve de Murville and P. Jenkins, *Catholic Cambridge* (London, 1983), pp. 98–105.

for London'. These do not necessarily refer to the church, although the entry for 2 May 1842 'Left London for Cambridge began church', is specific.[74] This was also the date of the meeting with Webb and his friends. However, it did not result in a notice in *The Ecclesiologist*.[75]

Pugin's church was built of stone, with slate roofs, and was of 3 bays with no chancel. As Pugin explained, 'In the church of St Andrew about to be erected in Cambridge, the space being exceedingly limited, the chancel is taken out of the east end compartment'.[76] It also had a two storey sacristy on the liturgical north side. The east and west elevations were of three lancets. There was a bell-cote and a porch containing the door with Early English foliate hinges and elaborately over-structured joinery. The first and second bay nave piers had rounded Early English drums with capitals and one octagonal Decorated type to the sanctuary with semi-octagonal responds at both ends, as Pugin varied his sources to suggest historic development.

Pugin was often at his best in simple buildings of local materials, whether brick or stone. Occasionally he used a specific model or source: here it is the thirteenth-century church of St Michael, Long Stanton, seven miles north-west of Cambridge. However, the buttressed west gable and bell-cote, and the relationship of the aisles to the clerestory-less nave and the triple lancets at the 'east' end, are modelled on – rather than quoted – from the original. It is unclear how Pugin chose his source, but significantly Long Stanton was noticed in *The Ecclesiologist* in June 1843 and later proposed 'to serve as a model for the Colonies'.[77]

As usual, Pugin was as much concerned with the furnishing and ritual arrangement of the church as with its architecture, and accounts for furniture occur in 1842.[78] The sum of £35 11s. 0d., charged to his account by Hardman, was presumably for the furnishings and vestments required for the consecration.[79] There was an elaborately carved altar with bas-relief font of

[74] Pugin, *Diary*, 21 and 22 July 1841 also 2 May 1842; A. Wedgwood, *Pugin, op. cit.*, pp. 49, 52.
[75] See below, notes 87–90. There were passing references to Pugin's publications, however: *Ecclesiologist*, I (1842), pp. 175, 192; *Ecclesiologist*, 2 (1843), pp. 12, 112.
[76] A. W. N. Pugin, 'Present State', *op. cit.* (1843 pagination), pp. 63–4.
[77] *Ecclesiologist*, 2 (1843), pp. 171–2 and 'Report of the Thirty-Ninth meeting on Thursday, November 7' [1844], *Ecclesiologist*, 4 (1845), p. 23, when 'full working drawings' of St. Michael Longstanton and two other churches were sent to the United States. See also P. Stanton, *The Gothic Revival and American Church Architecture, op. cit.*, pp. 91–98. It was published in R. and J. A. Brandon, *Parish Churches, Being Perspective Views of English Ecclesiastical Structures* (1848). Pugin used this model at Shepshed, Leics., St. Winifred (1842–3) and Barntown, Co. Wexford, Ireland, St. Alphonsus Ligouri (1844–1851) both with variations on the bellcote form and the chancel. R. C. Carpenter used it extensively. See Chapter 5.
[78] A. W. N. Pugin, *Diary*, quoted in A. Wedgwood, *Pugin Family, op. cit.*, pp. 53–4, items (g) and (i) between ff. 24–5 and opposite f. 30.

three quatrefoils, the outer two with seated angels, the centre with a cross and *Agnus Dei.* The baptistery had stone niches and a font. Parclose screens and a rood screen were provided as well as a triple lancet east window by William Wailes. At the centre was a Virgin and Child, and the two outer lancets showed St Andrew and St Felix. It was installed in 1845 at the cost of £20 and was made to Pugin's design.[80] The 'X' frame crucifix with a vested figure of St Andrew crucified set within a roundel with seated angels and stiff-leaf Early English foliage survives in the present church. It is one of Pugin's most original designs in wooden sculpture (Plate 25). The label in Gothic lettering reads 'the gift of A. Welby Pugin AD 1843 St Andrew Pray for us' and suggests not only the piety but also the self-advertisement Pugin often employed.[81] Traditionally, this gift was the result of a vow to St Andrew when Pugin was threatened with shipwreck off the Scottish coast, and Bishop Wareing referred to it as such at Pugin's funeral.[82] Superseded by the present church, Pugin's church firstly became a school, and in 1902 it was demolished and moved to St Ives, Huntingdonshire, where it was altered in re-erection as the Church of the Sacred Heart.[83]

Although obscurely situated, Pugin's church defined the new architectural faith: here for the first time in Cambridge 'the real thing' and 'correct' style and planning were allied with the Gothic antiquarianism which the Society preached. And it seems inconceivable that Society members did not visit it. Here was a church in the preferred Early English style, unlike the 'something between the Elizabethan and Debased perpendicular' of St Paul's.[84] The plan and elevation were congruent, the interior correctly planned with distinct nave and aisles, the roofs were open-trussed rather than ceiled and the porch and sacristy were distinct in plan.

Although as Pugin explained 'the chancel is taken out of the east compartment',[85] it was nevertheless dignified with a rood and figures, and

[79]   Hardman Order Book, Pugin account 11 February – 27 July 1843, quoted in D. Robinson and S. Wildman, *Morris and Company in Cambridge* (Cambridge, 1980), p. 22; Pugin's 'commission and expenses' was £25.00 Pugin, *Diary*, 30 February 1842, quoted in A. Wedgwood, *op. cit.*, p. 94.

[80]   A. W. N. Pugin, *Diary*, 27 January 1845, quoted in A. Wedgwood, *op. cit.*, p. 58, pp. 92–95.

[81]   Royal Commission of Historical Monuments (England) *City of Cambridge*, 2 vols (1959), I, Part 2, Plate II; Part 2, p. 300.

[82]   *The Tablet*, 2 October 1852, pp. 629–30.

[83]   The Church of the Sacred Heart, St. Ives. The surviving brick and stone building is recognisably Pugin's, although its architectural impact and liturgical arrangement were altered both at the time when the screens were sold on and in the recent re-ordering. *Diocese of Northampton Centenary Souvenir 1850–1950*, p. 109 and tablet in church; N. Pevsner, *The Buildings of England, Bedfordshire, Huntingdon and Peterborough* (Harmondsworth, 1968), p. 336 misdates to 1908.

[84]   A. W. N. Pugin, 'Present State', *op. cit.* (1843 ed.), p. 89.

provided with an altar and piscina in stone. Other ritual arrangements were equally elaborate. The porch had stone benches and holy water stoups and the baptistery was screened off with a stone font and two aumbries for chrism and holy oils for the sick. All these stone furnishings had Early English details like the St Andrew crucifix. Pugin had been publishing designs for church interiors of this elaboration since 1839, and especially in 'Present State' (1841–2), which must have fleshed out for the Camden men the neo-Gothic interiors they wished to see, and the furnishings they were fighting for at the Round Church. Using the new Puginian language, *The Cambridge Independent Press* described St Andrew's 'as a correct specimen of a beautiful English parish church of the Middle Ages: though plain, elegant, chaste and devotional ... every feature is real, genuine and natural "The screen" altar so beautifully carved – the open seats'.[86]

The day after he began the church, Pugin recorded in his *Diary* 3 May 1842 'Ely with the Camden men'.[87] Benjamin Webb's *Diary* for 1 May 1843 reads 'A. W. Pugin came on a visit, took him to King's [College], introduced him to Paley at S. Sepulchre's ... He, Paley, Stokes, Neale and Haskoll to supper' and 3 May 'took Pugin to the [Trinity College] Library and to Ely, after evensong found Pugin passionately weeping in Lady Chapel ... [at supper] Pugin in an awful state of mind'.[88]

Webb visited Pugin twice in the summer of 1842 and again in Cambridge on 29 May 1843 when Webb wrote 'lionized Pugin about ... delighted with his geniality and vigour'.[89] Webb was to meet Pugin in London in 1844, accompanying none other than Pusey himself.[90] But Webb's *Diary* makes no reference to the church of St Andrew, and *The Ecclesiologist*, for political reasons, resolutely ignored it, not on account of ignorance, but of fear of acknowledging Pugin's obvious hegemony. Despite Pugin's warm support, the 'Camden men' were coy in acknowledging his influence, and they were at pains to make distinctions between the 'advanced' architectural and religious views of the Society and those of the contemporary Catholic Revival as represented by Pugin.

The first criticism of Pugin was by Neale and Webb in the 'Introductory Essay, Sacramentality: a Principle of Ecclesiastical Design' in their 1843 translation of Bishop Durandus *Rationale Divinorum Officiorum*.[91] While

---

85   *Ibid.*, p. 64.

86   *Cambridge Independent Press*, 29 April 1843 quoted in *The Tablet*, 6 May 1843.

87   A. W. N. Pugin, *Diary*, 3 May 1842, quoted in A. Wedgwood, *op. cit.*, pp. 52, 87; Webb's address is noted p. 53.

88   B. Webb, *Diary, op. cit.*, 2 and 3 May 1842.

89   *Ibid.*, 29 May 1843.

90   B. Webb, *Journal* quoted in M. Belcher, *op. cit.*, p. 293. Pugin visited Cambridge, 23 March 1843; B. Webb, *Journal* quoted in *ibid.*, p. 293, p. 945.

91   J. M. Webb and B. Webb, *The Symbolism of Churches*, pp. xviii–cxxxii. See also: P.

quoting from *True Principles* they defended their refusal to give 'Mr Pugin
credit for several passages which seem to involve the principle now contended
for' and claimed to see Pugin's 'Reality' in architecture as inadequate,
proposing a 'Christian Reality [or] Sacramentality',[92] which they accused
Pugin of ignoring in his writings even if attempted in his churches. In fact the
'Introductory Essay' is full of derivations from Pugin, such as the claim that
the Society 'was the first who dwelt on the absolute necessity of a distinct and
spacious chancel, the first who insisted on, the re-introduction of the Rood
Screen'.[93] The description contrasting a contemporary galleried church with a
medieval building was obviously derived from *Contrasts*.[94]

The *Rationale Divinorum Officinorum* was a curiously impractical choice
of medieval liturgical commentary to recommend for the nineteenth-century
Anglican Revival, but it was wonderful to the translators for its endless
symbolism.[95] Pugin wrote 'indeed I am sadly misrepresented for they accuse
me of being indifferent to Symbolism in architecture !! after all I have written
and done this is too bad, and the introduction written by two Camden men
whom I greatly respect.'[96] The craftiness of the 'Camden men' was in contrast
to Pugin's open dealing and was reflected in their jesuitical refusal to allow
English Catholics to join the Society, while offering honorary membership to
French Catholics such as A-N. Didron, the editor of the influential *Annales
Archéologiques*, who accepted,[97] and the Comte de Montalembert, who refused
on the grounds that the 'Puseyites' were 'heretics'.[98]

Stanton, *Pugin, op. cit.,* p. 146; S. Muthesius, *op. cit.,* pp. 1–2, 4–18; M. Belcher, *op. cit.,* pp. 212–13.

[92] *The Symbolism of Churches, op. cit.,* pp. xix, xxvi and Postcriptum. They also referred to the Catholic Church in England as 'in a schismatickal position', p. xxviii. This view was not shared by Beresford Hope: see below, note 101 & 109.

[93] *Ibid.,* pp. xxii, liv–lix and cxviii. Pugin first described the deep chancel and rood screen in *Contrasts*, (1836) and first saw one at Phillipps private chapel at Grace Dieu Manor, Leicestershire, in October 1837.

[94] *The Symbolism of Churches, op. cit.,* pp. cxxviii–cxxxii, and pp. cxix–cxxvii on the rise and fall of Gothic styles.

[95] *Ibid.,* pp. xxxv–xl; xlviii–ix; lxxxix–cxiii.

[96] Quoted in P. Stanton, *Pugin, op. cit.,* p. 146.

[97] The *Annales Archéologiques*, 1–2 (1846–7) was first reviewed in *Ecclesiologist*, 4 (1845), p. 180. J-B-A. Lassus and E-E. Viollet-le-Duc were both elected late in 1849 or in 1850, see *Ecclesiologist*, 10 (1850), p. 399.

[98] Charles Forbes de Tryon, Comte de Montalembert: 'A Letter Addressed to Reverend Member of the Camden Society on the subject of Catholic Literary Societies, on the Architectural, Artistic and Archaeological Movement of the Puseyites' (Liverpool 1844). For his refusal to join the 'heretics', see *The Tablet*, 26 October 1844, p. 678; *Ecclesiologist*, 5 (1846), pp. 3–5; J. M. White, *op. cit.,* pp. 132–3. De Montalembert's *Du vandalisme et du catholicisme dans l'art* (Paris, 1839) was another plagiarist of Pugin, but de Montalembert described St. Andrew's Cambridge in his *Des interêts Catholiques aux 19e siècle* (Paris, 1860), II, pp. 243–4.

Although some critics had characterised the Camden Society as a fifth column of Popery since 1841, no major figures in the Society became Catholics until late in 1845 when Webb's fellow Honorary Secretary, Frederick Apthorp Paley,[99] and a committee member, Scott Nasmyth Stokes,[100] announced their intentions, adding to the crisis of the disruption of 1845-6. Neale agonised over the threat produced by the secession of Paley and Stokes, and replanned the January 1846 number of *The Ecclesiologist* to include the anonymous attack 'The artistic merit of Mr Pugin' which we now know to have been by A. J. B. Beresford Hope.[101] Neale warned that 'Paley and Stokes! suppose they were to go, and were to publish an *Ecclesiologist* what right have we to say that we are the genuine *Ecclesiologist*?'[102] The removal of the Society to London and the new partnership with Beresford Hope was intended to counter this threat; Beresford Hope for his part was to be a more open and effective critic of Pugin than Neale and Webb. What was the nature of the January 1846 attack on Pugin? It was first of all intended to distance the Society from any imputed discipleship with Pugin, as the editorial which preceded it made clear: 'The present ecclesiological movement was the spontaneous growth of the English Church'. The journal referred to the influence of *Contrasts* and *True Principles* but claimed an *a priori* movement within the Church of England in the winter of 1838-9, that is the constituent meetings of the undergraduate society.[103]

[99] Frederick Apthorp Paley (1815-1888), classical scholar and founding member of the Cambridge Camden Society, later honorary secretary and committee member. He 'resided in college 1836-1846 but was requested to give up his rooms in 1846 when he was suspected of having encouraged a pupil to join the Roman Catholic church'. See J. A. Venn, *Al Cant, op. cit.*, II, pp. 5, 9. He returned to Cambridge as a private tutor 1860-1874. Paley was cited as defending Pugin's reputation by Neale and Webb in their *Symbolism of Churches*, in the 'Postscriptum', *op. cit.*; P. Stanton, *The Gothic Revival and American Church Architecture, op. cit.*, identified Paley as author of 36 items in *The Ecclesiologist* as against Neale and Webb's 46.

[100] Scott Nasmyth Stokes (1821-1891) of Trinity matriculated 1840, BA 1844, called to the Bar 1852, Inspector of Schools 1853-1871. He became a Catholic in 1845. J. A. Venn, *Al Cant, op. cit.* II, pp. 6, 51. He was father of Leonard Stokes (1858-1925) the Catholic architect. See J. M. White, *op. cit.*, pp. 117-155.

[101] 'The artistic merit of Mr Pugin' in *Ecclesiologist*, 5 (1846), pp. 10-16; Beresford Hope was indentified in Neale's letter to Webb 5 November 1845 as 'Hope on Pugin's churches': *Letters of John Mason Neale DD selected and edited by his daughter* [Mary Sackville Lawson] (1910) pp. 86-7; the editor identifies the author of the article in a footnote. J. M. White, *op. cit.*, pp. 134, 179-80, however, does not identify Beresford Hope, nor do Stanton or Belcher. His name appears in Pugin's *Diary* in 1844, quoted in A. Wedgwood, *Pugin's Family, op. cit.*, pp. 67, 91.

[102] Neale to Webb 8 November 1845, *Letters, ibid.*, p. 88; see also pp. 84-9; 93-4.

[103] *Ecclesiologist*, 5 (1846), pp. 3-5, repeating certain claims to originality made in the 'Introductory Essay' of *The Symbolism of Churches, op. cit.*

RODERICK O'DONNELL

The review was technically of Pugin's 'Present State of Ecclesiastical Architecture in England'.[104] Pugin's descriptions of his own building – and even more his thirty-six plates – were analysed to show him puffing up his own reputation: 'Priory of St Gregory's Downside', in fact unexecuted, was compared with 'the gorgeous palaces of Mr Martin's pictures',[105] referring to the architectural fantasies of John Martin. Were St Chad's Cathedral, Birmingham (1839–1841) – which the author had clearly visited – or St Barnabas, Nottingham (1842–44), as executed, anything like the plates? Pugin was dismissed as 'an illustrator'[106] and, while his early influence was acknowledged, his buildings were guyed. Crucially but most indefensibly, he was accused of having founded no school, a point on which Pugin always prided himself, and which was evidently untrue as the case of R. C. Carpenter shows.

The Ecclesiologist refused to print Pugin's reply which came out instead in the *The Tablet*.[107] Pugin, always his own severest critic, agreed with some points, particularly over St Chad's; but he accused *The Ecclesiologist* of 'an impudent falsehood', and predicted that churches soon to open such as St Giles, Cheadle, would 'revive the desponding Ecclesiologists'. He explained his bewilderment to J. R. Bloxam: 'I Always opened [?] my library drawings everything for the ecclesiologist people, designing their seal for them gratis & served them in every way'.[108] The attack on Pugin was clearly intended to distance *The Ecclesiologist* from him – the 'Anglo-Romanist' in Beresford Hope's phrase – and to play down Pugin's reputation as a church-builder, the extent of which was causing some obvious embarrassment to the Society. The response to this was the only major review *The Ecclesiologist* ever gave to new Catholic architecture, which on internal evidence can also be attributed to Beresford Hope.[109]

The opening of Pugin's St George, Lambeth (1840–8) as the future Southwark Cathedral was often called, was given a review part defensive and

---

[104] *Ecclesiologist*, 5 (1846), pp. 10–16. A. W. N. Pugin, 'Present State', I, in *Dublin Review*, 20 (1841), pp. 301–48; *Ecclesiologist*, 1 (1842), pp. 80–183; thirty-six plates were announced, Part I illustrated over 12 church projects, and Part II nine ecclesiastical commissions; 24 Pugin churches are listed in the index of the 1969 reprint. 'Two prints of St. Chad's, Birmingham and Pugin's drawing 'S. Edmund', frontispiece to no. 14 of the 'Lives of the English Saints' were also reviewed.

[105] *Ecclesiologist*, 5 (1846), p.12. See also: R. O'Donnell, 'Pugin designs for Downside' in *Burlington Magazine*, cxxii (1981), pp. 230–3.

[106] *Ecclesiologist*, 5 (1846), p. 15.

[107] A. W. N. Pugin, 'Letter to the editor of the Ecclesiologist' in *The Tablet*, 31 January 1846.

[108] Pugin to Bloxam, quoted in M. Belcher, *op. cit.*, p. 242.

[109] These reviews, particularly their interest in the scale and use of large churches, anticipate much in Beresford Hope's, *The English Cathedral of the Nineteenth Century* (1861). However, M. Belcher, *op. cit.*, does not identify him.

part patronising: 'The Anglo-Roman communion has been put in possession of two of the largest [churches] in Pointed Architecture which have been raised in England we should be but cowardly if we were to attempt to blink it by silence'.[110] It was this church which Webb had first visited in 1842, and by which many London critics were to base their judgements of Pugin. The writer went on to claim that the Anglican Church's over-commitment to all sorts of church-building and restoration had by contrast 'prevented our having *yet* made that precise sort of demonstration, which Lambeth, Salford, [M. E. Hadfield's St John, Salford (1844-8)] Birmingham and Nottingham have afforded – the building of new Pointed churches, sufficiently large to have their claim to be cathedrals generally allowed to pass'.[111] The reviewer continued *'The Ecclesiologist* has already noticed two out of the number',[112] presumably, Beresford Hope's review of Birmingham and Nottingham in his 'Artistic merit' article . The review criticised the incorrect orientation of these churches, and contrasted current Roman Catholic use with the Anglican choir-use of sanctuaries as proposed by the Society. He also made an interesting comment that Pugin's high altar tabernacle at St George's, based on German 'Sacrament house' types, was too dominant.[113] The sanctuary of St George's was contrasted unfavourably with that of Hadfield's St John, Salford.[114] Pugin's St Mary, Liverpool (1844-9), was also disparaged, *The Ecclesiologist* not yet recognising it as a 'town-church' *avant le lettre*[115] There was also a notice of Pugin's church of St Joseph, St Peter Port, Guernsey.[116]

Pugin's Anglican commissions in Cambridge were noticed in a matter of fact way, and not held up as exemplars. He was specifically not named as *architect* for the restoration of Jesus College Chapel, but he was described only as being 'called in' to shore up the tower piers.[117] In contrast, the role of the patron was emphasised. 'All the works a donation of a very munificent member of the college, are designed by Mr Pugin. The screen, the work of Pugin, will be solid'.[118] But there was praise for the organ 'We have seldom

110 *Ecclesiologist,* 9 (1848), pp. 151–64; quotation, p. 151.
111 *Ibid.,* p. 151. Already associated with specific Catholic vicars apostolic, they became cathedrals in 1850 when the Pope appointed Catholic bishops with English titles, the so-called 'Papal Aggression'.
112 *Ibid.,* p. 151.
113 *Ibid.,* pp. 159–60. For Pugin's so-called 'Benediction' altars, see R. O'Donnell 'Pugin and Catholic London, an early divorce, I' in *True Principles* (Newsletter of the Pugin Society), Winter 1998.
114 *Ecclesiologist,* 9 (1848), pp. 151–64; referring to Hadfield 161-4, and to C. F. Hansom and J. J. Scoles.
115 *Ibid.,* p. 163. Pugin's St. Oswald, Old Swann Liverpool was also named.
116 *Ecclesiologist,* 8 (1848), p. 399, not in the 'New churches' column, but under 'Notices and Answers': 'The design, furnished by Mr Pugin a handsome building' but goes on to criticise the choice of stone (not noticed in M. Belcher, *op. cit.*).
117 *Ecclesiologist,* 9 (1848), pp. 145–50, quotation p. 146.

seen anything more graceful than his organ, which is due, mainly, to Mr Pugin'.[119] Oddly, Pugin was (incorrectly) named as architect for the restoration of the chapel at Magdalene, whereas only the Hardman east window was by him.[120] His *Floriated Ornament* (1849) was also reviewed.[121]

By December 1848, when Southwark Cathedral was noticed, the 'Rood Screen Controversy' had broken out in the Catholic church.[122] *The Ecclesiologist* was a not disinterested commentator, hoping to imply that the Gothic Revival was bound to fail in the Roman but succeed in the Anglican church. It was first noticed in August 1848 as 'a controversy in the Anglo-Roman body',[123] in the review of Southwark.[124] Subsequently, it was dismissed in a February 1850 review of 'The Address to the Irish Ecclesiological Society', identifying the influence of Newman and the Oratory,[125] and then in the April 1850 review 'Mr Pugin and *The Rambler*'.[126]

Beresford Hope, as identified by *The Rambler*, went further, not in *The Ecclesiologist*, but the *Christian Remembrances* in January 1851 under the perceptive title 'Oratorianism and Ecclesiology'.[127] In the June 1851 review 'Mr Pugin on chancel screens',[128] Pugin's 'modern Catholic ambonoclast'[129] or destroyer of rood-screens, was identified with the Oratorians whose 'all-seeing'[130] proposal for contemporary Catholic church-planning was equated

[118] *Ibid.*, pp. 146–7. The donor John Sutton, later third baronet, became a Catholic in 1856: see H. Davidson, *Sir John Sutton A Study in True Principles* (1992); M. Belcher, *op. cit.*, quotes from Pugin's letter to Sutton: 'I see the Ecclesiologist does not approve', p. 260.
[119] *Ecclesiologist*, 12 (1851), pp. 323–5.
[120] *Ibid.*, 12 (1851), p. 325: The reference 'fully restored, under the care of Mr Pugin'. See M. Belcher, *op. cit.*, p. 352.
[121] *Ecclesiologist*, 10 (1850), pp. 324–6; M. Belcher, *op. cit.*, p. 269.
[122] *The Rambler*, II (1848), pp. 227–8.
[123] *Ecclesiologist*, 9 (1849), p. 79. For the Rood Screen Controversy see B. Ward, *The Sequel to Catholic Emancipation* (2 vols, 1915), II, pp. 261–78; Josef F. Altholz, *The Liberal Catholic Movement in England: the "Rambler" and its Contributors, 1848–1864* (London 1962); J. M. White, *op. cit.*, pp. 182–3; R. O'Donnell, 'The Architecture of the London Oratory Churches' in Michael Napier and A. Laing (eds), *The London Oratory Centenary 1884–1984* (London, 1984), pp. 21–47; S. O'Reilly, 'Contrasting views of history: the Rambler's rejection of Pugin's historical validation of the Gothic revival' in *Architectural History* (JSAHGB), 41 (1998), pp. 179–81.
[124] *Ecclesiologist*, 9 (1848), pp. 156, 164.
[125] *Ecclesiologist*, 10 (1850), pp. 322–3; Pugin wrote to Hardman '[Beresford] Hope wrote the article it is far beyond Butterfield's calibre': M. Belcher, *op. cit.*, p. 271.
[126] *Ibid.*, pp. 393–9.
[127] *Christian Remembrancer*, xxi (1851), pp. 141–65.
[128] *Ecclesiologist*, 12 (1851), pp. 205–11.
[129] A. W. N. Pugin, *A Treatise on Chancel Screens* (London, 1851), p. 99.
[130] *Ecclesiologist*, 12 (1851), p. 207 (quoting Pugin).

by the Society with the '"all-hearing" principle of popular Protestantism'.[131] Anglicans, particularly Beresford Hope, were clearly watching the Catholic debate about the style and plan of churches appropriate for the Catholic Revival in the 'Town church' exchanges which began in January 1850 in *The Rambler*,[132] ideas which G. E. Street was to take up in December 1850 in his 'Town Church' paper.[133] In all these, *The Ecclesiologist* acted as somewhat as a Job's comforter to Pugin, then under attack from the more recent Oxford Movement converts who had followed Newman into the Catholic Church, and especially into the Oratory founded in 1848 and soon establish in London and Birmingham. It was they who thereupon 'put away the childish things' of the Gothic Revival, and who made *The Rambler* magazine their mouthpiece. Pugin, who might have expected support from his architectural disciples who had remained Anglicans, did not find it: the claim *The Ecclesiologist* was to make on his death that 'when Oratorianism arose in his own communion, and he found among Roman Catholics less sympathy and encouragement, he seemed to value the more the firm and consistent line advocated by our Society',[134] is not borne out by the facts. In fact there were only a few further references to him.[135] Extraordinarily, *The Ecclesiologist* did not publish its own obituary of Pugin. Instead a sort of editorial sufficed which acknowledged the influence of the 'Present State' (1841-2) articles and the encouragement Pugin gave: 'now that we have lost him, we can have with no hesitation in announcing [him] the most eminent and original architectural genius of his time'.[136]

The Ecclesiologist also made the distinction between a Pugin who was 'never perhaps quite able to understand how those who agreed with so hearty and profound an admiration of medieval art could tolerate any adaptation of its principles to modern requirements and altered ritual ... His own ideal ...

[131]   *Ibid.*
[132]   'Town churches' exchanges in *The Rambler*, V, January 1850, pp. 11–18; February 1850, pp. 124–6; June 1850, pp. 525–6.
[133]   G. E. Street 'On the proper Characteristics of a Town Church', in *Ecclesiologist*, 11 (1850), pp. 227–33, and later Beresford Hope: *The English Cathedral of the Nineteenth Century* (1861).
[134]   *Ecclesiologist*, 13 (1852), pp. 352–3.
[135]   *Ecclesiologist*, 9 (1849), pp. 289, 291, referring to St. Patrick's College, Maynooth; *Ecclesiologist*, 9 (1849), pp. 368–70 referring to Pugin's watercolours at the Royal Academy; *Ecclesiologist*, 11 (1850), p. 271, referring to the incomplete state of Pugin's Enniscorthy Cathedral, Co. Wexford, prompted by the 'desecration' of the Round Church. There were further minor references in 'Ecclesiological aspects of the Great Exhibition', *Ecclesiologist*, 12 (1851), pp. 178–90 and a review of Dr. Rock's *Heirurgia*, in *Ecclesiologist*, 12 (1851), pp. 426–7 refers in passing to Pugin.
[136]   *Ecclesiologist*, 13 (1852), pp. 352–3. An obituary reprinted from the *Morning Chronicle* followed, pp. 353–7; M. Belcher, *op. cit.*, pp. 292–4.

was an absolute copy of a mediaeval building ... this carried out ... in his most interesting church of St Augustine at Ramsgate',[137] an intriguing point they did not develop. It also claimed that Pugin was about to become an Anglican.

Perhaps moved to contrition later, Beresford Hope was prominent from 1860 on the Pugin Memorial Committee, acting as chairman and joint treasurer with G. G. Scott (and others). Beresford Hope, who gave £25, was the largest individual donor, Scott and Sir Charles Barry each donated £10; Webb, a committee member, gave one guinea; the name of J. M. Neale does not appear.[138] Although Pugin's Catholic patrons, friends and professional colleagues such as M. E. Hadfield, John Hardman and J. H. Powell contributed, neither of the Hansom brothers, nor Scoles, was involved. Catholics perhaps felt somewhat sidelined in the Memorial, and therefore proposed a specifically Catholic memorial by completing St Augustine's Church, Ramsgate; the 1860 committee seems to have contributed to the furnishings of the Lady chapel in 1862.[139]

Ferrey also gave further currency to the red-herring that Pugin was about to rejoin the Anglican Communion[140] to be repeated in popular Anglican histories of the Revival since such as B. F. L. Clarke's[141] and John Betjeman's.[142] But other nineteenth-century architects were more balanced: in 1862 the young R. N. Shaw was a contributor to the Memorial, and a visitor to Ramsgate in the 1890s,[143] while Scott himself insisted on placing Pugin on the plinth of the Albert Memorial where he remains frozen, ignoring Cockerell who is in conversation with Barry. The whole Bodley phase of the later nineteenth-century Gothic Revival was something of an Anglican homage to Pugin, and this respect for him was also reflected in some select Catholic circles.[144] Both Shaw and G. G. Scott junior modelled churches on St Augustine's itself, treating it almost as *The Ecclesiologist* had predicted 'an absolute copy of a medieval building.'[145]

[137] *Ecclesiologist*, 13 (1852), p. 352.

[138] B. Ferrey, *Recollections* (London, 1862), pp. 468–72.

[139] A subscription 'from the Catholic architects of England' opened in 1853 was unsuccessful. See *The Tablet*, 17 December 1853, p. 806; see also [anon] *St. Augustine's Ramsgate: the Church, the Abbey, the School* (Ramsgate, 1904).

[140] B. Ferrey in *Builder*, October 16 1852, p. 664; also B. Ferrey *op. cit.*, pp. 256–6.

[141] B. F. L. Clarke, *Church Builders of the Nineteenth Century*, (1938), pp. 67–8.

[142] John Betjeman, *'Coming Home' an Anthology of his Prose*, C. Lycett Green [ed], 1997, p. 275.

[143] A. Saint, 'Pugin's Architecture in Context' in P. Atterbury (ed) *A. W. N. Pugin: Master of the Gothic Revival* (New Haven, 1995), p. 97.

[144] R. O'Donnell, 'Thomas Garner and the choir of the Abbey church at Downside' in *The Raven*, no. 276 (1994), pp. 50–3.

[145] *Ecclesiologist*, 13 (1852), p. 352; G. Stamp 'Ramsgate cemetery chapel' in *Architectural History* (JSAHGB), 41 (1998), pp. 273–7.

'BLINK [HIM] BY SILENCE'

This paper expands the writer's contribution to the unpublished festschrift for the retirement of Professor Micheal Jaffe (1926–1997) as Director of the Fitzwilliam Museum, Cambridge. The writer wishes to thank Geoff Brandwood for his close reading and for the references to Neale's and Webb's diaries; he acknowledges comments from Anthony Symondson SJ, and Alexandra Wedgwood.

'The Stuff of a Heresiarch': William Butterfield, Beresford Hope, and the Ecclesiological Vanguard

CHRIS BROOKS

In February 1842 the fledgling *Ecclesiologist* published a letter from 'W. B.', who described himself as an architect hoping to become 'a member of the Camden Society ... when the opportunity offers'. The letter briskly dismissed the need for an altar rail where a chancel screen was provided: though sympathetic, the editorial response defended a practice authorised by the Jacobean Church.[1] In the autumn of the same year a second letter, this time signed 'W. Butterfield', urged the Society to 'engage some goldsmith in the manufacture of Chalices of the ancient form'.[2] In February 1843 *The Ecclesiologist* announced the Camdenians' intention of sponsoring church plate designed after the medieval fashion under the supervision of their own agent, 'W. Butterfield, Esq., Architect, of 4 Adam Street, Adelphi, London', whose 'zeal and skill' were gratefully acknowledged.[3] At a meeting of the Society on 5 December, Butterfield was present when plate and book-bindings he had designed were exhibited and 'much admired.'[4] Early in the following year, he agreed to provide the Committee with drawings for what became *Instrumenta Ecclesiastica, or, a Series of Working Designs for the Furniture, Fittings, and Decorations of Churches and their Precincts*. The *Ecclesiologist*'s review of the first part particularly praised 'the talent and accuracy of Mr. Butterfield'.[5] In the same May number of the journal, Butterfield's designs for the church of Coalpit Heath in Gloucestershire – in fact his very first Anglican church – were pronounced 'worthy of much commendation'.[6] At the Society's Anniversary Meeting on 11 May 1844, he was elected a member.[7] It had taken two years for Butterfield to move from an all-but-anonymous

---

[1] *Ecclesiologist*, 1 (1841–2), pp. 55–6.
[2] *Ecclesiologist*, 2 (1842–3), October 1842, pp. 25–6.
[3] *Ecclesiologist*, 2 (1842–3), 117; the Committee announced the arrangement with Butterfield, 'a gentleman of much taste and skill', at the meeting of the Society on 13 March 1843; *ibid.*, p. 126.
[4] *Ecclesiologist*, 3 (1843–4), p. 76.
[5] *Ecclesiologist*, 3 (1843–4), p. 118.
[6] *Ecclesiologist*, 3 (1843–4), p. 113.
[7] *Ecclesiologist*, 3 (1843–4), p. 132.

letter to working at the centre of the ecclesiologists' activities: yet he never fully belonged to the centre, and his route there is unclear. Personal contacts there undoubtedly were, but they remain obscure. John Mason Neale's diary mentions 'an architect named Butterfield' with reference to the 'W.B.' letter,[8] so his identity was at least known to the principal Camdenians at an early stage. But there are no further references to him in Neale's diary. Webb's diary, on the other hand, reveals a growing familiarity: after his first recorded meeting with Butterfield at dinner in Cambridge on 27 April 1843,[9] contacts steadily increased, and by 1845-6 the two men were meeting regularly.[10] Important as the friendship with Webb was, however, it served to consolidate rather than to establish Butterfield's relationship with the Camden Society. And that relationship was a peculiar one, for however he manoeuvred from February 1842 to get himself into the position he occupied two years later, it was not by publicly fostering the connection; nor, thereafter, did he maintain it by a public presence. With the exception of accompanying his plate on 5 December 1843, Butterfield never went to a meeting of the Society, not even in its later London years when all the leading Anglican Gothic architects were attending. Nor did he ever turn up to discuss his architectural designs, or donate drawings – both of which his contemporaries did regularly. The distance he maintained between himself and the social body of the ecclesiologists, so to speak, is striking because he was simultaneously positioning himself as one of their two most favoured architects, the other being Carpenter of course. In this context, it is highly suggestive that though Butterfield's letter of February 1842 expresses the desire to become a member of the Camden Society 'when an opportunity offers', this did not happen until May 1844. He was not awaiting a haphazard 'opportunity', one might conclude, so much as working for a change in his status relative to the Society. By May 1844, with little overt courtship, he had established himself at the forefront of the ecclesiologists' plans. That is, he was elected, or rather allowed himself to be put up for election, from a position of strength rather than as a suitor for Camdenian favour.

This is all very unlike other young architects who became members in the 1840s – George Gilbert Scott, for example, who joined after being 'greatly excited' by an article of Benjamin Webb's.[11] Scott was already well-established

---

8   Lambeth Palace Library, MS 3108, fol. 12v. The entry is dated 1 February 1842; I am very grateful to Geoff Brandwood for this reference, and for the citations from Webb's diary that follow.

9   Bodleian Library, MS. Eng.misc.e.406, fol. 47r.

10   Bodleian Library, MS. Eng.misc.e.408. Paul Thompson, in his seminal study *William Butterfield* (London, 1971), describes Webb as one of Butterfield's few close friends; the diary entries lend support to this.

11   Sir George Gilbert Scott, *Personal and Professional Recollections* (London, 1879); new edn, ed. Gavin Stamp (Stamford, 1995), pp. 87-8.

in architectural practice, whereas Butterfield had hardly started. Moreover, Scott had the kind of confidence necessary to recognise his own shortcomings, his need for instruction on somebody else's terms – to which we can probably add his ability to spot a potential market. When Butterfield joined the Camdenians it had to be on something like his own terms. The reasons were more than personal. They illuminate issues crucial to the leadership of the ecclesiological movement and the development of Victorian Gothic, and to the underlying issue of social class, so determinant a factor in the whole making of Victorian Britain. To get a sense of what was involved we must turn to Butterfield's life, scant though the details are, and to the effects of his upbringing and early career.[12]

The only personal memoir of Butterfield of any substance has cast a long shadow. In a paper given – appropriately enough – to the Ecclesiological Society in 1941, Harry Redfern, then aged 83, remembered his time in the offices of Henry Woodyer, briefly articled to Butterfield in the 1840s, and Butterfield himself, for whom Redfern worked in 1877.[13] Despite exaggerations, Redfern's account still matters, particularly for the social perceptions it reveals. In his comparison between the two architects, Woodyer, handsome and romantic with a yacht in the Mediterranean, wins hands down. Butterfield, by contrast, was withdrawn and wedded to an invariable routine: he never smoked, never took a holiday, drank tea in the Athenaeum Club every afternoon, allowed his staff no break for lunch, and gave them only three days off a year. Moreover, Redfern claims, Butterfield had been apprenticed to a builder, had no formal architectural training, was self-taught in his knowledge of medieval Gothic, and did not draw like a proper architect. Redfern's paper established a myth, given the aesthetic works in the following year by John Summerson: Butterfield was the untutored genius, harsh, uncompromising, in his soul a builder rather than an architect, to be celebrated for expressing – in Summerson's famous phrase – 'the Glory of Ugliness'.[14] Although the myth's grosser substance was largely dispersed by Thompson in 1971, one element, little discussed by commentators, remains crucial. Redfern tells us Woodyer's father was 'a well-known and greatly loved physician' – that is, a professional; and that Woodyer himself was 'a very great gentleman'. By contrast, Butterfield's parentage was wholly obscure and – a decisive detail that Redfern remembers

12 Most of the known biographical facts are given in the early chapters of Thompson's book, to which the reader should turn for the full picture, such as it is. The summary account that follows draws largely upon this source, though the emphases and interpretations are my own.
13 Harry Redfern, 'Some Recollections of William Butterfield and Henry Woodyer', *Architect and Building News*, 177 (1944), pp. 21–2; 44–5.
14 John Summerson, 'William Butterfield; or the Glory of Ugliness', *Architectural Review*, 98 (1945), pp. 166–75.

with something like indignation more than half a century later – he always called the money he paid his staff 'wages', not 'salaries'. As every Victorian knew, professional gents drew 'salaries': 'wages' were for workers. The implication is clear. Quite simply, William Butterfield was not a gentleman. It was a determinant factor of his career, his aesthetic, and his whole relationship with the indubitable gentlemen who ran the Cambridge Camden Society.

Butterfield was born in 1814, the eldest son of a London druggist, also called William, who had a shop in the Strand. His parents were nonconformists, in itself an indicator of social class, and most of his family were tradespeople. In this Butterfield was quite unlike those contemporaries of his who were also to become leading ecclesiastical Gothic architects. In keeping with this background, from 1831 to 1833, he was articled to a Pimlico builder, Thomas Arber, training which gave Butterfield a detailed grasp of construction and function. *The Ecclesiologist's* later reviews of his work often praised the practicality of his approach – his 'reality', to use a favourite (albeit overloaded) Victorian term.[15] When Arber went bankrupt in 1833, Butterfield – whose father's business was prospering – transferred to an architectural apprenticeship. This was a vital move: building was trade, but architecture was already emerging as a recognised profession, requiring scholarship and artistic ability as well as practical skills.[16] And to be recognised as a professional was at least to lay claim to being considered a gentleman. From 1833 to 1836 Butterfield was the pupil of E. L. Blackburne, a London architect with strong antiquarian interests,[17] and in 1838-9 became assistant to a Worcester architect – probably Harvey Eginton, whose practice included

[15] For a discussion of which see Chris Brooks, *Signs for the Times: Symbolic Realism in the Mid-Victorian World* (London, 1984), particularly pp. 145-65.

[16] There is an extensive literature on the emergence of the architectural profession. The importance of historically correct Gothic and of church restoration in advancing the social standing of architects has been stressed by Chris Miele, '"Their Interest and Habit": Professionalism and the Restoration of Medieval Churches, 1837-77', in Chris Brooks and Andrew Saint (eds), *The Victorian Church: Architecture and Society* (Manchester, 1995), pp. 151-72.

[17] Blackburne was a Fellow of the Society of Antiquaries, and had definite links with the ecclesiologists in the 1840s, though he was never a member of their society. At a meeting of the Camden Society on 24 April 1845, the Committee recommended 'a proposed work on Decorative Architectural Painting, by Mr. E. L. Blackburne', for which '[t]he Society will head the list of subscribers', *Ecclesiologist*, 4 (1845), p. 172. The first part of Blackburne's *Sketches Graphic and Descriptive for a History of the Decorative Painting applied to English Architecture during the Middle Ages* (London, 1847), was reviewed in *Ecclesiologist*, 8 (1848), pp. 49-51, and the latter part pp. 385-7. There is no indication of whether Butterfield was involved in any of this, but his connection with Blackburne is obviously suggestive, as too is the fact that the book dealt with decorative colour at precisely the time when Butterfield was beginning to be absorbed by the whole subject.

church building and restoration.[18] During this period Butterfield began to acquire his extensive knowledge of English medieval architecture: while in London he had visited, drawn, and measured churches in the home counties, and he pursued the same course of study around Worcester. He returned to London in 1840, moving in 1842 to 4 Adam Street, Adelphi, from whence he opened negotiations with the Camdenians and where he lived and worked with unvarying regularity until 1886. He never married and his private life, what little is known of it, was utterly uneventful. He clearly felt affection for the family of his elder sister, Anne Starey, and enjoyed friendship with the Coleridge family of Ottery St Mary in Devon – of whom more in due course.

Everything we know about Butterfield indicates a man locked into himself, achieving protection through routine, reticence, distance. Such strategies are diagnostic of the intense personal insecurity that derives from social vulnerability. And Butterfield, the gifted son of a lower middle class nonconformist shopkeeper, was highly vulnerable in the often rigidly stratified class system of Victorian Britain. It is this that makes his engagement with the Cambridge Camden Society so telling, so tense, and – ultimately – so poignant. For here was an organisation wedded to strict notions of social and political, as well as ecclesiastical, order: patrician, hierarchical, dictatorial in temper.[19] Its self-assumed authority offered Butterfield a means of legitimisation, a way of overriding the uncertainties of his class position. It was, of course, a dangerous attraction, for the authority derived ideologically from a deeply conservative, top-down societal model – precisely that most threatened by the kind of commercially-enabled class mobility exemplified by young Butterfield's rise from shopkeeping to aspirant professional.[20] Crucial, however, was the nature of ecclesiological Gothic, which not only had to be faithful to medieval precedent, but which the Camdenians constantly promoted as a science. That is, a discipline with objectively-verifiable rules and procedures, and thus, precisely because it was such, wholly authoritative. Such an understanding of style, and implicitly style's relation to and derivation from socio-political structures, was intensely important to

[18] Eginton crops up several times in passing in *The Ecclesiologist* in the 1840s, and the area around Worcester is clearly well known to the journal. Intriguingly, in the Rev. William Scott's 1848 paper 'On Wooden Churches', reference is made to a medieval wooden church formerly existing near Worcester, of which 'some drawings in Mr. Butterfield's possession have been made', *Ecclesiologist*, 9 (1848–9), p. 18.

[19] See, for instance, the passing remarks on social conditions in the England of the 'Hungry Forties' in Neale's *Hierologus; or, The Church Tourists* (London, 1843). For discussion see Chris Brooks, *The Gothic Revival* (London, 1999).

[20] Given such considerations it is unsurprising that Butterfield kept quiet about his background, let alone his first church, Highbury Congregational Chapel in Bristol of 1842–3, a commission obtained through his family's nonconformist connections.

Butterfield: as he wrote later in a private letter, '[we] are living in an age most terribly subjective and sensational.'[21] Where individual fancy is the artistic norm, the promotion of the extrinsically-derived values of precedent, the impersonality of process and product, becomes an oppositional, even radical cultural stance.

Ecclesiological Gothic in its early years demonstrates the paradox of a cultural practice that captured a vanguard position in architecture by prescribing an absolute orthodoxy. For Butterfield it was the precondition for the creation of his own architectural manner, uniquely expressive and individualist but able to claim all the impersonal values that had accrued to Gothic's famed 'reality' – structural integrity, honesty of materials, functional articulation, moral gravity, historical consciousness, and the rest. The fusion transformed historicism into modernity, stamped Gothic with progressiveness, and enabled Butterfield to centre his emotional and creative energies, with all their freight of class anxiety, outside himself – in short, to objectify them. In the invention of his own, idiomatic Gothic Butterfield both needed to be endorsed by the Camdenians and to be free of them. As designer for *Instrumenta Ecclesiastica* and the Society's agent for plate, his position was ambiguous, at once committed and disengaged: the designs were his, but all had to be approved by the Committee. And the Committee's function was ambiguous too: neither architect nor patron, but sinking some aspects of both into the role of stylistic-cum-theological arbiter. Running through this whole nexus of relationships were questions of aesthetic responsibility and leadership. In a movement impelled by reformist zeal, who was initiating developments and who was following? Who was in the van of the vanguard? Such questions largely remained in suspension during the Camdenians' period in Cambridge, but were precipitated by the crisis of the Society in 1845, the move to London, and the rise to supremacy of Alexander James Beresford Hope.

Heir to a family fortune built on diamond-trading, the son of the collector and connoisseur Thomas Hope, Alexander married into one of England's most powerful political dynasties, the Cecils, having begun his career as a Member of Parliament – on the right wing of the Peelite Tories – in 1841, when he came down from Cambridge. In due course he constructed a position for himself as the principal spokesman of High Anglicanism in the Commons: the Camden Society was his most important base. Although Hope

---

[21]   W. B. to the Warden of Keble College, 20 January 1873, quoted Thompson, *Butterfield*, p. 33. Butterfield was not alone in his views. See also *inter alia*, Pugin's diatribes against stylistic licence in *Contrasts* (1836) and *True Principles of Christian Architecture* (1841), Ruskin's attack on the Pathetic Fallacy in Volume 3 of *Modern Painters* (1856), and Arnold's onslaught on philistine individualism in *Culture and Anarchy* (1869). All three specifically related the dominance of the subjective to the prevailing moral condition of Victorian society.

had joined the Society while at Cambridge, beginning a lifelong friendship with Benjamin Webb,[22] he does not seem to have been closely involved in the early years, and is not mentioned in *The Ecclesiologist* until the report of the fourth Anniversary Meeting on 11 May 1843.[23] The context, crucially, was political. Hope seconded the adoption of the annual report, then helped fight off an amendment deploring the Camdenians' association with 'extravagant and untenable theories' before rounding off what was clearly a difficult evening by moving a vote of thanks to the President. Here, in fact, were the premonitory stirrings of the 1845 crisis, and it is no accident that they coincide with Hope's emergence in the Society. Though different in almost every other way, Hope, like Butterfield, came to the ecclesiological movement as an outsider: a plutocratic layman whose family was half-Dutch, with little claim to the historical alliance between land-owning gentility and the Anglican church. As we have seen, Butterfield needed to join the Camdenians on his own terms, and the class and social dynamics involved were closely tied to issues of leadership – what we might think of as vanguardism. Hope similarly chose his own moment to arrive as a central figure, the moment at which external political pressures and internal dissensions began to split the Society. After the fourth Anniversary, Hope vanishes from *The Ecclesiologist* until the account of the fifth Anniversary Meeting of 11 May 1844,[24] which notes his co-option to the Committee following the meeting – the same, incidentally, that elected Butterfield to membership. The Society's crisis arrived by the end of the year, triggered by the resignation of two of its episcopal patrons. On 13 February 1845, unannounced, the Committee recommended dissolution:[25] there is no doubt that it was a tactic. What followed was a strategic repositioning: the Society was 'weeded of some who never sympathised with it, and never gave it any assistance',[26] formally separated from *The Ecclesiologist*, moved to London, renamed the Ecclesiological late Cambridge Camden Society, then reunited with its journal.[27] Sometime in the summer of 1845 the Committee elected Hope as

[22]   Their correspondence is quoted extensively in Henry William Law and Irene Law, *The Book of the Beresford Hopes* (London, 1925), which remains the principal published source for biographical details about Hope. Unfortunately, all the letters between him and Webb have disappeared since the publication of the Laws' book.

[23]   *Ecclesiologist*, 2 (1842–3), pp. 147–50.

[24]   *Ecclesiologist*, 3 (1843–4), pp. 132–3.

[25]   *Ecclesiologist*, 4 (1845), p. 72.

[26]   *Ecclesiologist*, 4 (1845), p. 174; the words are those of the Committee.

[27]   The 'Advertisement' to *Ecclesiologist*, 4 (1845) is at pains to point out that the journal has been disconnected from the Cambridge Camden Society. The 'Preface' to *Ecclesiologist*, 5 (1846), records the adoption of the Society's new name at its Anniversary Meeting on 12 May 1846, and the subsequent return of the copyright from '"The Proprietors of the *Ecclesiologist*"' to 'the "Ecclesiological

Chairman:[28] it was an acknowledgement of where the motive power behind the changes lay.[29]

To explain what was at issue when Butterfield, Hope, and ecclesiological Gothic came together in the middle years of the 1840s, requires more than historical narrative or biographical speculation: it needs a model of cultural analysis. Particularly illuminating is Pierre Bourdieu's concept of the field of cultural production:[30] we must address it initially in theoretical terms.

For Bourdieu, artistic activity is a material practice taking place within the field of cultural production, which comprises cultural organisations, artistic coteries and movements, works of art, and individuals. The field is visualised as a rectangle which has two pairs of opposing poles: aesthetic autonomy at one positive or dominant pole, with mass market culture determined by commercial demand as its negative opposite; prestigious art and artists enjoying what Bourdieu calls a 'high degree of consecration' at the other dominant pole, with low prestige art and artists at its opposing negative pole. Beginning from a position determined by aptitude and the acquired skills provided by education, the careers of individuals or groupings operating in the field – 'trajectories' is Bourdieu's word – are dynamic, and can be mapped in terms of the sequence of positions they take up relative to the paired poles that structure the field. Although organisation within the field, its hierarchies of value and so forth, possesses a relative autonomy, the field of cultural production as a whole is contained within the field of power, where it is situated towards the negative pole: negative because the power exercised by cultural producers and consumers is clearly less than that of – for examples – governments and big business. At the same time, however, the field of power is itself placed at the dominant pole of the all-embracing field of class.

Bourdieu thus asks us to see cultural production as integral to the workings of the social and political power that is in the hands of the groups that make up the dominant class(es) of any given society. What particularly interests him is the interplay between cultural prestige and economic power. To explore this Bourdieu invents the concept of cultural capital, initially a non-economic asset made up of attributes like originality and artistic integrity, and skills such as critical discrimination. High cultural capital is found

---

late the Cambridge Camden Society'", with effect from the issue of July 1846.

[28] It is not possible to establish the exact date, but it is clear from the report of the Society for December 1845, that the Committee appointed Hope as Chairman soon after its election at the Anniversary Meeting in May; see *Ecclesiologist*, 5 (1846), pp. 18–19.

[29] Hope's ecclesiological *coup* has been well described in James F. White, *The Cambridge Movement* (Cambridge, 1962).

[30] See principally 'The Field of Cultural Production, or: The Economic World Reversed' in Pierre Bourdieu (ed.), Randal Johnson, *The Field of Cultural Production. Essays on Art and Literature* (Cambridge, 1993), pp. 29–73.

typically among *avant-garde* groups furthest from the commercially dominated mass market. Characteristically, such groups seek to maximise their cultural capital, thus enhancing their prestige in the field and their standing in relation to power and class, by – for examples – issuing manifestos, publishing specialist journals, promoting an esoteric aesthetic vocabulary. However, because cultural prestige is one of the badges of the socially elite it is frequently sought by individuals who are economically wealthy but who enter the field with initially low cultural capital. The result is one of the most characteristic transactions in Bourdieu's analysis: the exchange of economic capital for cultural capital. Typical would be the *nouveau riche* bourgeois who makes his name as a discriminating collector by buying old masters, or – more rarely perhaps – who supports new art movements in order to establish his reputation as a cultural patron. His own trajectory as an agent in the field, plotted against the pairs of opposing poles, would be shaped by such actions. But they would also affect the trajectories of other agents: of a dealer or gallery from whom he bought pictures, for example, or a group of young painters whom he supported. And the transactions between the parties involved would in each case be an exchange of economic capital for cultural capital.

Bourdieu's strategies afford some compelling insights into the development of ecclesiological Gothic and the roles of Butterfield and Hope. From the late eighteenth century, the cultural prestige of Gothic within the architectural field had risen dramatically. The Camdenians, dominated by clerics and clerics-to-be, set themselves to ensure that the cultural capital that had accrued to revived Gothic generally would be maximised in the specific instance of church-building. The warrant for this was claimed by the not unfamiliar ploy of appealing to an authority outside the formal realm of architecture, or indeed aesthetics: to the truths of Christianity as embodied in the traditions of the Church Catholic and Apostolic. Thus an early review of J. L. Petit's *Remarks on Church Architecture* castigates the writer for taking 'a merely utilitarian view of the subject', failing to recognise its 'most unvarying and exalted principles'.[31] Camdenian tactics were those of an artistic coterie: they issued what were effectively manifestos addressed to those responsible for designing or looking after churches;[32] published a highly contentious journal; and spent much time elaborating a specialist language to describe what they were doing – headed by coinages like 'rubrical planning', 'Sacramentality'[33]

[31]   *Ecclesiologist*, 1 (1841–2), p. 87.

[32]   For examples, *A Few Words to Church Builders* (London and Cambridge, 1841), *A Few Words to Church Wardens on Churches and Church Ornaments* (London and Cambridge, 1841), and *Twenty Three Reasons for Getting Rid of Church Pues* (London, 1843).

[33]   The principle of church arrangement invented – or discovered – by Neale and Webb, as detailed in the long introductory essay to *The Symbolism of Churches and*

and 'ecclesiology' itself. Combined with combativeness and a ready knack of irritating their elders and betters, such characteristics typify what Bourdieu identifies as *avant-garde*. They are the stuff of the conscious vanguardism noted earlier.

Unlike many of Bourdieu's examples, however, the Camden Society largely comprised members of a politically conservative and socially privileged class segment, their dynamic reformism committed to enhancing that privilege – a radicalism of the Establishment. The Camdenians' trajectory in the field of power was replicated in the architectural field, where professionalism was still struggling to define its territory and deny it to the host of builder-architects, contractors, and speculators whom Pugin had contemptuously lumped together as 'The Trade'.[34] Espousing Pugin's position, the Camdenians vigorously promoted the cultural prestige of ecclesiologically correct Gothic, at the same time denouncing – through *The Ecclesiologist*'s reviews – the Gothic efforts of existing, often highly reputable, practitioners. The result was the creation of a radical trajectory in the architectural field, both for the Society and for the young architects who joined it in the 1840s. For Butterfield, moving from the dominated end of the class field, that trajectory carried him into the vanguard of Gothic design, a position at the furthest remove from that part of the field occupied by 'The Trade' – and from his own past, of course, for he had initially been articled to a builder. Thus, the stylistic radicalism Butterfield developed was a kind of corollary of the class position from which he started. It was also an assertion of creative independence, the aesthetic autonomy that Bourdieu identifies with a high degree of 'consecration' and with cultural positions at the opposite pole to the commercialised mass market. Given the ambiguities in Butterfield's relationship to the Camden Society, such autonomy could consort with the creative leadership of ecclesiological Gothic, or finish up in divorce. This brings us back to Beresford Hope.

Despite his social standing, contacts, marriage and wealth – the determinants of his position in the field of power – Hope, as a young M.P. of undoubted ambition, had no 'natural' party, no obvious alliance of social and economic interests that he represented. But in the Camdenians, clearly sliding into disarray in the mid-1840s, he saw the opportunity to create such a party for himself. In the 1845 crisis, getting clear of the Anglican authorities in Cambridge University, moving to London, purging dissidents, even changing the name, were all means of reshaping the Society to Hope's purposes, making it more accessible to his management. But success needed something other than manoeuvres that were essentially political. Capturing the

---

Church Ornaments: a Translation of the First Book of the Rationale Divinorum Officiorum, written by William Durandus, sometime Bishop of Mende (London and Cambridge, 1843).

[34] In the notorious – and very funny – dedicatory plate of *Contrasts*.

Camdenians, by the very nature of the Society's objectives, required a specifically cultural trajectory: Hope had to enter the architectural field on his own account. As early as 1841–2, Hope began to furnish the distressingly Protestant chancel of his family's estate church at Kilndown, Kent, commissioning fittings designed by Carpenter and Butterfield, among others. By March 1845, amidst the Society's many tribulations, *The Ecclesiologist* was able to acclaim the completed *ensemble*: 'The chancel ... lighted up for evensong, is a sight which all ecclesiologists ought to see.'[35] The sense of Kilndown as a spectacular attraction is appropriate, for the chancel doubles as a showcase and a box of delights. It was a demonstration of what the Camdenians could do, and what Hope's patronage could do for the Camdenians. To suggest a measure of self-promotion in the Kilndown scheme is not unduly cynical: in 1843 – that significant year in Hope's trajectory – he was accused of self-advertisement, of 'puffing', because of the undue prominence given to his donation to the Gothic refronting of Trinity Lodge, Cambridge.[36]

In 1843–4, however, Hope found the perfect strategic object for his architectural patronage. A letter in the *English Churchman* lamenting the sacrilegious fate of the ruins of St Augustine's Abbey, Canterbury, urged 'some pious and wealthy Catholic' to purchase the site.[37] Hope did so, and was then approached by the Rev. Edward Coleridge, Master and Fellow of Eton and one of the Coleridge clan,[38] who had long dreamed of establishing an Anglican missionary college. Where could be more appropriate than the despoiled abbey founded by the first missionary to England? And what could speak more clearly of ecclesiology's determination to rebuild the English Church, in spirit as in fabric? Hope was convinced, donated the site and paid for the college chapel, while Coleridge raised the money to build the rest: work began late in 1844. The architect, by all accounts Hope's choice, was William Butterfield. It was a bold decision. Though he had provided fittings for Kilndown, Butterfield had not yet completed his first Anglican church and was still to embark on his first restorations. On the other hand, his trajectory had carried him – as we saw earlier – into the forefront of Camdenian design.

35 *Ecclesiologist*, 4 (1845), p. 92.
36 The College Fellows had actually paid for most of the work; the affair occasioned a squib from Tom Taylor, 'This is the House that Hope built'. See *Book of the Beresford Hopes*, p. 131.
37 The letter appeared on 13 September 1843: quoted in *Book of the Beresford Hopes*, p. 157.
38 He was a nephew of the poet Samuel Taylor Coleridge, and the youngest of seven brothers. 'There are more Coleridges than Herods in the Bible', remarked Benjamin Jowett, 'and I can never remember one from another': for a guide through the genealogical tangle see [Bernard] Lord Coleridge, *The Story of a Devonshire House* (London,1905).

In a single move, the St Augustine's commission now established him, along with Hope as the patron, in the vanguard of ecclesiological Gothic, and thus of Gothic Revival architecture as a whole.

On its completion in 1848, St Augustine's was widely and enthusiastically reviewed. In Butterfield's design, Gothic true principles were developed with a vigour verging on forcefulness – both an announcement of his markedly personal manner, and an anticipation of High Victorianism's formal vocabulary (plate 26). In a long leading article,[39] *The Ecclesiologist* applauded Butterfield's 'architectural success' and celebrated the College's creation through the efforts of an 'individual clergyman' and the 'munificence of an individual layman'. There is more than a hint of self-congratulation, 'considering who the almost-founder of the college is, and who the architect'. The close association made between Hope and Butterfield is an index of their perceived joint standing in the ecclesiological vanguard. Remembering Hope's trajectory, St Augustine's gave him architectural status to accompany his political weight: it was decisive, one might suggest, in helping him to the Chairmanship of the Society in the summer of 1845. And yet there was an uncomfortable truth acknowledged in *The Ecclesiologist*'s description of him as St Augustine's 'almost-founder'. At no point could Hope claim to have originated the project. A letter in a newspaper had prompted it, the idea of a college was Edward Coleridge's, the architecture Butterfield's. The whole process had been – in Bourdieu's terms – a classic exchange of economic capital for cultural capital. The unkindly disposed might well have said that Hope had bought his way to architectural and ecclesiological prominence.

For Butterfield, St Augustine's confirmed the trajectory initiated by his carefully managed relationship with the Camdenians: it established him as a leading Gothic architect in the forefront of ecclesiology, while the emergence of his personal style claimed the ground of creative independence. Other commissions for conventual complexes followed, such as Cumbrae College (1844–51) and St Dunstan's Abbey, Plymouth (from 1849), leading eventually to his great works at Rugby School (from 1858) and Keble College (1867–83). On a smaller scale, the success of St Augustine's asymmetrical composition influenced his management of parsonages, parish schools, and school-houses. The College's missionary purpose also brought Butterfield into direct contact with the people running Anglicanism's colonial project.[40] By 1847 he was already drawing up proposals for Adelaide Cathedral,[41] eventually built to the

[39] *Ecclesiologist*, 9 (1849), pp. 1–8.
[40] A project which the Cambridge Camden Society eagerly supported, and which formed part of its terms of reference. Apart from regular reviews of church-building in the empire, *The Ecclesiologist* also contains numerous references to plate and fittings derived from Butterfield's designs in *Instrumenta Ecclesiastica* being used by colonial churchmen.
[41] Reviewed in some detail and very positively in *Ecclesiologist* 8 (1848), pp. 141–2.

revised scheme he prepared in 1868-9; there were to be other works in Canada as well as Australia, and plans for New Zealand. In addition, St Augustine's introduced Butterfield to the Coleridges, who, in 1849–50, largely funded the restoration of the great Devon church of Ottery St Mary, their home town, with Butterfield as architect.[42] Butterfield's association with the family lasted most of the rest of his life, and brought commissions that ranged from designs for stained glass and memorials to the rebuilding of the Coleridge house, Heath's Court. For a withdrawn and solitary man, it also brought friendship. According to John Duke Coleridge's biography, Butterfield had become one of his 'close and intimate friends'[43] by the 1850s. His father, Sir John Taylor Coleridge, seconded Butterfield for membership of the Athenaeum in 1858,[44] and in 1867 was instrumental in Butterfield's election to an eccentrically elite dining club called – with poignant appropriateness – Nobody's Friends.[45] Butterfield certainly stayed with the family at Ottery, where hangs the fine portrait of him by Jane Fortescue, John Duke's wife. She died suddenly in 1878 and Butterfield designed the setting for her monument in the south transept of the church: it is one of the most moving of any of his works.

The comments are perceptive and very suggestive in terms of Butterfield's development. 'Nothing could be more severe than this design, and yet it has a character of its own which is perhaps impossible to describe: it has just that individuality which we admire in our ancient churches.'

[42] Enthusiastically described by John Duke Coleridge, 'On the Restoration of the Church of S. Mary the Virgin, at Ottery S. Mary', *Ecclesiologist*, 13 (1852), pp. 79–88, a longer version of which appeared in *Transactions of the Exeter Diocesan Architectural Society*, 4 (1853), pp.189–217. The money for the restoration came principally from Francis George Coleridge, a solicitor in Ottery, and Sir John Taylor Coleridge, Judge of the Court of Queen's Bench; both were elder brothers of Edward Coleridge, begetter of St Augustine's.

[43] Ernest Hartley Coleridge, *Life and Correspondence of John Duke Lord Coleridge Lord Chief Justice of England*, 2 vols. (London, 1904), 1, p. 217. Following his father into the law, John Duke Coleridge – 'Duke' was his grandmother's family name not a title – became Chief Justice of the Common Pleas in 1873, and Lord Chief Justice in 1880. He was ennobled in 1874, becoming – most confusingly – Sir John Duke first Baron Coleridge.

[44] The Certificate for Ballot is dated 8 February 1858; the members signing in support of Butterfield's eligibility included Benjamin Webb.

[45] The membership, which was strictly limited, largely comprised ecclesiastics, lawyers, and landed gentry: it included several Coleridges as well as Sir John Taylor, who became President in 1861. Butterfield was proposed by another friend-cum-patron Sir William Heathcote, squire of Keble's parish, Hursley. See *The Club of "Nobody's Friends" since its foundation on 21 June 1800 to 29 April 1902*, privately printed (London, 1938): I owe this extraordinary reference to Geoff Brandwood.

With the completion of St Augustine's College, Butterfield's relationship to the Ecclesiological (late Cambridge Camden) Society, the identification between his trajectory and theirs, was at its closest. Increasingly, however, this association became inseparable from his relationship to Hope, whose control of the Society grew ever more complete. From the mid-1840s, under the joint editorship of Hope and Webb, *The Ecclesiologist* – never, in any case a respecter of other people's opinions – set about eliminating, or at least subordinating, other rivals for the leadership of ecclesiastical Gothic. As early as 1843, in the introduction to their translation of Durandus, Neale and Webb had already claimed the ecclesiologists were out-distancing Pugin because he had failed to recognise the principle of Sacramentality. In January 1846 a piece on 'The Artistic Merit of Mr Pugin' relegated him to little more than a clever draughtsman.[46] Over the next few years *The Ecclesiologist* deprecatingly reviewed theoretical writings about Gothic by J. L. Petit and the former Secretary to the Society F. A. Paley,[47] ignored the important works of the Brandon brothers,[48] and picked holes in studies of the architectural arts such as Charles Winston's pioneering work on medieval stained glass.[49] Meanwhile Hope's brief *Essay on the Present State of Ecclesiological Science in England* was reported in detail, with lengthy quotations, at least one of which was reckoned to be 'full of thoughtful and comprehensive suggestions, most aptly and beautifully expressed.'[50]

At the same time, through the late 1840s and early '50s, *The Ecclesiologist* kept pace with Butterfield's rapidly expanding practice, in part reflecting a perception of him as the Society's own man, in part constructing him as such. Figure 1 plots the coverage of Butterfield in the journal throughout its existence, and should be compared with Figure 2, which charts his commissions for churches and church-related work over these years.[51]

[46]   *Ecclesiologist*, 5 (1846), pp. 10–16; p. 11. There was undoubtedly an element of political expediency in denying Pugin's importance: Newman's desertion in 1845 had made the whole High Anglican movement jumpy about any links with Rome.

[47]   *Ecclesiologist*, 6 (1846), pp. 67–8, and 4 NS (1847), pp. 75–7 respectively.

[48]   *Ecclesiologist*, 7 (1847), p. 205. The Brandons' *Parish Churches* appeared in parts in 1846–7, and their *Analysis of Gothick Architecture* came out in 1847.

[49]   See *Ecclesiologist*, 10 (1850), pp. 81–97.

[50]   *Ecclesiologist*, 7 (1847), p. 205.

[51]   Figure 1 includes all occurences of Butterfield or his works in the *Ecclesiologist*. Differential significance is reflected by an elementary system of weighting: a passing reference or brief notice equals 1 unit; a review of a building in 'New Churches', 'Churches Restored', or similar, equals 2 units, as also does a published letter from Butterfield, of which there are only three; a whole article – or most of one – about a Butterfield building equals 3 units. Albeit approximately, the graph provides an index of Butterfield's importance to the people producing *The Ecclesiologist*, and his visibility to its readers. Figure 2 is based on the catalogue of

CHRIS BROOKS

Very clearly, the former closely shadows the latter over *The Ecclesiologist*'s first decade or so. Contributing significantly are references to *Instrumenta Ecclesiastica* – shown by the earlier of the subsidiary graphs – which culminate in the peak coverage year of 1850, when the national Burial Crisis made Butterfield's cemetery designs in the *Instrumenta*'s Second Series immediately topical (plate 31). The high profile afforded Butterfield was integral to promoting the Society's vanguardism under Hope's leadership, and reciprocally related to *The Ecclesiologist*'s repudiation of any view of Gothic apart from its own – or Hope's. This interconnection provoked a particularly telling onslaught in 1850, the very year of maximum coverage.

In *The Ecclesiologist* for August 1850, 'New Churches' was headed by a perspective and plan of Butterfield's 'grave and stately' St Matthias, Stoke Newington, then being built (plate 27).[52] The next issue carried a letter attacking the design, written by Edward Augustus Freeman, later to become one of the nineteenth century's most heavyweight historians. Freeman was a member of the Society, but far more a luminary of the Camdenians' nervous sister, the Oxford Architectural Society. A High Churchman, an expert on Gothic, and decidedly tetchy, Freeman was uncomfortably positioned from the standpoint of *The Ecclesiologist* – a part-ally but also a rival authority. It printed his articles and reviewed his publications, usually with qualified approval, but disputed many of his conclusions about the history of Gothic, his views on restoration, and his architectural nomenclature. There was rigidity on both sides, Freeman was impatient of contradiction, and he may well have been irritated by the sometimes bantering tone *The Ecclesiologist* used towards him. Even so, his attack on St Matthias was surprisingly violent: 'one of the very worse designs I have seen', its silhouette 'the most unpleasant ... to be found in the whole range of ancient examples'; the tower a 'portentous erection', the porch 'absurd and ugly', the pinnacles 'ridiculous', the aisle walls 'ludicrously low', the west front 'a miserable failure'. But this was merely the lead-in to a larger target.

[The design's] entire want of architectural merit is rendered more conspicuous by its pretence, and its affectation of singularity. And I have deemed it a kind of duty to expose it at length, as I find that the productions of Mr Butterfield do not meet with the same just severity as those of other architects, though I am sure there is no one whose perpetual and ineffectual striving after originality more constantly deserves it.[53]

architectural works given by Paul Thompson, *William Butterfield*, pp. 428–52: it allows 1 unit for each year each commission was active. No claim is made for its absolute value: what matters is the overall shape of the graph, particularly as it relates to Figure 1.

52   *Ecclesiologist*, 11 (1850), pp. 142–3.
53   *Ecclesiologist*, 11 (1850), pp. 208–10.

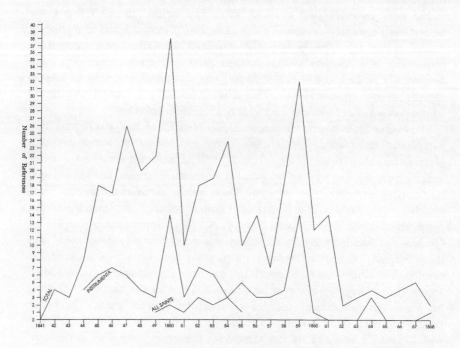

Figure 1: Butterfield in *The Ecclesiologist*.

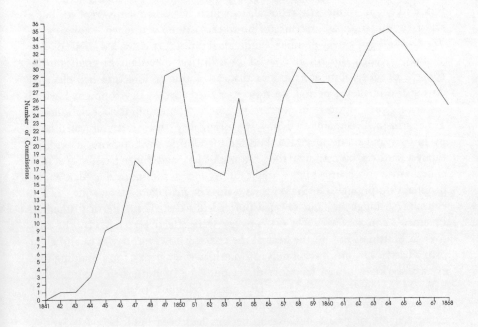

Figure 2: Butterfield: Total Ecclesiastical Architectural Commissions.

The mark at which Freeman aimed was not merely Butterfield, nor even *The Ecclesiologist*'s partiality for him, but the whole complex of positions and trajectories that made up the vanguard of ecclesiological Gothic, now derided as an 'ineffectual striving after originality'. Freeman's letter was followed by an immediate rebuttal, to which he subsequently replied, but a set-piece refutation – a measure of how seriously he was taken – appeared in *The Ecclesiologist*'s next number.[54] Individual points are defended in detail, but running through the whole is a use of historical precedent to vindicate the concept of 'development': the idea that, as Gothic architecture had changed during the medieval period, so now it invited further development beyond historical prescription in order to meet contemporary social needs. Vanguardism, Freeman's 'striving after originality', was thus vindicated both by history and modernity. The key site for Gothic development, at once its catalyst and its object, was the Victorian city, and the necessity for new churches to proclaim High Anglicanism and accommodate a dense and proliferating population. St Matthias, said *The Ecclesiologist*, was just such a church. Although he later savaged Butterfield's designs for Perth Cathedral, Freeman's contacts with *The Ecclesiologist* were effectively ended by the row over St Matthias. For all the heat of the contest, however, it was essentially a proxy battle. Or, more accurately, St Matthias was a proxy for a building that everybody knew was a far more direct outcome of Butterfield's connection with Hope and the Society, far more self-consciously a product of vanguardism and Gothic development, but which was not yet available for either censure or praise because no designs had been published: All Saints', Margaret Street.

The story of the construction and decoration of All Saints', Margaret Street has been told more often than that of any other Victorian church, most authoritatively by Paul Thompson.[55] The present discussion will focus on how All Saints' fits into the various positions and trajectories this chapter has described, particularly those of Hope and Butterfield, and how these changed during the protracted process of completing the church. As is well known, All Saints' was projected as the Camdenians' model town church, to exemplify Gothic's potential for development in a modern urban setting: precisely the principle defended so staunchly by *The Ecclesiologist* in the St Matthias controversy with Freeman. Credit for the original concept must go to Hope. As early as November 1845, just after he had become the Society's chairman, he wrote to Webb describing a new breed of Anglican urban churches.

> [They] must have a foreign character, lofty and apsidal, and domineer by their elevation over the haughty and Protestantized shopocracy of their respective towns. They must have a boundless area of nave to hold as many

---

54 *Ecclesiologist*, 11 (1850), pp. 233–6.
55 Paul Thompson, 'All Saints' Church, Margaret Street, Reconsidered', *Architectural History*, 8 (1965), pp. 73–94.

as possible of the adjacent all but heathen population. The windows should be lofty and space be afforded for mural painting, window tracery and painted glass being also developed to perfection.[56]

As we saw earlier, Hope's patronage of St Augustine's College gave him the kind of cultural capital needed to secure the chairmanship, but was at no stage his idea. The concept of a town church was different: this Hope could justifiably claim to have originated, and with it the idea of a new sort of ecclesiastical architecture predicated on Gothic development. If St Augustine's gave Hope a place in the vanguard, creating a model town church would establish a new forward position on his own initiative, confirming his trajectory in the architectural field as a leader – perhaps *the* leader – of ecclesiological Gothic. Discrediting other architectural authorities was part of the process. So too *The Ecclesiologist*'s coverage of Butterfield, the marked increase from 1848 to 1850 no accident, for these were the years in which Hope secured the site of the Margaret Street chapel, Butterfield drew up the designs for All Saints', and work began. That is, *The Ecclesiologist* expanded its publicity for Butterfield when he started the project intended to be the fulfilment of Hope's career. So defeating Freeman's assault on St Matthias was crucial, not only because of its substance but also its timing.

Hope was the co-patron of All Saints', and assumed a principal role in its building.[57] Despite some disappointment about the cramped nature of the site, he thought Butterfield had succeeded in developing 'a type of town Church original but good, striking and catholic'.[58] At this early stage Hope's intimate engagement with the designing of All Saints' is clear: the Laws, with full access to the Webb correspondence, claim it was 'a real labour of love to Alexander'.[59] Given the increasing individuality of Butterfield's architectural manner, and the personal and class issues involved in its creation, Hope's close involvement – or was it supervision? – made dispute inevitable. And the extent of Hope's economic and cultural investment, the absolute centrality of All Saints' to his trajectory in the architectural field, made it inconceivable that he would ever sufficiently distance himself from the project to allow Butterfield to assert his own creative position. Indeed, as Paul Thompson has

[56] Quoted in *Book of the Beresford Hopes*, p. 161; the strong class imperative behind Hope's missionary aspirations should be noted.
[57] Hope's contribution – substantial as it was – was outweighed by the £30,000 put in by the banker, Henry Tritton. But Tritton wished to remain anonymous, and of the two others nominally responsible for supervising progress, Sir Stephen Glynne and the incumbent W. Upton Richards, the first took little active part and the second was fully occupied arguing with Hope about the character of the services held in the church. As Thompson has remarked, 'Hope treated the responsibility as a piece of private patronage', 'All Saints' Reconsidered', p. 74.
[58] Hope to Webb, quoted in *Book of the Beresford Hopes*, p. 163.
[59] *Book of the Beresford Hopes*, p. 163.

pointed out, All Saints' was generally known in the press as "'Mr A. B. Hope's church'".[60] Conflict came principally over the decoration of the church's interior.

In April 1850, in a passage quoted many times since, *The Ecclesiologist* announced the decorative programme of All Saints'.

> The founders and the architect of this church are anxious to make it a practical example of what we are very anxious to see tested, viz., constructional polychrome. The material of the building, and of the appended clergy and chorister-houses is to be red and black brick, arranged in patterns, with stone windows and bonding in the church. Internally there is to be a use of coloured marble, which was of course impossible in the middle ages. Geometrical mosaic-work in tiles is to be introduced, and above all, the building is to be arranged with a view to frescoes of a high order of art.[61]

The statement implies the existence of an advanced body of opinion within the ecclesiological movement that had long pondered the merits of structural polychromy and had eventually decided to put the matter to the test. This was thoroughly misleading. Firstly, there is wilful redundancy in the artificial distinction between 'the founders', which really meant Hope, and the authorial 'we', which could only mean *The Ecclesiologist*, co-edited by Hope, and the Society, chaired by Hope. Secondly, despite the suggestion of extensive consideration, this is the first time the phrase 'constructional polychrome', or anything similar, occurs in *The Ecclesiologist*. True, the periodical had been advocating colour in churches for years, but this was invariably painted colour.[62] It had been frescoes Hope had intended for All Saints': structural polychromy only became the church's vertebrate decorative principle after John Ruskin's famous plea for constructional colour in *The Seven Lamps of Architecture*. Its review in October 1849 is one of the few instances of *The Ecclesiologist* extending approval to a writer positioned independently of Hope. Even so, structural polychromy is never mentioned by name, nor Ruskin's ideas addressed directly. If, as seems likely, *Seven Lamps* provided the theoretical grounding for All Saints' shift into constructional colour, Hope and *The Ecclesiologist* never acknowledged it.

The decorative *practice* of All Saints' was another matter again, for its sharp geometrical patterns, machined finishes, and artificial materials are wholly un-Ruskinian. The conception was Butterfield's, the first of the great

---

[60] 'All Saints' Reconsidered', p. 74.

[61] *Ecclesiologist*, 10 (1850), pp. 432–3; the only previous mention of All Saints' was in August 1849, stating that work was soon to start, *Ecclesiologist*, 7 NS (1849–50), p. 64.

[62] A review of Pugin's *Glossary of Ecclesiastical Ornament* in 1844 asserts 'We have always been of opinion that colour is an absolute essential to perfect beauty in a church', *Ecclesiologist*, 3 (1843–4), p.142.

polychromatic schemes of his mature style – individualistic, endlessly resourceful, as paradoxically impersonal as they are intense. There was painted colour, now gone, in St Augustine's chapel, and the tile pattern reredos at Ogbourne St Andrew, Wiltshire, may date from his restoration of 1847–8. Almost certainly, he read *Seven Lamps*, with its shimmering descriptions of Italian polychrome, and searched out illustrated sources, for many of the chromolithographs in Wyatt's *Specimens of the Geometrical Mosaics of the Middle Ages*,[63] which makes extensive use of Italian examples, show pattern forms and sequences that Butterfield was to use repeatedly. But in adopting them, he radically changed their scale. Thus precisely the kinds of variations on lozenge, triangle, and square sequences, with countercharged colours, that we find throughout his work occur as large-scale floor patterns in the Rome churches of Sta Maria in Trastavere and San Bartolomeo nell'Isola del Tevere, but also as arrangements of individual tesserae in Palermo Cathedral, each just a few millimetres wide and illustrated by Wyatt full-size.[64] Similarly: the open circles circumferenced by triangles from the choir floor of Rome's S. Marco appear on the font of Ottery (1850), Butterfield's first major polychromatic creation (plate 28); sextafoil forms in circles from the same floor turn up in the marble inlay of the All Saints', Margaret Street pulpit; a motif of ellipses around squares that is a border sequence from the nave floor of San Lorenzo Fuori le Mura is echoed on the chancel walls of Langley, Kent (1854–5) and Waresley, Cambridgeshire (1855–7).[65]

Such a recension of medieval precedents is almost mannerist in temper, but it is of a piece with the whole way in which Butterfield's mature style remade Gothic's historicist vocabulary, and its potential for meaning and expression. Butterfield's structural polychromy is independent both of the ecclesiologists and of Ruskin: meshed with his other idiomatic qualities it produced in All Saints' the seminal building of what we now know as High Victorian Gothic (plates 29 & 30). Here then was architectural vanguardism. But structural polychromy was not of Hope's making. Its theoretical articulation came primarily from Ruskin, its extraordinary practice from Butterfield, realised through the very building which, from Hope's perspective, should have been promoting his own claim to leadership in the architectural field.

Without the Webb correspondence the details of the disintegration of the relationship between Hope and Butterfield cannot be recovered, but the extracts given by the Laws are revealing when seen in terms of the larger

---

[63] Matthew Digby Wyatt, *Specimens of the Geometrical Mosaics of the Middle Ages* (London, 1848); the very publication of Wyatt's book indicates the currency of the whole subject.

[64] These examples occur as Wyatt's plates 3, 4, and 12.

[65] For the Italian originals see Wyatt's plates 2 and 7.

dynamics this chapter has explored.[66] Disagreements started as early as 1849 over Butterfield's insistence that the choir screen he had designed for All Saints' made a communion rail redundant. It was the very same issue he had raised in the letter that signalled his introduction to the ecclesiologists – a telling enough indication of the man's persistence. 'Butterfield', Hope wrote,

> has the stuff of a heresiarch in him, he is of the stamp of Tertullian, Eutyches, etc., stiff, dogmatical, and puritanical, and pushing one side of Catholicism into heresy ... He puts himself above the Western Church.

Despite the early spat, things went on amicably while the shell of the church was constructed, but once work shifted to the interior, its fittings and above all its constructional colour, deterioration was rapid. In 1852 there was a 'sort of controversy' over seating, Butterfield wanting chairs while Hope advocated moveable benches. Characteristically, Hope pursued a lengthy debate in *The Ecclesiologist* about it, signing his own pieces 'A Committeeman',[67] but Butterfield eventually got his way. Not so in an argument with the glass-painter Alfred Gerente about the tonality of the west window, which Hope – who had been keen on the Gerente practice since the 1840s – decided against the architect: Butterfield's defeat was temporary, for he supervised the window's replacement in 1877. By 1853 Hope was writing that Butterfield 'objects to being thwarted' and prophesying 'the beginning of the end' between them. Hope had 'lost respect for him', was vexed by having to tolerate 'his tomfooleries', and claimed it was 'not commonsense in him to suppose I would put £35,000 of mine and other folks' money at the arbitration of his autocratic taste.'

This last was the key, not just because the structural polychromy was proving hugely expensive, but because, as always with Hope, his grasp on economic capital was reciprocally related to his claim on cultural capital. He had thought up the idea of a model town church, and put a lot of money into All Saints', but the cultural return on his investment was being appropriated by Butterfield. His plaint to Webb was heartfelt.

> The artistic invention of the design is fully as much due to me as it is to him. I do not wish to rob him of any advantage in the eyes of the world which he may gain as architect of All Saints, but as between him and me I must have it understood how much of the work is due to me and in how much he has only been my executive. The following points are entirely my suggestion: the use of granite and alabaster and of brick externally, the frescoing of the east end, the German plan of a choir raised above the nave, and the vaulting

---

[66] All the quotations from the correspondence that follow are taken from *Book of the Beresford Hopes*, pp.175-7.

[67] His first letter appeared in April 1854, *Ecclesiologist*, 15 (1854), pp. 89-93: there is no doubt that the author was Hope, for the Laws quote a passage from his correspondence with Webb that recurs in this piece.

of the choir, and the fixed super-altar. I am certain that I am co-originator with him of the Church.

One could be more sympathetic to Hope were it not for the pervasive social arrogance. Despite what he says, he was not content to be *co*-originator with Butterfield because that would involve equality. Indifferent to Butterfield's professionalism, he is patronisingly magnanimous about any advantage that might accrue to him 'in the eyes of the world' as long as the man acknowledges he has been Hope's subordinate, that in much of the work 'he has only been executive'. These are the strategies of class, the field that in Bourdieu's model encloses the fields both of power and cultural production. And when things started to go wrong with 'his' architect, when Butterfield started to disagree, to insist on the pursuit of his own aesthetic, to claim both independence and equality, it was to the language of class that Hope resorted in his letters to Webb. Butterfield 'has been spoilt by his work in All Saints', ceased to 'act as a gentleman', and become 'an employé'. These were precisely the terms on which Butterfield was most vulnerable, and it is part of the ironic bind of class conflict that the more Butterfield asserted the professional and artistic independence that gave him a claim to the status of gentleman, the less Hope thought he was one. There is a further irony too. As was noted earlier, Hope's 1845 conception of a town church advanced ecclesiology's class objectives by overawing 'the haughty and Protestantized shopocracy': in the process of actually building that church he found the cultural credit for it taken from him by the son of a nonconformist shopkeeper. In the end, Hope could no more understand the visual and affective complexity of All Saints' than he could sympathise with the man who created it. The heart of the offence was the structural polychromy, not only epitomising the aesthetic that he found so objectionable, but doing so in a way that was at once idiosyncratic – Butterfield's own – and formidably consistent.

> Butterfield has so parricidally spoilt his own creation with the clown's dress, so spotty and spidery and flimsy as it looks in a mass now that it is all done, and worst of all the Church looks so much smaller than it used to do with nothing but the solemn columns to give scale. Butterfield on his side is honestly fanatical in his colour doctrines, and completely believes that I have marred the world's greatest work.

The broadening rift between Hope and Butterfield shaped *The Ecclesiologist*'s account of the architect's work during the 1850s (Figures 1 and 2). Following a pronounced fall in commissions in 1851,[68] Butterfield's output remained steady – excepting the sudden leap in 1854[69] – through to a marked and sustained rise after 1856. *The Ecclesiologist*'s coverage builds up to 1854, with a

[68] Probably the result of the hostility towards High Anglicanism that followed the re-establishment of the Roman Catholic hierarchy in 1850.

[69] This may be exaggerated by the statistical effect of a number of commissions being completed in 1854 coincidentally with the start of a number of others.

substantial article on one of Butterfield's buildings each year: Perth Cathedral in 1851, Coleridge's piece on the Ottery restoration in 1852, the final account of St Matthias, Stoke Newington, in 1853.[70] But the climax in 1854 is marked by an article about Sheen, the remote Staffordshire parish on the Beresford estates where Hope tried to set up an Anglo-Catholic settlement with Webb as the priest, and employed Butterfield to design the parsonage and finish the church.[71] The parsonage is a fine work, but the importance for *The Ecclesiologist* clearly rests with the whole scheme, and Hope's direction of it. 1853–4 brought the major rupture in relations at All Saints', so there was surely calculation in drawing attention to a project originated and run by Hope, with Butterfield as a subaltern. Especially as five other Butterfield works are reviewed in the same year, the most since 1850 and more than the total reviewed over the next three years, when his presence in *The Ecclesiologist* is reduced to little more than passing mentions.

This changes sharply in 1858, when Butterfield's new church of St John, Hammersmith, and the chapels of Balliol College and Battersea Training College, are reviewed, and the designs for St Matthew, Auckland, given a whole article to themselves.[72] *The Ecclesiologist* was gearing up for the imminent opening of All Saints', Margaret Street. Though he had quarrelled irreconcilably with Butterfield, Hope's prestige was bound up in the completion of All Saints', and the cultural status of its architect – lamentably wayward as he may have become – needed to be affirmed. All Saints' was consecrated on 28 May 1859, and in that year Butterfield and his works occur more often in *The Ecclesiologist* than in any year apart from 1850. As well as the article on the church itself – of which more shortly – there are: reviews of his restorations at Sudbury, Wavendon, and Milbrook; long accounts of Cumbrae and Perth in a piece on 'Ecclesiology in Scotland'; and more on St John, Hammersmith.[73] In all though – as can be seen from the subsidiary graph in Figure 1 – references to All Saints' make up nearly half of the total for Butterfield and his works in the 1859 *Ecclesiologist*. After that there is one important article comparing his church of St Alban, Holborn, with Street's St James the Less, Westminster, and a few reviews of minor works, but from 1861 Butterfield hardly exists in the remaining volumes of the periodical.

The manipulation of Butterfield's exposure in *The Ecclesiologist* was seconded by a steady shift in the journal's reaction to the architecture. In August 1849 a review of the restoration of West Lavington, Sussex, comments unfavourably on stylistic '*crotchets*'.[74] It was *The Ecclesiologist*'s first

[70] *Ecclesiologist*, 14 (1853), pp. 267–9.
[71] *Ecclesiologist*, 15 (1854), pp. 153–5; Butterfield's commission dated from 1852, when he took over the church from a local architect.
[72] *Ecclesiologist*, 19 (1858), pp. 341–2, 241–2, 340–41, and 91–2 respectively.
[73] *Ecclesiologist*, 20 (1859), pp. 75, 290, 291, 376–88, and 323 respectively.
[74] *Ecclesiologist*, 10 (1850), p. 67.

antipathetic response to Butterfield's work, and was contemporary with the first dispute at All Saints', the argument with Hope about the communion rail. In 1853, when things at All Saints' really started to go awry, the final review – ironically enough – of the much-defended St Matthias, Stoke Newington, animadverts on features that are 'positively ugly', and reveal 'a general tendency to uncouth and cumbrous ornamentation'.[75] Though Butterfield's architectural boldness continued to be praised, similar complaints crop up regularly over the next few years, with his internal structural polychromy particularly reprobated: at Hathersage, Derbyshire, the stone and tile reredos 'is heavy and the colours inharmonious'; the decorative scheme on the plans for All Saints', Margaret Street, shown at the 1855 Paris Exhibition, is 'needlessly coarse and altogether inharmonious'; the reredos of St John's, Hammersmith, is 'deficient in dignity and unpleasing in form'.[76]

All of this was effectively preparation for *The Ecclesiologist*'s review of All Saints' itself.[77] It is a curious, halting, and in parts mean-spirited performance. Butterfield is duly praised for 'the general force and power of the design', for being 'manly and austere', even for approaching 'the sublime of architecture'. Nevertheless, 'some of these merits have been carried to excess', so there is a 'dread of beauty', even a 'deliberate preference of ugliness'. Inevitably, however, the real spite is reserved for the internal polychromy. The polished granite and marbles, and some details, are commended, but 'we cannot extend our praise to the rest of the architect's own share in colouring the interior.'

> The patterns in the nave, and over the chancel arch, seem to us abrupt, and disproportionate, and ungainly. They are without flow or continuity: and the colouring throughout is fragmentary and crude. This too is a crying fault in the inlaying of the pulpit and chancel-screen: and the green voussoirs of the arches, in connection with the succession of other bald colours, are to us very displeasing. And there are some incongruities to be observed; such, for instance, as the comparatively rude brickwork of the nave edging itself up, so to say, among the more costly materials of the chancel. Lastly the grisaille of the clerestory, cold and flat and yet spotted with gaudy blots of colour, is surely in bad taste absolutely, as well as relatively to the rest of the interior.

By contrast, William Dyce's east end frescoes, which now seem the most conservative feature of the whole ensemble, are given fulsome praise: 'we ... wish that the whole interior had been coloured by the same hand.' Of course – for Dyce, gentlemanly and distinguished, was Hope's man,[78] and Hope had really wanted frescoes for his town church all along.

[75] *Ecclesiologist*, 14 (1853), pp. 267–9.
[76] *Ecclesiologist*, 15 (1854), p. 358; 16 (1855), p. 292; 19 (1858), p. 342 respectively.
[77] *Ecclesiologist*, 20 (1859), pp. 184–9; this is the source of all the quotations in the discussion that follows. As Thompson has pointed out, many details of the review were to be carried forward into the 'Glory of Ugliness' myth.

As was remarked before, Hope was incapable of granting Butterfield the equality of creative independence, and could never understand the architectural and decorative language through which that independence was so dynamically expressed. Confronted with the very vanguard that he had courted Hope stood uncomprehending: and what he could not comprehend · he denigrated. Butterfield is not even mentioned in the last two-thirds of *The Ecclesiologist*'s review of All Saints'. And at the end of it Hope's unsavoury desire to corner all the credit is gratified.

> To ourselves it is a source of no small pride and satisfaction that one of our most valued coadjutors has not only contributed with his proverbial munificence to the funds of the undertaking, but has been from the first to last the originator, and adviser, and the ultimately responsible director of the works.

Hope got something of what he wanted from All Saints', Margaret Street. 'The Church,' he wrote to Webb, in the immediate aftermath of the opening, 'this week seems the great fashionable fact. Ever so many people were talking to me about it at Lady Derby's ball last night.'[79] A month after the consecration, the ecclesiologists celebrated the twentieth anniversary of the founding of the Cambridge Camden Society. At the Anniversary Meeting, Archdeacon Thorp resigned as President and Hope was unanimously elected his successor. The timing could hardly have worked better if he had planned it: indeed, as Hope was responsible for the later delays in completing All Saints', I suspect he did. But his bid to become the leader of the Gothic vanguard had failed. Although *The Ecclesiologist* articles on Street and William White cut a new vanguard trajectory during the 1850s, it was they, not the Society and not Hope, who were leading. Eventually, in the comparison between St James the Less and St Alban's mentioned earlier, *The Ecclesiologist* was unsure whether it approved Street's powerfully personal manner any more than it did Butterfield's.[80] And White seemed determined to be unconventional.[81] In fact, by the time Hope became President of the Ecclesiological Society, ecclesiology itself had largely settled into respectability: what had been pioneering twenty years before was now close to the decent norm of Victorian Churchmanship. In 1865 Hope was elected President of the Royal Institute of British Architects. A signal distinction for a

[78] According to the Laws it was Dyce who provided Hope with the nasty phrase about 'the clown's dress', used to describe Butterfield's polychromy in the letter quoted earlier. For a decisive demonstration that Dyce's frescoes were an expression of Hope's aesthetic not Butterfield's, see Marcia Pointon, *William Dyce 1806-1864. A Critical Biography* (Oxford, 1979), pp. 128-35.

[79] Quoted in *Book of the Beresford Hopes*, p. 168.

[80] *Ecclesiologist*, 22 (1861), pp. 317-30.

[81] For example, the design of his fine church at Lyndhurst, Hampshire, was found to be 'deformed by great eccentricities', *Ecclesiologist*, 20 (1859), p. 288.

non-professional, it represented the final shift of his architectural trajectory away from experimentation and the vanguard to the cultural establishment. During his incumbency, *The Ecclesiologist* of course carried reports of the RIBA meetings. And very dull they are too.

What finally of Butterfield? Although personal contacts with Webb were maintained, Butterfield had ended his on-and-off engagement to the Ecclesiological Society by the mid-1850s. He submitted his last design for the Second Series of *Instrumenta Ecclesiastica* – mostly by other architects – in February 1854,[82] and in May wrote defending his woodwork at Dorchester Abbey.[83] As far as the record of *The Ecclesiologist* is concerned, it was his last direct contact with the Society: the connection ended as it had begun, with the formal distance of a letter. In December 1856, the Committee appointed Street to oversee the Society's plate: Butterfield was not mentioned.[84] By a peculiar irony, in 1853 and 1854, as relations at All Saints' disintegrated, the Society's Anniversary Meetings were held at 1 Adam Street, Adelphi, a few yards from where Butterfield lived and worked at number 4: needless to say, he did not take the half-a-dozen steps from his front door to join them.

Yet for Butterfield, the building of All Saints', Margaret Street, was a triumphant achievement, though he continued to fret about the interior, adding and amending, for the rest of his life. At All Saints', he created, complete in all essentials, an architectural language that was uniquely his, but that was felt as a dynamic influence across the whole, marvellously varied range of High Victorian Gothic. Other Victorian architects are sometimes like Butterfield: Butterfield is never like anyone else. Here was, and recognisably still is, the architecture of the vanguard. For Hope, the consecration of All Saints' was a carefully manipulated climax, from which he sought to extract the maximum yield of cultural capital. For Butterfield it was a stage in a continuing trajectory. As a comparison of Figures 1 and 2 shows at once, there is a total mismatch between his virtual disappearance from *The Ecclesiologist* after 1861 and the actual development of his practice. Through the middle years of the 1860s Butterfield had more work on hand than at any other time in his career, and by 1868, as *The Ecclesiologist* folded, he was embarked on his greatest group of buildings, Keble College. His continuing pursuit of his own style, indifferent to changes in architectural fashion, was inevitably solitary, but equally it was never anything other than aesthetically radical. This is probably why he took to the Coleridges, and they to him. Coming from impoverished artisan stock only a century before, they were in the forefront of a new nineteenth-century meritocracy: poets, writers and artists, as well as clerics and lawyers, a family of intellectuals and professionals with a marked streak of individualism and even radicalism. For something

[82] *Ecclesiologist*, 15 (1854), p. 120.
[83] *Ecclesiologist*, 15 (1854), pp. 180–81.
[84] *Ecclesiologist*, 18 (1857), p. 50.

like four decades, Butterfield was their architect: the final words can be left to John Duke Coleridge, in a letter of 1894.

> Architects and contractors are an unstable lot of fellows in general, though I have been spoilt by old Butterfield, who kept his time to an hour, never exceeded his estimates by a shilling, and whose work, some of which I have known for forty years, seems as if it would last for ages.[85]

---

[85] *Life and Correspondence of Lord Justice Coleridge*, 2, p. 381.

A Trusted Disciple: Richard Cromwell Carpenter

JOHN ELLIOTT

In the early years of the Cambridge Camden Society's existence, it was the designs of Richard Cromwell Carpenter (1812–55) which came closest to meeting the Society's ideals, Carpenter's church in London's Munster Square being described as 'the most artistically correct new church yet consecrated in London.'[1] With time the praise increased as the Cambridge Camden Society attempted to develop a distinctive position from that advocated by Pugin, and so it was no less a luminary than A. J. Beresford Hope, the Society's Chairman and later its President, who, in 1855, told the world of ecclesiology that the recently deceased Carpenter had been an architect who was 'superior even to Pugin'.[2] Further:

> Had his life been spared a little longer, he would at last have designed a church for the British Isles, of a size and dignity somewhat commensurate with the architectural ability of one who has proved himself of the metal of the old cathedral builders.[3]

More recently, the Rev. Basil Clarke, that cleric-cum-architectural historian, has described Carpenter as 'almost the ideal ecclesiological architect', his churches of St Mary Magdalene in Munster Square, and St Paul's in Brighton, coming 'nearer, perhaps, than any others to realizing the ecclesiological ideal'.[4] Perceptively it was the architect turned architectural historian, H. S. Goodhart-Rendel, who managed to differentiate between two of the Society's favourites, describing how the 'Puseyites saw RCC as *their* Pugin. Butterfield was their dangerous man, Carpenter their scholarly and safe one',[5] a man who was 'a true artist, without the fire or the precocity of Pugin, but perhaps with more discretion in design'.[6] Yet strangely there is little

---

[1]   *Ecclesiologist*, 13 (1852), p. 168.
[2]   *Ecclesiologist*, 16 (1855), p. 138.
[3]   *Ibid.*, p. 140.
[4]   Unpublished commentary on Carpenter written by Basil Clarke (Council for the Care of Churches).
[5]   Letter, 29 December 1945 from H. S. Goodhart-Rendel to Basil Handford (Lancing College Archive).
[6]   H. S. Goodhart-Rendel, 'English Gothic Architecture of the Nineteenth Century' in *RIBA Journal* (1924), p. 328.

reference to Carpenter in the modern texts on Victorian architecture, and where there is, the linkage is usually to Pugin. Crook describes Carpenter as 'worthy of the Puginian mantle' that the Ecclesiologists placed upon him.[7] Dixon and Muthesius describe him as 'a follower of Pugin who was favoured by the Ecclesiologists',[8] while citing his early churches as being 'very much in the manner of Pugin'.[9]

Both Carpenter and Butterfield were early favourites of the Cambridge Camden Society, and while the works of Butterfield are known and respected, those of Carpenter remain obscure. Why this dichotomy? Well, Carpenter died when he was just forty-two, and before he had developed his undoubted talents to the full. Further, unlike his contemporary and associate Pugin, who also died young, he was not a writer, and so did not bequeath to us his ideals in literary form. Perhaps more significantly, Carpenter's works have only recently been researched after many years of neglect,[10] whereas those of Butterfield were investigated by Paul Thompson almost thirty years ago,[11] and by others in more recent years.[12] This chapter aims to re-establish Carpenter as a leading Gothic Revivalist and ecclesiologist.

Richard Cromwell Carpenter (1812–55) belonged to the same generation as Benjamin Ferry (1810–80), George Gilbert Scott (1811–78), Augustus Welby Northmore Pugin (1812–52), Samuel Sanders Teulon (1812–73), William Butterfield (1814–1900) and Henry Woodyer (1816–96): a galaxy of nineteenth-century architectural talents.[13] Somewhat surprisingly, Carpenter's architectural career falls into two contrastingly different parts. The former – which is not discussed in this chapter – was dominated by his father, a cattleman turned property developer. He commissioned his son to produce non-Gothic secular designs for the development of Lonsdale Square in north London, arranged for him to be the surveyor who planned the

[7]   J. M. Crook, *The Dilemma of Style* (London, 1989), p. 64.
[8]   Roger Dixon and Stefan Muthesius, *Victorian Architecture* (London, 1978), p. 241.
[9]   *Ibid.*, p. 199.
[10] See J. P. Elliott, *The Architectural Works of Richard Cromwell Carpenter (1812–55), William Slater (1819–72) & Richard Herbert Carpenter (1841–1893)*, unpublished PhD thesis, London University (1995).
[11] Paul Thompson, *William Butterfield* (London, 1971).
[12] For instance, see chapter 6 in this book on Butterfield by Chris Brooks.
[13] Carpenter was born on 21 October 1812 and baptised at the Pentonville Chapel on 25 November. He was educated, at least in part, at Charterhouse, which he attended as a day boy from 1825 until 1827 or 1828. He married Amelia Dollman on 6 October 1840, and they lived at 99 Guilford Street, close to Russell Square, until about 1850, three children being born in the interim. In 1849 Carpenter's architectural business was relocated to Carlton Chambers at 4 Regent Street, the family moving to a house at 40 Upper Bedford Place around 1851. Some time between 1851 and 1854, the Carpenters had a fourth child, Amy, who died at the end of June 1854.

construction of Victoria Street from a point north of Holborn Bridge to Clerkenwell Green, and secured his appointment as a surveyor or architect with various railway companies: secular commissions which stand in stark contrast to that which was to follow. The second, much more important, part of Carpenter's career was dominated by the Cambridge Camden Society and its attempt to reform Anglican ecclesiology.

So how did a conventional secular architect who was very much under the influence of his father, achieve this transition to become a favourite of the Cambridge Camden Society, and a specialist in ecclesiology? The question is more easily asked than answered, much of the evidence which would support a reasoned argument having disappeared along with Carpenter's office papers and private correspondence. However, we have been left fragments of evidence which suggest what may have happened. For instance, Carpenter received his architectural training from John Blyth (1806–78), a surveyor rather than an architect, or as *The Ecclesiologist* put it, 'a gentleman of great practical experience',[14] who:

> early discovered in the mind of his pupil a strong inclination towards the study of ecclesiastical architecture, a bias which he encouraged by releasing him from the trammels of 'office routine', and afforded him full liberty and means for following the natural bent of his mind.[15]

Beresford Hope tells us that Carpenter and Pugin were friends,[16] at one time both lived in the same area of London, and, according to Beresford Hope, their friendship 'mutually encouraged their common zeal for the revival of medieval architecture.'[17] More important was the friendship between Carpenter and Nathaniel Woodard (1811–91), a man who was to spend his working life building schools for middle class boys. Their friendship is well attested in the Lancing College archive where there are numerous letters between Carpenter and Woodard which speak of their joint interests.

However, Carpenter's interest in ecclesiology pre-dates the foundation of the Society by at least seven years, the initial inspiration coming from the Rev. Thomas Mortimer who had developed a reputation for his advanced liturgical practices. As early as 1832, when Carpenter was just nineteen, Mortimer asked him to produce designs – sadly unexecuted – for a new church in Gray's Inn Road, London, which would hold 3,000, 'with double aisles, two western towers and spires, clerestory, and apsidal sanctuary'. As Beresford Hope later wrote: 'Judged by our present standard, the design and the arrangements would be thought very mediocre; but for its time of day, the case was far otherwise.'[18] Then in February 1836 Mortimer again

[14] *Ecclesiologist*, 16 (1855), p. 137.
[15] *Builder*, 16 (1855), p. 165.
[16] *Ecclesiologist*, 16 (1855), p. 139.
[17] *Ibid.*
[18] *Ibid.*

commissioned Carpenter to produce plans for a reordering of a proprietary chapel, the latter writing to Woodard saying 'The Newtown Street Chapel is going to be Episcopolized – We have made the designs &c for the same'.[19]

But, if any year was crucial to Carpenter's development as an ecclesiological architect it was 1841. Not only did he become involved with Nathaniel Woodard at Bethnal Green, where the latter had just been given charge of the newly formed district of St Bartholomew's, and where they both became acquainted with many of the supporters of the Hackney Phalanx, but it was also in that year that Pugin introduced Carpenter to the Cambridge Camden Society, where in the words of G. G. Scott 'Carpenter and Butterfield were [to become] the apostles of the high-church school'.[20] It was also in 1841 that Carpenter's first church design was executed – St Stephen in Birmingham – something Henry-Russell Hitchcock later described as 'perhaps the most "correct" example of the 14th century English parish church being built in 1841' by somebody other than Pugin.[21]

In the fourteen years which followed, Carpenter was responsible for designing twenty-eight new churches and three cathedrals, producing plans to restore another thirty-six churches and three abbeys or cathedrals, as well as building or reordering sixteen schools, nine parsonages and two great houses. Carpenter was made a fellow of the Royal Institute of British Architects in 1853,[22] and in 1893 that same organization posthumously described him as 'one of a small band of earnest thinkers who [had] caught the true spirit of medievalism'.[23] He died, aged 42, on 27 March 1855, from 'Tubercular disease of Lungs and Bladder',[24] and was buried at Highgate Cemetery.[25]

Carpenter's specific contribution to ecclesiology was directly related to the Cambridge Camden Society's early attempts to create a church form which was suited to the more sacramental and catholic form of liturgy which had emanated from the Oxford Movement. This was an architectural form whereby 'the material fabric symbolises, embodies, figures, represents, expresses, [and] answers to, some abstract meaning', a system which permits the expression of liturgy through structure.[26] The logic of such a system was

[19]   Carpenter to Woodard (Lancing College Archive). This was the chapel which Benjamin Webb attended in 1838, and possibly where he met Carpenter.

[20]   G. G. Scott, *Personal and Professional Recollections* (London, 1879), p. 112.

[21]   Henry-Russell Hitchcock, *Early Victorian Architecture in Britain* (London, 1954), p. 115.

[22]   He became a District Surveyor for St Luke's Old Street and the Liberty of Glasshouse Yard in 1847, and for East Islington in 1853.

[23]   *RIBA Journal* (1893), p. 339.

[24]   See the death certificate.

[25]   On 2 April.

[26]   J. M. Crook, *The Dilemma of Style* (London, 1989), p. 66 citing W. Durandus, *Rationale Divinorum Officiorum*, translated and edited by J. M. Neale and B. Webb (London, 1843), intro., xxxv–lxxvii.

described in an undated letter from the Cambridge Camden Society to the Incorporated Church Building Society.

> We cannot but think, for instance, that a chancel of fair proportions and separate from the nave, might lead men to a more reverent estimation of the Sacrament of the Eucharist; that the Font, of stone, in its ancient place, at the entrance of the church ... would be a standing memorial both of the Rock on which the Church is built and of the vows which bind those who have been brought into it, and that those who pass by our mean and unchurch-like modern temples in indifference, or come to them in compliance with public opinion, might sometimes be led to reflect on the power of religion, if our churches both internally and externally bore witness to the care and self denial and faith of those at whose cost they have been erected.[27]

Pugin had enunciated the new architectural principles this approach required, but his conversion to Roman Catholicism made it undesirable that his principles should be openly recommended by the Cambridge Camden Society, just as his membership of that Society, and that of other Roman Catholics, was considered a step too far.[28] What was more, the established Anglican architects who could claim any ecclesiastical specialism were, in the Society's eyes, tainted by the pre-Victorian traditions they had used in developing their practices. So the need was to find Anglican architects who were enthusiastic to embrace the architectural ideas that had emanated from Pugin and the religious ideals promulgated by the Oxford Movement; architects who were committed to the particular brand of structural sacramentalism which was advocated by the Cambridge Camden Society. Carpenter was one of these, and his particular contribution to ecclesiology has three strands: the evolution of a church design which was suited to town and city parishes; a separate design which was appropriate to rural areas; and the development of each of these paradigms so as to make them suitable for use overseas. Three ecclesiological models which could be copied as the 'High Church' ideals were spread outwards by the Cambridge Camden Society and its members.

In considering the first of these – Carpenter's urban church prototype – we are initially forced to confront an apparent contradiction, in that his precedents for this ecclesiological type were based on one particular church, that which had belonged to the Austin Friars in London; a church which was based, at least in part, on the German hall church arrangement, rather than on any medieval English example which the Cambridge Camden Society supposedly preferred and advocated.

The Austin (mendicant) Friars came to Britain in 1252 and initially settled in Wales. Their London house – including a church – was established

[27] Undated open letter from the Cambridge Camden Society to the Incorporated Church Building Society (Lambeth Palace Library, H5194.3).
[28] He converted to Roman Catholicism in 1835.

in the following year by Humphrey de Bohun, the Earl of Hereford and Essex and a Constable of England, the community being located on land between the London Wall, Throgmorton Street, Broad Street and Copthall Avenue. It seems likely that the first structure was in an Early English style with triple lancets, perhaps being based on the Temple Church which was under construction in 1240. The church was rebuilt by the Earl's successor a century later, this building being in the style associated with the time of Edward III, with four-light windows and curvilinear tracery. A third rebuilding, or restoration, most probably occurred in the fifteenth century, as according to Francis Bumpus 'The mouldings throughout, including the inner and outer arch and jamb-mouldings to the windows … [were] unmistakeably of this period'.[29] The plan comprised a chancel, plus a large nave, and separately gabled wide aisles which provided accommodation for a vast congregation. On 12 November 1538 the community was suppressed, the Friars' House and Cloister being demolished, while the chancel and transepts were turned into a stable. By an order of Edward VI dated 24 July 1550, the nave and aisles were given over to the Dutch Reformed Congregation, and remained in their possession until 10 October 1940 when they were destroyed by a German bomb.[30]

The overall plan – especially the great width which was achieved within the seven-bay nave and aisles – was similar to the German hall churches.[31] The nave was covered by a king-post roof, and by the early 1800s each aisle had a lean-to.[32] Slender compound piers supported the arcade, the circular bases being terminated by an octagonal plinth, the capitals by an octagonal abacus, all – according to Bumpus – identical to those in St Mary, Stamford. The aisles were lit by broad four-light windows topped by elaborate curvilinear tracery, precedents which Bumpus ascribes to the Latin Chapel in Oxford Cathedral, or the 'Bishop's Eye' circular window in the south transept of Lincoln Cathedral, though the clerestory of Ely Cathedral is just as likely.

This church provided the precedent for all Carpenter's town churches, and especially for his principal urban church, that dedicated to St Mary Magdalene and built in Munster Square, Camden, London between 1849–52

[29] See T. F. Bumpus, *London Churches Ancient & Modern* 1 (New York, 1908), pp. 125–27.
[30] For a history of the Dutch Reformed Church see J. Lindeboom, *Austin Friars: History of the Dutch Reformed Church in London 1550–1950* (The Hague, 1950). The church as it existed in 1800–30 is recorded in a water-colour by George Shepherd, while the interior pre-1940 is recorded in a range of photographs, all of which are in the Conway Library.
[31] See Paul Frankl, *Gothic Architecture* (London, 1962), pp. 60ff, 139ff & 154ff.
[32] Supposedly a modification which occurred during one of the restorations or rebuildings.

(plates 32 & 33). The linkage was confirmed by Carpenter's son in 1881, when, in a talk to members of the St Paul's Ecclesiological Society he said 'the principle aimed at in the church was spaciousness', and that as a precedent 'The ancient City church of Austin Friars was taken as an example, and worked out with necessary modifications'.[33] Specifically, 'The wide aisles and lofty arcades, with the absence of a clerestory, were like Austin Friars', while the separate high-pitched roofs for the nave and aisles were 'improvements on the flat aisled roofs of the older church'. The aim, Carpenter junior explained, of wide aisles as well as of a wide nave, was to make the arcade the chief feature, in contrast to contemporary churches which often had a wide nave and narrow aisles, an arrangement which made the arcade appear to be insignificant.[34]

However, the precedents were not all taken from the Austin Friars, the chancel arcading was copied from Exeter Cathedral – 'one of the finest examples of this Geometrical Decorated date' – while the design for the roofs had been taken from Sherborne Abbey.[35] The window traceries – Carpenter junior declared – were 'based on geometrical forms', the mouldings being 'very carefully proportioned to the larger and smaller mullions and tracery', Exeter Cathedral – and its west window – forming the precedent for part of the window at the eastern end of the south aisle.[36]

It was the Rev. Edward Stuart – curate at Christ Church, Albany Street – who commissioned the church in Munster Square sometime around 1848. The foundation stone was laid on 10 July 1849 and the church was consecrated on 22 April 1852. Both Carpenter and Stuart had been involved with the reordering of Christ Church, Albany Street some five years earlier, a conversion which was both architecturally and liturgically something of a compromise. Hence the aim in Munster Square was to achieve the perfect union of both without the constraints of an existing building, and as Basil Clarke so aptly put it, to create a church which was 'as near perfection as the handicraft of men, the skill of architects, and the experience and ingenuity of ecclesiastical art could make it'.[37]

Carpenter's original design – illustrated in *The Ecclesiologist* of February 1850 – was in the favoured Middle Pointed style, and comprised a

---

[33]   By naming the area Munster Square those responsible were perhaps declaring the ultimate source of the precedents.

[34]   *Building News*, 6 May 1881, p. 513.

[35]   Carpenter restored Sherborne Abbey between 1849 and his death in 1855, and so was well aware of its architectural details. His father was involved with extension of the railway connecting Exeter and Barnstaple, and presumably it was through this connection that Carpenter became acquainted with the details of Exeter Cathedral.

[36]   *Building News*, 6 May 1881, p. 513.

[37]   Basil Clarke, *Parish Churches of London* (London, 1966), p. 142.

chancel, nave, two separately gabled aisles, plus a tower and spire at the south western corner (plate 34). The *Ecclesiologist* reviewer predicted that all would be well pleased once the building was complete, declaring that the overall design was 'exceedingly good', the western façade being 'most dignified', while the proposed tower was 'beautifully enriched'. Perhaps more importantly everything inside would 'be very satisfactory', the structure 'excellently proportioned' and arranged in accordance with the latest Camdenian ideas,[38] and this despite any Germanic antecedents.

A shortage of funds required economies, and the erection of the north aisle, tower and spire were deferred; a decision which *The Ecclesiologist* regretted, as it called into question the practice of building 'very large churches in neighbourhoods like this', when had 'the founders of S Mary Magdalene been content with a smaller church, they might at once have finished the fabric, instead of leaving anything so imperfect as the part it is now proposed to raise in the first instant'.[39]

In 1902 Norman Shaw said that it was 'the width and height of... [the] aisles ... [which gave] the character and dignity to the Church', declaring that St Mary Magdalene was 'the beau ideal of a town church. It looks spacious, and yet it is by no means very large, and it certainly is not lofty. In general aspect it is very restful, and is entirely free from all affectation in design.'[40] Later, Basil Clarke described it as 'one of the best illustrations of the revolution in church building that the Ecclesiologists accomplished'.[41]

The praise flowed, and not surprisingly, as the stylistic precedents – window tracery, chancel arcading and the like which was derived from English precedents – were exactly what the Cambridge Camden Society had advocated. In his *A Few Words to Church-Builders* John Mason Neale had been quite explicit, declaring that 'The Decorated or Edwardian style, that employed, we mean, between the years 1260 and 1360, is that to which only, except from some very peculiar circumstances, we ought to return', and that is exactly what they got in Munster Square. However, there is no mention of a hall church plan in the Society's edicts, yet here we have one of that organization's favourite sons building to continental precedent. Perhaps the answer to this apparent contradiction lies with Pugin, and the peculiar relationship which existed between Carpenter, Pugin and the Cambridge Camden Society. Pugin showed the architectural way forward. He charted a route that many, including the Society, found attractive, a route that went

---

[38]   *Ecclesiologist*, 10 (1850), p. 352–54.
[39]   *Ibid.*, p. 353. The north aisle was added in 1882–3. The tower and spire were never added.
[40]   N. Shaw, 'The Church of St Mary Magdalene' in T. Sedgewick (ed.), *Description & History of the Church of St Mary Magdalene, Munster Square, London NW* (London, 1902), p. 7.
[41]   Basil Clarke, *Parish Churches of London* (London, 1966), p. 142.

back to an earlier medieval age. Yet there was a difference between Pugin's interpretation of the ideal past and that advocated by the Society. For Pugin that age predated the Reformation; it was a Roman Catholic age. For the Camdenions the age was Catholic but also Reformed. So while they admired much of what Pugin had to say, the realities of religious prejudice and the Society view of history required them to find architects of their own persuasion to execute that which Pugin advocated: in short they had to find an 'Anglican Pugin'.

The proof of this thesis lays closer to hand than one would imagine; it lies in a comparison of Pugin's St George, Southwark (1840–48), that much-debated church, which admirers and critics of Pugin closely followed the development of, with Carpenter's St Mary Magdalene, Munster Square (1849–52).[42] In both the plan was based on the German hall church arrangement, and on the Austin Friars' London church in particular, with separately gabled nave and aisles, an arrangement that allowed large numbers to be accommodated while also giving everyone an unobstructed view of the altar.[43] In short, it was Pugin who first developed a town church model which was based on the church of the Austin Friars' (in 1840–48), and Carpenter who then copied it at Munster Square (in 1849–52).

Two churches which were built at Brighton show how deep was Carpenter's commitment to this hall church plan. St Paul's was erected in West Street (1845–48) (plate 35), while All Saints was built nearer to the railway station (1847–52). Both were of knapped flint with Caen stone dressings, both were in the approved Middle Pointed style, and, as initially designed, both comprised a two-bayed chancel, a nave, two aisles, a tower and spire.[44]

---

[42] Pugin also used a similar arrangement in St Mary, Newcastle and St Thomas of Canterbury, Fulham.

[43] See R. O'Donnell, 'Pugin as a Church Architect' in Paul Atterbury and Clive Wainwright (eds), *Pugin A Gothic Passion* (London, 1994), pp. 68–9. For Pugin's comments on the Austin Friars' church see A. W. N. Pugin, *The Present State of Ecclesiastical Architecture* (reprinted, Oxford, 1969), p. 118.

[44] See *Ecclesiologist*, 5 (1846), p. 203 and a letter from Carpenter which says the spire of St Paul's should be 283 feet tall. The collapse of Chichester Cathedral spire in 1861 unsettled the church authorities, and ensured that the original design for St Paul's was never executed. Instead between 1873–5 Herbert Carpenter designed a wooden lantern tower. The tower and spire of All Saints were not finished. There were also marked dimensional similarities with what was to follow in London's Munster Square, the nave widths being 28' 6" at All Saints, 23' 6" at St Paul's, and 26' in London, while the north aisles were almost identical, 20' 6" in both Brighton churches and 21' 5" in London. The ratio of space between the nave and north aisles of these three churches comes close to the German 50/50 model, with the nave accounting for 58% of the combined width at All Saints, 53% at St Paul's and 55% in London. It was in the south aisle that the main difference occurred,

Throughout, the Camdenian influence remained unsullied. St Paul, Brighton was 'correctly' orientated with the chancel at the eastern end, and according to Charles Eastlake, its internal arrangement meant that it was 'one of the first modern county-town churches erected with a palpable recognition of those changes of ritual which were now openly encouraged by a certain section of the clergy'.[45] Similarly, when reviewing Carpenter's church at Milton (1854–6) *The Ecclesiologist* reported how:

> The chancel rises from the lantern by two steps, the sanctuary two more, and the altar stands on a footpace. There is a low screen at the chancel-arch, but no gates; and the chancel is seated stall-wise ... On the south side of the sanctuary is a single sedilia ... [while] The font stands at the west end of the nave, to the north of the door. The seats are all low and open, with a wide central passage paved with plain red tiles, as is the chancel; the sanctuary pavement being richer. There is an altar-rail of oak.[46]

Thus Carpenter's town church model seems to be one which combines the external recreation of a thirteenth- or fourteenth-century building with a hall church plan and an interior which was laid out to facilitate the more ceremonial form of worship which was advocated by the Cambridge Camden Society. Basil Clarke claimed that the church in Chichester which was dedicated to St Peter the Great (1848–52) was 'one of the best of its kind we have seen. The outside will one day be indistinguishable from a 14th-century church'.[47] In similar vein Goodhart Rendel pronounced the design for Christ Church at Milton (1854–6) as being 'beyond all praising'.[48] When it came to the internal arrangements *The Ecclesiologist* was initially thankful for small mercies, reporting how Carpenter's church at Bordesley (1844–6) 'reflects considerable credit on Mr Carpenter', not least because of the absence of internal galleries and the presence of low uniform seats.[49] However, expectations soon changed, and, in 1850, Carpenter's design for the chancel at Munster Square was initially considered to be below par, *The Ecclesiologist* complaining that the chancel arch had been 'corbelled off', while 'the choir

---

with a width of 21' 6" in London, 17' 3" at All Saints and just 14' at St Paul's, a variation which was most probably Carpenter's reaction to site restrictions, and an attempt to preserve the main elements of his design. In reacting to a restricted site Carpenter could either scale down the whole design, or alternatively restrict just one element (the south aisle), leaving the remainder of the scheme untouched. Figures for All Saints taken from ICBS File 4078 (Lambeth Palace Library) and those for St Paul's from drawings held at the RIBA.

[45] J. Mordaunt Crook (ed.), C. Eastlake, *A History of the Gothic Revival* (reprinted, Leicester, 1972), p. 224.
[46] *Ecclesiologist*, 18 (1857), p. 334.
[47] Basil Clarke Notebook No 7, p. 2 (Council for the Care of Churches).
[48] Goodhart-Rendel card index (National Monuments Record).
[49] *Ecclesiologist*, 3 (1844), p. 150.

JOHN ELLIOTT

stalls ... were both insufficient and not returned'.[50] They would also have preferred 'the dwarf stone wall' which separated nave and chancel to be topped by 'a light metal screen',[51] and hence the church was declared 'less perfect in some of its ritual arrangements ... than S Barnabas [Pimlico]'.[52] However, by the time the church was completed in 1852 all signs of serious criticism were gone, *The Ecclesiologist* complementing Carpenter on 'this noble church', whose 'architectural ornamentation generally is particularly good', and whose structure had 'fully succeeded in producing an imposing effect of height and space', the 'graceful arcades of five arches offer[ing] scarcely any encumbrance'. The sanctuary, they declared, was 'very spacious', being surrounded by 'an arcade of beautifully carved arches, resting on detached shafts of S Anne's marble', while a dossal with 'rich diaper of gilding' topped the altar and was itself 'emblazoned [with] a floriated cross'.[53] Overall this was 'the most successful modern architectural', and 'artistically correct new church yet consecrated in London',[54] and like St Paul, Brighton (1845–8), was 'just suited to the Anglican ritual' which could 'be solemnly and stately celebrated in the presence of such a congregation as its nave could contain'.[55]

Carpenter's country church genre was a more limited affair producing just four examples.[56] The architectural precedents are less complex than those used in the urban areas, though the internal arrangements remain identical if miniaturised. There is no longer any reference to the Austin Friars, or to the German hall churches, but instead a faithful replication of an ecclesiastical form that had graced the medieval English countryside.

In the Society's early years there was much attention paid to the medieval churches close to Cambridge. In 1843 *The Ecclesiologist* carried a report on the abuse which had been inflicted on St Michael, Long Stanton; a 'very beautiful little Early-English chapel' whose chancel was being 'used for a school.'[57] Then in 1845 *The Ecclesiologist* reported that tracings of this same

50 *Ecclesiologist*, 10 (1850), p. 354.
51 In 1881 Carpenter's son said that this was not his father's design, as he had recommended a stone wall. Carpenter Junior said he was partly responsible for the screen which then existed but that he would like to see it removed – see *Building News*, 6 May 1881, p. 514.
52 *Ecclesiologist*, 13 (1852), p. 168.
53 *Ecclesiologist*, 13 (1852), p. 167.
54 *Ecclesiologist*, 13 (1852), pp. 167–68.
55 *Ecclesiologist*, 10 (1850), pp. 204–7.
56 St James, Nutley (1842–4); St John the Baptist, Cookham Dean (1844–5); St James the Less, Stubbing (1849–50); St John the Evangelist, Bovey Tracey (1852–3).
57 *Ecclesiologist*, 2 (1843), p. 171. Pugin also used this church as the model for his Roman Catholic Church in Cambridge – St Andrew (1842–43). The Cambridge Camden Society must have known of Pugin's church though it did not publicly refer to it. Interestingly Carpenter also uses this same model as did Pugin's most

church had been sent to the United States so that they could be used as the basis of designs there.[58] St Michael, Long Stanton was almost certainly used as the model for St James the Less Episcopal Church in Philadelphia (1846–48), but closer to home it most probably also formed the basis of Carpenter's model church for rural areas.

Typical is the church which he designed to be built at Cookham Dean near Maidenhead (plate 36), an area 'abutting on and being part of Maidenhead Thicket', with a population of 'Nine hundred or thereabouts [people who were] ... almost exclusively ... Agricultural Labourers among whom ignorance and immorality have prevailed for some time past'. In 1843 a local committee sought permission to use a cottage 'for the performance of Divine Service', to appoint the Rev. George Hodson 'to have the spiritual charge of the said District',[59] and to commission Carpenter to produce designs for a new church. The style was Middle Pointed, with a dominant nave, subsidiary aisles, and an elevated Tractarian chancel. The foundation stone was laid in July 1844, and the church consecrated on 22 May 1845, *The Ecclesiologist* reporting:

> A church is just completed at Cookham Dean, near Maidenhead, dedicated in honour of S. John Baptist. It is a most satisfactory design; very simple, and yet not mean or starved; of unpretending but solemn character. The chancel is of a good size, with windows of excellent workmanship. The style is of the fourteenth century. The pitch of the roof is proper, and all the details are appropriate. The nave has a western bell gable, very ably treated, holding one bell. The aisles have lean-to roofs, low side walls, and square windows; the eastern windows of the aisles are like the side windows in the chancel. The south-western porch is of wood, well carved, and rather elaborate. The church holds 300 persons: the cost is about £1300.[60]

There is a great similarity in plan and style between the church at Long Stanton and those which were designed by Carpenter at Cookham Dean (1844–5); St James, Nutley (1842–4); St James the Less, Stubbing (1849–50); and St John the Evangelist, Bovey Tracey (1852–3). However, there is also a similar likeness to many of the small rural churches which Pugin designed, a similarity which suggests that both the Anglican and Roman Catholic followers of Pugin (Carpenter for the Anglicans and Hansom for the Roman Catholics) were basing their designs on the same source. As Roderick O'Donnell puts it, for Pugin there was only one architectural style, as there

---

adept Roman Catholic imitator – Charles Francis Hansom (1817–88) at St Alphonsus, Hanley Swan, Worcs. (1844–46). Information kindly supplied by Roderick O'Donnell.

[58]   *Ecclesiologist*, 4 (1845), p. 23.

[59]   Oxford Records Office c1033–1. Hodson was the second son of the Archdeacon of Stafford and Canon of Lichfield Cathedral and a Trinity College student between 1837 and 1843.

[60]   *Ecclesiologist*, 4 (1845), p. 138.

was for anyone 'who claimed descent from the Church of the Middle Ages',[61] and this idealised country parish church was to become the model not just for Pugin and his followers, but also for the Cambridge Camden Society.

It is interesting to see that for Pugin such stylistic similarity between what the Society would have claimed to be two different brands of Catholicism was not surprising. When commenting upon the efforts of his fellow Roman Catholic architects Pugin declared that 'in the present revival of Catholic architecture, the authorities for which can only be found in the ancient edifices of the country, it is very possible and even probable that two architects may erect precisely the same edifice', as 'When buildings are derived from a common source, it is very natural that they should greatly resemble each other'.[62] Hence, because for the Society Anglicanism was as Catholic as Roman Catholicism, the fact that both Carpenter and Pugin designed country churches with the same plan and in the same architectural style, that differing Catholic architects alternated 'two-light traceried Decorated windows with the Early English lancets',[63] that they placed 'belfreys, in the form of perforated gables' atop the western wall,[64] was not plagiarism but simply the consequence of such features being found in ancient churches.

The similarities are striking. Compare the churches Carpenter designed with Pugin's St Mary, Southport (1837–8); St Anne's, Keighley (1838–9); St Mary, Warwick Bridge (1840), St Lawrence, Tubney (1844-7)[65] – and even St Alphonsus, Barntown, Wexford (1844–51), where, as at Bovey Tracey, the bell-cote emerges from a western buttress. In all the designs the nave and chancel are dominant, the aisles being subsidiary spaces, the division between chancel and nave being structurally evidenced. The bell-cote summons the laity to worship and signifies the consecration. The naves have lean-to roofs, there is no clerestory, the nave and chancel roofs are steeply pitched, the chancel is elevated, and the altar elevated even more so. In each the materials are local, and honest, though the buttresses are usually symbolic as well as structural. Overall there is a similarity which attests to a common interest; though it was Pugin (whose designs originated in the 1830s and early '40s) who was the leader, and Carpenter (whose designs started in the 1840s) who was the follower, a position of which Pugin could hardly have complained.

[61] R. O'Donnell, 'Pugin as a Church Architect', P. Atterbury & C. Wainwright (eds), *Pugin: A Gothic Passion* (New Haven & London, 1994), pp. 65–6.

[62] A. W. Pugin, *The Present State of Ecclesiastical Architecture in England* (London, 1843), p. 108.

[63] R. O'Donnell, 'Pugin as a Church Architect', P. Atterbury & C. Wainwright (eds), *Pugin: A Gothic Passion* (New Haven & London, 1994), p. 67.

[64] A. W. N. Pugin, *The Present State of Ecclesiastical Architecture in England* (London, 1843), p. 19.

[65] The only Church of England church amongst those designed by Pugin.

British Imperial expansion provided a conduit which facilitated trade, emigration and the export of Christianity, especially Anglicanism; so much so that in his book *The English Cathedral of the Nineteenth Century*, Beresford Hope refers to the colonies as 'that great England beyond the seas', where 'the Church has to constitute itself in every particular, without the material advantage of being "established"'.[66] The early stages of the nineteenth century were unique in that during that period there was both a significant increase in overseas territories and in the number of overseas dioceses. While the Evangelical revival provided an initial rationale for domestic and overseas missionary work, Tractarianism was not slow in following, and as committed agents of Tractarian beliefs, the Cambridge Camden Society took a special interest in things colonial. Carpenter's contribution to the material presence of Anglicanism in the colonies represents an important aspect of his practice.

There was an early recognition that these overseas posessions comprised a diverse mix of races, cultures and climates, and that merely to export the ecclesiastical architecture of the mother country was inappropriate. As early as 1846 *The Ecclesiologist* suggested a north–south stylistic divide, with churches in the north being based on the native vernacular of the individual country, while those in the south would be styled upon a polychromatic variant of the Lombardic, as this was both suggestive of warmer climates and had been the style of the medieval Church.[67] These pre-set ideas never saw fruition, and there grew a recognition that such an eclecticism was not possible until a local architectural skill had been developed. In 1847 *The Ecclesiologist* shifted the emphasis towards educating the Colonial clergy and their local architects, declaring that overseas 'church-builders ... must learn Ecclesiology for themselves', they must learn to 'perfect Christian architecture' with 'correct arrangement', and to build churches which were 'suitable for Catholic worship'. However, while such ecclesiological skills were being learnt, the Mother Church and its church-builders could help – 'by circulating Ecclesiological works, and by furnishing accurate drawings of churches and their parts'.[68]

Publication of *Instrumenta Ecclesiastica* in 1847 was a response to this need, containing 'working drawings of details and fittings, appertaining to churches and their precincts', using precedents which the Society had copied from British models.[69] The object was to 'supply, in cheap and convenient form, some of those designs which experience has shown the conductors of the Ecclesiological late Cambridge Camden Society to be most generally

[66]   A. J. B. Beresford Hope, *The English Cathedral of the Nineteenth Century* (London, 1861), pp. 19–20.
[67]   See George L. Hersey, *High Victorian Gothic: A Study in Associationism* (Baltimore & London, 1972), pp. 74–75 for further details.
[68]   *Ecclesiologist* (1847), pp. 16–18.
[69]   The drawings were produced by Butterfield.

wanted'.[70] A second version of *Instrumenta Ecclesiastica* was published in 1856, and the change in emphasis is illuminating. Designs for decorative details were still included, but relegated to a less dominant role, while model designs were introduced for an iron church plus another for a wooden church which was 'suitable for a temperate climate'[71] – designs for which Carpenter was wholly or partly responsible.[72]

In October and November 1850 the Society approved Carpenter's 'designs for a wooden church ... intended for the island of Tristan d'Acunda' and 'determined to publish them in the next number of their *Instrumenta Ecclesiastica* (plate 37).[73] The accompanying narrative declared that 'The Church will be wholly of timber, with the exception of the foundations and a low basement, which may be formed of rubble-stone or brick'.[74]

The precedents were Carpenter's domestic designs for country parishes. The aisles were half the width of the nave, while the roof was similar to that used for St James, Nutley (1842–44), with one continuous – but variable angle – surface covering aisles, nave and chancel, and with a wooden bell-cote at the western end. The style was Early English – associational rather than structural – timber being used to create a form of nave arcade, while wooden cusped lancets pierced the walls and arcaded chancel. The chancel was elevated by one step at the arch giving access to a stalled choir, and by three more steps at the entry to the sanctuary, while the altar was elevated yet again. *The Ecclesiologist* said the design 'deserves the highest commendation',[75] though in *Instrumenta Ecclesiastica* the Society commented that it could be improved by 'break[ing] the long continuous ridge of the roof [and] by placing the bell-turret over the point of division between Nave and Chancel'.[76]

While *Instrumenta Ecclesiastica* may have helped to spread the Camdenian ideals, it was by word of mouth and personal contact that the

[70]   See the 'Prefatory Notice' dated 21 January 1847 for *Instrumenta Ecclesiastica* (London, 1847). The volume contained three ground plans, two for a church and one for a college (the three ground-plans were all of S Mary the Virgin, Cobham, Kent), but there were no external elevations, and the majority of the book was devoted to items such as decorative ironwork, lichgates, gable crosses and various internal artefacts.

[71]   See plate xix 'Wooden Church: Ground Plan', in *Instrumenta Ecclesiastica* (London, 1856).

[72]   Carpenter produced designs for a wooden church and was asked to also produce designs for an iron structure. However, he died before the latter could be completed and the task was taken on by his pupil and successor William Slater.

[73]   The meetings were held on 8 October and 9 November and were reported in *The Ecclesiologist* (1850), pp. 248 & 262.

[74]   *Instrumenta Ecclesiastica* (London, 1856), plate xix.

[75]   *Ecclesiologist*, 12 (1851), p. 221.

[76]   *Instrumenta Ecclesiastica* (London, 1856), plate xx.

greatest impact was achieved.[77] Especially important were the endeavours of the Colonial clergy, who when returning from visits to England, took with them copies of designs which had been produced for English churches. By 1847 the Rev. F. H. Cox, had obtained copies of Carpenter's plans for St John the Baptist, at Cookham Dean.[78] These he then modified, and embellished with designs taken from *Instrumenta Ecclesiastica* and with illustrations published in *The Ecclesiologist*, before he personally supervised the building of a new church in Tasmania (plate 38) – St John the Baptist, Prossers' Plains, near Buckland (1846–48). He wrote 'I have employed no architect – for architects here are anything but ecclesiastical; – nor contractor – for contractors here, or at least church-contractors, are proverbially not trustworthy'.[79] Cox revealed his precedents in a letter he sent to *The Ecclesiologist* during 1847,[80] writing that 'The plan, [had been] (adopted from one by Mr Carpenter, designed for S John the Baptist's, Cookham Dean)' the roofs being 'copied from Vol. iii of *The Ecclesiologist*'.[81]

The church was a model of Englishness, something Joan Kerr describes as 'a transported English church', which 'because of the rector's ecclesiastical connections', differed from the 'amateur efforts' at church building which had previously been attempted in that country.[82] The foundation stone was laid in 1846, the church was opened in 1848 and consecrated in early 1849. It was reviewed by *The Ecclesiologist* on several occasions,[83] being praised for the correctness of its internal arrangements, and for the 'excellent masonry of the walls, which, with their massive staged buttresses, present an appearance of great solidity'. Overall *The Ecclesiologist* described the design as 'characteristic of an English village church', with 'ornamental gable-crosses at the east end of the chancel and nave ... [a] simple bell-gable at the west', and windows of 'foliated tracery of the fourteenth century'.[84]

---

[77] For a discussion on Pugin's influence in Australia see Brian Andrews, 'Pugin in Australia' in Paul Atterbury & Clive Wainwright, *Pugin: A Gothic Passion* (New Haven & London, 1994), pp. 246–57.

[78] Plans had been sent to Tasmania by the Cambridge Camden Society in 1844. *The Ecclesiologist* reporting a meeting held on 11 May 1844 said: 'Three models of churches of different sizes, designed for the Society by R. C. Carpenter Esq to be sent out to the diocese of Tasmania were exhibited to the meeting by the Architect' – *Ecclesiologist*, 3 (1844), p. 133.

[79] *Ecclesiologist*, 8 (1847), p. 87.

[80] The letter was dated 9 March 1847 and sent from Prosser's Plains, Van Dieman's Land.

[81] *Ecclesiologist*, 8 (1847), pp. 87–8.

[82] E. J. Kerr, *Designing a Colonial Church: Church Building in New South Wales 1781–1888*, unpublished PhD thesis, York University, 1978, p. 195.

[83] See *Ecclesiologist*, 11 (1850), pp. 89–91 and 1853, p. 113.

[84] *Ecclesiologist*, 11 (1850), pp. 89–90.

Carpenter's church at Cookham Dean and its source at Long Stanton, was also the precedent for two other churches which it was proposed to build in Australia. One of these was at Cabramatta, near Sydney, New South Wales, where in 1848 a group of local residents were anxious to build a church which could be dedicated to the Holy Innocents, and where Carpenter's drawings were modified by Edmund Blackett,[85] who as Colonial Architect, was responsible for overseeing the building of all churches erected under the provisions of the Church Act 1836.[86] The foundation stone was laid in late 1848, and the church consecrated in 1850. In 1851 *The Ecclesiologist* contained a brief report stating that:

> Within the district ... there has lately been erected the little church of The Holy Innocents, Cabramatta, a mere nave and chancel, with bell turret and wooden porch, but its forms and details within and without showing a most satisfactory example of ecclesiological development.[87]

Joan Kerr refers to Holy Innocents as 'a perfect ecclesiastical church of the same type as Cox's building at Prossers' Plains', though it was built in English bond brickwork, with stone facings, rather than exclusively of stone as at Prossers' Plains. It was small, having just a two bay nave, with a disproportionately large chancel, a north vestry, a timber porch and a bell-cote. Inside there was a high-collar beam roof, and fittings which were 'perfectly correct according to the ecclesiological formula', being 'as perfect a medieval replica as was ever realized in the colony'.[88] There was:

> open seating throughout the nave, [a] pulpit at the south east corner... two steps up to the chancel (with chancel arch), and another step with some low altar rails to the sanctuary. The choir stalls are situated on the north side of the chancel, with two chairs for the clergy facing them to the south. There are carved stone sedilia on the south side of the sanctuary.[89]

Carpenter was also involved with plans for a church at Hagley in Tasmania, though this time the precedents were taken from his town church

---

[85] Blackett was born in Southwark on 25 August 1817. He acted as a surveyor of the Stockton & Darlington Railway, before emigrating to Australia. He quickly became associated with Bishop Broughton, and was appointed Colonial Architect in 1849. Surviving drawings show that Blacket designed a font for the church (See the Mitchell Library MC D216-1(134)), and it is possible that he also designed the chancel furniture and fittings. A full account of Blackett and his works is given in Morton Herman, *The Blacketts: An Era of Australian Architecture* (Sydney & London, 1963); Joan Kerr & James Broadbent, *Gothic Taste in the Colony of NSW* (NSW, 1980) and Joan Kerr, *Edmund T. Blackett, Architect* (National Trust of Australia, 1983).

[86] The act remained in force until 1862 and provided a pound-for-pound subsidy on churches costing between £600 and £2,000.

[87] *Ecclesiologist*, 12 (1851), p. 260.

[88] *Ibid.*, pp. 204–5.

[89] See Kerr, *Designing a Colonial Church...*, p. 204.

genre. Carpenter's drawings are still held at the church, and show the designs for a middle pointed structure with a four bay nave, a narrower and lower three bay chancel, a south porch, and a north aisle which terminated in a three stage western tower topped by a broached spire. The aisle windows were originally intended to be couplets below a curvilinear cinquefoil, but between design and execution the tracery style changed from curvilinear to geometric. The western end had four lancet lights below a wheel, a window that was copied from the clerestory at Exeter Cathedral,[90] while at the eastern end there was a stumpier five light version of the geometric light which was used for the east window at Milton and for the south chancel window at Munster Square. The tower and spire were derived from the design used at Monkton Wylde, the spire being broached with a lunette on each of the four faces, the lower stage of the tower having a single curvilinear light, the middle level a couplet below curvilinear tracery, while the upper level had a pair of couplets below a quatrefoil.

All very Camdenian, all very English, and perhaps a bit too much so, as there was a long delay before the foundation stone was laid in 1861, and then only the nave and aisle were built, the church being opened for service in January 1863. A chancel, tower and spire were added later to a different design produced by Henry Hunter, and the church was consecrated in 1871.[91]

However, the English prototype was not always welcomed with open arms. The Cambridge Camden Society provided copies of Carpenter's designs for All Saints, Brighton, to the Anglican diocese in Philadelphia, in the United States, hoping they could be used as the designs for what became St Mark's Church in the city of Philadelphia. However, the designs:

> were found inapplicable, to the climate and circumstances of the church, particularly from the aisles having separate gables, which it was thought would in that climate cause too great a lodgement for snow.[92]

Similarly, while mid-nineteenth-century outreaches of the Church of England on the Atlantic Islands, in Australia and even in the eastern part of the United States, all experienced some commonality of climate and served a population that was dominated by a European heritage, settlements on the Indian sub-continent were culturally and climatically another matter. In 1851 the Rev. Dr Garstin, who was responsible for those Anglicans living near Point de Galle in Ceylon, wrote to *The Ecclesiologist* saying that the area was 'very prominent ... all the steamers between Suez and India, China, the Straights of Malacca, and Australia, draw up ... [though the] fixed resident European population is very limited'.[93]

---

[90] But with the direction of spin reversed for a church in the southern hemisphere.
[91] See *Church News*, 20 January 1863, and September 1871.
[92] *Ecclesiologist*, 8 (1848), p. 285.
[93] He added that the Wesleyans and Baptists have chapels, the Dutch have their own church and the Portuguese have a Roman Catholic church – the Anglicans were

He requested 'a good sketch or two ... of a building strictly ecclesiastical', as 'We have a number of persons here who are able to work out the idea perfectly, if presented to them, but are quite incapable of conceiving it, for want of having seen any models'. His requirements were for a church which would hold '500 persons, equal, on account of our heat, to 750 in England'. He reiterated the need to amend any design so as to compensate for the heat, saying 'it is almost impossible for you to understand to what extent the necessity for admitting air, and yet excluding the sun's direct rays'. However, Garstin showed his European architectural background by suggesting Italy as a source of stylistic precedents, and by rejecting a verandah arrangement which he claimed 'destroys the effect of a church'. Instead the requirement was to 'find such a plan as will give abundance of air through doors and windows, and yet, by the help of judicial provisions, and perhaps well managed planting, afford shelter from the tropical glare and tropical rains'.[94]

Carpenter's designs were shipped to Ceylon, and *The Ecclesiologist* printed his accompanying memorandum, which explained how he had reacted to the major requirement for ventilation. Because the Bishop of Colombo preferred 'a surrounding cloister ... to serve as a verandah', so Carpenter had – despite Garstin's objections – 'generally adopted the same principle of design', combining the cloister with 'ample height in the building', and 'lucarne windows, which give light to the clerestory openings',[95] an arrangement that would generate a thorough vertical ventilation. However, he did take note of Garstin's plea for simplicity, saying 'the details are kept purposely very simple', consisting of single and double splays, and a teak timber roof covered with tiles.[96] Perhaps more importantly for the Cambridge Camden Society, *The Ecclesiologist* also reported how 'The ritual arrangements are quite correct', within a design that comprised an aisled nave,[97] an apsidal chancel,[98] and cloisters which extended 'along the north and south sides, with a sort of narthex along the west end'.[99]

Whatever its attempted climatic adaptations, the basic precedents of the design were clearly European, the saddle-back tower being described as reminiscent of the 'north-west tower of Rouen'.[100] Despite its liturgical correctness the design was rejected, partly because it ignored the stylistic

---

the 'only religionists who have not a place of worship'. See *Ecclesiologist*, 12 (1851), p. 20.
[94] *Ibid.*, pp. 20–1.
[95] These he suggested should be executed in galvanized metal.
[96] *Ecclesiologist*, 12 (1851), p. 23.
[97] 80 ft by 22 ft 6 ins.
[98] 40 ft long.
[99] *Ecclesiologist*, 12 (1851), p. 22.
[100] *Ibid.*, p. 23.

preferences of the patron, but also because it was 'not well suited to the climate':[101] when faced with the ferocity of tropical heat the need for an image of medieval England became less important than ventilation and comfort.

For Carpenter and many of his contemporaries, religion occupied a position of prime importance, a position which made regular church attendance the norm, and a career in church architecture both a practical and desirable proposition. So in pursuing his earthly pilgrimage Carpenter assumed his own form of religious vocation, one dedicated to the service of his God by the act of giving structural expression to the ideals of the Cambridge Camden Society. Perhaps more importantly he contributed to a wider culture, building model churches which could be copied by others. Without doubt he was one of the Cambridge Camden Society's favoured sons, and helped them to develop the ideal Anglican church; a style which with time was adopted throughout England, by the Anglican sister churches in Scotland and Ireland, and overseas.

Before Pugin and the Cambridge Camden Society had started to issue their fiery polemics, church architecture was often dominated by a love of the picturesque, just as its liturgy was often centred on the spoken word. While Christopher Webster and Simon Bradley have shown how the situation could not always be summarised so simply,[102] there is more than a grain of truth to the suggestion that it was these two – Pugin and the Cambridge Camden Society – that transformed the architectural and liturgical form of a large part of the Established church. Because of the Society's conscious desire to distance itself from Pugin, it was Carpenter who played a key role in this transformation. What is more, the similarities between the architectural arrangements used by Pugin and Carpenter are too striking to be ignored, and it was for this reason that Goodhart-Rendel christened Carpenter the 'Anglican Pugin'.

What was it about Carpenter's designs which made him such a favourite with the Cambridge Camden Society? Undoubtedly the answer is his faithful rendition of an arrangement that mirrored the requirements John Mason Neale had so eloquently outlined in his *A Few Words to Church-Builders*. So whatever church Carpenter designed *The Ecclesiologist* praises it, just as the efforts of certain other architects received continual condemnation. He was praised whether it be a town church built to a German plan, or a rural church built to an English one. However, perhaps there is evidence to suggest that Carpenter was more fulsome in his support of the Cambridge Camden Society than were others of its architectural members, and so perhaps his churches were seen as being better models which should be copied. The Society's edicts are well documented and even a brief

[101]   *Ecclesiologist*, 12 (1851), p. 400 and 13 (1852), p. 276.
[102]   See also Peter Nockles, *The Oxford Movement in Context* (Cambridge, 1994).

examination of Carpenter's churches quickly shows how complete was his adherence. Yet perhaps it was not so difficult to be considered a favourite son, for as Neale so eloquently put it in *A Few Words to Church-Builders*:

> It is not pretended that all the Decorations recommended ... can be adopted in every church ... But to describe a church as it *ought* to be, may perhaps have the advantage of showing how very far below such a model are most of the buildings to which we now by courtesy give that name.[103]

So how should we view Carpenter? Was he a plagiarist, a brilliant imitator, or merely a safe pair of hands? Without doubt Carpenter and Pugin both followed the same architectural Holy Grail; both sought a solution to the challenges of their day in the same remnants of the past, yet it is Pugin who seems to lead the way. But to classify Carpenter simply as a plagiarist or imitator is to misunderstand the complexities, prejudices and realities of Victorian religious life. Yes, Pugin had charted an architectural way forward, just as the Oxford Movement had charted a doctrinal pathway for Anglicanism, and so logic might have suggested that Anglicanism should embrace Pugin's architectural edicts. However, early Victorian Anglican sensibilities were tender; the Church of England felt under threat from growing secularism, and from the advances of both Roman Catholicism and Non-Conformity. With a declining market share the need was for uniqueness, and so the Cambridge Camden Society felt forced to distance itself from Pugin while simultaneously adopting his ideas; to adopt his principles and claim they were their own.[104]

While circumstances may have propelled Carpenter into the role of the 'Anglican Pugin', he was also much more. His buildings have a grace and balance that is completely missing from many of Butterfield's commissions: there is no straining for effect, no sharp contrasts; just balance, a perfect union between applied internal colour and structural colour and an internal arrangement that met the liturgical needs that the Cambridge Camden Society advocated. His St Mary Magdalene in Munster Square has a grace few other

---

[103]   *A Few Words to Church-Builders* (1849), p. 3.

[104]   Yet Carpenter, presumably with the approval of the Society, used Pugin's stained glass designs. The west window in Sherborne Abbey was designed by Pugin as part of Carpenter's restoration of 1849–55, as was the glass in St Paul, Brighton, which Carpenter designed (1845–9). The church had been commissioned by the vicar of Brighton, the Rev. H. M. Wagner, for his son, the Tractarian Rev. A. D. Wagner. Carpenter designed the structure and Pugin the glass which Hardman then manufactured. Clearly there was no shame in such a co-operative venture, Wagner senior even visiting Pugin at Ramsgate and reporting how 'I had the pleasure of passing an hour last week at Ramsgate with Mr. Pugin, who showed me some of the drawings' (Letter from H. M. Wagner dated 10 August 1849 in the Hardman Archive), while Pugin visited the Brighton church on 9 November 1850.

Victorian churches possess, as does his St Peter the Great, Chichester, St Paul, Brighton and St Nicholas, Monkton Wylde. A great sense of space is created by the hall church plan, the slender nave columns and the simple roof forms, while the chancel is decorated to create a visual focus towards the liturgically most important part of the building. Throughout the archaeological detail is precise; Carpenter had extensive knowledge of the differing Gothic styles and he used this knowledge to effect. At Butterfield's All Saints, Margaret Street the eye is continually distracted from the main event, the senses are assailed; at St Mary Magdalene, Munster Square there is peace and tranquillity, no extravagant gestures, simply a striving for eternity. Even when the finances and the congregation are more limited, as they were in the rural parishes, the essence of Carpenter is still there, the beauty, the charm, the simplicity: a work of art in miniature. As one modern commentator so aptly put it; 'Carpenter's churches are easy on the eye.'

But where does that leave Butterfield? Was Carpenter simply pipped at the post by a more upwardly mobile and ambitious man? The answer is most probably yes, and has much to do with the influence of Beresford Hope. As Chris Brooks has shown, both Beresford Hope and Butterfield shared a common interest which formed the basis of their initial activities within the Society. However, as Hope achieved the status to which he aspired, so he tired of Butterfield and his wildness, and instead adopted Carpenter as his preferred architect. In 1844, when Beresford Hope paid for the restoration of his church at Kilndown, Carpenter had been just one amongst many who effected 'a most marvellous change', Salvin, Carpenter, Butterfield, Willement and Thomas creating a chancel – 'so rich and beautiful in its fittings and decorations'.[105] Carpenter designed, and Thomas carved, the 'glorious rood-screen ... coloured and gilt to perfection',[106] the open benches which replaced the box pews, and the stalls which were erected within the newly created chancel. Butterfield designed a brass eagle and two six light coronas,[107] Salvin designed a stone altar and Willement decorated the walls with a riot of colour,[108] such that, according to *The Ecclesiologist*, the 'chancel of Christ Church, Kilndown, lighted up for evensong, is a sight which all ecclesiologists ought to see.'[109]

Beresford Hope's spat with Butterfield over the decoration of All Saints, Margaret Street reached its height in the early 1850s, and so when, in 1854, Beresford Hope wanted to modernise his own house at Kilndown, it was to Carpenter that he turned. It was also Carpenter that he used to design a

---

[105]   *Ecclesiologist*, 4 (1845), p. 91.
[106]   *Ibid.*
[107]   Which were manufactured by Potter of South Molton Street. See *Ecclesiologist*, 3 (1844), p. 127.
[108]   *Ecclesiologist*, 4 (1845), p. 92.
[109]   *Ibid.*

JOHN ELLIOTT

new parsonage at Kilndown (1854–5), to create a tomb for his mother and
step-father (1854) and to produce many of the designs which were to appear in
the 1856 edition of *Instrumenta Ecclesiastica*.[110] Carpenter died in 1855 and
Butterfield again started to enjoy something of his old importance, though the
recovery was short-lived. Carpenter's architectural practice was taken over by
one of his pupils, William Slater, who was joined by Carpenter's son, Richard
Herbert Carpenter in 1857, the two acting in partnership from 1863. So
rapidly the pendulum swung back to Slater & Carpenter who continued with
the modernisation of Bedgebury Park, the Hope seat; designed a new lychgate
to the church at Kilndown (1860); a tomb for the Rev. J. Murray of St
Andrew, Wells Street (1862–3); a tomb and memorial reredos to Beresford
Hope's daughter, Catherine (1870); and ultimately the memorial tomb for
Beresford Hope and his wife (1881–2). To commission one's memorial must
be the ultimate act of patronage, and the highest indicator of personal
preference. While Butterfield was given the commission to restore St
Augustine's College in Canterbury, and to design All Saints, Margaret Street,
it was the Carpenters – father first and then the son – and Slater that
Beresford Hope progressively turned for those commissions which were
closest to his heart.

So perhaps we should leave the final word on Carpenter to Beresford Hope,
and specifically to the obituary he wrote on Carpenter for publication in the
Ecclesiologist in 1855:

> It has become a hackneyed phrase to say, that the work of any artist will
> 'live'; nevertheless, we cannot find any words which will more accurately
> describe what we believe will be the verdict of posterity upon the
> productions of Carpenter. He never seemed to dream of producing a sudden
> or startling effect, and yet his works all tell, and are all eminently original
> and varied, and particularly devoid of mannerism. His success lay in the
> perfect keeping of everything he did, – the harmony of parts and general
> utility of proportion running through the entire building. The entire mass is
> broad and manly, and every detail beautiful, as a single study, and
> thoroughly finished but never frittered into inanity. Of the value of
> mouldings to give light and shade, he was thoroughly convinced, and from
> his extensive knowledge of their different characteristics in the successive
> styles of Pointed, be handled them with peculiar effect. In proof of his
> carefulness, we have been assured by one long intimate with Carpenter, that
> he was once for three days drawing a single set of mouldings from the
> dictation of his chief. Nor was Carpenter merely an architect: his
> acquaintance with symbolism and the *instrumenta* of worship was great, and
> his resources in them never at fault. But, above all, his eye for colour was
> exquisite. The harmony of his disposition naturally produced this excellence,

---

[110] The earlier edition of 1847 had been dominated by Butterfield's designs whereas
he is simply one designer amongst many in the 1856 edition.

171

in which (without hinting at any other comparison to the advantage or disadvantage of either ...), we think that he was superior even to Pugin, – safer and more equable.[111]

I am grateful to Dr Roderick O'Donnell and Dr Geoff Brandwood for having read a earlier version of this chapter and provided helpful comments and suggestions.

[111]   *Ecclesiologist*, 16 (1855), p. 138.

George Gilbert Scott and the Cambridge Camden Society

GAVIN STAMP

'Amongst Anglican architects, Carpenter and Butterfield were the apostles of the high church school – I, of the multitude.' So, in his *Personal and Professional Recollections*, did Sir Gilbert Scott distinguish himself from those particular architects who were the 'mouth-pieces – or hand-pieces – of the Cambridge Camden Society.'[1] Scott, in contrast, indeed ministered to the multitude, to the many vicars and rectors, deans and provosts who constituted the broad centre of the Church of England – so ensuring his phenomenal professional success as a builder and restorer of churches over four decades in a career which ended with his death and burial in Westminster Abbey in 1878.

Scott's relationship with the Cambridge Camden Society was sometimes strained – at least as far as he was concerned – and yet it was symbiotic, and crucial to his career. His success as a church architect, Scott later claimed, was 'in spite of every effort on their part to put me down by misrepresentation and flippant criticism of the most galling character. No matter how strenuous my endeavours at improvement, everything was met by them with scorn and contumely.'[2] Yet not only did Scott recognise that, 'with all its faults ... the good which the Society has done cannot possibly be over-rated,' he also acknowledged his own debt to its influence. Ever sensitive to the slightest criticism, ever anxious to exploit any means of advancing his own career, Scott worked hard to secure favourable notices in the pages of *The Ecclesiologist* – indeed there was hardly an issue in which his name did not appear.

And the Society, in turn, recognised his merits and his sincere commitment to the great crusade of the Gothic Revival. For the mature churches of Gilbert Scott, together with his restorations of ancient churches, more fully exemplify the principles of the Cambridge Camden Society,

[1] G. Gilbert Scott (ed.), *Personal and Professional Recollections by the Late Sir George Gilbert Scott, R.A.* (London, 1879), p. 112.

[2] Original MS of Scott's Recollections, published in Gavin Stamp (ed.), *Personal and Professional Recollections by the Late Sir George Gilbert Scott* (Stamford, 1995), pp. 103 & 445. On p. 105, Scott complained how they had 'criticized one of the very best churches I had ever built' on the basis of an erroneous lithographed view, but it is not known to which church he was referring: possibly it was St Mary, Stoke Newington.

perhaps, than the work of any other architect. 'Sir Gilbert Scott was neither by taste nor temperament an innovator,' concluded E. M. Barry. 'In the midst of controversy his works showed sobriety of design, and moderation of judgement. The Tractarian movement and the Gothic revival went, indeed, hand in hand; but he was too earnest a champion to wish his cause to be identified with any single party.'[3] This was surely true but, especially after the crisis of 1845 which brought the doctrinal prejudices of its committee into the open, the Ecclesiological late Cambridge Camden Society perhaps needed the connection with a well-established and broadly-based Gothicist like Gilbert Scott as much as he craved the approval of *The Ecclesiologist*.

George Gilbert Scott was a year older than Pugin, and his career as an architect preceded the foundation of the Society. Formally in partnership with William Bonython Moffatt from 1838 until 1846, Scott at first concentrated on securing commissions for the new union workhouses, but at the end of the 1830s he began to design churches. 'Church architecture was then perhaps at its lowest level,' he later considered, and, as the son and grandson of clergymen, and with many clerical connections, Scott was well placed to launch himself into this potentially fertile area of practice. He began at Lincoln – with St Nicholas's, in the Early English style – and was later ashamed of the result. 'My first church (except one poor barn designed for my uncle King) dates from the same year with the foundation of the Cambridge Camden Society, to whom the honour of our recovery from the odious bathos is mainly due. I only wish I had known its founders at the time. As it was, no idea of ecclesiastical arrangement, or ritual propriety, had then even crossed my mind.'[4]

No indeed; this church and the six which followed, were everything that the Camden Society was founded to excoriate. Scott's worst sin was 'the absence of any proper chancel, my grave idea being that this feature was obsolete. They all agreed too in the meagreness of their construction, in the contemptible character of their fittings, in most of them being begalleried to the very eyes, and in the use of plaster for internal mouldings, even for the pillars ... These days of abject degradation only lasted for about two years or little more, but, alas! what a mass of horrors was perpetrated during that short interval!'[5] But Scott was soon 'awakened to a truer sense of the dignity of the subject' and, in a celebrated passage in his *Recollections*, presented his acceptance of the true principles of Gothic architecture as a sort of Damascene conversion.

[3] Tribute by Edward M. Barry, quoted in *Recollections*, p. 384.
[4] *Recollections*, pp. 85 & 86. The 'poor barn' for his uncle, the Rev. Samuel King, was at Flaunden in Buckinghamshire.
[5] *Recollections*, pp. 86-7. The other churches were at Birmingham, Shaftesbury, Hanwell, Turnham Green, Bridlington Quay and Norbiton, as the editor, Scott's son, helpfully listed as a footnote.

This awakening arose, I think, from two causes operating almost simultaneously: my first acquaintance with the Cambridge Camden Society, and my reading Pugin's articles in the *Dublin Review* ... Pugin's articles excited me almost to fury, and I suddenly found myself like a person awakened from a long feverish dream, which had rendered him unconscious of what was going on about him.[6]

As for his acquaintance with the Society, Scott here displayed his unerring ability to meet the right people to advance his career.

I saw somewhere an article by Mr Webb, the secretary to the Camden Society, which greatly excited my sympathy. Just at the same time I had become exceedingly irate at the proposed destruction by Mr Barry of St Stephen's Chapel, and I wrote to Mr Webb and subsequently saw him on the subject. I was introduced, I believe, by Edward Boyce. Mr Webb took advantage of the occasion to lecture me on church architecture in general, on the necessity of chancels, &c., &c. I at once saw that he was right, and became a reader of *The Ecclesiologist*...

Writing of these two catalytic events, Scott confessed that 'I may be in error as to their coincidence of date,' but Benjamin Webb's diary confirms that, on 1st February 1842, 'G.G. Scott appealed to us to strive to save S. Stephen's Chapel, in the New Houses of Parliament, which Barry is about to destroy' and that, the very next day, 'Went over the New Houses with Scott: both of us disgusted with the design & the mouldings.'[7] And, on 7th February, Scott joined the Cambridge Camden Society – a year later than Carpenter, but two years ahead of Butterfield.

Scott's relationship with the committee of the Society can thence be traced by references in *The Ecclesiologist*, which, very soon after he had joined, was

favoured with several designs for New Churches, erected, or in course of erection, by ... the architect of the Bishops' Memorial at Oxford (plate 39). There is so much beauty in several of the arrangements, and we are so well persuaded that the faults are those of the age, the merits those of the architect ... We feel sure that Mr Scott will give us credit for the admiration which we feel for his talents, and the sincerity with which we hope that he may have full scope for their exercise; and impute our observations, if in any thing we seem to speak harshly, to the necessity which obliges us, as a Church Society, to judge of things absolutely, not relatively; which makes us say – not, 'this is good for the present age,' but 'this would not have been allowed in an age more pious than ours.'[8]

So, of course, such features as 'the absence or curtailed proportions of the chancel' in six of the nine churches was condemned. But, although Scott always felt unqualified praise was his due, he really had little to complain of.

6   *Recollections*, pp. 87–8.
7   Benjamin Webb's diary (Bodleian Library MS.Eng.misc.e.406).
8   *Ecclesiologist*, 1 (1842), p. 56.

And if he was not numbered amongst the 'Architects approved' in the notorious index to volume III of the journal, neither was he proscribed along with the 'Architects condemned.'[9]

Mentions of Scott were usually kind, if sometimes complaining of 'mannerism.' And the architect was clearly anxious to mend the error of his ways. Of Holy Trinity, Manchester, the editors found it 'impossible to speak without much satisfaction ... But although there is much to admire, there are also considerable defects ... The clustered pillars supporting the arches of the nave are stilted, which seems to be no uncommon fault of Messrs. Scott and Moffatt...' But soon after, in a notice of 1846 of St Mark's in Swindon New Town, built by the Great Western Railway, *The Ecclesiologist* was 'very glad to see that Mr. Scott has given up stilting the bases of his pillars,' while complaining that the spire was too small for the tower. More typical was a review in which 'We are glad to be able to speak favourably of the general effect of a design for a new church, at Wood Green, Tottenham' by Scott & Moffatt. And as for Holy Trinity, Normacott, near Stoke-on-Trent, 'The church is altogether deserving of great praise.'[10]

The church which really marked Scott's acceptance of the principles of ecclesiology – and made his name as a Gothicist – was St Giles, Camberwell, in South London (plates 40 & 41), a commission won in competition after the burning of the old church in 1840. *The Ecclesiologist* in 1842 pronounced the published design 'on the whole, a magnificent one' while complaining of the shortness of the chancel, but the design was subsequently revised and Scott's 'conversion to the exclusive use of real material came during the progress of this work, and much that was at first shown of plaster was afterwards converted into stone.' The building was finished in 1844, and, the following year, *The Ecclesiologist* was suitably impressed.

> We now turn to a church which is really conceived in a generous spirit, and which in spite of some drawbacks, which we shall feel bound to mention, is one of the finest ecclesiastical structures of modern days: the new parish church of S. Giles, Camberwell, a large cross church, with aisles, north and south porches, central spire, and well developed chancel, of the Middle pointed style. The altar is of stone...[11]

With that 'dogmatic spirit' which John Mason Neale considered 'the life and soul of *The Ecclesiologist* and the Cambridge Camden Society'[12] and which

9   *Ecclesiologist*, 3 (1844); the condemned architects were Barry, Blore, Carver, Cottingham and Kennedy; the approved Allen, Butterfield, Carpenter, Derick, Ferrey, Harrison, Hayward, Kirk and Sharpe.
10   *Ecclesiologist*, 5 (1846), p. 155; 6 (1846), p. 191; 4 (1845), p. 40; 9 (1849), p. 162.
11   *Ecclesiologist*, 1 (1842), p. 68, & 4 (1845), pp. 59–60.
12   *Letters of John Mason Neale, D.D., Selected and Edited by his Daughter* (London, 1910), quoted in James F. White, *The Cambridge Movement: The Ecclesiologists and the Gothic Revival* (Cambridge, 2nd ed., 1979), p. 105.

helped to make it one of the most powerful and influential pressure groups in architectural history, the anonymous author naturally found things to criticise.

> The font is incorrectly placed ... We are a good deal amused at the galleries (for the church contains galleries), because in the first place they are the least offensive galleries we have ever seen, and in the second place because they have purchased this inoffensiveness at the expense of a great part of their practical utility, that of holding people ... The worst fault of the church remains to be told, that it has got a show side. The north side, from facing the street, is much more elaborately decorated than the opposite one.

Nevertheless,

> no one can help being much pleased at so noble and, considering all things, so complete an attempt at better things, raised in the same town, and during the life-time of the same generation which saw the building of S. Pancras, S. Marylebone, and All Souls.[13]

But suffering from that sensitivity bordering on paranoia which seems characteristic of successful knighted architects, Scott remained convinced that the committee of the Society had turned against him. 'What I complain of is,' he wrote in 1860:

> their attempt just at this period, to crush those who were labouring strenuously in the same cause, and the same direction with themselves; and that, with the sole object, so far as I could ever ascertain, of the more easily elevating others whom they viewed as their own representatives. To expose the misdoings of ignorance and vandalism was their duty; to point out the shortcomings of their fellow-labourers would have been a kindness; but to treat friends and allies with studied scorn and contumely, through a series of years, because they had not sworn implicit allegiance to their absolute *régime*, was discreditable to the sacred cause which they professed to make the object of their endeavours, and ended in undermining their influence, through the obvious self seeking it evinced; thus damaging the movement they otherwise so ably advocated. Even Pugin himself could not escape their lash, his single sin *being his independent existence*.[14]

The Ecclesiologist certainly knew how to be rude. Of St Philip's in Leeds, erroneously attributed to Scott, the editors wrote in 1847 that 'On the whole, though there is no actual fault which we can find with the church (fittings and some of the windows excepted, and also the accommodation for the western gallery), its whole effect is somewhat tame and common-place ... It is more what we should have expected Mr. Scott to have built some years ago than now. Mr. Scott has the capacity of being a very good architect, but he has the

[13]   *Ecclesiologist*, 4 (1845), pp. 59–60. The galleries were subsequently removed.
[14]   *Recollections*, 1995, pp. 106 & 446.

habit of not doing himself justice.'[15] He was again damned with faint praise in the notice in 1848 of the design for St John's Cathedral in Newfoundland, for

> Under these conditions, a most impracticable climate, no available native materials, an unpliant ritual, and the need to retain a parochial character, – we think that such a combination, as in the parallel case of a tropical climate, would have justified an attempt at development. Mr. Scott, has, however, chosen to build by precedent: and the result, though scrupulously correct, appears to us deficient in the indescribable character, the moral feeling, if we may say – of originality. Under such circumstances, Christian art could afford to be plastic. S. John's Cathedral, as designed by Mr. Scott, reminds us of a first-rate University prize poem. There is authority for every detail and phrase; it is learned and dignified, but perhaps cold: it displays the artist's reading and study more than his genius.[16]

Yet, compared with, say, Edward Blore or E. B. Lamb, Scott got off lightly, and favourable references far outnumber dismissive ones in the pages of *The Ecclesiologist*. Criticisms of Scott's work, indeed, usually involved the aspects of church architecture the Camden Society was most concerned about: liturgical correctness and the choice of style. If a chancel was inadequate, or a font wrongly placed, the editorial committee would naturally point out the solecism. 'A new church is in progress of building at Barnet by Messrs. Scott and Moffatt in the Early Decorated style,' it was reported in 1845; but the chancel was incorrectly planned: 'There is enough good about this church to make us regret the unsatisfactory arrangements. Does it not seem a mockery to build a Catholick-looking church, and then make the priest pray to the people?'[17]

As for style, *The Ecclesiologist* in the 1840s unhesitatingly insisted upon Middle Pointed whether for a new church or a restoration. Coming across a new church at Sewerby, near Bridlington, in 1847, 'We are sincerely sorry that Mr. Scott should be the architect of this church. The style adopted is Romanesque ... if an architect will now-a-days build in Romanesque, he may make it like an old church in that style. This Mr. Scott has signally failed in, having produced a structure at once heavy and fantastical...' But while Third Pointed or Perpendicular was, of course, anathema, earlier First-Pointed Gothic was tolerated. With regard to St Andrew's, Bradfield:

> We hardly know whether we ought to notice this church as a new one or as a restoration ... We need not say that we should have advised the adoption of Middle-Pointed in the rebuilding of this as of every other church, from a preference founded, we believe, on reason and propriety. But next to

15 *Ecclesiologist*, 7 (1847), p. 110. The church was actually designed by R. D. Chantrell.
16 *Ecclesiologist*, 8 (1848), p. 277; this was presumably written by Benjamin Webb, whose diary records that he went to Scott's office to see the Newfoundland design on 17th January 1848 (Bodleian Library MS.misc.e.408).
17 *Ecclesiologist*, 4 (1845), p. 236.

Middle-Pointed, we believe, the style adopted is our favourite. It has a heiratic dignity and solemnity about it which makes itself strongly felt in Bradfield church.

And criticism was often tempered with praise, as in 1847:

We regret not to have previously noted the new church which is rising in the City Road, from Mr. Scott's design [St Matthew's]. The style adopted is, we are sorry to say, First-Pointed, and the architect has been miserably cramped by his site ... With all these disadvantages, this is certainly the best new church which has yet been built for our communion in London (perhaps the best absolutely).[18]

Scott himself, of course, was much exercised about the best style to employ, and he agreed that 'the revived style was one, and its unity was "Middle Pointed." I held this as a theory myself,' he wrote. 'They held it as a religious duty, though they now seem to have forgotten this phase in the history of their faith, and are very irate when it is referred to.' But Scott was less dogmatic, and he recalled with evident pleasure how the victory by Burges and Clutton in the competition for Lille Cathedral in 1856

was really the first occasion on which the Ecclesiological Society's law, as regards the 'Middle Pointed,' was set at nought ... One thing, however, never changed, the intolerance shown by them for all freedom of thought on the part of other men. Everyone must perforce follow in their wake, no matter how often they changed, or how entirely they reversed their own previous views. Nor was anything more certain than this, that however erroneous their former opinion might have been, their views for the time being were right, and that every one who differed from them was a heretic, or an old fashioned simpleton. It had many years before been a saying of mine, that there was no class of men whom the Cambridge Camden Society held in such scorn, as those who adhered to their own last opinion but one.[19]

Such rigid collective dogmatism is often encountered with political movements; Scott felt it was typical of a 'clique ... a superior class neglecting often their own special training, in the intensity of their self-satisfaction at belonging to the privileged party, whose great moral rule is to trust in themselves, and to despise others.'[20] And the trouble was that Scott was not part of that clique: he never became friendly with Webb or Neale, and remained wary of Beresford Hope despite close professional contacts.[21] He concluded – probably with good reason – that this distance was the result of his churchmanship, although he was also for once honest enough to admit

[18] *Ecclesiologist*, 8 (1847), p. 186; 9 (1848), p. 68; 8 (1847), p. 54.
[19] *Recollections*, pp. 203 & 206.
[20] *Recollections*, p. 207.
[21] In discussing criticisms of the Albert Memorial, Scott wrote that 'I believe that Mr Beresford Hope though nominally friendly, is only too glad to promote these attacks and it was, I dare say, he who set upon me one of the most vindictive and unscrupulous writers of the age.' – *Recollections* (Stamford, 1995 edn), p. 477

that, at that time in the 1840s, Scott & Moffatt 'were disliked by our fellow-professionals for our almost unheard-of activity and success.'[22] 'I suppose that I was not thought a sufficiently high churchman,' he complained in his *Recollections*, and his eldest son later recalled that 'he was an *Anglican* essentially and in the best sense of the term. Decidedly opposed to Roman practices on many points, principally upon the use of Images which he could not but think was *almost* if not quite Idolatrous.'[23]

It was certainly theology rather than architecture that was the issue in Scott's most serious argument with the Cambridge Camden Society. This occurred in 1845 after he had won the international competition for rebuilding the Nikolai-kirche in Hamburg (plate 42). Scott had seen off the *Rundbogenstil* of Gottfried Semper and the feeble essays in mediaevalism by other German architects with a rich and assured design with a tall steeple which showed that in all Europe only Pugin was his rival in such sophisticated mastery of Gothic. But *The Ecclesiologist* remained unimpressed:

> Now this building, as designed for the worship of one of the worst sections of an heretical sect (for the Hamburg ministers are notorious for neology), hardly comes under our notice. Mr Scott's lithograph presents a north-west view, and we are bound to confess that the spire is beautiful, and well managed ... But the question arises, how must we characterise the spirit that prostitutes Christian architecture to such a use? If this art means anything, – if it is not a hollow mocking of beauty, – a body without a spirit, – then it symbolizes the whole substance of Catholick teaching, the whole analogy of the Faith. How absurd then, in the first place, to apply it to those who reject that teaching and that faith! How absurd to build a nave and aisles for those who explain away the Adorable Mystery that they symbolize; to erect a choir for those who have no priests; to adorn a font for those who scoff at regeneration; to enrich wall and pinnacle with images and legends for those who cannot away with miracles! Truly absurd is this, in an aesthetical point of view; and what in a moral? It is like using the words of the Bible for the relation of some profane story: it *is* using the 'petrified' teaching of the Church for the propagation and ornament of heresy. We do earnestly trust that Mr. Scott's example will not be followed. We are sure that the temporal gains of such a contract are a miserable substitute indeed for its unrealness, and, – we must say it, – its sin.[24]

Scott, as always, responded at length to this attack and wrote a defence of his action in undertaking a Lutheran church, making the good point that 'it is to churches which are "occupied by the Lutherans" that we must look for examples of the movable fittings of our mediaeval churches,' noting that even Pugin had recognised that the Lutherans had looked after their mediaeval buildings better than either Anglicans or Roman Catholics.[25] But *The*

22   *Recollections*, p. 133.
23   *Recollections* (Stamford, 1995), pp. 104 & 492.
24   *Ecclesiologist*, 4 (1845), p. 184.

Ecclesiologist declined to print the full text of Scott's long letter; instead, as he complained, it 'gave a worse than garbled statement of it. This I suppose was the work of *Mason Neale*.'[26]

'We have received a calm and temperate letter of some length from Mr G. G. Scott, architect, in reply to our strictures upon his intention to build a – to appearance – Gothic cathedral, in Hamburgh, as a place of Lutheran worship...,' *The Ecclesiologist* informed its readers.

> The confession of Augsburg is, he says, as sound as the Thirty-nine Articles: Luther held baptismal regeneration: Lutherans have preserved more of the ancient furniture of the churches in their occupation than Anglicans or even than foreign Catholics have done. Mr Scott then quotes at length from a pamphlet, to show that his Gothic design was preferred to its Romanesque competitor from symbolical reasons; and concludes with an eulogy upon the zealous liberality of the citizens of Hamburg. The answer to all this lies in a nutshell. The question is not, whether Lutheranism retain some mixture of true religion; for upon this ground Mr Scott may as well build a Gothic cathedral for Mahommedanism, or Brownism, or any other form of superstition. Neither is the question whether Luther were less destructive than Latimer, nor whether the followers of the former retain much of church furniture; for upon this ground Mr Scott will prefer, not only Lutheranism, but Irvingism also, to the English Church. Still less is it the question, whether the meeting-house at Hamburg will be built by persons not altogether insensible to the beauty of the symbolical theory; for what fancy religionist is there who could not adapt – the exercise of private judgement being granted – the parts of a Gothic cathedral to the novel creed of his choice? Not that the use of such cathedral for schismatical purposes would become thereby less profane: on the contrary, it would become more so. No: the simple question is this: is the body for whose use Mr Scott erects this building, a part of the One Holy Catholic Church, in which the Faith teaches us to look for salvation?...'[27]

Given that pages of close type were regularly devoted to such dry subjects as lychnoscopes and credence tables, the refusal of *The Ecclesiologist* to publish Scott's wide ranging and intelligent letter was inexcusable. Perhaps this was because the architect gave as good as he got and defended the historical basis of Lutheranism with, as James F. White has written, 'considerable theological acumen.' He may have been arguing with Cambridge-educated clergymen, yet 'probably the Ecclesiologists knew very little about Lutheranism, but they did know that it was heretical and schismatic.'[28] Fortunately, George Gilbert Scott junior respected his father's wishes and published the whole of the letter in the posthumous volume of *Recollections* in 1879. Surprisingly perhaps, a

[25] *Recollections*, p. 138.
[26] *Recollections* (Stamford, 1995), p. 447.
[27] *Ecclesiologist*, 4 (1845), pp. 242–3.
[28] James F. White, *The Cambridge Movement: The Ecclesiologists and the Gothic Revival* (Cambridge, 2nd edn, 1979), pp. 126–7.

few years after this controversy *The Ecclesiologist* carried a long article on the Crystal Palace and Pugin's Mediaeval Court by August Reichensperger, who, although a Catholic, was a great supporter of Scott's Hamburg church and had been an ally of Ernst Zwirner, the German architect who had been instrumental in securing the commission for the English Gothicist.[29] But, sadly, the anathemas of the Camden Society were eventually effective, for Scott's Hamburg masterpiece was largely destroyed by British bombs during the Second World War.

If, as Scott insisted, the Society was cool towards his work during this period, this prejudice did not really manifest itself in *The Ecclesiologist*. And if the editors were sometimes critical of details of his new churches, they were almost always approving of his restorations of ancient ones. Scott's first restoration was of Chesterfield church and, as he himself confessed in his *Recollections*, he made mistakes. Only in 1846 did *The Ecclesiologist* notice this job, writing that

> The Liberality shown in the restoration of All Saints, Chesterfield, (a fine church, and one generally known for its twisted spire,) makes us sorry to have to record how unfavourable our opinion is of the manner in which it has been carried out. As an extenuating plea it must be recorded that it was completed in 1843. Messrs Scott and Moffatt must, we should fear, have left the work too much to take care of itself. There are galleries ... The font is overdone. The reading desk faces west. The reredos is patched up...[30]

Scott later stated that *The Ecclesiologist* had accused him of selling the rood screen, although the published notice does not in fact say this – suggesting that he was suffering as usual from professional paranoia rather than a genuine grievance.

And the Society was soon approving of his restorations. The first important one was of St Mary, Stafford, which was first noticed by *The Ecclesiologist* in 1842 as being 'designed upon the strictest architectural principles, and with equal judgement and good taste,' and by 1845, the editors were 'enabled to speak in terms of general commendation of this noble work.'[31] As if inaugurating the overwhelming wave of Victorian restorations which resulted in the partial or total rebuilding of almost every mediaeval church in England, this was far from being a matter of repair for Scott was happy to replace late work by new designs of a better date – hence the approval of *The Ecclesiologist*. However, the Rev. J. L. Petit, the architectural writer and illustrator, 'raised some considerable objections to certain parts of my proposed restorations, on the ground of their not being sufficiently conservative.' Scott, of course, disagreed – 'not in principle, but on the

---

29   See Michael J. Lewis, *The Politics of the German Gothic Revival: August Reichensperger* (New York & Cambridge, Massachusetts, 1993).

30   *Ecclesiologist*, 5 (1846), p. 83.

31   *Ecclesiologist*, 1 (1842), p. 65, & 4 (1845), p. 139.

application of the principles to the matter in question,' and was pleased that both the Cambridge Camden Society and the Oxford Architectural Society supported him.[32] Typically, Scott justified his changes by finding evidence of what he argued was the original design:

> the result was a happy one, for embedded in the later walling we found abundant fragments of earlier work, which enabled me to reproduce the early English south transept with certainty, and a noble design it is ... The pains we took in recovering old forms and details were unbounded, and though too little actual old work was preserved, I believe that no restoration could, barring this, be more scrupulously conscientious.[33]

Scott's treatment of St Mary, Stafford was praised by his friend, the historian Edward A. Freeman, in his *Principles of Church Restoration*, published in 1846, and this passage was quoted in a review of the book in *The Ecclesiologist*. Freeman was far too intelligent to subscribe to all the articles of faith of the Camden Society, and not only did he deny that any satisfactory general rule for restoring mediaeval churches could be found, but he was bold enough to admire both the Romanesque and even the Perpendicular.

> A more remarkable case, as affecting different parts of the same building, may be found in S. Mary, Stafford, the late noble restoration of which is one of the most glorious fruits of the improved feeling on these matters. Nothing therein reflects more credit on the judgement of the architect, than his restoring the chancel-roofs to their high pitch while he preserved the clerestory and low roof of the nave. A mere abstract consideration might have led to the enunciation of one or two canons according to the taste of the framer; either "that late Perpendicular clerestories added in place of high roofs should be removed," or "that they should be retained." Practice, however, shows that even in the same Church both may be found to fail; for assuredly the architect would not have done so well had he either retained the miserable clerestory of the quire or destroyed the noble roof of the nave.[34]

Freeman's anonymous reviewer used the occasion to discuss what he defined as the 'three systems of conducting a restoration, which we may respectively name the Destructive, the Conservative, and the Eclectic.' And, with its dogmatic insistence on an ideal in both style and theology, *The Ecclesiologist* naturally approved of the first of these approaches as

> it comes recommended by all the authority of the architects of better ages; for they, as all the world knows, never dreamed of working on any other principle. Again, it is the only system which offers the logical possibility of working a building into a state of abstract perfection; for, of course, it

---

[32] *Recollections*, p. 98; the whole matter was discussed in John Masfen's *Views of the Church of St Mary at Stafford* (London, 1852), with its title page drawn by Pugin.

[33] *Recollections*, p. 99.

[34] Review of E. A. Freeman, *Principles of Church Restoration*, 1846, in *The Ecclesiologist*, 7 (1847), p. 168.

logically follows upon the theory of architectural development that there can be only one perfect period of architecture, all others tending to or declining from it.

As for the Conservative approach, it was really the product of timidity, sentimentality and decadence.

> Because in the decline of Christian art various barbarisms were inflicted on churches, because the beautiful pitch of an early roof was sacrificed to make way for the clumsy addition of a late and heavy Third Pointed clerestory, because the east window of a magnificent Middle-Pointed chancel was replaced by the monotonous panelling of Tudor design, it is surely too much to be called on to perpetuate these barbarisms.[35]

But, in a rare confession of fallibility, the reviewer recognised that such dogmatism could be unfortunate – for what if churches had been treated in the Destructive manner a few decades back when Third Pointed was 'generally considered to be the most perfect? ... there is no telling what mischief might not have been perpetrated.' So, he concluded, 'the third or Eclectic system is the only one which will bear the test of examination.' – a middle course involving a judicious combination of restoring and remodelling. And this, in fact, was the approach Scott usually adopted, however cautiously. Naturally, he claimed otherwise: 'I venture forward as a champion of conservatism ... it is *the one* principle which needs to be constantly urged and enforced'. So he asserted in his *Plea for the Faithful Restoration of our Ancient Churches*, published in 1850 but written two years earlier. And, as far as he was concerned:

> It is much to be regretted that so highly influential a body as the Ecclesiological Society should have given an indirect sanction to this system of *radical restoration*, by the very unhappy discussion which took place at their annual meeting in 1847, in which the different members severally announced their adherence to what had been rather whimsically distinguished by a very talented writer in *The Ecclesiologist* as the 'Conservative,' the 'Destructive,' and the 'Eclectic' systems of restoration. If such unguarded conversations must take place, it would be better that they should be *in private*...[36]

Scott's *Plea* was wise and cautious, adamant that

> a restored church appears to lose all its truthfulness, and to become as little authentic, as an example of ancient art, as if it had been rebuilt on a new design ... It is against this system of so-called restoration, a system which threatens to deprive us of all authentic examples of the humbler forms of this sacred art, that I wish to take this opportunity of PROTESTING.

The Destructive argument he dismissed, as

[35] *Ecclesiologist*, 7 (1847), pp. 163 & 167.
[36] G. G. Scott, *A Plea for the Faithful Restoration of our Ancient Churches* (London, 1850), pp. 21–2.

our position is, in fact, *totally distinct* from that of the ancient architects ...
we have not originated a new style, but are called upon to re-awaken one
which has for centuries lain dormant; and it is absurd to argue that, because
those who originated it did not scruple, during its progress, at destroying
specimens of the earlier varieties, to make way for what they thought better,
we are equally free to destroy their works to make way for our own.

And as for the transcendent claims of Middle Pointed to extinguish other
phases of Gothic, 'rather should we view the remains of the whole range of
pointed architecture, whether in its earlier or later forms, in its humbler or
more glorious examples, as one vast treasury of Christian art, wonderfully
produced, and as wonderfully preserved for our use.'[37]

The Ecclesiologist gave Scott's *Plea* a long and favourable review, smugly
observing that 'Mr Scott, starting from independent premises, had by a course
of individual reasoning attained conclusions on the various points under
consideration almost identical with our own. It is, we can assure him, a great
gratification to us to record this.' Furthermore, the reviewer pointed out that

> Mr Scott belongs in Church Restoration to the conservative party, but he
> words his dogmas so very moderately, that in point of fact we can discover
> but little difference in him from that shade of the *Eclectic* theory of which we
> are the professors ... Mr Scott goes on to allow sufficient latitude of
> exception to the rigid canon of mere conservatism to entitle him, although
> he will probably himself repudiate the designation, to be admitted of the
> moderate eclectic party.[38]

Indeed, although in principle Scott may have been firmly against
conjectural restoration – on whatever grounds – neither life nor architecture
was ever so simple, so naturally there were qualifications, compromises to be
made. 'No one,' he admitted, 'who has not tried it, knows how easy it is to
admit the principle, but how difficult practically to realize it. However
earnest the restorer may be in his conservatism, he will find that in practice he
is often compelled to fall short of it.'[39] And so, in practice, in his many – far
too many – restorations, Scott or his assistants replaced more stonework and
woodwork than was strictly necessary and were quite happy to remove a
Perpendicular window if evidence could be found for the form of an earlier
one – and evidence often was, for Scott was an inspired and brilliant
archaeologist and historian. But it is also true that a mediaeval church was
likely to be more gently and tolerantly treated by Scott than by, say, G. E.
Street or by the Society's own darling, William Butterfield.

Even so, in concluding his article, *The Ecclesiologist*'s anonymous
reviewer repeated 'how much gratified we are with this volume' and soon
Scott became the Society's favourite restorer. 'To have to record its

[37]   Scott, *Plea...*, pp. 21 & 26.
[38]   *Ecclesiologist*, 11 (1850), pp. 12–13.
[39]   Scott, *Plea...*, p. 27.

restoration under the able superintendence of Mr Scott is no small pleasure to us,' *The Ecclesiologist* insisted in discussing St Mary's at Harrow-on-the-Hill that same year, 1850.[40] The editors were certainly happy to recommend that Scott should look after old churches – and not just mediaeval ones, for they praised his 'marvellous transformation' of Christopher Wren's St Michael, Cornhill by inserting (unfortunate) round-arched tracery in the windows. And they were glad to see him appointed to look after the great cathedral churches, with the great problems of restoration and reordering they presented. As for Westminster Abbey, 'It is with extreme satisfaction that we announce that Mr. Blore has resigned the post of "surveyor to the fabric," and that Mr. Scott has been appointed to succeed him. We wish that the change had taken place much sooner.' This was in 1849.[41]

Scott's first cathedral was Ely, where he was appointed surveyor in 1847, and the progress of the restoration was closely followed by *The Ecclesiologist* over the next two decades. And when, in 1866, J. C. Buckler savaged him in his *Description and Defence of the Restorations of the Exterior of Lincoln Cathedral, with a Comparative Examination of the Restorations of other Cathedrals, Parish Churches &c.*, the editors leapt to Scott's defence – by condemning the 'unscrupulous, unfair, and unprovoked attack upon Mr G. G. Scott' in this 'extraordinary book' and by publishing his letter to Beresford Hope in which he rebutted the accusations.[42] Buckler was in fact motivated largely by professional jealousy, for he had been working at Lincoln for some years and the way in which he had 'skinned' the west front had been causing concern in *The Ecclesiologist*, while Scott had supplanted him as architect elsewhere.[43] But Buckler's assertion that 'death and destruction to antiquities follow his footsteps,' however unfair, also anticipated the more objective and damaging attacks made on Scott's vast restoration practice in the following decade, by J. J. Stevenson, W. J. Loftie, John Ruskin and William Morris – and by then the Ecclesiological Society was no longer in existence to defend its hero.

In truth, after about 1850 Scott could do almost no wrong in the eyes of *The Ecclesiologist*, although it must have been galling for the architect that the editors tended to assume that they were his mentors. 'We can speak in terms of unmixed commendation of Mr Scott's recent volume,' began a condescending review of his *Remarks on Secular and Domestic Architecture, Present and Future* in 1857. 'In fact, most of his arguments might have

[40]   *Ecclesiologist*, 10 (1850), pp. 72–3.
[41]   *Ecclesiologist*, 9 (1849), p. 334.
[42]   *Ecclesiologist*, 27 (1866), pp. 280 & 290.
[43]   David Cole, *The Work of Sir Gilbert Scott* (London, 1980), p. 140. Murray's *Handbook to the Cathedrals of England: Eastern Division* (London, 1862), noted that 'Much of the west front is at present (1862) undergoing a scraping process which threatens serious injury to the sculpture and finer details.' (p. 274)

appeared in our own pages, and much that he has ably and vigorously said has, in substance, been anticipated in our own articles. Not that this detracts in any way from the merit and interest of Mr Scott's disquisitions...'[44] His only fall from grace was when he did as he was told by the Prime Minister – a sin almost as heinous as building for Lutherans. 'We have already expressed our regret that the eminent architect in question was not better advised,' opined *The Ecclesiologist* in 1861 about Scott's Italianate design for Whitehall.

> We cannot think that the Foreign Office which is to be built from his design will add much to his artistic reputation; and we fear that the carrying out of the Palmerstonian inspirations will be to him anything but a labour of love. Let us hope, at least, that this ill-omened meddling with the principles of a rival style will not affect the purity of Mr Scott's Gothic design.[45]

As for Scott's mature churches, *The Ecclesiologist* was unstinting in its praise. A first notice of All Souls, Haley Hill, Halifax, in 1856 announced that 'this church promises to be one of the richest and finest for its size, of modern times.'[46] A full description of it was published four years later in an article on 'Halifax and Doncaster' which discussed Scott's two finest churches of the decade. The second was St George, Doncaster, which Scott had rebuilt after the old parish church had been destroyed by fire in 1853. *The Ecclesiologist* throughly approved of the result, perhaps because Scott was eclectic rather than conservative in his approach; that is, he did not faithfully reproduce the old building but lengthened it, altered it, and changed its style in conformity with the principles of the Society. 'In rebuilding the noble cruciform church ... Mr Scott was limited by the condition that the new structure should reproduce in its essential features, the outline and ground-plan of the original building. This task he fulfilled with great ability; not slavishly copying the detail and style of the former church, but transmuting the whole conception, with much subtle felicity, into the characteristics of an earlier and purer architectural period.'[47] That is, Perpendicular was replaced by Geometrical Decorated.

All Souls, Haley Hill, was built for Colonel Edward Akroyd, M.P., the Halifax worsted manufacturer, and was, Scott considered, 'on the whole, my best church.' And, to a great extent, it was the complete and lavish embodiment of the ideals of the Cambridge Camden Society of ten years before, except that the style chosen was Geometrical Decorated – orthodox, if just a little earlier than the 'early late Middle Pointed' most favoured by the ecclesiologists. It has a nave separated from balanced aisles by noble arcades on clustered shafts, while taller arches announce the presence of short transepts. Above all, the square-ended generous chancel is structurally distinct and

---

44   *Ecclesiologist*, 18 (1857), p. 16.
45   *Ecclesiologist*, 22 (1861), p. 221.
46   *Ecclesiologist*, 17 (1856), p. 186.
47   *Ecclesiologist*, 21 (1860), p. 145

dominated by a fine sculptured reredos. Admittedly there was no rood screen, but the Society had had comparatively little success in making that feature mandatory; instead, there is a distinct chancel arch and, below it, solid rails and gates to emphasise the liturgical separation of nave from sanctuary. All furnishings are in their appointed places and are beautifully crafted, while the whole building is modelled with the extensive use of carving and figure sculpture. Externally, the asymmetrically placed steeple dominates the surrounding new suburb of Ackroydon and proclaims the necessary supremacy of the House of God. A decade after such ecclesiology was seen as subversively Popish, it had become almost conventional in a proud wool-manufacturer's church in the West Riding of Yorkshire.

The Ecclesiologist carried two plates of All Souls – an exterior and an interior view, drawn by J. Drayton Wyatt (plates 43 & 44) – and found practically nothing to criticise in its eulogy (after a visit, Benjamin Webb confessed himself 'amazed' — Ackroyd must have been pleased, for he joined the Ecclesiological Society in June 1860).[48] But although there was a mildly polychromatic effect in the use of two types of stone, Scott's church displays none of the apparent originality of interpretation achieved by Butterfield and Street in the 1850s through the use of Italian precedents and by the illumination of Ruskin's 'Lamp of Truth' in the handling of austere planes of masonry. The design of All Souls' was largely English in character, Picturesque rather than Sublime, and avoided demonstrative experimentation. All this was typical of the architect.

So had The Ecclesiologist turned its back on its earlier championing of Butterfield by now praising a more conservative Gothic? Surely not; the Cambridge Camden Society had really championed Butterfield more on account of his ecclesiological orthodoxy than because he was seen as progressive. Besides, modern historians can sometimes mistake exoticism for inventiveness, and while the polychromy and formal abstraction of Butterfield's architecture was highly personal, it nevertheless owed much to Gothic precedent. Those precedents were often Continental, although sometimes English. Scott was similarly dependent upon historical models, but he reinterpreted them in a different way, producing a church on Haley Hill which could never be mistaken for a mediaeval building. After all, there was more than one form of originality to be striven for in the 1850s. For not only did The Ecclesiologist 'warmly congratulate' George Gilbert Scott on his church for Akroyd, but it also insisted that

> in the extensive introduction of figure sculpture, externally and internally, he
> has opened a new era of church art. It is this which distinguishes All Souls,
> Halifax from every other modern work; and if All Saints, Margaret Street

---

[48]   Webb's diary for 20 May 1860: 'Mr E. Ackroyd met us. To his place. After lunch with him & Mrs A. to the Cemetery, the New Church, the Schools, Mill &c, &c. Amazed.' (Bodleian Library MS.Eng.misc.e.414).

was the first example of the highest pictorial art being introduced into church decoration, the church at Haley Hill will mark the epoch when the sculptor first made good his claim to admission within the sanctuary.[49]

Scott may not have belonged to that inner charmed circle of architects favoured by the Ecclesiological (late Cambridge Camden) Society and he felt aggrieved at the treatment he received in its journal. But a close study of its pages suggests that he really had little to complain about. And, after all, the editors had published a book review in 1849 which, in discussing the remarkable progress recently made in reviving the Gothic, concluded that, 'Bad as it may be, the Pointed of Wren is infinitely better than that of Soane and Wyattville, and yet the latter has within a single generation grown up into that of Pugin, and Carpenter, and Butterfield, and Scott.'[50] What greater praise could there be than to be placed in such exalted company?

The author wishes to acknowledge the help given him by Geoffrey Brandwood in the preparation of this essay.

[49] *Ecclesiologist*, 21 (1860), p. 152.
[50] Review of George Aycliffe Poole, *A History of Ecclesiastical Architecture in England*, in the *Ecclesiologist*, 9 (October 1849), p. 137.

Three Men in a Gondola: Ruskin, Webb and Street

DALE DISHON

> I can imagine nothing so delightful as to glide from island to island, and from church to church, in a gondola. Ecclesiology in Venice is made easy (Benjamin Webb, 1848).

Picture Venice, a gondola gliding 'softly and equably, over the deep green rippling water, through dark narrow canals, among stately palaces, and under countless bridges; while everything is bathed in a warm hazy light'.[1] In this imaginary gondola are three illustrious Victorians: John Ruskin (1819–1900), visionary art critic and author of *The Stones of Venice*; Rev. Benjamin Webb (1819–85), co-founder of the Cambridge Camden Society and author of *Sketches of Continental Ecclesiology*; and George Edmund Street (1824–81), leading Gothic Revival architect and author of *Brick and Marble in the Middle Ages*. This chapter is the story of their respective impressions of Italy, and the subsequent impact on the theory and practice of Victorian church building.

An article in *The Builder* of 1867, evaluating the influence of architectural theorists, concluded that 'Pugin has most influenced us in structure, John Ruskin in ornament'.[2] Ruskin's most important contributions to architectural theory were *The Seven Lamps of Architecture*, published in 1849, and *The Stones of Venice* whose first volume appeared in 1851 and the next two in 1853. Unlike Pugin, Ruskin was not an architect, still less an engineer. His architectural theories were based on artistic judgement, imaginative power, social psychology and aesthetic philosophy. The overwhelming impact he had on his generation was made possible by his literary virtuosity. The dry and practical nature of architectural treatises had already been changed by Pugin's fiery polemics; Ruskin took the model a step further by capturing the emotional complexity of architecture and conveying it to his reader through impassioned prose.[3]

---

[1] B. Webb, *Sketches of Continental Ecclesiology, or Church Notes in Belgium, Germany and Italy* (London, 1848), p. 299.

[2] W. C. James, 'On the Influence of Some Contemporary Writers on the Architecture of the Day', *Builder*, 25 (1867), p. 483.

[3] See M. W. Brooks, *John Ruskin and Victorian Architecture* (Rutgers University Press, 1987).

In *The Seven Lamps of Architecture*, Ruskin advocated the pursuit of a new style adapted from one universally accepted form. He considered four styles to be suitable for this purpose: Pisan Romanesque, early Sienese Gothic, Venetian Gothic, and Early English Decorated. Throughout his life he was to change his allegiance from one to the other; but after the publication of *The Stones of Venice* his name was forever linked with Venetian Gothic, and became synonymous with a particular kind of eclecticism known as 'Ruskinian Gothic'.[4]

The most widely-read and influential section of *The Stones of Venice* was the chapter on the 'Nature of Gothic' which appeared in the second volume. In this chapter Ruskin attempted to classify the Gothic style, its external forms and internal elements. Externally he defined Gothic as the architecture of the gable. A fine Gothic building would have a roof rising in a steep gable, pointed-arch windows and doors with gables over them, cusped or foliated apertures, and arches carried on true shafts with bases and capitals.[5] A superior Gothic building would also have a roughness and largeness about it, would be of irregular design, the ornament would be perpetually varied, and the sculpture would be intelligible and interesting.[6] Perhaps more importantly, Ruskin believed the soul of Gothic to be also made up of internal, or moral, elements which he defined (in order of importance) as Savageness, Changefulness, Naturalism, Grotesqueness, Rigidity and Redundance.[7]

Charles Eastlake, whose *History of the Gothic Revival* of 1872 provided an invaluable contemporary commentary, ranked *The Stones of Venice* as a work of the highest merit and importance: 'If we regard collectively the character of its contents, the nature of its aim, or the beauty and vigour of its language, there is no parallel in the range of English literature'.[8] He defined Ruskin's aim as 'not only to give an historical and artistic description of Venetian architecture but to incorporate with that description his ideas of what modern architecture should be: not only to illustrate, but to moralise, expound and advise'.[9] The influence of *The Stones of Venice* on the development of the Gothic Revival was therefore immense:

[4] See J. Mordaunt Crook, *The Dilemma of Style* (London, 1989), pp. 69–75; and *idem*, 'Ruskinian Gothic', *The Ruskin Polygon*, ed. J. Dixon Hunt & F. M. Holland (Manchester, 1982), pp. 65–93.

[5] J. Ruskin, *The Stones of Venice*, II, 4th edn (Orpington, 1886) [1st published 1853], pp. 228–9.

[6] *Ibid.*, pp. 229–31.

[7] *Ibid.*, p. 154.

[8] C. L. Eastlake, *A History of the Gothic Revival*, ed. J. Mordaunt Crook (Leicester, 1970) [1st published 1872], p. 274.

[9] *Ibid.*, p. 275.

Previous apologists for the Revival had relied more or less on ecclesiastical sentiment, on historical interest, or on a vague sense of the picturesque for their plea in its favour. It was reserved for the author of 'The Stones of Venice' to strike a chord of human sympathy that vibrated through all hearts, and to advocate ... those principles of Mediaeval Art whose application should be universal ... That he made many converts, and found many disciples among the younger architects of the day, is not to be wondered. Students, who but a year or so previously had been content to regard Pugin as their leader, or who had modelled their notions of art on the precepts of the 'Ecclesiologist,' found a new field open to them, and hastened to occupy it. They prepared designs in which the elements of Italian Gothic were largely introduced...[10]

Unfortunately, as Eastlake pointed out, 'Mr. Ruskin was continually advancing propositions, often excellent in themselves, which he as frequently failed to maintain – not for want of argument, but because his arguments proved too much.'[11] In attempting to prove his architectural theory, Ruskin

encountered endless difficulties, involved himself in many apparent contradictions and inconsistencies, and though it enlisted the sympathies of those whose opinions on art are based on sentiment rather than study, it was received with incredulity by a large proportion of his readers, while professional architects, as a rule, regarded him in the light of a vain and misinformed enthusiast.[12]

In what light did the Ecclesiological (late Cambridge Camden) Society view Ruskin and his impact on the Gothic Revival? One might suppose it would have disapproved of anyone who favoured Italian Gothic over English Decorated. After all, it had stated unequivocally that 'the greatest glory which Christian Architecture has yet attained was reached in the early part of the Decorated Style';[13] its recommendation to the Anglican architect was to 'choose the glorious architecture of the fourteenth century' as the sole language in which to 'express his architectural ideas'.[14] Indeed, *The Ecclesiologist* did voice some objection to being 'called upon ... to admire every distortion, and settlement, and false measurement in Pisa'.[15] It complained that by 'confining himself chiefly to southern Pointed, – and, indeed, knowing comparatively little of the northern Gothic, – Mr. Ruskin ... does injustice to the latter'.[16] But on the whole, it rather surprisingly reviewed Ruskin's works in highly favourable terms.

[10]   *Ibid.*, p. 278.
[11]   *Ibid.*, p. 270.
[12]   *Ibid.*, p. 269.
[13]   Cambridge Camden Society, *A Few Words to Church-Builders*, 3rd edn (Cambridge, 1844) [1st published 1841], p. 6.
[14]   J. M. Neale & B. Webb (eds), *The Symbolism of Churches and Church Ornaments* (Leeds, 1843), p. xxiv.
[15]   'Mr. Ruskin's Seven Lamps of Architecture', *Ecclesiologist*, 10 (1850), p. 116.

This was certainly not out of sympathy for his theological views, for he was as adamantly Protestant as Pugin had been devoutly Catholic. His 'monomania ... against Catholicity', his 'continual abuse of the Church of Rome, and, by implication, of the Church of England' was much lamented by *The Ecclesiologist*.[17] Yet it praised his 'eloquent and earnest pen',[18] his 'clear perception and vigorous statement of true principles' and his 'cutting exposure of shams and falsehoods in art'.[19] It recommended *The Seven Lamps of Architecture* as an 'eloquent and deeply instructive' volume, abounding with 'valuable lessons and thoughts'.[20] It described *The Stones of Venice* as being 'of extreme value in suggesting and directing thought, in forming and guiding a habit of observation and induction'.[21] It even went as far as to admit that Ruskin had come 'practically to much the same conclusions as ourselves'.[22]

Of course, the ecclesiologists could not endorse every single view that Ruskin propounded; no one could, for he was too emotive and contradictory, as well as 'needlessly minute and wearisome'.[23] Yet overall, they seemed happy to 'adopt, almost without reserve, Mr. Ruskin's principles of criticism without in the least degree sharing his hatred of Catholicity'.[24] This endorsement implies that Ruskin's views on architecture were not as far removed from those of Pugin and the ecclesiologists as might originally be supposed; it also confirms that the Society's ideals had themselves undergone a process of evolution.

Let us examine some of the points on which Ruskin and the ecclesiologists saw eye to eye. The first of these was *reality*. The Cambridge Camden Society had originally stated that 'the first great canon to be observed in Church-building is this: LET EVERY MATERIAL EMPLOYED BE REAL ... Let deal be seen to be deal, not painted to resemble oak; let brick be known to be brick, not stuccoed to imitate stone'.[25] Ruskin was entirely in agreement – so much so that *The Ecclesiologist* claimed his views on the subject 'might have been taken from one of our own pages'.[26] It declared his 'denunciation of all false representation of material – sham granite and marbling' to be 'most refreshing'.[27]

---

[16]   'Ruskin's Stones of Venice II', *Ecclesiologist*, 14 (1853), p. 424.
[17]   'Ruskin's Stones of Venice I', *Ecclesiologist*, 12 (1851), p. 275.
[18]   'Seven Lamps', *Ecclesiologist*, 10 (1850), p. 111.
[19]   'Stones II', *Ecclesiologist*, 14 (1853), p. 415.
[20]   'Seven Lamps', *Ecclesiologist*, 10 (1850), p. 119.
[21]   'Stones I', *Ecclesiologist*, 12 (1851), p. 276.
[22]   'Stones II', *Ecclesiologist*, 14 (1853), p. 415.
[23]   'Stones I', *Ecclesiologist*, 12 (1851), p. 276.
[24]   *Ibid.*
[25]   Cambridge Camden Society, *A Few Words to Church-Builders*, p. 29.
[26]   'Seven Lamps', *Ecclesiologist*, 10 (1850), p. 112.
[27]   *Ibid.*, p. 113.

Another point on which the Ecclesiological Society concurred with Ruskin was his censure of the Classical/Renaissance tradition. 'We can heartily adopt his powerful denunciations of "the pestilent Renaissance"', enthused *The Ecclesiologist*.[28] No doubt it recognised in Ruskin a powerful ally in the battle against the Classicists, who, hot in pursuit of Italy's Classical heritage, had ignored or maligned its Gothic monuments.

Ruskin's abhorrence of the soulessness of modern society as reflected in its architecture and design also found a strong resonance among the ecclesiologists. 'We thoroughly sympathize with him in the disgust he expresses at the modern shop architecture', they wrote, agreeing that 'every dictate of architectural common sense is violated in the modern specimen'.[29] Ruskin deplored the manufacture of unnecessary goods, production without practical or noble ends, and copying for any purpose other than documentation. *The Ecclesiologist* considered his discourse on the subject 'most truthful and useful ... full of sound and earnest thought'.[30] It pronounced his 'social disquisitions' to be 'worthy, if not of entire acceptance, of very careful thought and consideration'.[31]

The ecclesiologists were also in agreement with Ruskin over the fundamental importance of nature: 'Nature and the Church answer to each other as implicit and explicit revelations of God. Therefore, whatever system is seen to run through the one, in all probability runs through the other'.[32] But they could not agree with his anti-rationalist approach to ornament as based on nature: 'It would be difficult to defend from a charge of fancifulness much of Mr. Ruskin's argument when he comes to speak of the natural forms which he thinks most appropriate for types of ornamentation'.[33]

The Society's endorsement of Ruskin's views on the use of brick in urban building points to a process of evolution in its own theories. In the early 1840s, the Society had claimed that 'brick ought never to be used where building-stone can be obtained; since the effect of this material, however well it be treated, is mean and unsatisfactory'.[34] By 1850 – the year in which the tax on bricks was repealed – its views had changed sufficiently to allow its own flagship church, All Saints, Margaret Street (1850–1859), to be built of polychromatic brick. The need to adapt church building to urban surroundings had obviously necessitated the replacement of picturesque Puginian rough-hewn stone with sublime Ruskinian brick. By 1853 the ecclesiologists were pleased to 'find in Mr. Ruskin a supporter in

---

28 'Stones I', *Ecclesiologist*, 12 (1851), p. 279.
29 *Ibid.*, pp. 283–4.
30 'Stones II', *Ecclesiologist*, 14 (1853), p. 423.
31 *Ibid.*
32 Neale & Webb, *Symbolism of Churches*, p. xliv.
33 'Ruskin's Stones of Venice I', 2nd Notice, *Ecclesiologist*, 12 (1851), p. 343.
34 Cambridge Camden Society, *A Few Words to Church-Builders*, p. 12.

recommending the proper use of brick as a building material.'[35] They had obviously realised, as Ruskin had done, that brick was a better means of achieving their desired effect of 'appropriateness, solidity, grandeur, honesty, chasteness, boldness'.[36]

While the Society was able to acknowledge Ruskin's contributions to the debate on Victorian Gothic, Ruskin himself seemed unwilling to acknowledge any debt either to his predecessors or contemporaries. *The Ecclesiologist* complained that

> Mr. Ruskin takes no notice of the efforts and success of other architectural writers and thinkers in the same field. He has been often anticipated in many of the principles he lays down, and the arguments by which he enforces them ... He might well have been content with the credit of being the most forcible and eloquent, without implying that he is the only original, expounder of the laws and principles of the revived Christian architecture.[37]

Although Pugin's name is the only one specified in this context,[38] *The Ecclesiologist* may have been making a veiled reference to Rev. Benjamin Webb, co-founder of the Cambridge Camden Society whose writings on Italian Gothic in fact preceded Ruskin's by a number of years.[39]

Webb first visited Italy in 1844-5. His impressions were published in 1848 as part of *Sketches of Continental Ecclesiology, or Church Notes in Belgium, Germany and Italy*. His style of writing was the antithesis of Ruskin's: dry, concise and factual, with subjective comments kept to a minimum. His descriptions of Italian churches seem like mere inventories when compared to Ruskin's forceful and poetic prose. One can understand why it was Ruskin, and not Webb, who popularised Italian Gothic. Yet many of the ideas and impressions put forward by Ruskin were in fact formulated by Webb before him. For example, although Ruskin is credited with spreading the gospel of Italian horizontality among English church builders, it was Webb who first identified Italian churches as having 'greater breadth, flatter roofs, and many-storied towers'.[40] It is perhaps unsurprising to discover that Webb was responsible for the favourable review of Ruskin's *Seven Lamps of Architecture* in *The Ecclesiologist*.[41]

Crucially, Webb anticipated Ruskin's emphasis on *truth* and *reality*. His main criticism of Italian Gothic was its deployment of various devices to

35 'Stones II', *Ecclesiologist*, 14 (1853), p. 425.
36 Cambridge Camden Society, *A Few Words to Church-Builders*, p. 17.
37 'Stones II', *Ecclesiologist*, 14 (1853), p. 415.
38 *Ibid.*, p. 425.
39 See J. Mordaunt Crook, 'Benjamin Webb (1819-85) and Victorian Ecclesiology', *Studies in Church History*, 36 (1997), pp. 423-57.
40 Webb, *Sketches of Continental Ecclesiology*, p. 187.
41 The authorship of the review has been identified from Webb's diary by J. Mordaunt Crook. See *Studies in Church History*, 36 (1997), p. 445.

hide the true nature of structure and materials. In Como Cathedral, for example, he observed that 'the west façade is a sham front; as it nearly always is in Italian Pointed'.[42] In the Duomo in Milan ('one of the largest and most perfect examples of the Pointed style in Italy')[43] he condemned the 'very beautiful tracery of the most flowing kind' painted on the nave vaulting as 'an inexcusable unreality, however good in effect'.[44] In actual fact, he was placing truth above beauty – a moral standpoint which was later to become Ruskin's trademark.

To judge the extent to which Webb anticipated Ruskin, one need look no further than his impressions of two cities: Verona and Venice. 'I know no town more beautiful, and in all respects satisfying than this', wrote Webb of Verona.[45] It was there that he 'discovered' what was later to become one of the tenets of Ruskinism: patterned coloured brickwork. In S. Anastasia, for example, he was struck by the 'alternate voussoirs of stone and brick' around the windows.[46] In S. Fermo Maggiore his eyes were opened to another future tenet of Ruskinism – the use of natural materials in ornament:

> I could not help noticing in this church, that the variety and beauty of the marbles in Italy made a necessary change in the general ornament, particularly of tombs. A greater flow and capriciousness, and more freedom in a kind of arabesque became a natural consequence of the use of materials so easily cut, and which could be inlaid and contrasted with such facility and beauty.[47]

As for Venice, it seems to have bewitched him. His descriptions of it are almost as emotional and imaginative as Ruskin's:

> To feel oneself at Venice is like the realization of a dream ... Every common incident becomes poetical, and associated with all possible contrasts of sunlight and deep shade, and wavering reflections of proud buildings and white flashing marble domes ... In a word, everything is puzzling and fascinating.[48]

Unlike Ruskin, who had no specific interest in ecclesiology, Webb's chief aim was to study Venetian churches. He was not disappointed: 'Venice is a bewitching city, but must be more so to an ecclesiologist than any one ... I can imagine nothing so delightful as to glide from island to island, and from church to church, in a gondola. Ecclesiology in Venice is made easy'.[49] One of the highlights of his tour was St Mark's, which he declared 'unique in the

42 Webb, *Sketches of Continental Ecclesiology*, p. 196.
43 *Ibid.*, p. 200.
44 *Ibid.*, p. 201.
45 *Ibid.*, p. 242.
46 *Ibid.*, p. 247.
47 *Ibid.*, pp. 250–1.
48 *Ibid.*, p. 299.
49 *Ibid.*, p. 298.

world in almost every point of view in which it can be regarded'.[50] In his opinion, 'no language could adequately describe the singular effect produced by the extreme gorgeousness of the ornamentation of the interior. It is one complete blaze of beautiful marbles and mosaics'.[51] Five years later, in the second volume of *The Stones of Venice*, Ruskin did find the language to describe the interior of St Mark's. To this day his description is one of the richest passages in English literature. So while Webb deserves recognition for having 'discovered' Venetian Gothic, it is highly probable that without Ruskin's eloquence the merits of the style would never have reached such a wide audience.

Webb devoted much attention to the liturgical arrangements of Italian churches and considered it 'his duty and privilege' to 'recommend for thoughtful consideration among English Churchmen, anything in the practical religious system of the Roman Catholic body ... likely to be beneficial'.[52] He saw Italy as a source of inspiration for church builders because of its Catholicism, as well as its stylistic tradition. As a result, his readership was limited mainly to ecclesiologists. Ruskin had the opposite problem: while his Protestant sympathies enabled him to appeal to a wider audience, they prevented him from accepting the religious associations of Italian Gothic. There were times when he twisted himself up in knots trying to explain the moral appeal of an Italian Gothic building while denying the faith of the men who built it.

If Pugin had difficulty reconciling ideology with practice, Ruskin's Utopian theories proved even more impossible to fulfil. The architects of the Gothic Revival found that Ruskin did not provide them with a practicable solution for the dilemma of style, so they absorbed his visual recommendations into their own notions of style. The result was that 'Ruskinism' became largely independent of Ruskin himself and developed in ways with which he did not agree. The architects of the 1850s who attempted to absorb and apply Ruskin's ideas – Benjamin Woodward, George Gilbert Scott, George Edmund Street, John Pollard Seddon, and Alfred Waterhouse – inevitably transformed his ideas in the process. So while they moved from struggle to success, he proceeded from hope to disillusionment.[53]

Street was one of the few architects with whose work Ruskin was proud to be associated. He proclaimed him 'one of our quite leading Gothic architects' to whom 'we owe so much'.[54] Introducing a lecture by Street on

50   *Ibid.*, p. 268.
51   *Ibid.*, p. 269.
52   *Ibid.*, p. xiii.
53   Ruskin did approve of *some* of these architects' work. In a lecture at the RIBA on May 15 1865, he stated that the work of Scott, Butterfield, Street, Waterhouse, Godwin and Woodward was 'original and independent'. J. Ruskin, *Works*, XIX, ed. E. T. Cook & A. Wedderburn (London, 1905), p. 23.

Venetian architecture on February 15, 1859, he went as far as to pronounce Street's designs 'pure beyond anything he had ever seen in modern architecture, in exquisite propriety of colour and in fineness of line'.[55]

Eastlake upheld Ruskin's opinion of Street, stating that

> the rich fertility of this architect's inventive power is only equalled by the sagacious tact which guides its application. He is not only master of many styles, but he can give original expression to every one of them. Where decoration can be afforded, he invests his work with sumptuous refinement which reveals itself in every detail. Where simplicity is required, he makes simplicity attractive. This faculty of design belongs to that rare order which unites artistic instinct with practical ability.[56]

Street must have been a practical, talented and tactful man indeed, for he managed to be a firm favourite with the ecclesiologists as well as with Ruskin. In fact, he forms a vital link between Ruskinism and ecclesiology. He began his architectural career as a disciple of Pugin, influenced no doubt by George Gilbert Scott, in whose office he worked from 1844-9. In 1845 he became a member of the Cambridge Camden Society. This, and his restoration of Sundridge church in Kent in 1848, a few miles from Brasted where Benjamin Webb was then curate, 'brought him into intimate relations with that gentleman'.[57] Webb, recognising Street's capabilities, recommended him to Rev. W. J. Butler, vicar of Wantage 'as a young man of ability and originality, who, with a love for hard work, was sure to interest himself actively and personally in all he had to do with'.[58] As a result, Street obtained several commissions in Berkshire, including Wantage vicarage and schools, which enabled him finally to set up his own practice.[59]

By 1850, Street had been a highly active member of the Ecclesiological Society for some years, reading papers before its members and making designs for all manner of church fittings and furniture at their request. Consequently, when the firm of Newton, Jones and Willis of Birmingham asked the Society to name the best man to design church furniture for the Great Exhibition of 1851, it recommended Street. Webb wrote to him that 'these designs will be much in your way'[60] because Street had always upheld the Society's view that church fittings should be designed by an artist or architect and not left to chance. Ruskin was advocating similar principles of totality in art at the time,

---

[54]   *Ibid.*, p. 255.
[55]   Ruskin, *Works*, XVI, p. 462.
[56]   Eastlake, *History of the Gothic Revival*, p. 322.
[57]   A. E. Street, *Memoir of George Edmund Street* (London, 1888), p. 13.
[58]   *Ibid.*
[59]   See J. Elliott & J. Pritchard (eds), *George Edmund Street: a Victorian Architect in Berkshire* (Reading, 1998).
[60]   Quoted in A. E. Street, *Memoir of G. E. Street*, p. 17.

praising the comprehensiveness of design caused by the intimate association of painting, sculpture and architecture.

It was Webb who finally persuaded Street to leave Oxford in 1856, where he had been employed as diocesan architect to Bishop Wilberforce, and move to London. He insisted that Street's career would have a better chance of expanding there, and was proven right when Street subsequently received several important commissions.[61]

Street also had a close relationship with another founder of the Cambridge Camden Society, John Mason Neale. He began designing the convent of St Margaret, East Grinstead, Sussex, for Neale in 1853. Street's son, Arthur Edmund, attested that his father 'had long been on terms of intimacy with Mr. Neale ... and so strong were his sympathies for the welfare of the institution that he freely gave his services then and thereafter'.[62] Building work, supervised by Neale, began in 1865. In 1881, just before his death, Street attended the consecration of the chapel. The buildings – simple, unornamented and grouped in a picturesque manner – were in a Puginesque, vernacular style.

In fact, all of Street's designs in the early 1850s were in the Puginesque mould – picturesque, vernacular and very English. In 1850–1 he travelled to France, Germany and Belgium to study the forms of northern European Gothic. From then on he became a regular traveller to the continent and gradually also a crusader for the introduction of its architectural forms into English church building. He lectured and wrote profusely about continental ecclesiology, including such publications as *The Churches of Lübeck* (1854) and *Some Account of Gothic Architecture in Spain* (1865).

It was in 1853, as a result of the publication of the second volume of Ruskin's *Stones of Venice*, that Street first travelled to Italy. His impressions were published in 1855 as *Brick and Marble in the Middle Ages: Notes on a Tour in the North of Italy*. *The Ecclesiologist*, while acknowledging that Street's tour had not covered new ground, nevertheless hailed the book as a 'handsome and instructive volume', 'a useful and important contribution to an architectural library'.[63] It believed the book would give readers who had never been to Italy 'a better notion than it is easy to get elsewhere of the richness and beauty of the Pointed architecture of Italy'.[64] For although Street did not have Ruskin's imagination or literary genius, he had the great advantage of being a professional architect, which meant that his illustrations were more accurate and his observations geared towards members of the architectural profession.

---

[61]   See *ibid.*, p. 22.

[62]   *Ibid.*, p. 20.

[63]   'Mr. Street's Italian Tour', *Ecclesiologist*, 16 (1855), p. 299.

[64]   *Ibid.*, p. 302.

His impressions of Italy, while confined to architecture rather than wider artistic or social issues, were dominated by Ruskin nonetheless. He openly admitted his debt to Ruskin's writings:

> It is impossible to conclude this Preface without mention of the obligations which not only all who travel in Italy, but all who are interested in good architecture, owe to Mr. Ruskin. No man need or can profess his acquiescence in every one of the opinions which he has propounded, but as an architect I feel strongly that a great debt of gratitude is owing to him for his brilliant advocacy of many laws and truths in which every honest architect ought gladly to acquiesce.[65]

One of the points on which Street fully concurred with Ruskin, as did the ecclesiologists, was the preference for Gothic forms as opposed to those of the Renaissance. His opinion of Italian Renaissance architects was unequivocal:

> The same falseness of construction, and heaviness, coarseness, and bad grotesqueness of ornamentation, seem ever to attend their works, together with the same contempt of simplicity, repose, and delicacy which we are so accustomed to connect with them. In short, I see but little reason to differ from the estimate which Mr. Ruskin has given of their merits in the 'Stones of Venice,' and what he has so well said I need not attempt to enlarge upon.[66]

But Street was at first perplexed by Ruskin's preference for southern over northern Gothic. Judging Italian architecture by Puginian standards, he found it structurally clumsy, and was slightly disappointed on visiting Venice. He was bewildered by the exterior of St Mark's: 'To a mind educated in and accustomed to the traditions of northern architecture, there is something so very *outré* in the whole idea, so startling in its novelty, that it is hard at first to know whether to admire or not'.[67] Ruskin later came to agree with him; by 1859 his views had altered sufficiently to declare that 'he entirely accepted the condemnation of Mr. Street with regard to St Mark's. It was a building that certainly could not be compared in any respect with the magnificent cathedral of Chartres'.[68]

Street was, however, totally captivated by the interior ornament of St Mark's, as both Ruskin and Webb had been before him. He felt it pointed 'most forcibly to the absolute necessity for the introduction of more colour in the interior of our buildings ... Not till then, shall we see a satisfactory school of architects in England'.[69] The imagery he used to describe the patterned floor which 'swells up and down as though its surface were the petrified waves

---

[65] G. E. Street, *Brick and Marble in the Middle Ages*, 2nd edn (London, 1874) [1st published 1855], p. xvii.

[66] *Ibid.*, p. xiv.

[67] *Ibid.*, p. 152.

[68] Ruskin, *Works*, XVI, p. 463.

[69] G. E. Street, *Brick and Marble*, p. 163.

of the sea'[70] echoed Ruskin's description of 'the waves of marble that heave and fall in a thousand colours along the floor'.[71] In point of fact, Webb had recorded the marvels of this floor before either of them:

> The very floor is a mosaic of rich patterns and colours. Porphyry, jasper, serpentine and alabaster, verde, and rose antique, and a hundred others, give a truly eastern magnificence; to which art has lent its magic in every conceivable branch.[72]

Street much preferred the constructional polychromy of Bergamo and Cremona to Venetian incrustation. He believed coloured marbles were better employed in the actual construction of a wall, banded with bricks or other coloured stones, than in ornamental coating. He disagreed with Ruskin's view that 'the school of incrusted architecture is the only one in which perfect and permanent chromatic decoration is possible',[73] stating that 'the Venetian mode was rather likely to be destructive of good architecture, because it was sure to end in an entire concealment of the real construction of the work'.[74] In this he was also at odds with the Ecclesiological Society, who unconditionally accepted Ruskin's views on incrusted architecture.[75]

By the time Street stood in front of Strasbourg Cathedral at the end of his Italian tour, he had been converted to Ruskin's point of view concerning the merits of surface as opposed to linear Gothic:

> After seeing the simple unbroken façades of Italian churches, with their grand porches and their simple breadth of effect, there is something so entirely destructive to all repose in a front covered as this is with lines of tracery, panelling, niches, and canopies in every direction, that it leaves, I confess, a painful feeling upon the mind...[76]

His conclusion was that the future of Victorian Gothic lay in the synthesis of the colour and pattern of southern Gothic, learnt from Ruskin, with the structure and reason of northern Gothic, learnt from Pugin. He believed that the most important element to be gleaned from Italian Gothic was

> the introduction of colour in construction – which is managed generally with such consummate beauty, refinement, and modesty, that even where it accompanies faulty construction and unworthily sham expedients, it is impossible to avoid giving oneself up altogether to admiration of the result.[77]

The Ecclesiologist agreed, expressing its belief that Street's book would persuade its readers of 'the beauties and merits of [employing] constructional

[70] *Ibid.*, p. 159.
[71] Ruskin, *Stones of Venice*, II, p. 70.
[72] Webb, *Sketches of Continental Ecclesiology*, p. 269.
[73] Ruskin, *Stones of Venice*, II, p. 79.
[74] G. E. Street, *Brick and Marble*, p. 400.
[75] See 'Stones II', *Ecclesiologist*, 14 (1853), p. 420.
[76] G. E. Street, *Brick and Marble*, p. 360.
[77] *Ibid.*, pp. 380–1.

polychrome in our buildings, as well secular as religious'.[78]

Street subsequently became strongly opposed to the use of rough, rustic-looking stones in urban church building. In 1857, when practically the only brick-built church in London was Butterfield's All Saints, Margaret Street, he wrote an article in *The Ecclesiologist* protesting against the use of Kentish ragstone in London churches. He argued that 'this kind of material, whose fitness and beauty in its own district and among country scenes I should be the first to acknowledge, was entirely out of place in town buildings, among crowds of houses' where the purpose of these rough stones 'seems to my not very partial eye, to be that of soot-collectors'.[79] These ideas were a direct result of his study of Italian, particularly Veronese, brickwork (plate 45). Butterfield had of course used polychromatic brickwork before him; but, as *The Ecclesiologist* pointed out, 'Mr. Butterfield's works show, by their architectural detail, that in the mass they are decidedly northern and specially English. Mr. Street, on the other hand, has drunk deep of the Italian and Early French springs'.[80]

All Saints, Boyne Hill, Berkshire (1854–7), was the first church to bear the fruit of Street's Italian travels. His design, although far from Italian in outline, included Italian elements in the details. The walls were constructed of polychromatic red brick relieved by bands of stone and the spandrels of the nave arcade were filled with Ruskinian stone carvings. *The Ecclesiologist*, probably under the influence of Webb, hailed the church as 'a great success' and ranked it 'in the first class of the buildings which have grown under the combined revival of Pointed architecture and ritual correctness'.[81] It praised the 'admirable iron screen-work, copied from that round the tomb of one of the Scaligers at Verona'.[82] But it criticised the 'overpowering redness' of the brickwork and thought Street should have 'toned down the predominant hue'.[83]

It was less reserved in its praise of Street's first London church, St James-the-Less, Thorndike Street, Westminster, designed in 1859 and built 1860–61 (plates 46 to 50). This remarkable Italianate Gothic church was commissioned as a memorial to Dr. James Monk, Bishop of Gloucester and Bristol, by his three daughters. Its extraordinary existence in the heart of Pimlico's slums would have been unthinkable before the publication of Ruskin's *Stones of Venice*. *The Ecclesiologist*, in an article reviewing St James-the-Less in comparison with Butterfield's St Alban, Holborn, claimed that Street had

[78] 'Street's Tour', *Ecclesiologist*, 16 (1855), p. 305.
[79] G. E. Street, 'Kentish Rag and Black Pointing', *Ecclesiologist*, 18 (1857), p. 8.
[80] 'Churches and Schools in London', *Ecclesiologist*, 22 (1861), p. 317.
[81] 'Shottesbrook and Boyn Hill', *Ecclesiologist*, 19 (1858), p. 316.
[82] *Ibid.*, p. 317.
[83] *Ibid.*, p. 316.

stepped beyond the mere repetition of English mediaeval forms, to produce a building in which a free eclectic manipulation of parts has been grafted upon a system of polychromatic construction, having its basis in the fact that London is naturally a brick town.[84]

It was particularly impressed by the church's 'high, perfectly square, unbuttressed tower' (plate 47), which it considered 'thoroughly Italian'.[85] On the whole the article was most favourable, but did not recommend Street's style for general imitation since only an architect of his calibre and imagination would be capable of controlling such eclecticism.

Eastlake, reviewing the Gothic Revival's departure from English tradition, claimed that 'in no instance was this revolt from national style more marked than in the Church of St. James the Less ... The whole character of the building, whether we regard its plan, its distinctive features, its external or internal decoration is eminently un-English'.[86] He confirmed *The Ecclesiologist*'s view of the tower:

> If Mr. Street had never designed anything but the campanile of this church – and its Italian character justifies the name – it would be sufficient to proclaim him an artist. In form, proportion of parts, decorative detail, and use of colour, it seems to leave little to be desired. To form a just appreciation of its merits, let the architectural amateur walk down to Garden Street from any part of London, and note as he passes the stereotyped patterns of towers and spires which he will find to right or left of his road. How neat, how respectable, how correct, how eminently uninteresting they are! No one cares to look at them twice. They are all like each other, or so little different that if they changed places any day, by help of Aladdin's lamp, the London world would never find it out.[87]

In designing the tower, Street did not reproduce any particular model. His method was not to imitate but to create a personal synthesis out of the architectural languages of the countries he visited. St James-the-Less would probably seem as much out of place in Italy as it does in London because, as Street's son noted, in this church 'what is Italian has become so entirely absorbed in what belongs to the architect's own inspiration, that it is hard to put the finger on any actual features which recall Italian examples'.[88] The tower is a synthesis of several Italian campanili mixed with northern elements such as the roof. From the illustrations in Street's book it appears that his main sources were the campanile of Sta Maria Maggiore in Bergamo, which caused him to say that 'Italian campanili have quite a character of their own';[89]

[84] 'Churches and Schools in London', p. 317.
[85] *Ibid.*, p. 320.
[86] Eastlake, *History of the Gothic Revival*, p. 321.
[87] *Ibid.*, pp. 321–2.
[88] A. E. Street, *Memoir of G. E. Street*, p. 37.
[89] G. E. Street, *Brick and Marble*, p. 59.

San Giacomo del Rialto which he considered 'the best campanile in Venice';[90] and his favourite, the campanile of the Palazzo Scaligeri in Verona which he described as 'a lofty, simple, and almost unbroken piece of brickwork', adding that Italian tower-building 'need give no fairer example of its power than this simple and grand erection'.[91] Ruskin was to sketch the same campanile in 1869, noting its 'noble sweep of delicately ascending curves sloped inwards'.[92]

Street's admiration for the solid mass and breadth of Italian campanili was directly influenced by Ruskin's theories on sublimity:

> The relative majesty of buildings depends more on the weight and vigour of their masses, than on any other attribute of their design: mass of everything, of bulk, of light, of darkness, of colour, not mere sum of any of these, but breadth of them; not broken light, nor scattered darkness, nor divided weight, but solid stone, broad sunshine, starless shade.[93]

The exterior of St James-the-Less upholds these principles as well as exemplifying Ruskin's belief that 'a building, in order to show its magnitude ... must be bounded as much as possible by continuous lines'.[94] This method also met with the approval of the ecclesiologists, who were 'delighted to find in Mr. Ruskin a champion for the beauty, as well as the strict architectural propriety, of the Italian method of decoration by horizontal bands of colour'.[95] By adhering to Ruskin's principles on the power of architecture, Street managed to give the church an impression of great strength and magnitude in spite of its cramped urban site and tight budget. The total cost of the fabric was only £5,800, an achievement highly commended by *The Ecclesiologist*.[96]

The influence of Italian models can be seen to greatest advantage in the church's brickwork. Street was particularly fascinated by the patterned coloured brickwork of Verona, as Benjamin Webb had been before him, stating that 'one feasts uninterruptedly there on all that can delight the eye in form and in colour'.[97] He incorporated these forms and colours into the belfry windows of the tower (the emphasis on the top storey being a quintessential Italian feature), the patterned voussoirs of the transept windows, and the arches of the tower's ground storey (plate 48). These arches with their bold

---

[90]   *Ibid.*, p. 187.

[91]   *Ibid.*, p. 84.

[92]   Ruskin, *Works*, XIX, p. 457.

[93]   J. Ruskin, *The Seven Lamps of Architecture*, 2nd edn (London, 1855) [1st published 1849], p. 91.

[94]   *Ibid.*, p. 68.

[95]   'Stones I', 2nd Notice, *Ecclesiologist*, 12 (1851), p. 348.

[96]   *Ecclesiologist*, 22 (1861), p. 414. The overall cost, including glass-painting, carving and decorations, was less than £9,000.

[97]   G. E. Street, *Brick and Marble*, p. 121.

patterns of black brick, notched red brick and white stone are particularly vibrant and muscular.

The feature which appears to be most closely based on a particular Italian model is the circular west window, with its powerful compressed columns radiating from a central rose. It bears a remarkable resemblance to the east window of Sant' Andrea, Vercelli, where Street found himself 'in the rare state of mind (in an Italian church) of admiring without grumbling!'[98] The trefoiled cusping of the lancet windows in the transepts is based on a Venetian feature which was much admired and illustrated by Ruskin. A prominent Venetian feature which does *not* appear in this church is the ogee arch; Street considered it a debased form of the pointed arch derived from the East and refrained from using it in his designs.

The east end of the church exhibits a different set of continental influences. An apse is a feature most commonly associated with French Gothic, though in this case the absence of surrounding aisles or chapels might indicate some borrowing from early German examples.[99] The Cambridge Camden Society had originally stated that an apsidal east end 'in England, is very inadvisable. It is un-Anglican, it is unnatural'.[100] But by the time St James-the-Less was built, its views had changed; *The Ecclesiologist* noted that 'Mr. Butterfield ... stands alone among eminent architects in his refusal to accept the apse'.[101] The brickwork of the apse is in the same polychromatic Italian style as the rest of the church, but the plate tracery is in the early thirteenth-century French style of the Abbey of Bonport.[102] Street obviously believed in borrowing whatever elements of Gothic architecture he found most powerful, irrespective of their country of origin.

The interior of St James-the-Less (plate 49), like the exterior, would have been stylistically unthinkable before the publication of *The Stones of Venice*. The masonry supplies the savageness and rigidity which Ruskin considered essential elements of Gothic buildings, while the ornament provides the naturalism, changefulness and grotesqueness he required. The interior as a whole is an essay on Street's belief, echoing Ruskin, that 'we must have colour in our buildings ... Let it be the most beautiful, the most glowing, and the most poetical we can obtain'.[103] The apse therefore combines a French sexpartite ribbed vault with Italian polychromatic red brick banded with stone. 'The roof of the chancel is deserving of the utmost praise,' stated *The*

[98] *Ibid.*, p. 332.
[99] See 'Mr. Street on German Pointed Architecture', *Ecclesiologist*, 18 (1857), pp. 164–5.
[100] Cambridge Camden Society, *A Few Words to Church-Builders*, p. 14.
[101] 'Churches and Schools in London', p. 318.
[102] See N. Jackson, 'The Un-Englishness of G. E. Street's Church of St James-the-Less', *Architectural History*, 23 (1980), pp. 86–94.
[103] G. E. Street, 'On the Future of Art in England', *Ecclesiologist*, 19 (1858), p. 236.

Ecclesiologist, hastening to 'heartily congratulate Mr. Street on this stroke of artistic power'.[104]

The nave arcade, comprising three bays, was considered by *The Ecclesiologist* 'very clever' and 'the key to the entire composition of the church',[105] for it followed Ruskin's principles of breadth and mass. The arches are low sprung, with a wide span, and the polished shafts of red granite particularly short and stout. Their 'barbaric bulk'[106] marks the shift of taste in the 1860s to a more muscular type of Gothic.

Street believed that 'three-fourths of the poetry of a building lies in its minor details',[107] so he lavished attention on every inch of the interior, from the reredos with its rich mosaic of marble, to what *The Ecclesiologist* called the 'first really artistic adaptation of mastic incising' on the apse wall.[108] He also believed that since 'no other country ever boasted of the same abundant richness of artistic power' as Italy did, he and his colleagues should 'try to do what the Italian architects did: paint the walls we build'.[109] He therefore commissioned George Frederic Watts to paint a fresco on the chancel wall, and employed the firm of Clayton and Bell to paint a Jesse Tree on the roof of the nave according to his designs.

Unfortunately, his noble ideas did not translate well into practice. The fresco by Watts, of an enthroned Christ with attendant angels and evangelists, did not live up to Italian precedents in either quality (it had to be replaced by a similar mosaic in the 1880s because the paint had deteriorated) or style. 'We are no advocates for forced antiquarianism,' declared *The Ecclesiologist*, 'but there is a limit of modern feeling which the painter who works in a Gothic church ought not quite to touch'.[110] Watts, it seems, had overstepped that mark. His fresco contrasted too violently with 'the bright, strong, early coloration of the roof',[111] now barely visible under layers of grime.

The love of change that Ruskin termed 'that strange *disquietude* of the Gothic spirit that is its greatness; that restlessness of the dreaming mind'[112] can be found everywhere in the church. In the aisle walls, for example, each capital is different from the next, each marble column unique, each inlaid base of a different design. Ruskin's ideas on grotesqueness, or 'the tendency to delight in fantastic and ludicrous ... images'[113] created by the disturbed

---

[104] 'Churches and Schools in London', p. 321.
[105] *Ibid.*, p. 322.
[106] *Ibid.*
[107] G. E. Street, 'On the Future of Art in England', p. 238.
[108] 'Churches and Schools in London', p. 325.
[109] G. E. Street, 'On the Future of Art in England', p. 238.
[110] 'Churches and Schools in London', p. 326.
[111] *Ibid.*
[112] Ruskin, *Stones of Venice*, II, p. 181.
[113] *Ibid.*, p. 203.

imagination of the Gothic architect, manifest themselves in various carved capitals displaying dragons and devilish beasts.

Other carved capitals implement Ruskin's ideas on 'naturalism; that is to say, the love of natural objects for their own sake, and the effort to represent them frankly, unconstrained by artistical laws'.[114] Street agreed with Ruskin on naturalism, stressing the importance of 'a return to first principles and truth in the delineation of nature and natural forms'.[115] He made use of the liturgical ornaments recommended by the Cambridge Camden Society – birds, fish, lilies, demons[116] – but instead of treating them in a Puginian abstracted manner, he gave them the naturalistic form recommended by Ruskin.

The sculpted groups in the capitals of the nave arcade, representing the parables and miracles, pay homage to Ruskin's observations on the close relationship between sculpture and architecture in Italian Gothic. So does the pulpit, carved by Farmer to depict evangelists and saints. It was considered by *The Ecclesiologist* to be 'a bold experiment'[117] for its use of sculptural elements in combination with small coloured marble columns. These columns illustrate Ruskin's view that 'the colours of architecture should be those of natural stones; partly because [they are] more durable, but also because more perfect and graceful'.[118] Coloured marble was also used in the reredos and in the chancel floor (plate 50), where it was combined with encaustic tiles to create the kind of effect admired by Street, Ruskin and Webb in St Mark's, Venice.

Each material was used in its true form, without recourse to surface deceit, according to the doctrines of both Ruskin and Webb. Street reiterated their ideas:

The principle which artists now have mainly to contend for is that of Truth; forgotten, trodden under foot, despised, if not hated for ages, this must be their watchword. If they be architects, let them remember how vitally necessary truthfulness in construction, in design, and in decoration, is to any permanent success in even the smallest of their works.[119]

In 1843, Neale and Webb had complained that

architecture has become too much a profession: it is made the means of gaining a livelihood and is viewed as a path to honourable distinction, instead of being the study of the devout ecclesiastick... We do protest against the merely business-like spirit of the modern profession, and demand from them a more elevated and directly religious habit of mind. We surely ought to look at least for Church-membership from one who ventures to design a

[114] *Ibid.*, p. 181.
[115] G. E. Street, *Brick and Marble*, p. 407.
[116] See Cambridge Camden Society, *A Few Words to Church-Builders*, pp. 21–2.
[117] 'Churches and Schools in London', p. 326.
[118] Ruskin, *Seven Lamps*, p. 126.
[119] G. E. Street, *Brick and Marble*, p. 406.

church.[120]

In Street they found an answer to their prayers, for his search for architectural truth was inextricable from his religion. His son attested to the fact that

> his religion, not an acrid one nor ostentatiously worn, was intimately bound up with his work ... This was the secret of his love for the men of the Middle Ages and their handiwork. He saw that those glorious monuments, which are the boast of Europe, owe their pure and exalted type of beauty to the devotional and self-obliterating faith of the men who built them.[121]

In the words of Goodhart-Rendel, 'like almost every other Victorian, he insisted always upon ... truthfulness as an indispensable antecedent to beauty'.[122] This might explain how Street managed to please such diverse factions as Ruskin and the ecclesiologists at the same time. As Ruskin told the Ecclesiological Society at a lecture on 13 June, 1861: 'All good art was the expression of the whole man – of his soul and heart, of his intellect, and of the whole power of his body ... No great work of art existed which did not give some expression of the mind of the man at work'.[123] Street agreed with this view but did not make the same social deductions as Ruskin; he preferred to confine his 'medieval spirit' to architecture. It was left to Street's pupils, the younger architects of the Arts and Crafts movement, to inherit Ruskin's ideas on social reform and incorporate them into the next phase of the Gothic Revival. William Morris, Phillip Webb, Richard Norman Shaw and J. D. Sedding were all pupils of Street's in the 1850s; they may have learnt their brickwork from him, but they derived their social philosophy from Ruskin.

Although St James-the-Less marked the apogée of Street's Ruskinian phase, Italian Gothic features continued to appear in his buildings for some time. In St Philip and St James, Oxford (1860–2) he enriched the building with constructional polychromy, 'not by covering it over with stripes like a zebra, but by introducing bands of reddish stone at rare intervals and by marking the voussoirs in the same manner'.[124] The tower, although not a detached campanile, nevertheless retains an Italian feature in the louvred belfry windows.

Street ended his career in a vein which is best termed High Victorian Eclecticism. The Law Courts in the Strand, London (1868–82) were the crowning glory of his achievement.[125] In them he combined his favourite Gothic styles to create a new synthesis – one which answered Sir Walter

[120] Neale & Webb, *Symbolism of Churches*, pp. xxi–xxii.
[121] A. E. Street, *Memoir of G. E. Street*, p. 57.
[122] H. S. Goodhart-Rendel, *George Edmund Street* (London, 1983), p. 5.
[123] Ruskin, *Works*, XIX, p. 463.
[124] Eastlake, *History of the Gothic Revival*, p. 324.
[125] See D. B. Brownlee, *The Law Courts: The Architecture of George Edmund Street* (Cambridge, Massachusetts, 1984).

James's appeal to architects to take 'a *via media* between Pugin's view of ornamenting only those parts of a building which are constructive, and Ruskin's more licentious view of scattering beauty with a liberal hand wherever fancy dictates'.[126] The style owed much of its origins to French and English Gothic, but the influence of Ruskin and Italian Gothic were still there. The north-east tower on Carey Street demonstrates that Street never forgot Ruskin's lessons on the importance of colour or the strength of horizontal banding. Ruskin was reluctant to admit any connection with the majority of High Victorian architecture, but made an exception when he wrote to the *Pall Mall Gazette* in 1872: 'I am proud enough to hope ... that I have had some direct influence on Mr. Street; and I do not doubt but that the public will have more satisfaction from his Law Courts than they have had from anything built within fifty years'.[127]

The tides of architectural taste were returning to English shores once more, with Street in the vanguard. Eastlake found it

> remarkable that this architect, who was one of the first to set aside home traditions of style in favour of Continental Gothic, should be amongst the earliest of his professional contemporaries to return to English models. Among his admirers, who watched with interest the completion of St. James the Less, there was probably not one who foresaw the change which was destined to take place in the spirit of his design...[128]

The ecclesiologists were among Street's greatest admirers, but even they could not have foreseen the changes in his style. He was admired by other factions too: in 1874, the RIBA awarded him their Gold Medal (which denoted literary, not practical, excellence in the field of architecture) for *Brick and Marble in the Middle Ages* and *Gothic Architecture in Spain*. Ironically, Ruskin was intended to be the recipient of the medal that year, for *The Stones of Venice* and other architectural treatises; but in an unprecedented and embittered step, he refused to accept it. G. G. Scott presented the medal to Street instead, saying that he 'probably extended his studies and his wonderful powers of sketching to the mediaeval buildings of a greater number of countries and places than any other living man'.[129]

It was this ability to appreciate and assimilate a variety of Gothic forms, coupled with a deep spirituality, which made Street such a vital link between Ruskinism and ecclesiology. He had started his career as a firm disciple of Pugin and a strict adherer to the principles of the Cambridge Camden Society; but, following the publications of Webb and Ruskin, saw the need to revitalise Victorian church building through the introduction of continental Gothic motifs. He remained faithful to the Camdenian principles

126 James, 'On the Influence of Contemporary Writers', *Builder*, 25 (1867), p. 463.
127 Ruskin, *Works*, X (1904), p. 459.
128 Eastlake, *History of the Gothic Revival*, p. 326.
129 Quoted in A. E. Street, *Memoir of G. E. Street*, p. 227.

of truth and reality, but proved that they could be achieved through the employment of more than one style or material. He strengthened and advanced the ecclesiologists' position on the use of brick and the introduction of colour by bringing these away from Butterfield's maverick style into the mainstream of urban church building. Although by the late 1870s he was too set in his ways to succumb to the plurality of revivalist styles (such as Queen Anne) which had taken over from the Camdenian vision of a single Gothic form, he was in fact partly responsible for this widening of the ecclesiological horizons.

In 1877, during the course of yet another continental tour, he met up with Ruskin in Venice where he 'joined him in a chorus of lamentation over the evidences of the all-pervading spirit of the age, which ... is changing ... [the city's] whole character'.[130] Both men were then in their fifties and it appears that even Street was weary of the long battle waged by both Ruskin and the ecclesiologists to defend Gothic architecture from the evils of modernity, Classicism and restoration. He died four years later, exhausted by the strain of completing the Law Courts. Ruskin, probably to his regret, lived to see the twentieth century. Perhaps we ought to leave them in the city that brought out the poet even in Benjamin Webb – Venice, in the spring of 1877, stretched out in a gondola and watching how 'the strong tide, as it runs beneath the Rialto, is reddened ... by the reflection of the frescoes of Giorgione'.[131]

---

[130]   *Ibid.*, p. 255.
[131]   Ruskin, *Stones of Venice*, II, p. 79.

'One of Whom we Know but Little...'
John Loughborough Pearson and the Ecclesiologists

HILARY J. GRAINGER

In short, there never was such a church more completely built in independence of our society than this has been: when therefore in this church we behold the ideas for which we have fought and suffered obloquy so prominently exhibited, we can indeed thankfully and sincerely offer our *Deo gratias* as the only suitable expression of our feelings at such a result. It is not the first time we have been similarly placed, neither, we may venture to assert, will it be the last, but from all its contingent circumstances it is a very memorable occasion.[1]

The church referred to by *The Ecclesiologist* was Holy Trinity, Bessborough Gardens, London, designed by Pearson in 1849 and completed in 1852.

John Loughborough Pearson (1817–1897) was to hold a unique position within the development of the Gothic Revival in England. In the first appraisal of Pearson's work since the John Newberry articles in the *Architectural Review*, of 1896,[2] Herman Muthesius was swift to acknowledge in his *Neuere Kirchliche Baukunst*, published in 1901,

A figure surpassing all others in the history of the new English church architecture and in whom one must perhaps find the high point of its development is the great church builder J. L. Pearson. His activity as a church architect had begun in the 1840s and stretched without a break until his death in 1897 which cut off this extraordinarily vigorous man in full career. Thus he had not only experienced the whole course of the Gothic Revival from its beginning, but had also played one of the leading roles within it.[3]

Basil Clarke's laudatory critique of Pearson's work appeared in his *Church Builders of the Nineteenth Century*,[4] of 1938, David Lloyd's chapter on

[1]   *Ecclesiologist*, 13 (1852), p. 409.
[2]   E. Newberry, 'The Work of John Loughborough Pearson, R.A. Part I, Ecclesiastical', in *Architectural Review*, 1 (1896–7), pp. 1–11. Part II, 'Domestic', 1 (1896–7), pp. 69–82.
[3]   H. Muthesius, *Die Neuere Kirchliche Baukunst in England* (Berlin, 1902), p. 34.
[4]   B. F. L. Clarke, *Church Builders of the Nineteenth Century* (London, 1938), pp. 196–209.

Pearson was included in *Seven Victorian Architects*,[5] in 1976 and Anthony Quiney's pioneering and authoritative monograph was published in 1979.[6] These various evaluations of Pearson's achievements serve to locate his productions in the wider social, religious and architectural context of the nineteenth century, with all its concomitant complexities.

Given the existence of such detailed appraisals, this chapter concentrates on a smaller range of churches selected as a focus for examining the nature and depth of Pearson's engagement with the philosophy of the ecclesiologists. It has to be said from the outset that little is known about Pearson's relationship with the ecclesiologists. How he reacted to their comments and criticisms is more to be seen from his buildings than any other source. Quiney's contention that Pearson was

> the only great Victorian church architect whose career extended through the three phases of the Gothic Revival, and the only one to produce great works representative of each of them,[7]

provides a valuable starting point. St James, Weybridge, Surrey (plate 1), designed in 1845, with later additions, exemplifies Pearson's conformity with the ecclesiological ideal of the 1840s and 1850s, which was to reach consummation in Holy Trinity, Bessborough Gardens (1849–52). The latter established Pearson's position alongside Pugin, Scott and Carpenter. St Peter, Vauxhall, designed in 1860 and built 1863–64, made explicit the influence of Continental sources and confirmed Pearson's emerging personal style. St George, Cullercoats, Northumberland (1882–84), raises a series of issues about the ways in which Pearson carried the Society's ideal into his mature works, despite departing from strict adherence to ecclesiological authority; this departure resulting from the formulation of an entirely personal interpretation of Gothic architecture, informed by foreign study. Historical perspective allowed Nikolaus Pevsner to conclude

> the layman would be wrong, if he thought that the great church builders were copyists of the past. A man like Pearson was so steeped in the thirteenth century's elements that he could use them for buildings which taken as a whole had no period authority.[8]

Cullercoats, as we shall see, is a particularly fine testament to this view (plates 54 to 56).

However, Pearson's early commissions reveal a deep admiration for the Middle Ages, the orthodoxy proposed by Pugin and a close adherence to the principles of the Cambridge Camden Society. This warrants some

---

[5] D. Lloyd, 'John Loughborough Pearson, noble seriousness', Chapter IV in J. Fawcett (ed.), *Seven Victorian Architects* (London, 1976), pp. 66–83.

[6] A. Quiney, *John Loughborough Pearson* (London & New Haven, 1979).

[7] *Ibid.*

[8] N. Pevsner, Introduction, in J. Fawcett (ed.)., *op. cit.*, p. 6.

explanation, given his late membership, beginning in June 1859. In 1852, the Camdenians confessed that 'the architect [of Holy Trinity, Westminster] is one of whom we know but little – but still he is not one of those of his profession with whom we have been particularly thrown. We do not know if more than two or three of our committee have ever seen him'.

It would appear then that, as Basil Clarke observed, Pearson's 'understanding and appreciation of mediaeval work developed independently, and he did not involve himself in ecclesiological controversies.'[9] However, as Quiney points out, somewhat remarkably,

> Though he [Pearson] accepted Pugin as his master – who did not in the 1840s? – within a few years he had built churches which Pugin had aspired to but never really achieved, churches which fulfilled the ideal of the early phase of the Victorian revival of the Gothic style. 'Pearson's nearly perfect fourteenth-century church at Bessborough Gardens ... summarised it all.'[10]

Eastlake had been the first to argue that Pearson,

> like many of his fellow students, began his professional career with the fixed intention of adhering not only to the principles of Medieval art, but to national characteristics of style. His early churches in Yorkshire and other parts of England, many of which were erected between 1840 and 1850, exhibit those characteristics in an eminent degree.[11]

Eastlake's assessment is perhaps rather narrow and misleading. Pearson's early churches were indeed Gothic, often very good Decorated, as the Camdenians liked, but Eastlake ignores the fact that Pearson began his career learning the whole gamut of architecture, classical as well as Gothic, working in both and also in a kind of Tudor/Jacobean. He trained under the Durham County Surveyor, Ignatius Bonomi, whose father Joseph had established some distinction as a designer of Neo-classical country houses. Moving to London in 1842, Pearson worked for Anthony Salvin for six months before superintending the building, in 1843, of the new hall and library at Lincoln's Inn, Holborn, for Philip Hardwick, in which the Tudor style was applied to a modern building. Despite the strong Neo-classical flavour of much of his early training and his own heterogeneous architectural interests, Pearson was drawn increasingly towards the possibilities offered by the Gothic alternative. Through the almost exclusive Tractarian patronage at the start of his career (much of it from Camdenians), he was inevitably bound to the Gothic style, although he was never to abandon the broad base of his studies. He always harboured the hope that he might execute a Classical building. Indeed, in 1878 Pearson was to design in a sort of François Ier at

9   Clarke, *op. cit.*, p. 197.
10   Quiney, *op. cit.*, p. 17.
11   C. L. Eastlake, *A History of the Gothic Revival* (1872), reprinted in the Victorian Library (Leicester, 1970), p. 303.

Westwood House, Sydenham, and in the 1890s, in Elizabethan and Jacobean respectively, at Emmanuel and Sidney Sussex Colleges, Cambridge.

Eastlake's assessment can be accounted for partly by the fact that *A History of the Gothic Revival* was published in 1872 before many of Pearson's mature works had been executed. However, even at this early stage, Eastlake considered Pearson to be more than a competent and committed Gothic grammarian and placed him in the group of pioneers of the Gothic Revival who 'began to design with greater confidence', to be followed by those who 'profiting from their labours, advanced upon their taste'.[12] Eastlake was equally perceptive in recognising the significance of St Peter, Vauxhall, designed in 1860. By 1896, with the benefit of further historical purchase, Newberry contended,

> A careful and conscientious student of old Ecclesiastical Architecture, his early works bear rather the impress of his surroundings than of that vigorous and sometimes daring individuality which is displayed in his more mature efforts.[13]

It is therefore worth exploring first the issue of 'independent' development. Gothic was in the ascendant in the early 1840s and Salvin had introduced Pearson to its latest domestic manifestations – Tudor and Elizabethan. Furthermore, Pearson's tracings and copies of Salvin's churches, which were for a while favourites of the Cambridge Camden Society, provided him with an insight into both the aims of the Society and the newly defined discipline of ecclesiology. Clarke believed Pearson's early churches to be 'not particularly interesting', other than containing 'hints of his future developments'.[14] Indeed Quiney suggests that to date, Pearson had been involved only in church building of an 'indifferent' quality. So how did Pearson come to judge the Society's mood so perfectly, so early in his career? The answer lay with Pugin, who had undoubtedly influenced the prevailing climate of the 1840s. The ecclesiologists, however, with characteristic immodesty claimed much of the credit for the establishment of a genuinely Christian architecture and this was indubitably the case. Through *The Ecclesiologist*, they were, indeed, very influential. Benjamin Webb boasted as early as 1843, about 'the calm and steady diffusion of the views and principles advocated by the Society, and especially the growing adoption of them by professional architects'.[15] Some of this success can be attributed to the Society's publication, in 1841 *A Few Words to Church Builders,* one of a series of highly influential publications, which ran to second and third editions in

---

12 *Ibid.*, p. 209.
13 Newberry, *op. cit.*, p. 2.
14 Clarke, *op. cit.*, p. 198.
15 B. Webb, quoted in J. F. White, *The Cambridge Camden Movement, The Ecclesiologists and the Gothic Revival* (Cambridge, first published 1962, reissued 1979), p. 183.

1842 and 1844. It is fair to suppose that Pearson would have been aware of this iteration, heralded by Pugin as 'the first distinct publication which has issued from the present Establishment.'[16]

By all accounts a reticent man, Pearson displayed a reluctance to allow his early designs to be publicized, preferring instead to rely on personal contacts and friendships for patronage. In the first ten years of independent practice, from 1843, twelve churches were either built or rebuilt. His early connections with the landed gentry and, more importantly, the newly appointed Tractarian clergy, who doubtless kept him abreast of recent theological developments, formed the basis of his early commissions, all in the East Riding of Yorkshire.[17] As already suggested, this series bound him to Gothic. Built respectfully out of local stone and acknowledging local surroundings, these churches were representative of that type which, according to Eastlake, 'reproduced with more intelligence and with a better sense of adaptation'[18] than some contemporary work by other architects. Slavish imitation and copyism were never issues with Pearson.

The chapel at Ellerker (1843) was designed for Canon Townsend of Pearson's native Durham. Recent research by Anthony Quiney has established that the consecration was attended by a large number of Tractarians, many of whom were to play a crucial role in the subsequent pattern of Pearson's patronage. The initial design, however, was not by Pearson, but by William Hay Dykes. It immediately attracted the attention of the reviewer in *The Ecclesiologist*,[19] who commended it as 'extremely simple, but withal so ecclesiastical and correct in its character that it reflects great credit upon the taste and skill of the architect'.[20] The use of Middle-Pointed detail, of course, accorded entirely with the Society's preferences. *The Ecclesiologist* had, however, 'grumbled about the poor design of the gable cross over the east window and the lack of another cross over the nave gable; further it wanted the roof pitch to be raised to make it equilateral and carried up to the lower weathering on each side of the bell gable'.[21] The deficient pitch of the roof in the design by Dykes was unfortunate given the Society's assertion as early as 1841 that 'A high pitched roof is far more essential to the Christian effect of a church than a tower or spire'. Dykes was to be replaced by Pearson who, it would seem, 'had already included these features in his

16 A. W. N. Pugin, *Present State of Ecclesiastical Architecture in England*, republished from the *Dublin Review* (London, 1843), p. 61.
17 For a full account of early patronage, see A. Quiney, 'The Door Marked "Pull": J. L. Pearson and his First Clients in the East Riding of Yorkshire', *Architectural History* (1998), pp. 208–19.
18 Eastlake, *op. cit.*, p. 209.
19 *Ecclesiologist*, 2 (1843), p. 165.
20 *Ibid.*
21 Quiney, 'The Door Marked "Pull"', p. 212.

design by the time of the review, or, heeding the review at the start of construction, made certain that the finished church should display them'.[22] While Pearson's design followed Pugin's instructions in respect of 'lavish buttressing', the 'hints of future developments' are apparent. Quiney detects an independent element in Pearson's concern for Classical harmony in the proportions of the chancel arch. This interest in Classicism perhaps resulted from his training with Bonomi and Salvin. Classical elements in Pearson's work, anathema to the Society, were to develop further and were always destined to set him apart in some ways from his Gothic Revival contemporaries, including Butterfield, Street and Carpenter.

Ellerker was followed by the rebuilding of Elloughton (1844–6), in the neighbouring parish. The more generous patronage of this church, together with its chapel of ease at Wauldby, afforded Pearson greater scope for decoration. In both buildings there are pulpits approached by means of passages passing through the chancel wall, a feature which Quiney points out, had been illustrated by Pugin in *The Present State of Ecclesiastical Architecture in England*. Furthermore, the bellcote at Wauldby resembles that by Pugin at Warwick Bridge, also illustrated by its designer.[23] The roof pitch, however, is much steeper than Pugin's and the chapel at Ellerker, presumably in response to the criticisms of *The Ecclesiologist*. A third commission was at neighbouring St Mary, Ellerton, designed in 1848.

Without doubt, the most important of the East Riding commissions was that of North Ferriby, designed in 1846. In the same year, Pearson designed what was tantamount to a 'twin' church: St James at Weybridge in Surrey (plates 51 to 53). The drawings exhibited at the Royal Academy were jointly signed by Pearson and Arthur Johnson, who would appear to have been more than an assistant. Weybridge was not only typical in style to those illustrated in Pugin's *The Present State of Ecclesiastical Architecture in England*, but was also the perfect embodiment of the 'beau ideal' of the village church proposed by the Society, with aisles and complete with western tower and spire. Furthermore, the circumstances surrounding the establishment of this new church exemplify the problems encountered by the new breed of High Churchmen in their efforts to undertake any kind of reform.

The old church at Weybridge, designed in a picturesque Home Counties vernacular with a wooden belfrey, was to all intents and purposes, a preaching box, which had served its purposes unchallenged during the eighteenth century. However, William Giffard, newly appointed rector in 1846, was to initiate sweeping changes in Weybridge. He was well-connected, being the son of Sir Ambrose Hardinge Giffard, Chief Justice of Ceylon, cousin of Lord Halsbury, a Lord Chancellor, and brother-in-law of William

---

[22] *Ibid*. Quiney provides a full explanation of the background to this commission.
[23] Quiney, *John Loughborough Pearson*, p. 23.

Webb Follett, Attorney General. More importantly, 28-year-old Giffard was an ambitious Tractarian, intent upon making not only liturgical changes, but also in establishing an appropriate architectural expression for those changes. He had been married by Samuel Wilberforce,[24] Bishop of Oxford, for whom Street worked as diocesan architect, which raises the possibility that he may have been one of the new 'Good Churchmen', a movement of church reform, initiated by Bishop Wilberforce which had encouraged 'a raising of standards in priestly life, liturgical knowledge and competence and business administration.'[25] On arrival in Weybridge, Giffard began by radically altering the pattern of services. Communion, which had been celebrated once a quarter with a congregation of ten, was celebrated, after his appointment in 1846, once a month, with an average attendance of twenty or thirty. By 1847, there were sixty communicants. Giffard appears to have made friends with some of the richer and newer families in the village, including the Reverend Dr Thomas Spyers and Thomas Feetham, two wealthy men who had come to live in Weybridge. Spyers was a Doctor of Divinity from Hampshire, aged 41, who ran a school for young gentlemen in the High Street. He was not the curate of St James, despite his qualifications, but was the church treasurer and sometimes preached and conducted funerals. Feetham was older, hailed from Durham and had made a considerable fortune out of coal. These two men, together with Giffard, were largely responsible for the new church, which became known as 'the cathedral of the Thames Valley'.[26] Soon after his arrival, Giffard drew attention to the 'dilapidated condition' of the church, 'totally preventing the possibility of enlargement'.[27] This swept aside the option supported by Neale's publication of 1843, Church Enlargement and Church Arrangement, which stipulated that the removal of Georgian additions, such as pews and the inclusion of stained glass, gilt roodscreen and painted and frescoed walls was preferable to a total rebuilding. Giffard harboured higher ambitions. The parish of Weybridge had a population of 1064, for which 278 sittings were provided in the church. Of these 278, 60 were appropriated to two families, in galleries built by faculty, and 20 were in the chancel, the property of the rector, so that there were, at the disposal of the parish, only 198 sittings of which number only 65 – including 40 seats for the school – were free for the poor. Giffard asserted that

> The new church for which a new site has been given, is intended to contain 608 kneelings of which number 305 will be free and unappropriated for ever. The cost of erection will be £5,000, the whole of which sum it is impossible

---

[24]   Also present at the Ellerker consecration service.
[25]   For this and other information about St James' church, Weybridge, I am indebted to local historian Helen Kempster. See her A History of St James' Parish Church, Weybridge (Weybridge, 1997), p. 34.
[26]   Ibid., p. 31.
[27]   Ibid.

to raise in a small rural parish. It is hoped therefore that those who are desirous of promoting the Glory of God and the good of their fellow Christians will embrace this opportunity of offering to Him the abundance wherewith He has blessed them.[28]

It would appear that although subscriptions were forthcoming, there was a great deal of resistance to the idea of a new church. Indeed, such was the level of feeling that several parishioners were moved to write poetry in defence of the old, shabby original church. In 1848, when the new church was nearing completion, a statement of accounts showed that its cost had exceeded original estimates. The Rector and Dr Spyers made themselves legally responsible for the shortfall between subscriptions and payment, a sum of £1,721 8s. 7d. A letter was sent out to the townspeople suggesting that parishioners would not wish to occupy a church for which they had not made payment, especially in view of the fact that so many would no longer be paying any pew rent. This only served to inflame the situation. There was call for a referendum and a 'vitriolic letter' was issued anonymously accusing the Rector and Dr Spyers of 'incapacity and mismanagement of funds' and even more seriously, accusing them of misappropriating the collections for 'unusual and illegal uses which are repulsive to the feelings of the communicants'.[29] The high feeling prevailed long after Giffard's untimely death in 1855. It is clear that parishioners, in invoking adjectives such as 'illegal' and 'repulsive', were referring to the high church rituals which were being practised in the new church. Giffard and Spyers were blamed for the encouragement of High Church ritual and all that had ensued.

When the church was finally completed it had cost £7,334 16s. 11d., all but £500 of which was raised by donations and collections. A scrutiny of the subscription lists reveals that the church was paid for by a remarkably small group of individuals, sixty at most, and out of the total donations, very nearly half emanated from just seven people, The Rector, his sister Dame Jane Follett, Dr Spyers and Thomas Feetham then churchwarden, Nathaniel Milne, a local lawyer and the Misses Walker.[30]

It is not clear as to why Pearson was appointed as architect, but as a devout High Anglican, Pearson might have met Giffard through mutual friends and might well have been aquainted with Thomas Feetham, given the Durham connection. Pearson was certainly to remain close friends with Spyers, making extensive alterations to his houses in Weybridge and Hampshire.[31]

---

28 *Ibid.*
29 *Ibid.*, p. 32.
30 *Ibid.*, p. 33.
31 Spyers conducted Pearson's wedding ceremony in Hampstead in 1862 and Pearson went to stay with Spyers at Wallop Lodge after the sudden death of his wife Jemima in 1864. Pearson's only son Frank was sent to Dr Spyers' School. In

One of the things which must have infuriated opponents of High Church practices would have been the fact that Weybridge had been designed so explicitly for High Church ritual. As originally built, it comprised a five-bay aisled nave with a short chancel and a west tower. The nave and aisles were 63 feet long and 50 feet across, with north and south porches. The high pitched roof, with exposed rafters, was wholly acceptable to the ecclesiologists, as was the distinction made between the nave and chancel by the chancel arch.

Of considerable interest is the fact that Pearson was to be involved with additions and alterations to the church over a period of more than thirty years. The changes that were introduced parallel some of the developments in contemporary ecclesiological thinking. In 1858 Pearson added a small chancel aisle at the head of the south aisle and the large south chancel aisle in 1865, reflecting the needs of the growing congregation. However, the most interesting development was that of the enlargement and embellishment of the chancel. In 1883 the marble pavement in the chancel was laid, adding to the colour in the church, but more importantly, in 1885, the chancel arch was raised by ten feet, providing the spacious eastward vista. Later that year the benefactors asked the Rector if they could pay Pearson to make additional structural changes which would further enhance the east end of the church. He lengthened the chancel by ten feet and raised the roof and walls by six feet. The altar was lengthened, the steps were raised from three to five, and a new east window was designed. A new reredos was fashioned from red and white Derbyshire alabaster. The Society's early reluctance to sanction a reredos had been tempered and Pearson was anyway in tune with its insistence that niches should contain figures. At the reconsecration of the chancel sixteen clergy were reported to have processed and the Bishop of Guildford preached that it was the same spirit which led the woman in the Gospel to pour the valuable oil on Jesus' head, that had led to the beautifying of the chancel. This act, argued the Bishop, was a protest against niggardliness in worship.[32] The issue of the function and design of chancels had long exercised the Society and had been the source of a great deal of controversy. The issue of occupancy of the chancel to some extent had been resolved after 1841, with the design of Leeds parish church and the introduction of the cathedral form of choral service. John Jebb was convinced that the proper place for the choir was the chancel and the ecclesiologists had accepted this principle in 1843. Pearson and Giffard had ensured that the choir stalls were included in the original design for Weybridge. In 1846, the Society had called for further refinement, in the form of a distinction between chancel and 'sacrarium'. The latter was to be distinguished by its elevation or by the altar rail. Pearson employed both

the Pearson family he was always known as 'dear Dr Spyers'. My thanks to Anthony Quiney for this information.
[32] Kempster, *op. cit.*, p. 39.

devices and further distinction was secured by the new inlaid marble sanctuary floor (plate 2). In 1867 *The Ecclesiologist* contended that so long as this arrangement prevailed, 'so long will the living witness exist in the Church of England to the especial dignity of the Eucharist, to the antiphonal form of worship, and to the special attributes of the clerkly function'.[33] In 1893 Pearson was engaged again, to supervise the final alterations, which involved the chancel walls being covered with Derbyshire alabaster, intersected by bands of mosaic. The angels of the old and new testaments were added just below the roof. Great care seems to have been taken in selecting colours to harmonise with the stone with which the church is built. Weybridge is one of the few churches by Pearson to be decorated in this costly way, the finance coming from an anonymous donation. Basil Clarke argued that the chancel at St Augustine's, Kilburn, consecrated in 1880, 'suffers from an excess of ornamentation, and is less successful than many of Pearson's: he did better work when he had less money to spend'.[34] At Weybridge, the contrasting richness works well.

Of further interest are the tower and spire, features which were later to characterise Pearson churches. In common with its 'twin' in North Ferriby, Weybridge has a west tower with broached spire and a chancel with a north vestry. Churches such as these were illustrated by Pugin, 'but the example closest to them in elevation and detail as well as in plan is Pugin's church at Kirkham in Lancashire'.[35] North Ferriby follows the Puginian model closely whereas at Weybridge the obvious point of departure is the tower: 'its angled buttresses are carried up to the top of the belfry stage to join the broaches of the spire, resulting in an increased verticality which makes the tower appear unpleasantly thin'.[36] A lithograph[37] produced just before the church was built shows an intended parapet with corner pinnacles to the lofty, 200-foot spire, an arrangement favoured by Pearson as late as 1871 in the case of St Augustine's, Kilburn (spire completed in 1897). The spire at Weybridge, completed in 1856, soars directly from the tower, with no architectural features to break its line (plate 3). Its positioning was entirely in accordance with the Society's contention that, 'Every church, not being cross, should have its tower or bell-cote at the west end, unless there be some stringent reason to the contrary'.[38]

David Lloyd maintains that 'Neither North Ferriby nor Weybridge owes anything specific to the architectural traditions of the region in which it is set; both are modelled on the typical high medieval church of the east or

[33] *Ecclesiologist*, 28 (1867), p. 231.
[34] Clarke, *op. cit.*, p. 202.
[35] Quiney, *John Loughborough Pearson*, p. 23.
[36] *Ibid.*
[37] Illustrated in Kemspter, *op. cit.*, p. 21.
[38] *Ecclesiologist*, 4 (1845), p. 205.

south Midlands which the ecclesiologists of the time idealised'.[39] Although at
North Ferriby, Pearson in fact reset many of the stones from the former
parish church into his own. Eastlake, in suggesting that the peculiarity of the
structure of Weybridge 'is the use of chalk for all the pillars, arches and
ashlaring', the effect of which he felt to be 'very striking',[40] raises the issue of
local materials. The chalk, veined with white marble, was obtained from
quarries near Guildford and draws attention to the fact that Pearson
invariably employed local materials in his designs.

Pearson's continued involvement can presumably be explained by his
close personal friendship with Spyers. It is interesting to note, however, that
in 1872, to meet the demands of the increase in population, the thriving parish
turned instead to the Society's favourite, William Butterfield, for the design of
a daughter church, St Michael and All Angels. Pearson is recorded, however,
as giving a church bible.

In 1849, three years after the design of Weybridge, the attention of *The
Ecclesiologist* was drawn to the simultaneous laying of the first stones of Holy
Trinity, Westminster and St Matthew, Westminster. The former and costlier
was a gift of the 'single munificence of the Archdeacon of Westminster'[41] and
designed by Pearson, the second was to be built by subscription to the designs
of G. G. Scott. *The Ecclesiologist* felt that its readers 'must have rejoiced at this
striking sign of returning Christianity'.[42] Both churches were to be designed in
Middle-Pointed. 'London may yet become "la ville des beaux cloches"',[43]
waxed the commentator. Holy Trinity was so admired by *The Ecclesiologist*, it
was afforded not only a long paragraph when nearing completion in 1851,[44]
but a four and a quarter page article on completion in 1852,[45] perhaps
signalling the change of attitude, on the part of the Society, towards city
churches which was to become more apparent in the early 1850s.

> It is in short a structure of considerable architectural importance, and only as
> such would merit a detailed notice in any journal which interested itself in
> the artistic development of London. But, as we need hardly say for ourselves,
> we are ecclesiological before we are artistic, and there is another aspect of
> this church peculiarly our own, and particularly gratifying to us, under
> which we are called to notice it.[46]

The Ecclesiologist, while predictably lamenting the absence of a chancel
screen, was particularly struck by the fact that

[39]   D. Lloyd, *op. cit.*, p. 68.
[40]   Eastlake, *op. cit.*, p. 76.
[41]   *Ecclesiologist,* 10 (1849–50), p. 235.
[42]   *Ibid.*
[43]   *Ibid.*
[44]   *Ecclesiologist,* 12 (1851), p. 321–2.
[45]   *Ecclesiologist,* 13 (1852), pp. 409–12.
[46]   *Ibid.*, p. 409.

Holy Trinity church exhibits every distinctive feature of that system of church arrangement which it has been the constant and primary intention of our pages to advocate, as the embodiment of the Church of England, for which we have often been laughed at and often taken to task, and in which we have triumphed. Such a triumph of these principles as the church now before us, is far more striking, viewed *ab extra*, and more complete, than would be that manifested in a structure of even superior merit erected under our own more immediate influence. The founder of this church,[47] there can be no motive of delicacy for mentioning the simple state of things, is personally quite unknown to us. All that we do know of him is that he is a cathedral dignitary of some age, and therefore of a school antecedent to any we have helped to found. Whether hitherto esteemed to be high church or low church we cannot tell, we cannot even tell whether he has even read a single line of any of our publications, or if he has, what he thinks of their tone or their contents ... We first read of the intention of the Archdeacon of Westminster building a church in the public papers, and the actual works have been the only sources through which we have even acquired of ideas of its character.[48]

Together with the fact that the Society did not know if more than two or three of the committee had ever seen Pearson, arguing that 'he was not one of those of his profession' with whom the Society had been 'particularly thrown',[49] it was no wonder that Holy Trinity was seen as an overwhelming endorsement of the success of the Society's mission.

The argument was proposed that Holy Trinity, Westminster, might have been more spacious, more elaborately moulded, more richly decorated, but 'the crowning merit of this church is the very complete exhibition which it offers of the ritualism of the Prayer Book'.[50] With its cruciform ground plan, it is one of Pearson's most orthodox examples of Middle-Pointed, so favoured by the Society. It consisted of a nave with aisles and clerestory and north and south porches, transepts, and a chancel with aisles of one bay and sacristy to the north. There was a central tower and spire, nearly 200 feet high, an arrangement welcomed by *The Ecclesiologist*. The tower was open internally to a height of 55 feet and formed a lantern, which was groined over. Praise was not unbounded. The plan

has unfortunately necessitated lantern piers of such a bulk as seriously to impede sight between the chancel and the nave. The former is divided into two parts at the spring of the arches of the one bayed aisles projecting

---

47 Bentinck was a Tractarian and had been at the Ellerker consecration with his wife. He also commissioned works from Pearson. These included in 1856, the commission to design new National and Commercial Schools to adjoin the church and recommended him to some of his ecclesiological friends, among them the Champernownes of Dartington, who employed Pearson in Devon.

48 *Ecclesiologist*, 13 (1852), p. 409.

49 *Ibid.*

50 *Ibid.*

chapel-wise from the transepts, and at the division a considerable rise is indicated. This has unfortunately brought the east and two side sanctuary windows which are very long far too low.[51]

There were regrets that the ground plan had not brought the chancel into the lantern, an arrangement considered 'very dignified' and one which 'would have been eminently adapted to the general motif of this church'.[52] The commentator argued that with the lantern space left unseated, 'we fear that an erroneous impression might be given that the true arrangement takes up more room, otherwise available for congregational use, than is actually the case, at least in this church'.[53] The arrangement of open transept seats running east and west, was disapproved of because occupants were unable to see the altar, on account of the eastern lantern piers. They could only see one another. *The Ecclesiologist* mused, 'Further reflection the more convinces us that long transepts are not suitable to the parochial worship of the English Church'.[54]

The chancel roof was considered 'too thin, and striving too much after ornament'.[55] The pillars of the nave were alternately octagonal, consisting of clusters of four larger and smaller shafts, 'with a complexity too great for their size'.[56] The fittings of the sanctuary comprised three sedilia, first considered 'simply and well treated',[57] and admired for their being recessed in the thickness of the wall with stone elbows, but then, in a subsequent article deemed to be 'too much carved for that class of sedilia'.[58] The chancel was unusually wide, indeed wider than the nave. *The Ecclesiologist* argued that as a result of the awkward site and resulting dimensions, 'the whole aspect of the nave was that of an attempt after an effect not to be attained within the given dimension'.[59] Newberry later concurred that 'this treatment gives an effect of great spaciousness to the chancel without the reason for it being, at first sight apparent'.[60] The aisle windows were considered by *The Ecclesiologist* to be rather too short, the clerestory of three lights was considered to be 'injured by the roof overhanging, as no ancient roof of any church so large and ornate a character ever did'.[61] The stone carving inside was 'far too finely and thinly done, and we could detect many traces of Perpendicular feeling in the

[51] *Ecclesiologist*, 12 (1851), p. 231.
[52] *Ecclesiologist*, 13 (1852), p. 410.
[53] *Ibid.*
[54] *Ibid*, p. 411.
[55] *Ecclesiologist*, 12 (1851), p. 231.
[56] *Ibid.*
[57] *Ibid.*
[58] *Ecclesiologist*, 13 (1852), p. 410.
[59] *Ecclesiologist*, 12 (1851), p. 231.
[60] Newberry, *op. cit.*, fn. 2, p. 3.
[61] *Ecclesiologist*, 12 (1851), p. 231.

mouldings'.[62] The Society, of course, condemned Perpendicular decoration as 'meretricious enrichments',[63] arguing the style to be defective on moral grounds. The gravest criticism was reserved for the east window which had seven lights. It was considered to have been placed 'much too low' and therefore 'depriving the santuary, altar and window, of that solemnity which they would otherwise possess'.[64] The same criticism had been levelled at Ferrey's St Stephen, Rochester Row, despite the window standing higher than it did at Holy Trinity. *The Ecclesiologist* advised that 'even at the loss of having to sacrifice some of the actual glass, building up the lower portion of the window, so as to afford space for some kind of reredos however simple',[65] would have been wise. Sceptical readers were exhorted to visit the desired effect of the east window either at Thomas Cundy's First-Pointed church of St Barnabas, Pimlico (1850) extolled for 'its ritual completeness', or Carpenter's Middle-Pointed St Mary Magdalene, Munster Square (1849), a particular favourite of the Society, or the Third-Pointed St Andrew, Wells Street. The arrangement of the chancel and sanctuary, in terms of the number and distribution of the steps, as well as the fittings deserved praise, 'indicating as it does, that Mr Pearson felt how much is depending on this for maintaining the distinction between these two more sacred portions of a church'.[66]

The chancel rose from the crossing upon two steps, was stalled with stalliform seats with subsellae on either side and richly paved with encaustic tiles. At the west end, at either side, was an allotted stall for the incumbent and curate, described by *The Ecclesiologist* as being 'the legitimate reproduction for our times of the stalls decani and cantoris'.[67] The panelled wooden altar was deemed 'too small, an error, which it has been attempted to rectify, though not efficiently, and with an ungraceful result, by means of a mensa larger than the substructure'.[68] The font stood in the south aisle to the west of the porch and was elaborately carved with black marble shafts. In general, *The Ecclesiologist* considered that there was too much carving and that 'a simple treatment might have been more effective'.[69] Other commendable features, rewarding to the Society, included the treatment of the two storeyed vestry as a semi-circular pile attached to the southside of the chancel considered 'very felicitous' having been graced by a 'very pretty and well-placed chimney'.[70] There was a spacious two storeyed sacristy on the north side. The journal

[62] *Ibid.*, pp. 231–2.
[63] *Ecclesiologist*, 4 (1845), p. 270.
[64] *Ecclesiologist*, 13 (1852), p. 411.
[65] *Ibid.*
[66] *Ibid.*
[67] *Ibid.*, p. 410.
[68] *Ibid.*
[69] *Ibid.*, p. 411.
[70] *Ecclesiologist*, 12 (1851), p. 232.

commended 'the half domestic feeling thrown into this portion of the church'[71] which was deemed ingenious.

In conclusion, it was felt that Mr Pearson would excuse any critical remarks

> upon a church which we could not but regard with pleasure, indicative as it is of the great revival which has taken place in our church architecture, and which he has so laudably seconded in the present instance.[72]

Bolstered with an unswerving confidence in their convictions, the Society saw Pearson as a valuable ally, all the more so because of his acknowledged independence. The approval of Pearson's work by the Society would seem to have been secured.

Praise was widespread. Pugin is reputed to have considered Holy Trinity, Westminster, to be in advance of anything then accomplished by the Gothic Revival. Charles Barry admired it and George Gilbert Scott pronounced it to be the 'best modern specimen of a fourteenth-century English church' that London could then boast.[73] The nave, with its considerable height, was considered by some to be the most effective portion of the church externally. Newberry drew the inevitable comparison with St Stephen's, Rochester Row.[74]

Pearson's work between 1857 and 1862, involved the designs for twelve new churches and many major additions to others. Considered without foreknowledge of his later, mature works, they reveal an enthusiasm for those tenets of High Victorian architecture practised by Butterfield and Street and promoted by Ruskin. Although constructional polychromy and vigorous decoration are employed, there is evidence of Pearson's natural restraint, which was to become much more apparent in his later works, especially at St George, Cullercoats. Nevertheless, it has been remarked that had Pearson died at this stage of his career, he would have been regarded very differently, 'not as a gentle Late Victorian architect, but as a violent Mid Victorian one'.[75] Three of these new churches were reviewed by The Ecclesiologist in 1860. St Leonard, Scorborough, in the East Riding of Yorkshire, begun in 1857, St Peter, Daylesford, Worcestershire, designed 1857–59, built 1859–63 and St James, Titsey, Surrey, designed 1859, built 1860–61.

These reviews show that Pearson, unlike many of his contemporaries, was still very much in favour. This could be accounted for by the fact that the

[71] Ecclesiologist, 13 (1852), p. 412.
[72] Ecclesiologist, 12 (1851), p. 232.
[73] It is not clear whether these remarks were made personally to Pearson, but they are quoted in his obituary in the Building News (17 December, 1897), p. 866.
[74] Newberry, op. cit., p. 3.
[75] I. Nairn, in N. Pevsner and I. Nairn, Buildings of England, Surrey (Harmondsworth: Penguin Books, 1962), p. 409, quoted in Quiney, John Loughborough Pearson, p. 60.

Society was moving towards more original designs and away from the 'correct' fourteenth-century model. St Leonard, Scorborough, welcomed as 'a design of great merit and originality',[76] conformed to the ideal of a spacious chancel, a western tower, south-western porch and a vestry at the north-west of the chancel. The west window, comprising two trefoil-headed lancets with a foliated circle under a common hood, conformed entirely to the ideal. The Society had been considerably exercised by the inclusion by some architects, of triple lancets. The ensuing debate in the early 1840s came to typify their intransigence.

The style of St Leonard was the approved canon of very early Geometrical Middle Pointed, but as was the case with many Pearson churches, it was the tower which was of particular interest. The ecclesiologists considered it to be almost overwhelming, occupying as it did, almost the full breadth of the nave. There is no belfry stage, instead the lucarnes of the stone broach octagonal spire are so large as to become the belfry. The spire rises from between four lofty angle pinnacles capped with pyramidal spirelets. *The Ecclesiologist* conceded 'The whole composition, though unusual, is dignified and effective'.[77] They admired the constructional polychromy in both the steeple and the body of the church, in particular, the elaborate detailing of the angle shafts of the tower, the incised bands of panelling and the rich wall cornices. The 'generally rich ornament'[78] of the interior was, however, tempered in accordance with Pearson's natural refinement, which was soon to mark him apart from his more enthusiastic contemporaries. The tenor of the detailing was French, by now acceptable to the Society. As a result of Ruskin's 'pervasive' influence, 'any sign of foreign study was automatically considered meritorious'.[79] This detailing, together with the employment of colour, served to articulate the architectural structure, showing a point of departure from Ruskin, and altogether different from Butterfield. It is interesting to note that classical elements, to date restricted to the proportions of St Peter, Vauxhall, but to become such a significant ingredient in Pearson's mature work, appear in the interior details of St Leonard, Scorborough, although one would have expected these to attract adverse criticism, they escape comment, probably because what is Gothic is pretty overwhelming. *The Ecclesiologist* instead enthused about the treatment of the reredos, 'with sunk panelling and incised diaper work'.[80]

Restorations in general provoked some of the most barbed comments from *The Ecclesiologist*. The *Journal of the Royal Institute of British Architects* argued that 'It has been well said that Mr Pearson was better known to the

---

[76]   *Ecclesiologist*, 21 (1860), p. 49.
[77]   *Ibid.*
[78]   *Ibid.*
[79]   Quiney, *John Loughborough Pearson*, p. 53.
[80]   *Ecclesiologist*, 21 (1860), p. 49.

public as a 'restorer' than a producer.[81] Indeed after Scott's death, in 1878, Pearson inherited a great deal of well documented restoration work, much of it involved with cathedrals. *The Ecclesiologist* could often be dismissive or jejune, at worst vituperative in its reviews of restorations. Their first evaluation of three of Pearson's restorations, all for Sir Tatton Sykes, appeared in 1860 and once again, he fared well. St Martin, Nibley, Gloucestershire, involved the restoration of the chancel in 'a good First-Pointed style', the Society's second preference. The reviewer considered the ritual arrangements to be 'good, except that the subsellae are not continued to the westernmost stalls on each side, and that there is no screen',[82] always a point of contention with the Society. St Mary, Kirkburn, 1856–57 and St Michael, Garton-on-the-Wolds, 1856, both small Romanesque parish churches in the East Riding of Yorkshire, were also restored for Sykes. Guided by the existing remains and character of the nave of St Michael, Garton, Pearson rebuilt the chancel in Romanesque. *The Ecclesiologist* could not resist the opportunity of expressing its own preferences, 'We doubt whether enough remained to justify this course in preference to the choice of Middle-Pointed for the additions'.[83] In 1859–62, Sir Tatton further commissioned Pearson to redesign St Margaret, Hilston, in Yorkshire, another small, Norman rural church. The two original doorways on either side of the church and the north porch-door, were retained but Pearson designed the rest of the church in the 'Early-Pointed style'. The plan comprised nave, chancel, with north west sacristy, and western tower. The roofs were appropriately lofty and the tower was described as having 'a well developed belfry-stage (with a shafted pairs of lancets on each side) is roofed with a solid, quadrangular, pyramidal spire. This is likely to be effective'. *The Ecclesiologist* waxed,

> The ritual arrangements are correct; and the internal decorations are unusually sumptuous. In particular, there is an alabaster reredos of three recessed Romanesque arches, with dwarf marble shafts, sculptured behind with a representation of the supper at Emmaus. The east wall on each side of the altar (which by the way is richly and properly vested) is ornamented with incised patterns filled with cement, and with a rich horizontal band containing heads of saints in circular medallions.[84]

The floor of the chancel was laid with encaustic tiles, so admired by the ecclesiologists, which were arranged in carefully combined patterns. The church fittings, all designed as usual by Pearson, were in accordance with the Society's ideas.

---

[81] *Ecclesiologist*, 21 (1860), p. 52.
[82] *Ibid.*
[83] *Ecclesiologist*, 23 (1862), p. 181.
[84] *Ecclesiologist*, 23 (1862), p. 60.

As early as 1854, Pearson had discussed with Lord Hotham the possibility of enlarging, or even replacing South Dalton church. Contemporary accounts of the church make explicit reference to the fact that Pearson's recent commission for St Leonard, Scorborough, by his agent and local landowner, James Hall, acted as a catalyst for Lord Hotham's commissioning of the design for St Mary, Dalton Holme, Yorkshire in 1858. *The Ecclesiologist* described the style in its 1862 review as 'Middle-Pointed, of strictly English character, and of a very ornate type'.[85] There was a chancel arch, much favoured by the journal, dividing the 57-foot nave and the 34-foot-6-inch chancel. The roofs were of timber and this prompted the reviewer to remark that 'We can speak with high admiration of the design of this church. The absence of a stone roof (considering the sumptuousness of the structure) and of colour, constructional or otherwise, is to be regretted'.[86] The east and west windows however, are filled with excellent painted glass by Clayton and Bell, one of Pearson's favourite firms of craftsmen.

The tower and spire, rising to 200 feet, were considered to be 'exceedingly good'. The 'great simplicity', of the base was relieved by the west window, 'a geometrical composition of five lights'. The steeple was thought to be 'altogether most effective'. Eastlake considered the church to be 'a pure specimen of Middle-Pointed, treated indeed with more originality of detail than the Church of the Holy Trinity at Westminster'[87] completed in 1852. Internally, the quite ornate detailing distinguished it from Pearson's early Middle-Pointed style. In St Mary, Dalton Holme, High Victorian vigour is confluent with the elegance of the Decorated style.

In the five years that elapsed between St Mary, Dalton Holme (1858–61) and the design for the small church of Appleton-le-Moors, Yorkshire (1863–6), Pearson moved from 'pure Middle-Pointed' to the 'severest form of French Gothic, with an admixture of details almost Byzantine in character',[88] representing what Eastlake called 'the extraordinary vicissitudes' through which modern Gothic had passed. This is clearly apparent from the entirely different character of Pearson's Holy Trinity, Westminster (1849–52) and his St Peter, Vauxhall (1863–64). Standing on opposite sides of Vauxhall Bridge, only eight or ten years had elapsed, but in the interval the study of Medieval French architecture, 'fostered by the influence and example of ... Sir Gilbert Scott' had 'exerted a modifying influence on the Architecture of England'.[89] It was not only Scott's influence. Street had promoted the study of northern European Gothic and, following Ruskin's example, advocated Italian Gothic. During the 1850s and 1860s,

---

[85]   *Ibid.*
[86]   *Ibid.*
[87]   Eastlake, *op. cit.*, p. 303.
[88]   *Ibid.*, p. 304.
[89]   Newberry, *op. cit.*, p. 3.

Pearson had travelled extensively in Europe, visiting France, Germany, Belgium and Spain and the influence of his study of continental ecclesiology, which gave him the chance to look at other buildings and also scenery, became startlingly apparent in his designs for St Peter, Vauxhall. Described by Clarke as 'Pearson's first really fine church',[90] St Peter raises a number of issues, reflecting as it does, changes in the Society's thinking. As suggested above, from the early 1850s the Society appears to have revised its ideas about the appearance and decoration of churches, and admitted to taking a particular interest in metropolitan churches. Perhaps influenced by its move to London in 1846, it acknowledged the need for city churches to display 'distinctive' character. In 1850 Cundy's St Barnabas, Pimlico, was criticised by *The Ecclesiologist* as being 'too little like a town church', while Ferrey's St Stephen, Westminster had 'too much of a country-church look'.[91] In the same year Street, whose first London church of St James-the-Less, Westminster (designed 1859, built 1860–61) had received unreserved praise from the journal, lent weight to the argument with his contribution, *On the Proper Characteristics of a Town Church,* in which he established six points 'as of essential importance in town churches', namely the avoidance of rusticity, the relaxation of steep roofs, the advocacy of clerestories, the regularity of parts, the questioning of the 'invariable use of the spire' and finally, the issue of height which was 'of immense importance, and to be obtained at all costs'.[92] The subject was subsequently taken seriously by the ecclesiologists. A. J. Beresford Hope, by then President of the Ecclesiological Society, argued for the reconciliation of the needs of large congregations with those of preferred liturgical practices, expressed in Gothic form. In 1861 he published *The English Cathedral of the Nineteenth Century,* in which he made unashamed concessions to utilitarianism. He advocated the radical proposal for the cathedral system, forming a nucleus of evangelism in the large towns. He proposed: 'The religious institution which will undoubtedly grow out of rational and business-like endeavours to evangelize large populations, whether it is called so or not, will, in every large town, virtually be a cathedral, and it had therefore best be moulded openly and honestly into a cathedral shape'.[93] Pearson provided a response to Beresford Hope's call for such a building to include administrative accommodation as well as classrooms, those 'adjuncts' which have now developed into the parish hall.[94] In the same year, *The Ecclesiologist* made special mention of the schools and parsonage-house

[90] Clarke, *op. cit.*, p. 198.
[91] Quoted in White, *op. cit.*, p. 186.
[92] G. E. Street, 'On the Proper Characteristics of a Town Church', *The Ecclesiologist,* 11 (1850), pp. 230–3, quoted in White, *op. cit.*, pp. 186–7.
[93] A. J. Beresford Hope, *The English Cathedral of the Nineteenth Century* (London, 1861), quoted in White, *op. cit.*, pp. 190–1.
[94] *Ibid.*

JOHN LOUGHBOROUGH PEARSON

adjoining St Peter, Vauxhall, arguing that they would 'make the whole group one of singular merit and beauty'.[95] Addressing the Society's Annual Meeting of 1864, Hope recognised the limitations of the Church of England's view that a church should be a church and not a preaching-house. He thought instead that 'it ought to be a church and a preaching-house too'.[96] He cited Dutch examples and advocated the use of large, unified spaces, of wide naves, narrow aisles, or no aisles at all. High vaulted structures would pronounce by their heavy mass their place in the urban environment.[97] His ideas met with a largely favourable response, although Archbishop Thorp was 'staggered' and 'upset'. 'It is all new, all heretical ... exactly the contrary of what we used to say'.[98] The scale of churches was very important, if they were to stand as beacons above the architectural cacophony of the busy town streetscape and skyline. If St James, Weybridge, represented the 'beau ideal', then St Peter, Vauxhall, due to be consecrated a few days after the Society's meeting, 'embodied the new ideal of a massive, unified brick structure'.[99] Cited by Beresford Hope, St Peter shows strong Continental, particularly French, influence and yet the church and associated buildings were remarkably in tune with the modified orthodoxy of the ecclesiologists, who were by this time quite prepared to countenance foreign influences. Eastlake had declared Street's St James-the-Less, Westminster, in every respect 'eminently un-English'.[100] Pearson's Vauxhall church and associated buildings, their sources and the circumstances surrounding their commissioning and production, are well documented by Quiney. Briefly, the church's Romanesque plan consists of a nave and chancel of equal height and width, a western narthex and baptistry, narrow nave aisles, a low double aisle on the north side of the chancel, with the vestries beyond, and the organ chamber on the south side.

The inclusion of a triforium and a clerestory showed Pearson to be entirely in accordance with Street's belief that clerestories 'in town churches were the right place for the admission of light'.[101] The windows of the clerestory, together with the large double west windows serve as the almost exclusive light source. The main internal space was lofty, given the width, and yet the arcades and aisles were quite low. The arrangement also showed Pearson's homage to English abbey churches, the blank triforium of the nave (arcaded and glazed in the chancel), being particularly reminiscent of Tintern.

---

[95] *Ecclesiologist*, 22 (1861), p. 58.
[96] A. J. Beresford Hope, address to the Annual General Meeting of the Ecclesiastical Society, 1864, quoted in S. Crewe (ed.), *Visionary Spires* (London, 1986), p. 78.
[97] Crewe, *op. cit.*, p. 78.
[98] *Ibid.*
[99] *Ibid.*
[100] Eastlake, *op. cit.*, p. 321.
[101] *Ecclesiologist*, 11 (1850), p. 320.

This supports Goodhart-Rendel's view that 'those who had been the first to stray in foreign pastures – Pearson, Bodley, Street, were the first to return and crop their native fare ... patriotic stalwarts such as Micklethwaite and G. G. Scott junior, were few'.[102] Of great significance is firstly the fact that St Peter's is entirely vaulted with stone ribs and brick infill, following the example of the brick vaulting of the chancel and sanctuary in Street's St James-the-Less, Westminster (1859), described by *The Ecclesiologist* , as 'a stroke of artistic power',[103] on the part of Street. It was no less enthusiastic about Vauxhall, remarking that 'The speciality of the church is its groined roof, this feature gives this fine design unusual importance'.[104] This represented quite a departure from their original advocacy of open timber roofs! Secondly, Pearson introduced the apsidal termination so admired by the French, but conspicuously eschewed by medieval church builders in England, in preference to the square east end. *The Ecclesiologist* invoked Murano as a source, although Quiney proposes San Abbondio, at Como.[105] The important point was that it was unbuttressed. The Society had originally upheld the view that an apsidal east end 'in England, is very inadvisable. It is un-Anglican, it is unnatural'.[106] It has been argued that Pearson naturalized the apse:

> Gilbert Scott could not do it – his looks pinchbecked and Frenchy; Street could not – his looks mean and stupid. All the other masters avoided it; the minor men rushed at it with excruciating results. Pearson succeeded. His are the only truly English apses in existence. But he grew to love them less and less, and reverted to the square end with fine compositions of grouped lancets.[107]

Truro Cathedral (1880–1910) and All Saints, Hove (1889–1901), are good examples of apses, although the Catholic Apostolic Church, Paddington, Brisbane Cathedral and Woking Convent Chapel all have apsidal eastern ends.

    The Ecclesiologist's enthusiasm for St Peter, Vauxhall in 1861 also reflected its changing attitude, the reviewer concluding, 'We have seldom had a more important design – or one more thoroughly satisfactory – than this before us'.[108] Dixon and Muthesius conclude 'With its massive unbroken brick walls, strict horizontals and general heaviness, St Peter's belongs to High Victorian design proper; but the vault – a great rarity in Britain at the time – and the simplicity of the plan also point to Pearson's final style from 1870s

---

102 H. S. Goodhart-Rendel, *Architectural Review*, quoted in Clarke, *op. cit.*, p. 176.
103 'Churches in London', *Ecclesiologist,* 22 (1861), p. 57.
104 *Ecclesiologist,* 23 (1862), pp. 272–4.
105 Quoted in Quiney, *op. cit.*, p. 70.
106 'A Few Words to Church Builders', 3rd. edn. (Cambridge, 1844) [1st published 1841], p. 14.
107 Clarke, *op. cit.*, p. 207.
108 *Ecclesiologist,* 22 (1861), pp. 57–8.

onwards'.[109] The church not only presaged Pearson's later works, but provided a prototype for many urban parish churches in the later nineteenth century, including those of James Brooks, who Dixon greatly admired.

St George, Cullercoats is a comparatively late work commissioned by Algernon George Percy, the 6th Duke of Northumberland in commemoration of his father, George. In common with many mature Pearson churches, Cullercoats suggests the 'spaciousness of a small cathedral'. By the time Pearson was engaged to design St George, Cullercoats, between 1878 and 1881, the influence of the Society had waned. However, the church provides an opportunity to explore the ways in which Pearson's late works carried forward the ideals of the Society.

The 5th Duke, a notable builder of churches, exemplified the Society's ideal patron. In the Tynemouth area alone he is recorded as endowing five new parishes and building three new parish churches, these being St Paul, Whitley Bay, St John, Percy Main and the now-demolished St Peter, Low Shields. In continuing the tradition, his son evidently considered a new church to be a fitting tribute to his father. There had been plans put forward for the rebuilding of Tynemouth Priory and apparently George Gilbert Scott had been involved. The 6th Duke had thought that a share in such a project would be of interest as a memorial, but by 1877 he would appear to have decided otherwise. The choice of site for the new church was significant. The Duke was developing his estates in the area. The Winter Gardens and Aquarium, the Grand Parade and the impressive new streets in Tynemouth, all bearing Percy names, signalled expansion and the growing prosperity anticipated in the 1880s. The magnificent railway station at Tynemouth was designed to cater for the influx of visitors, particularly in the summer. The new church was intended to be the distinguished centrepiece of these developments.

The new parish of St George, Cullercoats, was created to serve the area of the seafront between Tynemouth and Whitley Bay and was accordingly taken from two of the 5th Duke's earlier parishes. The village of Cullercoats, hitherto part of the parish of St Paul, Whitley Bay, was joined with the new streets of Tynemouth, including Percy Park, Percy Gardens and Percy Park Road, taken from the parish of Holy Saviour, Tynemouth. St Paul had been designed in 1864 by the 5th Duke's favourite architect, Salvin, for whom Pearson had worked in the 1840s, but the church is without particular architectural merit. Holy Saviour was designed by local architects J. and B. Green, in 1841, as an aisleless nave, preaching box, with lancet windows.

The scheme for Pearson's new church progressed quickly, appearing in the Duke's Business Minutes in September 1877. By July 1879, the church was

[109]   R. Dixon and S, Muthesius, *Victorian Architecture* (London, 1978), p. 219.

named as St George and is quoted as 'containing about 800 sittings'.[110] Interestingly, the Duke's architect is first cited as being Mr Rich of Newcastle. The sites for the church and vicarage had to be extended and the entire enterprise is said to have cost the Duke nearly £25,000. However, the Duke's most significant legacy was the appointment of Pearson. Quite why Pearson was chosen is not clear, but it is of interest that he originated from Durham, the original Diocese of the Parish, before the establishment of the Diocese of Newcastle in 1882. It is likely that the Duke would have been attracted by Pearson's national reputation, built up since his move to London in 1842. St George was consecrated by the Bishop of Newcastle in December 1884. St Hilda, Darlington (1887–8) is now the only Pearson church in his native Durham diocese.

By the 1870s Pearson's career was firmly established and confirmed by his selection to design a new Cathedral for the revived See of Truro. This was to be the first Cathedral to be built in England since the Middle Ages. It was in the same year, 1878, that Pearson accepted the commission for St George and it is possible to find the detailing of Truro echoed at Cullercoats.

The Duke, a High Anglican, must have been aware of the strong Methodist and Non-Conformist tradition of the area – there were several Methodist churches in Cullercoats village alone – and so the appropriateness of style and liturgy would have been an issue.

Basil Clarke nominated St George as 'an example of Pearson's simpler and less ambitious style',[111] an extraordinary assessment, given its dramatic shape. He quoted Bishop Lightfoot, who argued that it 'set an ideal of something better in the way of church building than that to which we are commonly accustomed'.[112]

An undated plan, presumed to be by Pearson, shows a cruciform arrangement, in which only the nave has aisles. The plan is notable for its clarity and simplicity; there are no side chapels, and no complicated but characteristic vistas of columns. The lectern was positioned in the centre of the crossing in Pearson's plan and the pulpit on the corner of the south side of the chancel arch. Significantly, it would have been difficult for many of the congregation in the transepts to see the altar. It was not until 1909 that the seats were removed from the north transept to create the Lady Chapel.

The church as built has a six-bay nave with aisles and west porches, crossing with single-bay transept to the north, tower and spire to the south, a single-bay chancel and polygonal apse. The western narthex is treated as a baptistry, the font being placed between the entrances and central to the nave aisle. There were no projecting porches, the westernmost aisle bays are so

---

[110] 6th Duke of Northumberland, Business Minutes, Alnwick Castle, Northumberland, vol. 64 (April–September, 1879), p. 111.

[111] Clarke, op. cit., p. 207.

[112] Quoted in Clarke, op. cit., pp. 207–8.

designed to open to the outside, providing access on either side of the west end of the church (plate 4). There is a western gallery, a favourite in Pearson churches, often placed as a kind of canopy over entrances, over pulpits, or both. This espousal of galleries indicates the extent to which the influence of the Society had waned by the 1880s. At Cullercoats, the gallery acts as a canopy over the font. The dimensions of the church are on a grand scale, the tower and spire are 180-feet high and the nave is 98-feet long and the chancel 50 feet. The church is 55 feet in width and the underside of the stone vault is 42 feet above the floor. The church is marked on the original plan as having 705 sittings, 294 in the nave, 304 in the aisles, 45 in the north transept and 32 in the chancel.

Internally, there are explicit parallels with St Peter, Vauxhall. The nave has a three-storeyed elevation, and like Vauxhall has an arcade supported by substantial cylindrical piers, a blank triforium and a clerestory, taller than that at Vauxhall. The windows have plate tracery set in deep reveals. The arches of the quadripartite rib-vaulting spring from shafts with bases set on the capitals of the main arcade. As Quiney points out, 'there is an appropriate northern precedent in Whitby Abbey'.[113] Reference has often been made to the classical elements in Pearson's work, and it is the case, that although the proportions differ, the churches of both Vauxhall and Cullercoats are set out in a similar fashion, based on the Golden Section. Even in his earliest works, a sympathy with Classicism was always confluent with a love of Gothic, perhaps a legacy from his early training with Bonomi. These classical elements in Pearson's mature works, his feeling for proportion and the subtle employment of the Golden Section which account for the individuality of his style, would have been anathema to the ecclesiologists. The three-storeyed elevation extends into the chancel, the ground storey arcade becoming blind as there is no ambulatory, as was the case at Vauxhall. The apse at Cullercoats is polygonal and not semi-circular. The vaulting at St George's is interesting; the nave and the crossing have quadripartite vaults. The two bays of the sanctuary are constructed with one octopartite vault. A transverse rib divides the vault in order to accommodate the two bays of the side elevations. Pearson unusually employs a ridge-rib linking the crossing to the boss from which radiate the ribs of the apse. Optically, this feature serves to extend the length of the sanctuary. 'Through its simplicity and proportions, the interior has an almost archaically classical feeling'[114] (plate 5). The aesthetic effect of the church depends upon the subtle spatial perspective created by Pearson; 'the width and height slightly decrease first between the nave and the crossing, and then between the crossing and the sanctuary'.[115]

[113] Quiney, *op. cit.*, p. 154.
[114] *Ibid.*, p. 155.
[115] *Ibid.*, p. 154.

Stylistically, the church was thirteenth-century in character, severe and simple in plan, outline and massing, and indeed in detailing, qualities which seem entirely in keeping with its exposed position close to the sea. It was built entirely from sandstone quarried locally at Billy Mill, North Shields, although the vestries which were added in 1935, to mark the church's Jubilee, were built with stone from the demolished church of St Peter, Newcastle.

Of further interest are the external features. The symmetry is broken only by the tall, graceful steeple which rises above the south transept, of which Ruskin would have approved. This arrangement was used at St John, Upper Norwood, too. Towers, always subject to review and criticism by the Society, in terms of 'placement, height, openings and termination' were one of the most imposing features of Pearson's designs. At the International Exhibition of 1862 in London and later in 1867 in Paris, he exhibited a large sheet of designs for towers in his early manner, about half of which had been built. His later designs were far more accomplished, 'invariably vigorous and graceful, and many of them genuine masterpieces'.[116] Sadly, many remained unexecuted; these include St Michael, Red Lion Square, St Alban, Birmingham and St Stephen, Bournemouth, which lacks its spire. Pearson was most influenced by northern French models, particularly Early Gothic of Normandy, which often emphasised the square contour, confining any enrichments within this outline. His storeys are 'graded with enviable intuition', while the junctions of his towers and spires were 'always masterly'.[117]

The solid-looking spire at St George, built of stone, is all the more interesting for its lack of corner pinnacles. The buttresses are slight, but provide a strong vertical accent and the spire is typically short. The Society would once have disapproved of its position, favouring towers at the west end, but in the 1880s Pearson might well have recognised the 'stringent reason'[118] for relocating it to be one of creating an emphatic presence. Together with the dominant, unbuttressed and undecorated apse (plate 6) which rises uncompromisingly from the ground, the tower and spire serve to anchor the church to its rather precarious position, abutting the edge of the coastline, as it falls away to the beach below. Ruskin would have been pleased by its attempted sublimity. Pevsner maintains that 'it gives a fine accent to a drab sea front'.[119] The apse is relieved only by narrow shafts at its angles and string courses marking its storeys. The two lower storeys are blank. The clerestory lancet windows are linked by blind narrow arches to the vertical

---

[116] 'The Late John Loughborough Pearson, R.A.', *Journal of the Royal Institute of British Architects*, 3rd. series, 5 (1898), p. 120.

[117] *Ibid.*

[118] *Ecclesiologist*, 4 (1845), p. 205.

[119] N. Pevsner, *Buildings of England, Northumberland*, reprint (Harmondsworth, 1974), p. 120.

shafts. This lends a horizontality which accords visually with the horizontal division between the aisle and the clerestory of the south elevation. This continuity is interupted only by the dramatic intervention of the steeple.

One of the most significant aspects of St George's is that it remains an outstanding example of an unspoilt Victorian church. Over a century of changing liturgical fashions have left the building more or less unaltered. The font, the pulpit, the High Altar (though it is always covered except on Good Friday), the credence table, the altar rails, the choir screens and the pews were all designed by Pearson and are still in position today. The chalice, paten and flagon, which were the gift of the Duchess of Northumberland on the occasion of the consecration of the church in 1884, were also designed by the architect. The great standard candlesticks before the High Altar, together with the huge Altar Cross which now stands in the Choir Vestry, are also believed to be the work of Pearson. Compared with St James, Weybridge, there is no polychromy and the church decorations rely on spatial and proportional refinement. Indeed, originally there was no stained glass. Interestingly, a great burst of activity in the improvement of the church resulted from the arrival of Canon Blount Fry (1904–46). Although weekly celebration of the Eucharist had been the norm since the church's consecration Canon Fry was almost certainly the first vicar to wear vestments, although a finely woven chasuble stored in the sacristy hints at earlier attempts to impose vestments on an unwilling congregation.[120] The marble steps and mosaic floor in the chancel and sanctuary were brought from Italy during the course of Fry's incumbency.

Cullercoats was originally gas-lit, the holes in the roof through which the pipes conducting the gas to the mantles below are still visible. In 1905 the church was provided with mains electricity and Pearson's son Frank designed the distinguished and unobstrusive light fittings situated between the nave pillars. Dramatic and daring in its composition, sparing in its decorative detailing and above all, inimitative, St George, Cullercoats exemplifies Pearson's finest churches of the 1870s and 1880s which justifiably secured his position as one of the leading church architects in Europe.

In conclusion, it has been suggested that the Camdenians did

> directly beget a race of architects, beginning with Butterfield, who were far more than copyists, and whose works are of a beauty and grandeur that will endure. We do not count among them Sir Gilbert Scott, the supreme popularizer of the style. Nor even James Brooks, though he contributed noble brick and continental details to the revival in a series of Anglo-Catholic churches built from his heart. But Butterfield, Pearson, Bodley, Scott II and Micklethwaite are men who, though conforming ex animo to the Gothic canon, wielded the style with an originality, fineness

---

[120] I am indebted to Paul Ritchie, organist at St George, Cullercoats, for this and other material relating to the history of the church.

and power which redeemed and justified the Camdenist enthusiasm.[121]

Pearson's irrefutable contribution to the development of the Gothic Revival would appear to have been made independently from the Society and yet his work was invariably in tune with its vacillations. This was a remarkable achievement. As Scott was to realise, the Society 'demanded obedience, totally and unconditionally. When it changed its mind on any subject, architects were supposed to do likewise'.[122] Scott claimed 'It had many years before been a saying of mine, that there was no class of men whom the Cambridge Camden Society held in such scorn, as those who adhered to their own last opinion but one; and this sentiment has been the great inheritance and heirloom of their imitators'.[123] Pearson would seem to offer the antithesis, in that his work seemed almost to anticipate the vagaries of their thinking on such diverse issues as the admittance of foreign styles, the development of urban churches, the role of chancels, vaulting and apses. Pearson's own development, which was, in many ways a microcosm of the development of the Gothic revival, invariably concurred with the evolution of ecclesiological thinking, although that was not, of course, his avowed intention. The Society was probably quick to espouse success, rather than to initiate it. It certainly embraced Pugin who worked according to his own convictions. Butterfield did likewise, although his *Instrumenta Ecclesiastica* was, however, influenced by Ruskin. Pearson read heavily from both, but there is no solid evidence that he did what he was told, certainly not after 1857, by which time the Society was becoming a spent force anyway. Pearson certainly responded to various influences, but often did produce results of which the ecclesiologists disapproved. His family reported that he would consider an architectural problem from his own viewpoint, governed by propriety and, one suspects, more by an early reading of Pugin and later of Ruskin than the issues raised monthly in *The Ecclesiologist*. Unlike some other Victorian church architects, he was to remain in favour with the Society. Perhaps his escape from vitriolic attack can be accounted for by his representing, at the most fundamental level, the perfect embodiment of the type of architect so loved and sought by the Society. It is important to remember that Pearson produced some very fine non-ecclesiatical work, Treberfydd House, Quar Wood, Westwood and the Astor Estate Offices, but he was nevertheless conventionally religious and never entered into controversies, or even corrected public mis-statements relating to him and his work. It is undeniably the case that the Society stressed the importance of 'art for religion's sake' very vehemently, as a reading of Neale's *Hierologus* affirms. The Society saw the ideal architect as 'a single architect, alone, pondering deeply over his duty to do his utmost for the

[121] E. Milner-White, 'Architecture of the Oxford Movement', *Theology*, 27 (1933), pp. 25-6.

[122] White, *op. cit.*, p. 127.

[123] G. G. Scott, *Personal and Professional Recollections* (London, 1879), p. 206.

service of God's holy religion, and obtaining by devout exercises of mind a semi-inspiration for his holy taste'.[124] One of the fundamental beliefs of the Society was that architects 'must take a religious view of their profession', for a 'religious ethos, we repeat, is essential to a Church architect'.[125] Pearson was an architect who apparently made his Communion before picking up his pen to design a new church, declaring his aim 'to think what will bring people soonest to their knees'[126] Above all, Pearson observed that fundamental principle of 'Sacramentality', which Neale and Webb regarded as 'the clue to genuine Christian Architecture'.[127] The ecclesiologists' belief that only good men could build good churches, a contention shared by Pugin and others, was perfectly embodied in Pearson, a man of devout faith whose talents were 'all put to the purposes of achieving a noble monumentality, at once mysterious and thoroughly conceived, to serve the purposes of the Christian faith'.[128]

I am very grateful to Anthony Quiney for his help in the preparation of this chapter, to Helen Kempster and Paul Ritchie for material relating to St James, Weybridge and St George, Cullercoats, respectively and finally to my parents who brought me up to love Cullercoats and the North East.

[124] *Ecclesiologist*, 4 (1845), p. 277.
[125] White, *op. cit.*, p. 70.
[126] This oft-quoted anecdote relates to Pearson at Truro and was interpreted by Bishop Wilkinson's biographer, in what Anthony Quiney believes to be 'in a spirit of pious reverence that borders on the romantic'.
[127] White, *op. cit.*, p. 70.
[128] A. Quiney, 'St Stephen's Church, Bournemouth and John Loughborough Pearson', published in the *Festival Booklet to Celebrate the Centenary of the Architect John Loughborough Pearson* (Bournemouth, May 1997).

George Wightwick : a Thorn in the Side of the Ecclesiologists

ROSAMUND REID

George Wightwick, son of William and Ann Maria, was baptised on 16 November 1802, at St Mary, Mold, Flintshire. St Mary's was traditionally Low Church, but it was here, in April 1876, four years after Wightwick's death, that the noisy proceedings of the Easter Vestry were reported in the local press, and the vicar was accused of making the church a laughing stock. There were complaints that he had introduced unwelcome innovations: a surpliced choir, processions, crosses on the Communion table, and 'all those tawdry decorations we are acquainted with in Roman Catholic churches',[1] in fact all those excesses associated with High Church ritualism that George Wightwick, architect, critic and writer, came to despise.

This dichotomy between Low Church functionalism and High Church dogma is the key to understanding Wightwick's attitude towards ecclesiology and the theories that were the foundation of his church design. It was these theories that proved to be a thorn in the side of the ecclesiological establishment, while at the same time they were the cause of Wightwick's downfall as a church architect. To look at the situation more broadly, however, and with the hindsight of a century and a half, Wightwick's quarrel with ecclesiological principles represented a challenge to the Cambridge Camden Society that was eagerly and vituperatively taken up. It was a challenge that others might have made, and some in fact did make, as correspondence and comment in *The Ecclesiologist* confirms. But other architects, such as R. D. Chantrell of Leeds, more mindful perhaps of their reputations and the effect on their pockets of such censure, seemed unable or unwilling to sustain their arguments over a number of years in the way that Wightwick did.[2] For this reason he has a place in the history of the Camden

[1]   *Wrexham Advertiser*, Saturday 22 April 1876, Clwyd Record Office D/GW/1960.
[2]   Chantrell, already well established as a church architect in Leeds before the Cambridge Camden Society was formed, drew regular criticism from *The Ecclesiologist* in the mid-1840s. However, despite much of it being unwarranted or factually inaccurate, after his initial attempt to defend his position, he seems to have taken the line of least resistance, and done everything he could to adopt the

Society, not just as a protagonist, but as representative and guardian of one of a number of alternative perspectives on church design, all of which differed to some extent from the ideas of the Society. Moreover, it seems that Wightwick indirectly represented the community within which he lived, and that through his work he was expressing the views of 'the man on the Clapham omnibus'.

George Wightwick was born in Mold on 26 August, 1802. He was an only child and left fatherless at the age of nine when his father was accidentally drowned. Four years later his mother was married again, to William Damant, a widower with two children, a son and a daughter whom Wightwick was later to marry. The family moved to London and Wightwick attended school in Tooting for two years, before being articled in 1818 to Edward Lapidge of Grosvenor Square, where he completed his training as an architect in 1823. Two years later he travelled for some months in Europe, before taking employment with John Soane, as companion and amanuensis. This period lasted only eight months, punctuated by personal differences between the two men, although out of it came some mutual respect and a sharp and sensitive portrait by Wightwick of his difficult employer.[3] However, it is clear from Wightwick's diary that, even at this early stage of his career, he found himself challenging authority that he could not respect. It was this uncompromising characteristic that was later to be observed in his relationship with the Cambridge Camden Society.

In 1829, shortly after his time with Soane, Wightwick left London and followed his family to the West Country, where he established himself in Plymouth, and was later invited by John Foulston to join his practice prior to retirement. Although the terms and date of their partnership are not known, by 1832 responsibility for Foulston's commissions was being assigned to Wightwick, who went on to become the leading architect in Plymouth and Cornwall. It was only after his move out of London that Wightwick established his reputation as an architect, and he was undoubtedly successful in the public buildings and private houses that he was commissioned to design. After the Plymouth blitz some of Wightwick's work there remained, buildings that represented his contribution to Foulston's classical vision of the city, notably the Esplanade on Plymouth Hoe and the nearby Crescent, both designed early in his career. Wightwick was responsible also for the original

Society's principles. See C. Webster, *The Life and Work of R. D. Chantrell, Architect*, unpublished M. Phil. Thesis, University of York, 1985.

3   George Wightwick, 'The Life of an Architect', p. 107. Wightwick's autobiography was never published in its entirety, but only in parts, in *Bentley's Miscellany*, as 'The Life of an Architect': vols xxv, xxxi (1852–4) and vols xlii, xliii (1957–8). For the purposes of this essay reference is made to the bound edition of these parts held at the Royal Institute of British Architects Library, annotated by the author, and to which page numbers relate.

South Devon and East Cornwall Hospital and for the Devon and Cornwall Female Orphanage, both in Plymouth, neither of which is standing to-day. His noted Post Office and Public Library in Devonport, buildings in the Neo-classical style influenced by his own preference for Italianate, were destroyed in the Second World War. Further afield Wightwick was responsible for Calverleigh Court at Tiverton, Trevarno House at Helston and Watermouth Castle at Ilfracombe. He was also well known in the West Country as a raconteur, humorist and lecturer in the fine arts, and it was through these skills that he was able to build up the social network through which he promoted himself as an architect.

Wightwick designed a total of nine churches, of which eight were certainly built. Three were in west Devon: Holy Trinity, Plymouth (1840); Christ Church, Plymouth (1845) – both now demolished – and Brownston Chapel, Modbury (1844), which is now a private house. The others that were built were in Cornwall: St Michael and All Angels, Bude (1834); Lanner Chapel, Lanner (1840); St Mary, Portreath (1841), demolished; St John, Treslothan (1842); and St Peter, Flushing (1842). The ninth church was finally built at North Brentor, a village on the edge of Dartmoor, although the design was modified and it was not ascribed to Wightwick. He also designed two chapels, one Baptist and the other Congregational, as well as cemetery buildings which are still in use to-day, all in Plymouth. His designs were influenced by his love of Gothic, and inspired by his own ecclesiological theories, even though these did not conform to the increasingly ritualistic views of the established church. The philosophy that guided him throughout his life was based on an alliance of principle and pragmatism, which was confirmed in his architectural designs as well as in his extensive writing. As he himself explained, he left 'the *spiritual* fight in more fitting hands', while he confined himself to 'the mere combat *artistical*'.[4]

It seemed, however, increasingly difficult for Wightwick to separate the 'spiritual' from the 'artistical', as his arguments became more rigid and hostile to the ecclesiological theory that was becoming equally firmly established. Nevertheless he conceded that his church designs should be inspired by his love of Gothic, stating that it was only in this way that he could express his theories. Thus, of course, he supported to some extent the beliefs of the Camden movement. Wightwick confirmed this opinion through research, tracing the development of architectural choice, and quoting figures from the first fifteen Reports of the Church Commissioners. This research showed that Gothic was selected for 174 churches, only forty being designed in the Classical style. While maintaining that utilitarian requirements should be the first consideration, he believed that Anglo-Gothic was the most

[4] 'Modern English Gothic Architecture', *Weale's Quarterly Papers on Architecture*, 3 (1845), p. 2.

appropriate style, its keynote the reconciliation of richness and simplicity.[5] After he retired, in 1862, an article by Wightwick was published in the *Builder*, 'The Question of Classic and Gothic Architecture dispassionately considered', where he set forth his argument for the use of Gothic in all ecclesiastical buildings, stating:

> The purpose of the church is *so* especial that we require everything which fitness, expression, and association can bring to bear on the question; and, as the most direct means of answering *all* these, the whole country, without one dissentient, has declared at length for the Gothic, and nothing but the Gothic, as applied to church purposes.[6]

Mordaunt Crook, in his paper on Regency Architecture in the West Country, suggests that Wightwick allowed the Gothic wing of his practice to become hopelessly out of date.[7] Out of date his practice may have seemed, but this is partially to misread Wightwick's principles. In fact the nature and strength of his beliefs simply could not have allowed him to conform to the authority of *The Ecclesiologist*. As Wightwick said in his paper on ecclesiastical architecture, in the construction of a church mere utilitarian principle was not sufficient; indeed 'nothing shall be admitted which does not supply a convenience or symbolize a feeling'.[8] He discussed his views in *Weale's Architectural Papers*, stating that an architect must have both the feeling for the grand and the picturesque, as well as the executive abilities of an artist. Principles of convenience should ensure adequate space for public worship, within range of perfect hearing and with full and free view of the officiating clergy, and the chancel should be open to the general view, uninterrupted by either pulpit or desk, but not so deep as to render the clergy remote from the congregation. With his usual pragmatism Wightwick suggested that pillared aisles and 'extreme longitudinal extent' could be 'hostile' to free sight and hearing, and that, when vision was obscured space would be occupied by 'the idle or dissolute'.[9] The principles of expression should find their focus in the cruciform design, and wherever practicable the doctrine of the Trinity should be represented. Wightwick acknowledged Pugin when he agreed that, while

5   'On the Present Condition of Architecture in England', *Weale's Quarterly Papers on Architecture*, vol. ii, p. 6.

6   George Wightwick, 'The Question of Classic and Gothic Architecture dispassionately considered', from *The Builder*, 1 March 1862, p. 153, and March 15 1862, p. 180.

7   J. Mordaunt Crook, 'Regency Architecture in the West Country: the Greek Revival', *Journal of the Royal Society of Arts*, cxix (1971), p. 449.

8   George Wightwick, 'Ecclesiastical Architecture; on the Determination of some Principles for the Establishment of an Ecclesiastical Style of Architecture expressing the Reformed Church in England', December 1844, published as an article (periodical uncertain), offprint held at the RIBA Library.

9   'Modern English Gothic Architecture', *Weale's Quarterly Papers on Architecture*, vol. iii, p. 2.

there should be liberal sanction for decorative splendour, no feature of ornament should be employed that did not afford convenience or typify suitable feeling, so that the free employment of splendour would be consistent with the integrity of the building, thus adding to the 'truth-telling whole'.

As far as they went, therefore, these arguments were not so far removed from those opinions expressed in *The Ecclesiologist*, and were unlikely to give rise to quarrel. So far so good. The trouble, however, came when these theories were translated into reality, as it became clear that Wightwick's designs went beyond his published opinions, challenging Camden Society precepts and outraging ecclesiological sentiments. The ideas expressed both by his church design and through his published work caused mayhem within the ranks of the ecclesiologists; this response, articulated as it was through the pages of *The Ecclesiologist*, can only have drawn attention to Wightwick's simple and functional places of worship, and thus elevated them in importance.

Almost all Wightwick's churches had certain features in common. They were box-like in outline, with a bell-tower but without aisles or pillars. The most distinctive feature, however, was the shallow chancel. In not one of his churches is the chancel the prescribed one third the length of the church, and in two of them there is no chancel at all, so that the Church Militant is duly acknowledged, while the Church Triumphant is not so celebrated. Moreover, in several of Wightwick's plans the siting of the pulpit appears to reduce the importance of the altar, thus promoting the preacher and the spoken word, and seemingly to demote the sacramental aspects of worship. This practice was deeply offensive to the Camden Society. J. Mason Neale stated that:

> One of the great abuses of modern times is the position and monstrous state of the pulpit. It has often been placed, with the reading-pue and clerk's desk immediately before the High Altar, as if for the express purpose of hiding, as much as possible, the latter from the congregation. If there were any similarity between the two, such a position might be natural; but as the one is directed to God and the other to the people, a corresponding difference in the arrangement of the Church furniture is required... How symbolic is this in an age which puts preaching before praying![10]

Again, according to Neale, next in importance to the chancel is the porch, which he describes as 'indispensable',[11] but this feature is noticeable by its absence in Wightwick's designs. In only two of his churches is there a porch, and in each case it is but token and incorporated into the building.

It is significant that only one of the churches designed by Wightwick was not in part funded by the Incorporated Church Building Society. The CBS played a limited but important role in the financing of new churches and

[10]   J. Mason Neal, *A Few Words to Church-Builders* (Cambridge, 1844), p. 24.
[11]   *Ibid*, p. 9.

in the extension and restoration of old, in accordance with quite rigid recommendations.[12] Its munificence was restricted, and certain conditions and caveats applied. In the case of Wightwick's churches the contributions from the ICBS supplemented the grants made by the Church Commissioners, the local Diocesan Committees, and contributions of both patrons and parishioners.

While not absolute, the church design favoured by the ICBS followed certain theoretical principles. Most importantly, grants would be made only where extra seating was provided, carefully measured, and when such seating was free. Simplicity in design was favoured, and grants were not offered for the financing of architectural ornament or unnecessary embellishment. In fact these grants were intended for just such churches as Wightwick designed. The ICBS, founded in 1818, was incorporated by Parliament in 1828, and funded by voluntary contributions. It had a strong commitment to the spiritual welfare of the working classes. Perhaps it was inevitable also that a political component could be detected in the urgency and enthusiasm for the funding of these new churches. A letter published in the *Royal Cornwall Gazette* and signed by all the clergy of Plymouth, Devonport and Stonehouse, expressed gratitude to the Lord Bishop of Exeter for his advocacy of Holy Faith through support for the funding of these churches. They claimed that only the building of additional churches could check the fearful and insidious form of 'Atheism' as expressed through the 'demoralising and impious system of Socialism'.[13] Wightwick's church designs, simple and relatively cheap to build, were therefore appropriate for those areas where the need was greatest for functional churches, capable of accommodating large numbers of people, and for communities least able to raise money for themselves and which might otherwise have joined the ranks of the Dissenters.

The Church of St Michael and All Angels in Bude (plate 57), built in 1834, and altered by the addition of chancel and transepts in 1876, was the first church designed by Wightwick. Dismissed by Pevsner as 'unimportant',[14] it was, however, an important commission for Wightwick, and was described minutely and fervently by its designer in an article he wrote for the *Architectural Magazine*.[15] This chapel of ease to the fourteenth-century St

---

12 Records of the Incorporated Church Building Society are held at the Lambeth Palace Library, and reference is made to them as they relate to churches designed by Wightwick.

13 *Royal Cornwall Gazette*, 6 March 1840.

14 N. Pevsner and E. Radcliffe, *The Buildings of England: Cornwall* (Harmondsworth, 1970), p. 47.

15 George Wightwick, 'A few Observations on the Reviving Taste for Pointed Architecture, with an Illustrated Description of a Chapel just erected at Bude Haven, under the direction of the Author', *Architectural Magazine*, 2 (1835), pp. 345–8.

Andrew's church at Stratton in Bude, was commissioned by Sir Thomas Dyke
Acland. The Acland family was probably the oldest surviving family in the
county of Devon,[16] and was linked through the marriage of Dyke Acland's
cousin to Dr Pusey's elder brother, Philip. Dyke Acland was said by his son
to be 'on most intimate terms with Dr Pusey';[17] nevertheless as a younger man
Dyke Acland's main preoccupation had been with religious liberty and
tolerance. He was a Tory, politically middle-of-the-road, and with a
reputation for the philanthropic interest he took in his estates, which it was
said he ruled with 'benevolent despotism'.[18]

Wightwick would have known Acland through membership of the
prestigious and learned society, the Plymouth Athenaeum, but significantly
Acland later also became a member of the Diocesan Church Building Society.
This society represented the views of the Exeter Diocesan Architectural
Society, established in 1841 and stood for all the principles that were
anathema to Wightwick. The munificence of Acland in building the church is
commemorated at the entrance; also acknowledged, however, is his generosity
in the addition of chancel and transepts. Perhaps the church properly needed
to be enlarged, and perhaps also Acland's views changed, but it seems likely
that in any case these particular additions signified some dissatisfaction on the
part of Acland with the original church design by Wightwick. Ten years after
the church was built a letter from Wightwick to Acland, dated 5 October
1844, seems to confirm this; Wightwick stated that he believed himself to be 'a
marked man' as a consequence of his 'secession from, and determined
opposition to, the Diocesan Architectural Society'. He went on to state that
he had heard it said that any merit in the design of the chapel at Bude should
be attributed to the manner in which Wightwick had been '*drilled in to it*' by
his employer; moreover, that much trouble had been caused by the constant
necessity for alteration. His letter concluded:

> Now if such really were the case in your opinion, I have nothing to do but
> to submit to it. I venture, however, to speculate on your entertaining
> towards me more favourable feeling; and respectfully beg that you will oblige
> me by *expressing* it – if you conscientiously can. If *you* did not speak thus
> disparagingly of me, I care not who else may have done so; and all I therefore
> seek is your authority for enabling *my* informant to correct *his* informant on
> this point. The cessation of your employment I have hitherto attributed to
> reasons not affecting my professional repute; and I only hope you will be
> enabled to restore my comfort in respect to the precious value which I attach

---

[16] Anne Acland, *A Devon Family. The Story of the Aclands* (London, 1981), W. G.
Hoskins in Foreword, p. xv.

[17] *Memoir and Letters of the Rt Hon Sir Thomas Dyke Acland*, ed. Arthur H. D.
Acland (London, 1902), p. 96.

[18] Anne Acland, *A Devon Family. The Story of the Aclands*, p. 61. Acland joined the
Ecclesiological Society in 1846 as a life member.

to your good opinion.[19]

There is no evidence that Acland was in fact able to restore Wightwick's comfort, as it seems clear that Wightwick's reputation as a church architect was by 1844 quite flawed and his designs suspect in the eyes of the Camden Society.

The new doctrines permeated the architectural establishment and, in the West Country particularly, there was contention between, on the one hand, the High Churchman or Puseyite, and on the other hand, the Low Churchman, Non-Conformist or Evangelical. In his autobiography Wightwick describes an incident in Plymouth that could only have contributed to his reputation as an anti-ritualist and stubborn Low Churchman:

> To complete my downfall, I took some little part in a public meeting then held by the Anti-Puseyites of Plymouth ... my conduct being alluded to, by my lamenting clerical friends, with that sort of pitying censure which sensible admonition would bestow upon silly delinquency.[20]

Pusey was himself the director of a house for Sisters of Mercy at Plymouth, while Henry Phillpotts, Bishop of Exeter, was a High Churchman and prominent member of the Exeter Diocesan Ecclesiological Society. Both these men represented a theological view that Wightwick found impossible to accept.

Six years after Wightwick completed the commission for St Michael and All Angels he designed the first of his two churches in Plymouth, both of which were criticised for defects which arose from an adherence to the strictures of the ICBS. Neither of these churches is in existence to-day, but the records of the ICBS as well as those of the Church Commissioners give some historical background. Both were built in the parish of St Andrew; Holy Trinity Church was completed in September 1842, and Christ Church in November 1845. Holy Trinity in Friars Lane in the Barbican, was commenced in 1840 when five or six hundred people attended the foundation ceremony, reported in some detail in the *Royal Cornwall Gazette*,[21] and minutely by the *Plymouth and Devonport Weekly Journal*.[22] It had a capacity of 1200, and was described by Goodhart-Rendel as 'A galleried Classical Church lit by a Venetian window at the E. end and rows of lunettes above the Tuscan arcades of the interior'.[23] The *Civil Engineer and Architects Journal* reported, when the foundation stone was laid on 20 May, that the perspective of the interior would be 'boldly picturesque and ecclesiastical',[24] and further

19 Acland Papers, Devon Record Office, Exeter, 1148M/19/30.
20 George Wightwick, 'The Life of an Architect', p. 176.
21 *Royal Cornwall Gazette*, 29 May 1840.
22 *Plymouth and Devonport Weekly Journal*, 28 May 1840.
23 Goodhart-Rendel, card index at the National Monuments Record Library.
24 *Civil Engineer and Architects Journal*, iii (July, 1840), p. 25.

commented on the peculiar circumstances of its locality. This reference is likely to relate to the difficulties of building on such a restricted and steep site in the heart of the Plymouth Barbican. Goodhart-Rendel said of this church: 'Externally it has quite a pleasing elevation of the Italian kind. Small'.[25]

Holy Trinity church closed in 1939, both because of its dilapidated condition and the decreasing local population in this area of Plymouth; it was later destroyed in the Plymouth blitz, and all that now remains is one wall at the end of a parking lot. However, even before the foundation stone was laid, there had been critical comment particularly relating to the position of pulpit and reading desk. The Church Commissioners, having examined Wightwick's plans, had insisted that both should be moved in order that sight of the communion table was not impeded. Wightwick argued his case. Although the siting of pulpit and reading desk were clearly in accordance with his own theoretical views, he excused his stand by explaining to the Church Commissioners that he had no choice over where they should be located. He referred to difficulties relating to the site and also to the lack of light into the building.[26] Once more Wightwick's views were at variance with those of the established ecclesiology of the Church of England, in his belief that the spoken word should take priority over the spiritual representation of the altar.

In the same year that Holy Trinity church was consecrated another application was made, this time for assistance with the funding of Christ Church, again in the parish of St Andrew's.[27] In the letter accompanying the application, it was explained that the area was far from wealthy,

> and just now there is an amount of bankruptcy in the Town hitherto unknown. Dissent is rampant, and sad indifference pervades the minds of a very large portion of those who term themselves Churchmen, in addition to this, those who are attached to the Church have been very much called upon for Trinity church which was consecrated only in August.

In the records of the Church Commissioners there is correspondence relating to the financial constraints under which Wightwick worked, in particular referring to the responsibility for costs if the contractor were to become bankrupt.[28] In the ICBS records are Wightwick's drawings for the building of the church, and a description in *Kelly's Directory* states that Christ Church, Eton Place, with 880 sittings, was 'built of stone in the Perpendicular style, consisting of clerestoried nave, aisles, west porch and belfry containing one bell'.[29]

---

[25] Goodhart-Rendel, card index at the National Monuments Record Library.
[26] ICBS, file 2322, Lambeth Palace Library, London.
[27] ICBS, file 3160.
[28] Records of the Church Commissioners, file no. 18249 (Part 4).
[29] *Kelly's Directory of Devonshire and Cornwall* (London, 1939), p. 507.

With the rebuilding of Plymouth in 1966, the church was demolished. In the centre of the city, and originally part of the parish of St Andrew, it had become an independent parish in 1887, but by the middle of the twentieth century the congregation had dropped to 40 or 50.[30] Goodhart-Rendel was critical of this church, stating 'Not good at all: for its date, very bad. A Tudor thing with a show front – no steeple'.[31] On its completion, however, the *Plymouth and Devonport Weekly Journal* described Christ Church enthusiastically and in great detail, using an account written in Wightwick's style, and likely to have been by him.[32] This article was subsequently reproduced in *The Builder*.[33] Notwithstanding this, Christ Church was harshly judged and criticised by *The Ecclesiologist* as 'one of the worst that we have set eyes on out of Cambridge'. While conceding that the Church had some merits, 'features that indicate an improvement in cheap church-building ... the faults will be found greatly to preponderate'. Wightwick is not specifically named as the originator of the church design, but again a chancel of 'meagre proportions' is noted.[34]

In 1841 Wightwick was asked by Edward William Wynne Pendarves to design a chapel, later to be dedicated to St John, on the Pendarves Estate at Treslothan in Cornwall (plate 58), as well as a curate's house, school and associated buildings. This important commission represented a watershed for Wightwick, and one on which his reputation as a church architect was later to be judged. Pendarves was influential, he was a merchant banker, Justice of the Peace and Member of Parliament for Cornwall and later West Cornwall between 1826 and 1853. He was described at the time of his death as one of 'the old and staunch Reformers of the county', the last survivor of a small band of eminent men whose liberal principles and advocacy of great truths had profoundly affected public opinion.[35] Pendarves of Treslothan and his wife were referred to by Wightwick as prominent friends for some years; indeed he seemed to have been 'an industrious and liberally remunerated servant' until he lost their good opinion.[36] This remark most likely refers to an incident where he was blamed for faulty work and held responsible for a want of vigilance. His employer had been gravely annoyed and his lady 'furious'. However, the buildings were duly completed, and now present an attractive co-ordinated complex, even though the school has been demolished. In 1967 they were described by Professor A. C. Thomas of the Institute of

---

[30]   W. J. Power, *A Layman's Guide to Some Plymouth Churches* (Plymouth, 1977), p. 8.
[31]   Goodhart-Rendell, card index at the National Monuments Record Library.
[32]   *Plymouth and Devonport Weekly Journal*, 28 May 1845.
[33]   *Builder*, 3 (1845), p. 601.
[34]   *Ecclesiologist*, 3 (1844), p. 54.
[35]   *West Briton*, 1 July, 1853.
[36]   George Wightwick, 'The Life of an Architect', p. 157.

Cornish Studies at Redruth as 'all executed in a kind of Victorian granite Gothic which is wholly un-Cornish but which nonetheless possesses a charm of its own'.[37]

St John, Treslothan was in part funded by a grant of £200 from the ICBS,[38] but the records show difficulty throughout the negotiations. Wightwick's drawings were lost, and in a somewhat peevish tone, in a letter dated 31 August 1839, he refused to complete further drawings 'without the sanction of the Society'. Nevertheless, sent with this letter, and contained within the record, there is a drawing by Wightwick relating to St John's church and described by him as a 'sketch'. Later, in a letter from Wightwick dated 12 November 1839, he excused what he thought the ICBS may judge as excessive decoration. He explained that this was at the desire of Pendarves, who for that express purpose had increased his subscription from £300 to £500, as well as giving the land.

The laying of the foundation stone for this church on 10 March 1840 was described in the *West Briton* under the title 'New Episcopal Chapel',[39] and Wightwick's design was described as 'splendid'. In contrast to this detailed description, the *West Briton* commented only briefly, in one sentence, on the consecration by Bishop Phillpotts of Exeter two years later.[40] The church designs themselves illuminate the reasons for the apparent change in public approval, and there is further confirmation in the notes from a paper read in 1942 on the history of the church.[41] This document reported that in 1890 an entrance to the church was made through a door in the south-west corner. Until that time the entrance had been through the south-east corner, so that, as was drily observed, 'Late-comers faced the congregation'. The Pendarves family entered through a similar door on the north side of the chancel. Comment was made on the positioning of the two pulpits and on the screen, which stretched across the chancel about 6ft from the east wall, shutting off a small vestry. Even the roof trusses were the cause of censure, when Wightwick's design for the church at Treslothan was attacked vituperatively by *The Ecclesiologist* :

> This is one of those cases in which no mercy ought to be shown to the architect, who, with unlimited funds at his command, has shown that his signal failure is owing to nothing but his own insufficient acquaintance with the art which he professes. The building is meant to be of the First-Pointed style. It is in form an oblong without aisles, not even pretending externally to a chancel. ... The area of the church is occupied by a row of open benches

37 Charles Thomas, *Christian Antiquities of Camborne* (St Austell, 1967), p. 168.
38 ICBS, file 2352.
39 *West Briton*, 13 March 1840.
40 *Ibid.* 25 July 1842.
41 Unpublished 'Notes for a Paper on Parish History read by Miss L. A. Eustice, 1942', St John's Church Papers, Cornwall Record Office, Truro.

in the middle, and by pues at the sides. The font is at the west end: and there is a western gallery and organ. The roof resembles that of a railway station; and the lancets – our readers must remember the style – are about as large in proportion to the size of the building as the windows in King's College Chapel.[42] (plate 59)

The subsequent entry in *The Ecclesiologist* refers to the church at Wyke in Surrey by Henry Woodyer, and the warm praise for the architect of this church is in marked contrast to the condemnation meted out to Wightwick. Woodyer is commended for his design, and comment is made on the length of both chancel and nave. That the nave should be almost twice the length of the chancel is positively noted, and the south porch is remarked on for being 'excessively pretty'. *The Ecclesiologist* concludes with the remark 'On the whole, we have not seen a village church superior to this'.[43]

The design for a church at Lamerton was noted by Wightwick as the 'only one of my church designs that ever passed the *full* approval of my diocesan judges.'[44] The contract was taken, the working drawings made, and subsequently, on 19 February 1844, an application was put before the ICBS for funds towards the estimated cost of £805.[45] However, the church was not built at that time, and there were difficulties even from the beginning. In a letter to the ICBS, dated 8 December 1845, Wightwick confessed 'I fear I have been carelessly irregular in making use of the plans and papers of the intended church in the parish of Lamerton'. He stated that £1,000 had been bequeathed for the express purpose of providing tower and bells. The tower had been added, plans and specifications remodelled 'so as to unite the whole', the entire cost to be £1,900. Later that month the plans were approved and a grant of £75 was promised, but apparently the building went no further than the design stage. In a letter dated 2 December 1850, replying to an enquiry from the ICBS, the Rev. Edward Carlyon stated that work on the church had not commenced 'in the hopes that arrangements might be made to unite that part of my Parish with Brent Tor'.

There is some clarification of the difficulties of endowment and residence that had delayed Carlyon's plans in a letter from him to the ICBS, when he applied again for funds six years later in June 1856,[46] stating that a new and more appropriate site was available. He proposed that the building should be commenced according to the plans originally approved by the Society, but without a steeple, a parsonage house being built instead. The response to this request from the ICBS referred to the design and included the brief statement: 'The design is very inferior and it doesn't appear to be the

42 *Ecclesiologist*, 4 (1845), p. 185.
43 *Ibid*, p. 185.
44 George Wightwick, 'The Life of an Architect', p. 177.
45 ICBS, file 3397.
46 *Ibid*.

work of an Architect'. G. Rendle, architect and surveyor to Rev. E. Carlyon, staunchly defended Wightwick, who had by then retired, replying:

> The disparaging remarks at the conclusion of the Report which you have sent me to day ... [are] intended to apply not to the mere mechanical manipulation of the drawings but to the general design. The design was as of course you are aware the work of G. Wightwick Esq an Architect who long practised in the district – who was well known and deservedly esteemed; and the present plans are in conformity with my instructions rigid copies of his with the exception of some slight modifications most of which were rendered necessary by a change of site.

Dismay and indignation were expressed also in a letter from Carlyon to the ICBS, dated 8 November 1856, when he said that the plans were strictly in accordance with those previously submitted to the ICBS which had met with entire approbation. 'Of Mr Wightwick's character as an Architect I don't profess to be a judge, but I know that he was regularly educated for it and had an extensive practice both in this County and Cornwall by which he was enabled to realise a fortune and retire from business...' However, after twelve years the views of the ICBS had perhaps become more entrenched, influenced increasingly as they must have been by the ecclesiologists, but, notwithstanding the criticism, a grant of £100 was forthcoming, and the church was finally built, and consecrated on 24 September 1857 (plate 60).

Despite an attribution of Christ Church, North Brentor, to Richard Gosling of Torquay,[47] it nevertheless seems that Wightwick's plans were indeed the basis for the design that was finally accepted by the ICBS. A drawing is included in the ICBS records, not signed by Wightwick, but nevertheless showing the church that had originally met with full approval, although with modifications dictated presumably by the new site, particularly the porch and vestry which are transposed. The design of the tower is certainly not the work of Wightwick, but evidence of his theories may be seen in the simple interior, and particularly in the shallow and unimportant chancel. An account that Gosling rendered to Carlyon, now held by the West Devon Record Office, includes sums for the work of the masons and plasterers, with additional amounts for the tower, but with no design fee included in the total.[48] It seems likely, therefore, that Gosling may well have designed the tower, but was responsible only for modifications to Wightwick's original design in order that the church would fit onto the new site. Perhaps after all Wightwick's theoretical stance was indeed vindicated by the building of this church at North Brentor, attributed though it is to Richard Gosling, and to some extent confirmed by the account he submitted in 1857. It was perhaps poetic justice that Wightwick's church, the last that he

[47] Bridget Cherry and Nikolaus Pevsner, *The Buildings of England: Devon* (Harmondsworth, 1991), p. 210.

[48] West Devon Record Office, Plymouth, 824/5c.

designed, should thus finally have been built according to the requirements of ecclesiological theory.

The culmination of the Cambridge Camden Society's censure was reached in response to the publication of Wightwick's drawings and descriptions of the ideal Protestant cathedral in the pages of *Weale's Quarterly Papers*.[49] These seemed at first glance to embrace all those principles that were important to him, as well as to the Society. The ruling theme was the cross that should represent length, height and verticality, so that 'If altitude be one feature of the sublime, extent of longitudinal perspective is another'. However, Wightwick was not content to express himself thus simply, and went on to criticise European cathedrals, explaining how they all aimed at only some partial supremacy, extravagance of scale, or decoration, height of internal vaulting, altitude of towers. 'Only in England will you find genius curbed by judgment, and enthusiasm tempered with modesty'.[50] Wightwick drew on his respect for English Protestant cathedrals when he designed his own building, acknowledging elements that he took from those he particularly admired. He discussed principles of convenience and expression that coincided exactly with the recommendations of the Camden Society, but critically added the rider that there should be 'no architectural dispositions nor decorative details, which exclusively proclaim the peculiar ceremonies and tenets of the Church of Rome'.[51]

He went on to argue that, having paid due attention to antiquity through adherence to the principles and details of Gothic pointed architecture, which he described as 'unimprovable', altered circumstances and present necessities should be allowed to dictate deviation. In a previous article written for *Weale's Quarterly Papers on Architecture* Wightwick had already criticised the view that spires should commence from the ground, stating that in his own opinion the expression of the base was essential to the dignity of the building, as otherwise it would resemble a mining chimney. He had analysed the proportions of the great English cathedrals, and noted that commendation should be given particularly to those edifices with three spires. 'Thus, though there may be no actual crowning centre point, there will be that direction given to the imagination which will induce it to form one in idea, and the pointed principle will be carried out as far as *feeling* is concerned'.[52] He had taken his argument further when he had confirmed the sanctity of the church through the amount of light that was allowed to enter, and he had further defined the status of the worshipper by limiting the size of door through which he should enter. Rose windows were, for Wightwick,

[49]   'Modern English Gothic Architecture Continued', *Weale's Quarterly Papers on Architecture*, 3 (1845), pp. 1–18.
[50]   'Ancient English Gothic Architecture', *Ibid*, p. 6.
[51]   'Modern English Gothic Architecture', *Ibid*, p. 12.
[52]   'Ancient English Gothic Architecture', *Ibid*, p. 9.

unnecessary and distracting, as well as light-limiting. Full light should shine through great windows to the honour of God, which would thus 'symbolise the pervading expansion of the light of Truth, while the small doors typify the humility of truth's seeker'.[53] He therefore pointed out that the whole history of church architecture was a succession of such deviations, and then described his own plan:

> At the same time, equally regarding the spirit and necessities of our simplified worship, we invest the main body of our cathedral with the importance which formerly belonged only to a small part of it – rendering this as spacious and free as possible, to the entire exclusion of pillars, aisles, rood screens, and secluded recesses. Long processions are no more to move before us. The triforium is no more required for the nuns, or the hanging of pendent draperies. The nave is no longer required as an outer preaching place; nor is the chancel any more to be regarded as the 'Holy of Holies', in which the priests are to sit apart from their brother sinners.[54]

Subsequently, again in the pages of *Weale's Quarterly Papers on Architecture*,[55] Wightwick described his first article as being 'in opposition to the proclaimed view of the Camden Society', stating that, in his opinion, the Society was quite unable to consider architecture in any other light than as an historical language which was relevant only to preceding ages. He advocated that, after the demise of the present Society, which he considered to be imminent, another such should be formed more relevant to contemporary needs. He stated that 'a slavish obedience to *past* periods has tended to extinguish the chance of that respect which we should desire *future* periods to have for *us*'.[56]

The Society's reaction was predictable, and censured Wightwick through the pages of *The Ecclesiologist* in an attack that seemed to be more personal than theoretical.[57] It represented a lengthy and sarcastic review of Wightwick's article, mocking and criticising each and every statement that he had made, but noticeably making no attempt to substantiate its own theoretical perspective. Perhaps attack seemed to the Society more constructive than defence, but it could have been that by 1845 the Camden Society had nothing new to say, and was finding it difficult to maintain momentum. However, the Society undoubtedly understood Wightwick's article as an implied threat and a wish to annihilate the Society, as well as promoting his own design for a Protestant cathedral. Both ambitions should only meet with failure, according to the writer of the review. Sarcasm was heaped upon Wightwick's beliefs that windows should be large and doorways

53   'Ancient English Gothic Architecture', *Ibid*, vol. ii, p. 8.
54   'Modern English Gothic Architecture', *Ibid*, vol. vii, p. 16.
55   'Modern English Gothic Architecture (continued)', *Ibid*, p. 1.
56   'Modern English Gothic Architecture (continued)', *Ibid*, p. 6.
57   *Ecclesiologist*, 4 (1845), p. 77.

small, and that a third spire would be admirable: '(with all due deference to our modest emulator, the most hideous thing eyes ever beheld, – an extinguisher set on a crab's back)'. Wightwick's article was quoted extensively, and comment was made on the length of the chancel; '(it is unnecessary to inform our readers that the Vightvickio-Protestant cathedral has nothing that deserves the name of chancel)'.

This article effectively brought Wightwick's career as a church architect to a close. He clearly realised this when he said '...my imagined mission has proved a mission only imagined, that I have failed to keep the ground which I fondly fancied was entrusted to me; and that in consequence of my inadequacy fools (still) rush in where angels fear to tread'.[58] Speaking thus of his professional life in 1851 Wightwick left Plymouth for retirement in Bristol, where he continued to live and write for a further twenty-one years before his death in 1872. Here he turned his attention to local affairs, writing extensively in the press, with critical comment on the buildings in the city and its environs. Moreover, as well as the articles he contributed to *Weale's Quarterly Papers on Architecture*, in 1846 he published *Hints to Young Architects*, which was reprinted four times, and between 1852 and 1858 he wrote regularly for *The Critic, London Literary Journal*, as well as for the *Edinburgh Building Chronicle* between 1854 and 1857. He maintained his interest in the arts, and his critical comments on Ruskin's *Seven Lamps of Architecture* appeared in six articles for *Architect and Building Operative* in 1849–50. His essay 'A Critical Study on the Architecture and Genius of Sir Christopher Wren' gained him the RIBA Silver Medal in 1859.

On his death Wightwick left behind evidence of a lifetime's work; not only buildings, but writings, drawings and watercolours; most of his drawings and many of his papers, including the autobiography that he wrote in parts for *Bentley's Magazine*, were left in his will to the Royal Institute of British Architects, together with a copy of his *Palace of Architecture: a Romance of Art and History* (1840). There are, however, working drawings of a number of his houses held by the owners, and many drawings relating to his churches are held in the Record Offices of both Devon and Cornwall, as well as within the ICBS records at Lambeth Palace Library and the Church of England Record Centre. The Exeter Institution holds a number of pen and wash drawings by Wightwick and Archdeacon R. H. Froude relating to Devon church details,[59] only recently located and listed. The association between Wightwick and Froude may have come about through Froude's connection with the ICBS when Wightwick's church plans came before his attention; nevertheless it

58 Introduction to the bound edition of Wightwick's hand-written lectures to the Plymouth Athenaeum, held at the RIBA Library. These lectures were delivered from 8 January 1828.
59 Exeter Diocesan Architectural Society. Table of contents of Vol. 1 of the Society's Scrap Book. Sketches by Archdeacon Froude, n.d.

ROSAMUND REID

seems to have been a surprising association as Froude, described as 'an epitome of the old high churchmen of England',[60] was the father of Hurrell Froude, pupil to John Keble and close friend of Cardinal Newman. However, whatever the antecedents of the connection between Wightwick and Froude, the small and exact pen and wash drawings are the result, representing perhaps a rapprochement between Wightwick and the Anglican church.

Wightwick's theoretical stance may have been pragmatic and contained by reasoned argument, but above all it represented his awareness of the needs of the community, which he saw as paramount in his work as a church architect, as well as the requirement to work within the constraints of a limited budget. Some difficulty may indeed have arisen for him out of the adaptation of traditional pointed Gothic architecture to requirements that did not exist when Gothic churches were originally built, but in Wightwick's view the restitution of Gothic as propounded by the Cambridge Camden Society was a contradiction, a denial of contemporary requirements and a vain harking back to the past. Furthermore he made quite plain how strongly he felt that professional architects should be able 'to maintain that amount of independence which should appertain to them as professors, lest they become a mere body of architectural draughtsmen, with nothing but the laws of building societies to obey, and only "bookish theorick" to follow'.[61] This statement was significant for Wightwick; it expressed his own wish to pursue independent theory and to develop architectural skills unhindered by dogma. Such a view could not, however, have been countenanced by the Camden Society, who were swift in their retribution. Wightwick clearly understood his position and acknowledged in his diary that the papers he wrote for *Weale's Quarterly* 'did not advance my interests with the High Church party; and it is needless to say how that party predominated in the diocese of Exeter before it became so general as it now is'. He went on to state 'Others were soon in the places which had very likely remained mine had I consented to be the mere draughtsman of the Diocesan Architectural Society; and from this time I declined as a leading practitioner in the south-western counties'.[62]

Wightwick's capacity to influence ecclesiological opinion may indeed have been limited, but his views were widely read in the architectural press, where he discussed such matters as the appropriateness of design and style to the purpose of a building, approving or criticising the work of his contemporaries, and seeking to educate and inform. He was neither a

[60] William Owen Chadwick, *The Mind of the Oxford Movement* (London, 1960), p. 65.
[61] George Wightwick, 'Ecclesiastical Architecture; on the Determination of Some Principles for the Establishment of an Ecclesiastical Style of Architecture, Expressing the Reformed Church in England', December 1844. Offprint held at RIBA Library.
[62] George Wightwick, 'The Life of an Architect', p. 612.

philanthropist nor a philosopher, but some of the qualities of each inspired his work. Wightwick's sense of failure came from his disappointment when his ecclesiastical contracts ceased. Undoubtedly this was because he failed to change his views in accordance with contemporary opinion, thus isolating himself from those who could have maintained his previous reputation by offering him further commissions. His stubbornness may be either applauded as representing an honourable loyalty to his own beliefs, or criticised as a foolish and dogmatic insistence on his own prejudices. Without doubt Wightwick was an opinionated man. There were occasions when he provoked argument in the Plymouth Athenaeum, and from time to time he disagreed with his employers. He himself described in his diary his difficult early relationship with Sir John Soane. Nevertheless he was willing to risk both his livelihood and his friendships for his principles, and can be remembered for this, if not for his useful and unmemorable churches.

In practical terms, when he died in 1872, Wightwick left an estate of nearly £7000, and his extensive architectural practice must have been lucrative to have enabled him to retire at the age of fifty. Perhaps his final years confirmed him as a successful writer, in a way that his earlier life had not done as a church architect, and his writing and humour stand out to-day in the pages of the many architectural journals to which he contributed. Nevertheless, despite his difficulties with the High Church movement there remain six churches, five of which are still in use as places of worship, as well as a number of church monuments. In Plymouth and Devonport the dozen shops and shop-fronts that Wightwick certainly designed, as well as many terraces of houses and minor public buildings, were destroyed in the blitz or subsequently demolished. However, in Plymouth and the West Country there are still forty-seven surviving buildings, terraces and country houses, as well as eight significant additions, evidence enough of a successful professional life.

Re-Presenting the Church Militant: the Camden Society, Church Restoration, and the Gothic Sign

CHRIS MIELE

Church restoration was central to the Camdenian programme. The Society's first law is clear on this point: it exists to promote 'the study of Ecclesiastical Architecture and Antiquities, and the restoration of mutilated Architectural remains'.[1] And although new churches would very quickly take up more and more of the Society's time, restoration retained a special place, so much so that the official seal A. W. N. Pugin designed for it in 1843 makes no reference to church building at all[2] (plate 23). At the bottom is St Sepulchre, Cambridge, then just restored by Anthony Salvin acting on the instructions of the Society. Framing the Gothic tabernacle above are a pair of images showing an imaginary thirteenth-century church before and after a radical reconstruction.

It is easy to see why this refashioning of medieval architecture was so important. 'Restoration', 'rebuilding', 'reconstruction', the very terminology is rich in metaphorical possibility, implying spiritual as well as physical renewal. Archdeacon Thorp underlined the point in his first annual address to the Society. As he saw it ecclesiology was a 'practical' tool, just the thing to breath new life into England's musty, medieval churches, transforming them from picturesque accents in the landscape, fodder for Romantic tourists and artists, into blazing signs of faith, images, icons, even, of piety and high purpose.[3] Though Thorp did not say so, he might well have had in mind the shining example of St Francis himself, a fervent reformer who had laid the foundations for his ministry by rebuilding ruined churches around Assisi. But of far greater influence, and being so near to hand as to need no reference, was the example of the Tractarians themselves who had undertaken the editing of Patristic texts – a literary restoration – to endow their own programme with the authority of the Church Fathers. By studying and restoring ancient

---

[1]   From the *Report of the Cambridge Camden Society*, 1842, and quoted in J. White, *The Cambridge Movement. The Ecclesiologists and the Gothic Revival* (Cambridge, 1962), p. 235.

[2]   The insignia was published in *Ecclesiologist*, 3 (1843–4), pp. 184–5, where there is a full description of it, and in *Instrumenta Ecclesiastica* for 1843.

[3]   *Report of the Cambridge Camden Society*, 1840, pp. 4–5.

churches the Camdenians were associating themselves with the most tangible and conspicuous signs of British Christianity as it had been passed down over the generations, asserting a kind of proprietary right to it.

This desire to see the health of the Church as reflected in its monuments was not novel.[4] It is there in embryo form as far back as the Rev. James Bentham's 1771 essay on Ely Cathedral, where the study of church architecture is likened to religious meditation. Religious 'reformation' would only come when churches were 'restored to their proper dignity'. To round off the point Bentham quoted Horace's ode in which a ruin is presented as a sign of declining Roman virtue: *donec templum refeceris*.[5] Sixty years later the Camdenians adapted this clause so that the noun read in the plural, 'Until you have restored the temples'. Neale, Webb, and their cohorts must have known Bentham, but they did not acknowledge the source.[6] This was true to form. The Society was fond of stressing its own novelty. Indeed, so indifferent were the founder-members to their immediate context, that they did not scruple to use William Camden's name in their title even though a Camden Society had been founded in 1838 to publish archival sources. This desire to cover over the traces of influence, to sever ties with the immediate past, to invent a foundation myth, all are hallmarks of a classic *avant-garde* gambit.[7] This is not to say that the Society was merely following fashion, that its forebears explain its achievement. There can be no doubt that in the 1840s the CCS's advice on the care and furnishing of old churches was unsurpassed, standard-setting stuff.[8] Nor can anyone reasonably question the genius which the committee had for printed propaganda, twisting the tradition of the religious pamphlet to its own architectural and theological ends. But the Society's mastery in the field of 'monument discourse' was shortlived, confined to this first decade. Afterwards the ecclesiologists had to yield the palm to specialist church architects and a younger generation of militant, though less sectarian, county-based architectural societies.

---

[4]   See S. Bradley's outstanding *The Gothic Revival and the Church of England, 1790–1840*, unpublished Ph.D. thesis, University of London (1996).

[5]   J. Bentham, 'Historical Remarks on Saxon Churches', *Essays on Gothic Architecture*, ed. J. Taylor (London, 1800), xi, pp. 88–91, 94. First published in *The History of the Cathedral Church at Ely*, 1771, by J. Bentham and B. Willis.

[6]   *Ecclesiologist*, 2 (1842), p. 72.

[7]   See G. Pollock, *Avant-Garde Gambits, 1888–1893. Gender and the Colour of Art History* (London, 1992) for a discussion of these issues, and M. Calinescu, *Five Faces of Modernity. Modernism, the Avant Garde, Decadence, Kitsch, and Post-Modernism* (Durham, NC, 1987), esp. pp. 95–118.

[8]   White's account, pp. 156–77, is unsurpassed.

Beginnings

The Society's involvement with church restoration was at first modest, personal even. John Mason Neale's remarkable diary spanning November 1838 to March 1840 shows ecclesiology developing from picturesque tours of churches near to Cambridge.[9] Brass rubbing, sketching old tombs, admiring the landscape through the shifting light of the seasons and in the company of friends, none of this seems of a piece with the pious rigours of mature ecclesiology, and yet Neale's love of antiquity was formed in this context. It is easy to picture this handful of green, dreamy undergraduates, to imagine their desire to tinker with one minor feature or another in one of their best-loved churches, if only to leave some mark of their travels, not unlike the initials scratched by countless picturesque tourists on mouldering church tombs across the land.

The founding of the new Society in May 1839 provided the impetus and a new, more serious purpose. Soon afterwards preparations were under way to restore the decayed and defaced Romanesque font at Coton church. This the Trinity men probably knew from G. R. Boissier's 1827 *Notes on Cambridgeshire Churches*, where an engraving shows the stern, sublimely primitive font looking very much in need of care and attention. By November Neale was overseeing the work. This first attempt stayed close to his heart, and he chose to publish a vignette of the renewed Coton font as a kind of initial letter at the start of his preface to the Society's *Monumental Brasses* (1846), a book which could itself be seen as a sentimental memorial to the early days of the Society and published on the eve of its reconstitution in London. In that same November of 1839 Neale was also arranging to strip the 'modern plaister' from the tower of St Benedict's in Cambridge, which was then rightly thought to be of Anglo-Saxon origin. A local builder exposed six square yards of rubble masonry and made smaller trials elsewhere. Neale had hoped to renew any primitive decorations, and, when he found none, ordered the work to stop. Other members restored a font cover at St Edward's (since removed).[10] Another opportunity arose in the course of a Society outing. Stopping to inspect the beautiful Early English south door at Barrington church, roughly ten miles south-west of Cambridge, the vicar 'expressed his anxious wish to have it handsomely restored'. There and then the Society agreed to meet the expense.[11] A lithograph of the Society's design for the renewed door was published, like the St Edward's font, in *Memorial Brasses*.

[9]   Except where otherwise stated, what follows is drawn from Lambeth Palace Library Manuscripts, 3107, 8 November 1838, and 15, 19, 21–26 November 1839. The Coton font is discussed by E. J. Boyce in *A Memorial of the Cambridge Camden Society, Instituted May, 1839, and the Ecclesiological (late Cambridge Camden), May, 1846* (London, 1888), p. 23.

[10]   White, *op. cit.*, pp. 160–61.

[11]   *Ecclesiologist*, 1 (1841–2), p. 58.

But minor works in out-of-the-way places were no match for the Society's mounting ambitions. Neale wanted something more dramatic, because, as he put it, one perfect example is 'worth a thousand precepts'.[12] And by summer 1840 he was himself in the thick of it, advising on the restoration of the church of St Nicholas, Old Shoreham, in Sussex. Though he later claimed to have acted as a 'representative' of the Camden Society, it appears he asked for its support only later, when the funds provided by the patron of the living, Magdalene College, Oxford, were running down. Like St Benedict's, parts of St Nicholas were understood to be pre-Conquest in origin, though the bulk of the cruciform structure dates to the mid twelfth century.[13] According to Neale a churchwarden had set the noble work in motion late in 1839.[14] Soon afterwards John Chessel Buckler drew up plans. Buckler, who had been a practising Goth since 1826, was one of the most adept antiquarian-architects of his generation, and it would be interesting to know just what Neale contributed to the project. His published account records simply that Magdalene College had asked him 'to superintend the restorations'.[15] The offer very probably came from Dr M. J. Routh, then president of the College and also first president of the Oxford Society for Promoting the Study of Gothic Architecture (hereafter OAS – see below).[16] Routh had strong views on architecture, and as rector of Theale in Berkshire had been instrumental in the construction of Holy Trinity church in that parish; his sister, Mrs. Sheppard, paid for it. This was begun in 1820 to the designs of Edward Garbett who used a very advanced lancet style. Buckler's father, John, who would soon give up his practice to his son in order to pursue his antiquarian urges, later provided a design for a matching tower.

Neale visited St Nicholas in the first weeks of 1840 to fill out a Church Scheme for the building, one of several hundred he completed between 1839 and 1842.[17] There is no reference in this document to the condition of the

[12] J. M. Neale, 'An Account of the Late Restorations in the Church of Old Shoreham, Sussex', *Transactions of the Cambridge Camden Society*, 1–3 (1839–41), pp. 28–34, at p. 28.

[13] I. Nairn and N. Pevsner, *The Buildings of England, Sussex* (Harmondsworth, 1965), pp. 285–7.

[14] Apart from material relating to the restoration of the chancel in the archives of Magdalene College, there is no evidence relating to this restoration in the standard repositories at the County Record Office or amongst the Incorporated Church Building Society (hereafter ICBS) papers at the Lambeth Palace Library.

[15] Neale, 'Old Shoreham', p. 33.

[16] S. L. Ollard, 'Oxford Architectural and Historical Society, and the Oxford Movement', *Oxoniensa* 5 (1940), pp. 146–60, at p. 151.

[17] Lambeth Palace MSS. 1977, fos. 49–51. On schemes generally *see* also R. R. Kenneally, 'Empirical Underpinnings: Ecclesiology, the Excursion and Church Schemes, 1830s–1850s', *Ecclesiology Today*, 15 (January 1998), pp. 14–19. See also C. Miele, *The Gothic Revival and Gothic Architecture: the Restoration of Medieval*

church, but these were just the sort of details that ecclesiologists tended to overlook. If the typically hyperbolic description Neale offered in a paper to the Society that November is to be believed, then St Nicholas was the veritable archetype of a desecrated church: the nave was 'filled with pews of all sorts and sizes'; the walls 'reeked with moisture' and were draped with 'green mould'; the east window was unspeakably 'disfigured'. There was a catalogue of minor faults – various and sundry blocked lights, shoddy wooden casements, once venerable architectural features partially destroyed, and, finally, 'every moulding clogged with plaister or whitewash'. Walking from the nave to the chancel a visitor might imagine that, to quote Neale's wonderfully emotive account, 'he was descending into the dungeon of a criminal, rather than going up to the house of the Lord'.[18]

All this was undone over the course of the year, and for less than £1,000. This sum covered the cost of restoring the elegant little chancel screen and of seating the nave with a set of uniform poppy-headed open benches. Though poppy heads are most commonly found on choir stalls, they were unusual in naves. A number of seating schemes from the 1830s and early 1840s feature them – the Round Church in Cambridge, discussed below, was one such – but after 1845 or so it was more common for nave benches to be unornamented.[19] In any case, at Old Shoreham the most substantial part of the work was the rebuilding of the ruined north transept, which was well under way by September 1840, when Neale asked the Society for £100.[20] How much is Neale and how much Buckler? And what exactly did superintending the work entail? In the 1960s Nairn and Pevsner (quoting Nicholas Taylor) put everything save the chancel down to the young Camdenian, but Neale would not have been able to prepare contract drawings, a bill of quantities, or specifications.[21] He might easily have talked over the details with Buckler, even made a few rudimentary sketches, and he might have been responsible

Churches in Victorian Britain, unpublished Ph.D. thesis (New York University: 1992), pp. 60–81, and the same author's 'Real Antiquity and the Science of Gothic Architecture', in *The Study of the Past in the Victorian Age*, ed. C. Brooks (Oxford, forthcoming).

[18]   Neale, 'Old Shoreham', p. 32.
[19]   See the nave seats in Christ Church, Kilndown, Kent (A. Salvin, and others, 1840); St Thomas's, Compton Valence, Dorset (B. Ferrey, 1839–40); St Stephen's, Leverbridge, Lancashire (E. Sharpe, 1842); St Michael, Ashton-under-Lyne, Greater Manchester (unknown, 1840 scheme of seating); St Giles's Camberwell, LB of Southwark (G. G. Scott, 1841–4); St Saviour's, Tetbury, Gloucestershire (S. W. Daukes, 1848). This is the result of a selective survey of church furnishing schemes which Teresa Sladen carried out for English Heritage in 1997. See Historical Analysis and Research Team, Subject Files, 'Church Furnishings'.
[20]   Letter to J. G. Young, September [1840?], Lambeth Palace Library, Manuscripts, 3120, fo. 31.
[21]   *The Buildings of England, Sussex*, p. 287.

for the overall form of the benches. By summer 1841 his campaign against pews and in favour of open benches based on medieval examples was under way. In December he delivered a lecture which was published early in 1842 as *The History of Pews*, which came out in a second edition the following year as well as a supplement (in which the spelling 'pues' was used). Although earlier antiquarian literature as well as archidiaconal charges of the 1830s had objected to pews for aesthetic, archaeological, and liturgical reasons, no one had previously committed themselves so wholeheartedly to the reform of church seating.[22]

Whatever else he might have done, Neale clearly spent a great deal of time studying the Romanesque details. These helped to feed his theory that twelfth-century decorations were directly representative of the 'various methods of martyrdom'. Thus began the Camdenian quest to develop the theory of the architectural sign which culminated in Neale and Webb's *Durandus* of 1843.[23] Neale's description of what the Romanesque mouldings at Old Shoreham represented is worth quoting:

> The saw toothed, the nail-head, the reticulated, the chain, the cable, tell a plain tale as to their derivation, and others which may at first sight appear more obscure, are in reality as emblematic as above. The chevron may well symbolise either impalement or exposure to the teeth of wild beasts ...[24]

Neale had been helped to this rather extraordinary position by George Lewis's splendid monograph on Kilpeck Church, which had been circulated in draft form to the OAS and then CCS early in 1840, although the two men disagreed as to the specific content of medieval signs.[25] Neale saw such 'emblematic' details as referring to church doctrine as it had developed over centuries. Lewis saw things differently. He believed that Romanesque decorations had precise scriptural correspondences and so could be read as truncated stories; this was another instance of the Romanesque being embraced by protestant Anglicans anxious about the Catholic connotations of the Gothic.[26] Nevertheless, Lewis was the first to publish translations from the chapter on church symbolism and ornaments written by William Durandus in

22   Bradley, *op. cit.*, p. 190.
23   *The Symbolism of Churches and Church Ornaments. A Translation of the First Book of the Rationale Divinorum Officiorum written by William Durandus, Sometime Bishop of Mende...* (Leeds, 1843). This was dedicated to the Society.
24   Neale, 'Old Shoreham', p. 30.
25   *Illustrations of Kilpeck Church, Herefordshire... with an Essay on Ecclesiastical Design* (London, 1842), ii–ix, pp. 7–8, 16–8, *et passim*.
26   T. Mowl, 'The Norman Revival', in *Influences in Victorian Art and Architecture*, ed. S. Macready and F. H. Thompson (London, 1985), pp. 41–8, at pp. 46–7. On the more pervasive Victorian mistrust of Catholic imagery see S. Gilley, 'Victorian Feminism and Catholic Art: The Case of Mrs. Jameson', in *The Church and the Arts*, ed. D. Wood (Oxford and Cambridge, USA, 1992), pp. 381–92.

1286.[27]

A Model Restoration in Cambridge

Old Shoreham was a worthy project, but the Society had not taken a leading role in the work, probably because it was cut off from the world in a sleepy little corner of the south coast. Just as Buckler's work was being completed the Society was presented with a perfect opportunity to make a much more prominent, practical demonstration of its principles, and as luck would have it not 300 yards from Trinity's own front gates. In the second week of August 1841 part of the south aisle of the round nave of St Sepulchre, Cambridge collapsed. Generations of burials too close to the shallow Romanesque foundations had sapped the underlying gravel. Ominous bulges in the outer walls suggested worse to follow. At once 'some members of the University approached the parish vestry' offering to pay for the repairs.[28] This soon expanded into a full-scale restoration sponsored by the Camden Society. In exchange for providing most of the £1,000 then estimated for the job, the Society secured places for representatives on the Restoration Committee which also included the two churchwardens, the curate, the Rev. James E. Dalton, and the incumbent, the Rev. R. R. Faulkner, who was non-resident and took very little interest in the parish.[29]

The vestry was grateful. The parish was small and poor, and the congregation was said by one Camden supporter to be dominated by the 'anti-rate' party.[30] True or not, it is certainly significant that the Round

[27] Bentham had referred to Durandus in his 1771 essay. Later R. Simpson at Oriel College, Oxford, delivered a paper on the ancient text to the 2 December 1840 meeting of the OAS. See *Rules and Proceedings* of the Society for this date, 1 (1840), p. 4. Simpson declared the views expressed in the Durandus to be 'fanciful' but of historic interest because 'the architects of our Gothic cathedrals and churches had some such objects in their minds when forming their designs'. Although Lewis did not publish until 1842, he sent a complimentary proof to the OAS on 26 October 1840. In the accompanying letter he praised the Oxbridge societies. See OAS Calendar of Correspondence, Bodleian Library Manuscripts, Dep.d.538. Neale's 1840 paper on Old Shoreham makes it clear that he read an advance copy or draft of the text.

[28] Subcommittee for the Restoration, *The Church of the Holy Sepulchre or the Round Church, Cambridge* (Cambridge, 1842), p. 4.

[29] Richard Rowland Faulkner was admitted to St John's in 1818, he was the son of the Rev. E. L. Faulkner, rector of St John's, Clerkenwell, and was vicar of Holy Sepulchre from 1825 until his death in 1873. Faulkner was installed at Havering, where he took up permanent residence in 1834. See *Alumni Cantabrigiensis, 1753–1900* (Cambridge, 1954). According to Thomas Thorp's *A Statement of Particulars connected with the Restoration of the Round Church by the Chairman of the Restoration Committee* (Cambridge and London, 1845), p. 4, Rowland did not attend any early meetings of the Restoration Committee.

[30] J. O. Halliwell, 'St Sepulchre's, Cambridge', *The Archaeologist and Journal of*

Church had a long-standing association with charismatic, evangelical preaching. In the early 1780s Henry Coulthurst had established a Sunday evening service here for the poor and helped to inspire the great Charles Simeon. By 1784 the Round Church was one of three in Cambridge where, according to Wesley himself, 'true Scriptural religion is preached'.[31] It is not clear whether a more Protestant strain of Anglicanism was still being practised at the Round Church in 1841, but the shadow of Simeon (who died in 1836) and his followers was very long, and it certainly took in Trinity College. There remains the possibility, then, that the recent history of the Round Church was as important to the Camden Society as the splendid twelfth-century architecture. Here the stripping out of galleries and pews would have had a very particular ideological charge. And in this struggle for the symbolic high ground, as in so many others, the decisive factor was money. The Society had it, the parish didn't. The vestry promised £300, but in the end even this had to be borrowed from the President of the Camden Society, Archdeacon Thorp, who acted as a kind of modern-day project director.[32] Neale was otherwise occupied during the early stages of the restoration.[33] Thus opened a drama that would eventually contribute to the crisis of the Camden Society, its dissolution, and reconstitution in London.[34]

The Round Church

The Round Church had long been recognised as a rare and somewhat enigmatic monument, one of four surviving ancient British churches with western rounds.[35] In 1781 James Essex read an important paper on the building to the Society of Antiquaries, in which he dismissed the idea that round churches had been built as synagogues (Holy Sepulchre was in a part of Cambridge known traditionally as the Jewry). He concluded that this and the

---

Antiquarian Science, 1 (1842), pp. 105–14, at pp. 111–2.

[31] H. E. Hopkins, *Charles Simeon of Cambridge* (London, 1977), pp. 44, 174. I am grateful to Geoff Brandwood for drawing my attention to this.

[32] The parish paid the money back in instalments between 1844 and 1850. See Cambridge Record Office (hereafter CRO), Holy Sepulchre, Vestry Minutes, P21/8/1, 1844, 1845, 25 April 1848, and Easter 1850.

[33] In August 1841 he was appointed tutor and chaplain at Downing College, but after only three weeks he resigned because he had not been able to persuade the Master and Fellows to attend chapel. By the end of the year he had taken up a temporary curacy at St Nicholas, Guildford. See L. Litvack, *John Mason Neale and the Quest for Sobornost* (Oxford, 1994), p. 15.

[34] E. Rose, 'The Stone Table in the Round Church and the Crisis of the Cambridge Camden Society', *Victorian Studies*, 10 (1966–7), pp. 119–144.

[35] There are round naves at Little Maplestead Church, Essex, the Temple Church, London, and the Church of the Holy Sepulchre, Northampton. The chapel at Ludlow Castle in Shropshire has a round nave, but the exact reason for this is not clear, and the Victorians did not class it with the parochial examples.

other round churches were typological copies of the original Holy Sepulchre in Jerusalem, a building which had been built in the fourth century by Constantine the Great and was in turn based on that greatest of round temples, the Pantheon.[36] Thus the circular form had crossed from Western Christendom to the East, and been brought back again by the Crusaders. On the basis of stylistic evidence he concluded that the round plan had been established in c.1125, which is what Pevsner said two centuries later.[37] The original form of the east end has never been determined. The chancel and its north aisle were rebuilt in the fifteenth century, when the top stage of the drum was also replaced by a bell stage with Perpendicular tracery. Essex's paper concluded with a paper reconstruction of the round as it would have appeared when newly built (plates 61-2). In the accompanying text he put a plea for this to be realised, and for the interior to be improved. It was then

> as much deformed as the outside: a gallery has been built above the arches, which reduces the circle to a square [in plan], and by its projection hides the pillars and arches... Pews, which are no ornament to any church, and never intended in this, fill the area below, and not only encumber the pillars, so that they appear much heavier ... but destroy the real form and apparent magnitude of the building.[38]

The gist of Essex's paper found its way into later guidebooks, including an anonymous one published by Deighton's of Cambridge in 1837 – Boyce and Neale matriculated in 1836 – which decried the condition of the building as it was then:

> On account of its singular shape [the Round Church] excites the curiosity of the antiquary; though its primary form has been much disfigured by subsequent rebuildings, and in its present state it appears under many disadvantages.[39]

The Templars were not known to be associated with the site, and so it was surmised, again on the strength of Essex's 1781 paper, that the church had been built by some lay fraternity or prince as a prayer offering for success in the Crusades.

[36] 'Observations on the Origin and Antiquity of Round Churches; and of the Round Church Cambridge in Particular', *Archaeologia* 6 (1782), pp. 163-72. Read to the Antiquaries on 24 May 1781.

[37] Though the Royal Commission on the Historical Monuments of England was more circumspect. After noting that the Abbot of Ramsey had granted the site to the fraternity of the Holy Sepulchre sometime between 1114 and 1130, its fieldworkers would only venture a date of sometime in the first half of the twelfth century. RCHME, *An Inventory of the Historical Monuments in the City of Cambridge* 2 vols. (London, 1959, 1988), I, p. 255.

[38] Essex, p. 177.

[39] *The Cambridge Guide including Historical and Architectural Notes of the Public Buildings*, new edn (Cambridge, 1837), p. 200.

In the meantime several views had been published. Arguably the best is Samuel Prout's which John Britton issued in 1805 and later reprinted in *Architectural Antiquities of Great Britain and Ireland* (1826–33) (plate 62[a]). Augustus Charles Pugin drew St Sepulchre's for Ackerman's 1815 *History of the University of Cambridge*. Storer published another view in 1830, and so did the Rev. J. J. Smith in the *Cambridge Portfolio* of 1840. But what really sparked interest in the building was an 1836 publication by the architect and fellow of the Society of Antiquaries, William Wallen. Although this specifically concerned the round nave at Little Maplestead, Whallen's book considered the whole category of building and provided a detailed history of the Crusades, which he illustrated with rather charming and Romantic knights in authentic dress. Anthony Salvin, who would be appointed architect to the restoration, subscribed and so did the young George Gilbert Scott, Benjamin Ferrey, and A. W. N. Pugin himself. Wallen did not venture exact dates, except to say they all came after 1095 – which was quite obvious, since that was when the Council of Clermont declared the First Crusade.

Then, in November 1839, James Orchard Halliwell delivered a paper on the church to the Society. Halliwell had matriculated at Trinity soon after Neale but was by this time at Jesus studying mathematics and working as librarian; in 1844 he started the work for which he is remembered today, the first modern, critical biography of Shakespeare. His position *vis à vis* the Society is not clear; he was only briefly a member. In any case, after hearing Halliwell's paper on the Round Church, Neale set about scraping at the fabric in search of emblematic mouldings.[40] In November 1841, two months after the Society had got involved with the building, Halliwell published an enlarged version of the paper on St Sepulchre's in his own short-lived *Archaeologist and Journal of Antiquarian Science*.[41] He concluded that there was no hard evidence to date the round nave precisely, but soon after would report a document to the Society that gave the consecration date as 1101.[42] He echoed the speculation put in the 1837 guide, hinting that the church had been built as a private prayer offering for success in the Holy Land. All this echoed the Camdenian world view perfectly, and what was more it meant that the building the Society had tied itself to was arguably the first round church in England as well as being an early specimen of the Norman style.[43]

[40] Lambeth Palace MSS. 3107. fo. 72, entry for 23 November 1839.
[41] 1 (1842), pp. 105–14.
[42] T. Thorp, *The Church of the Holy Sepulchre, Cambridge* (Cambridge, 1844), pp. 8–9.
[43] Anon. [Cambridge Camden Society Subcommittee for the Restoration of the Round Church/Thomas Thorp], *The Church of the Holy Sepulchre or the Round Church, Cambridge* (Cambridge , 1842), p. 4. Yet even Thorp, fired by enthusiasm for the project, grew more circumspect, and by 1844 he had settled on a date of *c.*1130, partly on stylistic grounds and partly because be believed that the

But the symbolic potency of the Holy Sepulchre, whether the date was a precocious 1101 or a more sober 1130, made it especially attractive. Neale's interest in architectural symbolism, his desire to isolate that moment when architecture slipped from being a literally mimetic art form into a conventionalised language, was well established. What building could be more susceptible to semiological analysis than one whose essential and defining characteristic was a typological resemblance to the Temple of the Holy Sepulchre in Jerusalem, and through this to an even more ancient precedent, the Pantheon? Constantine's round building, supported by twelve columns (the Cambridge example has eight), was meant to symbolise the heavens and the passage of Christ's Resurrected Body from the Sepulchre itself into the eternal firmament.[44] In 1844 Thorp spoke openly about this chain of resemblances, calling Holy Sepulchre at Cambridge a 'facsimile' of the Early Christian example by which he meant not a literal copy but a rough formal one capturing the essence of the original.[45] The fundamental idea of the building was profound, echoing across the centuries and at a single stroke conflating Pagan, Early Christian, and medieval traditions as well as Eastern and Western Christendom. St Sepulchre's was a manifestation of that continuous Christian tradition which the Tractarians had in their own rather different way been seeking to establish. Thorp hoped that the thoroughness which the Society brought to this one project would inspire visitors to emulate the example, and thus bring about the success of the Camdenian's own architectural crusade against national apostasy.

Anthony Salvin was retained to survey the building and oversee the restoration. He had probably got the job through the intervention of Alexander James Beresford Hope, whose church at Kilndown in Kent Salvin had just finished refurnishing, providing both stained glass designs and a stone altar, as well as orchestrating other works by Butterfield, Carpenter, and Willement.[46] His only previous brush with restoration had been in 1830, when he was charged with restoring the south transept at Norwich Cathedral and coming up with a furnishing scheme for the choir. Yet there is no denying that he was pushing the Gothic Revival in new directions. In the late 1830s he had departed from the modular symmetry which was so characteristic of the Gothic employed in the Commissioners' Churches.[47]

---

dedication to the Holy Sepulchre was first used by the Knights Hospitallers at Clerkenwell to commemorate the 1134 massacre of the Knights Templar in Jerusalem. Thorp, *op. cit.*, p. 8.

[44] The Camdenians planned to cover the vaults of the restored building with frescoes depicting zodiacal symbols.

[45] Thorp, *op. cit.*, pp. 6-7, 11.

[46] J. Allibone, *Anthony Salvin, Pioneer of Gothic Revival* (Cambridge, 1988), pp. 115-6. See also White, *op. cit.*, pp. 156-7. Thomas Willement designed the stained glass at Kilndown and at the Round Church.

Holy Trinity, Darlington (1836–8) was a breakthrough building; its asymmetrically-placed tower was ahead of anything that had gone before, but the promise of this commission was not realised. The 1840 church at Spittlegate in Grantham is disappointing, and the scheme of furnishing is crowded and unsophisticated.[48] The roughly contemporary design for Sewstern church in Leicestershire is little better; the chancel is barely expressed.[49] All this begs the question of just who exactly was responsible for what at the Round Church, the architect or his opinionated client? Salvin's drawings for the project, identified in the 1970s in a private collection, have since been lost, though from a published description it is clear that these included contract drawings for the open benches.[50] But was the overall form of the benches his or the CCS-dominated restoration committee? In the absence of new documentary evidence, we may never know.

Salvin did at any rate produce the perspective view of the building as restored, a lithograph of which was published by the Society in 1842. He also wrote a detailed fabric report which concluded that the entire church would have to be underpinned with concrete in order to avoid further collapse. The Romanesque groin vaulting in the round aisle was in very poor condition, the result, he surmised, of the vibrations set up by bell ringing. As for the round belfry itself, this was said to be on the verge of ruin and was in any case in a Gothic style that detracted from the purity of the Romanesque original. It was eventually taken down to the corbel table.[51] The present bell tower at the west end of the north aisle was not initially planned but came later that year.[52]

The evidence for the original appearance of the top stage of the round was slight to say the least – precisely one clerestory window on the north side, which was in turn replaced during Salvin's work.[53] Essex's paper reconstruction of 1781 seems to have exercised a strong influence (plates 61 and 62[b]). There is of course the possibility that the two architects, working from the same evidence, drew similar conclusions. Both have a conical cap, and the drum heights are broadly similar. But there are differences, and these are

---

47   Bradley, *The Gothic Revival*, pp. 408–9.
48   Papers of the Incorporated Church Building Society, Lambeth Palace Library (hereafter ICBS), 2710.
49   ICBS 2807. See also ICBS 3240 and 3297.
50   John Loughborough Pearson was set to copying them when he joined Salvin's office in autumn 1841. Pearson also made drawings for the Kilndown furnishing scheme. See A. Quiney, *John Loughborough Pearson* (London & New Haven, 1979), p. 13, and *ex info.* the author, 1997.
51   [CCS, Subcommittee for the Restoration], *Holy Sepulchre* (1842), p. 4. See also Thorp, *Holy Sepulchre*, pp. 1–5. The old bells were sold in 1845 to the Rev. H. Winsor of St Paul, Armitage Bridge, Huddersfield. Cambridge County Record Office (CCRO), P21/24//12a.
52   Thorp, *Holy Sepulchre*, pp. 19–20.
53   [CCS, Subcommittee for the Restoration], *Holy Sepulchre* (1842), p. 4.

telling. Take the eaves. Salvin went for a primitive touch, exposing the rafter ends, whereas Essex covered them over with a neat, and very Georgian-looking, parapet. The string courses do not run over the buttresses in the earlier reconstruction but they do in Salvin's, thus binding the various elements together in a characteristically Victorian way. Essex gave the entrance a tympanum, Salvin did not.

The Ecclesiologist published regular reports on the progress of the works. By November 1841 (when Salvin was made an honorary member of the CCS) the bell tower with its late Gothic windows had been taken down to the nave corbel table. The new drum of masonry was raised and the timber frame of the conical cap constructed by December. On the inside of the church whitewash was removed. By January 1842, the nave was ready to receive encaustic paving; a pattern based on ancient examples was being discussed but action was deferred until the building work was completed. That spring the workmen were building the tower groining; the decision was taken to replace the ancient arch into the chancel with a modern design in the late Gothic style to match the surviving east end. The new south chancel aisle, designed to match that on the north, was roofed over by this time.[54] This aisle was meant to provide space for seatings lost when the pews in the round had been cleared.[55]

The first snag came in May 1842.[56] Up until then Salvin had been intending to keep the north chancel aisle and the east wall of the chancel, both in a late Gothic style. However, once workmen had started to cut back the plaster it was clear that the brick and rubble core was beyond repair.[57] There was no choice but to rebuild them in facsimile as well, so that by the close of 1842 the east end was entirely new.[58] Excavations had turned up earlier foundations and some twelfth-century carvings under the present east end.[59] Had members on the Restoration Committee known from the start that the entire east end was going to be rebuilt, they would have opted, it was admitted at the time, for a Romanesque design. But the stylistic die had been cast. The east end was to be Perpendicular in style. It was not that the Society objected to the lack of stylistic unity, it was just that with such an

54 *Ecclesiologist*, 1 (1841–2), pp. 5–6, 29–30, 51–2, 115.
55 This method of enlargement was exactly in line with what Neale would advocate in the 1843 Camden publication *Church Enlargement and Church Arrangement* (Cambridge), pp. 8–9, in which the building of an aisle is reckoned to be more consistent with the original character of an ancient church than the extension of the chancel or nave, though on the tiny Holy Sepulchre site neither of these was a serious option.
56 *Ecclesiologist*, 1 (1841–2), pp. 143–4.
57 [CCS, Subcommittee for the Restoration], *Holy Sepulchre* (1842), pp. 5–6.
58 *Ibid.*
59 *Ecclesiologist*, 1 (1841–2), pp. 143–4.

exceptionally important medieval church, consideration would have been given to removing later work which was unexceptional. But as if this were not bad enough, rebuilding the chancel and north aisle was going to put the project even further over budget. The initial estimate had shot up from £1,000 to £2,400, and there was still a considerable sum to spend on the furnishing.[60] When the roofs on the east end were on, in March 1843, the Society's funds were exhausted, but at least most of the purely architectural work was finished.[61] As the scaffolding came down it would have been clear to anyone who had known the church before that something in the order of 80% of St Sepulchre's had been rebuilt (plate 62[b]).[62] No one seemed to mind. Scrupulous regard for surface and authentic material would not become an issue for at least another decade, and even then only amongst a minority of progressive architects, critics, and archaeologists.[63]

There remained the interior fittings, not an added extra but absolutely essential to the project. The restoration committee had first discussed them in August 1842: encaustic tiles, a mixture of ancient and modern stained glass, a new font, and oak poppy-head benches.[64] There would be no compromising, and no delay. Until the money could be raised by subscription, the work would proceed 'on the personal security of those engaged in conducting it' in order to 'set an example, in this as well as other particulars, of the duty incumbent upon all church restorers, of doing every one of his own works as well, and as far, as he can'.[65] Salvin's designs were received in March, but the final decision was held over to give the incumbent, the Rev. Faulkner, the chance to comment.[66]

It is to be regretted that this furnishing plan has been lost; however, a seating plan made at the turn of the century[67] and a careful analysis of the

---

[60]   [CCS, Subcommittee for the Restoration], *Holy Sepulchre* (1842), pp. 6–7. There was an application to the Incorporated Church Building Society, but sadly this file survives neither in the ICBS archives at Lambeth Palace nor amongst the smaller collection of Society material at the Antiquaries in Burlington House.

[61]   *Ecclesiologist*, 2 (1842–3), p. 130.

[62]   There has never been a proper inventory of surviving stonework of the kind carried out a few years ago on the west front of Rochester Cathedral. This figure is based on the author's analysis of the standing fabric. It appears that the only authentically ancient stones remaining are those composing the lower drum, the transverse arches in the nave aisle, the arcade and gallery sections of the nave itself, and perhaps a few of the mouldings to the main entrance.

[63]   See Miele, 'Real Antiquity', *passim*, and the same author's '"Their Interest and Habit": Professionalism and the Restoration of Medieval Churches', in C. Brooks and A. Saint (eds.), *The Victorian Church: Architecture and Society* (Manchester, 1995), pp. 151–72.

[64]   *Ecclesiologist*, 1 (1841–2), pp. 202–3.

[65]   [CCS, Subcommittee for the Restoration], *Holy Sepulchre* (1842), p. 7–9.

[66]   Thorp, *A Statement of Particulars* (1845), p. 7.

surviving fabric and furnishings allows it to be reconstructed with a fair degree of accuracy. The round was left entirely clear except for the font for which Salvin designed a six-foot high cover, unusually large for this date and looking forward to those elaborate font covers designed in the last quarter of the century.[68] The church was paved throughout with Chamberlain's encaustic and glazed tiles, an early example of a complete scheme. The tile manufacturer had sent samples of his revived medieval tiles to the Oxford Architectural Society in October 1841, making them available to members of the sister societies for the same 20% discount extended to the trade.[69] Because of the awkward plan, the benches had to be accommodated in the east end but were not permitted to encroach on the chancel, a cardinal rule of Camdenian church arrangement. To achieve this the chancel was raised one step above the rest; a wood panelled divide, which doubled as the back rest for a bank of stalls, was run between the westernmost arches of the two-bay chancel. The seating in each chancel aisle was broken into two banks entered from the northeast and southeast bay of the round aisle. Additional benches were set down along the east wall of each chancel aisle facing north and south respectively. The area of greatest interest was of course the chancel. This was installed with three stalls on each side; the outermost was merely that bench run between the piers (noted above), which also provided a clear physical barrier between the aisles and chancel. In front of these plain benches was a linked pair of benches with no frontals (the present frontals were added later, probably in the early part of this century) and no returns. At the east end of each innermost bench was a lectern facing inwards, that to the north was more elaborate and broader. The octagonal wood pulpit was probably placed against the south pier; it has a shallow stone base and was originally entered by stairs from the southeast. The area between the choir stalls was paved in encaustic tiles; there was a clear space to the west of the sanctuary, and two steps up into it, where there stood a stone altar table.

As for the benches themselves, they are of oak and economically constructed. Each bench end finishes in a tenon secured by screws into sleepers which were not fixed to the floor. Benches abutting the outside walls are fixed to them. The average depth of each bench is 16", and the seats roughly 11⅜". The backs are low, some 12¾", and finish well below the poppy heads which stand proud. The bench itself is placed 18" above the tile pavement, and the seat back is vertical. There is a book board of 7¼" to the

[67] CCRO, P21/6/4. This is not to scale.
[68] RCHME, *Cambridge*, vol. 2, p. 254.
[69] Calendar of Correspondence of the Oxford Architectural Society, Bodleian MSS., Dep.d.538, 14 October 1841, *Rules and Proceedings of the Oxford Architectural Society*, 3 November 1841. 'We are much obliged,' Chamberlain's wrote, 'by your kind assurance of giving our tiles notoriety, and in no quarter do we feel more anxious to stand well than at the University of Oxford'.

rear of most. The height of each bench end from tile pavement to the tip of the poppy head is 46¾" and the distance from back to back roughly 38". These dimensions are broadly in line with what Neale and *The Ecclesiologist* had been recommending for some time. The January 1843 number of the journal contains an analysis of the dimensions of medieval seating.[70]

The seating plan and bench design were unusual for the 1840s, but neither unique nor controversial. The stone altar was. This was installed, it was said, at the request of an anonymous donor, who also paid for a stone credence table. Salvin's drawings for everything were ready by 4 May 1843, but when the Committee presented costed designs to the incumbent, the Rev. Faulkner, on the very next day, the stone altar design was held back.[71] Faulkner wrote to Thorp on 8 May to express his gratitude to the Society:

> It is certainly a matter of much moment that now all parties concerned in the internal arrangements be of one mind, and after your remarks of the happy and friendly meeting the other day there cannot, I think, be much doubt respecting it. I am sure that I shall be delighted with the restoration.[72]

In his 1845 account of these events Thorp is suspiciously silent about why Faulkner was not told about the altar table, and yet it can only have been that the Restoration Committee had decided to gamble on Faulkner's indifference to it all – he spent most of his time at his other living – or on his reluctance to object to a *fait accompli*. Things went ahead smoothly, and the furnishing was almost done by September.[73] On 25 October 1843, Queen Victoria herself was led around the church in the company of Faulkner as part of a royal visit to Cambridge. Only minor points remained, principally an oak roof to the new south chancel aisle to match the original one in the north. Faulkner himself paid for this in 1845.

Two weeks after the Queen's visit, Faulkner wrote Thorp a somewhat hysterical letter, in which he lambasted the Society for installing a stone altar contrary to the canons of the Church of England. Thorp tried to mollify Faulkner, or so Thorp claimed. The lines between opposing camps quickly hardened. Faulkner brought a suit at the Ely Consistory Court alleging that the stone altar was illegal and asking the Chancellor to overturn his earlier faculty.[74] The case was heard in April 1844. In July the Chancellor found against Faulkner and issued a special licence to sanction the altar and credence table. He also awarded the churchwardens' costs. There was a long report of the judgment in the Anglican *British Magazine* with quotations from

[70]   'Open Seats', *Ecclesiologist*, 2 (1842), pp. 122–5, at pp. 122–3.
[71]   Elliot Rose, 'The Stone Table in the Round Church and the Crisis of the Cambridge Camden Society', *Victorian Studies*, 10 (1966–7), pp. 119–44, at pp. 127–8.
[72]   Thorp, *A Statement of Particulars* (1845), p. 13, as quoted in Rose, *op. cit.*, p. 128.
[73]   *Ecclesiologist*, 3 (1843–4), p. 21.
[74]   Rose, *op. cit.*, p. 130.

Faulkner's ranting testimony – the stone altar was such 'as are used for idolatrous and heretical purposes in popish churches'.[75] He went on in this way at some length. Beresford Hope, Thorp, Benjamin Webb, the young William Butterfield, and Sir Stephen Glynne had all sworn affidavits to the effect that nothing precluded the use of a stone altar table in the Church of England.[76] Meanwhile support for the Society was coming unstuck amidst charges of crypto-Romanism. Victory in the Consistory Court galvanised the Evangelical party which counted *The Times* amongst its supporters. The paper thundered against the Society, declaring itself the enemy of all 'innovations' in matters of religion. Faulkner was given space to accuse the Camdenians of 'the abominations of Popery'.[77] With financial backing from this new coalition Faulkner appealed to the Court of the Arches. Meanwhile Thorp's May 1844 address to the Society hinted that it might soon have to be dissolved.[78] The committee survived a motion calling for it to be wound up, but confidence was shaken, and the chorus of Evangelical disapproval did not stop.[79] Faulkner's claims had become something of a *cause celebre*. His appeal was upheld. In January 1845, Rt. Hon. Herbert Jenner Fust delivered judgment. The Archdeacon of Ely was instructed to order the removal of the offending items in April 1845.[80] It should be stressed that Fust did not think that the material from which the altar was made mattered all that much; for him the case turned on whether or not the feature was fixed to the east wall of the chancel and therefore immoveable. He established it was, but only just, by virtue of some lime putty between the horizontal slab and the wall.

The long-demolished Camdenian altar is recorded in two images. One is a rather plain engraving published in *The Ecclesiologist* of 1845 and showing only it and its immediate setting. The other is a very good lithograph of the finished interior, which was published in the 1846 edition of *Monumental Brasses* as a record of the Society's work (plate 63). The *Cambridge Chronicle* for 14 June reported that a new communion table, rails, and other unspecified decorations would be completed shortly by a local man, one J. Wentworth.[81] *The Ecclesiologist* described the new wooden table as having 'flimsy buttresses for legs, and cockniy [sic] spandrels'.[82] This is not very fair to the handsome

[75] *The British Magazine*, 26 (1844), pp. 204–11.
[76] Rose, *op. cit.*, pp. 125–33.
[77] *The Times*, 3 and 7 August 1844, pp. 3 and 6.
[78] Rose, *op. cit.*, p. 132.
[79] *Ibid.*, pp. 135–7.
[80] Judgment of the Rt Hon. Herbert Jenner Fust, Kt., Dean of the Arches, *The Stone Altar Case*, ed. from the Judge's notes by J. E. P. Robertson, DCC Advocate (London: W. Benning and Co., 1845), p. 2. See also *English Reports*, vol. 143 (1845).
[81] As quoted in *The Ecclesiologist*, 4 (1845), pp. 194–5.
[82] *Ecclesiologist*, 4 (1845), p. 217.

piece of oak furniture which survives in the church today. But on the other hand, and with the benefit of art historical hindsight, there can be no denying that Wentworth's new work, which included altar rails and a priest's chair, was behind the times, looking more like the frilly Gothicism of Pugin's suite of Windsor furniture than anything authentically medieval. Remarkably, apart from minor alterations in the early part of this century, the interior fittings survive as an eloquent witness to the first of many architectural disputes which were linked to ritualism. 1845 was a turning point in the history of the Victorian Church of England; in January there was the Round Church decision and in early October Newman's conversion.[83]

Practical Advice

The Society would never again become directly involved in the restoration of an ancient church, but this did not stop it from pronouncing on the subject. The forthright, sometimes outspoken, reviews published in *The Ecclesiologist* are generally well known, but another area of the Society's work, that of giving advice, less so. According to E. J. Boyce, admittedly writing years after the fact, the Society received a total of 98 requests 'respecting the reparations of old Churches, designs for new ones, details in connexion with the internal arrangement of existing churches, and designs for Church Plate and Ornament' in 1842-3 alone.[84] The most significant intervention from this early period concerned the Church of St Mary, Stafford. The rector of Stafford invited G. G. Scott to survey his church and make plans for its restoration in 1840 or 1841. Still new to this sort of work Scott needed the help of an expert, so he employed Edwin Gwilt. He had gained experience of old buildings in the office of his father, George, a London architect-antiquary who had rebuilt the choir and Lady Chapel of St Marie Overie in Southwark (now the Cathedral).

At Stafford the crossing piers were near to collapse and the rest of the church was in need of embellishment. The nave had been rebuilt in the Perpendicular style with a fine clerestory. Here Scott's work was confined to repairs and a few decorative flourishes to enhance the overall aspect of the ancient fabric. The chancel and south transept were somewhat later and in a 'debased' version of the style, at least according to Scott. On the basis of archaeological evidence the architect proposed rebuilding the east end so that it had three matching gables in an early thirteenth-century style. No one quarrelled with this, but Scott's plans for the south transept were more invasive and controversial. Working from a few surviving details, the architect concluded that this transept actually predated the chancel. Scott was keen to

---

[83]   O. Chadwick, *The Victorian Church*, 2 vols. (London, 1970 edition), 1, pp. 212-21, esp. pp. 213-4, 221. Chadwick's conclusions about the history of ritualism come in vol. 2, p. 242.

[84]   *Memorial*, p. 22.

establish his credentials as an archaeologically-minded church architect whose restorations were based on scholarship and the eternal verities of medieval style, not on personal whim, and he was very proud of this transept. His reconstruction drawing shows a steeply pitched roof – the angle was known by weather mouldings on the tower – and three distinct lancet lights, each separated by narrow offset buttresses.

This design was displayed along with the rest of the drawings for the project in the west end of the church in 1841, where they came to the attention of the Rev. John Louis Petit. He had just published *Remarks on Church Architecture* and would, over the coming decade, contribute to the battle of the styles.[85] Petit was also an accomplished, if somewhat eccentric, draughtsman. His style was formed on that of Samuel Prout, Ruskin's favourite, and may have influenced Street's mature style. In any case, Petit was the kind of critic who would not go away. He had a personal interest. His brother-in-law was Thomas Salt, a leading Stafford citizen and prominent banker who had made a generous contribution to the restoration fund.

Petit had no quarrel with the stylistic transformation of the chancel, its reorientation from the Perpendicular into something in the Early English, nor with the frilly overlay of Gothic details that Scott was proposing for the rest, but he strongly disapproved of what was planned for that south transept. It was less a question of details, which Petit disputed in any case, than it was with the general principle of the thing. Although the existing transept was a late example of a 'debased' style, it was nevertheless authentically Gothic and furthermore a prominent local landmark. The citizens who had known the church for generations would never accept the reconstruction as old. It was as simple as that. Petit was being a little disingenuous here, merely using the local residents to raise one of the perennial problems of philosophy. They stood for the innocent eye, in this case the eye that knows antiquity by patina, wear, and personal memories. Still, it was fair comment and neither the first nor the last time that the question of authenticity would be raised in such a context.[86]

For five months, from October 1841 to January 1842, letters crossed, until finally the disputants agreed to be bound by the decision of a committee of experts drawn from the Society and its sister group at Oxford. The resounding endorsement of Scott's transept stung, and this was not the first time Petit had been crossed by the Camdenians. *The Ecclesiologist* had given his first book a decidedly mixed review (see below). In an appeal to posterity, and perhaps to preserve his self respect, Petit decided to publish the correspondence.[87] The Society for its part made much of this intervention.

[85]   N. Pevsner, *Some Architectural Writers of the Nineteenth Century* (Oxford, 1972), pp. 95–101.

[86]   Miele, 'Real Antiquity', *passim*; also Pevsner, *Some Architectural Writers*, p. 96.

[87]   See J. L. Petit, *On the Proposed Restorations of St Mary Stafford* (privately printed,

The anonymous reviewer was for once explicit about the level of involvement: a representative visited the site and inspected plans, then reported back to the committee in Cambridge, who debated the matter. They discussed it with colleagues at Oxford and issued a judgment. The end result was the nearest thing to a statement of restoration principles that the Camden Society published before 1847, and so is worthy of quotation. In such buildings, with remains from several phases,

> two principles offer themselves as guides. We must, either from existing evidences or from supposition, recover the original scheme as conceived by the first builder, or was begun by him and developed by his immediate successors; or, on the other hand, must retain the additions or alterations of subsequent ages, repairing them when needing it, or even perhaps carrying out more fully the idea which dictated them ... For our own part we decidedly choose the former; always however remembering that it is of great importance to take into account the age and purity of later, the occasion for its addition, its adaptation to its uses, and its intrinsic advantages or convenience.[88]

More than a century later, in 1976, Nikolaus Pevsner would quote these same words, without any regard for their original context, in order to prove that the Society routinely counselled the removal of late Gothic work and, furthermore, was committed to returning ancient buildings to one moment in their history.[89] He was seeking to turn the Camdenians into the foil for the rise of a modern conservation philosophy as espoused by Ruskin and Morris. But as we have seen in the case of the Round Church, the Society did not unswervingly demand stylistic unity. Instead it was guided by that presumption in favour of the historic building as it has been passed down through the generations, showing due regard for the stylistic heterogeneity which was, and remains, so characteristic of medieval churches. Of course this inclusive definition of what constituted the historic interest of a church did not extend to any feature that was remotely classicising, nor did it lead to a scrupulous regard for authentic fabric. Such prejudices would take a very long time to shift.

Nevertheless, this point is worth stressing, because it is still widely believed that the Society advocated stylistic purification, the 'correction' of any features which did not fall into that narrow band of stylistic rectitude – the Middle Pointed or Decorated. In fact notices of church restoration

---

1842). The dispute is recounted in an excellent memorial publication by J. Masfen, *Views of the Church of St Mary Stafford...* (London, 1852). Scott himself devoted several pages to this project in *Personal and Professional Recollections*, new edn, ed. G. Stamp (Stamford, 1995), pp. 97–100, *et passim*.

[88]   *Ecclesiologist*, 1 (1841–2), pp. 60–2.

[89]   'Scrape and Anti-scrape', in *The Future of the Past*, ed. J. Fawcett (London, 1976), pp. 35–54, at pp. 41–2.

CHRIS MIELE

published in *The Ecclesiologist* in the first half of the 1840s have very little to say about style at all, and focus largely on the clearing of church interiors, their refurnishing, and 'repairs' as distinct from reconstructions or restorations. It was if the act of merely exposing the ancient fabric was sufficient. Often, as in the favourable review given to the restoration of Binstead church on the Isle of Wight, there is merely a recitation of the different parts, roof, chancel, tracery and furnishings, as if they had been rediscovered by lifting away post-medieval accretions.[90] And there are many other instances to which one could refer to expand on this theme. Consider the high praise which the Society lavished on Pugin's work at Peper Harrow church in Surrey, where the architect had made a reconstruction of a long-gone Norman chancel arch based on fragments embedded in the walls. The contrast between its rude chevron mouldings and the fine Decorated tracery in the restored east end did not ruffle the anonymous reviewer in the slightest (plate 64). Likewise was Scott praised for adopting what was then a radical approach to Spratton church at Northamptonshire, retaining virtually every authentic 'feature', even those which were arguably bad of their kind, for example, the 'debased windows in the south chancel aisle'.[91] That statement of principle which Pevsner quoted, out of context, in 1976, was actually so broad as to commit the Camden Society to nothing so comprehensive as a theory. It was more a question of every case being judged on its merits, a deeply pragmatic approach that comes across in the countless notices of church restorations published in *The Ecclesiologist*.[92] The Society was dogmatic, true, but more so in relation to the style of new churches, church furnishing, and the vexed question of church symbolism.

What, then, are we to make of Boyce's claim that the Society advised on nearly 100 cases in 1842-3? Sadly it is hard to draw firm conclusions, because the Society's papers do not survive. James White, whose pioneering study of the Society has been so influential, took Boyce at his word, judging this level of activity to have been more or less constant. He does not ask how many of these 100 or so requests of 1842-3 were answered with substantial,

90 *Ecclesiologist*, 2 (1842), p. 167. See also the review of Pugin's work at St Mary, Wymeswold, 4 (July and November 1845), pp. 194, 286-7; St Michael, Sowton *et al.*, 5 (1846), pp. 84-6.

91 *Ecclesiologist*, 6 (1847), pp. 118-20.

92 In principle the Society disliked clerestories which it deemed 'mostly a Perpendicular introduction' because these lessened the impression of height which was deemed essential to the 'character and effect of ancient churches'. The resulting increase in light was also troubling. However, that said, the Society was careful to add that many late Gothic clerestories, particularly in East Anglia, were excellent works of art in their own right and ought always to be kept, thus once again allowing the individual design merits of a building to outweigh dogma. *Ecclesiologist*, 4 (1845), pp. 103-5.

detailed advice.[93] Nor does he speculate why, if this level of advice continued, did later Society publications make no mention of it? The Society was not slow to trumpet its successes. Its close involvement with Stafford was unusual, like the work itself. Scott's scheme was one of the most comprehensive, extensive, and expensive restorations of its day.

This is not to say the Society wielded no influence, only that very detailed work, on a carefully defined study sample, is needed to see how ecclesiology spread at the local level. Was the diffusing agent the Society itself or rather one of its affiliated groups, and if so was the message passed on unchanged? If an architect or clergymen sent in a design for critique – for such was routinely noted in *The Ecclesiologist* – this itself implies they were already broadly in sympathy. Does this count as influence? Generalisations will only go so far. Most of Boyce's 100 or so requests could well have been answered by a pamphlet or by a review in the journal. The loss of the Society's papers has left us with more work to do. It is possible, however, to get some idea of the way the Camdenians might have managed their caseload by examining the records of its sister society at Oxford, which fortunately do survive in the manuscript collection at the Bodleian.

Parallel Developments at Oxford

The Oxford Society for Promoting the Study of Gothic Architecture, or Oxford Architectural Society (OAS), was no less active than the CCS, and just as advanced in many respects, though it has not attracted the same scholarly attention.[94] The OAS was actually founded three months before the CCS, in February 1839. The Heraldic Society at Oxford from which it sprang was older still. Although one modern scholar has traced its foundations to a series of papers written by Hurrell Froude on Gothic architecture in the early 1830s, and despite eleven of the 16-strong committee being Tractarians, the OAS was in its official pronouncements rather mild on the sacramental side of church architecture.[95]

---

[93]   White, *op. cit.*, pp. 158–9.

[94]   See S. L. Ollard's excellent 'The Oxford Architectural and Historical Society, and the Oxford Movement', *Oxoniensa* 5 (1940), pp. 146–60, and also W. A. Pantin, 'The Oxford Architectural and Historical Society', *Oxoniensa* 4 (1939), pp. 174–94. The OAS's early calendars of correspondence survive in the Bodleian Manuscripts collection along with miscellaneous papers (Dep.d.518, 538 and 539). *The Rules and Proceedings of the OAS* were published from December 1840, almost a full year before the first number of *The Ecclesiologist,* though the former contains only summaries of papers and occasional annual addresses. Because surviving collections of this publication at the British Library and Society of Antiquaries are bound into volumes differently, the references to the *Proceedings OAS* which follow are given by date of meeting, not page or volume number.

[95]   Ollard, pp. 152–7.

The first request for practical advice came within days of the OAS's founding from the incumbent of Sydling church in Dorset. He invited comments on his own design for a new nave timber roof, and wanted advice on how to repair the ancient chancel screen.[96] Interestingly, many of these early requests concerned furnishings and church carpentry; the letter written by John Ward, a London architect, seeking advice on the design of open benches in a restored interior was typical.[97] Most of the rest were for small, almost trifling details, the sort of work that an incumbent or curate might carry out on his own – repairing or exposing a sedilia, laying down tiles, or instructing a local mason to repair damaged window tracery to follow a surviving example elsewhere in the church.[98] Apart from the Stafford case, the only other large-scale, highly publicized controversy into which the OAS was drawn in these early years was generated by proposals to demolish the medieval church of Blackbourton in Oxfordshire.[99] Small scale or not, the OAS very quickly established a reputation for itself. The Archbishops of Canterbury and York offered themselves as patrons in November 1840.[100] Within a year Thomas Thorp was writing to suggest an affiliation with the CCS.[101] Chamberlain's sent samples of their new line of encaustic tiles for approval to the OAS – not the CCS.[102] In 1844 George Godwin, editor of *The Builder*, asked permission to insert notices of the Society's transactions in his paper.[103] When the *Koelner Dombauverein* began to raise money from abroad, its first approach was to the OAS.[104] And like the CCS, the OAS cultivated close relationships with professional architects in order to satisfy members' requests. At first it turned to J. M. Derick, Pusey's architect for the building of St Saviour, Leeds. In 1843–44 he was replaced by Butterfield and a little

---

96 Bodleian MSS., Dep.d.538, 10 May 1839.

97 Bodleian MSS., Dep.d.538, 26 November 1840, John Ward, architect of 34, Brook Street, London.

98 Bodleian MSS., Dep.d.538, 21 September and 21 October 1841, 13 September 1842, 5 August 1844.

99 The incumbent, the Rev. J. Lupton, enlisted the OAS's help against the vestry. The OAS was asked to provide detailed advice on repair, presumably in order to show that it was viable. Bodleian MSS., Dep.d.538, 1 November 1843.

100 Bodleian MSS., Dep.d.538, 2 November 1840, November 1841.

101 Bodleian MSS., Dep.d.538, 1 July 1841.

102 Bodleian MSS., Dep.d.538, 14 October 1841, and *Proceedings OAS*, 3 November 1841.

103 Bodleian MSS., Dep.d.538, 20 February 1844.

104 This came from a Professor Scholz at the University of Bonn who seems to have spent time at Oxford. Bodleian MSS., Dep.d.538, 24 March 1843. The OAS refused to contribute but promised to publicise the great project, although in the long term Reichensperger ties with the Ecclesiological Society would prove to be deeper.

known architect by the name of James Cranstoun.[105]

The published *Rules and Proceedings* of the OAS show that it had the same intellectual range as the CCS, though sadly only extracts or summaries of papers read at meetings were ever published. There was a paper on Durandus' *Rationale* delivered two years before Neale and Webb's translation of 1843; a paper on 'the principles to be followed in church restoration'; another on church arrangement by James Barr (this was expanded into the OAS's only handbook).[106] There was also a paper by Pugin on spires and a corresponding member discussed the symbolism of German medieval churches.[107] The OAS led the way in making contacts with Continental movements. As early as June 1842 it had initiated a debate on the various state-sponsored systems for historic building control, spurred by the exciting work being undertaken by the French *Comite Historique des Arts et Monuments*, the forerunner of the *Commission des Monuments Historiques*.[108] The Oxford Society did not, however, even begin to come close to matching the acerbic wit of the Camden Society's infamous 'reviews', and on the whole had a rather more respectful attitude to architects.[109]

In addition, the OAS published, although again its style was less combative than the CCS, and it did not use the pamphlet or review as polemical vehicles. Instead the OAS concentrated on architectural monographs. Its series of early works is impressive: J. M. Derick on Stanton Harcourt church (1841), James Harrison on St Giles, Oxford (1842), J. C. Buckler on Wilcote church (1844), Butterfield on Shottesbrooke (1844), James Cranstoun on the chapel of St Bartholomew, near Oxford (1844), and a study of Great Haseley church (1846) by the Rev. Henry Addington. Most of these

---

[105] *Proceedings OAS*, 27 June 1843, 13 November 1844.
[106] *Anglican Church Architecture, with Some Remarks upon Ecclesiastical Furnishing* (Oxford, 1843).
[107] *Proceedings OAS*, 2 December 1840, 9 June and 3 November 1841.
[108] *Proceedings OAS*, 3 November 1841, 2 March and, especially, 6 June 1842. The latter, the third AGM, was dominated by discussions of the different European systems. This was most likely prompted by the Select Committee on National Monuments and Works of Art, which had started taking evidence in June 1841, having come about through pressure brought to bear by the Society for Obtaining Free Admission to Public Monuments. This group had been specifically motivated by developments in France. See *Art Union*, 1, 2, and 4 (1839, 1840, and 1842), pp. 43, 128, and 175–6 respectively, and also *Parliamentary Papers*, 1841, 4, 437–635. I am very grateful to Peter Mandler for these references. For the Camden Society's response to monument care abroad see C. Miele, 'Victorian Internationalism and the Victorian View of Monument Care on the Continent', in J. de Maeyer and L. Verpoest, eds., *Gothic Revival*, forthcoming (KADOC, Catholic University Leuven), pp. 211–22.
[109] See, for example, responses to designs submitted for review by John Plowman and Benjamin Ferrey. *Proceedings OAS*, 2 March 1842.

fed in one way or another into a restoration. It certainly helped that the Society secretary was the Oxford publishing dynamo John Henry Parker, whose press also put out a study of Kirkstead church, compiled by the Lincolnshire Architectural Society and underwritten by the OAS.[110]

And just as the CCS had sought to undertake a model restoration as a practical demonstration of its principles, so too had the OAS. In truth the OAS was first in this field as well, though like the CCS its practical work began in a small way. In 1840 members asked Derick to make a paper restoration of the east window of St Giles, Oxford. They subsequently put him on a kind of retainer, commissioning small designs and six full building surveys prior to restorations, on all of which the OAS committee advised.[111] There were in addition not one but two model restorations on the scale of the Camden Society's work at the Round Church. The first commenced in April 1841, when the Chapel Clerk at Windsor granted the Society permission 'to take under their auspices and under the direction of their own architect the whole of the work for the restoration of the Church of Great Haseley' in Oxfordshire.[112] The possibility of working here had first been raised by a paper read at an ordinary meeting in November 1839.[113] Derick restored the steeply pitched roof to the chancel and the east lights, but did very little else.[114]

The Oxford Society oversaw the complete refurnishing of the church at the same time, publishing a plan of the new arrangement in Barr's *Anglican Church Architecture* of 1843 (plate 65). The comparison between this scheme and the ideal church plan published by the Camden Society in *A Few Words to Church Builders* of 1841 is revealing, and to see why it helps to understand a little of the church arrangements were being changed under the influence of the Incorporated Church Building Society (plate 66). Amongst the ICBS' papers at the Lambeth Palace Library are dozens of seating plans from this

[110] See the preface to *An Architectural Description of St Leonard's Church, Kirkstead* (Oxford, 1846).

[111] *Proceedings OAS*, 2 December 1840 for his restoration of the east window of St Giles Church, Oxford; also 23 November 1842 and appended accounts, which refer to detailed surveys made prior to the restoration of six different churches – Kingham, Bladington, St Nicholas Abingdon, Daglingworth, Ambrosden, and Steeple Ashton – all of which were said to be under the direction of the OAS Committee, although this should be interpreted loosely.

[112] Bodleian MSS., Dep.d.538, 23 April 1841. The patronage was split between the Queen and the Dean and Chapter of Christ Church Oxford.

[113] T. W. Weare, *Some Remarks upon the Church of Great Haseley, Oxon.* (rev. ed. 1848), x. This was first published in 1840 and again, somewhat revised in 1847. The book was offered as a kind of architectural primer for prospective members. The Rev. Weare had, incidentally, been an active member of the older Heraldic Society; the church is rich in emblems, containing more than 200.

[114] Bodleian MSS., Dep.d.538, 21 October 1841.

period, valuable records of how furnishings were set out before the ecclesiological movement took hold.[115] The ICBS required regular, closely spaced seating in benches, not pews, which is hardly surprising as its remit was the extension of free seats in churches. The Society also tried to encourage greater respect for medieval architecture, a sensibility matched by the rise of antiquarian architects in the 1820s and 1830s. The ICBS-sponsored approach should be seen as a transitional stage between what we now think of as the typical Georgian church interior, heavily pewed and galleried, and the ecclesiological arrangements which became ubiquitous in the last third of the nineteenth century. Derick's plan for Great Haseley is absolutely typical of the sort of scheme the ICBS was grant-aiding, and it represents the concensus on furnishing which had emerged in the 1830s. In addition to packing the church with benches, he close coupled the pulpit and 'reading pew', and set the pair in a sea of benches. As for the new benches themselves, these were low and in a Gothic style, but essentialy of box construction and so still redolent of pews (plate 87). The open benches which were installed at Old Shoreham and the Round Church were something new. They have that simplicity of design and construction that characterizes the most advanced Gothic furniture of the period, in particular Pugin's designs for the Oscott College furniture of 1838-9.[116]

The overall arrangement of furnishings in the Society's ideal plan was also new. (plate 66) An extraordinary amount of space is alloted to each functional element or liturgical zone. There has been a disaggregation, and although this is the result of studying medieval layouts, the effect is to underscore the symbolic potential of each element. This is most striking in the chancel, which has been cleared of everything but the altar and separated from the nave seating by a kind of *cordon sanitaire*.

The OAS's work at Dorchester Abbey was even more ambitious, commensurate with the quality of the building, which has a splendid chancel in the early Decorated style and a noble nave arcade.[117] Once again the idea to get involved with the building came from a paper delivered at an ordinary meeting, in this case one read by the incumbent, the Rev. Henry Addington, on 17 June 1844. Cranstoun's design for the chancel was ready by late October, when E. A. Freeman, whose star was fast rising in the Society, forced through a rule change which enabled the OAS actually to commission architectural works. No one had apparently given any thought to whether or

---

[115] On the ICBS see T. Parry's excellent 'The Incorporated Church Building Society, 1818-1851', M.Phil. thesis (Trinity College, Oxford, 1984).

[116] C. Wainwright, 'Furniture', in *Pugin. A Gothic Passion*, ed. P. Atterbury and C. Wainwright (London and New Haven, 1994), pp. 127-42.

[117] See H. Addington's study published for the OAS, *Some Account of the Abbey Church of Ss. Peter and Paul, Dorchester* (Oxford, 1845; rev. ed. 1860). See also ICBS file which chronicles the reseating of the nave in 1852-4.

not the OAS was able to enter into a contract, and this was typical of Freeman's deeply pragmatic strain. The Dorchester Abbey scheme included new oak seating, a pulpit, as well as a nave roof and miscellaneous repairs, and was estimated at £2500. A special subcommittee was formed the following May and various contracts were signed early in 1845.[118] The size of the job meant it would run and run, and in 1858 Scott was called in to finish it off; in the meantime, certainly by spring 1847, Butterfield had replaced Cranstoun on this job and as the OAS's most favoured architect.

Regionalisation

Together the Oxbridge sisters provided the model, and in some cases the impetus, for many of the regional architectural societies which were set up during the 1840s. Thorp himself helped to found the Bristol and West of England Archaeological Society in 1842; the secretary, J. R. Woodford, was *ex*-Pembroke College and a CCS member.[119] The BWEAS committee got involved in the ongoing restoration of St Mary Redcliffe in Bristol, and tried to undertake the restoration of St James's nearby, but this came to nothing. The Bristol Society could at least boast of smaller successes, the restoration of the south porch of Slimbridge Church and also the re-erection of the Norman font at All Saints in Bristol.[120] The Architectural Society of the Archdeaconry of Northampton worked somewhat differently, using a roving committee that made inspections along the lines of archidiaconal visitations.[121] The Down and Connor and Dromore Church Architecture Society and the Yorkshire Architectural Society, both founded in 1842, and also affiliated with the CCS, were committed to promoting church restoration as well,[122] though by far the most successful of these second tier societies was the Exeter Diocesan Architectural Society, established in the spring of the 1841. Its links with the Society were close; Philip Freeman, who undertook a detailed study of open timber roofs for the Society was a key member of EDAS.

The Exeter Society promoted church building and restoration in southeast Devon. According to Chris Brooks it forged an 'alliance between clergy and powerful laity', the sort of union which the 'Cambridge Camden Society was urging on Anglicanism nationally'.[123] The EDAS *Transactions* was

---

[118]   *Rules and Proceedings*, 30 October, 13 and 30 November 1844, 14 May 1845. See also Bodleian Library MSS., Dep.d.540.
[119]   T. Thorp, *Charge Delivered at the Visitation of the Archdeaconry of Bristol* (Bristol, 1842), p. 25, and *Ecclesiologist*, 2 (1842), p. 28.
[120]   *Bristol and West of England Archaeological Magazine*, 1 (1843), pp. 1–15, 82.
[121]   The results were published in the *Associated Architectural Societies. Reports and Papers*, 1 (1850) pp. 18–19.
[122]   *Ecclesiologist*, 2 (1842), pp. 28, 45–7, 53, 68–9.
[123]   'Building the Rural Church', in *The Victorian Church*, eds. C. Brooks and A. Saint (Manchester, 1995), pp. 51–81, at p. 64.

an ambitious, illustrated series, printing both papers read at ordinary meetings and as well as short notices of advice given. The Society never undertook a 'model restoration' as such, although the decision to devote the entirety of its first volume of *Transactions* to the magnificent church at Ottery St Mary should perhaps be seen as a declaration of intent realised by important members of the EDAS if not the EDAS *per se*.[124] Nevertheless, being in effect a creature of the Diocese, it wielded terrific influence.

The Oxbridge Societies tried to bring these other groups under their joint umbrella, with some success, but by the late 1840s, with the CCS in London and the OAS becoming less of a Gothic Revival presure group, the different provincial groups required a new focus. The Bucks Architectural and Archaeological Society, founded in 1847, was one of the last to seek affiliation with the Oxbridge groups.[125] Architectural societies founded after this date came together under the aegis of the Associated Architectural Societies, set up in 1850. The prospectuses of these various later groups, while they often refer to the pioneering work of the university societies, were careful to declare themselves neutral on matters of doctrine; this caution was the result of the Durandus and of the stone altar affair; the re-establishment of Roman Catholic hierarchy fanned the flames further. Thus, it became usual for the prospectuses of societies to have one or two lines which were intended to function as a disclaimer. The Northampton Society's was typical: its aim was to restore medieval churches 'to their original state, as far as may be consistent with the Reformed worship now carried on within them'.[126] Nevertheless, this groundswell of activity meant that by the early 1850s churches in even remote corners of the country were likely to be within easy reach of some faction or other of a now more broadly-based ecclesiological movement.

Towards a Theory of Monument Care?

For all that the Camden Society was in the thick of things – advising, criticising, doing – it never expounded a theory of monument care. That pronouncement, printed at the time of the Stafford dispute (see above) was exceptional. No, the striking thing about the early volumes of *The Ecclesiologist* is just how little one finds in them about the effect a restoration might have on a church's status as a monument, or on, to be more precise and piously academic, its ontology as an ancient thing. To be fair, this is partly explained by the fact that transformations as sweeping as Scott's at Stafford

---

[124] The Butterfield restoration commenced in 1848–9.
[125] Interestingly the Society secretary used Cambridge Camden Society not Ecclesiological Society. There are papers relating to the BAAS in the County Museum at Aylesbury. The official publication, *Records of Buckinghamshire with the Transactions of the BAAS*, did not appear until 1858.
[126] *First Report of the Architectural Society of the Archdeaconry of Northampton*, text of address read at a public meeting held on 16 October 1848, pp. 9–10.

were actually pretty rare. Spending on church restoration would not really take off until the 1850s and, in more remote dioceses, the early 1860s.[127] But even allowing for this pattern of expenditure, there remains something to be explained. After all the Camdenians were not theory-shy, and there was already a nascent tradition of writing on this subject, both in England and across the Channel.[128] This silence on what one would think were burning questions – the matter of authenticity primarily, or the extent to which a building's art historical importance ought to dictate the way it was cared for – was actually the product of the Camdenian ideology. For to construe a church as a monument, one has to accept that a distance has opened up between its original purpose and the way it is used in the present.

Monuments are static things, often ruinous, and even where they are not quite crumbling, they tend to wear their age on their sleeves. History and aesthetics, not religious fervour, are the operative concepts. They are essentially secular endeavours, and as such are foreign to high-minded ecclesiology. The Society's science of church architecture was based on the assumption that ancient churches should be seen first and foremost as living vessels of faith, emblems of fundamental Christian truths as these have been revealed through history. And yet, and here was the rub, the most ardent ecclesiologists saw some merit in antiquity. Age lends a church, and hence the Church by law established, a certain gravity, a density and importance. In short, the Camdenians wanted to eat their cake and have it too. They wanted the sheer power conveyed by antiquity, the magic worked by invoking ancient precedents and forms, but they wanted this power without having to be saddled with the burdens that arise from something attaining monument status. The Camden Society had really no choice but to pass over any detailed discussions on the right way to restore ancient churches, because this would be tantamount to saying that they were not merely functional units, symbolically articulated worship machines.

The essence of the Camdenian approach to the historical aspect of medieval churches comes across most clearly in Neale's 1843 *Church Englargement and Church Arrangement*. It is a fascinating little book, engagingly written and clear, but underlying it is the assumption that all ancient churches really need is a decent maintenance programme, that and an appropriate set of furnishings. If replacing Georgian pews and galleries with new, efficient open benches does not produce enough room, then and only then will Neale recommend new work, but even this must follow the lead set by the ancient building itself. Hence, a Romanesque church consisting of a chancel and nave with a Decorated aisle should only be extended by the

[127] Miele, 'Gothic Architecture', pp. 4–7.
[128] The English background is discussed at length by Bradley. For the Continent, see W. Denslagen, *Architectural Restoration in Western Europe: Controversy and Continuity* (Amsterdam, 1994), pp. 84–94, 151–5, *et passim*.

construction of another aisle not by a pair of transepts. These would be appropriate, according to Neale, if the original building had been planned to take a crossing tower. Neale was inviting his readers to group churches according to a limited range of normative types, each of which required a different strategy for its care, based on medieval precedent. There was thus an objective measure to be applied to all church restoration, a measure established not by reference to modern perceptions of interest and quality but one entirely circumscribed by antiquity itself. The system as laid down in *Church Enlargement and Church Arrangement* is all very orderly, and there is much to recommend it.

As for the style of new work, Neale had precious little to say, except that, of course, the modern architect had to take care to base the design of any new work on details found in the church or locally and, furthermore, that the style of an addition should make sense in historical terms. Hence, it would be a nonsense to add a Romanesque aisle to a Decorated nave. Fictive historical narratives were fine so long as they were internally consistent. Taken each on their own, it is possible to find the elements of Neale's argument in earlier literature. His achievement lay in codifying and regularising what had gone before, making sure that each precept was clear and tallied with the rest. Thus, Neale and the Camdenians put paid to the notion that taste should dictate the way ancient churches are maintained.

This belief in the archaeological record as the final arbiter lies at the heart of the dispute between the Society and the Rev. Petit's 1841 *Remarks on Church Architecture*. In a chapter on 'modern repairs and alterations' Petit urged architects to improve the proportions of ancient churches according to the sophisticated artistic principles of the modern picturesque movement, a set of values which, he freely admitted, were wholly unknown to the medieval architect. Petit showed himself to be a believer in the idea of progress, and, what was more, an admirer of that thoroughly Georgian concept, the picturesque. The anonymous reviewer for *The Ecclesiologist* was incandescent: 'We have uniformly insisted on attention to the *ancient* forms and arrangements of our churches, and have never listened to any unauthorised though specious proposals for "adaptation".'[129]

It should be stressed that what the Camden Society was striving after was accuracy not authenticity. The line from the review just quoted makes it plain: the over-riding concern was for integrity of 'forms and arrangements', abstract notions essentially, which by their nature devalue material integrity. In practice this meant that the Society did not rate untouched fabric higher than accurate copies, indeed if anything such copies were superior because they recorded the original design more clearly than a worn or decayed original. Again there was nothing particularly new in this view of antiquity.

[129]   *Ecclesiologist*, 1 (1841–2), pp. 91–105, at p. 103.

The fixation on the formal characteristics of medieval architecture had been growing since Bentham's day, helped along by the Rev. John Milner and John Carter in the 1790s, and perfected in 1817 by Thomas Rickman. His *Attempt to Discriminate the Styles of English Architecture* was a complete taxonomy of medieval style, a method for studying, dating, and conceptualising antiquity which was one of the cornerstones of ecclesiology. The Society's first publication – which was also one of its most succcessful – *A Few Hints on the Practical Study of Ecclesiastical Antiquities* (1839, and later editions) was really a recasting of Rickman. It posited a method for studying and understanding antiquity.

The effect which this method had upon the ontology of ancient buildings has been discussed by this writer at length elsewhere, and so the point will not be laboured here.[130] Here it is sufficient merely to note that the quest for a system which could sort medieval architecture and its constituent parts according to formal types, and then relate these types to a chronological sequence, had tended to shift the emphasis away from the surface characteristics of medieval building towards an understanding of medieval architecture as a system of design, an eternally valid grammar of form which was regular, predictable and transparent. The Society made this translation by means of the 'Church Scheme', a blank reporting form printed at the end of the 1839 *Few Hints...* handbook. The Society printed thousands, selling them at bulk discounts to members and affiliated societies. The CCS, OAS, and EDAS started a joint Scheme library. Building archives covering every ancient church in the country were imagined, each serving a programme of collaborative research that was thought to be essential if the science of church architecture was to advance.[131] The Church Scheme was designed to teach those who had no drawing ability, but were otherwise familiar with architecture, how to describe any ancient church according to a stylistic shorthand, the familiar sequence of Norman, Early English, Decorated, and Perpendicular with all the associated terms.

The Scheme worked by filtering out picturesque incident, leaving in its place an image of pure, unadulterated medieval style. This process powerfully affected the way antiquity was understood, and in turn set priorities for church restoration. Consider a comparison. Set an 1815 engraving of St Dunstan, Stepney, then fast being absorbed into greater London, against a Church Scheme for the same building which Neale completed in 1839. (plates 68-9) In the perspective view St Dunstan's appears as one single entity, an organic whole comprehended in an instant, and conveying age as much by the

130 C. Miele, 'Real Antiquity and the Ancient Object', in C. Brooks (ed.), *The Study of the Past in the Victorian Age* (Oxford, 1998), pp. 103-24.
131 C. Miele,. *The Gothic Revival and Gothic Architecture: The Restoration of Medieval Churches in Victorian Britain*, unpub. Ph.D. thesis (New York University, 1992), pp. 75-81. See also R. R. Kenneally, pp. 14-19.

RE-PRESENTING THE CHURCH MILITANT...

style of its parts as by its rambling outline and worn surfaces. Indeed, the very manner of representation is riddled with codes and devices calculated to signal age. The Scheme strips all this away, breaks the church down, parses it into constituent parts, reducing it to a sequence of cues which by the very act of being separated from the unique building take on a generic existence. It pretends to greater accuracy and truthfulness, but then this is a blind. In fact all that has happened is that one representational stratagem has given way to another. Thus a particular traceried light in the perspective becomes a specimen illustrative of some larger stylistic grouping or trend, and so on, until the unique combination of elements that made up the building are transposed into the universal vocabulary of style. This way of describing radically delimits the historic interest of St Dunstan, confining it to a series of characteristic forms, which are presented as having the same value. There is no hierarchy in the Scheme's representational strategy, except of course that all post-medieval features and furnishings have been excluded.

For the Society, restoration was a way to make ancient buildings more legible as sequences of stylistic cues as these were captured in a Church Scheme. This could be achieved in any number of ways: by exposing hidden elements, repairing or reproducing damaged ones, or reconstructing lost features on the strength of evidence. A church refashioned in this way, harshly brought into line with the sharp focus of taxonometric vision, was still historic, no one could deny that; the fabric still appeared to be a collection of distinct building phases, but the historical narrative was strangely flat. The loss of irregularity, of quirky picturesque incident, reduces the number of meanings that can be attached to this particular ancient building. The setting of St Dunstan, the subtle marks of time which play over its surface in this engraving, the eccentricity of its outline and form, in short its unique character, all this encourages flights of fancy, intimate associations and memories. Such an image humanizes a building, gives it the widest possible range of signification. This comparison between perspective view and its Church-Scheme rendering highlights a difference which is exactly similar to that between seeing a butterfly speared and spread out under the harsh light of a natural history display case, and seeing that same creature flitting from flower to flower on a blazing June day. The scientific image might be as true a picture as can be achieved, but despite this higher order of objectivity, it lacks emotional depth.

Accuracy requires a single standard, one interpretive strand. The Camdenian obsession with it explains why the Society showed no interest in any talk about how elucidating the style of a building might affect its historic character. And this obsession also explains why the Society was so troubled by the views of the Comte de Montalembert and Didron in France, two figures for whom otherwise they had the highest regard. Generally, the Society disapproved of the involvement of the French state in monument care, although this involvement did occasionally produce results that far outstripped what could be achieved in England where the voluntarist principle held sway. The announcement of stupendous plans for the restoration of Notre Dame, funded by the State to the tune of 2,650,000 fr (then close to £40,000), demanded a response from the Society, and it warmly approved. But Didron's published advice on the scheme was shocking to ecclesiological sensibilities because it was too secular – 'antiquarian' was how the Society termed it. Didron seemed happy 'to treat medieval churches as preserved objects of architectural and archaeological curiosity rather than as living things, the Cathedral temples of THE EVERLASTING'.[132] Another case in point was Rheims, where both the editor of the *Annales Archeologiques* and the Comte had opposed the restoration of the north spires because the towers had stood without them for six centuries. From the point of view of *The Ecclesiologist* such respect for the 'time-honoured aspect' of a building was

> a death blow to Christian art! But what a gross material judgment this is. We are not to measure our ideas of buildings by what the original design was, the highest archetype of their *'poietes'*, but by the fragment which war, and tumult, and insolvency may have permitted the completion of!...
>
> [A] cathedral is in one sense as truly existent when its architect has conceived the whole entire majestic plan in his mind, as a sonnet of Wordsworth's or a hymn of St Ambrose was when its author should have composed it in his mind, though as yet he might not have committed one of it to paper.[133]

To see how restoration should be done properly, readers were directed to Cologne Cathedral, where the majestic ancient choir and the modern works of completion stood as a testament to the confluence of medieval and modern ambitions.[134] The *Dombauverein* and its architect Zwirner were not so much piling stone upon stone as realising a 'mystical substance'.[135] The responses to these two great restoration projects on the Continent bring us closer towards the Camdenian view of church restoration, but again this was not theory as such. It was part and parcel of a theological position. There was still no higher criticism, no systematic engagement with the problem of how to reconcile the historic and liturgical character of medieval churches, no grappling with that much more elusive concept, authenticity.

All this changed in response to E. A. Freeman's *Principles of Church Restoration*, first conceived as an OAS lecture and then published in a small

---

[132] *Ecclesiologist*, 5 (1846), pp. 55–67, at p. 64.

[133] *Ecclesiologist*, 5 (1846), p. 64.

[134] On which see M. J. Lewis, *The Politics of the German Gothic Revival. August Reichensperger* (Cambridge, Mass., USA and London, 1993), 25–57 *et passim*. See also N. Borger-Keweloh, *Die mittelaltliche Dome im neunzehnjahrhundert* (Munich, 1986).

[135] *Ecclesiologist*, 5 (1846), p. 75.

print run in 1846. Freeman's *Principles* is one of those books which is more widely known through a famous review than first hand. It was the subject of a lengthy Society debate and a detailed review in *The Ecclesiologist* for May 1847. The anonymous author tried to do *Principles* justice, but in fact ended up crudely schematizing the system it presented. Freeman sorted ancient buildings according to how he believed they should be treated; the reviewer boiled these rather complex constructions down into three 'approaches': the Destructive, the Conservative, and the Eclectic.[136]

The Destructive approach was, according to *The Ecclesiologist*, founded on the premise that all new work should be in a new style. The justification for it was medieval precedent; ancient builders, the argument ran, had by and large torn down structures that had served their purpose and rebuilt them in the best modern style, showing scant regard or sentiment for what their forebears had wrought. The Conservative approach, by contrast, called for the scrupulous retention of every single ancient feature, irrespective of its quality or regardless of how much it spoiled an earlier, better design. Finally, there was the Eclectic or middle way, the one which the Society officially endorsed because it allowed each work to be judged according to its merits. This course of action was based on qualitative decisions, the artistic interest of a particular feature, say, or its rarity. The Eclectic approach was founded on the belief that the modern Gothic was a living, vital architectural style which should be developed, although not at the expense of the archaeological record.

For the first time in English there was a consistent critical vocabulary, and the Society latched onto this triad of terms. Unfortunately, the definitions were more *The Ecclesiologist*'s than Freeman's, and in this the book has been misrepresented. Freeman was deeply intellectual, and had not intended his little essay to lead to cut-and-dried categories. *The Principles* was not so much a practical handbook as a rumination on the historical self-consciousness which its author believed firmly distinguished the modern industrial age from everything that had gone before. Hence, it really was not fair for *The Ecclesiologist* to justify the Destructive approach by appealing to medieval authority. Freeman saw the gap between past and present as unbridgeable. For him the question of how to treat any ancient building or monument turned on its potential audience or audiences. This in turn led him to doubt that any ancient building, be it Stonehenge, a ruined abbey, or a functioning parish church, could necessarily have a fixed meaning. Significance was socially constructed, but here he, being a devout Churchman, drew the line. For although Freeman was willing to accept that ancient churches might in some senses be described as monuments, the needs of modern liturgical practice

---

[136] *Ecclesiologist*, 6 (1847), pp. 161–8. See the account in S. Tschudi-Madsen, *Restoration and Anti-Restoration* (Oslo, 1976), pp. 38–50, and W. Denslagen, *Architectural Restoration in Western Europe: Controversy and Continuity* (Amsterdam, 1994), pp. 62–3.

could never be sacrificed. Church restoration was then a complicated balancing act taking into account the artistic and historical importance of the building, sentimental associations, picturesque values, and, last but far from least, the requirements of its owners.

There was nothing to match *Principles* except, that is, for the heavily revised edition which Freeman brought out in 1852 under the title *On the Preservation and Restoration of Ancient Monuments*, where church architecture comes near to being subsumed into that larger and essentially secular category 'historic monuments'. The issues of audience response and semantic variability were developed here at length. The spur to the new edition had been partly Ruskin's aphorisms on restoration in the 1849 *Seven Lamps of Architecture* and to a lesser extent Gilbert Scott's *A Plea for the Faithful Restoration of Our Ancient Churches* of 1850.[137] Scott, who deserves more credit for advancing the debate than he is usually given, saw the gist of Freeman's 1846 work clearly and sought to answer whether and to what extent buildings could be seen to be historic monuments. Having fallen foul of the Society one or two times in his early career, the by-now well-established Goth must have enjoyed the chance to identify himself with the 'Conservative' approach, declaring himself in sympathy with Freeman's 1846 work against the Society. Freeman, for his part, was eager to respond to the way his work had been misinterpreted by the Society in 1847.[138]

From these debates, inaugurated by Freeman's two treatises on restoration, it is possible to trace the development of a modern preservation theory in English, a line of thought leading to William Morris's SPAB manifesto of 1877 and beyond. But hereafter the Ecclesiological Society would be standing on the sidelines, an interested spectator but not a key player. Through its journal the terms Destructive, Conservative, and Eclectic were widely adopted, continuing in use after *The Ecclesiologist* ceased publication in 1868. *The Ecclesiologist* extolled *The Seven Lamps* in general but when it came to the section on church restoration the anonymous reviewer refused to take on Ruskin directly because his response to buildings was at bottom that of an artist.[139] Ecclesiologists did not have that luxury. Freeman's 1852 book was merely politely received.[140] How odd that the Society which had once claimed church restoration as its special province was letting the initiative slip, although, admittedly, practitioners on the leading edge of monument care – Bodley, Burges, Scott, Street, and White principally – continued to revere the Society and to contribute papers on the restoration question. But by this point there were other interested parties.

---

[137] Freeman, 1852, pp. 6–10, 19, 24–5, 42–5.
[138] *Ecclesiologist*, 12 (1853), pp. 40–2. Freeman, 1852, pp. 7–10.
[139] *Ecclesiologist*, 9 (1850), pp. 111–20, at p. 118.
[140] *Ecclesiologist*, 12 (1853), pp. 40–2.

The Next Generation

By 1850 a second generation of local architectural societies were taking the initiative, and they, not the Oxbridge societies, would in the coming decade mount some of the most interesting debates on church restoration and preservation. At Lichfield, Northampton, and York, on daytrips, after lectures, and during annual general meetings, new voices were heard arguing along the lines of Freeman and Scott, who had bravely steered a course between the Scylla of restoration and the Charybdis of preservation as represented by Neale and Ruskin. George Aycliffe Poole, Henry Dryden, J. H. Markland, and other still less well known figures took Ruskin to task for being unrealistic, precious, absurd.[141] Their views were more constructive, more pragmatic, as they tried to puzzle out how it might be possible to square modern liturgical requirements with the claims of history, to treat ancient churches both as working buildings and as museum pieces. One of the strategies put forward at this time was to vary the rate of commission which architects charged on restoration work, perhaps doubling the normal 5%, and thus to discourage professionals from over-restoring merely to increase their fees. It was also suggested that only builders with experience of ancient buildings should be invited to tender. Some even said that the system of competitive tendering should be abandoned altogether. There were also various discussions about the setting up of a national repository of drawings of unrestored buildings.[142]

The cause for stricter standards of care was taken up from the centre by George Godwin, editor of the influential *Builder* magazine. In the early fifties he gave free rein to authors and correspondents who were like himself broadly in favour of Freeman's approach, and he was willing to turn over pages of the influential journal to disputes concerning one scheme of restoration or another.[143] Most of these pieces, which tended to be either anonymous or submitted under a pseudonym, called for clear critical categories and corresponding principles. One writer, who styled himself 'Architecturus', said their collective aim should be to derive a 'scientific system' of restoration, an ambition which was broadly in line with Godwin's positivist philosophy.[144] The debate grew so impassioned that even the Society of Antiquaries, which had previously been silent on these matters, published a 'Memorandum on Restoration' in 1855. This is redolent of Ruskinian idealism:

---

[141] See *Associated Architectural Societies. Reports and Papers*, 1 (1850–51), pp. 231–44; 2 (1852–53), pp. 1–13; 3 (1854–55), pp. 11–28, 130–6. See also Miele, 'The Gothic Revival', pp. 125–40.

[142] Miele, 'The Gothic Revival', pp. 438–531.

[143] *The Builder*, 10 (1852), pp. 226–7, 473–5; 13 (1855), pp. 468, 479, 502, 514, 613; 14 (1856), p. 20; 17 (1859), pp. 229, 257, 273, 287.

[144] *The Builder*, 10 (1852), pp. 226–7.

Restoration may possibly, indeed, produce a good imitation of an ancient work of art; but the original is thus falsified, and in its renovated condition is no longer an example of the art of the period to which it belonged.

The Ecclesiological Society moved with the tide of the 1850s, drifting slowly towards the 'Conservative' school but stopping well short Ruskin's formulations. Perhaps the Society, like many others, was coming to realise that unrestored churches were now an endangered species.[145]

Meanwhile, a younger generation of architect-members were challenging the older orthodoxies, treating churches as monuments rather than engines of doctrine. In 1857 Street wrote an article titled 'Destructive Restoration on the Continent'. Year on year he had seen one monument after another shrouded in scaffolding. When finally the work was done, he observed, 'there remains not the glorious old work, grim with ages, weather-beaten, here or there damaged or broken, but a clean smart copy of the old work'.[146] He was trying to bring his own practice into line with this sensibility, and in 1860 offered restoration of Stone Church near Dartford as an example of a new ethos. Three years later William White presented his restoration of Newland Church in Gloucestershire as an example of best practice, delivering papers on it to the RIBA and Ecclesiological Society.[147]

A mark of just how far the Society had travelled in twenty years was a debate initiated in 1861 by George Frederick Bodley in the pages of *The Ecclesiologist*. It began with an impassioned letter decrying what he called the 'destructive school of restoration' as practised on the Continent and particularly in France. This was followed by a paper read to the Society which was reported in the architectural press.[148] This former pupil of Scott himself wrote passionately about the 'poetry and mellowed grace' that was inevitably lost in a typical restoration abroad, a kind of atmosphere, the 'pensive effect of time on old buildings' which painters captured so perfectly. Bodley called on his countrymen to protest against large-scale reconstructions and rebuildings which were seen by some as characteristic of Napoleon III's absolutist regime. The Society threw its weight behind the cause and later that year arranged a joint meeting with the Royal Institute of British Architects and the Oxford Architectural Society to consider whether French restorers

[145] C. Miele, '"Their Interest and Habit". Professionalism and the Restoration of Medieval Churches, 1837–1877', *The Victorian Church* (Manchester, 1995), ed. C. Brooks and A. Saint, 151–72, at pp. 156–9.
[146] *Ecclesiologist*, 16 (1857), pp. 342–5.
[147] G. E. Street, 'Some Account of St Mary Stone, near Dartford, and Its Recent Restoration', *Archaeologia Cantiana*, 3 (1860), pp. 97–132. W. White, 'Notes on Newland Church. Gloucestershire, with Remarks on Church Restoration and Arrangements', *Sessional Papers of the RIBA 1863–64*, pp. 29–42. See also the latter's 'Cathedral Restoration', *Ecclesiologist*, 23 (1864), pp. 140–2.
[148] *Ecclesiologist*, 20 (1861), 22, 70–8.

were really going too far. One camp wanted the Institute to lodge a formal complaint with the French government using British diplomatic channels. There were remarks about the sins of Revolutionary iconoclasm being revisited on monuments which in fact belonged to Europe not any one country. Cooler heads prevailed. What was needed was a committee on European monuments, overseen by the French and English jointly. The debate ended when a faction led by John Ruskin observed that standards in England were no better than in France, and that British architects would be advised to put their own house in order before presuming to criticise anyone else's.[149] To be fair, the Institute of British Architects promptly did just that. In 1862 it established a pressure group called the Committee on the Conservation of Ancient Monuments, though its operations were strictly limited to the United Kingdom and based on the voluntarist principle.[150]

Bodley's swipe at the French provides a fitting postscript to this tale, because in this lecture he used 'protection' to describe the approach he hoped to see widely adopted. 'Conservative' had run its course. Bodley coined 'protection' to describe a new way of treating ancient churches, which means we have him and the ecclesiologists to thank for the title of William Morris's own Society for the Protection of Ancient Buildings, founded in March 1877, an episode which is usually presented as both the antidote to ecclesiological excesses and the forerunner of the modern ethos.[151] Morris was of course close to Bodley in the 1860s, but there is no hard evidence of the young designer following this debate. Indeed, we know very little of what Morris thought about the great restoration debate before the founding of the SPAB, which is odd because the success Morris, Marshall, Faulkner and Co. achieved was partly through commissions for stained glass and painted decorations for church restorations.[152] So it came about that Bodley, the architect who brought perfection to the ecclesiological ideal in the realm of new churches, came at the same time to adopt a position on church restoration which was antithetical to that developed in the early years of the Camden Society.

[149] *Ecclesiologist*, 20 (1861), pp. 213–14, 250–63. Also reported in *The Builder* 21 (22 and 29 June 1861) 19, 422–4, 440–1.

[150] C. Miele, '"Their Interest and Habit"', pp. 159–65.

[151] I am grateful to Michael Hall at *Country Life* for first pointing Bodley's use of this word to me.

[152] C. Miele, 'The Conservationist', in L. Parry (ed.), *William Morris* (London, Victoria and Albert Museum, 1996), pp. 72–9.

Ecclesiology in Scotland

JOHN SANDERS

The Cambridge Camden Society did not cause a single coherent ecclesiological movement in Scotland. Its effects were diverse, with antiquarians and the
various church denominations adopting the elements of ecclesiology which
suited them. The strands of influence on these groups developed independently and were only brought together after the foundation of the Aberdeen
Ecclesiological Society in 1886. Two factors inhibited the acceptance of
ecclesiology; the Presbyterian Church of Scotland and the nature of Scottish
medieval architecture.

The Anglican and Presbyterian churches in England and Scotland had
more in common at the end of the eighteenth century than they did after
ecclesiology had begun to affect the design of new churches. The invective of
the Cambridge Camden Society against the unhealthy state of religious
architecture and observance was applicable to the churches of both countries
before 1830. Large Georgian preaching boxes with galleries could be found
anywhere in Britain. During the seventeenth and eighteenth centuries
Scotland had developed some specifically Presbyterian centralised plan forms
which expressed the nature of reformed worship. A particularly popular form
was the 'T' plan with three galleried wings facing towards a pulpit on the wall
at the junction of the 'T'. The pulpit was the primary focus of the church and
considerably less emphasis was given to the communion table which was
located to the front or to the side of the pulpit.

An ecclesiological point of view on this unsatisfactory state of the
church in Georgian Scotland was expressed by Dr George W. Sprott, Minister
of North Berwick, in his book *The Worship and Offices of the Church of
Scotland* written in 1882. It is possible that his mocking description of
churches at the turn of the nineteenth century was influenced by the tone of
The Ecclesiologist:

> Huge square barns with immense galleries, and seats crowded close to the
> pulpit ... The interior of some of these Churches resembles a circus,
> class-room or music-hall. If the last, on entering you see a stage or platform,
> with a reading desk and sofa in place of an ecclesiastical pulpit, while behind
> there is a huge organ – the principal object in the building, – and you tremble
> for the Clergyman in front, who reminds you of those unfortunate Sepoys
> who, after the Indian Mutiny, were lashed to the mouths of cannon and

blown into a thousand fragments. Strange devices, too, one sometimes hears of for the administration of the Sacraments, such as a font on top of which a board is screwed to do duty as a table at times of Communion.[1]

It was felt that this kind of arrangement and the poor state of repair of many churches was indicative of a malaise in churchmanship; 'people got to think that to have mean and ugly sanctuaries was an article of religion with the Scotch!'[2]

Perpendicular Commissioner's Gothic was equally popular in Scotland and England and in both countries it was used to disguise plans inherited from the eighteenth century. William Burn's village church at Stenton of 1828 is one example from many which illustrates this compromise (plate 70); the plan is a typical Scottish 'T' arrangement with the pulpit placed at the centre of the south wall. The gallery in the central arm was for the exclusive use of the laird, it carried greater ornament and had a withdrawing room below with a separate entrance. In the design of the exterior, Burn concealed the way the church was used. It was intended to look like a Perpendicular chapel; the laird's arm of the T was placed out of sight from the road, the church was given a west tower with belfry openings, but without bells, and the west gable wall was given a Perpendicular window to suggest the position of an altar.[3]

Some significant Gothic Revival churches were built well before the influence of the Cambridge Camden Society. Two prominent Episcopal churches in Edinburgh, St John, of 1815 by William Burn, and St Paul, of 1816 by Archibald Elliot, are as advanced in their use of Perpendicular as any contemporary church architecture in Britain. A later account by the incumbent of St Paul's described its style as 'English Perpendicular ... generally an imitation of St Mary, Beverley.'[4] James Gillespie Graham's large Catholic chapels in Edinburgh and Glasgow, designed in 1813 and 1814, are also competent revivals for their date. All four of these buildings use crisp Perpendicular detailing and have naves and aisles with well articulated bays and buttresses. The plans, however, are late Georgian; aisled rectangles with galleries and only minimal altar recesses rather than chancels. The style of these churches may be significant in the development of domestic Gothic in their respective authors' country house practices but they do not seem to have influenced later church architects. Commissioners' Gothic waned in Scotland and England at the same time but the Gothic of Pugin and the Cambridge

[1]   George W. Sprott, *The Worship and Offices of the Church of Scotland* (Edinburgh: Blackwood, 1882), pp. 232–4.

[2]   James Cooper, 'Ecclesiology in Scotland', *Transactions of the Aberdeen Ecclesiological Society* [TAES], II (1895), p. 42.

[3]   The implied liturgical orientation is that the west window is at the 'East' end. The 'West' tower and entrance is, in fact, at the east.

[4]   *Transactions of the Architectural Institute of Scotland*, 4.1 (1854), p. 3, Introductory address by Bishop Terrot who officiated at St Paul, York Place.

JOHN SANDERS

Camden Society which replaced it in England did not gain the same hold in Scotland. Burn's Gothic churches after 1840 are less convincing and Gillespie Graham came to rely on anonymous help from Pugin to supply authoritative Gothic detail.[5]

In the early 1840s, when the influence of the Oxford Movement was spreading in England, entirely different forces were at work in the Scottish Established church. In the Disruption of 1843 half of the ministers and two thirds of the members left the Church of Scotland to form the Free Church of Scotland. The issues which caused the division were not doctrinal controversies but political concerns about church government. The dispute focused on the right of a landowner, or heritor, to choose a minister without regard to the wishes of the congregation. The Church of Scotland had been prone to schism for its entire history and the Free Church became one of several groups, generally from the more Protestant wing, which had split from the established church.

Although the majority of Scottish people belonged to the various Presbyterian churches, two smaller denominations must also be considered. The Scottish Episcopal Church was disestablished in 1689 by William of Orange to penalise its bishops for their political allegiances. It retained an episcopal structure throughout a period of suppression during the eighteenth century. At the start of the nineteenth century it began to merge with congregations of English Anglicans living in Scotland and it is generally regarded as being similar to the Church of England. The history of the Roman Catholic church in nineteenth-century Scotland is one of radical change. At the start of the century the Catholic Church consisted of the populations of the residual Catholic areas in the north-east and some areas of the Highlands. Irish immigration brought a new Catholic population to the south-west of Scotland. By 1885 it had become the largest non-presbyterian church in Scotland with 340,000 baptised persons, concentrated in Glasgow and the central lowlands.

The relative numerical strengths of the church denominations was the subject of a statistical survey published in 1885.[6] Its conclusions can be summarised as follows:

[5] James Macaulay, 'James Gillespie Graham and A. W. N. Pugin: Some Perthshire Connections', *Architectural Heritage: the Journal of the Architectural Heritage Society of Scotland*, 8 (Edinburgh, 1997), pp. 22–36.

[6] *Distribution and Statistics of the Scottish Churches* (Edinburgh, 1885), pp. 55–6. The denominations listed under 'Other' consist of; Congregational 12,000, Evangelical Union 13,210, Baptist 9,688 and Methodist 4,653. Membership of Unitarian churches is not listed in these statistics but accounted for a very small number of people. The figures for the Scottish Episcopal Church represent a much greater number who considered themselves to be Episcopalian. In 1900 about 116,000 people were Episcopalian of which about 46,000 were communicants. The

Presbyterian:	Church of Scotland	members	540,061	14 %
	Free Church of Scotland	members	329,541	9 %
	United Presbyterian	members	177,517	5 %
Roman Catholic Church		baptised	342,500	9 %
Scottish Episcopal Church		communicants	29,744	1 %
Other denominations			39,551	1 %
Total			1,458,914	39 %

The figures are expressed as a percentage of the total population of Scotland, which was 3,736,000.

In the Presbyterian churches, the fundamental upheaval of the Disruption left little room for ecclesiology. The Church of Scotland retained all the church buildings but, with only half of its former congregation to occupy them, it had little need for new ideas in new church architecture. The seceding Free Church of Scotland and similar, smaller Free denominations embarked on a considerable building programme in deliberate competition with the Church of Scotland. Some of their architecture is remarkable but, as the more Protestant party in the split, it was the least likely to be concerned with innovations which were inspired by Catholic or medieval practice.[7] Even when architects designed in a Gothic style, they found good Presbyterian reasons to depart from medieval precedents. Their interpretation of the Gothic style can be seen as part of movements all over Britain; muscular, Early French, Ruskinian and 'Go'. Dr Sprott identified a Scottish characteristic in this unfettered use of Gothic:

> The Scottish intellect in such departments is apt to show an excess of vigour, and styles of architecture have been invented which were never before heard of … much stupid and expensive ornamentation has often been lavished upon misshapen structures, the effect being to remind one of a deformed figure, heavily laden with jewellery and rich apparel.[8]

Perhaps the most ecclesiological of the architects who built for the Church of Scotland was John Honeyman (1831-1914). His churches of St Philip, Joppa, 1875, and St Michael's Parish Church, Edinburgh, 1881, are competent exercises in First Pointed with ecclesiological massing of nave, aisles and chancel. However, in his planning of the interiors, Honeyman deliberately departed from ecclesiological principles with the provision of galleries and unrestricted views.

---

percentage calculations are my own.

[7]   Gavin Stamp, 'The Victorian Kirk: Presbyterian architecture in nineteenth-century Scotland', Chris Brooks and Andrew Saint (eds), *The Victorian Church* (Manchester, 1995), pp. 98–117. The various free denominations tended to be the more enlightened and adventurous patrons. The churches of F. T. Pilkington and Alexander Thomson are notable examples.

[8]   Sprott, *op. cit.*, p. 233.

The Scottish Episcopal Church, as the Scottish denomination which most closely matched the Anglican church, was directly influenced by the Cambridge Camden Society.[9] The architectural development of the Scottish Episcopal church between 1830 and 1860 is comparable with that of the Church of England in any large English county. There was a similar mix of local and London based architects, the same general acceptance of ecclesiology with occasional serious attempts to meet all of the principles of the Cambridge Camden Society, and similar occasional references to local precedent within an architectural language set by George Gilbert Scott and William Butterfield.

St John, Jedburgh was one of the earliest of the new churches built in Britain to receive unqualified approval in the pages of *The Ecclesiologist* (plate 71).[10] It was designed by John Hayward of Exeter in 1844 for the Marchioness of Lothian who consulted the committee of the Cambridge Camden Society about its design. Butterfield designed the lychgate and the school. The consecration service of 15 August 1844 was an extraordinary event for such a small church and it seems that leading Tractarians decided to grasp the opportunity to promote their movement in Scotland. Four Scottish bishops and thirty-two clergy took part including some important Oxford Movement figures such as John Keble, William Dodsworth and Dr W. F. Hook. Six sermons were preached, all by English clergy; Hook twice, Robert Wilberforce, Dodsworth, Keble and W. H. Teale. The sermons were published with a description of the church which emphasised its ecclesiological correctness. The reviews in *The Ecclesiologist* were enthusiastic; in 1844:

> The noble founders have spared neither personal trouble nor money in making this church ... worthy of its purpose. We believe that few modern churches can compete with it in the ecclesiological propriety and decorative richness of their internal fittings and enrichments[11]

and in 1846:

> St John, Jedburgh, is by no means unimportant as a step in the present growth of ecclesiological knowledge: and will bear its part in the history of the revival of Christian art, should it ever be written. We hope, before long, it will be honourably rivalled in Scotland by the erection of more churches

---

9   The path of ecclesiology in the Episcopal church has been discussed in recent articles by Allan Maclean and by Tristram Clarke: Allan Maclean, 'The Scottish Episcopal Church and the Ecclesiological Movement', *Architectural Heritage...*, 8 (Edinburgh, 1997), pp. 47–59; Tristram Clarke, 'A Display of Tractarian Energy: St John's Episcopal Church, Jedburgh', *Records of the Church History Society*, 27 (1997), pp. 187–219.

10   Almost all of the information about St John, Jedburgh is taken from Dr Tristram Clarke's article for *Records of the Church History Society*.

11   *Ecclesiologist*, 3 (1843), p. 113.

by the holders of land in that country.[12]

Later architects of Scottish Episcopal churches could not live up to this optimism. The most prolific Scottish architect of Episcopal churches was John Henderson (1804–62) who built thirty churches. From 1844 his churches show a willingness to adopt the principles set in the first few years of the Cambridge Camden Society. But Henderson's work was criticised in *The Ecclesiologist* because he was not able to keep in step with the development of ecclesiological opinion about the arrangement of chancels or the choice of style. His later church designs at St Mary, Arbroath, 1854, and St Mary, Port Glasgow, 1857, could be mistaken for the work of R. C. Carpenter.

About a quarter of the eighty-eight Episcopal churches built between 1840 and 1860 were designed by English architects including most of the larger commissions. Butterfield and Scott received some significant opportunities. Butterfield built two cathedrals, at Perth and the country parish church sized Cathedral and College of the Isles on the island of Cumbrae. In 1855 Scott built St Paul, Dundee for Alexander Penrose Forbes, the Bishop of Brechin (plate 72). Forbes intended St Paul to be the principal church in his Diocese which had become centred on urban Dundee and it did eventually become its Cathedral. It is generally held that Forbes had a strong influence on the form of St Paul; a broad hall church nave with a full apsidal chancel without a screen. The plan suggests that Forbes was in sympathy with Beresford Hope's eclectic brand of ecclesiology, where European spaciousness and visibility were seen as legitimate modifications to national Gothic forms. These interests were expressed with greater sophistication at St Salvador, Dundee by G. F. Bodley from 1865, a near perfect embodiment of G. E. Street's description of a model church for Victorian towns.[13] St Salvador marks a crucial point in Bodley's transition from mid to late Victorian Gothic but this change did not have a significant influence in Scotland until the 1880s. It is possible that the new attitudes in London took some time to reach Scottish architects but Bodley's return to the English Decorated of Pugin had little meaning in Scotland. The revival of Decorated would have been a more radical stylistic leap because Scotland does not share England's rich stock of Decorated churches to act as a precedent. In the last two decades of the 19th century, younger architects such as Rowand Anderson, Robert Lorimer and Ninian Comper, who had worked in the offices of Scott, Bodley and Garner, or had been influenced by their work, began to construct a Scottish response to the late Gothic Revival.

[12]   *Ecclesiologist*, 5 (1846), p. 32, review of W. H. Teale, *Six Sermons Preached at the Consecration of the Church of St John the Evangelist, Jedburgh, in the Diocese of Glasgow, with an Introduction* (Edinburgh, 1845).

[13]   Anthony Symondson SJ, 'St Salvador, Dundee, and the Fulfilment of the Puginian Ideal', *Architectural Heritage...*, 8 (1997), pp. 108–116.

However, the Episcopal church had more than regional significance for the ecclesiologists. Many of the clergy and some major patrons had been educated at Oxford and Cambridge, in the thick of the Oxford Movement. It was seen as an Anglican Church which was less tainted by Protestantism than the Church of England and had freedom from state establishment so that it could develop towards the Tractarian goal. J. M. Neale considered joining the Scottish Episcopal Church during the first doctrinal controversy on baptismal regeneration.[14] The Scottish Episcopal church took a major part in the second doctrinal controversy about the real presence of Christ in the Eucharist which culminated in a charge of heresy made against Forbes by the other Scottish bishops.[15] Throughout the nineteenth century, the Episcopal church had its own tension between Tractarian and Evangelical parties which centred on the use of the Scottish Liturgy. The English rite was favoured by the low church party. The Scottish Liturgy of 1637 was considered to be a better setting for sacramental worship and was promoted by the Tractarians. The choral Scottish Communion service at the consecration of St John Jedburgh caused considerable disquiet within the Diocese of Glasgow.

The ambitious building programme undertaken by the Roman Catholic church in Scotland to meet the needs of a rapidly expanding population between 1860 and 1914 came too late to show any direct ecclesiological influences. The churches fit well into the standard pattern of basilican plan in Gothic dress which had been established by E. W. Pugin and his contemporaries around 1860. Only a few churches represent an earlier generation of more faithful medieval revival in the tradition of A. W. N. Pugin. The best of these churches are by Joseph Hansom for aristocratic patrons; for the Lovats in the Highlands and St David, Dalkeith for the same Marchioness of Lothian who had built St John, Jedburgh and contemporary with her conversion in 1853.

Just as the fundamental difference between the Church of England and the more diverse religious scene in Scotland had a limiting effect on the acceptance of ecclesiological principles, the different nature of medieval architecture in the two countries had a similar effect on their application. The stock of medieval buildings is quite different; England has over nine thousand medieval parish churches,[16] but in Scotland the total number of cathedrals, abbeys and parish churches, from Early Christian chapels until the Reformation, is around three hundred and fifty.[17] The Cambridge Camden

[14] James F. White, *The Cambridge Movement* (Cambridge, 1962), p. 211.
[15] Symondson, *op. cit.*, pp. 111–13.
[16] White, *op. cit.*, p. 2.
[17] These figures were reached by considering the entries in MacGibbon & Ross which I consider to be the first reliable and illustrated national survey of churches in Scotland. That churches are of limited interest clearly represents a subjective viewpoint but in using this source I intend to make a comparison with the

Society complained about the desecration of English churches but at least the majority were roofed and in use. In the mid-nineteenth century only about a quarter of Scottish medieval churches were still in use and many of these had been radically altered or substantially rebuilt since the Reformation. The total of three hundred and fifty surviving Scottish churches includes a significant number of buildings, possibly about fifty, where only fragments or founda- tions remain and which would have given little evidence of Pre-Reformation architecture or ritual. The ecclesiological appreciation of Scotland's churches was further restricted by the loss of some significant buildings; the two largest thirteenth-century cathedrals, at Elgin and St Andrews, were so ruined that only a limited understanding of their architecture was possible, and all of the abbey churches were partially or entirely in ruins. The Society's preference for cruciform churches with aisled naves in the Decorated style disqualified the majority of Scottish parish churches from acting as sound precedents for new architecture. Most Scottish medieval parish churches were long and low, on a rectangular plan with nave and chancel under one roof.

The stock of Scottish precedents was lacking in ambition and poorly preserved but for an ecclesiologist the greatest deficiency was in architecture of the right period. A lecture by the noted antiquary Joseph Robertson, given in 1856, illustrates the general contemporary opinion about the history of Gothic architecture in Scotland.[18] He considered the 'Anglo-Scottish era' from the end of the eleventh century to the end of the thirteenth to be 'The great age of ecclesiastical architecture in Scotland, the noontide, at once the spiritual glory and the earthly grandeur of the Medieval Church in the north.' There was strong influence from England; 'The ecclesiastical edifices of Scotland ... differ from those of England only as the churches of one English shire may differ from another.' The Second Pointed or Decorated style flourished in England between 1272 and 1377 but, 'By this time Scotland and England were antagonists, politically, socially and ecclesiologically. There was the Papal Schism and a gradual connection with France'. Church building in Scotland was virtually suspended between 1293 and 1406 because Scotland was exhausted by the war with England. The few Decorated churches which were built, such as Melrose Abbey and Fortrose Cathedral were destroyed by the English army or during the Reformation. During the 15th century, Scottish and English Gothic diverged; 'Soon after the appearance of the Third Pointed or Perpendicular Style on the southern side of the Tweed, Scottish churches began to show the Flamboyant window-tracery, the double doorways with

average English parish church as discussed in the pages of *The Ecclesiologist*.
18 Joseph Robertson, 'Sketch of the History of Architecture in Scotland, Ecclesiastical and Secular, previous to the Union with England 1707', *Archaeological Journal*, 13 (1856), p. 228. The paper was read to the Architectural Section of the Meeting of the Institute, Edinburgh July 1856.

flattened heads under one pointed arch, the large richly-crocketed pinnacles, the polygonal apses ... of the contemporary architecture of France.'

So, despite encouragement in the pages of *The Ecclesiologist* that Scottish churches should contain Scottish precedents, there were no Scottish medieval churches which passed the strict ecclesiological criteria which would make them worthy of emulation. Some Scottish buildings were admired but writers and lecturers on the surviving artistic achievements of medieval Scotland were able to give a finite list of church buildings. Ecclesiology possibly played a part in moving attention away from the Romantic enthusiasm for the small number of landmark buildings made famous by Walter Scott but not typical of Scottish medieval architecture, such as Rosslyn, Melrose and Holyrood.[19] According to general mid-nineteenth-century antiquarian opinion, the highest point of Scottish Gothic had been reached in the thirteenth century at Glasgow, Dunblane and Elgin Cathedrals. Ruskin's enthusiasm for the west front of Dunblane Cathedral; 'I know not anything so perfect in its simplicity, and so beautiful ... in all the Gothic with which I am acquainted'[20] must have helped to promote the cause of Scottish First Pointed. Three vaulted bays of the otherwise entirely demolished Fortrose Cathedral were praised by antiquarians, including Neale, as Scotland's one fragment of real Decorated. Beauty in later buildings was not recognised; Rosslyn was peculiar and probably foreign, the choir of Melrose was imported English Perpendicular and the large town churches of the fifteenth and sixteenth centuries at Perth, Stirling, Linlithgow, Edinburgh and Haddington were considered stylistically debased.

Despite the differences in the nature of the Scottish legacy of medieval churches, it is arguable that the most widespread effect of ecclesiology in Scotland was on the development of Scottish archaeology. The early transactions of the Ecclesiological Society show an interest in Scottish churches with the publication of articles on the Ecclesiological Antiquities of Argyll by J. S. Howson.[21] References to medieval church architecture in Scotland tail off after this but Neale's *Ecclesiological Notes on the Isle of Man, Ross, Sutherland and the Orkneys* considered some church ruins in northern

[19]   References to Walter Scott appear frequently, for instance; *Ecclesiologist*, 2 (1842), p. 83.

[20]   Quoted from Ruskin's Edinburgh Lectures (1853) in Charles McKean, *Stirling and the Trossachs* (Edinburgh, 1985) p. 81. McKean notes on p. 83 Rowand Anderson's comment that Ruskin's description of the west front of Dunblane had made it famous. In 'Ecclesiology in Scotland', *Ecclesiologist*, 20 (1859), p. 377, the west front of Dunblane Cathedral is described as being 'In the small first class of European Art'.

[21]   J. S. Howson, on Scottish architecture, *Ecclesiologist*, 1 (1842), p. 56; on bibliographical sources for Scottish church research, *Ecclesiologist*, 2 (1842), pp. 83, 105; 'Ecclesiological Antiquities of Argyll', *Transactions of the Cambridge Camden Society*, 2–3 (1842).

Scotland.[22] By concentrating on the Highlands and Orkney these articles failed to cover a representative sample of Scottish medieval architecture.

A more comprehensive survey had to come from archaeologists and antiquarians based in Scotland; R. W. Billings, T. S. Muir, Joseph Robertson, Joseph Anderson and MacGibbon & Ross. Billings and Muir represent opposite extremes. Billings undertook a general survey of Scotland's old buildings, both ecclesiastic and domestic. His choice of subjects reflects the desire of his sponsor, William Burn, that the book should promote a Baronial revival in domestic architecture. Billings' beautiful illustrations are accurate but steeped in romantic pictorial effects. Muir single-mindedly pursued the prosaic recording of churches. According to his obituary, 'He was possessed by an intense desire to popularise the subject of ecclesiology in Scotland.'[23] His publisher called him 'the father of Scottish Ecclesiology' and his work was a major source for later writers on Scottish church architecture.[24] Muir wholeheartedly adopted the classifications of style and prejudices of the Ecclesiological Society and applied them to Scottish buildings. A hostile review of his 'Notes on Some Ancient Parochial Collegiate Churches' in the *Archaeological Journal* illustrates some of the pitfalls of this approach as well as the animosity which existed between antiquarians and ecclesiologists.[25] The reviewer complains of 'Speculations and conceits of the Ecclesiological School' and devotes a page to a dismissal of the ecclesiological interest in eastwards orientation. Some of the points seem valid; the 'Notorious fact' that 'Scottish architecture is more like France than England' meant that the 'Old fashioned names of First, Middle and Third Pointed' were not applicable in Scotland.[26] In the reviewer's opinion, 'A fatal confusion is the result' because Muir cannot distinguish Decorated from Flamboyant and identifies buildings of the fifteenth century as Second Pointed.

[22] J. M. Neale, *Ecclesiological Notes on the Isle of Man, Ross, Sutherland and the Orkneys; or a Summer Pilgrimage to St Mangold and St Magnus* (London, no date), Reviewed in the *Archaeological Journal*, 5 (1848-9), pp. 351-3. In 1859 *The Ecclesiologist* published an article entitled 'Ecclesiology in Scotland' which reviewed: Butterfield's St Ninian Perth and Cathedral of the Isles, Cumbrae; Glenalmond College; three churches in Dundee, St Paul, St Salvador and St Mary Magdalen; and two churches by William Slater, St Andrew, Dunkeld and St Peter, Edinburgh. The article does not discuss Scottish medieval architecture except for short remarks on Dunblane and Glasgow cathedrals (*Ecclesiologist*, 20 (1859), pp. 376-87).

[23] *Architect*, 30 (19.10.1888), p. 225. Obituary of Thomas S Muir.

[24] Margaret Stokes, review of T. S. Muir, 'Ecclesiological notes on some of the Islands of Scotland', *The Academy*, 29 (1885), p. 207.

[25] *Archaeological Journal*, 5 (9.1848), p. 238. White, *op. cit.*, p. 30; the ecclesiologists felt that they had superseded antiquarianism.

[26] White, *op. cit.* [note 14], p. 88. The terms 'First, Middle and Third Pointed' were ecclesiological, and were first used in *Ecclesiologist*, 4 (1845), p. 52.

The effect of these antiquarian opinions on architects is not easy to assess. A greater proportion of Gothic revival churches are First Pointed in Scotland than in England and this might represent a revival of the medieval churches which were considered to be Scotland's best precedents in ecclesiological terms. The west front of Dunblane was the most frequently used specific source but details from Pluscarden Priory and Glasgow Cathedral were also quoted. Pugin and *The Ecclesiologist* excused First Pointed in 'remote' areas such as the Scottish highlands, Ireland and New Zealand on the grounds that a more primitive style is appropriate to the environment and the stage of development of religion. The use of Decorated tracery was rare, at least until the 1880s when some architects had the courage to revive Scottish fifteenth-century precedents but by this date the Late Gothic architecture of G. G. Scott junior, Sedding and Bodley & Garner had become influential. However, these suggestions of a direct influence from the Ecclesiological Society can be balanced with the probability that most Scottish architects were not particularly concerned by the fussy strictures of an Anglican architectural society except when employed to build Episcopal churches. The architecture of G. G. Scott and Butterfield, who could work successfully in First Pointed, was probably an influence and the lancet style of Pearson certainly was. First Pointed was practical for the competitive church building boom of the 1850s and '60s, when money which could be spent on more seats or a prominent tower would be wasted on tracery.

By far the most important figure in the creation of an overt ecclesiological movement in Scotland was James Cooper (1845–1922). Cooper was born in Elgin and studied at Aberdeen University. His early life in the north-east of Scotland and his affection for its religious history and architecture was to be a strong influence throughout his life. Aberdeenshire, Banff and Buchan were the areas of Scotland which most strongly retained their native Catholic and Episcopalian traditions and this sense of a diverse religious culture seems to have led Cooper to become one of the leaders of the Catholic movement within the Church of Scotland. Cooper's first ministry was at St Stephen, Broughty Ferry near Dundee from 1873, where he added a chancel and introduced Christmas and Holy Week services, possibly for the first time in the Church of Scotland.[27] In 1881 he became the minister of East St Nicholas church in Aberdeen where he introduced controversial innovations in worship and furnishing. Cooper's rush to install a communion table, font, organ and lectern led to a petition of complaint to the Aberdeen Presbytery by eleven East St Nicholas elders in May 1882. The decision of the Presbytery that Cooper's 'High Church' doctrine and practices were in accord with the tradition of the Church of Scotland was a strong indicator of

[27]   Henry R. Sefton, 'The church in James Cooper's Day', *The Record of the Church Service Society*, 29 (Edinburgh, 1995), p. 4.

changing opinion. However, the Presbytery censured Cooper for the over-hasty introduction of these practices. He managed to implement further changes to the nature and frequency of the celebration of Holy Communion without controversy.[28] Cooper's status within the Scottish ecclesiological movement was stressed in the tributes which followed his re-election as president of the Scottish Ecclesiological Society in 1911. He was described as the 'The founder of modern Scottish ecclesiology in the widest sense' and 'the true and only begetter of the Society, and without his influence, example and enthusiasm, the Society could not be what it was, the largest of its kind in Great Britain.'[29]

Cooper instigated the Aberdeen Ecclesiological Society in 1886. His first move was to discuss it with Charles Carmichael, a young architect.[30] They drew together a group of twelve founder members consisting of Church of Scotland ministers and the architects William Kelly and A. Marshall Mackenzie. Cooper became the president and remained so until the amalgamation of the Aberdeen and Glasgow Ecclesiological Societies to become the Scottish Ecclesiological Society in 1903.

The Aberdeen society grew steadily from 186 members in 1888, two years after its foundation, to 389 members in 1897, the last complete year before amalgamation. Notable early members included the architects William Smith of Aberdeen and T. S. Robertson of Dundee. There were fewer architects than clergy. The clergy included leading members of the High Church party; Cooper's mentor, Dr William Milligan was an early member. Dr Sprott joined in 1887 and Rev. John McLeod of Govan in 1891. Episcopal clergy were also represented. New members joined from other parts of Scotland: the Glasgow architects J. A. Campbell in 1887, John Honeyman in 1890 and Campbell Douglas in 1891, W. L. Carruthers of Inverness in 1892, the Edinburgh architects Rowand Anderson in 1892 and John Kinross in 1894, Alexander Cullen of Hamilton in 1896. There were significant architectural patrons; John Ritchie Findlay who joined 1891, Lord Bute 'Of Cardiff Castle' in 1894 and Sir John Stirling Maxwell in 1895. John Comper was a member at least since 1889 and his son, Ninian Comper, was the earliest member to be based outside Scotland. The list of office holders for 1897, gives

28 Douglas M. Murray, 'The Ministry of James Cooper at Aberdeen', *Record of the Church Service Society*, 29 (Edinburgh, 1995), pp. 6–13. Douglas M. Murray, 'James Cooper and the East Church Case at Aberdeen, 1882–3: The High Church Movement Vindicated', *Records of the Scottish Church History Society*, 19 (1977), pp. 217–33.

29 *Transactions of the Scottish Ecclesiological Society* [TSES], 3 (1911–12), pp. xix–xx. Speeches by James Balfour Paul and F. C. Eeles respectively in Edinburgh, 14.1.1911.

30 *Transactions of the Aberdeen Ecclesiological Society* [TAES], 5 (Aberdeen, 1891), pp. 75–76.

JOHN SANDERS

an idea of the status which the society had reached in eleven years; Cooper was the president and William Kelly the secretary, as they had been from the beginning; the vice presidents were Dr Sprott and A. Marshall Mackenzie an established minister and architect respectively; the honorary vice-presidents were Lord Bute, a prominent Roman Catholic, Rev. Wilkinson, the Episcopalian Bishop of St Andrews, Principal Geddes of Glasgow University, J. W. Legg, founder of the St Paul's Ecclesiological Society and Rowand Anderson, by that time the 'pre-eminent' architect in Scotland.

The Glasgow Ecclesiological Society was formed in 1893. The development of the membership followed a similar pattern to the Aberdeen society with notable clergy from all denominations outnumbering architects. Many members were common to both societies. Cooper addressed the first general meeting of the Glasgow society[31] and in 1894 members of the two societies met in Glasgow to see the Cathedral and Barony Church and to share a convivial dinner. The two societies merged in 1903 to form the Scottish Ecclesiological Society. Cooper had left Aberdeen in 1898 to accept the chair of the Divinity Faculty of Glasgow University and was elected the first president of the united societies.[32] The membership of the new society is familiar from the lists of the earlier societies and it seems that the society had difficulty attracting new members. In 1901 a series of popular lectures on ecclesiological subjects was not well attended by the younger clergy.

When the Aberdeen Ecclesiological Society was formed, Cooper expressed his hope that it should have a similar effect to the Cambridge Ecclesiological Society.[33] In a later review of the work of the Aberdeen society he noted that it 'Never faltered in its advocacy of a worship in which the supremacy of the Eucharist shall be clearly recognised ... the restoration of the Holy Communion to its right place in relation to the worship of the Church, and the spiritual life of the baptised.'[34] There were other echoes of the Cambridge Camden Society; the stated aims of the new society were the 'Study of the principles of church worship and of church architecture with its allied arts' and the 'Diffusion in the North of Scotland of sound views and the creation of truer taste.'[35] The need for a review of ecclesiastical architecture was expressed by William Kelly; '*We* in this Society claim to be in the succession. They, in the old days, criticised in the pages of the *Ecclesiologist* architectural exhibitions as well as completed works of architecture, and so influenced public appreciation. The continuance of the work is greatly needed in these days.'[36] The transactions contain a similar balance of articles on

[31] *Transactions of the Glasgow Ecclesiological Society* [TGES], 1 (Glasgow, 1895), p. 4.
[32] H. J. Wotherspoon, *James Cooper, A Memoir* (London, 1926), p. 192.
[33] *TAES*, 1 (1886), p. 7.
[34] James Cooper, *op. cit.*, p. 48.
[35] *TAES*, 1 (1886), p. 7.
[36] *TAES*, II (1895), p. 2.

307

religious and architectural history with reviews of new churches and notices of excursions. The debate over the symbolic nature of Gothic architecture was re-enacted by the Glasgow Ecclesiological Society nearly fifty years after Neale and Webb's publication of Durandus.[37] As with the Cambridge Camden Society, theological discussion was avoided but for different reasons; in Cambridge to avoid charges of extremism, in Aberdeen because the society was interdenominational.[38]

Other differences between the two societies were due to their existence in a different time and place; the single-minded undergraduate fervour and fearless denunciations of late 1830s Cambridge would not have been appropriate for a group of Late Victorians drawn from various established political and religious points of view. The church building boom in Scotland had passed, so the society had to devote most of its reviews to reorderings, extensions and restorations. Members of the Church of Scotland felt protective over their democratic system of government, as Cooper had experienced in his own ministry, and would resist changes in modes of worship which could be associated with patronage. For the architectural development to take place the society had to present authoritative arguments without causing offence. Cooper felt that the working classes found it easy to accept change. It was the 'middle classes' and the 'nobility' who were resistant and his understanding of this target audience affected the way that the society presented its argument; 'In order to take the people with us – in order to avoid schism and disaster – we must train them by degrees.'[39] Cooper felt that the progress towards sacramental worship in the Church of Scotland should be gradual, an idea which parallels the English Anglican interest in 'development'.[40]

The Aberdeen Ecclesiological Society developed links with England. In 1893 Dr Wickham Legg was present to hear Comper's 'Practical Considerations on the Gothic or English Altar and Certain Dependent Ornaments' in which the 'English altar' was justified.[41] Other English speakers travelled north to give papers sometimes of little relevance to Scotland. Cooper lectured in England at least twice; he read 'The revival of

[37]   John Charleson, 'The Rationale and Symbolism of Christian Churches', TGES, 2 (1898), p. 46. Alex MacGibbon on symbolism, TGES, 2 (1898), p. 7.
[38]   White, op. cit., p. 35.
[39]   James Cooper, 'The Arrangement and the furnishing of a Scottish parish church', Transactions of the Edinburgh Architectural Association, 4 (1905), p. 30. Lecture delivered to the EAA 15.11.1905.
[40]   'Development' could be defined as the slow and progressive revelation of God's truth to Victorian society. This definition was suggested to me in a lecture by Michael Hall to the Victorian Society 'Late Gothic' symposium in November 1995.
[41]   TAES, II (1895). pp. 61–104.

church principles in the Church of Scotland' to the North Test Clerical Society in Hampshire in 1895,[42] and, more significantly, a review of 'Ecclesiology in Scotland' to the St Paul's Ecclesiological Society in 1893.[43]

One of the Aberdeen Ecclesiological Society's most persuasive arguments for sacramental worship in the Church of Scotland was in the reinterpretation of the history of the Reformation. Post-Reformation examples of the continuation of medieval practices were as valuable in Scotland as they were for the English ecclesiologists. Cooper would have been well aware that the publication of the *Hierurgia Anglicana* was intended to show that Pre-Reformation practices continued in Post-Reformation worship and in several lectures he tried to make a similar position for Scottish church history. His case was that the Post-Reformation church in Scotland had a liturgy which was enshrined in the Knox Liturgy of 1564. He stressed that John Knox, the hero of the Scottish Reformation, was instrumental in writing the immediate Post-Reformation Liturgies of the Church of England. Knox left England to escape Queen Mary's intolerance of Protestants and settled at Frankfurt where he ministered to a largely English Protestant congregation. They had to assemble quickly a prayer book which was acceptable to all parties. Knox's opinion on this compromise seems to have been more flexible than Calvin, but even Calvin felt that the English Prayer Book could be tolerated. This Frankfurt draft of the *Book of Common Prayer* had immense significance. Cooper was able to link Knox with an acceptance, albeit reluctant, of the same forms of prayer book worship which the Ecclesiologists promoted in England:

> here is a document to which our great Reformer not merely put his hand, but which he actually helped to compile, which he accepted, which he used in public worship, and urged others to comply with. It remains a monument not alone of his accepting *the principle* of a Liturgy ... [The draft] shows us how far John Knox was able ... for the sake of harmony, to go in the way of approving *that* Liturgy which has unquestionably the first claim on the Anglo-Saxon race, the *Book of Common Prayer*.

A Canadian Presbyterian writer, R. G Murison, saw the period between the Reformation and the Westminster Assembly of 1643 as 'The period when the Church was purest Reformed'[44] and contained much that would be recognisable in an English Anglican church; 'Knox's Liturgy advised that the Lord's Supper be celebrated once a month or as often as expedient. The Reformers believed in frequent celebration; to them the Holy Supper was the central rite, and a blessed means of grace. Calvin denounced annual

---

[42] *TAES*, III (1897), p. 262.

[43] *TAES*, II (1895), pp. 31–48.

[44] R. G. Murison, 'Worship in the Church of Scotland from the Reformation to the Westminster Assembly', *TAES*, III (1898), p. 341. This article was originally prepared for the Knox College Monthly and Presbyterian Magazine of Toronto.

Communions as the invention of the devil.'[45] John Knox's pulpit at St Salvator's chapel, St Andrews, allowed for addressing prayers eastwards.[46] Nineteenth-century resistance to sacramental worship was caused by a misconception of the spirit of the reformers. The characteristic barrenness of Presbyterian church services was a seventeenth-century change which could be blamed on England. According to Sprott, this change had been inspired by 'English Brownism', one of 'Those fanatical sects which sprang up during the Commonwealth.'[47] Murison summarised this case by contrasting the use immediately after the Reformation with the forms of worship which developed during the seventeenth and eighteenth centuries:

> the Church was not always chained to her present bare and unattractive mode of service, but had elements of greater richness and beauty ... Such, then, was the use and wont of our Mother Church before, in the Seventeenth century, by Brownism and sectarianism, by narrow-minded ignorance, bigotry, spiritual pride, and self-righteousness, she was stripped of her garments of beauty, and afterwards hardened to her shame by the rationalistic Moderatism of the Eighteenth century.[48]

The conclusion that the churches of England and Scotland were practically the same at the Reformation led Cooper to suggest that the Churches of Scotland and England might eventually reunite.[49] This must be considered a brave opinion given that many Anglicans considered that union with Rome was imminent and that some Protestant churches had set up committees to publicise these unwelcome Romish tendencies.[50]

The ideal state of the reformed Church of Scotland at the time of its foundation was possibly the most admissible argument for liturgical worship in the Presbyterian Churches but the Ecclesiological Societies were prepared to find ecclesiological comparisons in Early Christian and medieval practice. The model of the Early Christian church in Scotland was attractive for Sprott; 'St Columba and his followers maintained the form of Christianity, free in great measure from Romish error, and substantially the same as our own'.

[45] R. G. Murison, *op. cit.*, p. 346.
[46] *TGES*, 1 (1895), p. 22.
[47] The Brownists were a group similar to the Plymouth Brethren who split from the Anglican Church.
[48] R. G. Murison, *op. cit.*, p. 348.
[49] James Cooper, *op. cit.*, p. 31.
[50] Lord Halifax, Address to the English Church Union, 42nd Anniversary of the Union. Newspaper cuttings in the Evelyn Murray of Polmaise papers, Stirling County Records Office, Ref. 12/42/3. The press cuttings also contain acrimonious correspondence between the Secretary of the United Free Church Committee of Romanism and Rev. H. Erskine Hill, Episcopal Rector of Maryhill, Glasgow on the subject of a possible union between the Church of England and the Roman Catholic Church.

JOHN SANDERS

The memory of a Celtic church before the influence of Normans or Anglo-Saxons was attractive to nationalist sentiment in Scotland as it was in Ireland.

The liturgy of the medieval church could also be analysed in nationalist terms. Scottish ecclesiologists could claim that Scottish medieval liturgy was based on the Use of Sarum, the favourite medieval precedent for the Ecclesiological Society.[51] Very few Scottish office books survived the Reformation. One of these, the Arbuthnot Missal, had been adopted at St Andrew's between 1147 and 1164 and had became the general form throughout Scotland by 1249. According to the Rev. T. Newbigging Adamson, the Use of St Andrews was the same as the Use of Sarum. 'The very fountainhead of, therefore, the English *Book of Common Prayer*, which represents today the devotional practice of the overwhelming majority of the Anglo-Saxon race.'[52] The only significant difference in the St Andrews liturgy was that it commemorated Scottish saints[53] and omitted some English ones. The medieval church in Scotland preferred the Use of Salisbury to the use of York because the Archbishop of York had claims to jurisdiction over Scotland. In the ecclesiological view, therefore, the Sarum Use could be associated with the highest point of achievement of Scottish Gothic, its First Pointed of the thirteenth century. In the fifteenth century the Sarum Use was popularly but wrongly believed to have been 'Forced on Scotland by the hated Edward I.'[54] Opposition to the Sarum Use could be associated with the decline of the church into corruption and the consequent debasement of its architecture. At the Reformation the Scottish church was subjected to a more radical change than in other countries because 'The practical corruptions of the Scottish Church were more pronounced and virulent than anywhere else in Europe.'[55]

The Scottish Ecclesiological Societies were not able to promote an 'ideal' church with the dogmatism of the Cambridge Camden Society. The variety of views and faiths of their members made this impossible. Nevertheless, all the members seem to have agreed that worship should be sacramental and that the architecture of churches should reflect this as their primary purpose. Cooper advocated that churches should be orientated

[51] White, *op. cit.*, p. 207.
[52] T. Newbigging Adamson, on the Arbuthnot Missal, *TGES*, 1 (1895), p. 63. The Rev. T. Newbigging Adamson was the minister of St Margaret, Broughty Ferry. The use of the loaded term 'Anglo-Saxon' is curious for a Church of Scotland minister.
[53] Saints Fillan, Kentigern, Colman, Monan, Adrian, Baldred, Duthac, Kessog, Constantine, Rule, Margaret of Scotland, Ternan, Bride, Botolph, Ninian and Palladius.
[54] James Cooper, *op. cit.*, p. 36.
[55] David Watson, 'Some Aspects of Recent Church Architecture', *TGES*, 3 (1901), p. 41.

eastwards, that the chancel should be given architectural distinction and that churches should have spires.[56]

The members of the Aberdeen society visited and reviewed churches which embodied their aims. Two Aberdeenshire churches by Matthews & Mackenzie, at Crathie (plate 73) and Pitsligo, were considered to be ecclesiologically correct. As the parish church for Balmoral, Crathie church received particular attention and the support of the Royal Family as benefactors was noted with some satisfaction.[57] It is a country church for a small congregation with a cruciform plan and a squat tower over the crossing. In Mackenzie's description of his new church for the Aberdeen Ecclesiological Society he noted that the cruciform plan 'Greatly adds to the picturesqueness of the building'[58] but it seems clear that the plan was adopted to hide the Royal Family from the general view of the nave, in the manner of a traditional Scottish family aisle. The style of the church is significant. Mackenzie drew on Scottish sources; Pluscarden for the gable elevation of the royal transept and 'Decorated period' windows from Melrose for the nave.[59] These windows, together with the general massing of the church, give Crathie a Late Scots Gothic character and can be read as an attempt to provide a Scottish answer to the ecclesiological preference for Decorated.

Urban churches were also praised. Rev. John Mcleod's new church at Govan was seen as a highly significant statement of Scottish ecclesiological principles; 'Probably the most magnificent reared in connection with the National Church since 1560.' Together with the Barony Church and William Leiper's Hyndland parish church it marked 'A new era in the character of the parish churches of Scotland ... The prominence accorded in all three to the chancel and the altar (features hitherto rarely and grudgingly admitted) points no less to a revival of sounder views as to the place of the Eucharist in the Church's worship.'[60] A supportive view was taken on the effects of the movement in the Free Church and the limitations to progress were noted with an understanding which would not have been found in *The Ecclesiologist*:

> They, too, have done no little for fostering of Ecclesiastical Art: churches of theirs at Morningside, at Glasgow, Crieff, Ellie, Perth and Broughty Ferry exhibit a careful study of old work, and an intelligent effort to adopt old

---

[56]   James Cooper, *op. cit.*, p. 33.

[57]   Pitsligo; *TAES*, II (1892), p. 3; 'It represents the first attempt in Buchan to carry out in Presbyterian church-building the principles for the promotion of which our Society exists.' Crathie; *TAES*, III (1897), p. 256. The princesses gave jewels to be built into the furnishings and the Queen attended the dedication; *TSES*, 2 (1909), p. 21. Edward VII was credited for his taste in the building of Crathie church.

[58]   A. Marshall Mackenzie, 'The New Church at Crathie', *TAES*, III (1897), p. 257.

[59]   Ibid.

[60]   *TAES*, I (1888), p. 37.

arrangements to a form of service which they make it a point to cherish.[61]

This tide of reordering reached some of the early nineteenth-century churches mentioned at the beginning of this chapter; St John and St Paul Episcopal churches both had their galleries removed and received extended chancels, Stenton church lost its pulpit and gained the altarwise communion table and stained glass which Burn's exterior had always suggested it should have (plate 70).[62]

Although many of the early reviews of new churches appear to have been written by Cooper, we can guess that some of his architectural opinions were those of the architects who were involved in the foundation of the society: Charles Carmichael, William Kelly and A. Marshall Mackenzie. The general assumption in discussions of style was that churches should be Gothic. A few dissenting voices, notably in Glasgow, suggested that Early Christian styles would be more appropriate. Despite a scholarly interest in Scottish medieval churches, there seems to have been no requirement that new Gothic churches should be Scottish in character or that any phase of Gothic should be favoured.

The plans of new churches were praised if they were medieval in form. Auditorium features such as galleries and an organ positioned behind the pulpit were always criticised.[63] However, it was never suggested that medieval parish church planning should be followed exactly for Presbyterian churches. Dr Sprott shared the eclectic and European attitudes of Beresford Hope:

There is nothing in our system [of worship] inconsistent with the noblest style of architecture, nothing to prevent our utilising of all parts of a Gothic Cathedral; though perhaps the earliest form of the Christian Church, the Basilica, suits best our worship, the means at our disposal, and our traditions. The finest Reformed Churches in the world are the old Swiss Cathedrals, such as that of Basel. In Holland there are also many noble and stately cruciform Churches, the chancel or head of the Cross, being used for the Communion, as was the case in Scotland after the Reformation.[64]

Cooper agreed with the need for short chancels so that the congregation could see and feel involved in the ceremonial. He referred to S. Clemente in Rome

[61] James Cooper, op. cit., p. 46.
[62] Colin McWilliam, The Buildings of Scotland: Lothian (Harmondsworth, 1978), p. 440. Reordering in 1892 by James Jerdan, 'East' window Glass by C. E. Kempe, 1888. A bell was placed in the belfry in 1922.
[63] For instance; TAES, III (1896), p. 11; the new parish church at Largs was considered 'A beautiful church, designed with much skill, yet sadly marred in the very central point, by the organ occupying the whole of the choir ... that the organ, thus promoted to the place of highest honour, now dominated the entire services completely as it did the building': TAES, II (1892), p. 5; William Kelly's objections to the proposed east position of the new organ at St Machar's Cathedral, Aberdeen. These objections were not heeded.
[64] Sprott, op. cit., p. 234.

as an ideal plan. Similar calls for basilican planning came from the speakers to the Glasgow Ecclesiological Society.[65] Ironically, this meant that the ideal ecclesiological Presbyterian church could have exactly the same plan as the standard canonical Roman Catholic church. Some suggestion that architects wished to push beyond ecclesiological orthodoxy is evident in the transactions of the Glasgow Ecclesiological Society. In 1897 the architect H. D. Walton proposed a more radical alternative on the grounds that 'New forms of worship need new plans'.[66] He felt that the Byzantine or Greek cross centralised plan offered a

> Compromise between an Ecclesiological ideal [Gothic] and the hard practical congregational utility ... The most important objective in the planning of a modern Protestant church should be to place the officiating clergy in close touch with the whole congregation ... Medieval church buildings represent the highest development of Medieval Sacerdotalism ... A dispassionate consideration of the subject undoubtedly points to the ideal church of the future as one conceived on some centralised plan, with less aggressive pretentiousness outside and with more attention to convenience and impressiveness inside...[67]

The plan of the building need not be reflected in its style, however; 'There seems to be no adequate reason why any of the styles of Christian architecture, from the earliest Byzantine onto the latest period of Gothic, should not lend itself to the Oriental ground plan.'[68]

The Society could be even less proscriptive on the matter of church furnishing. It was felt that the communion table should occupy a permanent and prominent position. Stone or marble altars in Presbyterian churches were given favourable notices.[69] Cooper felt that any medieval precedent could be permissible; 'I hope there is nothing Christian or truly Catholic that we may not use (or hope to use) in the worship of the Church of Scotland.'[70] Provision for weekday worship in a side chapel was considered essential as was 'A reverent atmosphere for prayer'.[71] But Cooper's description of an ideal sanctuary seems tame when compared with the Cambridge Camden strictures on the same subject. Cooper felt that a chancel should have

> Handsome panelling, or hangings, higher than the Minister's head as he stands behind the Table ... [to] ... form a rich but quiet background. If flowers are to be used, there should be a sufficient shelf, or niches, in the reredos to enable large vases to be set with safety and effect behind the Holy

---

[65] *TGES*, 1 (1895), p. 3. *TSES*, 3 (1911–12), p. 32. Mr W. Baird Smith on the effects of early canon law on the architectural arrangement of a parish church.

[66] H. D. Walton, 'Church Planning from Byzantine examples', *TGES*, 3 (1901) p. 16.

[67] *Ibid.*

[68] *Ibid.*

[69] *TAES*, I (1887), p. 44.

[70] James Cooper, *op. cit.*, p. 30.

[71] *TGES*, 1 (1895), p. 22.

Table. Nothing should be on the Table, except its appropriate coverings, but the Bible, the Almsdish and the Sacramental Vessels.[72]

Restorations of churches were of considerable importance to the Scottish ecclesiological societies. Scotland's depleted stock of medieval churches had to be protected and restoration allowed Presbyterian worship to take place in a Pre-Reformation setting. There was concern over the quality of past restorations, at St Giles, Edinburgh, for instance, 'Whose monumental features were destroyed in the vandal 'restoration' of 1829–33.[73] For this and other drastic early nineteenth-century restorations at Dundee and Dunfermline Abbey, William Burn earned the title the 'Scottish Wyatt'.[74] In 1889 the Aberdeen society signed a petition against Lord Grimthorpe's work at St Albans.[75] The first restoration which was carried out according to ecclesiological principles was St Veigan, Arbroath, in 1871 by Rowand Anderson for Rev. Duke, 'The pioneer of the sound and practical Ecclesiology in the Church of Scotland'.[76] Anderson was to become the main figure in the restoration of Scottish churches. His restoration of Kings College Chapel, Aberdeen (plate 74), re-roofing of the nave of Dunblane and his project for the completion of Paisley Abbey received more attention from the Scottish ecclesiological societies than any new church.[77] Restoration projects by John Honeyman of Iona Abbey, St Michael, Linlithgow and Brechin Cathedral were also welcomed as was the internal restoration of St Giles, which finally removed the subdivision into four churches and restored a plan with a pulpit, stalls and reredos, which was almost indistinguishable from an Anglican church (plate 75). Sir James Balfour Paul noted that the deep chancels at Linlithgow and Paisley provided an opportunity to restore 'The administration of Holy Communion of the Long Table of old Scottish Rite.'[78] The Scottish Ecclesiological Society was strongly supportive of the proposals by Thomas Ross to re-roof the nave of Holyrood Abbey with a stone vault.[79] As late as 1913, Cooper gave evidence to the Select Committee on the Ancient

---

[72] James Cooper, *op. cit.*, p. 39.

[73] *TAES*, I (1890), p. 74.

[74] *TAES*, III (1897), p. 127. Rev. John Turnbull on the Parish Church of St Monan Fife, 'One of the churches which Burn "the Scottish Wyatt" inflicted to terrible injury.'

[75] *TAES*, I (1889), p. 11.

[76] *TSES*, 2 (1908), p. 341. Dr Sprott suggested Revd William Duke to be the new president, Duke declined on the grounds of age. Sprott said that St Veigans was, 'The first church in Scotland to be restored on the right lines'.

[77] *Architect*, 42 (1889), p. 191. Note of Anderson's report to Kings College Aberdeen Committee. *TAES*, II (1892), p. 64.

[78] *TSES*, 2 (1908), p. 409. The remark was made in response to the proposal to build a new chancel for Paisley Abbey. The practice was already in place at St Michael, Linlithgow following its restoration.

[79] *TSES*, 2 (1906), p. 275. The issue was discussed during a visit to Restalrig.

Monuments Consolidation and Protection Bill. He was generally supportive but careful to avoid anything that would prevent ruined churches from being re-roofed.[80] In 1905 Cooper was able to take a retrospective view of most of the major restoration projects. The modifications to medieval church planning in some of these restorations to accommodate Church of Scotland worship were a disappointment; he criticised Dunblane for its lack of a screen and felt that 'Our Church can hardly be said as yet, except in the case of St Giles, to have begun to realise the proper use of these noble piles.'[81]

Cooper's criticism of Dunblane for lack of a screen indicates the extent to which the Scottish ecclesiologists had met their aims. He was able to suggest that a loaded symbol of Anglo-Catholicism should be erected in a prominent church where it had no meaning in contemporary Presbyterian worship and know that his opinion would be respected.[82] The Scottish ecclesiological societies had been instrumental in the change of opinion which allowed such a suggestion to be made without being considered outrageous. Cambridge Camden Society attitudes and methods had survived into the twentieth century. They had been consciously employed to create a shift towards sacramental worship and more fastidious revivals of Gothic architecture. The strong membership of established clergy meant that the main effect of the Scottish ecclesiological movement was on the restoration and reordering of existing churches. The movement took place after the Mid-Victorian church building boom and so there are relatively few new churches which can be directly attributed to the influence of the Scottish ecclesiological societies. Most Scottish Late Victorian architects learnt their ecclesiology during their training in London or from periodicals but the Scottish ecclesiological movement helped to provide a more enlightened climate for these architects to bring contemporary church architecture to Scotland.

Acknowledgements. I am very grateful to Dr Gavin Stamp and to Rev. Tom Davidson Kelly who read and commented on a draft of this chapter. I am also grateful to Dr Tristram Clarke for giving me a copy of his article on St John, Jedburgh before its publication. I would like to thank Emma Plant and Susan Smith for their help with the text.

---

[80]   *TSES*, 4 (1912–13). He noted the desirability of re-roofing the nave of Dunkeld Cathedral.

[81]   James Cooper, *op. cit.*, p. 31.

[82]   Dunblane Cathedral had a screen by Lorimer installed in 1912.

Nonconformist Architecture and the Cambridge Camden Society

CHRISTOPHER STELL

When, according to Horace Walpole, the Earl of Bedford demanded of Inigo Jones that his new church of St Paul, Covent Garden should be made 'not much better than a barn', his architect gave him 'the handsomest barn in Europe'.[1]

About 1792, that great London demagogue the Rev. William Huntingdon ('Sinner Saved') gave *his* advice on the building of an Independent chapel at Welwyn, he recommended 'build as plain as you can, to keep out the wind and the rain is all we want'[2] – and he probably got just that. Nonconformists, as a whole, have been wary of ostentation, though there are many and varied exceptions to this rule.

In his much quoted description of Thomas Ivory's new octagonal meeting-house in Norwich, which John Wesley visited on 23 November 1757, Wesley admired the architecture and marvelled at the quality of the fittings – but then wryly remarked 'how can it be thought that the old coarse gospel should find admission here?'[3] Wesley copied the octagonal plan in several of his Methodist chapels, but always without the elaboration of detail which he so much distrusted.

Barns, and buildings of barn-like proportions, have played a significant part in the history of many nonconformist congregations. Large, readily available, these buildings could be used as temporary meeting-places or converted into regular places of worship and a few of these have survived in use to the present day. But it must not be supposed that dissenters, of whatever persuasion, were entirely lacking in appreciation of the finer points of architecture. Economic factors were, however, an overriding consideration: the need to house as large a congregation as cheaply as possible, often with very limited means, was a primary concern. Where money was available, either from the circumstances of the members or the presence of a wealthy

---

[1] J. Summerson, *Georgian London* (London, 1945), p. 15.
[2] R. L. Hine, *The History of Hitchin*, 2 vols (London, 1927–9), II, p. 132n.
[3] N. Curnock (ed.), *The Journal of the Rev. John Wesley, A.M.*, 8 vols (London, 1938), IV, p. 244.

benefactor within their midst, then some very presentable architecture often resulted.

The mid eighteenth-century Congregational chapel in Coombe Street, Lyme Regis, now demoted to a public spectacle under the name of 'Dinosaurland', was typical, in many ways, of the better class of nonconformist meeting-house at that time. The broad-fronted proportions of its plan follow those which Christopher Wren recommended for an auditory building with the pulpit set against the longer rear wall opposite the entrance. The construction of this large space, barn-like only in the simplicity of its proportions or in the eyes of its detractors, is externally explicit and representative of many others of its age, with its double roof upheld internally by a pair of posts dressed up as classical columns, while its external features of oval gallery windows with taller round-arched windows below follow the accepted style of the day.

In the fashionable watering place of Bath, the Countess of Huntingdon, a reluctant dissenter, but one none the less, attracted the polite and the curious to the ministrations of her Calvinistic Methodist preachers with a chapel in the Gothick style of Strawberry Hill. It was a building which, at least in its architecture, drew the praise of Horace Walpole. The big chapel, hidden behind the minister's house, he calls 'very neat, with true Gothic windows'.[4]

Even in the busy port of Poole in Dorset the hard-headed merchants who formed the nucleus of a new Independent church introduced a fashionably Gothick touch when they built their chapel in Skinner Street in 1777. Although the Georgian key-stones sit uncomfortably over pointed arched windows, and the obelisks on the parapet have an ill-concealed desire to evolve into pinnacles, the wind of change in what was to become architecturally acceptable was beginning to be felt.

Nineteenth Century

The early years of the nineteenth century saw many changes affecting nonconformists: political, religious and architectural. The older denominations began to develop a greater sense of corporate existence and all exhibited an increased willingness to stand up and be visible. Chapels came to be more prominently sited; some, such as the former Wesleyan 'Ebenezer Chapel' of 1823 in Acorn Street, Sheffield (plate 77), by Joseph Botham, even proclaiming their presence with a tower. Ebenezer was exceptional for its serious attention to Gothic detail in the front, of which the tower was intended to be completed with an open-work corona. Another Wesleyan chapel by Botham, Eastbrook, Bradford, of 1825, was only vestigially Gothic,

---

[4]   Letter to John Chute, 10 October 1766, quoted in J. Aitken (ed.), *English Letters of the XVIII Century* (Harmondsworth, 1946), pp. 109–10.

'approaching to the gothic'[5] was as much as was said at the time, but in both instances it was the suitability of the 'meeting-house' behind which was of greatest concern to the congregation.

Possibly the most outstanding of these pre-Camdenian Gothic chapels was the 'Regent Square' Scots Presbyterian church in Tavistock Place, London, built in 1824-7. This had an imposingly Gothic North front to the street, stone clad with two tall square towers, pinnacled and battlemented, with broad glazed and traceried windows in the upper stage, and a doorway in the centre bay below an impressively tall window. The church was designed by Sir William Tite and the front was claimed to be based, with some allowance for scale, on that of York Minster. Unfortunately, as was so often the case, the site was cramped between terraces of four-storied houses which concealed the brick-built, though buttressed, preaching house behind.

This kind of façadism was roundly condemned and lampooned by A. W. N. Pugin to whom the very name of 'meeting-house' was sufficiently anathema (plate 76); but many nonconformist chapels, and some Anglican churches too, were built on confined sites and economy as well as common sense called for a less ambitious touch to parts which were beyond the public view. Less excusable were the steep Gothic gables concealing cheap low-pitched roofs, a striking feature in two of Pugin's sketches,[6] which were no fiction – one example of which was to be seen in Hereford in a former Wesleyan chapel in Bridge Street, built in 1829. When enlarged and refronted in 1866 it was given a pedimented stone front and pointed arched windows with minimal tracery, concealing the brick building behind.

Baptists

It may be thought from such examples of façadism that nonconformists had no architectural conscience. Doubtless this was one of the impressions which Pugin sought to convey; but it was misleading. They had a different agenda and different priorities. To keep out the wind and the rain may have been a matter of primary concern; to accommodate large numbers of people was often a necessity, and the ability, even given the desire, to employ fashionable architects or to reach further than the utilitarian minimum was often beyond their means. The majority of nonconformist congregations, particularly those in rural areas, continued throughout much of the first half of the nineteenth century to build within the simple Georgian tradition of plain rectangular structures pierced as necessary by sash windows and one or two domestic-looking entrances in the front wall. But once 'style' in a self-conscious way was added to the equation anything might happen. In the 1840s the Roman-

---

5   W. W. Stamp, *Historical Notes of Wesleyan Methodism in Bradford and its Vicinity* (London, 1841), p. 102 and illus.

6   A. W. N. Pugin, *The True Principles of Pointed and Christian Architecture* (London, 1841), plate G, fig. 1.

esque style was briefly in vogue. It was a style which *The Ecclesiologist*[7] regarded as good enough for New Zealand, though hardly so for any more civilized society – which presumably did not include nonconformists in the eyes of the architectural pundits. Several chapels were built in this style, one of which, Cavendish Street Chapel, Ramsgate (plate 78), built in 1840 by James Wilson, was the subject of a long letter in the *Baptist Magazine*, in which the minister set out his reasons for its greater elaboration though he says nothing directly about the style.[8] He seems to have wanted a tower at the centre of the elevation and, though he refers to one as if it were built, the chapel has only a gable with a strange parapet supporting a rather grotesque finial. The writer of the letter concludes with the plea that Baptists should in the erection of their chapels 'keep pace with the times'. The internal fittings, the pulpit and its surroundings, which survive though re-sited, match the style of the exterior and are a riot of semi-circular arches, nook shafts and arcading.

Baptists of the 1840s seemed more concerned with matters of internal arrangement than with external appearance. In the same edition of the *Baptist Magazine* is an article on high pulpits, which are condemned as conducive to a formal style of preaching as well as being a source of bronchitis and other ailments affecting the preachers; there is also a letter on the 'construction of places of worship' in which acoustics are the main point of concern.[9] In the following issue we find these topics pursued by Philip Sambell, an architect of Truro, and by J. Wilson of Clerkenwell.[10] In the volume for 1842, a Mr Trickett of Bristol Baptist College takes up the cudgels in a long article 'on Baptist chapels'.[11] His opinions on style seem to be rather ambivalent: 'too strict an adherence should not be maintained' he says 'to architecture of a Gothic kind' because he finds the ornament grotesque and unnecessary; the copying of Grecian architecture he similarly condemns because of its paucity of windows. Mr Trickett then immerses himself in the evidently more interesting topics of seating, heating, general internal layout and so forth.

A few years on we find the Secretaries of the Baptist Union concerning themselves with a proposed 'Manual of Chapel Building' and asking for guidance on model chapels. And we may well wonder what became of that. But perhaps the most telling remark in this Baptist source is in the 1850 review of Frederick Jobson's classic book on *Chapel and School Architecture*.[12] Jobson was a Wesleyan minister and the reviewer notes the closeness of the Wesleyans to the Established church and Jobson's evident preference for the Gothic style which he 'endeavours strenuously to promulgate, but for which'

7   *Ecclesiologist*, 1 (1842), pp. 4–5.
8   *Baptist Magazine*, 32 (1840), pp. 673–5.
9   *Ibid.*, pp. 568–9, 672, 673.
10 *Baptist Magazine*, 33 (1841), pp. 243, 355–6.
11 *Baptist Magazine*, 34 (1842), pp. 411–17.
12 *Baptist Magazine*, 42 (1850), p. 683.

says the reviewer 'we have not the slightest sympathy', adding 'we should greatly regret the prevalence of this taste in the Baptist denomination'. He goes further, to claim that, in his view, 'a Gothic edifice cannot be ... an outward and visible sign of that simplicity which ought to characterize religious services under the Christian dispensation'.

The view that Gothic architecture was inappropriate for Baptist chapels was one which continued for many years and was shared by the popular Baptist preacher, Charles Haddon Spurgeon, whose Metropolitan Tabernacle in London was built in 1859–61 in a grandiose Classical pedimented and porticoed style by W. W. Pocock. In his speech at the laying of the foundation stone[13] Spurgeon made clear his view on the style appropriate for Baptist worship – 'The standard of our faith is Greek; and this place is to be Grecian. I care not that many an idol temple has been built after the same fashion. Greek is the sacred tongue, and Greek is the Baptist's tongue; we may be beaten in our own version, sometimes; but in the Greek, never. Every Baptist place should be Grecian, never Gothic. We owe nothing to the Goths as religionists. We have a great part of our scriptures in the Grecian language, and this shall be a Grecian place of worship'. Of course the Tabernacle was more Roman than Greek, and more Renaissance than either, but by his own admission, Spurgeon saw buildings 'from a theological point of view, not from an architectural one' – a view not far removed in its conclusions from that of the Camdenians.

There were of course exceptions to the general rule, one being a small village chapel at Bourton in Berkshire (plate 79) built in 1851 which might even have met with the approval of the Cambridge Camden Society, had it not been built for the Baptists. It has a gabled front with stepped diagonal buttresses, a pointed-arched doorway with a relatively modest circular traceried window above, and a single bell in a bell-cote at the apex of the gable. The chapel was built by Henry Tucker of Bourton House who must have been a gentleman of taste and who employed as his architect W. F. Ordish. It was opened, rather significantly, by the Hon. and Rev. Baptist Wriothley Noel who had left the Established church in 1848 and joined the Baptists in the following year.

Congregationalists

Congregationalists[14] or Independents seem on the whole to have been slightly more ready than Baptists to experiment with architectural style and this may be accounted for by the increased connexionalism within the denomination which came about in the early nineteenth century. This brought with it a

13 Mrs C. H. Spurgeon et al. (eds), C. H. Spurgeon's Autobiography, 4 vols (London, 1899–1900), II, pp. 327–8.
14 See C. Binfield, So Down to Prayers: Studies in English Nonconformity 1780–1920 (London, 1977), pp. 145–61.

greater concern for the appearance of its chapels. The newly-established *Congregational Year Book*[15] in its second number for 1847, carried an important though anonymous article 'Remarks on Ecclesiastical Architecture as applied to Nonconformist Chapels'. The religious origins of both Grecian and Gothic architecture are dismissed as irrelevant, being associated 'with two potent systems of false religion': the first with the 'idolatries of Classical mythology', the second with 'the shrines, and high altars, the sacristies and Lady Chapels, of Popish superstition'. It is assumed that at the Puritan reformation both styles were cast aside in favour of what the writer calls 'the religion of barns'. But the author expresses little sympathy with that either, or for many of the chapels of his own time. Those which do meet with his approval are in the styles whose origins were earlier denounced, but no opportunity is lost to distance himself from their roots. 'We have our Protestant character to maintain in its integrity and in these times of fearful apostasy to the church of Rome, it would afflict many honest Christians in other denominations, as well as in our own, if they should see our taste leading us to questionable conformities.' And so, having satisfied his Protestant Nonconformist conscience, the author leaves the reader to suppose that the Gothic style, as exemplified by Highbury Chapel, Bristol, which is singled out for praise, is at least to be tolerated or even encouraged. It is interesting to note that the Congregational 'Highbury Chapel' was an early work of William Butterfield who is said later to have expressed his regret at having assisted in the erection of what he described as 'a schism shop'. The writer of the article was aware of, and clearly sympathetic to, some of the publications of the Cambridge Camden Society and he quotes extensively from the advice which the Society had published on the use of suitable building materials.

In the same year, 1847, *The Ecclesiologist*[16] chose to notice the New Independent Meeting-house at Manchester, in a lengthy article mostly given up to attacking a party which had begun to steal its architectural clothes. This was the Congregational chapel in Cavendish Street, designed by Edward Walters, then in process of erection. Unwilling to leave unqualified the praise for a Gothic chapel comparable 'with many a well-intentioned Church of the "Movement"' the commentator offers it as either a hopeful sign, or 'a piece of unreal pageantry, a proof of deadness of heart, and obtuseness of sense, a hollow and sickening thing, like the laughter of idiocy, or a drunken revel in a charnel house'; naturally the latter conclusion was assumed and doubtless the writer would have been gratified to know that this chapel, a major development in nonconformist architecture, ended its days as a theatre workshop!

15   *The Congregational Year Book* (1847), pp. 150–63.
16   *Ecclesiologist*, 7 (1847), pp. 171–4.

Of course the design, or at least the general style of chapels, was determined by chapel building committees or occasionally by individual benefactors, some of whom continued to prefer buildings in the older Classical idiom; but increasingly as the century advanced the Gothic style prevailed. In Luton, Bedfordshire, the first Independent place of worship was not built until 1865, when, with the help of the English Congregational Chapel Building Society, the leading nonconformist architect of the day, John Tarring sometimes described as 'the Gilbert Scott of the Dissenters'[17] was brought in to design something suitable for the town. The new chapel seated over 1,000 persons, many in side galleries above the aisles, and it had a large school-room in the basement. These were necessary features of any large nonconformist chapel, but the steeple – usually at one corner and seldom containing anything resembling a bell – became almost *de rigeur* for any chapel of consequence.

Gothic chapels did not please everyone, and Reginald Hine records in his *History of Hitchin* that the Independent minister there, after attending the opening of the Luton chapel, commented disapprovingly in his church book 'this is the first nonconformist place within 25 miles or so with a *spire* and called a *church*'.[18]

Later still, Congregationalists were to express their architectural awareness in an even more robust manner, as in Emmanuel Church, Cambridge.[19] This large town chapel, with a substantial tower facing Trumpington Street, was designed in 1874 by Fuller and Cubitt; in its avoidance of internal columns it follows the precepts set out by James Cubitt in his book *Church Design for Congregations*, published in 1870.

Unitarians

If Congregationalists still felt some residual distrust of a style associated at least with the church establishment from which they had long separated – and the dreaded ritualism and 'Popery' against which they continued to inveigh – the Unitarians seemed to have few qualms in matters of style. Although for the most part the legal successors of the English Presbyterians, they had so far departed from Trinitarian beliefs that as 'free-thinkers' innovation or novelty had become second nature. When a society meeting in a fine Corinthian-columned chapel of 1780 in Mosley Street, Manchester, decided to relocate they employed no less a man than Charles Barry – then engaged on the Houses of Parliament – to design their new chapel in Upper Brook Street. This was opened in 1839, the year in which the Cambridge Camden Society was formed, and it seems to presage the efforts of nonconformists in

17   *Dictionary of National Biography.*
18   R. L. Hine, *The History of Hitchin*, II, pp. 132-3.
19   C. Binfield, 'James Cubitt and Emmanuel Congregational Church', *Chapels Society Newsletter*, 1 (December, 1992), pp. 80-4.

subsequent decades to present an architecturally fashionable and socially acceptable public image.

Barry gave the Manchester Unitarians a preaching-house which might have been the nave of a larger building, but it was complete in itself, and with its ribbed and vaulted ceiling and only minimal galleries it represents a remarkable change from the more usual appearance of a chapel.

During the early nineteenth century old nonconformist congregations which had become Unitarian were being challenged for the possession of their buildings by Trinitarian dissenters. In the 1840s Parliament put an end to these unseemly wrangles and several of these Unitarian congregations took the opportunity to rebuild. One of these was in Leeds where the big Mill Hill chapel (1847–8) in the centre of the city, by Bowman and Crowther, is one which attracted the notice of *The Ecclesiologist*, which reported that Unitarians, '*horribile dictu*, are building a meeting-house in florid Middle-Pointed. We hear that they intend to establish in it a kind of choral service, with vestments for their ministers'.[20] Mill Hill Chapel is a long building of seven bays with a central transept and the pulpit and choir at one end. The broad symmetrical front to the street bears some resemblance in its parts, though not in its style, to the Baptist Chapel in Ramsgate – but internally this is quite different and designed for a much more formal service than the Baptists might have tolerated. Today, shorn of its pinnacles and subdivided internally, the chapel is but a shade of its former self; but in architectural terms it still bears witness to the freedom which Unitarians exercised to express the new status they enjoyed following the passing in 1844 of the Dissenters Chapels Act.

Bowman and Crowther had, about the same date, designed another chapel, at Gee Cross in Cheshire (plate 80), for an old established and now also Unitarian, congregation. There, on the site of the old meeting-house, within a large burial-ground, they constructed what to all appearances is a parish church, with its nave and aisles, chancel and west tower and spire. It looks like an act of defiance, but it was rather a positive assertion of their newly-acquired religious equality. The interior still retains traces of the Protestant tradition, notably in the seating which fills the nave without any central aisle to tempt ministers into processional excesses. But in the chancel the communion table, provocatively daring the unwary to describe it as an altar, is an elaborate gilded affair, and surely a sore temptation to the ritualism to which it seems the Leeds Unitarians were laying themselves open.

The most ambitious of the later Unitarian chapels, the gift of wealthy manufacturers, a grade I listed building now undergoing expensive repairs by the Historic Chapels Trust, is at Todmorden in Yorkshire. It was designed by John Gibson of Westminster, paid for by the Fielden brothers in memory of

[20]   *Ecclesiologist*, 9 (1849), p. 144.

their father, and completed in 1869. It stands high up on a steeply sloping site overlooking the town and has all, or almost all, the attributes which might reasonably be expected of a truly Gothic church, even to a ring of eight bells in the tower. The nave arcade has piers of polished marble; the chancel has a stone vault, and the 'east' window is filled with stained glass by Capronnier.

Catholic Apostolic Church

An exceptional development amongst nonconformist denominations was the rise of the Catholic Apostolic Church, whose origins can be traced to charismatic practices within the Scotch church in Regent Square during the ministry of Edward Irving, and to a remarkable interest in the study of prophecy in the 1820s and '30s. 'Irvingism', called 'a novel delusion' by *The Ecclesiologist*,[21] was nevertheless a strong force for a time and very attractive for its rapid development of ritualism when the practice within the Established Church was still strongly contested.

The main centre of activity was based at Albury in Surrey where Henry Drummond had convened a series of conferences for the study of scriptural prophecy and where in 1832 he established a separate congregation. Albury became the seat of twelve divinely-appointed latter-day apostles and Drummond built, seemingly at his own expense, what is now known as 'The Apostles' Chapel', together with an octagonal annexe or 'chapter house' suitable for the meetings of the Apostles. The chapel, begun about 1837, was designed by William Wilkins and completed after Wilkins' death in 1839 by W. McIntosh Brooks. It was opened in 1840, a date rather too early to have been influenced by Camdenian notions though it served a ceremonial which, at its height, required a very considerable number of participants and far out-classed anything of which the Leeds Unitarians might have been thought guilty.

The interior of the Apostles' Chapel is relatively Spartan when compared with such later churches as the Central Church in Gordon Square, London, of 1853 by J. R. Brandon, or the much later one in Maida Vale of 1891–2 by J. L. Pearson, but it must be remembered that the Apostles were constantly feeling their way, increasing their ceremonial and adding to their architectural requirements, to all of which the Gothic style seems to have proved most suited.

Although the Catholic Apostolic Church is hardly representative of the general run of English nonconformity one further chapel of theirs, in Catherine Street, Liverpool, must be cited for its comparatively early date. The eastern arm of this was built in 1840 and was given the full treatment of ambulatory, clerestory and flying-buttresses, all on a diminutive scale. The completed building, as depicted in a lithograph of 1851 (plate 81), was

21   *Ecclesiologist*, 15 (1854), pp. 83–8.

intended to have a central tower and spire, and a nave of four bays, but sadly the work was only finished, after much delay and in a less ambitious manner, in 1857. Unfortunately the original architect's name is unknown. The *Ecclesiologist* of December 1853 refers to the building in an article on Liverpool churches, but claims facetiously, that 'it would have been an awkward building to criticise; as the plan, we hear, was revealed to the minister by inspiration' – whatever that may mean.[22] It is, of course, built to a quite acceptably Gothic plan, one probably inspired by some Continental cathedral and much reduced in scale.

Methodists

The largest of the nonconformist denominations in terms both of number of members and of chapels is the Methodist. Throughout the nineteenth century they were divided into several factions, the result of internal dissent or of enthusiastic revivals. The Wesleyans remained the largest of these and the one closest to the Established church from which they sprang. It is natural that the Wesleyans should have been inclined to express this position architecturally and to have been more inclined than some of their fellows to do so in a fashionable style.

The Wesleyan chapel in Newbury, Berkshire, built in 1838, is a representative example of its day; the gabled front with its lancet windows is divided, in a way which continued for a long time, by two tall octagonal buttresses, and possibly a bit out of period. Inside, it is a typical galleried chapel, but with one feature carried over from the eighteenth-century church; it had, and still retains, a central pulpit with a communion area in a recess behind. Such was the arrangement used in Wesley's Chapel, City Road, London, and Newbury is one of the least altered examples of this once popular layout.

The Rev. Frederick Jobson whose book *Chapel and School Architecture* – or rather his support for the Gothic style – was so swiftly dismissed by the Baptist reviewer, met with a better reception amongst his co-religionists. One of the chapels he praises is Poplar Chapel, London, built in 1848. It is, says Jobson, 'among the most ornamental of Methodist chapels'. Unfortunately its subsequent history of 'improvement' deprived it of any merit which it originally possessed. The denominations have never given much sign of respect for their own architecture, and the resulting alterations at Poplar were predictable, and typical. First the chapel was shorn of its pinnacles and parapet; then, in the twentieth century it was 'modernized' to look like a 1930s cinema from which it is only distinguished by having a large cross erected on the front gable. Poplar Chapel may not have been as remarkable as

---

[22]   *Ecclesiologist*, 14 (1853), p. 409. A longer and more favourable description had been published earlier in volume 9 (1849), p. 143.

Jobson supposed and, but for its historical connection with the popular preacher 'Lax of Poplar', its subsequent demolition is no great matter for regret. Jobson also published suggestions for the design of village chapels, one of which was built at Fordham, Cambridgeshire; these were in a very simple Gothic style, suited to the needs of cheapness and architectural propriety.

A much more ornamental and deserving Wesleyan chapel was built at Summerseat in Lancashire between 1844 and 1847, of which the demolition in the 1970s was much more tragic. This was no cheap effort by a building committee but a chapel erected by a wealthy manufacturer who knew what he wanted and was prepared to pay for it. John Robinson Kay employed the Methodist architect, James Simpson, to design a Gothic chapel suitable for Wesleyan worship using the *Book of Common Prayer* where the Methodist squire could be as much at home as any Anglican squire in a rural parish. Here, though it had a wide aisleless preaching nave, there was a substantial chancel and transepts; and later a small octagonal mausoleum was added as a burial place for the founder. This was the epitome of a squire's, or mill-owner's chapel, but it can not be claimed to be really representative of the denomination as a whole. On the contrary Methodists continued, as did Baptists, to build large Classical chapels throughout the nineteenth century; many of these were also designed by James Simpson who was prepared, and sufficiently stylistically versatile, to give clients what they asked for. All the Methodist groups seem to have felt more secure in chapels of that kind, possibly from reasons of cost but also because it had become almost a hallmark for them. One of many examples of the kind is the Wesleyan chapel at Snaith in Yorkshire, a building of 1862 by Edward Taylor of York, but a list of them could be extended almost indefinitely.

Society of Friends

And where should one look for that nonconformist architectural conscience which would stand firmly against any mediaeval style unrelated to their own history than to the Society of Friends; the Quakers? It used to be held that Quakers were unaffected by the Gothic revival. But did they not produce Thomas Rickman, though he parted from them in time? And Alfred Waterhouse, too, had a Quaker ancestry. Although these may not have had much influence on the inherent simplicity which Quakers required of their buildings, nevertheless Waterhouse did design one meeting-house, at Cartmel in the Lake District, in which stepped buttresses and a gabled porch indicate the lengths to which he felt able to go. Only a few other meeting-houses exist with anything approaching Gothic details. The one most likely to have raised the Camdenians' ire is at Scholes near Cleckheaton, Yorkshire (plate 82) which has the appearance of a typical small village chapel, good enough for a chapel-of-ease, just perhaps wanting a bell-cote. It was built in 1883 for a meeting supported by the Crossland family, perhaps one explanation for the choice of style, and designed by William Henry Thorpe of Leeds.

Fontlets

There remains to be considered one item of church furnishings in which the Cambridge Camden Society may possibly have had some influence on nonconformist practice. With the exception of Baptists and Quakers infant baptism continued to be observed; for this, in the eighteenth century, a small bowl or sometimes a substantial silver vessel, sufficed. From about 1840, however, miniature versions of Gothic fonts appear, the date coinciding with the growth of the Cambridge Camden Society. In 1841 *The Ecclesiologist*[23] was at pains to insist on the uncanonical nature of the artificial stone fonts manufactured by Austin and Seeley, a contention firmly denied by the makers, and in 1844[24] the question of portable fonts came under adverse criticism, especially when of 'stone and imitating church fonts'. However, a model of such a 'fontlet' exists at Hawkshead in the Lake District for which an attribution to the Society seems to be made.

The 'pue-dish' spelt P U E for increased ugliness, was anathema to ecclesiologists; but a baptismal or Christening basin of pewter or silver was considered a quite adequate vessel for the purpose by most nonconformist paedobaptist congregations; however, it had no parallel in the mediaeval church and so it could not be countenanced by ecclesiologists. Big mediaeval stone fonts were all that could properly be tolerated, though they were intended for the proper dipping of infants as the Prayer Book prescribes, a practice which even John Wesley, in his un-reformed days in America, discovered to his cost that his flock would no longer tolerate.

Not all nonconformist churches needed or could afford full-blown fonts, particularly in the early period of the Gothic Revival, and it seems that some compromise between the demands of Gothic architecture and the practicalities of the situation was being looked for just about the time when the Cambridge Society was in its formative years.

In a small Methodist chapel in Hawkshead in the Lake District, part of a house converted in 1862 as 'Union Chapel', is a plaster model, 8¼ ins high, with an inset china bowl, of the well-known font in Winchester Cathedral (plate 83). Around two sides of the base is an incomplete black-letter inscription 'Font in the / Cathedral Church of Winch'. It breaks off in the middle of the word 'Winchester' and the other sides of the base are blank. With it is a paper claiming that it was made 'for the "Cambridge Cambrian Archaeological Society" in the year 1840 and was later in the possession of Professor F. W. Rudler FGS JSO (1903) by whose brother it was presented to

---

[23] *Ecclesiologist*, 1 (1842), pp. 127–8.
[24] *Ecclesiologist*, 3 (1844), p. 127.

this chapel together with a copy of the order of service and other appointments in the year 1925' The attribution seems most likely to be a garbled reference to the Cambridge Camden Society. If so, was this then intended as a possible substitute for the despised pue-dish, and how does it square with the denunciation of artificial stone fonts which appeared in the pages of *The Ecclesiologist* in 1842, or of so-called 'portable fonts' imitating Gothic fonts in the issue for May 1844? Be that as it may, it was surely intended as a model for reproduction, as several pottery versions of this attest.

One fontlet most nearly resembling the Hawkshead model, made by Copeland, is in Park Lane Chapel, Ashton-in-Makerfield, Lancashire (plate 84). It is a little damaged at the base but the lettering around it is identical in style and breaks off in the same manner. The two fontlets vary slightly in some minor details, the Park Lane version is also somewhat smaller as might occur in the process of mould-making and casting. But in general and especially in the lettering these two vessels must be closely related.

Five further examples of the Winchester type, presumably of later date, are known to the writer. One in a chapel at South Milford, Yorkshire, by Shaw and Sons of Congleton (plate 85), has a separate domed cover. Another at Newport, Shropshire, maker unnamed, has a pyramidal cover.

Two other mediaeval fonts also served as models: that at the church of St Mary Magdalene, Oxford, and one in St Mary, Nottingham. The earliest dated copy of the Oxford font is in King Edward Street Chapel, Macclesfield (plate 86). This is inscribed below its octagonal base 'Font in Saint Mary Magdalene Church Oxford 1842 Style Decorated Circa 1350, Scale ⅛'. It also has a separate cover from which the finial is missing. Another Oxford style fontlet was purchased for the Wesleyans in Otley in 1841 by a Mrs Maude from John Yates of Bond Street, Leeds for 16s. 6d.[25] Nine others of this type are known, three by Minton and one by J. Flack.

The five known specimens of the Nottingham fontlet (plate 87), and many more which probably exist, are of the late nineteenth century and most have separate covers with finials. None is signed. Several other fontlets in a mediaeval style are known but it is not yet clear whether these were based on actual examples.

If, as it appears, the origin of these fontlets may lie with the Cambridge Camden Society then the influence of the Society undoubtedly reached out to those parts which it might hardly have been expected to touch. In the wider field of architecture, too, nonconformists were prepared to be swayed by prevailing fashions, but neither the ecclesiologists nor the Free Churches were under any delusion that external appearances told the whole story. Nonconformists were well aware of the dangers of being, what Ruskin called, 'blown into a change of religion by the whine of an organ pipe; stitched into a

[25] W. F. Seals, *Methodism in the Otley Circuit, 1744–1974* (1974), p. 26.

new creed by gold treads on priests' petticoats; [or] jangled into a change of conscience by the chimes of a belfry'.[26] but at times they came close to being singed by the fire whose flames had been so successfully fanned by the Camdenians of Cambridge.

[26]   J. Ruskin, *The Stones of Venice*, 3 vols (Orpington, 1898), I, Appendix 12.

'A Mass all Sung to Ancient Music': the Society's Influence on Church Music

DONALD WEBSTER

It was the opinion of A. W. N. Pugin that in our churches 'the altar and the arch may belong to the Age of Faith, but the singing drags us down to the level of the concert-room of the nineteenth century.'[1] It is hardly surprising then that early in its existence the Society should have devoted serious attention to the sung service, both in its congregational and choir-led formats. By 1847 John Mason Neale declared, 'Ecclesiology is the Science of Christian Aesthetics'[2] embracing all the arts, working in complementary fashion. This implied the inclusion of music in the Society's range of interests, and as early as 1843 it was making authoritative statements on the art.[3] 'The glorious architecture of the fourteenth century' was the preferred style for churches, but finding appropriate contemporaneous musical idioms for adoption was problematic. Plainchant was the obvious choice, but arguably it was too austere, and since it was sung chiefly in unison it offered little to those who were interested in choral singing. To satisfy the latter, a suitable compromise between the emotional restraint of plainchant and the alleged worldliness of modern idioms (i.e. those of the period since c.1750) was to be found in sixteenth-century polyphony, as exemplified by compositions of Thomas Tallis (1505–85), William Byrd (1543–1623) and their followers. The Society believed that this group of composers had produced work of outstanding musical quality, whilst sharing a spirituality with the plainsong tradition. Additionally, it was sufficiently distant in time to be thought of as 'archaic'. Thus the initial aims of the Society were as follows: the use of Plainsong rather than modern Anglican chants for the psalms; ancient, i.e. Pre-Reformation hymns sung to their associated plainsong tunes; and the use of sixteenth-century polyphony for such choral singing as could be attempted. In addition, it wished to introduce intoning of the prayers; strong congregational participation in the services; and a robed choir placed in the chancel whose

[1]   A. W. N. Pugin, *An Earnest Appeal for the Revival of the Ancient Plain Song* (London, 1850), p. 8.
[2]   E. J. Boyce, *A Memorial of the Cambridge Camden Society* (London and Cambridge, 1888).
[3]   *Ecclesiologist*, 3 (1844), pp. 1–5, 83–4.

primary aim was to lead the worshippers rather than appear as performers in their own right. Although the Society was at pains to distance itself from accusations that it was opposed to elaborate choir music, its desire for this to be drawn exclusively from sixteenth-century polyphony meant that only a handful of parish and cathedral choirs could attempt it. However, in the very year of the Society's formation a perfect liturgical and musical illustration of their principles was provided when the Rev. Frederick Oakeley introduced a choral service at Margaret Chapel, Margaret Street, London, and this proved to be a potent model for members to follow. Those who were at the forefront of these reforming initiatives included men like J. M. Neale (1818–66) and Benjamin Webb (1819–85) who were Cambridge men, and possessed of broad culture, sound learning and a deep spiritual outlook. They believed that the Church of England's Catholic inheritance – including its musical traditions – had been dissipated, notably in the century before 1840. This was partly by neglect and partly by the evangelical revival. Twentieth Century writers have tended to agree with them.[4]

There is ample evidence that music in the late-Gregorian church left much to be desired. In terms of that provided in Cathedrals the period was described as 'another very lean one ... Only three names are to be found here that rise even to the level of mediocrity, Jonathan Battishill (1738–1801) Thomas Attwood (1765–1838) and Samuel Wesley (1766–1837)'.[5] The canticles were sung to a small group of settings that were repeated frequently, and anthems were chosen, often with a cynical disregard of their seasonal appropriateness. Holy Communion was celebrated infrequently and with minimal choral input.

The lack of provision for music and clerical parsimony is told with much sadness by John Alcock (1715–1806) who was appointed Organist at Lichfield Cathedral in 1750.[6] He complained that the choir men would not attend practices, and that boys had to be retained after their voices had broken, since they at least knew the limited repertory. In the Preface to a collection of his anthems (1771) he wrote, 'All the time I was organist, which was upwards of ten years, there was not a book in the organ loft fit for use, but what I bought or wrote myself (for which I was never paid one half penny). It is not greatly to be wondered at that there are now no more subscribers to these anthems, considering how much the cathedral service is at present disregarded. I have received letters from several organists which mention that their choir music was never at so low an ebb'.[7]

[4]   These are too numerous to mention, but they include the writings of C. Henry Phillips, Kenneth Long, Erik Routley, and Ernest Walker. Note especially: P. M. Young, *A History of British Music* (London, 1967), pp. 456–63.
[5]   E. H. Fellowes, *English Cathedral Music* (London, 1941), p. 192.
[6]   P. A. Scholes, *Oxford Companion to Music* (London, 1942), p. 144.
[7]   *Ibid.*

In parish churches, the restoration of organs following this long period of neglect led to greater vocal discipline, especially where ornate hymn tunes in triple time were concerned.[8] Equally popular were anthems that used glee idioms, and fuguing psalm tunes.[9] Where there were choirs, these were situated in west galleries, alongside a motley collection of instrumentalists, when there was no organ. The musicians' ribald antics are described with relish by Thomas Hardy in *Under the Greenwood Tree*. In some churches charity children, whose singing was noteworthy more for its volume than its refinement, led the metrical psalms.[10]

From the foregoing there emerges a picture of an irreverence, neglect and apathy towards the state of music at places of worship at the end of the Georgian period. Such a situation existed in many churches, despite some notable attempts to introduce improvements, if only to compete with the Methodists. The responsibility for this unacceptable state of affairs was seen by some members of the Society as resting to a large extent on the poor standards condoned by the universities; in the middle decades of the nineteenth century eighty per cent of Anglican clergy were graduates of Oxford or Cambridge, and regular chapel attendance was compulsory for all undergraduates. Despite unmatched resources, their performance of religious music was deemed to have been of very poor quality.[11] Of the seventeen Cambridge colleges, choral services were held only at King's, St John's and Trinity. The two latter had shared an organist since 1799 and a boys' choir since 1819. Though it was averred that none of the boys could sing at sight, no one seemed to care.[12] However, the acoustics at King's were so flattering to the singing that even such incompetence as this attracted appreciative congregations who departed after the anthem.

Thomas Attwood Walmisley was only nineteen years old when he took up his organist appointments at Cambridge in 1833. In addition to directing the music at Trinity and St John's he had to play for services at King's and the University Church of Great St Mary, where the organists were elderly and infirm. From the start Walmisley attempted several praiseworthy and necessary reforms, notably in the enlargement of the choral repertory, though he never became a member of the Society. However, of the 302 anthems listed in his *Anthem Book*, only four compositions, those by Orlando

---

[8]   C. Burney, *History of Music* (London, 1789), p. 57.

[9]   Scholes, *op. cit.*, p. 33; see also *Lyngham* in *Hymns and Psalms*, no. 120.

[10] Scholes, *op. cit.*, p. 34.

[11] B. Rainbow, *The Choral Revival in the Anglican Church* (London, 1979), p. 206.

[12] Matthew Camidge, Organist of York Minster (1799–1842) is commonly credited with the distinction of being the first cathedral organist to attempt to teach his choristers to read music. See J. Webster. unpublished M.A. Thesis: *The Camidges – Paternalism or Nepotism?*, University of Leeds, 1991.

Gibbons, ante-date the Great Rebellion.[13] Moreover, it is unlikely that the choirs sang from pointed psalters during Walmisley's tenure, and disagreements over the allocation of notes to words must have been frequent. His compositions such as the Evening Service in D Minor 1854 shine like beacons in a sea of appalling mediocrity during the early years of Queen Victoria's reign.[14]

Webb and Neale were highly critical of the ordering of church services, particularly in their University. They believed that the clergy were those who could best implement the musical reforms the Society desired. Consequently it was to them rather than to the musicians that their work was directed. In particular, the CCS wished to lay stress on the Anglican church's apostolic descent and the sacraments, rather than on preaching. They were not interested in mere antiquarian research, as their critics averred, nor did they want elaborate contemporary choral music, tinged with secular influences, from which the congregation was excluded. In the absence of appropriate pre-Reformation models for the musical content of parochial services, the Society was forced into making the best of what they had. Their ideal was for a style of music that was restrained, archaic and holy. In this context Walmisley was criticised for his collection of 177 Anglican chants with high reciting notes, thus precluding congregational participation.[15] It was pointed out that if psalm singing were an exclusively choral activity, there would have been a Prayer Book rubric to that effect.

Writing many years later, W. E. Dickson praised the influence of the Society at the University for awakening students to the relation between Theology and the Ecclesiastical Arts, but he lamented their leaning towards severe and colourless music. 'Mortification of the flesh was applied to music of the Church, and was held to exclude the elements of Grace and Beauty from compositions dedicated to Religion as ministering only to sensuous pleasure'.[16] Such criticism of the CCS came from increasingly influential quarters as the century progressed. However, Dickson welcomed an association of Art and Religion to which, he believed, England had been a stranger for so long.

In the first number of *The Ecclesiologist* a comprehensive attitude was shown to the Arts. Much of the writing in subsequent issues had a combativeness that was designed to counter complacent attitudes. This inevitably created internal controversy, which tended to centre around Neale. His impulsive dogmatism was greatly at variance with Webb's calmer judgement. Neale's musical opinions were also highly suspect. He had the

---

[13] D. Adelmann, *The Contribution of Cambridge Ecclesiologists to the Revival of Anglican Choral Worship 1839–62* (Aldershot, 1997), p. 52.

[14] Fellowes, *op. cit.*, p. 212.

[15] *Ecclesiologist*, 5 (1846), p. 172.

[16] W. E. Dickson, *Fifty Years of Church Music* (Ely, 1894), p. 42.

effrontery to deliver a paper on church music in 1840, yet a year later he enthused over the Jackson *Te Deum*, 'which I have been studying diligently'.[17] This is a notorious piece, which Percy Scholes described somewhat charitably as, 'a composition that rises to the height of a curious sublimity of commonplace'.[18] It certainly accorded ill with other ecclesiological tastes. In contrast, Webb, with disarming modesty, had joined a singing class in Cambridge, so that he could obtain enough skill to teach others in his future parishes. His role in the Society's musical deliberations has not received sufficient esteem, and he never showed a predilection for ultra conservatism or antiquarianism of which his associates were accused so frequently.[19] Yet as early as 1841, despite Webb's well-known moderation, the Evangelical publication, *The Record*, attacked the Society and accused him of being a Roman Catholic in disguise.[20]

In an enthusiastic letter to Neale dated 31 December 1847 Webb wrote, 'At Margaret Chapel they have now got up a complete musical Mass ... all sung to ancient music ... nothing so solemn since the Reformation.' By this time Oakeley had been hounded out of his incumbency there and had joined the Church of Rome. However, his influence remained during the time of his successor, the Rev. Upton Richards. Ever since then, the pattern of its worship, and that of its replacement, Butterfield's All Saints', Margaret Street, has upheld ecclesiological principles faithfully. At both St Paul, Knightsbridge and at St Barnabas church, Pimlico, which he built in 1850, the high church ministry of the Rev. W. J. E Bennett proved similarly controversial and for similar reasons.

Timely support for the ecclesiologists' attempts to foster congregational singing had come from the National Society for Promoting Education of the Poor, an organisation that enjoyed support from the Church of England. This Society sponsored evening classes in sight singing for schoolmasters. John Hullah, who became a member of the CCS in 1843, did similar teaching at Exeter Hall, but on a much grander scale, attracting widespread support from the general public. This was part of a national campaign to encourage singing as a means of improving the nation's health. It began on 1 February 1841, and a year later an assembly of 1,500 people was able to give a public demonstration, thus showing the effectiveness of Hullah's methods.[21]

The ecclesiologists also had a desire for a restoration of medieval piety in church services. This could be attributed in part to the Romantic revival

[17] M. S. Lawson, *Letters of John Mason Neale, D.D.* (London, 1910), p. 24.
[18] Scholes *op. cit.*, p. 479. Other historians have been more forthright in their condemnation.
[19] Adelmann, *op. cit.*, p. 18.
[20] B. Webb's *Diary* 18 December, 1841, unpublished manuscript: Oxford, Bodleian Library, MS. Eng. Misc. e. 406.
[21] Adelmann, *op. cit.*, p. 8.

and an associated wish to return to the values of the past that manifested itself in many different ways. For instance both Webb and Neale were members of the Musical Antiquarian Society (1840–7). Out of this, the Motett Society evolved in 1841.[22] Its aims were not merely to publish but to perform Latin motets and English compositions by Gibbons, Blow and Purcell. E. F. Rimbault edited the music, and where necessary the words were translated by William Dyce.

The Motett Society and the reverent ordering of services in the chapel of St Mark Chelsea, an Anglican Teacher Training College, which had been opened in 1841, exercised an additional profound influence on the Society's musical thinking. This was due to the appointment, in 1842, of the Rev. Thomas Helmore as Vice Principal and Precentor at the College.[23] His duties involved the training of the students to sing the daily services. Their sight singing was in the expert hands of John Hullah and Edward May. Helmore was closely associated with the Motett Society and his four-part, all-male chapel choir performed several of its publications. Trebles were recruited from the College's Model School.[24] It was hoped that when they graduated, students would take back to their own parishes something of the experience they had enjoyed at Chelsea, including a love of, and skill in the performance of, plainsong. Helmore's work at the College of St Mark, Chelsea, achieved widespread recognition, and in 1846 he was appointed Master of the Children of the Chapel Royal, St James. He was the first clergyman since the Reformation to hold the post. In 1850 he was invited to join the Ecclesiological Society's Committee, having been previously described as 'the most accomplished church musician of our time'.[25] He was also appointed secretary of the Committee of Music. From that time until 1856, musical matters were mentioned frequently in *The Ecclesiologist* as a result of his initiatives. However, for all his undoubted sincerity and skill in a narrow field, he was a musician of limited attainments. It may be said that the Society had to be contented with second best because it had failed to attract the leading professional musicians, such as Wesley, Goss, Ouseley and Smart, who were

22   It will be noted that the musical reforms favoured by the ecclesiologists were drawn almost exclusively from pre-Reformation and sixteenth-century music, largely of Catholic provenance, thus laying themselves open to the charge made by their opponents of being crypto-Roman Catholics.

23   D. Coleridge, *Second Letter on the National Society's Training College* (London, 1844), p. 24.

24   Some students had unbroken voices when they came to College, see Rainbow *op. cit.*, p. 55.

25   Rainbow, *op. cit.*, p. 51. Arthur Sullivan became one of Helmore's Chapel Royal Choristers in 1854. In his biography of Sullivan (Oxford, 1984) Arthur Jacobs gives a delightful yet scholarly account of Helmore and his work, and of Sullivan's indebtedness. P. M. Young, *op. cit.*, describes Helmore as a relative nonentity.

hostile to plainchant,[26] and the ritualism – a word which was gradually entering liturgical discussions at this time – with which the Society was associated to an increasing extent in the public mind. Helmore argued that there were two kinds of church music, choral and congregational, and that the latter was most in need of attention. It implied singing in unison. Gregorian chant and hymn melodies were most suited to this in that they provided a severity and a penitential tone that was especially important in Christian worship. He wished to point out that because the Puritans had introduced metrical psalms there had grown up a prejudice among high churchmen against all kinds of hymns.[27] He appealed for the use of the Latin hymns of St Ambrose and St Gregory. The idea of their being translated into English had been mooted by the Rev. John Jebb as early as 1843.[28]

The publication of Part 1 of the *Hymnal Noted* in 1850 represented 'the first fruits of the Society's increased musical labours'.[29] It was the outcome of Neale and Helmore's initiatives and drew heavily on the Sarum Rite – an order of service used in the pre-Reformation diocese of Salisbury – as an appropriate source of words and music.[30] The second part of the *Hymnal Noted* followed in 1854 and, according to Adelmann, 'remains among the ecclesiologists' most significant and enduring gifts to the English-speaking Church'.[31] However, its publication came at an unfortunate point in the on-going conflict between the High- and Low-Church Anglicans. Cardinal Wiseman's announcement in 1850 concerning the restoration of the Roman Catholic hierarchy in Britain aroused the Anglican Bishop of London's denunciations of the Ecclesiological Society.[32] There was much rioting and a general refusal to accept the hymnal's pre-Reformation words and music, because it was suspected that the Society's members had Roman Catholic sympathies. Helmore argued that Plainsong was used in both the pre- and post-Reformation Anglican Church. 'That which is in accordance with the genius of our common humanity, consonant with our perceptions of the sublime and the beautiful ought to please ... in every age alike, unless some unhappy perversion of taste contravene'.[33] However, the book was too

[26] P. A. Scholes, *Mirror of Music*, vol. 2 (London, 1947), pp. 553–5.
[27] *Ecclesiologist*, 8 (1849), p. 208.
[28] J. Jebb, *Choral Service of the United Church of England and Ireland* (London, 1843), pp. 396–7. This shows an erudite broadmindedness on Jebb's part, since it was written only a year after S. S. Wesley took up his appointment as organist of Leeds Parish Church, the ordering of whose services, on Jebb's recommendation, was greatly at odds with that at Margaret Chapel, which represented the ideal so far as ecclesiologists were concerned.
[29] Adelmann, *op. cit.*, p. 65
[30] *Ibid.*, p. 66.
[31] *Ibid.*, p. 68.
[32] O. Chadwick, *The Victorian Church* (London, 1981), pp. 291–4.
[33] *Ecclesiologist*, 11 (1850), pp. 346–7.

limited and doctrinaire to be widely adopted, and only three London churches, St Alban, Holborn; All Saints, Lambeth; and St Columba, Haggerston, are known to have used it exclusively between 1866 and 1894.[34] Helmore's use of archaic notation, including the four lined stave and neumes – the traditional plainsong notation – made its deciphering difficult for the average singer and organist. Long melismas on certain syllables caused further problems. Whilst the book as a whole made limited impact, and perhaps Adelmann has overestimated its importance, it nevertheless remained influential in that almost every subsequent hymnal drew upon some of its contents.[35]

Perhaps as a response to fiercely Protestant critics, and as a demonstration of his own wide musical tastes, Helmore, in 1854, suggested to Neale that they collaborate in producing a supplement to the *Hymnal Noted* containing 'modern' i.e. non-plainsong tunes, and recently written verse.[36] However, nothing came of this proposal.

A further example of Helmore's lack of dogmatism was his long association with the gifted church music composer, the Rev. Sir F. A. G. Ouseley, Bart., Mus.D. (1825–89) who later became Professor of Music at Oxford University. Ouseley showed an active antipathy to Gregorian chanting of the psalms and was a wholehearted supporter of Jebb's view that the choral service was something to be witnessed silently, rather than an occasion for congregational participation. Helmore, for his part, regarded plainchant as the traditional song of the Church, hallowed by centuries and regrettably neglected in recent years. Despite their opposing views of this crucial topic, Helmore secured the performance, by the Motett Society, of five of Ouseley's anthems, including *How goodly are Thy tents*.[37]

The Society's aims also received powerful support from Dr Robert Druitt, a Mayfair physician and an amateur church musician who presented a *Popular Tract on Church Music* in 1845, which received favourable notice in *The Ecclesiologist*.[38] He followed this by forming the Society for the Promotion of Church Music the following year. Until 1851 he published and edited its journal, *The Parish Choir*, wherein one reads the most remarkable anticipation of the *Principles and Recommendations of the School of English Church Music* that were compiled by its founder and director, Sir Sydney Nicholson, nearly a century later. Druitt stressed the importance of clergy and musicians receiving proper education in church music and the reverent

[34] N. Temperley, *Music of the English Parish Church*, vol. 1 (Cambridge, 1979), p. 264.
[35] Notably the *English Hymnal* (London, 1906).
[36] Yet in his *Manual of Plainsong* he describes modern hymn tunes as 'nauseous'.
[37] This was a particular favourite of Helmore's and much of its musical language accords with sixteenth century convention.
[38] *Ecclesiologist*, 4 (1845), p. 182.

ordering of services.[39] Supplements of suitable parochial music for choir and congregation were issued with *The Parish Choir*, showing that Druitt had no desire to ban *choral* music from services. However, he condemned the organ, 'which had contributed as much as anything to the decay of congregational singing'.[40] He deplored the current state of church music and made sweeping condemnations of Tate and Brady's metrical psalms of 1696, which were still widely used. He wanted music that wore well and was free from secular influences, and proposed that every parish church should have a parochial association for the promotion of church music. Ideally Gregorian chants were to be preferred, but Anglican ones had to be sung until congregations become used to the whole concept of chanting.[41] This view reflected probably an enforced moderation, following the large number of secessions to Rome after Newman's decision in 1845. Arising from Druitt's membership of the Motett Society, he joined the ecclesiologists in 1853.[42] Early in 1846, John Hullah, who had been a member of the Society since 1843, delivered a lecture in Leeds at the behest of the vicar, the Rev. Dr W. F. Hook, whose devotion to the fully-choral cathedral-type service was well known.[43] Perhaps the setting gave colour to Hullah's remarks. He felt that the zealousness of some members for plainsong in unison led them to exclude other types of music from worship. Such a view he firmly rejected, maintaining that harmony was an inherently Christian science. Nevertheless, he shared the widely believed view that the art of composing truly appropriate church music was lost at the time of the Great Rebellion and never wholly regained. This was also the view of William Crotch (1775–1847), one of Ouseley's predecessors at Oxford, and it was an issue taken up by *The Parish Choir*.

It is easy to see how F. R. Wegg Prosser's paper at the Society's eleventh anniversary meeting on 16 May 1850, which demanded the exclusion of modern Protestant anthems from contemporary worship, would have alienated the leading church composers from everything the ecclesiologists stood for. Moreover, his blanket condemnation of their anthems – 'they are not the highest, nor the best, nor the most edifying, nor the most devotional kind of church music'[44] – did not suggest that his opinions justified so influential a platform. A similar dogmatism lies behind *The Ecclesiologist*'s four classes of anthems:

1. Those that predated the mid-seventeenth century, and a few full anthems of later date;
2. English verse anthems from the previous two hundred years;

39   Rainbow, *op. cit.*, p. 99.
40   R. Druitt, *A Popular Tract on Church Music* (London, 1845), pp. 52–4.
41   *Ibid.*, p. 46.
42   Adelmann, *op. cit.*, p. 145.
43   D. F. Webster, *Parish Past and Present* (Leeds, 1988), p. 33.
44   *Ecclesiologist*, 11 (1850), pp. 28–31.

3. Extracts from the oratorios;

4. Adaptations from the foreign church music of Haydn, Mozart and others.

The writer believed that the first class constituted a valuable stock for daily use, and that the second contained a handful of few worthy pieces. However, he thought that few oratorio excerpts were appropriate for liturgical use, and rarely did the cathedral choirs have adequate personnel for their performance. Suitably solemn pieces of Viennese church music should be performed only as voluntaries, since their design was 'thoroughly instrumental'.[45]

Curiously enough, S. S. Wesley shared *The Ecclesiologist*'s dislike of solos in church, arguing that they made for exhibitionism rather than true devotion.[46] Yet few composers for the English Church wrote so many solo passages in their anthems!

Can it be said that the ecclesiologists were entirely fair in upholding the repertory of the Motett Society as the only suitable choir music for use in church, knowing that the necessary expertise would be available at very few churches? They pointed out that at St Barnabas, Pimlico, the scene of riots in the 1850s against high church practices, there was a first-class choir *and* congregational singing, indicating that the two *could* co-exist.[47] But to imply that such favourable conditions could work everywhere was wholly unrealistic. Moreover, it also implied that choir-led congregational singing remained their ideal.

All this shows an uncertainty in outlook and an inconsistency, as does their statement that on the one hand it was reasonable for choral services to be more elaborate in cathedrals than in parish churches,[48] and on the other hand their maintaining that the Prayer Book rubrics remained the same for cathedrals as for parish churches.[49]

The Ecclesiological Society welcomed newly-composed work by its supporters, the Rev. S. S. Greatheed and H. J. Gauntlett among others, because it was deemed to be consonant with the ideal of earlier centuries. Sadly, virtually none of it has survived to our own day, save for a handful of the latter's hymn tunes. However, the works of S. S. Wesley, John Goss and Gore Ouseley, which never enjoyed comparable esteem by most ecclesiologists, still occupy a respected place in the late twentieth century. This undoubtedly stemmed from the major composers' dislike of plainsong. Wesley, who revelled in controversy wrote, 'Some would reject all music but unisonous chants of a period of absolute barbarism – which they term

---

[45]   *Ecclesiologist*, 14 (1853), pp. 340–1.

[46]   S. S. Wesley, *A Few Words on Cathedral Music* (London, 1849; reprinted Hinrichsen, 1961), p. 37.

[47]   *Ecclesiologist*, 14 (1853), pp. 129–31.

[48]   *Ecclesiologist*, 17 (1856), p. 13.

[49]   T. Helmore in J. Purchas' *Directorium Anglicanum* (London, 1858), p. 180.

"Gregorian". These men would look a Michael Angelo [*sic*] in the face and say that Stonehenge was the perfection of architecture'.[50] His compositions were singled out for special condemnation by the Society. 'If there were such a thing as Dis.Doc. (Doctor of Dissonance) Wesley should be the first recipient'. He was further accused of a 'want of intellectual cultivation'.[51] Yet his six-part *a capella* anthem *Cast me not away from Thy presence* and the accompanied full anthem, *Thou wilt keep him* must be numbered among the church music masterpieces of any period. Neither the sentiments of Wesley's published attitudes nor their mode of utterance justifies such a charge. For instance 'It courts no external favour of loud applause – has no strongly marked rhythm – nothing to quicken pulsation and excite spirits. It bends the mind to devotion, removes all impressions of subluminary things and brings home to a man an overwhelming sense of his own insignificance and the majesty of the eternal'.[52] In the face of all his composing ideals, criticisms of Wesley must reflect severely on the aesthetic perceptions of those who made them.

Wesley's zeal at Leeds Parish Church complemented Hook's desire 'for a good service even if I have to go to prison for it'.[53] Hook's determination was shown by his willingness to forego the services of another curate and use the money thus saved in the creation of that great tradition which the church has enjoyed ever since.[54] Hook relied heavily on the advice of John Jebb (1805–86) a leading authority on the choral service of the Anglican church, who argued forcefully for a cathedral-type service with minimal congregational participation.[55] Plainchant he looked upon as the product of an age of musical infancy. He contended that Anglican chants preserved the gravity of an ancient style and were better able to give varied expression to the psalms. In addition, he believed that uniformity in pointing was neither necessary nor desirable. Jebb was an Anglo-Irish clergyman who was Prebendary of Limerick Cathedral from 1832 to 1843. He was regarded as a leading authority on the choral service of the Anglican church. 'Because of his own background as a Cathedral dignitary and his consequent predilection for the cathedral form, Jebb persuaded Hook to introduce an imitation of that style at Leeds, rather than to adopt the alternative model first demonstrated in 1839 by the

50   S. S. Wesley, *op. cit.*, p. 49.
51   *Ecclesiologist*, 15 (1854), pp. 307–10. P. M. Young in *A History of British Music* (London, 1967), p. 460, describes Wesley as the one church musician of the period touched with genius. Joseph Barnby, Webb's much admired organist at St Andrew's Church, Wells Street, receives no mention.
52   Wesley, *op. cit.*, p. 45.
53   W. R. W. Stephens, *Life and Letters of W. F. Hook*, vol. 2 (London, 1878), p. 124.
54   D. Hunt, *Samuel Sebastian Wesley* (Bridgend, 1990), p. 36.
55   J. Jebb, *The Choral Service of the United Church of England and Ireland...* (London, 1843), pp. 284–7.

Rev. Frederick Oakeley at Margaret Chapel, London, where the choir's role was to lead the people in response, hymn and psalm.[56] It will be noted that no mention is made of anthems, yet it says much for the breadth of Jebb's musical outlook that he had mooted the idea of the ancient Office Hymns being translated into English as early as 1843. A mechanical delivery of the psalms, Jebb contended, was less preferable than that majestic roll of the chant that resembles the voice of many waters.[57] He advocated that the priest's versicles and prayers should be wholly intoned, as stipulated in the rubrics of the *Prayer Books* of 1549 and 1552, 'to the end that they may the better heare. In such places where they doe syng there shall the lessons be songe to a playne tune after the manner of distincte reading, and lykewise the Epistle and Gospell'. In all this Jebb was wholly supportive of Helmore and the ecclesiologists. Thus despite divergent outlooks on some matters, in others they shared common ground. Letters between them were generally courteous, and Jebb's standing as a liturgist freely acknowledged.[58] His balanced views were shown by his acceptance of an invitation to preach at the dedication service at St Michael's College, Tenbury, which Ouseley founded to promote the best church music practices as he saw them, in 1856, and Jebb's becoming a member of the Committee of the Society in 1860.[59] However, the Leeds example of choral services was greatly admired for its beauty and dignity, becoming highly influential throughout the English speaking world. In many respects it represented an important alternative to the model proposed by the Society. A similar philosophy to that at Leeds, prevailed at the Temple Church, London, where E. J. Hopkins tended the music with loving care from 1843–98.

The Society's increasing influence rested to a large extent on individual effort in the most unlikely and unpromising places. Comparisons were made between the perfunctory choral standards at St Paul's Cathedral and Westminster Abbey with those at a dedication festival at the small country parish of Kemerton, whose rector, Archdeacon Thomas Thorp, was the Society's first president. His assistant curate, the Rev. C. T. Heartley claimed, 'We now have a full choral service every night and are masters of about 50 anthems and of such a number of chants and psalm tunes as are necessary for performance of the service'.[60] Later that year Thorp wrote that ten times as many people attended the *sung* evening service as came in the afternoons to the *plain* service.[61] Thorp also led the protest against the governing committee of the College of St Mark's College, Chelsea who wished to discontinue intoning in

56 *The New Grove Dictionary of Music and Musicians* (London, 1980), vol. 9, p. 581.
57 Jebb, *op. cit.*, p. 304.
58 Adelmann, *op. cit.*, pp. 36, 148.
59 *Ecclesiologist*, 21 (1860), p. 238.
60 Letter to *Guardian*, 21 December 1853.
61 Letter to *Guardian*, 7 November 1855.

the services. Their specious reasoning included cost, its being offensive to London clergy, and that it would lead to the students acquiring Romish sympathies. In fact no additional cost had been incurred, and not one student had been converted to Rome since choral services had been instituted.[62]

Similar objections to the choral service were made at Brasted, and on 27 August 1851 *The Guardian* reported that the Archbishop of Canterbury intended to prosecute clergy in his diocese for intoning the service. Benjamin Webb received a monition dated 15 September of that year. In a letter to Dr Mill, Archbishop Sumner explained that his objection to intoning stemmed from St Paul's injunction to pray with understanding, and his concern for illiterate worshippers who would have difficulty in following a sung service.[63] This view is wholly contrary to the rubrics of the first and second *Prayer Books* of King Edward VI.

Very frequently it was through the independent initiatives of key individuals that the musical views of the Society were moved forward. A. W. N. Pugin's eminence as an architect gave an additional authority to his *Earnest Appeal for the Revival of Ancient Plainsong* (1850).[64] It represented a powerful endorsement of the Society's ideals. J. D. Chambers published a psalter, together with hymns, antiphons, and collects for the principal festivals and seasons, with appropriate music from ancient sources, including York and Hereford usages. It was intended for private devotion, but such a publication undoubtedly put temptation in the path of those who sympathised with pre-Reformation worship. However, its use required courage in the face of strong episcopal disapproval.

The Rev. William Dodsworth was the first incumbent of Christ Church, Albany, St Pancras, in 1837. In that year he published *A Selection of Psalms to which are added Hymns chiefly ancient for the use of the Chapel.* He had officiated previously at Margaret Chapel and from 1833 had been attracted to Puseyism. There was no chancel in his new church, and, interestingly, the organ was placed above the altar. Both the Rev. (later Cardinal) H. E. Manning and the Rev. Edward Pusey had accepted invitations to preach there. From 1843 Dodsworth set about improving the internal arrangements by raising the chancel, placing the organ at the back of the church, and installing new plain choir stalls just below the altar rails. In 1849 *The Ecclesiologist* congratulated him on the 'great musical amelioration',[65] especially the new accommodation for the surpliced choir. Psalms were sung to Gregorian chants. Dodsworth was one of only a handful of priests who worked for the choral revival in London.

[62] Adelmann, *op. cit.*, pp. 98–102.
[63] Lambeth Palace, MS 1491 fl 62–3, 18 October, 1851.
[64] Pugin, *op. cit.*, pp. 7–8.
[65] *Ecclesiologist*, 9 (1849), p. 378. See also Rainbow *op. cit.*, p. 126.

Any attempt to assess the extent of the Society's influence on church music is hindered by the manifest lack of consistency in its initiatives. Not only does theory often differ from practice, but the views of individual members were susceptible to staggering change. No one illustrates this more than Benjamin Webb. The ordering of services at St Andrew Church, Wells Street, where he became Vicar in 1863, seems to have entailed a repudiation of almost everything that the Society had earlier held most dear. Modern hymns were used, the psalms were sung to Anglican chants, and a professional choir performed twice daily. Their repertoire included canticles in modern settings, and spectacular settings of the Mass – by Gounod and Mozart – and elaborate anthems.[66] A few weeks after his arrival, Webb appointed Joseph Barnby as organist. His secular compositions, of which the part song, 'Sweet and Low' is typical, had the saccharine values that he also expressed in sacred pieces. It seems that these were also very much to the taste of the church's affluent congregation. Their participation in the service was minimal, and many departed after the anthem. After all the excuses that have been made, Webb showed a serious confusion of principle, in that the Barnby regime upheld neither ancient nor modern values that were wholesome. All that can be said in defence of Webb's apparent lack of principles is that, in displaying his well-known capacity for moderation, he was anxious not to offend his wealthy and influential parishioners, many of whom were habitués at the Royal Opera House, Covent Garden, where they enjoyed Gounod's secular compositions.[67]

The careers of other Society members suggest that alternative musical sympathies could produce a pragmatic solution when authoritative Society pronouncements were absent. The spirit of compromise is to be seen in the appointment of W. H. Monk and his work at St Matthias, Stoke Newington. Though not a member of the Society, his career shows much sympathy with its aims. Evensong was sung daily by a large choir, one third of whom attended in turn. They were happy to sing congregational music in unison. It was Monk who suggested *Ancient and Modern* as the title for the world's most famous hymn book. He was its musical assessor in 1868 and its joint musical editor for the editions of 1875 and 1889 to which he contributed many specially composed and deservedly popular tunes. Initially its contents were

[66] Webster, *op. cit.*, p. 51. Though superficially akin to the pattern of musical worship at St Andrew, Wells Street by Webb and Barnby, that at Leeds Parish Church – though reflecting a different type of churchmanship – was both more aesthetically wholesome and longer lasting in its influence. At his next appointment, St Anne, Soho, the service there enjoyed the popular nickname, 'the Sunday Opera'.

[67] It is difficult to understand how, presumably because of his association with Webb, Barnby's music could have been tolerated by the very people who were so ready to condemn Wesley. Fellowes' assessment of the two composers in *English Church Music*, pp. 203 and 227, represent twentieth century consensus views.

heavily weighted in favour of the 'ancient' but as the book expanded its contents, it veered towards the 'modern' and towards a more evangelical type of churchmanship.[68]

What was the long-term impact of the Society's initiatives? Scholars are agreed that musical composition for the English Church, from the 1880s onwards, began to attain a quality that equalled the best of that written during the preceding two hundred years, and in some instances had gone beyond it. Such compositions as C. V. Stanford's set a standard for his successors to follow.[69] However, the extent to which any of these musical developments can be attributed to the Society's initiatives is questionable. Gradually the ecclesiologists realised the difficulty of persuading ordinary churchgoers to accept their musical opinions. Whilst everyone was familiar with, and admired Gothic cathedrals, few knew anything of plainsong and High Renaissance polyphony. They could evaluate neither content nor mode of performance. Professional musicians remained aloof. The general public could now hear music in the newly-built town halls more easily, on a bigger scale, and of a better standard of performance than had existed before. So far from it having deteriorated, they believed that the resources of music had advanced, and found it difficult to accept the notion that the achievements of nineteenth-century church composers were inferior to those of previous eras, particularly when their secular compositions were taken into account.

Progress in the general acceptance of plainsong and polyphony, from 1900 onwards, especially in cathedrals and Anglo-Catholic churches was then all the more remarkable. It was attributable chiefly to the work of scholarly editors of this century such as R. R. Terry, A. Ramsbotham, E. H. Fellowes, C. B. Rootham, J. H. Arnold and W. H. Frere rather than to the legacy of the Society.

The practice of church music was greatly strengthened by the establishment of diocesan choral festivals in the nineteenth century. These enjoyed the blessing of the Ecclesiological Society not least for their propaganda value, and the active participation of individual members. Beginning with that in Cheadle, Staffordshire on 4 October 1849 they became annual events in some dioceses. At Lichfield Cathedral, on 14 October 1856, twenty-six choirs participated and there were forty-seven the following year. Plainsong was a feature of the Southwell festivals, bringing them still closer to the Society's heart's desire,[70] whilst *The Guardian*[71] congratulated the ones at Ely for choosing music that avoided any drawn from a period when the art was in its infancy, as well as rejecting poor contemporary works. However the size of the Canterbury Festivals from 1862 compelled their promoters to

[68] D. F. Webster, *Our Hymn Tunes* (Edinburgh, 1983), p. 106.
[69] Fellowes, *op. cit.*, p. 237.
[70] *Ecclesiologist*, 19 (1858), pp. 175–6.
[71] *Guardian*, 29 May 1861, p. 501.

respond to public taste and popularity rather than to the doctrines and desires of individual pressure groups, including those of the Society. By this date, its musical preferences formed only one of a number of equally acceptable alternatives. Indeed, it could be argued that by this time its views were supported by only a minority, even among the reformers.

The average Victorian choirman strongly objected to singing in unison, and this was clearly an inhibiting factor in his acceptance of plainchant. In an attempt to popularise it and the compositions of John Merbecke (c.1505–85) they were often published in metrical and harmonised fashion, even in such prestigious compilations as the *Cathedral Prayer Book*, 1875, edited by Sir John Stainer, organist of St Paul's Cathedral. This was of course totally at variance with their proper mode of performance. Richard Redhead's *Hymns and Canticles as used at morning and evening prayer at All Saints' Church, Margaret Street*, where he was organist from 1839–64, set Gregorian chants to four-part harmony, using a vocabulary that included dominant sevenths and other ear-tickling chords.[72] All this was counter productive. It did nothing to promote a general endearment of plainchant, and one suspects that many clergy supported its use more out of a sense of misguided historicity, and to curb excessive choral zeal, than out of genuine aesthetic appreciation.

Thomas Helmore's approach was more enlightened. He was helped no doubt by having a captive, educated congregation at St Mark's College, Chelsea, and frequent opportunities for rehearsal. This resulted in his pointed psalters for use with plainchant, plainsong manuals and *The Hymnal Noted* remaining influential among high Anglicans for well over a century.

The Society no doubt hoped that following the passage of the Catholic Emancipation Bill in 1829 and the establishment of the Roman Catholic hierarchy in 1850 they might be able to exercise some influence in the newly liberated church. Unfortunately there was a reluctance on the part of Roman Catholics to use Anglican music in any form, or to be influenced by its idiom, even of the better kind. On the contrary, Anglican churches that were given over to extreme High Church practices were not uninfluenced by Roman Catholic parochial music,[73] which all too often complemented visual gaudiness in the ornaments.

Instances of its emotional over-ripeness can be seen in the various editions of the *Mirfield Mission Hymn Book* dating from the early years of this century, which were designed for use in the Community of the Resurrection. F. W. Faber was a Catholic convert, and in some of his hymns and the tunes they attracted, such as *Hark, hark, my soul* set to Henry Smart's *Pilgrims*,[74]

72   Temperley, *op. cit.*, p. 256.
73   As for instance in the *New English Hymnal* (Norwich, 1986) where we encounter Victorianism of the most debased kind in *Soul of my Saviour* and its tune *Anima Christi* by William Maher: no. 305. Or was this a shrewd editorial move designed to secure Roman Catholic usage for the book?

similar tendencies are to be seen. Nicholas Temperley has pointed out that congregations supported by a large surpliced choir and a powerful organ were able to feel that they were taking part in real musical performances on the only occasions in their lives.[75] Such a thrill inevitably led to a dulling of the critical faculty where quality was concerned. It is perhaps worth noting that though Henry Smart was a leading mid-nineteenth-century church composer,[76] he was one of the few who showed real commitment to the congregation's contribution to church services, in his accompaniment of modern hymns at St Pancras, London, where he was organist from 1864 until 1879. When one considers the inartistic way in which plainsong was edited and performed the hostility it engendered is hardly surprising. Even the 1906 *English Hymnal* was not free from stylistic blunders which were not remedied until 1933, when the *New Music Version* incorporated J. H. Arnold's infinitely more musical arrangements. In its churchmanship the *English Hymnal* may be regarded as the *Hymnal Noted's* successor. Although its preface claims that 'it is not a party book expressing this or that phase of negation or excess',[77] that is precisely how it has come to be regarded, both by its admirers and its detractors. Nor can the great artistic esteem that it has enjoyed over *Hymns Ancient and Modern* be wholly justified.

Despite the limited popularity of plainsong, it was not until the liturgical reforms of the last decades of the twentieth century that it was threatened with wholesale removal from Anglican services. Its inclusion in the *New English Hymnal* of 1986, though smaller in quantity than in the 1906 edition, shows that the plainsong revival which the society had done so much to initiate was still a living issue among High Churchmen. As has been noted from the 1880s onwards, there were unmistakable signs of compositions for the church being written by men of superior general education, artistic taste, technique and liturgical sensitivity, whose work reached out to choirs and congregations. Most of their writing was for cathedrals but inevitably their influence percolated to the parish church, and Charles Wood and Basil Harwood showed a love of plainsong and High Church practices.

Thus the nineteenth century closed with the church and its music in better heart than at the beginning. The challenges of Darwin, Marx and Huxley had produced a fair quota of agnostics and atheists, but Sunday observance for most people meant more than negative proscriptions. If the Society's support for musical medievalism had been largely neglected, except as symbols of uncompromising Anglo-Catholicism, its support for the decent ordering of services and for high musical standards generally has remained and for this it deserves much credit.

---

[74]   *Hymns Ancient and Modern*, Standard Edition, no. 223 (London, 1916).
[75]   Temperley, *op. cit.*, p. 306.
[76]   *Ibid.*, p. 274.
[77]   13th impression, 1960, p. iii.

Postscript

CHRISTOPHER WEBSTER

It is appropriate to return here to a pertinent question almost implicit in the title of this book: just how influential and important was the Society in the context of the Victorian Anglican Church and its architecture? Anyone having read this far will, no doubt, be struck not so much by an obvious answer as by a realisation that such a question defies a simple, compact response. This final section of the book aims not so much to attempt to answer this essentially unanswerable question as to bring together some of the key issues which help inform any serious debate on this subject. However, even establishing parameters for a debate is by no means unproblematic. Indeed, it could be claimed that such a discussion is largely redundant since the Society itself claimed with disarming modesty that its aim was merely 'the study of Gothic architecture and of ecclesiastical antiquities'.[1] Only away from the public glare of the printed page was it usual for the Society to pursue its much wider agenda, and historians are handicapped by the absence of a clear policy statement. Furthermore, assessing the extent to which there was broad agreement with its objectives is difficult for several reasons. Firstly, on a whole range of topics, the Society's pronouncements did not remain static. For instance, in the early 1840s *The Ecclesiologist* was encouraging architects to study English Decorated examples and follow them faithfully: 'It is no sign of weakness to copy acknowledged perfection', it said.[2] However, within a few years, drawing inspiration from a much broader range of examples – including those from the Continent – was not only acceptable, but often encouraged. Webb's *Sketches of Continental Ecclesiology or Church Notes in Belgium, Germany and Italy*, of 1848 was important and in 1855, in an article on 'Mr Street's Italian Tour', *The Ecclesiologist* could confidently refer to 'the richness and beauty of the Pointed architecture of Italy'.[3] Even Archdeacon Thorp, the Society's first president, was moved to complain that he was 'staggered' and 'upset' by the Society's later stylistic sympathies: 'It is all new, all heretical ...

---

[1]   E. J. Boyce, *Memorial of the Cambridge Camden Society, Instituted May, 1839, and the Ecclesiastical (late Cambridge Camden) Society, May, 1846* (London, 1888), p. 35.

[2]   *Ecclesiologist*, 1 (1842), p. 134.

[3]   *Ecclesiologist*, 16 (1855), p. 299.

exactly contrary to what we used to say.'[4] While late twentieth-century historians might see this as inconsistency and as weakening the Society's authority, the Society itself had no difficulty in viewing this as a perfectly proper evolution in its thinking. Certainly it did not cause it to dilute the conviction with which it made its pronouncements. As Scott put it, 'One thing, however, never changed, the intolerance shown by them for all freedom of thought on the part of other men. Every one must perforce follow in their wake, no matter how often they changed, or how entirely they reversed their own previous views – there was no class of men whom the Camden Society held in such scorn, as those who adhered to their own last opinion but one'.[5] However, rather than agreeing with the hypersensitive Scott, perhaps it would be more reasonable to conclude that this is not so much 'inconsistency' as a valid philosophical development, especially in view of the relatively long period – almost thirty years – over which the Society remained active.[6] Given the vast changes that can be found in other aspects of Victorian society, it is hardly surprising that the Society's attitudes underwent significant revision. In addition, we can identify changes in key personnel within the Society as a further cause of shifts in its principal aims; the move from Cambridge to London in 1845 and the election of Beresford Hope as chairman was particularly significant in this respect.

A second reason for thinking that a straightforward answer to the question of the Society's influence is likely to prove to be simplistic arises from the fact that it agitated for change on such a relatively broad range of issues: reform of the Church of England as an institution; the restoration of High Church principles; a more serious commitment to the Gothic style; greater emphasis on the sacraments; the encouragement of greater piety among both clergy and worshippers; reform of church music; a revised emphasis on the arrangement of churches to include sacramental symbolism, etc. Given this diversity, one may expect that in some of these areas the Society's influence was considerable, yet in others it was less so.

In seeking to pursue further the question of the Society's influence, it may therefore be beneficial to follow a series of more specific lines of enquiry. So far as the Church of England as an institution is concerned, it is clear that pressure for reform, for the removal of sinecures and absenteeism, and for it to take on a more spiritual and less political role in society, were all well established before 1839. These were themes that occur frequently in Radical

---

[4] Quoted in S. Crewe, *Visionary Spires* (London, 1986), p. 78.

[5] G. G. Scott, *Personal and Professional Recollections* (London, 1879, reprint Stamford, 1995), p. 206.

[6] These three decades coincided with the spread of the railway network and its impact on ecclesiology should not be overlooked. The Society's early antiquarian excursions around Cambridge relied on horse-drawn transport but within a generation, train travel to the Continent had become commonplace.

literature of at least a generation earlier. For anyone seeking evidence of corruption, idleness or inappropriate secularisation in the late-Georgian church, John Wade's *The Extraordinary Black Book,* of 1831 – containing over one hundred pages of small, tightly packed text listing abuses of power and privilege – is just one of a number of such sources. Wade's chapter headings and sub-headings include: 'The un-Christian conduct of the clergy; more than one-third of incumbents pluralists; sinecurism – non-residence – pluralities.'[7] In addition, the concept of 'church reform' in the pre-Victorian period went well beyond denouncing examples of greed or idleness among the clergy; there was agitation from both the Evangelical and High wings of the Church of England for a renewed emphasis on ministry and spirituality.

How far was the Society instrumental in the Church of England's rediscovery of its Catholic heritage, in re-establishing the authority of the rubrics found in the *Book of Common Prayer* and in the wider shift away from Evangelicalism? Certainly the initiative of the Society was an important factor in this, but in any assessment of the Society's influence in this, it is clear that the earlier initiatives of the Oxford Movement must assume pre-eminence. As Nigel Yates has observed, in older histories of the Oxford Movement the impression was often given that every reform in the Victorian Church of England, and every pastoral and theological advance was the result of the Oxford Movement and its legacy, although he goes on to point out that such an assessment is nonsense.[8] However, it is the case that even among more recent histories of Victorian religion, the Movement has had whole chapters or sub-sections devoted to it, whereas the Cambridge Camden Society tends to be seen as an interesting – but essentially minor – player in the wider picture of the period's religious developments.[9]

Perhaps the central question in the context of this book is, 'what was the role of the Society in the Gothic Revival?' Once more, the picture is complex. There is ample evidence that antiquarianism at both the amateur and professional level was very well established before 1839. There were numerous late-Georgian publications aimed either at the specialist or more general reader which testify to the level of sophistication that studies in the subject had reached. Elsewhere, the popularity of Walter Scott's writings and

---

[7]   However, in other respects the Society would have had little sympathy with Wade's views, containing as they did an explicit agenda of secularism and Enlightenment philosophy.

[8]   N. Yates, *The Oxford Movement and Anglican Ritual* (London, 1983), p. 36.

[9]   For instance, see: O. Chadwick, *The Victorian Church* (London, 1966); G. Parson, *Religion in Victorian Britain* (Manchester, 1988); H. Davies, *Worship and Theology in England* (Princeton, 1970). One need look no further than the index of Chadwick's authoritative study where Neale is mentioned on seven pages, Webb on just one, but Newman appears on over sixty pages and Pusey on more than forty.

of Gothic novels points to a widespread, if superficial, acquaintance with medievalism. In addition, while it is fair to say that around 1840 Gothic was only one of a number of fashionable styles for secular buildings – and generally one less popular than the various classical alternatives, especially for urban structures – there was almost universal agreement that Gothic was the most appropriate style for churches well before Victoria came to the throne. Perhaps a sound pragmatic solution to the issue of the Society's importance in the Gothic Revival is that it gave a new impetus and substantial *gravitas* to an already established ideal. In particular, it encouraged any debate on the issue of style to go beyond the usual aesthetic criteria and include questions of morality. Yet, once again, the picture is more complex, this time as a result of what we might term 'the Pugin factor'. On a whole range of issues, including the belief that Gothic was the only Christian architecture, the desirability of church architects being deeply religious, on the inappropriateness of the mechanics' institute as a source of training for craftsmen intending to execute ecclesiastical furnishings and decoration, Pugin seems to anticipate the Camden men. Furthermore, one might argue that while the Society may well have 'borrowed' a number of key aspects of its early manifesto from Pugin's writings, arguably its most important debt to him was in terms of the language used to advance its ideas. The single-mindedness, the apparent unwillingness to consider alternatives, and the reliance on the vague concept of 'Christian commitment' as justification for a point of view where no more rational explanation existed, can all be traced to Pugin. As Crook put it, he was 'the godfather of Anglican ecclesiology'.[10] Of course, the Society was at pains publicly to distance itself from any link with him both because he was a Catholic and because any acknowledgement of a debt to him weakened the Society's own importance and authority, yet such a debt is hard to overlook.

To what extent were the clergy directly influenced by the Society's initiatives? It is probably unlikely that it actually *led* many in the direction of 'higher' forms of worship but it certainly helped to provide part of the intellectual framework and the appropriate physical setting for those who were drawn in such a direction. It afforded an important outlet for those with interests in architecture and the arts of the Church, and the orientation of the Society was such that it appealed most readily to clerics touched by the influence of the Oxford Movement. However, the ideas put out so forcibly reached far beyond those who were paid-up members of the Society. During its early years county architectural societies were only just coming into being and the only comparable organisation was the Camden Society's sister society in Oxford. The publications emanating from Cambridge found an eager market as the astonishing sales of the Society's cheaper publications reveal.

[10]   J. M. Crook, *The Dilemma of Style* (London, 1987), p. 54. As John Elliott has pointed out, it was Pugin who introduced Carpenter to the Society.

Clear guidelines were given on how to deal with the arrangement of churches and those guidelines would form the basis of the way churches were reordered over the subsequent decades, accepted as they were by a remarkably broad consensus of clergymen and their architects.

On the question of the Society's influence of church music, it seems that it had only a limited long term influence. Its almost excessive fondness for simple, dignified music, especially plainsong, and its unwillingness to recognise the quality and value of contemporary music, especially where it could be performed by a proficient choir, caused much resentment and alienation amongst professional musicians who might have proved useful allies in different circumstances.

The one area where the Society's influence is undeniable is in the arrangement and the decoration of churches. While a small number of churches with long chancels, accurately detailed windows, and elements of medieval construction and craftsmanship can be identified in the late Georgian period, the Society can be seen to have influenced church design in an important new way. Where reasonably convincing pre-Victorian copies of medieval churches were produced, usually they were the result of antiquarianism, and an antiquarian approach from a secular perspective. The Society's real innovation may be ascribed to its belief that the form of a church had to be dictated primarily by its function.[11] That is, the plan and arrangement were to be the products of the pre- and immediately post-Reformation ritual, and a more rigorous interpretation of the Prayer Book rubric, supported by medieval or sixteenth-century precedent. In addition, the form of the church needed to be symbolic of the Christian faith. Thus can the Society's commitment to long structurally-separate chancels, or the inclusion of a sedilia or chancel steps be explained. Yet, once again, the historian encounters the Society's inconsistency. The strict reproduction of a medieval plan was not always compatible with the mid-sixteenth century *Book of Common Prayer*. The Society's fondness for archaeological fidelity might dictate the inclusion of chancel aisles yet such features – built originally as side chapels – were redundant by the time of Cranmer's prayer book. To what use could they be put in the mid-nineteenth century? Often they served as an appropriate location for an organ yet the Society could hardly claim historical precedent for what was essentially pragmatism, and more importantly, it is symptomatic of the Society's muddled thinking on this and other aspects of church arrangements. It should have anticipated that an equally studious reproduction of every element revealed through ecclesiastical archaeology was likely to deny it an entirely clear or wholly convincing argument on questions of church arrangement. The Society also had a profound and revolutionary

[11] Yet here again it could be claimed that the Society did little more than adapt Pugin's philosophy of design, as set out in his *True Principles,* for Anglican consumption.

influence on the nave. Here, however, its passionate denouncement of box pews and galleries, and huge, centrally-placed pulpits may be ascribed essentially to the absence of pre-Reformation models, the need to focus on the altar and, importantly, the belief that if the lay members of the Church of England were to be made more pious, the luxury and self-satisfaction that pew ownership represented, needed to be removed. In the same vein, the Society had a passionate dislike of flat, plastered ceilings and, instead, advocated open, high-pitched roofs. This was all part of the desire to remove worship from the comfort of domesticity to the solemnity of true religion – from the drawing room of the Lord to the temple of the Most High.

The issue of the Society's role in the Church of England's rediscovery of its Catholic heritage has already been opened; it is helpful to return to it here. Rather than seeing Oxford and Cambridge as presenting rival claims for prominence in this, perhaps it is more useful to see the universities' initiatives as being complementary. There is general agreement that it was Oxford that gave the theological lead but it should be acknowledged that it was Cambridge ideas that provided the appropriate physical setting for the shift to 'higher' forms of worship. Indeed, leaders of the Oxford Movement generally avoided any involvement with questions of architectural decoration and ritual, believing that it was likely to compromise more important doctrinal priorities. Pusey even complained that he 'never had any sympathy ... [with] any innovations in the conduct of Services, anything of Ritualism, or especially any revival of disused Vestments.'[12] As Nockles has pointed out, 'it was not the Tractarians but the Ecclesiologists ... who applied the principles of the Catholic Revival to church architecture, furnishings and rubrical observance.'[13]

There was then a clear commitment by the Society to specific aspects of church arrangement, for instance, a dignified chancel designed to allow the celebration of Communion in accordance with the rubric of the *Book of Common Prayer*, and a nave – perhaps with aisles – where the congregation would be accommodated on east facing, supposedly classless benches, where all were, in theory, equal in the sight of God. Yet beyond these basic principles of planning, identifying a clear Camdenian 'line' on other architectural matters is more difficult. Although *The Ecclesiologist* devoted much space to the question of a model church, none was ever formally agreed on; All Saints, Margaret Street was, perhaps, the nearest the Society ever came to an official consensus, yet ironically, this church is probably the most idiosyncratic of all those with which the Society was ever associated. Trying to decide where the Society stood on most architectural questions is made

---

[12] H. P. Liddon, *The Life of Edward Boievecie Pusey* (London, 1893–4), vol. 4, pp. 211–12, quoted in P. B. Nockles, *The Oxford Movement in Context: Anglican High Churchmanship, 1760–1857* (Cambridge, 1991) p. 213.

[13] *Ibid.*

difficult by the speed with which its attitudes changed. In the early 1840s, unquestionably, the preference was for 'the glorious architecture of the fourteenth century [in England]',[14] yet only a few years later, the delights of Continental examples had been discovered, opening the way for German, French or Italian churches to be plundered in the search for useful ideas. Even the commitment to Gothic did not remain unquestioned; there was some interest in Romanesque among certain sections of the Society, and there was a parallel debate which challenged the early ubiquitous demand for stone and soon enabled the modern industrially-produced brick to be equally acceptable. How is one to classify a church like All Saints? The plan of the church itself is unproblematically derived from fourteenth- or fifteenth-century English examples, but the total arrangement of the whole complex including the clergy house and school is highly novel; there is a similar dichotomy that can be perceived between the church's pre-Reformation plan and the modernity of its rich polychrome external elevations.

A further cause for confusion in trying to classify the Society's architectural beliefs comes from the fact that at almost exactly the same time that Butterfield began All Saints, Carpenter commenced St Mary Magdalene in nearby Munster Square.

In these two churches – each the work of one of the Society's two most favoured sons – the contrasts are remarkable, yet the almost uniform enthusiasm for them revealed in the pages of *The Ecclesiologist* suggests nothing of their stylistic diversity. Carpenter – the 'Anglican Pugin' – specified Kentish ragstone and in selecting sources for the design displayed impeccable archaeological scholarship: the Austin Friar's church; Exeter Cathedral; and Sherborne Abbey. Meanwhile, Butterfield chose polychrome brick and drew on Continental – and especially Italian – examples. One building looks backwards to a glorious past, the other forward to a modern age of new materials and new horizons. They are, in short, incompatible as paradigms of an organisation with a clear architectural agenda.

In the second half of the Society's existence, as a new generation of architects like Pearson and Bodley came to the fore, each attempting to wring new life from the tiring flesh of the Gothic Revival, and producing exciting compositions far removed from the accepted models of the early 1840s, where did the Society stand? Had it become a spent force, merely a toothless observer of an architectural juggernaut it could no longer control, or should we see it as the upholder of a series of unalterable truths and as a continuing authority whose views were sought and respected? Here it is important that a distinction is made between stylistic issues and those concerned with planning and ritual arrangements. This new generation of architects did indeed take

[14] J. M. Neale and B. Webb, *The Symbolism of Churches and Church Ornaments* (Leeds, 1843), p.xxiv.

Gothic in directions that could hardly have been dreamed of in the early 1840s, but the type of worship for which they were designed was entirely in keeping with the Society's pronouncements. In addition, both the near monopoly which ecclesiastical commissions had in the careers of these architects, and their conspicuous piety were entirely in accordance with the ideal church designer the Society had sought to promote.

In seeking to understand what appears to be an absence of a clear line on architectural questions shown by the Society, it may be instructive to place its expressed views, inconsistent as they may be, within the context of the wider architectural debates of the period. Perhaps the key question which exercised Victorian architects and writers was whether they should be looking backwards or forwards. To look backwards seemed comfortable and re-assuring in a time of social upheaval. Yet few could accept historicism without ambivalence; surely the mother country of the world's greatest empire should have its *own* style. For others, finding a modern architectural language to reflect what was universally seen as an era of immense change, and scientific and technological progress was felt to be necessary. Examples of the dilemma are easily identified, perhaps none clearer than the frequently rehearsed case of St Pancras Station in London, built in the 1860s. The immense train shed of iron and glass, designed by the engineers Barlow and Ordish, had the largest uninterrupted span of any building in the world and was indeed one of the most technologically advanced structures of the age. Yet it was not allowed to remain exposed; as it neared completion, a competition was held to select a design for the hotel, waiting rooms and booking offices which would eventually hide it from the main approach. The winning design by Scott – who was, significantly, an architect not an engineer – presented the public with a swagger Gothic façade. Reassuring historicism might be said to have triumphed over a *tour de force* of engineering. In selecting their winning design, it seems the directors of the Midland Railway Company had little interest in an explicit celebration of the scientific achievements of the age and were certainly unconcerned that railway travel was without medieval precedent.

Central to the Victorian stylistic debate was the question of 'development'. Critics might point out that the use of medieval sources for St Pancras's front were inappropriate, but they were heavily outnumbered by those who could claim that this was *adaptation* rather than *plagiarism;* that the whole process of secularising Gothic in this way was not only a legitimate, but a desirable activity. In the wider debate on this issue, *The Ecclesiologist* came down firmly on the side of development; just as Gothic architecture had changed during the medieval period, so now it invited further development beyond historical prescription in order to meet contemporary social needs.[15]

[15] *Ecclesiologist,* 11 (1850), pp. 223–6. The writer is grateful to Chris Brooks for this

Development might also involve consideration of new materials and technology; Street claimed that 'every modern architect should exploit "the intelligence of this modern age"'[16] Even Beresford Hope who, as the self-proclaimed leader of the High Church Conservatives, might have been expected to promote a reactionary line, was well aware of the problem of identifying an appropriate architectural language for Victoria's reign, and was conscious of the need to find a solution. Writing in 1855, he claimed he could identify in Italian Gothic a 'key ingredient in the creation of a new synthesis'.[17] Here, he noted was 'a contribution to the solution of that great problem – an architecture of the future'.[18]

In the Janus-like stylistic uncertainty of the period, to which the examples above seem to point, was the Society in the vanguard of debate or merely a confused schizophrenic participant? Indeed, it is not just in the context of architecture that the mid-nineteenth century seemed unsure of whether it should be looking backwards or forwards. Examination of a range of contextual standpoints may lead one to conclude that the Society's apparent inconsistency should be seen not as some sort of lack of conviction, but as an entirely typical Victorian way of thinking. In the field of painting, the Pre-Raphaelite Brotherhood had many parallels with the Cambridge Camden Society: both were started by young men fired with idealism; both pursued a radical agenda; both reflected High Church principles. More importantly in the current discussion, the range of subjects explored by the Brotherhood shows a more-or-less concurrent concern with the historical and the modern. In their case, the common theme was religious and moral didacticism. Some of the group's work illustrates scenes from the time of Christ, for instance, Millais' *Christ in the House of His Parents* (1849), or Rossetti's *Girlhood of the Virgin Mary* (1850). In the former especially, the High Church agenda of the chancel dominated by the altar, and a liturgy dominated by the sacraments is only thinly disguised. However, at almost the same time, the group was also concerned to address the question of a contemporary application of Christian teaching in such works as Hunt's *The Hireling Shepherd* (1851–2) or his *The Awakening Conscience* (1853–4). The latter two both place their unambiguous moral message in a modern setting, and the Brotherhood seemed to see no contradiction in such chronological diversity of its chosen subjects.

Historians seeking further examples of the Victorian age's apparent ease in reconciling the traditional and the modern may point to the case of Darwin's *The Origin of the Species,* first published in 1859. It was the product of the best of the age's new-found scientific and empirical research; it also contained what were probably the most revolutionary conclusions published

---

material.
16   Quoted in S. Crewe, *op. cit.,* p. 78.
17   J. M. Crook, *op. cit.,* p. 89.
18   *Ibid.,* quoting *Saturday Review,* 2 (1856), pp. 68–9.

in the century. It enjoyed an enthusiastic welcome from certain sections of the intellectual middle class and was easily available in cheap editions. However, in the decade following its publication, rather than there being any decline in a commitment to Christianity, as Chadwick points out, 'the churches flourished as almost never before'.[19]

In seeking to evaluate the Society's influence, one conclusion at least seems safe if perhaps a little unexpected. It is that the real impact of the Society came not while it was at its most militant and crusading, but after what was, in effect, its demise. While its influence in the middle of the nineteenth century is open to debate, there can be no doubting its importance in the last quarter of the century and in the first half of the next; in those seventy-five years, it is unlikely that a single Anglican church was built which was not, in some way or another, affected by ecclesiology. The ideals of the Society were aided by the general shift in Anglicanism in a more Anglo-Catholic direction especially in the new century, and even more so following the Anglo-Catholic Congresses of the 1920s and '30s.

The final edition of *The Ecclesiologist* claimed that 'we have the satisfaction of retiring from the field as victors', and this was largely true.[20] However, in view of the profundity of much of the change the Society sought, it is hardly to be expected that change could be brought about quickly and without controversy. Among regular worshippers today, how many have not been touched by the resentment that something as simple as the introduction of a new tune to a familiar hymn can generate? And while few English Anglicans live in anything but complete harmony with their Catholic neighbours, the sad example of Northern Ireland should help us understand the early nineteenth-century distrust – often hatred – of the merest hint at Catholicism. No matter how vehemently the Society defended itself against charges of closet Popery, it must have been difficult for the man in the street not to equate Camdenian reforms with a shift towards Rome. Yet from the 1860s onwards, it is hard to find a new church which did not conform to the Society's principles, and by the end of the century, few pre-Victorian churches retained their pre-Camdenian arrangement and fittings. However incongruous the result, Georgian churches – regardless of their original style – gained Gothic chancels, stained glass and new benched seating.[21] By the early twentieth century, Camdenian principles had become an orthodoxy. Even the reforming zeal of the Modern Movement in the 1930s could offer no popular alternative, although there were several notable experiments. Only in the

---

[19] Chadwick, *op. cit.*, p. 2.

[20] *Ecclesiologist*, 32 (1868), pp. 315–16.

[21] Geoff Brandwood's research has confirmed that in most areas (including Cambridgeshire) restorations and re-orderings peaked only after 1868, usually in the 1870s and '80s. See G. K. Brandwood, 'Church Building and Restoration in Leicestershire and Rutland, 1800–1914 (Leicester University, Ph.D thesis, 1984).

second half of the twentieth century has there emerged a creditable alternative to the Society's principles of church arrangement, especially in the siting of the altar. Encouragement for change came from a variety of sources including the Liturgical Movement and the Parish Communion Movement, and culminated in the Liturgical Revival of the 1950s and '60s. All of them sought to remove the old hierarchical relationship between the priest and his congregation and, generally, make the conduct of services seem less remote for worshippers; moving the altar towards – or sometimes into – the nave was an important part of these initiatives. The Second Vatican Council of 1963 had the effect of confirming Anglican developments. The example of the two cathedrals in Liverpool is a helpful illustration of the change in thinking on matters of church arrangement. The Anglican cathedral, although initially planned in 1903, took on its final form only after the adoption of the revised design of 1942, and to the end, it is clear that Camdenian thinking underpinned its composition. However, the Catholic cathedral, conceived in 1959–60, uses a radical circular plan in which the seats surround the altar; not only does the design preclude a chancel, but there is no longer a function for one.

Yet even as we enter the new millennium, throughout most of the English speaking world, there remains an unmistakable idea of what a church should look like; it is held at least as firmly by those who rarely enter a church as by those who are regular worshippers. Remarkably, this consensus conforms almost exactly to the ideal promoted by the Cambridge Camden Society more than a century and a half ago when it spoke approvingly of 'a church as it should be'. When Neale and Webb visited Archdeacon Thorp's rooms on that momentous evening in 1839, could they possibly have dreamed of what would eventually be achieved?

Appendix: A Camdenian Roll-Call

GEOFFREY K. BRANDWOOD

The following pages aim to provide as complete a list as possible of members of the Cambridge Camden and Ecclesiological Societies from their beginnings in May 1839 to the election of the last known new member (Ellacombe) in 1867. Whenever possible brief biographical details are provided. In all there are 1,243 entries for known ordinary and honorary members plus a number of men who appeared at various meetings but whose membership is unrecorded (and is by no means certain). At the end is a list of over 60 sometime patrons – mainly bishops (a few of whom, in less exalted days, had been ordinary members of the Society). Some attempt at analysis is made in my chapter on the origins of the Society, but it is certain that there is much more to be found out, particularly in regard to clerical patronage, connections between individuals, and the details of the churchmanship of individual clergymen. The question naturally arises as to why certain people joined and others did not. It is curious, for instance, that although three well-known early-1840s architects – Edward Blore, L. N. Cottingham and R. C. Hussey – were members of the Oxford Architectural Society, they never figured in the Cambridge lists.[1] Equally one might have expected advanced churchmen, such as the Revs W. J. E. Bennett or Robert Liddell, to have joined but they did not. In some cases further work may provide suggestions, in others the distance of many years will leave the answers cloaked in obscurity. Quite obviously the Society was not prone to advertise desertions so, whatever else this list can do, it can only very rarely say exactly when an individual left. This tends to be with high-profile figures such as J. O. Halliwell and Professors Whewell and Willis. To partly remedy the problem, the dates of election are supplemented with information on whether the member was still on the books in 1846 (a particularly key year), 1856 and 1863.

---

[1]   It might be thought that Blore and Cottingham's non-appearance is related to the fact that they are included in *The Ecclesiologist*'s infamous index in volume 3 (1844) which lists 'Architects approved' and 'Architects condemned'. However, the categorisation was based on reviews of individual works within the volume, rather than blanket approval and disapproval.

GEOFFREY K. BRANDWOOD

Sources

The list has been assembled from two groups of sources which require a short explanation: The first is material published by the Society (shown in roman type) and includes what was the starting point for this project, the names and dates of election of members contained in the pages of *The Ecclesiologist*. The first such list details members elected on 8 November 1841. However, by that time the Society was 2½ years old and had been recruiting actively. So, to obtain more detail on the early period, use has been made of the membership lists printed in the CCS *Reports* for 1840 and 1841. The 1840 *Report* gives the membership in the middle of that year and it is supplemented with a further list of members elected during the Michaelmas term. Subsequent *Reports* also contain lists and these have enabled a few names, omitted from *The Ecclesiologist*, to be added (perhaps the most striking example is that of the architect, S. S. Teulon). The final key primary source was E. J. Boyce's *Memorial of the Cambridge Camden Society* of 1888 which, apart from reproducing the membership lists for 1842 and 1843, has the only known list of the 118 members as they were in December 1839. Very conveniently Boyce asterisks the 39 members who he claimed 'joined the C.C.S. *immediately* upon its institution, at the Meeting in May, 1839.'[2] In the period before *The Ecclesiologist* appeared (and in a few cases afterwards) it is not possible to give an exact joining date for most members so the ranges stated here have been made as close as the evidence allows.

Secondary sources – material indicated by italics – are many and varied. By far the most important is *Alumni Cantabrigienses ... 1752-1900 (AC)*, a staggering work of scholarship compiled by J. A. Venn, and giving summary biographies of Cambridge graduates. Without Venn's achievement the present list could never have been made up in the detail that it has. Oxford men are less well served by *Alumni Oxonienses (AO)* but this nonethless provided a good starting point for further research. Where extra information was needed on clerical careers this came from various editions of the *Clerical Guide, Clergy List,* and *Crockford*. Most of the details on architects' careers has been derived from the RIBA's *Biographical Dictionary of British Architects, 1834-1900* (ed. A. Felstead *et al.*, 1993), supplemented from published biographies where they exist and the *Compendium of Pevsner's Buildings of England on Compact Disc* (1995). No attempt has been made to provide lists of their works. The membership list for the Oxford Architectural Society for 1845 and the lists of Fellows of the Society of Antiquaries for 1840-5 have also

---

[2] *Memorial*, p. 40. Boyce's work has remained the most accessible source for lists of members in the early days until the present time. In preparing this new list, the present writer's task was aided greatly by possessing a complete run of *The Ecclesiologist*. It is a nice accident of history that this set once belonged to Boyce himself. After his death in 1897, his family presented it to the library of Church House, whence it was dispersed along with much other material.

360

been consulted. A little otherwise unknown information has been gleaned from the diaries of Benjamin Webb (BWD) and J. M. Neale. In addition, a considerable range of published sources has been used, including local directories, reference works on the peerage and gentry, the *Dictionary of National Biography*, and the *Army* and *Navy Lists*. The vast bulk of the information is to be found in fairly accessible and obvious sources and, therefore, in the interests of space, references have only been given when the source is obscure or it seems helpful to give it for one reason or another. Many individuals have kindly given advice and pieces of information and they are acknowledged at the end of this Appendix.

The Completeness and Accuracy of the List

Constructing a list like this has its hazards. First, there is the problem of simple errors in the primary sources. Not infrequently *The Ecclesiologist*, and sometimes the membership lists, get names wrong. The usual cause is a straightforward transcription error of, say, Fs, Js, and Ts (e.g. Astley, Tyssen) or an easy spelling mistake (e.g. Jenkins). Every effort has been made to identify such problems and they are commented upon in the biographical details. Occasionally it has been impossible to identify an individual precisely and this list can do no more than state the facts as best it can (e.g. Line, Marshall). Whether the list is entirely complete is a question that cannot ever be answered with certainty. In the volatile early months of the Society, a few people may have joined and quickly left (as did Halliwell) without leaving a trace. The occasional omissions from *The Ecclesiologist* have already been mentioned but the safety net of the membership lists has enabled escapees to be traced. It is just possible (especially in the period 1856–63) that there may be the odd case of someone being omitted from *The Ecclesiologist and* ceasing membership before the publication of the next membership list through death, resignation or lapsed subscription. In the opinion of the compiler, it is very unlikely that the omissions run into double figures.

Key to symbols

+   Committee member or officer in the Society
\#   Architect, artist or craftsman
*   Listed as a Tractarian clergyman in G. W. Herring's Ph.D thesis, 'Tractarianism to Ritualism: a Study of some Aspects of Tractarianism outside Oxford, from the Time of Newman's Conversion in 1845, until the First Ritual Commission in 1867' (Oxford, 1984)
§   Fellow of the Society of Antiquaries of London in 1845
•   member of the OAS in 1845
~   mentioned in mid-1846 membership list
¢   mentioned in mid-1856 membership list
¤   mentioned in mid-1864 membership list
‡   mentioned as a life member in 1864 membership list
<   before

GEOFFREY K. BRANDWOOD

Abbreviations

AC	J. A. Venn, *Alumni Cantabrigienses, Part 2, from 1752 to 1900,* 6 vols (London, 1940-54)
Adm.	admitted to or as
AL	*Army List*
AO	J. Foster, *Alumni Oxonienses; the Members of the University of Oxford 1715-1886,* 4 vols (Oxford and London, 1888)
Archbp	Archbishop
Archd.	Archdeacon (of)
A(R)IBA	Associate of the (Royal) Institute of British Architects
Bp	Bishop
BWD	Benjamin Webb's diaries in the Bodleian Library (MSS.Eng.misc.e.406-16)
can.	canon (of)
CAS	Cambridge Antiquarian Society
CCS	Cambridge Camden Society
CL	*The Clergy List*
D	ordained as a deacon (only stated when the person did not pursue a career in the Church or there is a substantial delay between ordination and his first clerical appointment)
dio.	diocese or diocesan
Eccl	*The Ecclesiologist*
ES	Ecclesiological Society
F	Fellow
F(R)IBA	Fellow of the (Royal) Institute of British Architects
FSA	Fellow of the Society of Antiquaries of London
GS	Grammar School
I	incumbent
ICBS	Incorporated Church Building Society
NL	*Navy List*
OAS	Oxford Society for Promoting the Study of Gothic Architecture (usually known as the Oxford Architectural Society)
P	ordained as a priest (only stated when the person did not pursue a career in the Church or there is a substantial delay between ordination and his first clerical appointment)
PC	perpetual curate
POD	*Post Office Directory*
POLD	*Post Office London Directory*
preb.	prebend (of)
R	Rector
RC	Roman Catholic
RD	rural dean (of)
RIBA	Royal Institute of British Architects
T	Tutor
V	Vicar

The Society generally used the (High Church) abbreviation 'S.' instead of St, and this usage has been followed here.

APPENDIX

Conventions

Roman type denotes information gleaned from CCS and ES sources, plus Boyce's *Memorial*.

Where a clergyman moved on to another appointment in the same county in the interests of space, the name of the county has not been repeated. The counties in which well-known places lie are not stated.

Dates and date-ranges have the obvious meaning that this is when something occured or when an individual was at a certain place or in a certain appointment. But when I say 'in 18xx' or 'in 18xx–yy' in relation to an appointment or an address, this means I have not traced the complete period involved (e.g. Bostock may have been at Warrington Grammar School before 1846, there between 1847 and 1857, and, indeed, afterwards).

Name	Date elected	Cambridge college/other college & university	Addresses/location given in *The Ecclesiologist*/ career details
Abraham, *Charles Henry Fox*	14.11.43 ~ ¢	Queens'	*Adm. Middle Temple 1845; Eccl has initials wrongly as 'C. H. J.'; of East India Rooms, 8 S. Martin's Place in 1849–56*
Abraham, Rev. *Charles John*, M.A.	1847¢	King's	*C Headley Down, Hants c.1839, ass. master Eton 1839–49, Divinity Lecturer S. George's chapel, Windsor 1848, went to New Zealand 1850, chapl. and Principal S. John's College, Auckland, Archd. of Waitamata 1853, 1st Bp of Wellington: 1858–70, returned to England 1868, Ramsden Preacher 1869, coadjutor to his friend Bp Selwyn of Lichfield 1870–8, preb. Lichfield 1872–6, R (non-resident) Tatenhill, Staffs 1875–6, can. and Precentor Lichfield 1876–90, helped organise Selwyn College, Cambridge as memorial to Bp Selwyn, +1893*
Ackland, Rev. *Thomas Suter*, M.A.	Founder ~	S. John's, F (1842–52) Clare	*Mathematical master Royal Institution School, Liverpool 1840–7, PC S. Stephen, Liverpool 1842–53, asst master S. Peter's College, London 1854–64, V Balne, Yorks 1864–75, V Wold Newton 1875–92, author of theological works*
Acland, *Thomas Dyke*, M.P.	1846 ~ ¢¢‡	*Christ Church, Oxford*	*B.A. 1808, 10th baronet, M.P. for Devon 1812–18 & 1820–31, for N. Devon 1837–57*
Adcock, Rev., *Halford Henry*, B.A.	<mid-40 ~ ¢¢‡	Trinity	*C Evington, Leics, C Humberstone 1841–51, V there 1856–61 (restored church under R. Brandon (q.v.), lived in Brighton 1876, then London, +1901*
*Addison, Rev. *William Fountaine*, M.A.	7.11.44 ~ ¢	*Wadham, Oxford*	*B.A. 1840, C Birtles, Alderley, Ches 1843–probably 1850, PC Dorchester, Oxon 1850–6, C S. Giles, Reading Berks, 1853–63, V Christ Church, Reading 1863–9, civil chapl. Gibraltar 1869–77, V Ossett w. Gawthorpe, Yorks 1877–93*
Ady, Rev. *Francis William*	22.6.52¢¤		*V & patron Market Street (Markyate), Herts 1847–85 where he had the church restored 1874, changed name to Adye 1869, –1910*
Ainger, *George Henry*	6.12.41 ~ ¢¢‡	S. John's	*C Alford, Som 1847–8, T S. Bees College, Cumb 1849–57, principal 1858–70, PC S. Bees 1858–70, hon. can. Carlisle 1870–82, R Rothbury, Northants 1871–86, RD 1872–86, proctor in Convocation 1874–86, surrogate & can. Dio. Newcastle 1882–6*
Ainslie, *Henry*	10.11.42 ~	Trinity	*C Bury, Lancs 1848–56, V Easingwold, Yorks 1856–72, V Applethwaite, Cumb 1873–92*
Airy, Rev. *William*	8.11.41 ~ ¢¤‡	Trinity	*R Bradfield St Clare, Suff 1833–6, V Keysoe, Beds 1836–74, R Swineshead, 1845–74, chapl. to Duke of Manchester, RD, noted locally as an antiquary, prolific writer (notably a facsimile edition of Domesday (posthumous, 1881), gave paper on the Keysoe font (Eccl 1 (1842), 120, 124–5)*
+Akroyd, Col. *Edward*	11.6.60¢¤		*Bank Field, Halifax, joined the committee on election, worsted mill-owner and sometime M.P., founder and benefactor of All Souls, Haley Hill (built 1856–9 to design by*

name	date elected	Cambridge college or other	Addresses/location given in *The Ecclesiologist*/ career details
#Akroyd, James Lloyd	10.11.42~		*Scott* (q.v.) *and the model suburb of Akroyden for his workers*, on ES committee 1860–probably 1868
Alford, Rev. Henry, M.A.	7.11.44	F 1834 Trinity	*Architect*, Coventry, *in 1850 ('appraiser and architect') Palace yd'* (Lascelles & Co's Directory) *C to his father at Ampton, Suff 1833 , Hulsean lecturer 1841–3 , V Wymeswold, Leics 1835–53 (restored the church under Pugin 1844–6), examiner in logic & moral philosophy, London University 1841–57, Minister Quebec Chapel, Marylebone 1853–7, Dean of Canterbury 1857–71, poet, musician, composer, author of various biblical works and hymns e.g. 'Come ye thankful people come'*
#Allen, *Charles Bruce*	10.53¢		*Architect*, present at 1852 anniversary meeting but not elected until Oct. 1853; *Eccl* 12 (1851), 399 reports his 'scheme for founding a "School of Art for Artist-workmen"'; 13 (1852), 178, 277–8 reports the proposal (supported by G. G. Scott) to form a museum of casts and details; pp. 283–4, 423 report how the 'casts and models' of the Society were handed over to the 'School of Art and Museum', *entered the Notre Dame de la Treille, Lille competition 1854 when address was* Architectural Museum, Canon Row, Westminster
Allen, Mr T. W.	7.2.42		Maidstone, Kent; POD (1846) *mentions a 'Wm. Hart Allen, surgeon, dentist & chemist'*
Allott, Rev. Richard, M.A.	1.5.41~¢	Senior F 1807 Trinity	*B.A. 1805, R Killery, dio. Armagh till 1858, Precentor Armagh Cathedral 1834–58*
Anderdon, John Leviscount	1845~¢¤‡		*Gentleman, The Retreat, Reigate, Surr, a sponsor (with B. Webb) at baptism of J. M. Neale's baby (BWD 8.5.46)*
Anderson, Mr C.	7.11.44~		Camberwell, Surr
+ Anderson, *Charles Henry John*	Late 40 ~¢¤‡	Oriel, Oxford	*Lea, Gainsborough, Lincs, B.A. 1826, succeeded as 9th baronet 1846, on ES committee 1846–probably 1868, wrote Ancient Models: Containing Some Remarks on Church-Building Addressed to the Laity (1840), important client of J. L. Pearson (see A. Quiney, John Loughborough Pearson (1979)*
André, J. L.	13.7.54¢		25 York Place, City Road, *London, an antiquarian; however, in* 1855-6 *the* ES *committee inspected apparently architectural designs by 'Mr. André' (Eccl 17 (1856), 214–5*
Andrew, George	Early 1846 ~	Trinity	*Adm. Trinity 1845, no other details in AC*
#Andrews, Geo. Townshend	8.5.45 ~ ¢		*Architect (1804–55), York, mostly designed in an Italianate style (esp. stations), before 1840 a partner of P. F. Robinson*

#Apsley, Alexander	1848		'Builder' in directories, 'architect' in ES membership list 1849 and 1853, Ashford, Kent, by 1853 of Red Lion Square, London
Archer, D.	7.11.44		Kingsdowne House, Swindon, Wilts
Arnold, Rev. Thomas Kerchover, M.A.	11.5.43 ~	F 1823 Trinity	R Lyndon, Rutl 1830-53, distinguished educationalist and prolific theological writer, wrote reply to Francis Close's attacks on the CCS
Arundell, Hon. Robert Arthur	6.3.45 ~¢		Burley, Oakham, Rutl, 11th child of 9th Lord Arundell, in 1849-56 of Haughton Lodge, Stockbridge, Hants
Ash, Jervis (or Jarvis) Holland	22.5.43 ~	S. Peter's	LL.B 1849, LL.D 1854, C S. Marychurch, Dev 1847-50, thereafter unbeneficed, of Hungershall Park, Tunbridge Wells, Kent, +1895
*Ashwell, Arthur Rawson, B.A.	1848¢☐	Caius	C Speldhurst, Kent 1848-9, C S. Mary-the-Less, Cambridge 1849-50, Vice-Principal S. Mark's College, Chelsea 1851-3, Principal of Oxford Dio. Training College, Culham 1853-62, C Holy Trinity, Hanover Sq, London, Principal Durham Training College 1865-70, can. Chichester and Principal Theological College there 1870-9, R S. Andrew, Chichester 1871-5, S. Martin, Chichester, 1872-5, Chancellor of Chichester Dio. 1879
Ashwell, James	14.11.43	S. Peter's	Engineer, one of the founders of the Royal Institution of Civil Engineers, +1881
Astley, Rev. John Wolvey, M.A.	13.2.43 ~¢	F 1828-49 King's	Eccl seems to have the initials 'T. W.' in error, appears to rejoin 1848; C Priors Quarter, Tiverton 1832-8, R Chalton w. Clanfield & Idsworth, Hants 1847-75
Atlay, Rev. James, B.A.	1.5.41	F 1842-59 & T 1846-59 S. John's	C Warsop, Notts 1843-6, V Madingley, Cambs 1847-52, Whitehall Preacher 1856-8, Select Preacher 1858, 1862, 1870, 1873, 1890, Lady Margaret Preacher 1859, 1887, V Leeds 1859-68 (succeeding Hook (q.v.) where he organised church extension schemes, can. Ripon 1861-8, Bp of Hereford 1868-94
Atkinson, Rev. Michael Angelo	<mid-40	F 1838 & asst T 1838-55 Trinity	R Fakenham w. Alethorpe, Norf 1855-87, RD Burnham 1868-87, bon. can. Norwich 1881-90
#Audsley, George Ashdown	14.12.64☐		Architect (1838-1925), Liverpool, in office of A. & W. Reid, began practice with brother, W. J. Audsley 1863, (q.v.), FRIBA 1876, emigrated to USA 1892, continued working there till c.1910
#Audsley, William James	14.12.64☐		Architect, Liverpool, same career as G. A. Audsley
Austin, Rev. Anthony	10.11.42 ~	Oriel, Oxford	Matriculated 1808, R Hardenhush, Wilts from 1823, R Alderley, Glos 1831-46, R Littleton Drew and PC Alderton, Wilts 1846-8, disappears from CL 1849
Babington, Charles Cardale, M.A.	6.12.41	S. John's	Eminent naturalist, Professor of Botany 1861-95, interested in archaeology, helped found CAS, declined to serve on CCS committee 1843, +1895

name	date elected	Cambridge college or other	Addresses/location given in *The Ecclesiologist*/ career details
*Babington, Thomas Arthur	8.11.41 ~ ¢	Trinity	C Compton Valence, Dorset 1849–57, R Wanlip, Leics 1860–75, + 1896
Bacon, Hugh Ford	Late 40 ~ ¢¤‡	Christ's	C Fen Drayton, Cambs 1836–41, C Bourn 1841–50, resigned for ill-health, V Castleton, Derbys 1853–71, + 1882
+Bacon, Robert William, M.A.	<mid-40 ~ ¢	F 1830–55 King's	Adm. Lincoln's Inn 1828, called to the Bar 1835, CCS auditor 1840–1, on committee 1842–3, PC Wattisham, Suff 1846–51, PC Bricet 1846–55, R Ewhurst, Surr 1854–62
Badger, Albert	1842–3	Trinity Hall	Asst. minister Charlotte Chapel, Pimlico, London 1843–4, chapl. Brompton Cemetery 1866–72
Badger, Thomas Smith	13.2.43	Trinity Hall	Adm. Middle Temple 1841, called to the Bar 1847, specialised in conveyancing, took additional name of Eastwood 1863, +1866
Bagge, Theodore James	13.2.44	S. John's	C Patrixbourn, Kent 1850, C Weyhill, Hants 1851–4, then apparently unbeneficed, + 1861
Bailey, Rev. Henry	Founder	F 1842 S. John's	Lecturer in Hebrew 1848, Warden S. Augustine's College, Canterbury 1850–78, Select Preacher Cambridge 1851, commissar for Bp of Jamaica 1866, R West Tarring, Suss 1878–92, hon. can., Canterbury 1863–1906, RD 1886–92, can. S. Augustine, Canterbury 1888–1906
*Bailey, James Sandford	13.2.45 ~ ¢¤	Jesus	C Nutfield, Surr 1847–9, V S. Clement's, Cambridge 1849–52, C S. Paul, Brighton 1852–76, resided at Eastbourne, + 1912
Bailey, W. R., see Bayley, W. H. R.			
Baird, John Forster	28.11.44 ~	Trinity	Adm. Inner Temple 1847, called to the Bar 1850, +1882
Baker, Rev. A.	?		Present at 1852 anniversary meeting, the only candidate seems to be Arthur Baker, C Aylesbury, Bucks in 1848–50, C All Saints, Marylebone in 1852, in CL 1858 but without benefice or cure, not in Crockford 1860
Baker, Rev. Hugh Lefroy	8.5.45 ~ ¢¤		Ballygawley, Armagh, Slater's Directory … of Ireland (1846) has Rev. J. L. Baker, Crew Cottage, Ballygawley, CL (1862) has H.L.C. as PC at Ballygawley
+Baker, Rev. Henry Williams	<mid-40 ~ ¢¤‡	Trinity	C Great Horkesley, Ess c.1844–51, V Monkland, Heref 1851–77, succeeded father as 3rd baronet 1859, ES auditor 1860–1, promoter and compiler of Hymns Ancient & Modern and wrote some of them (e.g. 'The king of love my shepherd is' and 'Lord, thy Word abideth'), edited other hymn-books and a devotional manual
+Baldwin, Alfred	14.12.64‡		Stourport, Worcs, ES auditor 1865–7
+Baldwin, Rev. John, M.A.	<mid-40	F 1825–41 Christ's	D 1825, P 1826, held various College offices, Mildmay preacher 1835–7, CCS auditor 1840–1, +1855

Name	Date	College	Notes
Ballard, Captain V.	1845–6		Danbury, Ess, probably Capt. Volend Vashon Ballard, 44th (The East Essex) Regiment of Foot, became captain 1844, disappears from AL 1846, see also Ballard, G.F.
Ballard, Rev. Edward Humphrey	1846 ~	Wadham, Oxford	B.A. 1842, C Pucklechurch, Glos in 1846, listed in CL 1843–50 but no appointment stated
Ballard, George Frederick	11.5.43		Cavendish Crescent, Bath, Som: Silverthorne's Bath Directory (1837) has a 'Mrs Admiral V. V. Ballard' at no. 11; although no Admiral V:V. Ballard has been traced in the Navy List, the unusual 'V. V.' initials suggest a family link. A James Vashon appears as an admiral in 1815–26, of Cavendish Cres. in 1837 (but an Admiral Ballard not yet traced)
Balston, Rev. Edward, M.A.	5.3.44 ~	F 1839–50 King's	Asst Master Eton 1840–60, F Eton 1860–2, 1868–91, Headmaster 1862–8, R Hitcham, Berks 1868–9, V Bakewell, Derbys 1869–91, RD 1872, Archd. Derby 1873–91
Bamford, Robert	14.11.43 ~	Trinity	C Uttoxeter, Staffs 1848–9, C Norbury 1849–50, C Highworth, Wilts 1850–4, C Abbotts Ann, Hants 1855–7, C Mickleton, Glos 1857–65, V Little Dewchurch, Heref 1865–72, C St Mary Redcliffe, Bristol 1878–80, V Poulton, Glos 1881–4, retired, +1893
Bampfield, Rev. J.	?		Present at 1856 anniversary meeting, probably John William Lewis Bampfield, of Trinity, Oxford, B.A. 1844, chapl. Royal Navy Hospital, Malta, retired 1880, formerly of Fowey, Corn
Banks, Rev. Samuel Horatio, LL.D	8.11.41	Trinity Hall	V Dullingham, Cambs 1828–82, V Cowlinge, Suff 1828–52
Barber, R. O.	1850–1¢		Tulse Hill, a Mr Barber present at 1856 anniversary meeting
Barker, Joseph	6.12.41 ~ ¢¤‡	Christ's	C Ecclesball, Staffs 1844, C Berkswell w. Barston, Warks 1845–67, V Eardisland, Heref 1867–1901
Barnes, Rev. Henry F.	Founder ~ ¢‡	Clare Hall	C Doulting, Shepton Mallet, Som 1841–3, C S. Luke, Chelsea 1843–4, asst minister S. James, Ryde, I.O.W 1844–9, V Bridlington, Yorks 1849–74, R Birkin 1874–93, assumed additional name of Lawrence 1877 can. & preb. York 1886–96
Barnes, Rev. Joseph Watkins, M.A	Late 40 ~ ¢	F 1830 Trinity	V Swineshead, Lincs 1840–3, V Holy Trinity, Kendal, Westm 1843–58 where he had the church restored
Barnewall, W. G. V.	5.3.44 ~ ¢		81 Jermyn Street, London (Cavendish Hotel according to POLD where 'G. V. Barnewall' perhaps a long-term resident)
Barr, Alfred or Arthur	6.12.41 ~	Emmanuel	Alfred in AC, Arthur in Crockford, C Croydon, Surr 1847–8, C Glaston, Rutl 1849–65, in CL 1866 but no appointment given, disappears from CL 1867
Barraud, J.	?		Present at the 1862 anniversary meeting, not the stained glass maker whose initials were F. P., though it is quite possible that the J. is a mistranscription of F.
Barrett, G.	28.11.44 ~ ¢		247 Tottenham Court Road, London, of Wood & Barrett 'Ironfounders &c'

369

name	date elected	Cambridge college or other	Addresses/location given in *The Ecclesiologist*/ career details
Barrett, J.	21.2.42 ~		Town Hall Buildings, Manchester
#Barry, Charles	7.57¤		Architect (1823–1900), in office of father Sir Charles Barry (q.v.) 1840–6, ARIBA 1846, in partnership with R. R. Banks 1847–72, FRIBA 1854, President RIBA 1876–7, FSA 1876, Royal Gold Medal 1877
#Barry, Sir Charles, R.A.	21.6.59		Architect (1795–1860), hon. member, commenced practice 1820, FIBA 1834
Barry, Rev. Charles Upham, M.A.	8.11.41	Trinity Hall	C.S. Edward, Cambridge, 1841–7, PC S. John, Oakfield, Ryde, I.O.W 1847–55, then lived unbeneficed at Ryde, +1883
#Barry, Edward Middleton	6 or 7.58¤	King's, London	Architect (1830–80), Palace Yard, in offices of T. H. Wyatt and his father, Sir Charles Barry, ARIBA 1855, FRIBA 1860, assisted father till 1860, RA Professor of Architecture from 1873
Barry, T. D.	13.2.45 ~ ¢		Taunton, Somerset
Barton, Rev. Henry Jonas	Late 40 ~	Brasenose, Oxford	B.A. 1818, D 1822, P 1823, V Latton w. Eisey, Wilts 1830–8, R Wicken, Stony Stratford, Bucks 1838–72, hon. can. Peterborough, RD Preston 1841–52
#§Basevi, George, junior	<mid-40		Architect (1794–1845), 17 Savile Row, hon. member, pupil of Soane 1811–16, in practice from 1820, FIBA 1834, FSA, F.R.S.
+•Bastard, Edmond Rodney Pollexfen	28.11.44	Balliol, Oxford	B.A. 1846, membership lapsed by mid-1846, re-elected early 1849 when address is Kitley, Yealmpton, on ES committee 1849 perhaps until c.1856, +1856
Bateman, James	22.5.43		Congleton, Ches, probably of The Grange, Biddulph, not a member in mid-1844
Battley, Rev. C. Beynon	23.4.56¢	Worcester, Oxford	In CL 1852–67 but no appointment stated, of 48 Russell Square, London in 1856, of Braunton, Dev. in 1865, disappears from CL 1868
Bayles, Rev. Philip	22.11.41	Corpus Christi	R S. Mary-at-the-Walls, Colchester, Ess 1804–55
Bayley, Ven. Henry Vincent	8.11.41	F 1802 Trinity	Chapl. to Bp of Chester, R Stilton, Hunts 1804–6, V Hibaldstow, Lincs 1806–14, sub-dean & preb. Lincoln 1805–28 (active in beautifying and renovating the cathedral), V Messingham nr Bottesford, Lincs 1810–26, V Great Carlton 1812–44, Archd. Stow 1823–44, R West Meon & Privett, Hants 1826–44, repaired Privett church and built a new one at West Meon
Bayley, Rev. William Henry Ricketts, M.A.	1.5.41 ~ ¢	S. John's	Name given wrongly as Bailey and his place of education as 'Oxon.' in 1841 membership list, C Littleton-on-Severn, Glos 1831, PC Stapleton, Bristol 1842–7, C Lugwardine, Heref's 1854–60, V Nailsea, Bristol 1860–72
#Bayne, Robert Turnill	26.3.63¤		Stained glass maker (1837–1915), 24A Cardington Rd, Hampstead, N.W., joined Heaton & Butler Mar. 1862

Bayne, William Joseph, M.D.	10.11.42	F 1821 Trinity	M.D. 1830, Southampton, *later lived near Regent's Park*, +1844
Bayning, Rev. Lord *Henry Townsbend* M.A.	<mid-40	S. John's	*R Brome w. Oakley, Norf 1821-47, R Honingham w. East Tuddenham, Suff 1851-66, bon can. Norwich, 3rd Baron Beynon from 1823, lived at Honingham Hall, assumed name of William-Powlett 1842*
Beadon, Hyde Wyndham	8.11.41 ~ ¢¤‡	S. John's	*RD Latton, Cricklade, Wilts, V Haselbury Plucknett, Som 1837-69, V Latton w. Eisey, Wilts 1838-91, bon. can. Bristol 1859-91*
Beal, C. B.	1846 ~ ¢¤‡		*Hanley Road, London, of Stoke Newington in 1849-64, Eccl gives initials as E. B. but membership lists say C. B.*
*Beanlands, *Charles*	28.11.44 ~	S. Catharine's Hall	*C S. Paul, Brighton 1852-60, PC S. Michael, Brighton 1860-98, chapl. to Earl of Crawford & Balcarres 1868-98*
Beauchamp, Rev. William Henry, M.A.	7.11.44	Christ's	*PC Langley and R Chedgrave, Norf 1843-53*
Beaufort, Rev. *Daniel Augustus*	?	Trinity & Jesus	*Present at 2.5.55 meeting, chapl. to Portman Chapel 1843-8, R Lymm (Warburton mediety), Ches 1849-72, preacher Rochester dio.1872-98*
+*Bedford, Rev. Henry, M.A.	1848	S. Peter's	*5 Devonshire Terrace, New North Road, B.A. 1839, C Ilford, Ess in 1844, C Welton, Northants in 1846, C Christ Church, Hoxton 1847-50, ES auditor 1849-50 became RC 1850, resigned from ES 2.51 (BWD 11.2.51)*
Belaney, Andrew Lockhart	14.11.43	S. Peter's	*No career details in AC*
*Belaney, Rev. Robert	21.2.42	S. Catharine's Hall	*C Alwinton & Holystone, Northumb 1833, other curacies till 1843, V Arlington, Suss 1843-52, became RC 1852, at death 1899 was the oldest RC P in Great Britain (born 1804)*
Bell, Thomas	8.11.41 ~ ¢¤‡		*'Surgeon dentist', 17 New Broad Street, London*
#Bellhouse, Francis Taylor	5.12.43 ~ ¢		*Architect, Manchester, of 58 King St in 1850, of 39 Princess Street in 1856*
Bellman, Augustus Frederick	<mid-40 ~	S. Peter's	*C Hemsby, Norf 1843-53, V Moulton 1853-96, chapl. to Blofield Union 1888*
Benifold, John Smith	14.11.43 ~	Pembroke	*Master at a private school in Brighton*
Bennett, Henry Edward	6.12.41	S. John's	*Adm. Inner Temple 1845, called to the Bar 1848, lived in Canada for some years, of Sparkford Hall, Bath, J.P., +1897*
Bennet, W.	<mid-1840	S. John's	*BWD notes one Bennett was at what was probably the foundation meeting of the CCS, appears in Appendix 1 of Boyce's Memorial (not as a founder) but in no other list*
Bentinck, George Augustus Frederick *Cavendish*	Late 40 ~ ¢¤‡	Trinity	*Adm. Lincoln's Inn 1842, called to the Bar 1846, legal and political career, M.P. for Taunton 1859-65, for Whitehaven 1865-75, +1891*

name	date elected	Cambridge college or other	Addresses/location given in *The Ecclesiologist*/ career details
Beresford, Field Marshal Viscount, *William Carr*	11.5.42 ~		*Bedgbury, Kent, military career, distinguished commander in the Peninsular War, M.P. for Co. Waterford 1811–14, became Baron Beresford 1814, and Viscount 1823, purchased Bedgbury estate 1824, step-father of A. J. B. Hope (q.v.), + 1854*
Berger, Lewis	1846–7		*Hounslow, Middx*
Berners, Rev. *Ralph*	22.11.41 ~	*Magdalen, Oxford*	*B. A. 1823, D 1826, P 1827, R Harkstead, Suff 1833–58, R Erwalton w. Woolverstone (succeeding his father and patron H. D. Berners) 1835–58, RD Samford 1843, hon. can. Norwich 1845*
Berthon, *Edward Lyon*	6.12.41	Magdalene	*C Lymington, Hants 1845, V Fareham 1847–57, V Romsey 1860–91 (restored church), RD, surrogate dio. Winchester 1860–99, also an accomplished engineer, designed an observatory at Romsey*
Bertles, *William Dodsworth Bates*	11.5.42	Pembroke	*Eccl apparently wrongly gives 'Birtle, Rev. J. Oake, Milverton, Somersetshire'; W.D.B.B. was C Oake, Som 1842–4, evening lecturer at Milverton, 1844–6, V Dronfield, Derbys 1846–62, R Sevington, Kent 1862–9, chapl. to Earl of Mountcashel 1842–69*
Betham, *Charles Jepson*	1842–3	Emmanuel	*C Hugglescote, Leics 1847–8, C Farcet, Hunts 1850–9, R Brettenham, Suff 1859–1906, surrogate 1878–1906, hon. can. Ely 1886–1906, RD Lavenham 1889–1901*
Betham, James	22.5.43		*Congleton, Ches.*
Bevan, Alured	2 or 3.51¢‡		*16 Devonshire Place, London, the address of a Mrs Charles Bevan in 1850*
+ ●Bevan, Beckford, B.A.	1845 ~ ¢‡	Christ Church, Oxford	*Adm. Inner Temple 1845, ES auditor 1853–4, of 16 Devonshire Place, London in 1849–56, of Bury S. Edmund's 1864*
+ Bevan, *James Johnstone*	< mid-40 ~ ¢‡	Trinity	*On ES committee 1845–6, 1847–probably 1868, Treasurer 1850, of Calverly Park, Tunbridge Wells, Kent in 1849, of Bury St Edmund's in 1856–64, J.P., + 1898*
Birch, *Henry Mildred*	10.11.42	F 1841 King's	*Asst. master Eton 1844–9, T. to Prince of Wales 1848–51, R Prestwich w. Oldham, Lancs 1852–84, hon. can. Manchester, surrogate, RD Prestwich & Middleton, chapl.-in-ordinary to the Queen & Prince of Wales 1852, can. Ripon 1868, proctor in Convocation*
Birkett, *Edmund Lloyd, M.D*	1849–50	Caius	*M.D. 1847, 3 Cloak Lane, London, + 1903*
Birkett, Rev. Robert	6.12.41	F 1832–51 Emmanuel	*P 1833, + at Kelloe vicarage, Durham 1851*
Blackall, Rev. *Samuel*	8.11.41	F S. John's	*Not recorded as a F in AC, C Ixworth, Suff 1846–67, chapl. to Bp of Ely 1866–73, bon. can. Ely 1866–99, V Earls Colne, Ess 1867–89, chapl. to Bp of Winchester 1873–99, RD Halstead, Ess 1877–89, chapl. to General Hospital, Bury S. Edmund's, + 1899*
Blades, J., Mr	6.12.41		*Cambridge*

Name	Date	College	Details
Blake, William	5.12.42 ~ ¢	Trinity	C Cam, Glos 1846-8, PC High Leigh 1849-53, C S. George, Liverpool 1854-6, Head Penrith School 1857-9, C Dalston, Cumb 1859-61, R Wetheral w. Warwick nr Carlisle 1861-1904, + 1905
Blakesley, Rev. Joseph Williams, M.A.	28.11.44	F1831 & T 1839-45 Trinity	D 1833, P 1834, Select Preacher 1840 & 1843, V Ware, Herts 1845-72, can. Canterbury 1863-72, Dean of Lincoln 1872-85, Master of Mercers' Company 1864
*Blanchard, Henry Dacre	28.11.44 ~	Trinity	C Great Yarmouth 1849-51, C S. John, Worcester 1851-3, PC Kilnwick juxta Watton, Yorks 1853-8, C Beaminster, Dors 1859, R Middleton-on-the-Wolds, Yorks 1862-1904
•Blandy, Charles	14.11.43 ~ ¢¤‡		Reading, Berks
Blathwayt, Wynter Thomas	14.11.43 ~	Trinity	C Tean & Croxden, Staffs 1848-50, C Fisherton Delamere 1850-4, C Langridge, Som, 1854-61, R there 1861-7, C Leigh, Staffs 1869-75, R Dyrham, Glos 1875-1909
Blencowe, James, LL.B	1845 ~ ¢	Christ's	Adm. Lincoln's Inn 1844, +1888
*Blew, Rev. William John, M.A.	7.2.42	Wadham, Oxford	B.A. 1830, 16 Warwick Street, Pall Mall, London, I St. John-next-Gravesend, Kent 1842-50, thereafter no clerical appointment (Warwick Street remained his address in 1880), author of hymn books and books on prayer
Blick, Rev. Charles	8.11.41	F 1807-49 S. John's	R Wentworth, Cambs 1821-47, R Brandesburton, Yorks 1847-52
Bliss, Frederick	10.11.42 ~ ¢	Trinity	C Taverne Courtney & Farington, Dors 1848-58, R Hammoon, Dors 1858-61
Blofeld, Rev. Thomas Calthorpe	10.11.42	S. John's	Hoveton, Norfolk, V Bishop's Norton, Lincs 1802-19, V Felmingham, Norf 1804-19, V Hoveton S. Peter & S. John 1815-51, RD Waxham 1842-51, R Drayton w. Hellesdon 1851-5, FSA
•Bloxam, Matthew Holbeche	< mid-40 ~ ¢¤		Rugby, hon. member, writer on church architecture including The Principles of Gothic Ecclesiastical Architecture (first ed. 1829)
Blunt, Rev. John James, B.D	< mid-40	F n.d. S. John's	For many years C Hodnet, Salop and chapl. to Rev. Reginald Heber and his successor, R Great Oakley, Ess 1834-9, Lady Margaret's Professor of Divinity, 1839-55
Blunt, Rev. Walter, M.A.	1845	F 1824-7 King's	V Longstock, Hants 1843-9, then no appointment stated in CL but address given as Wallop House, Longstock till 1868, disappears from CL 1869, his career is wrongly given in AC which states he was V Newark whereas the V there was one J. G. Bussell
*Blunt, Rev. Walter, M.A.	1846	Caius	D 1838, P 1841, C S. Botolph without, Aldgate (n.d.), C Cheadle, Staffs, 1843-4, C Helston, Corn 1844-5 or '46, at Kemerton, Tewkesbury 1846-50, C S. Mary's Chapel, Sobo, London 1851, R Bicknor, Kent 1858-68 where he proposed to restore the church under 'my friend, Mr Bodley' (q.v.) (Eccl 20 (1859), 140-1), prolific ecclesiastical author
#Blyth, John	1848¢¤		Architect & Surveyor (in 1843-9), 113 Aldersgate Street, London

name	date elected	Cambridge college or other	Addresses/location given in *The Ecclesiologist* / career details
#Bodley, George Frederick	1849–50¤		Architect (1827–1907), Brighton, *first pupil of G. G. Scott 1845–50, began own practice 1856, in partnership with T. Garner 1869–97, A.R.A 1882, FRIBA 1899, Royal Gold Medal 1899, F.S.A.*
Boissier, George Richard M.A.	<mid-40 ~ ¢	Magdalene	Hon. member, *C Chiddingstone, Kent 1828–36, PC Oakfield, Penshurst 1836–58; author of Notes on the Cambridgeshire Churches (published anonymously, 1827), +1858*
Bolton, Frederic Samuel, B.A.	<mid-40 ~ ¢¤‡	S. John's	*Asst master Bridgenorth G.S., Salop 1839–50, V Salt, Staffs 1851–76, preb. Lichfield 1869, RD Stafford 1871–6, R Tattenhill 1876–80*
Borman, Chevalier de	?		Present at 1862 anniversary meeting, *probably did not become a member; possibly Camille de Borman (b. 1837) bibliophile and heraldist or Stanislas Bormans (b. 1835), conservator of the state archives, university administrator*
Bostock, Rev. Henry, M.A.	21.2.42 ~ ¢	Wadham, Oxford	Aylesbury, Bucks, BA 1830, *at Warrington G.S. in 1846 and 1858, not in Crockford 1865*
Boultbee, Thomas Pownall	8.11.41	F 1842 S. John's	*C Oldberrow, Worcs and of Morton Bagot in 1848, C Cheltenham in 1852, T & chapl.Cheltenham College 1852–63, Principal S. John's Hall, Highbury (or the London College of Divinity) 1864–84, preb. S. Paul's 1883–4*
Boulton, Matthew Piers Watt	13.2.43 ~ ¢¤‡	Trinity	*Of Tew Park and Haseley, Oxon, High Sheriff 1848, J.P., +1894*
Bowden, John William, M.A.	13.2.44	Trinity, Oxford	*Roehampton, B.A. 1820, adm. Lincoln's Inn 1819, a commissioner of stamps 1824–40, a close friend of Newman, +1844*
Bowdler, Rev. Thomas	22.5.44 ~ ¢	S. John's	*4 S. Martin's Place, London, C Leyton, Ess 1803–6, R Hopton Wafers, Salop 1806–20, R Ridley & Asb, Kent 1811–22, R Addington 1820–34, PC S. Bartholomew, Sydenham 1834 (CL says 1832–43), Secretary ICBS 1846–56, can. S. Paul's 1849–56, chapl. to the Club of Nobody's Friends' 1851–6, chapl. S. Katharine's Hospital, Regent's Park*
+Boyce, Rev. Edward Jacob, B.A.	Founder	Trinity	*Born 1814, adm. sizar S. John's 1836, migrated to Trinity 26.10.36, associate of Neale and Webb whom he accompanied to persuade T. Thorp (q.v.) to be President of CCS, CCS Treasurer 1839–40, at Holy Rood, Southampton in 1841, C Godalming, Surr 1841–7, V there 1847–65, R Houghton, Hants 1865–97, wrote to Memorial of the Cambridge Camden Society (1888)*
#Boyce, Philip	<mid-53		Architect (fl. 1856–9), 40 Albion Street, Leeds, *(designed Maltby, W. Yorks church, 1859)*
Boyce, William	22.11.41 ~ ¢¤	Emmanuel	*Master Cheltenham College in 1845–79, C Swindon, Wilts in 1846, R Elkstone, Glos 1888–93, +1904*
Brackenbury, Rev. John Matthew	11.6.60¤	S. John's	*Asst master Collegiate School, Huddersfield 1838–41, C S. Mary Magdalene nr Downham, Norf 1841–3, asst master Marlborough College 1843–9, kept a military school at*

Name	College	Date	Notes
Bradley, Rev. *Charles Richard*, M.A.	Queens'	7.11.44~	Wimbledon *with a partner 1850-60, Head Wimbledon School with Rev. C. J. Wynne 1860-82, +1895*
Braithwaite, *Thomas Lawton*	S. Peter's	1845~	C New Chapel-in-Ash, Canterbury, Kent 1841-4, no appointment listed in CL 1845-8, C Elton-on-the-Hill, Notts 1849-50 C Staveley, Derbys *according to AC but not traced in CL, +1851*
Brakyn, *Harriss Carr*		10.53¢	Asst surgeon, Army medical staff, *in Sierra Leone 1852-3, Gold Coast 1855, disappears from AL 1856*
#Brandon, *David*		16.6.63a	Architect (1813-97), 24 Berkeley Sq, *articled to G. Smith 1828-33, ARIBA 1839, partner of T. H. Wyatt 1838-51*
#Brandon, *Joshua Arthur*		1845	Architect (1822-47), *worked with brother J. R. Brandon (q.v.)*
#Brandon, *John Raphael*		1845a	Architect (1817-77), 11 Beaufort Buildings, London, *also elected 13.5.57 when address is Clements' Inn, Strand, pupil of J. Dedeau of Alençor and J. T. Parkinson of London, FRIBA 1860, worked with brother J. A. Brandon (q.v.)*
Braybrooke, The 3rd Lord, LL.D., *see Neville*			
Brecknock, Earl of, *see Pratt, G. C.*			
Brereton, Rev. *Randle Barwick*, B.A.	S. John's	1845~	C Pilton & North Wotton, Som 1843-5, R Stiffkey w. Morston, Norf 1845-83, + 1897
Brewer, Rev. *James Sherren*, M.A.	King's, London	11.5.43¢a	Professor of English Literature, *King's, London in 1858-70, preacher at Rolls Chapel, Chancery Lane in 1865-70, editor of Field on the Church*
Bridges, Rev. *Alexander Henry.*	Oriel, Oxford	3.12.66	C Spitalfields, London 1836-8, C Beddington, Croydon, *Surr 1838-41, C Horsham, Suss 1841-8, bought manors of Bandon and Beddington 1859, RD 1873-89, C Horsham, Suss 1841-58, PC Southwater 1858-64, R & patron there 1864-91, RD 1873-89, hon. can. Winchester 1873*
Brien, *George*	Trinity	7.11.44~	Adm. Inner Temple 1846
Briggs, *John Henry*		13.2.45~	3 Gloucester Road, Victoria Gate, London, *same address in 1849*
Bristol, Marquis of, *see Hervey*			
§Briton, *John*, F.S.A		<mid-41~¢	Antiquarian, topographer, writer *(1771-1857), hon. member, Burton St, London, author of the Beauties of England, Antiquities of Great Britain, Cathedral Antiquities, and, with A. C. Pugin, Specimens of Gothic Architecture (1823-5)*
Brocklebank, *Thomas*	F 1847-78 King's	28.11.44	D 1850, P 1851, *held various offices at King's (e.g. bursar), +1878*
Brodie, *William*, B.A.	Trinity	<mid-40	D 1844, P 1845, R New Alresford, Hants 1851-68, V East Meon 1868-82

name	date elected	Cambridge college or other	Addresses/location given in *The Ecclesiologist*/ career details
Brodrick, George-Alan, 5th Viscount Midleton	11.5.43 ~		Peper Harrow, Godalming, *Surr, succeeded 1833*
Brodrick, John Robert, M.A.	<mid-40 ~	Trinity	+ 1848
Brogden, Rev. James	<mid-40 ~	Trinity	R Great Henny, Ess 1841–5, C S. Michael, S. Albans 1845–8, V Dennington w. Clifton, Oxon 1848–64, author of Catholic safeguards against the errors, novelties and corruptions of the Church of Rome (1851) and other works
Bromhead, Alexander *Leslie*	13.3.43 ~ ¢¤‡	Caius	Married daughter of John Kaye, Bp of Lincoln 1847, R Winwick, Northants 1848–76, RD Haddon 1861, hon. can. Peterborough 1863
#Brooks, James	21.6.64¤	University, London	Architect (1825–1901), 11 Serle St, Lincoln's Inn, articled to L. S. Stride from 1847, pupil at R.A. Schools, began practice 1851, FRIBA 1866, architect to Canterbury dio. from 1888, in partnership with his son James Martin Brooks as James Brooks & Son and with G. H. Godsell of Hereford in c.1900 as James Brooks, Son & Godsell
Brooks, W.	13.2.45 ~ ¢	Clare or Jesus	Not traced in AC as Brooks or Brookes
Brooks, William Cunliffe	25.11.57‡		Barlow Hall, Manchester, banker of Cunliffe, Brooks & Co.
Broughton, Henry Vivian	<mid-40	S. Peter's	Left CCS <mid-1841, V Wellingborough, Northants 1842–71, hon. can. Peterborough 1869, R. Polebrook 1871–5, RD Oundle 1873, V S. Mary, Leicester 1875–93
Brown, Mr C. E.	18.4.42 ~		Cambridge
Brown, Rev. John, M.A.	<mid-40	Senior F 1801–48 Trinity	Vice-Master Trinity in 1840, career at Trinity, V Bottisham, Cambs 1828, + 1850
Brown, Samuel Christmas	<mid-40	S. John's	Appears in Appendix 1 of Boyce's Memorial (with surname wrongly given an 'e') but not traced in any other list, C Stapenhill, Derbys 1842–5, C S. Clement, Ipswich 1845–6, C Walton-in-Gordano, Som, 1847–8, C Shenfield, Ess 1848–52, C Marshfield 1852–8, C Gipping & Shelland, Suff 1858–70, V Great Clacton w. Little Holland, Ess 1870–91
Browne, Rev. *Edward Harold*	8.11.41 ~ ¢	F 1837–40 Emmanuel	PC Holy Trinity, Stroud 1837, PC S. James, Exeter 1841–2, PC S. Sidwell, Exeter 1842–3, vice-principal S. David's College, Lampeter 1843–9, V S. Kenwyn-cum-Kea, Corn 1849–57, preb. Exeter 1850, Norrisian Professor of Divinity 1854–64, V Heavitree, Dev 1857–64, can. Exeter 1857–64, Bp of Ely 1864–73, Bp of Winchester 1873–90, prelate of the Order of the Garter 1873, + 1891
Browne, Rev. *Thomas Murray*	8.11.41	Trinity	Standish, Glos, C All Hallows, Bread St, London, 1826, R Great Whitcomb, Glos 1837–9, V Standish w. Hardwick 1839–64, RD, bon. can. Gloucester 1844–58, V Almondsbury 1864–79
Brownlow, The Earl, *see* Cust			

Bryan, Reginald Guy	6.12.41 ~	Trinity	C Yelden, Beds 1844-6, PC Brightside, Sheffield , Yorks 1846-7, Vice-Principal Protestant College of Malta 1847-56, V Fosbury,Wilts 1856-75, Principal Monkton Combe School, Bath 1875-1900, +1912
•Brymer, Ven William, M.A.	<mid-41 ~	Trinity	R Charlton Mackrell, Som (own patron) 1821-52, can. Wells 1834, Archd. Bath 1839-52, residentiary can.1840-52
#Buckeridge, Charles	28.3.55¢¤		Architect (1832 or '33-73), 118 College Street, Camden Town. The initial is given wrongly as 'E.' in Eccl; in 1854 adm. studentship at R.A. school of architecture and also working in Scott's office, moved to Oxford and began practice 1856, ARIBA 1861, moved back to London 1869
Buckland, Rev. Josiah Rowles., D.D.	13.3.43	Sidney Sussex	D 1810, P 1811, Head Uppingham School 1824-39, V Peasmarsh, Suss 1833-58, +1858
•Buckle, George	1845~	F & T 1843-52 Oriel, Oxford	B.A. 1842, D 1846, P 1848, V Twerton, Bath, Son (patron Oriel) 1852-76, preb. Wells 1868, can. Wells 1887, examining chapl. to Ep of Bath & Wells 1872, R Weston-super-Mare 1876-88
Buckle, William H.	1845~		Ramsgate, Kent
Buckman, Mr J.	7.11.44 ~ ¢		Cheltenham, Glos
Buller, J. E.	7.11.44 ~ ¢		Chase Lodge, Enfield, Middx
Bumpsted, James Jeffries, B.A.	30.4.44	F 1843-57 King's	Second name 'Jeffreys' in AC and 'Jeffrey' in Crockford, C S. Mark, North Audley St 1848-51, lived at Guildford, +1874
Bunch, Rev. Robert James	6.12.41	F 1829 Emmanuel	C Toft, Cambs 1841-6, R Loughborough (patron Emmanuel College) 1848-70, can. Peterborough 1850-70, RD
Bund, Rev. Thomas Henry Benjamin, B.A.	<mid-40	Trinity	Stroud, Glos, called to the Bar 1835, +1846
#Bunning, John Bunstone	6.12.41 ~ ¢		Architect (1802-63), 34 Guildford Street, London, in office of father, D. J. Bunning (surveyor), articled to George Smith. FRIBA 1849
Burford, Arthur Howard	13.2.44 ~ ¢¤		49 Charing Cross, London, POLD (1844) gives Drummond & Co, bankers at this address
Burge, William, Q.C.	1845~		1 Paper Buildings, Temple, London
#Burges, William	1845 ~ ¢¤	King's, London	Architect (1827-81), 2 Lambeth Terrace, Lambeth, articled to E. Blore 1844, joined M. D. Wyatt as an improver 1849, joined H. Clutton 1851 first as asst, then partner till 1856, FRIBA 1860
Burkitt, Rev. William, M.A.	7.11.44 ~ ¢¤	S. Edmund Hall, Oxford	Bromfield, Maidstone, PC Leeds, Maidstone, Kent 1843-74, not in Crockford 1878

name	date elected	Cambridge college or other	Addresses/location given in *The Ecclesiologist*/ career details
#Burleigh, *Charles Walklett*	1847		Architect (*fl. 1840s–50s*), Leeds, probably working with Philip Boyce (q.v.), a design praised in Eccl 5 (1846), 82
§•Burney, Ven. *Charles Parr*, D.D.	1-5.41	*Magdalen, Oxford*	R Sible Hedingham, Ess 1838–48, RD, Archd. S. Albans 1841, Archd. Colchester 1845, R Wickham Bishops 1848–64
*Burney, Rev. *Henry*, M.A.	1848¢a	*Exeter, Oxford*	R Wavendon, Newport Pagnell, Bucks (*probably responsible for Butterfield's restoration 1848–9) 1847–92, RD Bletchley 1866*
Burns, Mr James	1846 ~		Bookseller & stationer, 17 Portman Street, London
Burrell, *Richard*	13.2.45 ~ ¢	Christ's	C Horbury, Yorks 1848–51, V Stanley S. Peter, nr Wakefield 1851–8
Burridge, *Richard*	Founder	S. John's	No longer a member in 1841–2, R Milton, Hants 1850–60, chapl. to the troops at Fort Cumberland, not in Crockford 1865
Burton, Rev. *Thomas Jones*	Founder	S. Peter's	*Paradoxically BWD (20.5.39) notes he joined but later (19.10.39) says he declined to join (but he was at a meeting a week later). Guestling, Hastings, not noted as 'Rev.' in AC, CL or Crockford, BWD (26.9.41) notes 'Rumours of Burton's Perversion to Rome'*
Bussell, Rev. *John Garrett*	13.2.43	*Trinity, Oxford*	V Newark, Notts 1835–74, preb. Lincoln from 1859–74
§Butler, Rev. Dr. *George*	6.12.41 ~	T Sidney Sussex	Adm. Lincoln's Inn 1794, Head Harrow School 1805–29, R Calverton, Bucks 1814–21, R Gayton, Northants 1814–53, Chancellor of Peterborough 1836–42, Dean there 1842–53, brilliant mathematician and classical scholar
*Butler, Rev. *William John*, B.A.	10.11.42 ~	Trinity	Crondall, Farnham, C Dogmersfield, Hants 1841–3, C Puttenham, Surr 1843–4, C Wareside, Herts 1844–6, V Wantage, Berks 1846–80, RD, founder & warden of the Sisterhood of S. Mary's, Wantage 1850, hon. can. Christ Church, Oxford, can. Worcester 1880–5, Dean of Lincoln 1885–94
#Butterfield, *William*	11.5.44 ~ ¢¢‡		Architect (*1814–1900*), 4 Adam Street, Adelphi, London, apprenticed to Thomas Arber, a builder in Pimlico 1831–3, then an architectural student till 1840 when he set up office at Lincoln's Inn Fields, FSA 1881, RIBA Gold Medal 1884
Caddy, Rev. *Thomas*	13.2.45		PC Whitbeck, Cumb 1825–47. Eccl has the Rev. Caddy Thomas of Brandiston, Norwich; this seems reversal of his names but there is no apparent connection between T.C. and Brandiston; no C.T. has been traced in AC, AO or CL 1841–8
+*Caffin, Rev. *Charles Smart*	22.6.52¢a	*Caius*	C Chislehurst, Kent 1841–7, PC Holy Trinity, Crockham Hill 1849–52, V Milton-by-Sittingbourne 1852–62, ES auditor 1855–6, V Broadway, Worcs 1862–87
Calthrop, *Henry*	<mid-40	Senior F 1826 & T Corpus Christi	Archd. Derby 1840–1, R Great Braxted, Ess 1841–75, preb. S. Paul's 1841, preb. Lichfield 1841–76, +1887
Camden, 2nd Marquis & Earl, *see Pratt, G. C.*			

Campden, Viscount, see Noel

*Campion, Rev. Charles Heathcote, M.A. | Christ Church, Oxford | 1847–8¢¢‡ | Eccl gives second initial as 'W', apparently wrongly, B.A. 1836, C 1840, P 1841, I Westmeston, w. Chiltington, Suss (patron G. Campion) 1848–89, preb. Chichester 1870

Cane, Edward, B.A. | Trinity, Oxford | 14.11.43 | 105 Piccadilly, London, adm. Lincoln's Inn 1832

Capel, George, B.A. | Queens' | Founder~ | B.A. 1840, no other details in AC

Carington, Lady Charlotte Augusta Annabella | | 21.6.64¤ | 2nd wife of the 2nd Baron Carington of Upton, Notts, one of only two female members, see also Gibbs

Carlos, Edward John | | <mid-40~ | Hon. member, antiquary, solicitor in Lord Mayor's Court Office, 7 Old Jewry, London, also at 3 Gloucester Buildings, Walworth, various contributions to Eccl, e.g. 2 (1843), 49, 96, 7 (1847), 141–2

Carlyon, Rev. Philip | Emmanuel | 22.11.41~¢¤‡ | 3 High Street, Colchester, PC S. James, Exeter 1842–56, PC Revelstoke, Dev 1856–61, V Widecombe-in-the-Moor 1861–9, R Wisbech, Cambs 1869–81, chapl. to Bp Winchester, +1913 aged 102

Carpenter, George, B.A. | S. John's | <mid-40~¢¤‡ | C S. George's-in-the-East in 1846 C Cirencester, Glos in 1847–52, V Stapleford, Wilts 1854–65, V S. Luke, Christchurch, N.Z c.1868–70, V Moka, Mauritius & Dio. Secretary (S.P.G) Mauritius 1871–85, chapl. to Sir R. Menzies 1884–5, +1893

#•Carpenter, Richard Cromwell | | 1.5.41~ | Architect (1812–55), 99 Guildford St, Russell Sq, London, articled to J. Blyth, FRIBA 1853, in 1853 of 4 Carlton Chambers, Regent St & 40 Upper Bedford Place, Russell Sq.

#Carpenter, Richard Herbert | | 17.3.66 | Architect (1841–93), 4 Carlton Chambers, Regent St, London son of R. C. Carpenter (q.v.), articled to W. Slater 1857, was Slater's partner 1863–72, partner of B. Ingelow 1878–93, ARIBA 1863

Carter, William Adolphus, M.A. | F 1837–45 King's | 5.3.44~ | Asst master Eton 1839–57, lower master 1857–64, F. & Eursar Eton 1864, V Burnham w. Boveney, Bucks 1869–78, R Worpledon w. Burnham, Surr 1878–86, V S. Alban, Wood St, London 1886–1901, R S. Olave, Silver St & S. Michael, Wood St & S. Mary, Staining, Middx 1896–1901

Cartmell, Rev. James, M.A. | F 1833 & T 1839–49 Christ's | 1.5.41 | Master of Christ's 1849–81, Vice-Chancellor 1849, 1865, 1866, chapl. to the Queen 1851–81

#Castellani, Sig. | | 24.6.62¤ | Probably Fortunato Pio Castellani (1794–1865), hon. member, began in business in Rome 1814, founding a dynasty of goldsmiths, collectors, antiquarians and ceramicists, started a goldsmith's workshop in Rome c.1840 to revive ancient styles and methods for young goldsmiths. Possibly his son, Alessandro, who carried on the business was a distinguished antiquary and collector who sold his collection to the British Museum 1876.

name	date elected	Cambridge college or other	Addresses/location given in *The Ecclesiologist*/ career details
#Cates, A. H.	14.11.43 ~		Architect, York, designed *Markington church* (*W. Yorks*, 1844)
Cattley, W. C., B.A.	<mid-40 ~ ¢	Trinity	*Probably William Esdale Cattley, adm. Lincoln's Inn 1840*
*Cavendish, *Charles William*	14.11.43 ~	Trinity	*C Christ Church, S. Pancras, London 1847, R Little Casterton, Rutl 1848–50, became a R.C., +1890*
+Cavendish, Lord Richard	25.5.64□	*Trinity*	On ES committee 1864–probably 1868, grandson of 1st Earl of Burlington
Cayley, *Arthur*, B.A.	<mid-40 ~ ¢□‡	F 1842–52 Trinity	*T. 1843–6, adm. Lincoln's Inn 1846, conveyancer, called to the Bar 1849, Sadlerian Professor of Mathematics 1863–95*
+Cecil, Lord *Robert Albert Talbot Gascoigne*, M.P.	17.1.55¢□	*Christ Church, Oxford*	*F 1853 All Souls*, on ES committee 1855–65, M.P. Stamford 1853–68, Chancellor of Oxford University from 1869, succeeded as 3rd Marquis of Salisbury 1868, political offices, Prime Minister 1885–6, 1886–92, 1895–1902, +1903
*Chambers, *John Charles*, B.A.	7.2.42 ~ ¢□	Emmanuel	*C Sedbergh 1842, missionary priest Perth, Australia 1846–50, can. & Chancellor of Perth Cathedral 1850–5, V Harlow, Ess, 1853–6, Warden of House of Charity, Soho 1856–74, PC S. Mary the Virgin, Soho 1857–74*
+Chambers, *John David*, M.A.	13.2.43 ~ □	Oriel, Oxford	*Barrister, 3 Old Square, Lincoln's Inn, London 1831, Recorder of Salisbury from 1842, ES auditor 1846–7, Treasurer 1847–50, on committee 1850–probably to 1868, author of Divine Worship in England in the Thirteenth and Fourteenth Centuries contrasted with that in the Nineteenth (2nd. ed, London, 1877), Eccl wrongly gives his name as 'J. D. Chamberlain' but this is corrected in Boyce's Memorial*
+Chandler, Rev. *George*, D.C.L.	11.5.42 ~ ¢	New College, Oxford	Bampton Lecturer 1825, R All Souls, Marylebone in 1825–7, Dean of Chichester 1830–59, a ES vice-president 1845–58
#Chantrell, *Robert Dennis*	11.5.43 ~ ¢		Architect (1793–1872), Leeds, *pupil of Soane 1807–14, practised in Leeds from 1819, moved to London 1846*
#Chantrey, Sir *Francis Legatt*, Bart	<mid-40 ~	Trinity	*Sculptor (1781–1841), hon. member, knighted 1835*
Charles, Rev. *Samuel*, B.A.	Founder ~ ¢□‡	Trinity	*D 1842, P 1844, C Ringshall, Suff 1848–65, then career in education, disappears from Crockford 1892*
Charlton, *Charles*	10.39	St John's	Election date from BWD (29.10.39), C Slapton, Northants 1842–3, C Cranford 1843–4, PC Alvrick, Northumb 1846–68
#Chester, Francis	1846 ~ ¢		Architect (c.1812–81), Manchester
Chevallier, Rev. *Temple*	8.11.41	F 1819 Pembroke, F& T 1820	S. Catharine's Hall R *S. Andrew the Great, Cambridge 1821–34, Hulsean Lecturer 1826, PC Esh, Durham, 1835–69, RD 1858, Professor of Mathematics, Durham 1835–71, Registrar 1835–72, Professor of Astronomy 1841–71, hon. can. Durham 1846–65, can. residentiary 1865–73, also a classical scholar*

Name	Date	College	Description
Chidley, Richard	13.2.45 ~¢¤		Cheesemonger, 118 Whitechapel Road, London
Chisholm, Alexander	6.12.41	S. John's	B.A. 1841, apparently, returned to Australia
Cholmondeley, Charles	1846	Balliol, Oxford	Became a can. in the RC Church
Churchill, Rev. John, M.A.	13.2.45	Worcester, Oxford	Sholapore, Bombay, chapl. of Bombay Presidency 1843-69, R Croxall, Oxon 1874-79
Clapham, Rev. Charles, M.A.	13.2.44	Trinity	C Leeds, PC Armley, Leeds, 1822-48
#Clark, John Medland	10.11.42 ~		Architect (1813-49), Ipswich, Eccl apparently wrongly adds an 'e' to his surname
+Clark, John Willis, M.A.	2.5.60¤	F 1858 Trinity	On ES committee 1860-5, superintendent of Museum of Zoology 1866-91, President CAS 1883-4, FSA, completed and partly rewrote Willis's Architectural History of the University and Colleges of Cambridge, +1910
Clark, Philip	7.11.44	Queens'	Surname incorrectly given as 'Clarke' in Eccl, +1845 aged 24
Clark, Rev. William, M.D.	1.5.41 ~¢¤‡	Trinity	Professor of Anatomy 1817-66, V Arrington, Cambs 1824-5, V Wymeswold, Leics 1825, R Guiseley, Yorks 1826-59 (non-resident but restored the church and rectory and built new schools), F.R.S.
Clark, William George	6.12.41 ~	Trinity	F 1844-78, D 1853, P 1854, T 1857-66, Lady Margaret Preacher 1868, traveller, translator and writer, relinquished orders 1870, +1878
Clarke, J., M.A.	1.5.40 ~¢	Queens'	Possibly James Langton Clark, B.A. 1829, migrated to Australia c.1855
Clarke, J.	5.3.44	S. Peter's	Not traced in AC
Clarke, J. M., see Clark, J. M.			
Clarke, James Sanderson	6.12.41 ~¢¤‡	S. John's	C S. George's-in-the-East, London 1844-7, C Denham, Suff 1848-54, C Lewisham, Kent 1857-8, V All Saints, Blackheath, Kent 1858-64, V Goudhurst 1864-1911
Clarke, Joseph	22.11.41	Corpus Christi	Probably the subject was C Sowerby Bridge, Yorks 1844-6, C S. Margaret, Leicester 1846-8, C Leyton, Ess 1848-58, C S. Mary, Woodford 1858-73, V Eling, Hants 1885-97. Another Joseph Clarke of Corpus Christi was F 1839-54, C Middleton Tyas, Yorks 1841, Mildmay Preacher 1849-51, R Kegworth, Leics w. Isley Walton 1853-93, + 1894
#•Clarke, Joseph, FSA	15.12.53		Architect (1819 or '20-1888), articled to J. Griffith, ARIBA 1841, FRIBA 1850, diocesan surveyor to Canterbury and Rochester, and to S. Albans 1871
#Clayton, John Richard	11.6.60¤		Stained glass artist (1827-1913), Cardington St, Hampstead Rd, London, joined by Alfred Bell as a partner in 1855

name	date elected	Cambridge college or other	Addresses/location given in The Ecclesiologist/ career details
Clifford, John	14.11.43 ~	Trinity	C Fladbury, Worcs in 1854, no clerical appointment in 1858, in 1860 described as late C Standish w. Hardwicke, Glos and formerly of Guilsborough, Northants, PC Chipping Sodbury, Glos 1859–61, V Alderton, Wilts 1864–7, then without cure till + 1894
Clive, Viscount see Herbert			
Close, Thomas	13.2.43 ~ ¢		Nottingham, in 1854 mentioned as a 'proprietor' in S. James's St
#Clutton, Henry	6.54¢		Architect (1814–95), 26 Charles St, London, pupil of E. Blore 1835–40, in practice by 1844/5, FRIBA 1854, paper on Ste Chapelle, Paris Eccl 17 (1856), 247–53
Cochrane, Alexander Wishart Baillie M.P.	10.11.42	Trinity	Public service and political career, well-known in society, was the 'Buckhurst' in Disraeli's Coningsby
#§Cockerell, Charles Robert, B.A.	< mid-40		Architect (1788–1863), hon. member, Bank of England, in office of father, S. P. Cockerell from age of 16, and of Sir Robert Smirke 1809–10, architect to Bank of England from 1833, hon. FRIBA 1836, FRIBA 1849, President RIBA 1860–1
+*Codd, Rev. Edward Thornton	Founder ~ ¢¤‡	S. John's	A CCS secretary 1839–40, committee member 1840–1, 1842–4, but not a member from mid-1844, C Minchinhampton, Glos 1840, at S. Giles, Cambridge in 1842–3, PC Cotes Heath, Staffs 1844–59, V Bishop's Tachbrook, Warks 1859–77, disappears from Crockford 1878
Coddington, Rev. Henry, M.D., F.R.S	< mid-40	Late F 1820 & T 1822–33 Trinity	V Ware w. Thundridge, Herts 1832–45, RD, F.R.S 1829, good linguist and an excellent musician
Cole, Augustus William	Founder	S. John's	C Sundridge, Kent 1846, PC Ide Hill 1847–50, PC Langcliffe, Yorks 1852–4
Coleridge, Rev. Edward, M.A.	1845 ~ ¢¢‡	Corpus Christi, Oxford, & F 1823–6 Exeter	Of Ottery, Dev, gentleman, asst master Eton College 1824–50, lower master 1850–7, F 1857, assisted A. J. B. Hope (q.v.) to convert S. Augustine's, Canterbury into a missionary training college, V Mapledurham, Berks 1862–83
+Collison, Rev. Frederick William	Late 40 ~ ¢¢‡	F 1838–55 S. John's	On CCS committee 1841–2, Treasurer 1842–4, auditor 1844–5, senior dean 1845–53, PC Horningsea, Cambs 1842–4, R Marwood, Dev. 1853–86, restored the chancel there, RD, +1889
+Colson, Rev. Charles, M.A.	Founder ~ ¢	F 1840 S. John's	A CCS secretary 1839–40, committee member 1841–2, C S. Giles, Cambridge 1841, PC Hoddesdon, Herts 1842, R Great Hormead 1842–74 (restored the church there under Blomfield 1872–3), RD Rochester 1874–9, R Cuxton, Kent 1874–1901, can. Rochester 1874–1901
Colvile, Joseph William, M.A.	18.4.42	Trinity	32 Curzon Street, Mayfair, London, distinguished legal career, +1880
Compigné, J. Henry	13.2.45 ~ ¢		Middle Temple, London, the initial 'J.' is not accounted for in POLD which gives address as 24 Bucklersbury in 1845

Compton, Paulet Mildmay	Trinity	10.11.42 ~ ¢	C Milford (county not traced) 1847–8 (not traced in CL 1848), R Mapperton w. Witherstone, Dors 1848–1906
§•Compton, Spencer Joshua Alwyne, 2nd Marquess of Northampton, LL.D	Trinity	<mid-40	President of the Royal Society, succeeded 1828, +1851
Constable, J. C.	Jesus	<3.41	BWD (21.3.41) notes 'Constable of Jesus, a Camdenian, died of scarlet fever', 1841 Report notes his death on 20.3.41
Constable, Marmaduke		8.11.41	Walcot, Brigg, Lincs, BWD (6.9.41) notes that Marmaduke Constable, a Roman Catholic, proposed for CCS.'
Conybeare, Rev. William John	F 1839 Trinity	8.11.41	Adm. Lincoln's Inn 1840, Whitehall Preacher 1841–3, 1st Principal Liverpool Collegiate Institution 1842–8, succeeded his father as V Axminster, Dev 1848–54, author of a life of S. Paul, +1857
Cook, Edward Richard	Trinity	<mid-40	Left CCS <mid-41, adm. Middle Temple 1837, called to the Bar 1843, +1886
Cooke, T. B.	Trinity	28.11.44 ~	Possibly Thomas Henry Cooke of Stourport, Worcs, M.P. for E. Worcs 1832–5 and 1835–7, + 1901
Cooke, William, B.A.	Trinity Hall	Late 40 ~ ¢¤‡	C Hillingdon, Middx 1844–6, C Brantham, Suff, 1846–8, PC S. John, Charlotte St, London 1848–50, Examining Chapl. to Bp of Chester 1849–57, Select Preacher 1850, PC S. Stephen, Shepherd's Bush 1850–6, V Gazeley, Suff 1856–66, hon. can. Chester 1854–94, FSA 1874, editor of The Church Hymnal, and, with Webb, The Hymnary, author of various works e.g. Of Ceremonies, Lights and Customs etc.
Cookson, Rev. Henry Wilkinson, M.A.	F 1836 & T 1839 S. Peter's	10.11.42	Master of S. Peter's 1847–76, five times Vice-Chancellor, V Glaston, Rutl 1847–61, prominent in University affairs distinguished geologist, +1876
Coombe, Thomas, B.A.	Trinity	11.5.43 ~	C All Saints, Brighton 1844–52, PC here 1852–86, surrogate
Coombe, Rev. Thomas, M.A.	S. Peter's	7.2.42 ~	D 1821, P 1822, C Frittenden, Kent, C Waterbeach, Cambs, R Girton 1846–9, then no clerical appointment, + 1876, on election Eccl wrongly suggests he was an Oxford man. (corrected in the membership lists)
Cooper, George Henry	Trinity	22.11.41 ~	Adm. Inner Temple 1844, called to the Bar 1848, legal career, +1890
Cooper, Rev. John, M.A.	F 1837–9 & T 1837–55 Trinity	<mid-40	Senior Dean 1855–8, BWD (26.11.41) notes his resignation from CCS, V S. Andrew the Great, Cambridge 1843–58, Proctor in Convocation 1858–65, V Kendal, Westm 1858–96, hon. can. Carlisle 1861–83, Archd. Westmorland 1865–96, can. Carlisle 1883–96
Cope, Sir William Henry, 12th Bart	Trinity, Dublin	1.7.62¤	B.A. 1831, M. A. Magdalen Hall, Oxford 1840, minor can. Westminster Abbey and librarian there 1842–53, chapl. Westminster School 1843–51

name	date elected	Cambridge college or other	Addresses/location given in *The Ecclesiologist*/ career details
Corbett, *Edwin*	<mid-40	Trinity	*Adm. Inner Temple 1843, diplomatic career overseas, +1858*
Corles, Rev. *Harry*, M.A.	5.12.42	Trinity	*Initial given as 'A.' in Eccl, 3rd master Bury S. Edmund's G.S. c.1832-52, R Langham, Suff 1852-85, +1897*
Cornish, Rev. *Richard Pering*	1849-50	Christ Church, Oxford	*B.A. 1846, D 1847, P 1848, Lanreath, Looe, Corn, C Ashburton, Dev in 1852, PC Ivybridge from 1855, in 1865 Crockford describes him as formerly of Ivybridge*
+Corrie, Rev. Prof. *George Elwes*	Founder	F 1817 & T S. Catherine's Hall	*Norrisian Professor of Divinity 1838-54, a CCS vice-president from 1840, Master of Jesus 1849-85, a founder of CAS, R Newton, Cambs 1851-85, RD Wisbech 1851-78*
Cory, Rev. *Robert*	6.12.41	F 1825 Emmanuel	*C Barton, Cambs 1831, V Stanground w. Farcet, Hunts 1842-85*
Cotton, *Alexander*	8.11.41		Hildersham Hall, Cambs
Cotton, Rev. *George Edward Lynch*	8.11.41	F 1838 Trinity	*Asst master Rugby (the 'young master' of Tom Brown's Schooldays) 1837-52, Head Marlborough School 1852-8, Bp of Calcutta 1858-66*
•Courtenay, Viscount *William Reginald*, M.A.	10.11.42~	*Christ Church, Oxford*	*F (1828-31) All Souls, Oxford, Powderham Castle, Exeter, styled Lord Courtenay 1835 till 1859 when he succeeded as 11th Earl of Devon , M.P. S. Devon 1841-9, 1859, Chancellor of Duchy of Lancaster 1866-7, +1888*
Coward, *Thomas*	<mid-40 ~ ¢¤‡	Queens'	*No details available*
Cox, *Frederick Holdship*	Late 40 ~ ¢¤‡	Pembroke	*C Iping, Suss 1844-6, chapl. Tasmania, Warden of Christ's College 1846-9, V S. John, Hobart 1849-67, Dean of Hobart 1872-4, V Tilney All Saints w. S. Lawrence, Norfolk 1874-7, R Fen Ditton, Cambs 1877-83, V Elm 1883-96, RD Wisbech 1886-96, hon. can. Ely 1898-1906*
Craig, Rev. *John*	10.11.42~	Trinity, Dublin	*R Fetcham, Surr 1836-9, V Leamington Priors, Warks 1839-77*
+Cranborne, Viscount	<1865		On ES committee by 1865 (date of original election unknown), brother-in-law of Beresford Hope (*q.v.*), +1865
Crawley, *Charles*	1845 ~ ¢¤‡		Littlemore, Oxon
§Cripps, Rev. *John Marten*, M.A.	7.11.44 ~ ¢	S. John's	*R Great Yeldham, Ess 1843-87, +1893*
Crispin, *Alfred Trevor*	1848¢		70 Welbeck Street, London, *not traced in* POLD, in 1853 of Treasury, Whitehall, London
Crompton, *George*	13.2.43~	Trinity	*No details in AC*
Crompton, Rev. *John Laker*	10 or 11.50¢		Member of the Musical Committee in 1854, C Marylebone All Saints, London 1840-53, can. Maritzburg Cathedral 1875-89, V S. Andrew, Pinetown, Natal, +1889
Crosse, Rev, Dr	6 or 7.58¤		S. Leonards-on-Sea, *not traced in Crockford 1858*

Name	College	Date	Notes
#Crossland, William Henry		5.12.61¤	Architect (c.1834–1909), Halifax, pupil of G. G. Scott, began practice in Halifax c.1860, in Leeds by 1863, FRIBA 1867
#Cundy, Thomas, jun.		6 or 7.50¢¤	Architect (1820–95), assisted father, Thomas, from late 1840s, then practised alone, FRIBA 1857, various surveying posts
+Currey, Rev. George, M.A.	F 1839 S. John's	8.11.41	On CCS committee 1843–4, Whitehall Preacher 1845, Preacher of the Charterhouse 1849–71, Hulsean Lecturer 1850–2, Master 1871–85, preb. S. Paul's 1872–85
Curzon, Hon. Edward Cecil, M.A	Christ Church, Oxford	18.4.42	17 Connaught Terrace, adm. Lincoln's Inn 1840, barrister-at-law, Registrar of Companies 1855–76, +1885
Curzon, Hon. Robert, jun.		1847¢	Parham Park, Steyning, Suss
Cusack, Henry Thomas	Caius	<mid-40	Adm Lincoln's Inn 1842, +1865
§Cust, Hon. & Rev. Henry Cockayne, M.A.	Trinity	<mid-40 ~ ¢	R Cockayne Hatley, Beds 1806–61 (repaired church in 1820s, adding Continental furnishings 1826–7), R Sywell, Northants 1806, V Middle Rasen, Drax, Lincs 1806–32, can. Windsor 1813-61, R Scott Willoughby, Lincs from 1823–61, FSA
Cust, John, The Earl Brownlow, LL.D	Trinity	13.2.43	Cavendish Square, London, B.A. 1301, 2nd Baron, created Earl 1815, +1853
#Cuypers, Petrus Josephus Hubertus		24.6.62¤	Architect (1827–1921), graduated from the Koninklijke Akademie, Antwerp 1849, began practice in Roermond where he founded a workshop of artists and craftsmen, undertook building contracts in addition to making the designs, moved to Amsterdam 1865 but kept the workshop in Roermond, developed the largest Dutch C19 practice, was especially active in the N. of the country, awarded the RIBA Gold Medal 1898, particularly noted for his RC churches, the Rijksmuseum and Central Station in Amsterdam, present at 1862 anniversary meeting
*Dale, Thomas Pelham	Sidney Sussex	13.2.43	C Camden Chapel, Camberwell, London 1845–7, R S. Vedast, Foster Lane 1847–81, Librarian Sion College 1851–6, gaoled at Holloway for ritualistic practices at S. Vedast Oct. 1880–Jan. 1881, R Sausthorpe-cum-Aswardby, Lincs 1881–92
Dance, Henry Anderson	Queen's, Oxford	1845~	C Pucklechurch, Glos 1848, C Westerleigh, Glos in 1849–50, C Pattishall (1st mediety), Northants 1851–4, C Heyford, Northants in 1858-9, in CL from 1860 but no appointment listed, disappears from CL 1868
Darnell, Captain R. M. or R. B.		28.11.44 ~ ¢¤	Clifton, York (address confirmed in Slater's Directory (1848) but not traced in AL 1825–48 or NL 1823–45)
Darnell, Rev. William Nicholas	Corpus Christi, Oxford	1845 ~ ¢	B.A. 1796, preb. Durham, R Stanhope, Darlington, Co. Durham 1831–65
Daukes, Henry	Caius	13.2.43 ~	C Toft, Cambs 1846–7

name	Cambridge college or other	date elected	Addresses/location given in *The Ecclesiologist*/ career details
#Daukes, *Samuel Whitfield*		22.5.44 ~ ¢¤	Architect (1811–1880), Gloucester, *pupil of J. P. Pritchett of York, commenced practice c.1837, moved to London 1848*
Davenport, *Arthur*	Christ's	8.11.41 ~ ¢¤‡	C.S. Matthew, Ipswich 1845–6, V Holy Trinity, Hobart, Tasmania 1846–80, Archd. Hobart 1880–8, can. S. David's Cathedral, Hobart 1888–92, returned to England, + 1907
*Dawson, *William*	*Exeter, Oxford*	?	Present at 1862 anniversary meeting, C Hopton, Norf 1859–62, C S. James mission, Great Yarmouth 1862–9, C Chardstock, Dev. 1869–70, I S. John, Clerkenwell, London 1870
Daymond, Rev. *Charles*	S. Mark's, Chelsea	< mid-56 ¢¤	*Normal* mastership S. Mark's, Chelsea 1850–8, Principal S. Peter's Training College, Peterborough 1858–92, minor can. Peterborough from 1865, sacristan 1867–9, Precentor 1869, disappears from Crockford 1899
Dealtry, Rev. & Worshipful, *William,* D.D. 1-5.41	F 1798, T 1801–16 Trinity		Professor of Mathematics, Haileybury College 1805–13, R Clapham, Surr 1813–47, R Hatfield Broadoak, Ess 1814–16, R Watton, Herts 1816–30, R Clothall 1816–30, Chancellor, Dio. Winchester 1830–45, Archd. Surrey 1845–7, *unusually, be was a prominent Evangelical who joined the CCS (perhaps briefly)*
*•Dean, Rev. *Edward Brietzcke*	*Christ Church, Oxford*	1847	F 1836–55 All Souls, Oxford, V Lewknor, Oxon 1842–55, became RC 1855
§Deane, Rev. *John Bathurst*	Pembroke	6.12.41 ~ ¢¤‡	Finsbury Circus, London, *asst master Merchant Taylors' School* 1836–55, C S. Benetfink & of S. Michael, Wood St (n.d.), Bishopsgate 1855–87, R S. Helen w. S. Martin Outwich 1855–87, *author of various archaeological works*
Dearden, James		5.3.44 ~	*Magistrate,* Rochdale
Deck, Mr Norris		6.12.41 ~ ¢¤‡	Cambridge, received subscriptions for the CCS in 1843 while based at Stevenson's *(the publishers) read paper on the ecclesiology of Cambs to the ES* 1859, *of 11 Trumpington St in* 1865
Deighton, *John,* Mr		< mid-40	Cambridge, *'bookseller, stationer, publisher and agent to the University' in 1851, published* Hierurgia Anglicana
Deighton, *J.J.,* Mr		< mid-40	Cambridge, *possibly a duplication of the above, but clearly shown separately from the above in the membership lists*
de la Warr, Earl, LL.D., *see West*			
Dennis, *Samuel*	Trinity	< mid-40	*B.A.* 1842
Devoucoux, L'Abbé		1846 ~	Can. Autun; hon. member
de Winton, Henry	Trinity	14.11.43 ~ ¢¤	R Broughrood, Radnors 1849–81, RD Brecon 1864–80, Proctor of S. David's 1865–75, surrogate, Archd. Brecon 1875–95, R Cefnllysw Llandrindod, Radnors 1881–95

Name	Date	College	Details
Dickenson, E.	10.11.42 ~ ¢¤‡	Trinity	*Probably Edmund Henry Dickenson, B.A. 1843, adm. Inner Temple 1843, called to the Bar 1849, J.P., +1896*
Dicker, Hamilton	7.5.50		*Lewes, Suss*
+Dickinson, Francis Henry,	<mid-40 ~ ¢	Trinity	*Adm. Inner Temple 1835, a founder of Wells Theological College 1840, M.P. W. Somerset 1841–7, on ES commitee 1845–6, 1847–probably 1868, Treasurer 1846–7, contributed to The Guardian 1846–90, in 1853 of 8 Upper Harley St, rebuilt church at Kingsweston, Som. 1854, + 1890*
Didron, Adolphe-Napoléon	1846 ~ ¢¤	Trinity	*Hon. member (1806–67), founder and editor of the Annales Archéologiques (1844–65), secretary of the Comité Historique des Arts et Monuments, began a stained glass works in 1849 and a brass foundry in 1858, obituary in Eccl 29 (1868), 340–9*
Dobinson, Francis,	30.4.44 ~	S. John's	*Adm. Lincoln's Inn 1847, called to the Bar 1850, assumed name of Logan in lieu of Dobinson 1866*
Dobson, Thomas William	10.11.42	Corpus Christi	*Of Lancashire, no other details available*
+*Dodsworth, Rev. William, M.A.	8.11.41 ~	Trinity	*Gloucester Gate, Regent's Park, London, minister Margaret St Chapel, Cavendish Sq., London 1829–37, PC Christ Church, S. Pancras 1837–51, ES auditor 1846–7, a vice-president 1849–50, became RC after Gorham judgement, +1861*
Domville, Charles Compton William	1847		*5 Grosvenor Sq., London, succeeded as 2nd Bar't Domville 1857, also seat at Templeoge and Santry House, Co. Dublin*
Domville, David Edward, B.A	<mid-40 ~ ¢¤‡	Christ's	*C Devizes, Wilts 1845–6, C Semington 1847–8, PC S. Ives, Corn 1851–5, chapl. to the Fleet, +1866*
#Donthorn, William John	14.11.43 ~		*Architect (1799–1859), Hanover Street, Hanover Square, London, pupil of Sir Jeffry Wyatville 1817–20, FIBA 1835*
Douglas, Rev. Herman	11.6.60¤		*C Studley, Warks 1857–8, V S. Mark, Victoria Docks, London 1859–63, PC Newborough, nr Peterborough 1863–7, V Sandall Magna, Yorks 1867–76*
*Dove, Thomas Dove Jones	13.2.42 ~ ¢¤	Emmanuel	*C Briston, Norf in 1851, chapl. to the Union, Stamford, Lincs 1852–6, C Frome Selwood 1856–62, became R.C. + 1883*
Dowell, Rev. Stephen Britton, M.A.	1.5.41	F 1830–64 S. Peter's	*D 1815, P 1821, minister Arrington, Cambs 1843–61, +'864*
Drake, Rev. William, M.A	1.5.41 ~ ¢¤‡	F 1837–40 S. John's	*Head Leicester Collegiate School 1838–41, examiner in Hebrew, London University 1840–65 second master Coventry G.S. and lecturer S. John, Coventry 1841–57, V Holy Trinity, Coventry 1857–64, RD 1859–64, hon. can. Worcester 1860–85, chapl.-in-ordinary to the Queen 1862–96, R Sedgbrook w. East Alington, Lincs 1864–96*

name	date elected	Cambridge college or other	Addresses/location given in *The Ecclesiologist*/ career details
Druitt, Robert, M.D.	10.53¢¤		*Surgeon, 39A Curzon St, London, member of the Motett Society, founded the Society for the Promotion of Church Music 1846, published and edited The Parish Choir until 1851*
Drury, Rev. Benjamin Heath	5.12.42	F 1842–97 & T. Caius	*Asst master at Harrow 1840–63, President Caius 1868–75, & 1877–94, classical scholar, + 1902*
Dry, William, B.A.	<mid-40 ~ ¢¤‡	Caius	*C S. Stephen, Camden Town 1843–4, in charge of Minster-in-Thanet & of Little Valence, Kent probably 1844, chapl. Elphin, Launceston, Tasmania 1845–60, resigned, disappears from Crockford 1878*
•Dryden, Sir Henry, Bart, M.A.	<mid-40	Trinity	*Canons Ashby, Northants, succeeded as 4th baronet 1837 (also succeeded Sir E. M. Paget-Turner as 7th baronet 1874), J.P, High Sheriff 1844, FSA, distinguished antiquarian, contributed numerous articles to the Soc. of Antiquaries of Scotland, Architectural Soc. of the Archdeaconry of Northampton, + 1899*
du Boulay, Rev. Francis	6.3.45 ~	Clare	*C Stockleigh Pomeroy, Dev 1833–5, C Shobrooke 1835–9, sometime chapl. to Bp Philpotts of Exeter and married his daughter Sybella 1836, R Lawbitton, Corn 1839–92*
Duffield, Rev. Roger Dawson, M.A.	Late 40 ~	Downing	*Wivenhow, Colchester, changed name to Dawson-Duffield, chapl. to Duke of Cambridge (probably till the latter's death 1850), C Lamarsh, Ess in 1846, sinecure R Calcethorpe, Lincs 1852, V Great Eversden 1854–63, surrogate in courts of Bp of London and Archd. of Middx and of Colchester, R Sepbton, Lancs 1863–71, RD 1865, author on antiquarian, heraldic and genealogical subjects*
Duke, William, M.D.	1845 ~		*Hastings, of 22 Grand Parade in 1858*
Duncombe, Hon. & Rev. Augustus, D.D.	<1861	Worcester, Oxford	*Dean of York 1858–80, an ES vice-president from 1861, declined bishopric of Argyll & the Isles*
Dupuis, Henry, M.A.	11.5.42 ~	F 1830–52 King's	*Asst master at Eton 1835–52, V Richmond, Surr 1852–67, surrogate and RD 1858–67*
#Dyce, William, A.R.A.	1846 ~ ¢		*Painter (1806–64), A.R.A. 1844, Professor of the Theory of Fine Arts, King's College, London, R.A. 1848, painted reredos and ceiling at All Saints, Margaret St., obituary in Eccl 25 (1864), 91–4*
#Earp, Mr Thomas	21.6.64¤		*Stone carver (1828–93), Lambeth, hon. member, moved from Nottingham to London to work for George Myers c.1848, set up own business c.1852*
Eastwood, Jonathon	7.11.44 ~	S. John's	*C Ecclesfield, Yorks 1847–54, C Eckington, Derbys 1854–62, V Hope, Staffs 1862–4*
Ebrington, Viscount, M.P., M.A., *see Fortescue*			
+Eddis, *Arthur Shelley*	<mid-40 ~ ¢¤‡	F1840–4 & Asst T 1840–3 Trinity	Treasurer CCS 1840–2, on committee 1842–3, auditor 1848–9, 1856–7, 1861–2, adm. Lincoln's Inn 1842, called to the Bar 1845, legal career, +1893

Name	College	Date	Notes
Edlin, Mr Henry E.		22.5.43 ~ ¢	Cambridge, kept Bull Inn & Hotel in 1846, and owned the station refreshment rooms in 1858
Edwards, Rev. Edward Justinian George, M.A.	Balliol, Oxford	13.3.43	B.A. 1835, V Trentham, Staffs 1841–84, preb. Lichfield 1859, proctor 1868, 1874, +1880
Eitelberger von Edelburg, Prof. Rudolf		24.6.62¤	Art historian (1817–85), Vienna, hcn. member, doctorate in art history 1847, taught at Akademie der bildenden Künste 1850–64, professor Vienna University from 1852, founded the Österreichische Museum für Kunst und Industrie, instrumental in founding Zentralkommission für Kunst und historische Denkmale
§Ellacombe, Rev. Henry Thomas, M.A	Oriel, Oxford	2.4.67	C Cricklade, Wilts1816–17, C Bitton, Som 1817–35, V there 1835–50, R Clyst S. George, Dev 1850–85, writer on bells, contributor to Eccl (e.g. 19 (1858), 419; 22 (1861), 211–13, 374–5; 25 (1864), 67–9), his is the last recorded election to the ES (Eccl 28 (1867), 183)
Eller, Rev. Irvin	Queens'	10.11.42	R St Clement's, Saltfleetby, Lincs 1841–8, R Faldingworth 1848–78, secretary of Lincs Architectural Soc. in 1878, writer of religious and architectural works
Ellicott, Charles John, B.A.	S. John's	14.11.43	R Pilton, Rutl 1848–58, Professor of Divinity, King's College, London 1858–61, Dean of Exeter 1861–3, Bp of Gloucester & Bristol 1863–97, of Gloucester 1897–1905, member of Royal Commission on Ritual and the Rubrics 1867–70, biblical scholar and author
+Elliott, William, B.A.	Queens'	<mid-40	R All Saints, Worcester 1854–60, ES auditor 1859–60, PC Tranmere, Ches 1860–8, V S. Mark, Horselydown, Southwark 1870–82, disappears from Crockford 1893
Elliot, W.		28.11.44 ~ ¢¤	3 Adelaide Place, Stepney Green, London, in 1864 of 11 Chatham Place, Hackney
Elliott, W. F.		28.11.44 ~ ¢¤	Bishop's Hull, Taunton, in 1864 of Osborne House, Wilton, Taunton
+Ellis, William Henry, Mandeville, M.A	S. John's	19.3.64¤	Trafalgar Terrace, Monkstown, Ireland, ES auditor 1865–7, letter to Eccl 23 (1862), 22, +1911
Escott, Rev. George Sweet	Lincoln, Oxford	<mid-46 ~	R Brompton Ralph, Som (own patron) 1842–54, V Barnwood, Glos 1844–71
Evans, Edward	Corpus Christi	14.11.43	C All Saints, Northampton 1849, C Eriswell & Eccles, Norf 1849–53, 1853–6 (presumably a slight gap in 1853), V S. Stephen, Norwich 1856–62, R Lyng 1862–3, R Swanton Morley w. Worthing 1863–95, RD S. Brisley 1884–93, assumed name of Lombe in lieu of Evans 1860, disappears from Crockford 1910
Evans, Rev. Robert, M.A.	Trinity	Late 40	V Normanton, Notts, 1803, V Everton 1803–47, V Misson 1829–47, R Coveney, Cambs 1847–52, RD East Retford, J.P.
Evans, Rev. Robert Wilson	F 1813 Trinity	Late 40	V Aysgarth, Yorks 1825 (or perhaps 1836), Select Preacher 1830, 1833, V Tarvin, Ches 1832–42, V Heversham, Westm 1842–66, first Archd. of Westmorland 1856–66, various religious writings

name	Cambridge college or other	date elected	Addresses/location given in *The Ecclesiologist*/ career details
+*Evans, Rev. *Thomas Simpson*, M.A.	S. Alban's Hall, Oxford	1848	C & lecturer Kensington 1824, V S. Leonard's, Shoreditch 1841-80, ES auditor 1850-1
Evans, Rev. William Edward	Clare Hall	5.12.42	C Llanymynech, Salop 1825-9, PC Criggion, Montgom 1829-37, C Monkland, Herefs 1832-50, preb. Hereford 1841-61, V Madley w. Tibberton 1850-69, RD Leominster by 1842, Praelector of Hereford Cathedral 1845-69, residentiary can. 1861-9
Evans, William Sloane	Trinity	22.11.41 ~ ¢¤‡	*Became Sloane-Evans 1849, C S. David's, Exeter, Dev 1847, C Holy Trinity, Barnstaple 1848, V there 1851-2, C Townstall, Dartmouth 1849-51, C Cornworthy 1852-4, C East Allington 1854-6, chapl. Kingsbridge Union and lecturer at Kingsbridge 1856-77, C Sherford 1875-7, V Egloskerry w. Tremaine, Corn 1877-96, +1899*
Evelyn, *William John*, B.A.	Balliol, Oxford	1845 ~ ¢‡	Wootton, Surr, J.P., High Sheriff, Surr 1860, M.P. W. Surrey 1849-57 and Deptford 1885
•Falkner, *Thomas Alexander*	S. John's, Oxford	30.4.44 ~	B.A. 1842, C North Newnton, Wilts in 1857-8, chapl. to Bournemouth Sanitorium 1859, C Holy Trinity, Dorchester 1860-70, C Melcombe Regis 1871, V Winterbourne Monkton w. Berwick Bassett 1871-2, no clerical appointment known 1873-9, C Buckland Ripers, Dors 1880-7
*Fallow , Rev. *Thomas Mount*	S. Edmund Hall, Oxford	1846 ~	B.A. 1830, C All Souls, S. Mary-le-Bone, London in 1841-6, I S. Andrew, Marylebone 1847, a founder of the Society for Promoting Church Music, founder member of the Mottett Society, +1847
Fane, *William Dashwood*, M.A.	S. John's	21.2.42	Adm. Lincoln's Inn, London 1838, called to the Bar 1841, legal career, +1902
Faulkner, Henry Martyn	Trinity	11.5.43 ~ ¢¤	C Stroud 1844-7, chapl. at Buenos Aires 1848-59, chapl. in Falkland Islands
Fawcett, Rev. *Joshua*, M.A.	Trinity	<mid-40 ~ ¢¤‡	Low Moor, Bradford, Yorks, C Pannal, Yorks, C Everton, Lancs, PC Wibsey, Yorks 1833-64 (built church and parsonage there), chapl. to Lord Dunsany 1842 and to Lord Radstock, 1849, bon. can. Ripon 1860-4
#Fawcett, *William Milner*	Jesus	13.6.61	*Architect (1832-1908), Cambridge, pupil of Charles Walklett, began practice 1859, FRIBA 1867, member of Council 1871-3, 1884-9, vice-president 1896-1900, Ely Diocesan Surveyor from 1871, FSA 1874, President CAS 1884-5, partner of T. D. Atkinson from 1906*
Fearon, Rev. *William Charles*	S. John's	10.11.42	C Grimstone, Norfolk 1841-7, V Hunstanton 1847-61, R Ringstead Parva (sinecure) 1849-65, disappears from Crockford 1868
Featherstonhaugh, Rev. *Walker*, M.A.	F 1850-2 Durham University	1846	C Ovingham, Northumb 1845-8, C Eaglescliffe, Durham 1848-51, chapl. Durham County Gaol 1851-3 (Crockford) or 1855 (CL), C Stonegrave nr York 1854-5, C Hartburn nr Morpeth, Northumb 1855-6. R Edmundbyers, Co. Durham 1856-1904
Fell, Rev. *John*, M.A.	Trinity	1.5.41 ~ ¢¤‡	PC Wilburton, Cambs 1822-61, Head Huntingdon G.S. 1823-69, R SS. Mary & Benedict, Huntingdon 1861-9, R Thoresby, Lincs 1868-9

Name	College	Date	Notes
Fenton, J.		<mid-40 ~ ¢	Grove End Place, S. John's Wood, London, although the name is the same as that in the next entry, the two are shown separately in the printed membership lists from 1841 but in 1849–56 they have the same address of 79 Mark Lane
Fenton, James	Trinity	1.5.41 ~ ¢	Adm. Lincoln's Inn 1841, called to the Bar 1845, landowner, J.P., FSA, +1902, see also previous entry
Ferguson, Richard, M.A.	F 1839–59 Pembroke	7.11.44 ~	V S. Matthew, Smethwick nr Birmingham 1859–72, RD Handsworth 1869–72, R Durley, Hants 1873–90
#●Ferrey, Benjamin		6 or 7.58α	Architect (1810–80), Trinity Place, Charing Cross, pupil of A. C. Pugin, studied under W. Wilkins, began practice c.1834, FRIBA 1839, dio. architect of Bath & Wells 1841–80, F.S.A 1863, author of Recollections of A. N. Welby Pugin, and his father Augustus Pugin (1861)
Field, James William	S. John's	6.12.41	C Draughton, Northants, 1845–8, C Layham, Suff 1849–51, C Pidley w. Fenton, Hunts, 1852–7, C to his father at Braybrooke Northants 1857–67, succeeded father as R and patron 1867, resigned and + 1885
Field, Thomas	F 1847–58 S. John's	22.11.41	V Madingley, Cambs 1858–62, V Pampisford 1863–8, R Bigby, Lincs 1868–96, RD Yarborough 1886–94, preb. Lincoln 1893–6, antiquarian writer
#Fielding, Charles		23.4.56¢α	Architect, 1 New Street, Huddersfield, in 1864 of Buntingford, Herts
Finch, Rev. William	Christ Church, Oxford	8.11.41	R Warboys, Hunts 1828–71, +1880
*Fish, James Leonard	S. Mary Hall, Oxford	4 or 5.51 ¢α	Wantage, various curacies 1853–65, R S. Margaret Pattens w. S. Gabriel, Fenchurch St, London 1866
Fisher, Edward		13.1.52¢	16 Compton St E., Brunswick Sq., London, not traced in POLD
Fisher, George		10.11.42	Cambridge
Fisher, Osmond	F 1844–58 Jesus	8.11.41	C Writhlington, Som 1844, C All Saints, Dorchester 1846–53, V Elmstead, Ess 1857–67, R Harlton, Cambs 1867–1906 (the last two in the patronage of Jesus), F.G.S, hon. F King's College, London 1880–1914, hon. F Jesus 1892–1914
Fisher, William Webster, M.D.	F 1834–44 Downing	Late 40 ~	Downing Professor of Medicine 1841–74
Fitzpatrick, Richard William	S. Peter's	<mid-40	Adm. Inner Temple 1841, called to the Bar 1844, C Holy Trinity, Bedford 1851–8, PC there 1858–71
Fitzroy, E. A.			Present at 1862 anniversary meeting
Fleming, John	S. John's	6.12.41	C Whaplode, Lincs 1848–52, V S. Mary Wiggenhall, Norf 1852–68, resigned, chapl. to the gaol, King's Lynn 1863–8, +1869

name	date elected	Cambridge college or other	Addresses/location given in The Ecclesiologist/ career details
Fletcher, John	30.4.44 ~		Vale Bank, Bolton-le-Moors, *no doubt introduced through Edmund Sharpe (q.v.) whose patron he was for the building of Little Lever church and whose sister Sharpe married*
*Flower, Rev. William Balmbro, M.A.	1847¢	Magdalene	Enfield Highway, V Knutsford, Ches 1844–5, chapl. Training School, Swinton, Manchester 1845–6, can. Calcutta 1847, asst master Christ's Hospital, London 1846–50, C Stoke Damerel, Dev 1851, PC Kingskerswell 1852–5, R Crawley, Suss 1855–6, later lived in London, editor The Churchman's Companion, prolific religious writer, +1868 at Labuan
Foot, Jeffrey Robert	<11.12.39	S. John's	Neale's diary (11.12.39) notes him as a 'Camdenian' but he is not in 1840 membership list, C S. Mary Magdalene, Southwark 1843–7, school chapl. 1848–52, C Moreton, Dors 1853, C Woodsford and Tincleton 1854, C Hanbury, Staffs 1854–60, R there 1860–93
Forbes, *Walter, 18th Lord*	1845 ~ ¢		Castle Forbes, Aberdeenshire, succeeded 1843, +1868
Forbes, Sir Charles, 1st Bart	11.5.42 ~		Fitzroy Square, London and of Newe and Edinglassie, Aberdeenshire, M.P. Beverley 1812, Malmesbury 1818–32, created a baronet 1823, +1849
+Forbes, James Stewart, M.A.	Late 40 ~ ¢¤‡	Christ's	On CCS/ES committee 1841–2, 1844–6, from 1848, B.A. 1841, 4th son of Sir Charles Forbes (q.v.), FSA, +1871
Ford, William	7.2.42	F *n.d.* King's	Gray's Inn, London, legal career, President of the Law Society 1870–1, +1889
*Forrest, Rev. *Thomas Guest*	3.11.54¢	S. Peter's	C Leigh, Lancs 1849–50, C S. Paul, Birmingham 1850–4, C Market Bosworth w. Carlton, Leics 1854–6, C Wotton-under-Edge, Glos 1856–8, C Falfield 1858–62, C Portsea, Hants 1862–3, C Moulsham, Ess 1863–5, C Devoran, Corn 1865–70, C Sutton Cheney, Leics 1870–6, C S. James the Great, Stratford-upon-Avon 1876–7, V Upton, Northants 1877-1903, Eccl wrongly gives initials as W.G.
Fortescue, Hon. Dudley Francis, M.A.	1.5.41 ~ ¢¤‡	Trinity	M.P. for Andover 1857–74, Lunacy Commissioner 1867–83, J.P., High Sheriff of Waterford 1870
Fortescue, Hon. Hugh (Viscount Ebrington M.P., M.A.)	13.2.43	Trinity	Styled Viscount Evrington 1841–61, M.P. for Plymouth 1841–52 and Marylebone 1854–9, public service career, +1905
Fowell, Richard Drake	Late 40 ~	Christ's	C Great Snoring, Norf 1843–5, C Wisbech, Cambs 1845–7, C Chobham, Surr 1847–53, first V New Brighton, Ches 1856–87
#Fowler, Charles Hodgson	14.12.64 ~		Architect (1840–1910), pupil of Scott, ARIBA 1863, FRIBA 1870, moved from London to Durham
Fowler, Rev. Hugh, M.A.	18.4.42	Sidney Sussex	C Lamerton, nr Tavistock 1840–7, master Liskeard G.S. 1841, Helston G.S. 1847–9, Bideford G.S. 1849–54, Head Cathedral G.S. Gloucester 1854–71, C Matson, Glos 1867–70, V Barnwood, Glos 1871–7

Name	College	Date	Details
		1846–/¢‡	Cadogan Place, Chelsea, on ES committee from 1849–probably 1868, Treasurer in 1864–probably 1868, FSA
Francis, Clement	Trinity Hall	22.11.41 ~ ¢‡	B.A. 1843, of Quy Hall, Cambs, Solicitor to Cambridge University, +1880
Francklin, W., B.A.	Balliol, Oxford	11.5.42	North Petherton, Somerset, not traced in AO
+Franks, Augustus Wollaston	Trinity	1845-6 ~ ¢‡	Archaeological career especially at the British Museum, ES auditor 1859-60, +1897
Franks, Rev. James Clarke, M.A.	Chapl. 1819 Trinity	8.11.41	C Lolworth & Boxworth, Cambs 1817, chapl. at Trinity 1819, Select Preacher 1819–20, Hulsean Lecturer 1823, V Huddersfield 1823–40, C S. Mary, Whittlesey, Cambs 1844–54, R S. Margaret, Canterbury 1859–63 and 1867, theological writer, +1867
•Freeman, Edward Augustus	F 1845-7 Trinity, Oxford	1846 ~ ¢‡	Historian and writer (1823–92), with a particular interest in churches, wrote A History of Architecture (1849), and many other works, most famously A History of the Norman Conquest of England... (6 vols, 1867–79), prominent in the Oxford Architectural Society, Regius Professor of Modern History, 1884, J.P.
Freeman, Gage Earle	S. John's	14.11.43	C Geddington, Northants 1846–54, PC Emmanuel, Bolton 1854–6, V Macclesfield Forest w. Clough, Ches 1856–89, V Ashbam Weston and chapl. to Earl of Lonsdale 1889–1903, writer on falconry
Freeman, Rev. John S.	S. Peter's	8.11.41 ~ ¢‡	East Winch, Norfolk, C Barham, Suff, R (& patron) Ashwicken w. Leziate, Norf 1841–77, J.P., no second name in AC
+Freeman, Philip, M.A.	F & T 1842-53 S. Peter's	1.5.41 ~ ¢‡	On CCS committee 1841-4, Chairman CCS 1844-5, auditor 1845-6, Principal Chichester Theological College 1846–8, can. Cumbrae, reader in theology there 1853–8, V Thorverton, Dev 1858–75, preb. Exeter 1861-4, can.1864–75, Archd.1865–75, active in restoration of Exeter Cathedral, author of Rites and Ritual; a Plea for Apostolic Doctrine and Worship (c.1864)
French, G.J.		10.11.42	Bolton-le-Moors, Lancs
Frere, Rev. John	Trinity	<mid-40 ~	C Wakes Colne, Ess, C Hadleigh, Suff, R Cotenham, Cambs 1839–51
Frere, Philip Howard	F 1837 & T 1839 Downing	Late 40	Boyce's Memorial gives initials wrongly as 'P. J.'; bursar at Downing from 1839, in orders but unbeneficed
Frere, Rev. Temple, M.A.	Trinity	1.5.41 ~	C Woodbridge, Suff 1804–5, C Roydon & Burston, Norf 1805–20, C Little Marlow, Bucks 1815–21, R Roydon & Burston 1820–59 (patron, his brother John), chapl. House of Commons 1833, preb. Westminster, can. 1840–59, resided Roydon Hall 1821–46, J.P.

393

name	date elected	Cambridge college or other	Addresses/location given in *The Ecclesiologist*/ career details
Frost, Rev. Percival	6.12.41~	F 1839–41 S. John's	D 1841, P 1842, adm. Inner Temple 1839, mathematical lecturer at Jesus 1847–9, at King's 1859–89, +1898
Fussell, James George Curry	8.11.41~¢‡	Trinity	Eccl gives initials as 'J. C. G.'; D 1845, P 1846, became a H.M. inspector of schools, of Frome, Som in 1846–64 + 1883
Fyssen, J. R. D., see Tyssen, J. R. D.			
Gabb, Baker	5.12.43~¢	Christ's	Held various curacies, R Llanfihangel Ystum Llwern, Mon 1858–73
Galland, Thomas Spicer	30.4.44~	S. John's	Adm. Lincoln's Inn 1849, called to the Bar 1852
Galton, Francis	6.12.41~	Trinity	Scientist (1822–1911), wide scientific interests including devising the system of fingerprint identification, began research into heredity 1865, founder of the school of 'eugenics', F.R.S 1856, knighted 1909
*Galton, Rev. John Lincoln, M.A	14.11.43~	S. Edmund Hall, Oxford	Chapl. to Lord Roden 1832–73, C Leamington Priors, Warks 1843–8, C Cubbington, 1850–1, PC S. Sidwell, Exeter, Dev 1851–78
Galton, Theodore Howard	1.5.41~	Trinity	Adm. Inner Temple 1843, called to the Bar 1847, legal career, +1881
Gandy, James Hunter	7.11.44~¢	Trinity	C Goatburst, Som 1850, C North Petherton 1851, V Old Cleeve 1851–8, PC Upton, Peterborough 1858–62, R Stanwith, Northants 1863–73, V S. John, Angell Town, North Brixton, Surr 1873–7, R Chesterton w. Haddon, Hunts 1877–1900, +1905
Garfit, Rev. Mark, M.A.	10.11.42~¢¤‡	Trinity	C West Deeping, Lincs 1838–42, C Maxey, Peterborough 1842, R Stretton, Rutl 1842–63, R Coningsby, Lincs 1863–72
Garland, Thomas Lorance	<mid40~	S. John's	B.A. 1843, D 1855, P 1856, C Little Eaton, Derbys 1855–7, +1879
•Gaunt, Rev. Charles, M.A.	1846~¢	Brasenose, Oxford	B.A. 1812, R Isfield, Suss 1835, V West Wittering, Suss 1836–67
Geldart, George Cooke	21.2.42~	S. Peter's	D 1843, P 1844, C Itteringham, Norf 1848–54, lived at Leeds 1855–61, disappears from CL 1878.
#Gérente, Alfred	1849–50¢¤		Stained glass artist (1821–68), 13 Quai d'Anjou, Paris, hon. member, originally a sculptor, took up stained glass on death of his brother Henri, made the W and other windows for All Saints, Margaret St
#Gérente, Henri	1847		Stained glass artist (1814–49), 13 Quai d'Anjou, Paris, hon. member, brother of Alfred
Gibbs, Anthony	1847¢		11 Bedford Square, made his fortune in the Peruvian guano trade, POLD lists Anthony Gibbs & Sons as 'merchants, 47 Lime St' in 1843–7, in 1853 of Frogmore, Hampstead
Gibbs, Mrs	14.12.64¢¤‡		Berrow Cottage, Sidmouth, Dev, one of only two lady members (see also Carington)

Name	College	Date / code	Notes
...son, William Sidney, FSA		11.5.43 ~ ¤α	Newcastle upon Tyne, of Royal Arcade (Slater's Directory... (1848), of Bankruptcy Court (FSA membership list 1847)
Gilbert, Rev. George	Corpus Christi	?	Possibly a member in 1850, second master Grantham School 1820-51, C Grantham 1821-3, C Syston, Lincs 1826-30, V ?here 1830-74, chapl. to Bp of S. Helena 1862, preb. All Saints, Thorngate, Lincoln 1863-74, chapl. to Bp of Lincoln 1869
Gildea, Rev. G. R.		10.11.42	Newport Mayo, Tuam, Ireland, preb Tuam and a minister at Kilmaine, Tuam in 1860-5
•Gladstone, Rt Hon. William Ewart, M.P. 6.12.41 ~ ¤¤‡	Christ Church, Oxford		Politician (1809-98), made first important speech 1833, Chancellor of the Exchequer 1852-5, four times Prime Minister, brother-in-law of Sir Stephen Glynne (q.v.)
§Glover, John Hulbert, B.A.	F 1843 Clare Hall	5.3.44 ~ ¤α	D 1849, P 1851, member of Brotherhood of S. Katharine, Royal Hospital 1854-1912, V Kingsthorpe, Northants 1856-84
+§•Glynne, Sir Stephen Richard, M.P., M.A. 6.12.41 ~ ¤α	Christ Church, Oxford		Hawarden, Flintshire, succeeded as 9th bart 1815, B.A. 1828, M.P. for Flint Burghs 1832-7, for Flintshire 1837-41, 1842-7, Sheriff of Flints 1831-2, Lord-Lieutenant of Flints 1845-74, ES committee member 1845-6, a secretary 1846-50, a vice-president 1850-at least 1864, first president of Cambrian Archaeological Soc 1847, his sister Catherine married Gladstone (q.v.) 1839, wrote notes on over 5,000 churches
Godolphin, Lord, see Osborne F.			
#Godwin, Edward William		5.4.65	Architect (1833-86), Bristol, articled to W. Armstrong, FRIBA 1863, present at 1862 anniversary meeting
Goldsmid, Nathaniel	Exeter, Oxford	22.5.43 ~	Called to the Bar 1831, + 1860
Gooden, Alexander Chisholm	Trinity	<mid-40	Adm. Lincoln's Inn 1838, +1841 at Bonn
•Goodenough, Very Rev. Edmund, D.D. 5.12.43	Christ Church, Oxford		V Warkworth, Northumb 1818, sub-almoner to the King and Head. Westminster School 1819-28, preb. York 1824, of Carlisle 1826 and Westminster 1826-31, Dean of Wells 1831-45
+Goodwin, Rev. Harvey	F 1841-5 Caius	Founder ~ ¤¤‡	CCS/ES auditor 1839-40, 1845-6, on committee 1840-2, Treasurer 1844-5, V S. Edward, Cambridge 1848-58, Hulsean Lecturer 1855, Lady Margaret Preacher 1858, Dean of Ely 1858-69, Ramsden Preacher 1861, Bp of Carlisle 1869-91, member Royal Commission on Ritualistic Practices 1867-70
Goodwin, Rev. James, M.A.	F 1829-47 Corpus Christi	10.11.42	D 1829, P 1831, Bursar & T Corpus Christi 1842-7, R Lambourne, Ess 1846-74, Select Preacher 1851, RD 1854-74
Goodwin, Charles Wycliffe	F 1840-7 Catherine Hall	<mid-40	Left CCS <mid-1841, adm. Lincoln's Inn 1840, called to the Bar 1848, student of ancient texts, Egyptologist, the only lay contributor to Essays & Reviews (1860), edited Literary Gazette 1860-3, legal career in China 1865-78

name	date elected	Cambridge college or other	Addresses/location given in *The Ecclesiologist*/ career details
Gordon, Rev. Anthony, M.A.	< mid-40	*Trinity*	*P 1822*, chapl. Trinity College 1838–58, on ES committee 1854–c.1859, *disappears from CL 1859*
+Gordon, Hon. Arthur Charles Hamilton , M.A	10.53¢	Trinity	*M.A. 1851, political and public service career, M.P. Beverley 1851–7, overseas appointments 1861–90, + 1912*
Gordon, The Hon. Douglas Hamilton	13.2.43 ~	Trinity	*C Addington, Surr and domestic chapl. to Archbp Howley 1847, R Great Stanmore, Middx 1848–60, V Nortbolt 1860–80, preb. Calne, can. & Treasurer Salisbury Cathedral 1860–98, Prior of S. John's Hospital, Burcombe, Wilts 1894–1901, chapl.-in-ordinary to Queen 1857–1901 and King 1901*
+Gordon, G. J. R.	14.11.43 ~ ¢□		*Hampton Wick, Middlesex; apparently a diplomatic career with appointments in Rio in 1843, Stockholm in 1844–6, of Ellon Castle, Aberdeenshire in 1849–64, ES committee member 1849–probably 1868, 'our valued friend' (Eccl 22 (1861), 330), wrote on Scottish ecclesiology (Eccl 7 (1847), 190–3, 10 (1849), 362–71), Eccl and membership lists in 1844 and 1846 wrongly give second initial as 'E.'*
Gordon, Rev. Robert Augustus,, M.A.	22.5.44 ~	Pembroke	*Initials given wrongly as 'R. O.' in Eccl, C Charing, Kent 1839–40, C Sundridge 1840–6, R Avington, Berks, 1846–53, R Barley, Herts 1853–90, RD Buntingford 1854–82, + 1895*
+Gosling, F. S.	8 or 9.50¢□‡		*ES auditor 1852–3, on ES committee 1853–65, probably of of Gosling & Sharpe's Bank, 19 Fleet Street (see also M. J. Lomax and J. C. Sharpe)*
Goulburn, Rt Hon. Henry, M.A.	< mid-40	Trinity	*Political career, M.P. various constituencies 1808–31, Chancellor of the Exchequer 1828–34 & 1841–6, M.P. for the University 1831–56, friend and executor of Peel*
Goulburn, Henry, M.A.	< mid-40	F 1835 Trinity	*Son of the above, called to the Bar 1840, + 1843*
Gould, Rev. Edward	22.11.41 ~ ¢		*C Horringer (Horningsheath), Suff 1830-6, R Sproughton, Suff 1836–49, chapl. to Sheriff of Suffolk 1847*
Gower, Stephen Stock B.A	Founder	S. John's	*C Kingston-on-Thames, Surr 1844–52, C All Saints, Wandsworth 1852–73*
*Grant, Rev. Alexander, B.A.	10.11.42 ~ ¢	Trinity	*C Weston-sub-Edge, Chipping Camden, Glos 1842-5, R Manningford Bruce, Wilts 1845–80, disappears from Crockford 1881*
Granville, Rev. Augustus Kerr Bozzi, M.A.	7.11.44 ~ ¢□	Corpus Christi	*Piccadilly, London, C Chilton-super-Polden, Som 1841–2, C Dunston, Lincs 1843–3, V S. James, Hatcham, Surr 1845–68, sometime chapl. to Earl of Ripon, C.S. Margaret, Durham 1874–5, clerical organiser for CETS for Durham dio. 1875–6, C-in-charge Bearpark & Broom in parish of S. Oswald, Durham 1877–9, V S. Edmund, Durham 1879–84, author of religious works*
#Granville, Walter Long Bozzi	5.6.52¢		*Architect (1819 or '20–74), Putney, Surr, ARIBA 1842, went to India 1858 as architect to Eastern Bengal Railway, consulting architect to Government of Bengal 1864–9*

Name	College	Date	Details
......, (......)	Clare Hall	6.12.41~	*Matriculated 1840, no other details available*
Gravatt, W., F.R.S.		13.2.45~¢a	34 Parliament Street, Manchester
# Gray, Charles		13.6.65	*Architect (1827 or '29–81), 22 Westbourne Place, Eaton Sq., FRIBA 1860, lapsed 1872, a founder and secretary of the Architectural Association, Eccl wrongly reverses the addresses of Gray and C. F. Hayward who joined at the same time*
Gray, Rev. Horace Faithfull, M.A.	Corpus Christi, Oxford	10.11.42	RD 1837, preb. Wells 1842, dio. inspector of schools 1841–4, Warden & Professor of Pastoral Theology, Queen's College, Birmingham 1849–52, V Pilton, Som 1841–79, can. Wells
Gray, Samuel	S. John's	22.11.41~¢	V Dacre, Yorks 1846–9, I Cradock, Cape Colony 1850–3, C Holy Trinity, Marylebone 1858–9, C Kirkby Overblow, Yorks 1860, V Cundall 1861–4, V Pateley Bridge 1864–80, R Scorborough w. Leconfield 1880–9, P Bepton, Suss 1889–90
Gray, W.		6.12.41~¢¤‡	Thirsk, Yorks; in 1853–64 the Rev. W. Gray, Cradoc, South Africa is a member
+*Greatheed, Rev. Samuel Stephenson, M.A.	F 1837 Trinity	13.2.43~¢¤‡	C West Drayton, Middx 1840–1, not in CL 1841–3 or 1847–52, C Westhoe Hill, Norwood 1844–6, on ES committee 1852–probably 1868, Treasurer 1853–probably 1868, C Tonbridge in 1858, R Corringham, Ess 1862–87, no doubt the 'S.S.G.' in Eccl 19 (1858), 181–2, 321–6; 20 (1859), 11–17; 22 (1861), 99–103, 171–6
*Greatheed, Stephenson	Corpus Christi	1.7.62¤‡	Tunbridge, C Brampton, Derbys 1863–6, C Haywards Heath, Suss 1866–77, C Folkestone, Kent, C Prestbury, Glos (n.d.), C Peasedown, Som 1880–3, +1913
Greaves, Joshua	Trinity	Late 40	C S. George, Birmingham 1845–6, C S. Martin, Birmingham 1847–51, V Great Missenden, Bucks 1852–85
§Green, Thomas Abbott, FSA		7.2.42~	Pavenham Bury, Bedford, landowner, restored Pavenham church at own expense, furnishing it with old carved woodwork, rebuilt The Bury, moved his seat to The Grange, Felmersham c.1853 which he enlarged, restored chancel at Felmersham, 1853, High Sheriff 1848, +1855
Greene, Rev. Henry Burnaby	Corpus Christi	13.2.43~	V Long Parish, Andover, Hants, 1821–82
Gregory, Gregory		13.2.43	Hungerton Hall, Grantham, Lincs, bibliophile and collector, built Harlaxton Manor under Salvin (q.v.) to house his collections but may not have lived there until three years before his death in 1854
Gregory, Samuel		Late 40~¢	Solicitor (of Carter & Gregory), Lo·d Mayor's Court Office, London
Grenside, William Bent	S. Peter's	6.12.41~¢¤‡	C Claughton, Lancs 1846–55, V Melling 1855–1913, hon. can. Manchester 1905–13

397

name	date elected	Cambridge college or other	Addresses/location given in *The Ecclesiologist*/ career details
*Gresley, Rev. William, M.A.	1846¢¤	Christ Church, Oxford	B.A. 1823, preb. Lichfield 1840–57, lecturer S. Mary, Lichfield in 1841, sometime C S. Paul, Brighton (presumably in 1846 when address is S. Leonard's-on-Sea), PC S. John, Glastonbury, Dors in 1848, V Boyne Hill, Berks 1857–76
Grey, Hon. & Rev. Francis Richard	8.11.41 ~ ¢¤‡	Trinity	Eccl incorrectly gives initials as 'F. C.'; C Acton, Suff 1836, C Sapcote, Leics 1837, PC Buxton, Derbys 1837–42, R Morpeth & PC Ulgham, Northumb 1842–90, bon. can. Durham 1863–82, RD Morpeth, Northumb 1879–90, bon. can. & chapl. to Bp of Newcastle 1882–90
Grey, Hon. & Rev. John, M.A.	10.11.42 ~	Trinity	C Chenies, Bucks 1835–6, R Wooler, Northumb 1836–43, R Houghton-le-Spring, Durham 1836–95, R Wolsingham 1843–7, bon. can. Durham 1848–95, chapl. to the Bp 1879–90
+Griffin, Rev. William Nathaniel, M.A.	Founder	F 1837–48 S. John's	*Successful private T 1837–47, elected CCS Chairman till Neale took his degree (BWD 29.10.39), on CCS committee 1839–44, Chairman 1843–4, V Ospringe, Kent 1848–92 where he restored the church, RD Ospringe 1872–92, bon. can. Canterbury 1872–92*
Griffith, Edward George	8.11.41 ~	Trinity	Downshire Hill, Hampstead, adm. Inner Temple 1841, D 1849, P 1850, C Tollesbunt Major, Ess 1849–52, C Burrough-on-the-Hill, Leics 1852–3, V Winterbourne Cherborough (or Gunner) Wilts 1853–89
Griffith, John, B.A.	<mid-40 ~ ¢	S. John's	C Darley Abbey, Derbys 1843–53, PC Trinity Chapel, Brighton 1853–6, master Brighton College 1856–71, V Sandridge, Herts 1872–91, restored the church there and extensively remodelled the village, +1892
Griffiths, John	<mid-40 ~	Christ's	C Astbury, Congleton, Ches 1842–4, T Hawarden, Flint, V Aberdare w. S. Elvan's, Glam 1846–59, R Merthyr Tydfil 1859–85, local secretary of Cambrian Archaeol Soc.
Grigson, Rev. William, M.A.	1-5.41	Corpus Christi	C Little Cressingham, Norfolk in 1841–2, R & patron Whinburgh w. Westfield 1843–77, lord of manors in Saham Toney, Norfolk, disappears from Crockford 1880
Grimshawe, Samuel	7.2.42 ~	Brasenose, Oxford	B.A. 1830, Errnwood, Buxton, Derbys
Grose, John C.	5.3.44	S. Peter's	In AC be is without the initial 'C.'; C Leamington Priors, Warks 1849–52, disappears from CL 1853
Grote, John	<mid-40 ~ ¢¤‡	F 1837–66 Trinity	D 1842, P 1844, PC Wareside, Herts 1847, V Trumpington, Cambs 1847–66
Gubbins, John P.	1845 ~ ¢¤		Delhi, still there in 1864
Guffens, Godfried	15.7.62¤		Historical and portrait painter (1823–1901), hon. member, Antwerp, present at 1862 anniversary meeting, a lithograph of a picture of the Crucifixion by him shown athe committee meeting when he was elected

Name	Date	College	Notes
Guillemard, Rev. William Henry,	1.5.41 ~ ¢¤‡	F 1838 Pembroke	*Lecturer in classics & private T, Head Royal College of Armagh 1848–69, V S. Mary-the-Less Cambridge 1869–86, AC notes him as an active CCS member & active in introducing the Oxford Movement into Cambridge, +1887*
Haden, Rev. John Clarke, M.A.	10.53¢	Corpus Christi	*Dean's Yard, Westminster, minor can. S. Paul's 1834–49, R Hutton, Kent 1839–69, minor can. & precentor Westminster Abbey 1846–69, preist-in-ordinary to King 1834–7 and to Queen 1837–69, member of the Motett Society on election*
Haggitt, Frederick	Late 40	S. Peter's	*C Welwyn, Herts 1847–50, R Wallasey, Ches 1850–67*
+Haggitt, Francis Richard, M.A.	1847	Balliol, Oxford	*Belmont, Hereford, assumed name Wegg-Prosser 184? in lieu of Haggitt, on ES committee 1850–probably mid-1850s, High Sheriff of Heref's 1855, M.P. 1847–52*
Haigh, D.J.	1846 ~		Leeds
Hailstone, Rev. John, M.A.	Late 40 ~	F 1783 Trinity	*Woodwardian Professor of Geology 1788–1818, V Arrington, Cambs 1796, V Shudy Camps, 1798–1817, V Trumpington 1817–47*
Hailstone, Rev. John, M.A	< mid-40 ~	Trinity	*V Shudy Camps, Cambs 1834–7, V Bottisham w. Lode 1837–61, resigned, RD, antiquarian & archaeologist, active in restoring Bottisham church and building one at Lode, restored Anglesey Abbey, Cambs*
#Hakewill, John Henry	16.12.63¤		*Architect (1810–80), 50 Maddox St, W., son and pupil of Henry Hakewill, partner of brother E. C. Hakewill by 1840, FRIBA 1842*
Hales, Richard Cox	< mid-40 ~ ¢‡	Magdalene	*C Itchen Stoke, Hants 1841–3, C S. Peter-le-Bailey, Oxford 1847–55, City lecturer at S. Mark, Carfax, Oxford 1850–72, R Carfax 1862–60, R Woodmancote, Suss 1860–88, surrogate dio. Chichester 1875–1906*
Halkett, Rev. Dunbar Stewart	6.12.41 ~ ¢‡	Trinity	*Richmond Hill, Surr, D 1841, P 1842, R Little Bookham, Surr 1848–87*
Halkett, Henry, B.A.	6.12.41 ~ ¢	Trinity	Adm. Lincoln's Inn 1842
Hall, Hawkesley	7.11.44 ~ ¢		*In 1853 bank manager, The Square, East Retford*
#Hall, John	1848¢		*2 Argyll Place, Regent Street, London, not traced in POLD, in 1856 'Architect, New Zealand' (it has been assumed these are the same person who emigrated to pursue his career)*
Hall, Rev. Samuel William, M.A.	Late 40 ~ ¢	S. Mary Hall, Oxford	*Cottingham, Hull, Yorks, B.A. 1823, C Kirk Ella until + 1860*
Hallam, J. H. or J. W.	13.2.45 ~ ¢		*Cheadle, Manchester, in 1863 at 2 S. Paul's Crescent, S. Paul's Road, London NW*
§•Halliwell, James Orchard	10.39	Jesus	*Neale's diary (24.10.39) says 'our grand opponent originally' joined 10.39 and BWD (9.11.39) notes he joined the C.C.S. committee; on 24.11.39 Neale says ' be declined any further connection with the C.C.S', 1st secretary CAS, adm. Lincoln's Inn 1850, Shakespearian scholar, F.R.S, FSA (14.2.39), + 1889*

name	date elected	Cambridge college or other	Addresses/location given in *The Ecclesiologist*/ career details
Halson, *Charles Augustus*	1.5.41 ~	Pembroke	C.S. Mark, N. Audley St, London 1845–7, C Enfield, Middx 1848–9, lived at Monmouth from 1850, disappears from CL 1860
Hamilton, *Robert*, B.A.	<mid-40	Trinity	Adm. Lincoln's Inn 1839, M.D. 1859, medical career in Jamaica, member of Privy Council, +1880
Hand, R. W.	7.1.44 ~¢¤		Stafford, probably *Robert William Hand who had been an attorney's clerk in 1834*
Hare, Ven. *Julius Charles*, M.A	<mid-40	F 1818 & asst. T 1822–32 Trinity	Adm. Lincoln's Inn 1816, legal career, R Hurstmonceaux, Suss 1832–55, Archd. Lewes 1840–55, preb. Chichester 1851–5, chapl. to Queen 1853–5
Harford, J. S.	1.5.41		Blaise Castle, Bristol, no longer a member by mid-1842
+ Harington, Sir John E., Bart	8 or 9.50¢¤		First churchwarden S. Barnabas, Pimlico, close friend of the Rev. W. J. E. Bennett, on ES committee 1850–probably 1868, joined the ES musical committee
Harness, Rev. *William*, M.A.	1.5.41 ~¢‡	Christ's	19 Heathcote St, Mecklenburgh Sq., London, C Kilmeston, Hants 1813, C Dorking, Surr 1814, preacher at Trinity Chapel, Conduit St & minister S. Anne, Soho 1816, C Hampstead 1823–6, 1st PC S. Peter, Regent St 1826–44, clerical registrar of Privy Council 1841–69, minister Brompton Chapel 1844–7, R Pilton, Northants 1845–6, PC Holy Trinity, Knightsbridge 1846–8, 1st V All Saints, Knightsbridge 1846–69, preb. S. Paul's 1866–9, moved in literary circles, restored Shakespeare's monument at Stratford
Harper, *Francis Whaley*	8.11.41	F 1839–47 S. John's	D 1844, P 1846, Select Preacher 1848, V Selby 1850–88, can. & preb. York 1869–95
Harper, W.	30.4.44 ~		Bury, Lancs
Harris, *Charles P.*	<mid-40 ~ ¢		Newnham, Cambridge
*Harrison, Rev. John Newman, B.A.	<mid-40 ~ ¢¤‡	Caius	C Epsom, Surr 1843–4, C Reigate 1846–7, V & patron there & surrogate 1847–1901
*Harrison, Rev. Henry, M.A.	7.2.42 ~	Trinity Hall	Bedgebury, Lamberhurst, Kent, C Goudhurst, Kent 1836–40, V Kilndown 1840–92, chapl. to Viscount Alresford 1843–92
Harrison, Rev. *Thomas*, M.A.	11.5.42 ~	S. John's	Head Maidstone G.S. 1829–39, PC Holy Trinity, Maidstone 1839–54, R & V Newchurch, Kent 1854–69
#Hart, Charles	19.5.63¤		Ecclesiastical metalworker (+1880), Wych Street, W.C., London, of Hart & Son, had been joined by Thomas Peard 1853, who set up his own business 1860 and was soon joined by Frederick Jackson, but the two firms amalgamated c.1866 to form Hart, Son, Peard & Co. with works in London and Birmingham
Hartley, Leonard L.	13.2.43 ~ ¢	Durham University	Middleton Lodge, Richmond, Yorks
Hartnell, *Edward George*	6.12.41¢¤‡	Trinity	B.A. 1845, M.A. 1848
Hartnell, J.	5.12.42 ~		Hawkhurst, Kent

Name	College	Date	Details
§Hartshorne, Rev. Charles Henry, M.A.	S. John's	Late 40	Left CCS by mid-42, C Benthall, Salop 1827-8, C Little Wenlock 1828-36, PC Cogenhoe, Northants 1850-65, chapl. to Duke of Bedford, RD E. Haddon, FSA 1839, hon. member Société Française pour la Conservation des Monuments Historiques, *a founder of British Archaeological Association*
+Harvey, Rev. William Wigan	F 1831-44 King's	<mid-40	*Lecturer in Divinity 1836-44 & 1862-3, lecturer in algebra 1837-44, on CCS committee 1840-1, C. S. Botolph's, Cambridge in 1841-2, C Oakington, Cambs in 1841-3, C Trumpington 1844, surrogate, R Buckland, Herts 1844-72, I.P., R Ewelme, Oxon 1872-83*
Harward, John Frederick	S. John's	Founder	C Westerleigh, Glos, V Middleton-by-Wirksworth, Derbys 1848-55, V Little Maplestead, Ess 1855-1912
Haskoll, Joseph	Clare Hall	6.12.41 ~ ¢¤‡	*Son of the following, C S. Peter, Walworth, Surr 1843-7, C Leigh-on-Mendip, Som 1847-8, can. Perth Cathedral 1850-6, I S. Laurence, Laurencekirk, Kincards 1853-4, R Barkwith, Lincs 1854-71, an close friend of J. M. Neale (his literary executor)*
Haskoll, Captain William, R.N.		7.2.42 ~	*Walworth, Surr, father of the above, friend of family of B. Webb (q.v.), NL notes him, as a lieutenant on the brig Cruizer in the E. Indies 1841, BWD (25.1.42) notes he returned from war in China 1842, of St Peter's, Radley, Oxford in 1853*
Hasted, Rev. Henry John	Christ's	8.11.41 ~	Bury St Edmunds, D 1831, P 1832, R & patron Bradfield Combust & R Little Welnetham, Suff 1838-49, R Stoughton 1849-80, RD Sampford 1857-77, hon. can. Norwich 1877
Hauteville, Rev. Rawdon William	University, Oxford	16.12.62a	C Hay, Brecon 1847-9, C Woolavington, Som 1850-1, C Milverton 1851-6 C Weston-in-Gordano, Som and R Yatton Keynell, Wilts 1857-66, R Walton, Clevedon, Som 1866-80, author of 'The Character of the Church of England as opposed to Romanism and Puritanism' (1855), election date 16.12.62, not 16.12.63 as stated in *Eccl.*
Hawks, Rev. William, M.A.	Trinity Hall	7.2.42	R Gateshead Fell, Durham 1825-38, PC Saltash, Corn 1838-70, (the foregoing dates differ from Crockford and have been checked against CL), disappears from Crockford 1872
Hawtrey, Rev. Dr Edward Craven	King's	7.11.44 ~ ¢	*Asst master Eton School 1814-34, Head Eton 1834-53, Provost 1853-62, R Ewhurst, Suss 1835-54, V Mapledurham, Oxon 1854-62, R Farnham Royal, Bucks 1854,*
Hawtrey, Rev. John William, M.A.	F 1840-5 King's	30.4.44 ~ ¢	D 1843, asst master Eton 1842-69, Head St Michael's School, Westgate-on-Sea, Kent 1869-89, +1891
Haynes, Edward Cragg	Trinity	13.2.45	Adm. Middle Temple 1842
#Hayward, Charles Forster		13.6.65	*Architect (1830-1905), 8 Adam St, London, asst to P. & P. C. Hardwick, ARIBA 1855, FRIBA 1861, a secretary of RIBA in 1864-5, practised with T. R. Smith, Eccl has C. Gray's and Hayward's addresses reversed and wrongly gives Hayward's second initial as 'H', elected again 3.12.66 when address is 20 Montague St*

name	date elected	Cambridge college or other	Addresses/location given in *The Ecclesiologist*/ career details
Headlam, John, B.A.	1-5.41 ~	Pembroke	*Stated as being in holy orders and C to father at Brighton but not found in CL, became RC shortly before death in 1871*
Heale, Henry Newton	8.11.41 ~¢¤‡	Christ's	Highfield, Hemel Hempstead, Herts, J.P., 'dead' in June 1872
Heales, Alfred	25.11.57¤		Proctor, 8 Carter Lane, Doctors' Commons, *London in 1853–65*, FSA
Heath, John Moore	<mid-40 ~¢¤‡	F 1831 & T Trinity	*Adm. Inner Temple 1825, called to the Bar 1830, D 1836, asst T Trinity 1837–9, T 1839–44, P 1838 but no clerical appointments*
Heathcote, Rev. George	8.11.41	S. John's	R Steeple Gidding, Hunts 1835–59, R Conington, Hunts 1835–84 (patron J. Heathcote), RD Leightonstone (Div. 2) 1845–73, hon. can. Ely 1868–95, JP
Heathcote, Sir William, Bart, M.P.	11.5.43 ~	All Souls', Oxford	F 1822–5 Oriel, Hursley, Winchester, 5th Baronet, M.P. Hants 1826–31, N. Hants 1837–49, Oxford University 1854–68, patron of Hursley where Keble (q.v.) was V, + 1881
Hedley, Rev. Thomas Alcock	8.11.41 ~¢	Trinity	C S. Mary de Lode, Gloucester 1838, PC S. James, Gloucester 1841–8, then lived at Clifton, Bristol and no appointment given in CL, + 1854
#Hellyer, Thomas	11.5.43 ~¢¤		Architect (1811–94), Isle of Wight, pupil of William Gower of Winchester
+*Helmore, Rev. Thomas, M.A.	1849-50¢¤‡	Magdalen Hall, Oxford	*Church musician and composer (1811–90), D 1840, P 1841, C S. Michael, Lichfield for two years, priest-vicar Lichfield Cathedral 1840, vice-principal S. Mark's College, Chelsea 1842, Precentor there 1846–77, Master of Children in Chapels Royal 1846, on ES committee 1849–probably 1868, ES secretary for music 1852–6, Precentor of Mottett Choir 1856–62, sometime P-in-ordinary to the Queen, R Beverstone, Glos 1872 but resigned immediately on appointment, author of The Psalter Noted (1849) and the influential* A Manual of Plainsong *(1850)*
+Hemery, Rev. Jas, M.A.	5.3.44 ~	F 1839 & T 1839–44 Trinity	On CCS committee 1844–5, R S. Helier, Jersey 1844–9, Dean of Jersey
Herbert, Hon. Algernon, M.A.	Late 40 ~	Exeter, Oxford	Ickleton, Cambs, F Merton 1814, Dean 1828, adm. Inner Temple 1813, called to the Bar 1818, + 1855
Herbert, Edward James	<mid-40 ~¢¤‡	S. John's	*Styled Viscount Clive till he succeeded as 3rd Earl of Powis 1848, M.P. for Ludlow 1852–4, Salop 1854–9, an ES vice-president from 1857, M.P. for N. Salop 1843–8, succeeded 1848, as Lord-Lieut. of Montgomery 1877–91*
Herbert, Hon. George	28.11.44	S. John's	*Brother of the above, C Kidderminster, Worcs 1850–5, preb. Hereford and V Clun w. Chapel Lawn, Salop 1855–7, Dean of Hereford 1876–94, Master of S. Ethelbert's Hospital, Hereford 1887–94*
Hereford, Dean of, see Merewether, J.			
Hervey, Frederick William, M.P., M.A., Earl Jermyn 13.2.43 ~¢¤‡ Trinity			Ickworth, Bury S. Edmund's, styled Earl Jermyn till be succeeded as 2nd Marquis of Bristol 1859, M.P. for Bury S. Edmund's 1826–59, + 1864

Name	College	Date	Notes
Heslop, Andrew	Trinity	10.11.42 ~ ¢	C Holy Trinity, Preston, Lancs 1845–6, AC says + 1847 but remains listed in CL till 1849 and is in ES 1856 membership list
Hewett, John William	Trinity	1845–6 ~ ¢	F & T S. Nicholas' College, Shoreham, Suss 1849–52, C Bloxham, Oxon 1853–6, Head Bloxham G.S. 1853–6, C S. George, Whitwick, Leics 1857–66, C-in-charge Scropton, Derbys 1866–70, C All Saints, Hampstead 1870, C S. John, Clerkenwell 1871, C S. Paul, Finsbury 1872, C S. Saviour, Hoxton 1873, C S. Mary. Primrose Hill 1874–5, senior classical master North London College School 1874–8, + 1886
Hewett, Rev. Philip	S. John's	30.4.44 ~	R Abdon, Salop 1828–9, R Binstead Ryde, I.O.W. 1833–79
Hey, Robert, B.A.	S. John's	Founder	C Shirley, Derbys 1842–4, C Ashbourne 1844–5, PC Belper 1845–85, RD Alfreton 1854–64, preb. Lichfield 1862–85, serrogate, dio. Lichfield 1845–85
*Heygate, Rev. Thomas Edward	Queens'	6 or 7.58¤	C Brasted, Kent 1849–52, C Sheen, Staffs 1852–62, V there 1862–91, RD Alstonfield 1874–86, + 1900, re-election date 15.12.62, not 16.12.63 as stated in Eccl.
§Heywood, James	Trinity	<mid-40	Adm. Inner Temple 1829, called to the Bar 1838, F King's London 1856–87, M.P. N. Lancs 1847–57, J.P., FSA, + 1897
Hickes, Charles Robert	Trinity	<mid-40 ~ ¢	Adm. Middle Temple, legal career, of Bristol
#Hicks, John		14.11.43 ~	Architect, Bristol, designed a number of 1840s churches in Bristol and was partner of S. B. Gabriel, then moved c.1850 to Dorchester where Thomas Hardy was his pupil 1856–9 then assistant till 1862, + 1869
+Hildyard, Rev. James	F 1833–47, T 1840–7 Christ's	<mid-40 ~ ¢¢‡	Hebrew lecturer 1840, on CCS committee 1841–2, Mildmay Preacher 1841–3, senior proctor 1843–4, R Ingoldsby, Lincs 1846–87, restored the church there and built new rectory, J.P.
*Hill, George James, B.A.	Trinity	1847–8	C Lower Easton, Glos 1848, C Bitton & Oldland 1850–?, R Saltford, Som 1853–4, became RC c.1855
Hill, Rev. Henry, M.A.	Wadham, Oxford	1845 ~	Heacham, V Aston Cantlow, Warks 1846–9
Hill, Rev. Thomas	Clare	9.12.58	Asst master Mercers' School 1832–50, R Holy Trinity, Minories 1850–65
#Hills, Gordon M.		26.1.58¤	Architect (1826–95), hon. member, John St, Adelphi, articled in Southampton, asst to J. Butler, Cathedral architect of Chichester, managing asst to R. C. Carpenter (q.v.), began practice 1854, ARIBA 1857, dioc. surveyor to London, Rochester and S. Albans, contributions in Eccl 20 (1859), 80, 217–32
Hinde, Rev. Thomas, M.A.	Christ Church, Oxford	1.5.41 ~	B.A. 1822, C Cockerham, Lancs, C Winwick, Head Winwick G.S. by 1841 until 1851
Hine, Rev. Thomas Cooper		10.11.42 ~	D 1833, P 1835, C S. James, Bury S. Edmund's, R Quarrington, Lincs 1844–61

name	date elected	Cambridge college or other	Addresses/location given in *The Ecclesiologist*/ career details
#Hine, Thomas Chambers	11.5.44		Architect (1813-99), Nottingham, *articled to M. Habershon till 1834, partner of W. Patterson (builder of Nottingham) till 1848 and R. Evans, a former pupil 1857-67, practised with his son, George Thomas from 1867*
Hirst, Rev. Thomas	23.11.52¢	Clare	C *Wakefield* 1850-2, *minor can. Canterbury*, 1852-74, R S. Martin w. S. Paul, Canterbury, 1859-74, R Bishopsbourne, Kent 1874-1901
Hodgson, Rev. Edward Franks, B.A.	13.3.43 ~	S. John's	C *Bayford, Herts*, 1841-3, R Holton Beckering, Lincs 1844-82, RD Wraggoe
+*Hodson, Rev. George Hewitt, M.A.	Late 40 ~ ¢¤‡	F 1840-60 Trinity	PC Cookham Dean, Berks 1845-69, on CCS/ES committees 1843-4, 1846-probably 1868, V Enfield, Middx 1870-1904, RD Enfield 1882-1904, preb. S. Paul's 1883-1904
Hodson, Rev. James Stephen, M.A.	1845 ~ ¢¤‡	Merton, Oxford	R Edinburgh Academy 1854-69, Head S. Andrew's College, Bradfield 1870-2, R South Luffenham, Rutl 1877-81, + 1881
Holden, Hubert Ashton	7.11.44	Trinity	D 1848, P 1858, educational career, + 1896
*Hole, Rev. Samuel Reynolds, B.A.	13.2.45 ~ ¢	Brasenose, Oxford	Eccl wrongly gives initials as 'R. S.'; Caunton Manor, Newark, V Caunton 1850-91, RD Southwark 1873-87, can. Lincoln, preb. Lincoln 1875-87, proctor in Conocation 1883-4, chapl. to Archbp of Canterbury from 1883, Select Preacher, Oxford 1885-6, Dean of Rochester from 1887
Holmes, Rev. William Sancroft (or Sandcroft), M.A.	10.11.42 ~	Emmanuel	Gawdy Hall, Harleston, Norfolk, B.A. 1839, M.P. for Eastbourne, J.P., + 1849
Holt, Thomas	10.11.42~		Registrar Gloucester and Bristol Dio.
Hollway, John George	13.2.44 ~	Trinity	Adm. Middle Temple 1843, called to the Bar 1847, on the S.E. Circuit
Hook, Rev. Walter Farquhar, D.D.	10.11.42 ~	Christ Church, Oxford	Elected hon. member 5.12.42, chapl.-in-ordinary to King 1827 & to Queen 1839-75, V Leeds 1837-59 *(restored the church there)*, Select Preacher, Oxford 1833-4, 1858-9 & 1875, Dean of Chichester 1859-75, author of many historical and other works incl. Dictionary of Ecclesiastical Biography (8 vols 1845-52), and Lives of the Archbishops (12 vols 1860-76)
Hooper, Richard	8.11.41 ~	Trinity	C Holy Trinity, Exeter 1845-9, C S Stephen, Westminster 1849-55, R & V Upton & Aston Upthorpe, Didcot, Berks 1862-94, surrogate Oxford diocese 1878, author of a life of Dryden
Hope, Adrian John	1.5.55¢		Brother of the following, military career *(various regiments rising from captain 1844 to major 1855, lieut.-col. 1856)*, placed on half pay 1856, V of Bosbeck Haarlem, Netherlands in 1856, disappears from AL 1859
+•Hope, Alexander James Beresford, M.P., M.A.	<mid-40 ~ ¢¤‡	Trinity	President of the Union 1839, B.A. & University prize for Latin verse 1841, purchased S. Augustine's Abbey, Canterbury and influenced by E. Coleridge (q.v.) made it into a missionary college 1844, on CCS committee 1840-1, 1844-5, ES Chairman 1845-59, a trustee from 1845, President 1859-68, appointed B. Webb (q.v.) to the living of Sheen,

Name	College	Date	Notes
Hope, James Robert, B.C.L.	Christ Church, Oxford	10.11.42 ~¢	Staffs 1850, patron of Butterfield for rebuilding Sheen church and building All Saints, Margaret Street, assumed additional name of Beresford on succeeding to his stepfather's estates in 1854, M.P. Maidstone 1841–52 & 1857–9, for Stoke 1865–8, for Cambridge University 1868–87, established the Saturday Review 1855, President RIBA 1866–7, seats at Bedgebury Park Kent & Beresford Hall, Staffs, FSA, +1837
Hope, Robert John, B.A.	S. Catharine's Hall	13.2.44 ~	F (1833–47) Merton, Oxford, Chancellor Salisbury dio., added surname of Scott 1853, called to the Bar 1838, Q.C. 1850, +1873
Hope, William	S. Catharine's Hall	11.5.44 ~ ¢□	D 1841, P 1842, C S. Peter, Derby w. Normanton 1847–50, C S. Sepulchre, London E.C. 1851–7, C Scarborough, Yorks 1861–2, I in Madura, Madras, C S. Michael & All Angels, Princetown, Dev c.1877–9, +1898
Hopkins, Thomas Marshland	S. Peter's	22.5.43 ~¢	C Whitwick, Leics 1846–7, PC S. Peter, Derby w. Normanton, Derbys 1847–89, chapl. to Earl Ferrers from 1847, surrogate dio. Lichfield 1847
+Hopkins, William, M.A.	S. Peter's	<mid-40	C S. Giles-in-the-Field, London 1849–51, C S. Paul, Knightsbridge 1852, C Paddington 1853–5, PC S. Saviour, Paddington 1857–62
#Hopkins, William Jeffrey		5.3.50¢□	CCS auditor 1843–4, distinguished geology and mathematics teacher, President Geological Association 1851–3, +1866
Hopkinson, W.		7.2.42 ~¢□	Architect (1820 or '21–1901), Worcester, articled to H. J. Underwood, FRIBA 1861, Worcester Dio. architect
Hopper, Rev. Augustus MacDonald	F 1841–5 S. John's	<mid-40	Stamford, Lincs
Hopwood, John James	S. Peter's	Founder	Chapl. Horningsea, Cambs 1844–5, R Starston, Norf 1845–78, hon. can. Norwich 1854–72, Proctor in Convocation, Dio. Norwich 1857–68, RD 1565–8, Archd. Norwich 1868–78, J.P.
Hornby, Rev. Edward James Geoffrey	Merton, Oxford	22.5.43 ~	+1842 aged 23
*Horne, Rev. Edward, M.A.	Queens'	11.5.42 ~	B.A. 1839, R Walmersley, Bury, Lancs, 1850–80, hon. can. Manchester, 1855, RD Bury from 1850
*Horner, Rev. John Stewart Hippersley	Exeter, Oxford	13.1.52¢□‡	R S. Lawrence w. S. John, Southampton 1835–46, became RC 1847
Hough, Rev. Thomas George Pattinson	Caius	Founder	R (& patron) Mells w. Leigh-on-Mendip, Som 1835–74 : V Vobster 1835–60, preb. Wells 1842
Houghton, Baron, see Milnes			C Coltishall, Norf 1842–7, V Ham, Surr 1848–95

name	date elected	Cambridge college or other	Addresses/location given in *The Ecclesiologist*/ career details
Howard, William Watben	11.5.44 ~	S. John's	*C Brasted, Kent 1861–3, C Westerham 1863–6, asst chapl. at S. Petersburg 1866–8, C Basingstoke, Hants 1868–74, V Blackmoor 1874–80, R Market Deeping, Lincs 1880–1910, RD Stamford 1884–1909, Dean of Stamford 1884–1919, RD Ness 1888–1909, preb. Lincoln 1911–23*
Howe, John	28.11.44¢	Trinity	*C S. John. Coventry 1849–50, C Solibull 1852–5, V Knowle 1855–89, bon. can. Worcester 1882–9*
Howell, Rev. Alexander James	22.5.44	Magdalen Hall, Oxford	*C Jesus Chapel, Southampton 1841–6, C S. James, Enfield, Middx and chapl. to Duke of Cleveland 1845–6, V Darlington, Co. Durham 1846–60, autbor on classics*
Howlett, Rev. John Henry	8.11.41	F 1834–45 S. John's	*Chapl. Horningsea, Cambs 1837–9, R Meppershall, Beds (patron – S. John's) 1845–96 (restored the church 1875–7), RD Shefford 1869–93*
+Howson, Rev. John Saul, M.A	1839	Trinity	*On CCS committee 1839–40 (but not listed in Boyce's Memorial as a founder member of the Society), educational career incl. Principal Liverpool Collegiate Institution 1849–65, also V Wisbech, Cambs 1866–7, Dean of Chester 1867–95 where be restored the cathedral, wrote hymns, sermons etc and a life of S. Paul*
+Hubbard, J. G.,	6 or 7.50¢¤‡		*ES auditor 1854–5, 1857–8, of 24 Princes Gate, London in 1857*
Hubbard, Rev. Thomas	10.11.42	Trinity	*R Stondon Massey w. Aytborp Roding, Ess 1841–9, RD 1847–9, C Fairlight, Suss 1850–3, +1878*
Hubbock, G. B. or T. B.	28.11.44 ~		*Ponder's End, Enfield, POD (1846) lists a Geo. Parker Hubbock among the gentry in Ponder's End*
#Hugall, John West	7.12.59¤		*Architect (fl. 1849–78), King William St, W.C, addresses in Oxford and Reading in 1871, FRIBA 1872*
§Hughes, Rev. Thomas Smart, B.S.D.	Late 40	Emmanuel	*F & T Trinity Hall, F & Dean Emmanuel 1817, asst master Harrow 1809–11, Christian Advocate 1822–9, C All Saints, Cambridge 1826, can. Peterborough 1827–47, R Hardwycke, Northants 1832–6, R Fiskerton, Lincs 1829–46, PC Edgware 1846–7*
Hullah, John Pyke	14.11.43 ~ ¢¤	Royal Academy of Music	*Composer and teacher (1812–84), S. James's Place, London; in charge of musical training at S. Mark's College, Chelsea from 1841, Professor of Vocal Music, King's College, London by Feb. 1846*
Hulton, Arthur Emilius	5.3.44 ~ ¢¤‡	Trinity	*Southampton, C Threlkeld, Cumb 1849–53, PC Ivegill w. High Mead 1853–68*
Humble, Rev. Henry, M.A.	1845–6 ~ ¢¤	Durham University	*Newcastle upon Tyne, C Newburn, Northumb 1842–7, chapl. to Lord Forbes 1844–83, can. S. Ninian's Cathedral, Perth, Precentor there, disappears from Crockford 1884*
*Hunter, Rev. Evans Haynes	13.3.43 ~ ¢	Trinity	*C S. Matthew's, Bethnal Green 1843–5, C S. Anne, Limehouse 1845–8, C S. George, Southwark 1846–8, C S. John the Evangelist, C S. Pancras 1850–1, Ickham, Kent 1851–3, C*

Name	Date	College	Notes
Hutchinson, Rev. James	8.11.41 ~	S. John's	S. Thomas, Stamford Hill 1854–8, C Lymm, Ches 1858–61, C Little Drayton, Salop 1861–2, disappears from Crockford 1865
Hutchison, Aeneas Barkly	13.2.43 ~ ¢¤	Queens'	Asst master Blackheath Proprietory School, 1841–2, PC Pleskey, Ess 1843–66
Hutchison, William	14.11.43	Magdalene	6 Lime Street Square, London, C S. James, Devonport 1848–50, PC new church of S. James 1850–66, various posts, e.g. schools inspector, hon. local secretary & treasurer of Exeter Dio. Architectural Soc., hon. local secretary for the ICBS, 'monograph' on Callington church, Corn reviewed in Eccl 22 (1861), 228–9
Hutton, J. D., M.A.	28.11.44 ~	Trinity	Became R.C. 1845, ordained 1847, + 1863, left all his property to Brompton Oratory
*Ingle, John	22.5.43 ~	Trinity	Not traced in AC
Inglis, James	14.11.43 ~		C S. Olave, Exeter 1846–52 & 1861–7, R there 1867–91, Head King's School, Ely 1852–61, +1901; Colchester
Ingram, Rev. George, B.D.	18.4.42 ~ ¢	Queens'	R Chedburgh, Suff 1839–50, various writings including one on the state of the Church of England
Ingram, Thomas	23.11.52		Professor of music, 16A Walcot Place, Kennington Road, London in 1849–53
*Irons, Rev. William Josiah, B.D.	1841–2	Queen's, Oxford	C S. Mary, Newington 1835–7, V Barkway, Herts 1838–40, V Brompton, Middx 1840–70, Bamford Lecturer 1870, R Wadingham, Lincs 1870–2, R S. Mary Woolnoth, London 1872–83
*Irvine, Rev. James, M.A.	7.11.44 ~ ¢¤	Trinity	V Leigh, Manchester 1839–74
*Irving, Rev. John William	<mid-40 ~ ¢¤‡		C Broughton, Bucks 1843–54, R there 1854–93
+Isaacson, Rev. John Frederick	Founder ~ ¢¤‡	F & T S. John's	Lecturer King's 1829–39, R Freshwater, I.O.W 1839–86, a CCS vice-president 1840–at least 1864, hon. can. Winchester 1874–86
Isaacson, Rev. Stephen, M.A.	14.11.43 ~ ¢	Christ's	Dymchurch, Hythe, R S. Paul, Demarara, W.I. 1826–32, C S. Margaret Lothbury, London c.1832–4, C Dorking 1834–7, C W. Hackrey, Middx in 1841, resided at Dymchurch 1843–7, chapl. to Elham Union, Dymchurch
Izard, William Chantler	8.5.45	Christ's	C Low Toynton, Lincs 1845–8, C S. Dunstan, Stepney 1848–50, Head Stepney G.S. 1850–65, R Slindon, Suss 1865–96
#Jackson, A. Williamson	11.5.44 ~ ¢		Architect, King's College, London
+Jackson, Rev. John Charles, M.A.	3.1.60¢‡	S. John's, Oxford	5 Chatham Place, E. Hackney, London N.E., Head Hackney Church of England School 1854–74, on ES committee in 1854–probably till 1868

name	date elected	Cambridge college or other	Addresses/location given in *The Ecclesiologist*/ career details
#Jackson, J. G.	13.3.43 ~		Architect, Newbold Lodge, Leamington; Buildings of England: Warwicks *(1966) has 3 1830s buildings by J. C. Jackson'*
James, Herbert	13.2.45 ~	King's	C Aldburgh, Suff 1848–52, C Christ Church, Dover 1852–5, PC Goodnestone, Kent 1855–65, R Livermere, Suff 1865–1909, RD Blackburne 1886–94, lecturer in pastoral theology, Cambridge 1889
James, Rev. Richard Lee	3.12.56¤	Clare	C S. Peter, Portsea, Hants 1850–2, C Great & Little Kimble, Bucks 1853–4, V Watford 1855–1914, + 1921
James, Rev. Thomas	?	Christ Church, Oxford	Present at 1862 anniversary meeting, *a secretary of the Architectural Society of the Archdeaconry of Northampton*
+*Jebb, Rev. John, D.D.	11.6.60¤	Trinity, Dublin	B.A. 1826, R Dunerlin, Ireland 1831–2, preb. Limerick 1832–43, V Peterstow, Herefs 1843–86, preb. Hereford 1858 (restored church under Scott, 1866), Praelector 1863–70, can. residentiary 1870, added to committee on joining ES, friend of W. F. Hook, influential in reviving choral services (wrote The Choral Service of the United Church of England and Ireland (1843), Hebrew scholar, numerous contributions to Eccl e.g. 23 (1862), 36–40, 29 (1868), 35–9, 92–8
Jeffray, Rev. William Lockhart	< mid-1846 ~	Balliol, Oxford	PC S. Thomas, Preston, Lancs in 1841, PC Ashton-on-Ribble 1842–3, R Aidford, Ches 1853–62
Jenkins, Rev. Robert Charles, B.A.	< mid-40 ~	Trinity	*Surname wrongly given as 'Jenkyns'* in Eccl, C Willesden, Middx 1841–3, PC Christ Church, Turnham Green 1843–54, R & V Lyminge w. Paddlesworth, Kent 1854–96, hon. can. Canterbury 1869, hon. curator Lambeth Palace Library 1881
Jenner, Arthur Rice, B.C.L.	5.6.52¤		Brighton, of Tilehurst, Berks in 1857, in Canada in 1864
+*Jenner, Rev. Henry Lascelles, LL.B.	22.5.44 ~ ¢¤	Trinity Hall	C Chevening, Kent 1843–6, C S. Columb Major, Corn 1846–9, C Antony 1849–51, C Brasted, Kent 1852, minor can. Canterbury 1852–4, on ES committee 1851–66, ES secretary for music 1856–62, auditor 1856–7, V Preston-next-Wingham 1854–98, 1st Bp of Dunedin 1866–71, Bp of Église Catholique Gallicane, Paris 1882–93, letter to Eccl 7 (1847), 102–4 on flowers in churches, +1898
Jenner, Montagu Herbert	1846 ~ ¢		Chiselhurst, Kent, ES auditor 1856–7
Jephson, Rev. John M., M.A.	28.11.44	Trinity, Dublin	C Wilby w. Hargham, Norf 1846–7, C Leeds in 1848, disappears from CL 1849
Jermyn M.P., M.A., The Earl, see Hervey			
*Jerrard, Rev. Joseph Henry, M.A.	28.11.44 ~	F 1828 Caius	D 1841, first Principal Bristol College 1831–8, F & Classical Scholar London University, became RC 1851, + 1853

Jervis, William George, B.A.	S. Peter's	5.3.44 ~	*C Bengeo, Herts 1845-7, C Willington Spain & of Nor-on Mandeville, Ess 1848-53, founder and secretary of Poor Clergy Relief Corporation 1856-63, C Kingston-on-Thames, Surr 1853-8, PC East Molesey 1858-63*
Jessop, W.	Christ's	5.3.44 ~ ¢	*Not traced in AC*
Johnson, Rev. J., M.A.	Oriel, Oxford	14.11.43	*Hursley, Winchester, Hants, not traced in AO or CL*
#Johnson, John, F.S.A		2 or 3.51¤	*Architect (c.1807-78), 9 John Street, Adelphi, London, strained in Italy 1836-40*
Johnson, Rev. John Barham,	Corpus Christi	1.5.41¤‡	*Weston-super-Mare, C Nailsea, Som 1842-3, R Welborne, Norf 1845-83, +1894*
#Johnson, Robert James		19.3.61	*Architect (1832-92), 10 Belgrave St S., pupil of J. Middleton, asst in Scott's office 1849-58, ARIBA 1861, FRIBA 1865, moved to Tyneside and, with T. Austin, purchased John Dobson's practice, in partnership also with W. S. Hicks from 1875*
Johnson, William	F 1845-72 King's	10.11.42 ~	*Asst master Eton 1845-72, took surname of Cory 1872, +1892*
Johnson, William F.		1845~	*8 Connaught Square, London*
Johnston, Rev. George	Sidney Sussex	8.11.41 ~ ¢	*R Broughton, Hunts, 1839-86, J.P*
Jones, Rev. Dennis Edward	Lincoln, Oxford	11.5.43	*R S. John's w. S. Clement's, Stamford 1833-81, chapl. to Stamford & Rutland Infirmary, +1883*
Jones, Ven. Hugh Chambres, D.D	Christ Church, Oxford	1.5.41 ~ ¢¤‡	*Chapl. & secretary to Duke of Porland 1807-9, V West Ham, Ess 1807-45, examining chapl. to Bp of London 1813-28, R Aldham 1823-40, Treasurer S. Paul's Cathedral 1816-69, Archd. Ess 1823-61*
Jones, Herbert Walsingham	Trinity	12.45 ~ ¢	*C Runton, Norf 1850-9, R Sculthorpe 1859-89, hon. can. Norwich 1873*
#Jones, R. J.		21.6.59¤	*Architect, Milton-next-Gravesend Kent, possibly Richard James Cornewall Jones (1835 or '36-1912)*
Joseph, Nathaniel	Trinity Hall	5.12.42 ~ ¢	*Adm. Lincoln's Inn 1846, called to the Bar 1849, +1864*
Jowett, William	S. John's	10.39	*Election date in BWD (29.10.39) but not a member in mid-41, in holy orders, first Anglican clergyman to volunteer for foreign service of Church Missionary Soc. 1813, worked around the Mediterranean 1815-24, clerical secretary to the society 1832-40, lecturer at S. Mary, Aldermanbury, London, at S. Paul, Cornhill, at Holy Trinity, Clapham, V S. John, Clapham Rise 1851-5*
Joy, Rev. William, M.A.	F 1811-16 Trinity	< mid-40 ~ ¢¤‡	*C Oxenhall, Glos 1842-6, chapl. Trinity College 1844-6, resident in London 1846-58, C Springthorpe w. Heacham. Lincs 1858-63, V Shudy Camps, Cambs 1863-98*
Kay, Joseph	Trinity	13.2.43 ~	*Adm. Inner Temple 1844, called to the Bar 1848, Q.C. 1869, +1878*

name	date elected	Cambridge college or other	Addresses/location given in *The Ecclesiologist*/ career details
*Keble, Rev. John	14.11.43 ~ ¢¤	*Corpus Christi, Oxford & F. 1812–35* Oriel, Oxford *(1792–1886), B.A. 1810, D 1815, P 1816, T Oriel 1817–23, assisted his father at Coln S. Aldwyn, Glos, in charge of E. Leach & Barthorpe, C Southrop, C Hursley, Hants 1825–6, Professor of Poetry, Oxford 1831–42, V Hursley w. Otterbourne 1836–66, a leading figure in the Oxford Movement, author of 'The Christian Year (1827), co-operated with Newman on Tracts for the Times and wrote several himself*
*Keble, Rev. Thomas	<mid-46	*F 1820–5 Corpus Christi, Oxford*	*Younger brother of above, junior dean 1822, V Bisley, Stroud, Glos 1827–73, + 1875*
Keeling, Rev. William	8.11.41	F 1829–47 S. John's	*Senior Dean S. John's, R Barrow, Suff 1845–91*
Kemp, Charles	21.6.59¤		*Sydney, active in promoting Sydney Cathedral, hon. member by mid-1864, +, 1865, a C. Kemp wrote to Eccl from Islington 1861 (22 (1861), 153)*
Kennedy, Rev. George John, M.A	<mid-40	F 1835–43 S. John's	*D 1838, P 1839, no ecclesiastical appointments, asst master Rugby 1844–7*
Kent, Alfred	14.11.43 ~ ¢	Christ's	*Minor can. Gloucester 1849–53, V Coln S. Aldwyn, Glos 1853–95, RD Fairford 1880–95, hon. can. Gloucester 1891–5*
*Kerr, George Putland	28.11.44	Queens'	*Initials wrongly given as 'G. K.' in Eccl, C Mirfield, Yorks 1848–61, V (Upper) Horton 1861–91*
Killpack, William Bennett, B.A.	5.3.44	Corpus Christi	*V S. James, Devonport, Dev 1846–50*
+Kinder, John, B.A.	21.2.42 ~ ¢	Scholar of Trinity	*D 1846, P 1848, educational career in England and, from 1855, New Zealand, CCS committee member 1843–5*
King, Frank Bowers	11.5.44 ~ ¢	Clare Hall	*Also elected 13.2.45, C Burstwick w. Skeckling, Yorks 1846–52, V there 1852–90*
King, Rev. Henry, M.A.	5.12.43 ~ ¢	Christ's	*V Kirkby Stephen, Westm 1843–62*
King, J. E.	7.11.44 ~ ¢		*Angley House, Cranbrook, Kent, POD (1846) has Hon. Capt. King here*
King, Richard	10.11.42 ~	Christ's	*C S. John Hampstead, London 1843, chapl. to Bp. of Fredricton in 1848–9, C Butleigh, Som 1850, chapl. to asylum Prestwich, Lancs 1851–82, & 1906*
King, William Bowes	<mid-49¢	Clare	*B.A. 1846*
+Kingdon, George Renorden	Late 40 ~	Scholar of Trinity	*On CCS committee 1844–5, at S. Bartholomew's Hospital 1845–7, became RC & Jesuit 1847, various professorships, +1893*
+Kingdon, Rev. Samuel Nicholson	8.11.41	F n.d. Sidney Sussex	*Asst C Great S. Mary, Cambridge in 1841–3, V Bridgerule, Dev 1844–72*
Kingsley, Rev. William Towler	10.11.42	F & T n.d. Sidney Sussex	*D 1842, P 1844, R South Kilvington, Yorks 1859 till 1916 when + aged 101*
#Knightley, Thomas Edward	16.12.62¤		*Architect (1823 or '24–1905), 25 Cannon St, London E.C., articled to J. Wallen, ARIBA 1856, FRIBA 1860, in partnership with former pupil Thomas Battersby from 1901, Eccl wrongly gives first initial as 'F.'; election date 16.12.62, not 16.12.63 as stated in Eccl*

Name	Date	College	Notes
Knox, *Thomas Francis*	8.11.41	Trinity	*Became RC 1845, helped found the London Oratory, + 1882*
Laishley, *George New*	8.11.41 ~	Trinity	*Adm. Lincoln's Inn 1842*
Lambert, *Daniel*	6.54¢		*Banstead, Surr, gentleman*
Lambert, *Frederic*	6.54¢		*Banstead, Surr, probably son of the above, 'Frederick Lambert' listed as of Garratts Hall in Kelly's (1883)*
Landon, Rev. *Edward Henry*, M.A	13.2.45 ~	S. John's	*C Kelvedon Hatch, Ess 1838–41, C S. Philip, Dalston 1841-4, in Madeira in 1846, author of religions and other works, +1877*
Lane, Rev. *Charlton*	10.11.42	Trinity	*Kennington, chapl. in Brussels, C S. Margaret, Westminster, C Lambeth, London, PC S. Mark, Kennington 1832-64, RD Southwark 1832-64, V Hampstead 1864–72, +1875*
Lane, Rev. *Thomas Leveson*, M.A.	11.5.43 ~ ¢¤	S. John's	*V Kings Bromley, Staffs 1828–9, R Withington, Glos 1828–34, V Wasperton, Warks 1835–83, V Baswick (or Berkswich) Staffs 1836–83*
#Lassus, *Jean-Baptiste-Antoine*	1849¢		*Architect (1807–57), hon. member, enthusiast for the Gothic Revival, contributor to the Annales archéologiques*
Laurie, *A.J.D.*	10.11.42	Trinity	*Westwood House, Sydenham, possibly the Andrew James Charles Lawrie of Sydenham Hill listed by POD (1846)*
#Lavers, *Nathaniel Wood*	3.56¢¤		*Stained glass maker (1828–1911), began own practice 1855, took on F. P. Barraud as a partner 1858*
Law, The Worshipful & Rev. *James Thomas*	1.5.41	F 1814–17 Christ's	*R Tattenhall, Ches 1816, V Childwell, Lancs 1818, V Bowdon, Ches & King's Preacher, Lancs 1818–21, preb. Chester 1818–28, preb. Lichfield 1818, Chancellor Lichfield 1821–73, V Harborne, Staffs 1825–45, Special Commissary Dio. Bath & Wells 1840, Master S. John's Hospital, Lichfield, +1876*
Law, *Robert Vanbrugh*, M.A.	1.5.41 ~ ¢¤‡	S. Peter's	*V Weaverham, Ches 1823-34, R Wallasey 1825–34, can. Chester 1826, preb. & Treasurer Wells from 1829, R Yeovilton, Som 1834–5, R West Camel 1835, R Christian Malford, Wilts 1835–77, +1884*
Law, Rev. *William*	22.11.41 ~ ¢	Queens'	*C Great Linford, Bucks in 1838–42, R Marston Trussell, Northants 1842–1900, an early photographer c.1855*
Lawrence, *S.*	10.39	Trinity	*Election date from BWD (29.10.39), Bedington, Surr, likely to be Sydney Lawrence whose career was on the London Stock Exchange, + 1895*
Lawrie, *Andrew James Charles*, M.A.	10.11.42 ~ ¢¤‡	Trinity	*Third name given as Charles in AC but all CCS/ES lists give 'A. J. D.'; Westwood House, Sydenham, adm. Lincoln's Inn 1834*
Lawton, *R.*	1845–6 ~		*Chertsey, not listed in POD (1846)*

411

name	date elected	Cambridge college or other	Addresses/location given in *The Ecclesiologist*/ career details
#Lee, Francis Goodall	7.12.59¤		Architect, 3 Adam's Court, Old Broad St, London E.C., present at 1862 anniversary meeting
Lee, Newton Bolle Colbourne	11.5.43 ~ ¢	Trinity	Medical career, +1870
Lee, Rev. James Prince, M.A.	Late 40 ~	F 1839 Trinity	Asst master, Rugby 1830–8, R Ayot S. Peter, Herts 1837, Head King Edward's School, Birmingham 1838–47, hon. can. Worcester 1847, 1st Bp of Manchester 1847–69 (and as such fiercely opposed ritualist practices)
Lee, Rev. Samuel Lee, D.D.	<mid-40	Trinity	Professor of Arabic 1819–31, Regius Professor of Hebrew 1831–48, R Bilton, Yorks 1825–31, can. Bristol 1831–8, V Banwell, Som 1831–8, R Barley, Herts 1838–52, a great linguist, as an undergraduate had worshipped at Charles Simeon's Evangelical Holy Trinity, Cambridge, resigned from the Society 1845
Lefevre, see Shaw-Lefevre			
*Le Geyt, Rev. Charles James	?	Exeter, Oxford	Present at 1862 anniversary meeting, chapl. Magdalene, Oxford 1853–8, C Clifton Hampden, Oxon 1854–7, C Hursley, Hants 1857–8, I S. Matthias, Stoke Newington from 1858
Legh, Rev. John	?		Present at 8.5.45 meeting
Leith, Alexander, B.A.	10.39 ~ ¢¤‡	Trinity	Election date from BWD (29.10.39), Free Field, Aberdeenshire, legal career in Scotland, +1886
Lemann, Rev. Francis Gregory	8.11.41	F 1826–31 King's	R Merton, Norf 1839–51, V Langford w. Little Faringdon, Berks 1855–86, +1896
*Lendrum, Rev. Alexander	?	King's, Aberdeen	D & P 1832, present at 2.5.55 meeting, PC Crieff & Morthill, can. S. Ninian, Perth, I Warburton, Ches 1870–2, C Benefield, Northants 1872–6, R Blatherwyke 1876–90
+#Le Strange, Henry L'Estrange Styleman	13.2.43 ~ ¢	Christ Church, Oxford	Amateur artist (1815–62), Hunstanton Hall, Norfolk, painted ceiling of W tower Ely Cathedral 1854–5 and engaged on nave ceiling at death in 1862, on ES committee 1851–62, helped judge the ES annual colour prizes, obit Eccl 23 (1862), 282
#Lewis, Thomas Christopher	23.4.56¢¤		(c.1833–1915), trained as architect (and so described on election, no details of career known) but chiefly an organ-builder at Brixton, also cast bells 1878–8, opposed Lord Grimthorpe's views about them
+ *¹Lewthwaite, Rev. William Henry, B.A. Founder	8.11.41 ~	Trinity	On CCS committee 1840–1, C Adel, Yorks 1840–2, PC Clifford 1842–5, became RC 1851
Lewthwaite, Samuel	F n.d. Magdalene		C Elsworth, Cambs 1846–8, disappears from CL 1849
Liberty, Rev. Nathaniel	3.11.54¢	King's, London	C Kildwick, Yorks 1850–3, C Barking, Ess 1853–4, C S. Mary, W. Brompton, Middx 1854–67, chapl. Cancer Hospital, Brompton 1854–93, chapl. Brompton Cemetery 1855–93, C Holy Trinity, Brompton 1867–93, disappears from CL 1907

Lightfoot, John	8.11.41	S. Catharine's	4 Grove St, Liverpool, Lancs
#Lightly, William	16.12.62¤		Architect (d.1865), 23 Bedford Row, restored the Austin canons' church (Eccl 24 (1863), 235–7, 26 (1865), 184); election date 16.12.62, not 16.12.63 as stated in Eccl
+Lindsay, Hon. Colin	<mid-40 ~ ¢¤‡	Trinity	Haigh Hall, Wigan, ES auditor 1852–3, 1862–3, churchwarden at Wigan at the time of the 1856 restoration, founder & 1st President Manchester Church Society which, in 1860, became the English Church Union, became RC 1868, + 1892
Lindsell, John	1850–1¢		10 Torrington Place, London, the street numbers stop before 10 in POLD which gives a John Lindsell as a barrister at 24 Old Square, Lincoln's Inn in 1849–53
Line, Rev. R. T., M.A.	1845 ~	Christ's	Not traced in AC or CL 1841–8
Lingham, Rev. John Fentiman, B.A	Founder~	Trinity	V Northbourne, Kent 1849–52, V Margate 1852–4, R Lambeth 1854–83, RD Lambeth 1854–81, chapl. to Lord Londesborough 1876–93
+Lloyd, Rev. Francis Llewelyn, B.A.	Founder ~ ¢¤‡	F. 1840–58 S. John's	On CCS committee 1840-2, C Wilnecote, Warks 1841–53, V Aldworth, Berks 1858–88 where he restored the church and built the porch and vestry
Lloyd, John Philip	8.11.41 ~	Christ Church, Oxford	Dan-yr-alt, Llangadoch, Carmarthenshire, gentleman
Lloyd, Thomas Bucknall	5.12.42 ~ ¢	S. John's	C Lilleshall, Salop 1848–51, V Meole Brace 1851–4, surrogate dio. Lichfield 1854, V S. Mary, Shrewsbury 1854–87, preb. Lichfield 1870–96, Archd. Salop 1886–96, RD Shrewsbury 1873–8, R Edgmond 1888–96
#§Lockwood, Henry Francis	18.4.42 ~ ¢¤‡		Architect (1811-78), Kingston-upon-Hull, articled to F. F. Robinson, began practice c.1834, FRIBA 1844, moved to Bradford 1849, partner of William Mawson (1828–89) & Richard Mawson (1834–1904), moved to London 1874
Lockyer, Edmund Leopold	5.12.43 ~ ¢¤‡	Emmanuel, formerly S. Mary Hall, Oxford	C Bletchingley, Surr 1846–9, C Yatesbury, Wilts 1849–52, R Westcot Barton, Oxon 1852–1900
+Lodge, Rev. John, M.A.	<mid-40 ~	F 1818 Magdalene	Librarian of Cambridge University 1822–45, R Anderby, Lincs 1835–50, a CCS vice-president 1840–3, Vice-President Magdalene 1849–43
Lomax, M. J.	?		Asst secretary at meeting 26.7.66, no note of election found and probably not a member; the inside cover of the ES 1863–4 report says subscriptions and donations are to be sent to him at Gosling & Sharpe's Bank (see also F. S. Gosling and J. C. Sharpe)
Lott, H. W.	1845 ~		Tracey House, Honiton, Dev
*Lowder, Rev. Charles Fuge	29.7.52	Exeter, Oxford	C Tetbury, Glos 1848, C S. Paul, Knightsbridge in 1850, later C S. George's-in-the-East, then V S. Peter, London Docks 1866–80
*Lowe, Richard Thomas	<mid-49	Christ's	Chapl. Madeira 1832–52, R Lea, Lincs 1852–74

name	date elected	Cambridge college or other	Addresses/location given in *The Ecclesiologist*/ career details
#Lower, *Edward Ward*	13.2.44		*Architect (d. 1878), 8 Upper Ranelagh Street, London, in Guildford 1868*
Lower, *Henry Martyn*	6.12.41 ~ ¢¤‡	S. Peter's	*C S. Paul, Wolverhampton 1845–8, C S. George, Kidderminster 1848–9, C Sidmouth, Dev1850–4, can. Montreal 1854–7, chapl. to Bp of Montreal 1854, Archd. Newfoundland 1857–63, Principal S. John's Theological College, Newfoundland 1863–9, PC Wolverton, Bucks 1869–70, R Fowlmere, Cambs 1873–97, +1900*
Loxham, Richard, B.A.	11.5.44 ~ ¢¤	Durham University	*PC Formby, Lancs 1846–8, then addrss given as Bolton but no appointment stated*
Luard, *Henry Richards*	5.12.43 ~ ¢¤	F. 1849 Trinity	*University career, also V Great S. Mary, Cambridge 1860–87 where be had removed the east gallery nicknamed 'Golgotha' occupied by the Vice-Chancellor and beads of houses, President CAS 1864–5*
+Luard, William Charles	1846 ~ ¢¤‡		*10 Upper Wimpole Street, POLD (1847) lists a Henry Luard bere; W.C.L on ES committee 1849–probably 1868, Treasurer 1851–3, of Cardiff in 1856, of Llandaff in 1864*
Lucas, Rev. St. John Wells, M.A.	Late 40	Downing	*Early military career, P 1832, chapl. Downing 1840, R E. Hatley & V Tadlow, Cambs 1840–53, not a member by mid-1842*
Ludgater, Rev. *Henry*	11.5.43 ~ ¢¤	Trinity	*C Aythorp Roding, Ess 1842–9, R there 1849–95*
+*Luke, Rev. William Henry Colbeck*	5.12.61¤	Oriel, Oxford	*On ES committee 1849–51, Treasurer 1851–3 at Wells Theological College 1853–4, C Oundle, Northants 1854, C Carlton, Cambs 1855–7, C E. Retford, Notts 1857–60, C Chislehurst, Kent 1861–3, R Elmswell, Suff 1863–78, Diocesan Inspector, Ely 1868–83, V S. Matthias, Earl's Court, London 1878–92*
Lukis, Rev. *William Collings, B.A.*	< mid-40 ~ ¢¤‡	Trinity	*Semington, Melksham, C Bradford-on-Avon, Wilts 1841–6, PC East Grafton 1846–50, V Great Bedwyn 1850–5, R Collingbourne Ducis 1855–62, chapl. to Marquess of Ailesbury 1850–81, R Wath-juxta-Ripon, Yorks 1862–92, an authority on bells*
*Lunn, Rev. John Robert	5.12.61‡	F 1855–64 S. John's	*Sadlerian Lecturer in mathematics 1857–64, V Marton w. Grafton, Yorks 1863–99, musician and composer*
Luxton, John	5.3.44 ~	S. Peter's	*PC Brushford, Dev 1849–52, R Bodleigh 1855–92, disappears from Crockford 1894*
+*Lyall, Rev. William Hearle*	10.2.54¢¤	S. Mary Hall, Oxford	*17 Park Crescent, London, C Christ Church, S. Pancras, London 1852–3, R S. Dionis Backchurch 1853–77, ES auditor 1855–6, 1857–8, President Sion College 1876, became RC 1880*
Lyall, The Ven. *William Rowe, M.A.*	14.11.43 ~ ¢	Trinity	*C Fawley, Hants 1812–15, chapl. St Thomas's Hospital 1817, asst preacher Lincoln's Inn, R Weeley, Ess 1827–33, Arch. Colchester 1824–42, Warburton Lecturer Lincoln's Inn 1826, R Fawstead, Ess 1827–33, R Hadleigh, Suff 1833–42, Archd. Maidstone & preb. Canterbury 1842–5, R Great Chart, 1848–52, Dean of Canterbury 45–57.*

Name	Date	College	Notes
+Lygon, Hon. Frederick	?28.3.55¢	Christ Church, Oxford	F 1852 All Souls, Oxford, added to ES committee 28.3.55 but no earlier evidence of election, probably on committee till 1865, of Madresfield Court, Worcs, M.P., succeeded as 6th Earl Beauchamp 1866, FSA
Lynn, Rev. John M., B.A.	30.4.44 ~	Trinity, Dublin	Chapl. to the Union, Cleobury Mortimer & C there 1844–8, PC Thornthwaite, Cumb 1851–57
Lyon, Rev. Charles Jobson, M.A.	1845 ~ ¢α‡	Trinity	Minister Episcopal church, S. Andrews, Scotland
Lyon, Rev. Ralph, D.D.	1–5.41	Trinity	Head Sherborne G.S. 1823–45, R Bishop's Caundle, Dors 1841–56, V Haydon 1845–56
Lyons, George Joseph	6.12.41 ~	Trinity	Adm. Lincoln's Inn 1845, called to the Bar 1850
Lyttleton, Lord George William M.A.	< mid-40 ~ ¢α‡	Trinity	Hagley Park, Worcs, succeeded 1837, active in education promotion, Greek scholar, FSA, married second daughter of Sir Stephen Glynne (q.v.), Lyttleton, N.Z. named after him, +1876
*Maberley, Rev. Thomas Astley	?	Christ Church, Oxford	Present at 2.5.55 meeting, C.S. Andrew, Holborn, London 1836–41, I Cuckfield 1846–77
Macculloch, R.	13.2.43 ~ ¢		Guernsey
M'Ewen, Rev. Archibald	6.12.41 ~ ¢α‡	Magdalene	C Semington, Melksham, Wilts 1840–6, S. John, Dumfries 1846–83, +1904
•Mackarness, Rev. George Richard	13.6.65	Merton, Oxford	C Barnwell nr Peterborough 1848–54, F. S. Columba's College, Ireland 1846–7, V Ilam, Ashbourne, Derbys 1854–74, Bp of Argyll & the Isles 1874–83, articles in Eccl 19 (1858), 385–6, 27 (1866), 376–9
Mackenzie, A., B.A.	1845 ~ ¢	Exeter, Oxford	Not traced in AO, of 12 Southwick Crescent, Hyde Park Gardens, London in 1857
MacLeod, W. H, B.A.	Late 40 ~	Trinity	Not traced in AC
Maine, Henry James Sumner	1.5.41	Pembroke	Adm. Lincoln's Inn 1847, called to the Bar 1850, Oxford & Cambridge professorships, Master of Trinity Hall 1877–88, +1888
§Maitland, Rev. Samuel Roffey	10.39	Trinity	Adm. Inner Temple 1809, called to the Bar 1816, C S. Edmund, Norwich 1821–3, PC Christ Church, Gloucester 1823–7, travelled abroad, Librarian & Keeper of MSS to Archbp of Canterbury, Lambeth Palace 1838, editor of the British Critic, his joining the CCS noted in BWD 19.10.39, Neale's diary 20.10.39, hon. member, FSA (20.5.41), +1866
Majendie, Lewis A.	17.12.60α		Great Dunmow, Ess, probably a son of the Rev. Henry Lewis Majendie listed in POD (1846)
•Major, John Richardson, M.A.	1846	Exeter, Oxford	Head of King's College, London 1846–56, Head Crypt School, Gloucester 1863–7, Master Wye College 1867–71
Mandley, George Frederick	13.2.45 ~ ¢		34 Charlotte Street, Manchester, in 1853 'commission merchant', Mount St, Manchester

name	date elected	Cambridge college or other	Addresses/location given in *The Ecclesiologist*/ career details
Manners, Lord John James Robert	6.12.41 ~ ¢¤‡	Trinity	Adm. Lincoln's Inn 1840, M.P. Newark 1841–7, joined the Young England Party', M.P. Colchester 1850–7, for N. Leics 1852–85, for Melton 1885–8, various public service appointments, succeeded as 7th Duke of Rutland 1888, +1906
Manners-Sutton, Rev. Thomas, M.A.	18.4.42	Trinity	Sub-dean of Lincoln 1831-4, preb. Westminster Abbey 1817–31, R Tunstall, Kent 1827–36, R Great Chart 1818–36, preb. Lincoln 1831–44, R Averbam w. Kelham, Notts 1837–44
Manning, Charles Robertson	14.11.43 ~	Corpus Christi	D 1848, P 1850, R & Patron Diss, Norf 1857–99, RD Redenball, 1868–99, hon. can. Norwich 1895–9, J.P., F.S.A
*•Manning, Ven. Henry Edward	8.11.41 ~	Balliol, F 1832-7	(1808–92). A leader of the Oxford Movement, Petworth, Suss, C Woollavington-cum-Graffham, Suss 1833, R there 1833–51 (rebuilt both bis churches), RD Midhurst 1837, Archd. Chichester 1840–51, became RC 1851, succeeded Wiseman as Archbp of Westminster 1865, cardinal 1875, +1892
Mare, William Salmon, M.A.	5.12.42 ~ ¢	Magdalene	C Morpeth, Northumb 1843–53, chapl. to Earl of Durbam, PC Owslebury, Hants 1853–62, V Bramham, Yorks 1862–98
§•Markland, James Heywood, F.S.A.	10.11.42 ~ ¢¤		Bath; elected hon. member 1846 or '47, student Inner Temple 1814, FSA (2.1.09), F.R.S. 1816, author on ecclesiastical archaeology, Eccl wrongly suggests he was an Oxford graduate, + 1864
Markwell, Rev. James William, B.A.	1–5.41 ~	Christ's	Initials wrongly given as 'J.S.' in Eccl, C S. Matthew, Manchester 1842–4, PC Coldhurst, Lancs 1845, C S. Clement Danes, London 1846–50, PC S. James, Curtain Rd, London 1851-67
Marriott, Fitzberbert Adams	13.3.43 ~	Oriel, Oxford	Sydenham, Kent, R Cotesbach, Leics 1842-3, Archd. of Tasmania and chapl. to Bp there 1843–54, C S. Paul, Knightsbridge, London 1856–8, no appointment 1859, V Chaddesley Corbet 1860–90, disappears from Crockford 1891
Marshall, Rev. F. W. or F. S.	<mid-40~	Caius	Probably Frederick Anthony Stansfield Marshall, C Pulham, Norf 1843–5, C Peterborough & chapl. to the Union 1846–57, can. minor Peterborough 1850–69, Precentor 1865–9, V Bringhurst w. Great Easton, Leics 1869–74
+Martin, Rev. Francis, M.A	9.39	F1825–68 Trinity	Career within Trinity, Neale's diary (25.9.39) notes he agreed to be a CCS vice-president which he was till 1843, +1868
Martin, John, F.L.S	13.2.43		(1791–1855), Froxfield, Eversholt, Beds, F.S.A., bookseller in London, then librarian to Duke of Bedford at Woburn 1836–55, as 'W.A.' (for Woburn Abbey) wrote articles on the condition of Bedfordshire churches in Northampton Mercury (reprinted in the Bedford Times) 1845-54.
*Maskell, Rev. William, M.A.	1846-7	University, Oxford	Broadleaze, Devizes, Wilts, B.A. 1836, V S. Marychurch, Dev 1847–50, chapl. to Bp of Exeter in 1849, became RC 1850

Mason, Alfred William, B.A	Trinity	<mid-40 ~ ¢‡	Stratford Green, Ess, C Bocking, Ess 1843-48, C S. Thomas, Stamford Hill, London 1848-52, C Loughton, Ess 1854-8, C Chelmsford 1858-9, V S. Moulsham, Ess 1859-77, V Dedham 1877-84, RD Dedham 1879 bon. can. S. Albans 1885, + 1890
Masters, Algernon		11.5.44 ~	Wine and spirit merchant, Tunbridge, Kent, Eccl gives name as 'Master'
Masters, Mr Joseph R.		1846 ~ ¢□	Printer & bookseller, 33 Aldersgate Street, London, publisher of Eccl 1846-68
Mather, George	Trinity	5.12.42 ~	PC S. Chad, Freehay, Staffs 1847-37, PC Oakamoor 1854-65, RD Cheadle 1857-79, +1892
Mathison, William Collings		10.39	F 1840 & asst T 1840-50, T 1850-68 Trinity Election date from BWD (29.10.39), Trinity career till 1868 (incl. Vice-Master 1866-8), R Dickleburgh, Norf 1868-71
+Matthew, Henry James, B.A.	Trinity	17.12.60□	C Kilndown 1861-7, on ES committee 1862-probably 1867 or '68, chapl. Bengal Establishment, Allahabad 1867, at Fort William, Calcutta 1868, C All Saints, Hampstead 1874-7, chapl. Simla 1877, Archd. Labore 1888-98
Maude, George Skilbeck	S. Catharine's Hall	6.12.41	+1844 leaving £600 to CCS (BWD 25.6.44)
May, Rev. Frederic Schiller, B.A.	Caius	21.6.59□	Rifle Terrace, Bayswater, C Ashweltborpe, Norf 1856-9, Christ Church, Paddington, London 1859-84, chapl. to Bp of Dunedin 1878, T in family of Duke of Teck 1885-8, R High Laver, Ess 1895-19, surrogate of Doctors' Commons 1872-1909, author of works on the Swedish and Oriental Churches
Mayor, Charles	S. John's	<mid-40 ~ ¢‡	C South Cove, Suff 1845-8, C Wavendon, Bucks 1848-76, disappears from Crockford 1877
Mayor, Charles, M.A.	Trinity	1.5.41	D 1840, asst master Rugby School 1840-6, +1846
Mears, Charles		30.4.44 ~ ¢	Tredegar Square, Bow Road, London, brother of the next, + 1859
#Mears, George		30.4.44 ~ ¢	Bell-founder (1806 or '07-65), joint owner of the Bell Foundry, Whitechapel with the above, traded as C. & G. Mears 1844-59, cast 'Big Ben' 1858, from 1861 traded as George Mears & Co., Robert Stainbank joined as partner 1864 and bought the business in 1865 shortly before George's death that year, thence known as Mears & Stainbank
Meadows, Mr E.		22.5.44 ~	Cambridge
Meggison, Augustine	Trinity	6.12.41 ~ ¢	C Lanchester, Dur 1846, C Bottesford, Leics 1847-56, disappears from CL 1857
Mercier, Rev. Jerome John	S. Mark, Chelsea	16.6.63□	T S. Mark's College, Chelsea 1856-c.1867, C Hanwell, Middx 1867-76, R Kemerton, Glos 1877-1901, not in Crockford 1902

417

name	date elected	Cambridge college or other	Addresses/location given in *The Ecclesiologist*/ career details
Meredith, Rev. Robert Fitzgerald, M.A.	1845 ~	*Trinity, Dublin & Worcester, Oxford*	C *Woolbridge, Dors* 1842–3, V *Halstock, Dors* 1843–69, R *there* 1870–93, chapl. to Lord Monteagle in 1846–52, inspector of schools 1853–5, R (& patron) *East Chelborough alias Lewcombe, Wilts* 1849–57
§•Merewether, Very Rev. John	Late 40 ~	*Queen's, Oxford*	Chapl. to Duchess of Clarence 1824 and the Queen 1830, R *New Radnor* 1828, Dean of Hereford 1832–50, Deputy Clerk to the Closet 1833, V *Madley* 1836–50, keen antiquarian and practising archaeologist
Middleton, M.A., Viscount, *see Brodrick*			
+Mill, Rev. Dr William Hodge	<mid-40 ~	*Trinity*	First Principal Bishop's College, Calcutta 1820–38, chapl. to Archbp of Canterbury 1839, Hulsean Advocate 1839–44, a CCS/ES vice-president 1840–53, V *Brasted, Kent* 1843–53, his daughter married B. Webb (q.v.) 1847, can. Ely 1848–53, Regius Professor of Hebrew 1848–53, vice-president of CAS in 1851, Ramsden Preacher 1853
*Miller, Rev. Charles, M.A.	10.11.42 ~ ¢	*Magdalene, Oxford*	V *Harlow, Ess* 1831–85, RD
Miller, John Joseph	22.5.44 ~	*Trinity*	C *Guilsbrough, Northants* 1849–50, PC *Bockleton, Worcs* 1858–64
Miller, Rev. Joseph Kirkman	8.11.41 ~	F *1808 Trinity*	V *Walkeringham, Notts* 1819–55, PC *Laysters, Herefs* 1830–55, PC *Bockleton, Worcs* 1830–55
Mills, Henry	5.12.42	*Trinity*	Matriculated 1842, no other details in AC
Mills, Thomas, B.A.	13.2.43 ~	*Trinity*	C *Hanham, Glos* 1844–6, chapl. to *Keysham Union* 1846–8, R *Bulpban, Ess* 1848–55, disappears from CL 1857
Mills, Thomas, M.A.	8.11.41 ~ ¢‡	*Christ Church, Oxford*	Re-elected 1845, chapl.-in-ordinary to the King 1816, R *Little Henery, Ess* 1821, R *Great Saxham* 1821 w. Stutton, Ipswich, etc 1829–79, bon. can. Norwich 1859
Milnes, Richard Monckton, M.A.	Late 40 ~ ¢‡	*Trinity*	Monkfryston, Pontefract, M.P. for Pontefract 1837–63, succeeded as Baron Houghton 1858, author of various books of poetry and essays, +1885
Miniken, William, B.A.	11.5.42 ~ ¢□	St Catharine's Hall	Asst C *Chipping Camden, Glos* 1842–8, C *Dursley, Glos* 1849, disappears from CL 1850
Mitchell, Francis (or Frank) Jobmstone	13.2.44 ~	S. John's	*Eccl* wrongly has initials as 'F.T.', in 1846–9 of 12 Upper Wimpole Street, London, AC notes him as a businessman in S. Wales, the rebuilder of Llanfrechfa church and FSA and FGS
Mitchell, Thomas	5.12.43 ~	*Trinity*	C *Piston, Herts* 1843–7, C.S. *Pancras, London* 1847, V *Long Clawson, Leics* 1848–85
Moate, Charles R.	1847 ~		*Ponder's End, Enfield, Middx*
•Moberley, Rev. Dr George D. D.	1845 ~ ¢□‡	*Balliol, Oxford*	T. & senior dean Balliol 1830, catechetical lecturer, public examiner 1830, 1833–5, Select Preacher 1833, 1858, 1863, Head *Winchester College* 1835–66, F 1866–70, R *Brighstone, I.O.W.* 1866–9, can. Chester 1868–9, preb. Salisbury 1869, Bp of Salisbury 1869–85

Name	College	Date	Notes
Molesworth, Rev. Hugh *Henry*	S. John's	5.12.43 ~ ¢	C Ervan, Corn 1842-7, R Little Petherick 1848-62, succeeded as 9th Baronet 1855
Molesworth, Paul *William*	S. John's	22.5.43 ~ ¢	C Buckland-in-the-Moor, Dev 1845-6, R Tetcott, Corn 1847-54, became RC 1854, still of Tetcott in 1857
*Molyneux, Rev. John William *Henry*, B.A.	Trinity	<mid-40 ~	BWD (24.5.39) notes he was at what was probably the CCS foundation meeting but Boyce's Memorial does not record him as a founder, C Donoughmore, Co. Tyrone 1849, C Christ Church, S. Pancras 1850-1, PC S. Gregory w. S. Peter, Sadbury, Suff 1855-79, where he instituted advanced Anglo-Catholic worship, hon. can. Ely 1875-9, succeeded as 8th baronet 1879 but died same year
Money, Rev. James Stoughton, B.A	Emmanuel	13.2.43 ~	C Alderley, Glos 1841-3, R Yatesbury, Wilts 1843-52, FSA 1840, from c.1846 styled Money-Kyrle
Monk, *Charles James*	Trinity	11.5.44	Adm. Lincoln's Inn 1845, called to the Bar 1850, Chancellor of Bristol Dio. 1855-85, of Gloucester 1859-85, M.P. for Gloucester 1859-85 & 1895-1900, J.P.
Monkhouse, Cyril Joseph	Trinity	22.11.41	+1842
Montalembert, Le Comte *Charles-René Forbes* de	Paris	Late 40	*Writer* (1810-70), hon. member, enthusiast for medieval architecture and advocate of the Gothic Revival in France, withdrew from the Society objecting that membership had not been conferred in the proper manner and Society's use of the word 'catholic' in relation to its aims
Moore, Rev. Arthur	Probably University, Oxford	5.12.43 ~	B.A. 1825, R Walpole S. Peter, Lynn, Norf 1832-52, chapl. to Lord Melbourne, disappears from CL 1852
Moore, Rev. *Edward*, M.A.	S. John's	18.4.42	V Weston, Lincs 1835-66, PC Moulton chapel 1835-7, PC Whaplode Drove 1837-66, Head Spalding G.S. 1866-89, preb. & can. Lincoln 1870-59, FSA 1858
Morrell, James *Wright*	Trinity, Oxford	10.11.42	Tewkesbury, no career details available, +1873
Morrice, Rev. William *David*, B.A.	S. John's	Founder ~ ¢¢‡	C Leeds, 1840-2, C Clovelly, Dec 1842-7, C S. Andrew, Plymouth 1847, C Probus, Corn 1847-9, C Westbury, Wilts 1850-1, C Oldland, Glos 1852, V Longbridge Deverill w. Monkton Deverill & Crockerton, Wilts 1852-74, V S. Thomas, Salisbury 1874-85, can Salisbury 1863-98
Morris, John	Trinity	1845 ~	Distinguished career as a RC (converted 1846), including private secretary to Cardinal Wiseman, +1893
Mortlock, Rev. Edmund Davy	Christ's	<mid-40¢	C Pampisford, Cambs 1810, T. to son of Marquess of Bute, V Great Abingdon, Cambs 1835-45, R & V Moulton, Suff 1845-73, author of various religious works

name	Cambridge college or other	date elected	Addresses/location given in *The Ecclesiologist*/ career details
Mortlock, *Thomas*, M.A.	S. John's	<mid-40 ~	*Adm. Middle Temple 1799, senior partner of bankers John Mortlock & Co., Cambridge, J.P., High Sheriff, +1859*
Morton, *James*, M.A.	S. John's	Late 40	*Left CCS by mid-1841, R Stockleigh Pomeroy, Dev 1830, V Holbeach, Lincs 1831-65, preb. Lincoln 1831-65*
Mould, *Ralph Aller*	Trinity	8.11.41 ~ ¢¤‡	*C Cheadle, Staffs 1848-9, C Cam, Glos 1850, PC Holy Trinity chapel, Warrington 1851-60, disappears from CL 1861*
Mould, R. A.		1847¢¤	*Liverpool, a different person from the above (perhaps his son)*
Mouncey, *Daniel Burton*	S. Peter's	8.11.41 ~	*Matriculated 1840, no other details in AC*
•Murray, *Charles Robert Scott*, M.P., B.A.	Christ Church, Oxford	11.5.42	*Lived at Danesfield, Bucks, M.P. for Bucks 1841-5, +1882*
*•Murray, *Francis Henry*	Christ Church, Oxford	10.11.42 ~	*R Chisleburst, Kent 1846-c.1870, restored the church there under B. Ferrey (q.v.) 1848-9, author of various religious works*
Musgrave, Ven. *Charles*, D.D.	F 1816 Trinity	8.11.41	*V Whitkirk, Yorks 1821-6, PC S. John, Roundhay, Leeds 1826-7, V Halifax 1827-75, preb. York, first Archd. of Craven*
Musgrave, Rev. *William Peete*, M.A.		<mid-40	*C Trumpington, Cambs 1837-40, chapl. Trinity 1838-42, V Eaton Bishop 1841-54, can. & preb. Hereford 1844-92, chapl. to Archbp of York, R Etton, Yorks 1854-77, Warden S. Catherine's Hospital, Ledbury, Heref's 1877-92*
Napier, *The Lord Francis*	Trinity	10.39~	*Election date from BWD (29.10.39), political career, +1898*
Naylor, *Frederick Leeds*, B.A.	Trinity	14.11.43 ~ ¢	*C Chignal Smealey, Ess 1845-6, C S. Botolph, Aldersgate 1847-50, C Merstham, Surr 1852-60*
+*Neale, *John Mason*	Trinity, migrated to Downing Oct. 1840	Founder ~ ¢‡	*(1818-66), with Webb the driving force in setting up the CCS, Chairman 1839-42, on committee 1843-4, a secretary 1845-59, then an ordinary committee member, B.A. 1840, then asst T. and chapl. at Downing, D 1841, P 1842, C S. Nicholas, Guildford 1841-2 but not instituted, accepted living of Crawley, Suss but not instituted due to ill-health, for same reason spent winters in Madeira 1843-5, Warden Sackville College, East Grinstead 1846-66, inhibited by Bp of Chichester 1847-63, founded nursing sisterhood of S. Margaret at Rotherfield 1855, relocating it to East Grinstead 1856, prolific hymn writer and author, obituary in Eccl 27 (1866), 265-6*
§Neeld, *Joseph*, M.P., M.A.		10.11.42 ~	*Gritleton Hall, Chippenham, inherited a £900,000 fortune from his uncle in 1827 and used part of it to rebuild Gritleton House, the churches of Leigh Delamere and Alderton; for these and other works he employed J. Thomson (q.v.), legal and political career, FSA (31.1.28), MP for Chippenham, +1857*

Name	Date ~ mark	College	Notes
+Nelson, Earl *Horatio*	21.2.42 ~ ¢¤	Trinity	*Succeeded to title 1835, an ES trustee from 1845, a vice-president from 1864, of Trafalgar, Salisbury, +1913*
Nelson, Hon. John Horatio	5.3.44	Trinity	*C Eartham, Suss 1847–51, C Speen, Berks 1851–3, R Trimley S. Mary, Suff 1853–7, R Belaugh w. Scottow, Norf 1857–72, R Shaw w. Donnington, Berks 1872–1909, +1917*
Neville, Ralph, M.P	13.2.43 ~ ¢	Magdalene	*M.P. for New Windsor 1841–7, for E. Somerset 1865–8, for mid-Somerset 1868–76, + 1886*
§Neville, *Richard, 3rd Lord Braybrooke LL.D* Late 40		Magdalene	*Audley End, M.P. Thirsk 1805–6, Saltash 1806–7, Buckingham 1807–12, Berkshire 1812–25, succeeded 1825, assumed additional name of Griffin 1825, FSA (10.5.1838), +1858*
*Neville, Rev. William Frederick, M.A.	13.2.43 ~ ¢¤	Magdalene	*C Butleigh, Som 1841–5, V Butleigh w. Baltonsborough 1845–82, preb. Wells 1851, RD Glastonbury 1851–82*
Neville-Rolfe, Edward Fawcett, B.A.	<mid-40 ~ ¢¤‡	Trinity	*C Great Amwell, Herts 1846–50, R Morningthorpe, Norf 1950–3, C Great Amwell (again) 1854–62, chapl. of Cannes & Bordighera for 17 years, can. Gibraltar 1875–83*
Neville-Rolfe, Rev. *Strickland Charles Edward, M.A.*	<mid-40	*Wadham, Oxford*	*V Heacham, Norfolk 1838–52*
Newbould, William Williamson	Founder ~ ¢¤‡	Trinity	*C Bluntisham, Cambs 1844–5, C Comberton 1848–64, resided in London 1860 and Kew Green 1879–86, noted botanist*
Newcome, Rev. William	8.11.41 ~ ¢¤‡	Christ Church, Oxford	*Hockwold Hall, Brandon, Norfolk, B.A. 1799, R Belaugh, Norf 1810–24, C Mundford from 1815, Langford w. Ickburgh from 1824, V Sutton, Isle of Ely 1838–46*
#Niblett, Francis	6.3.45 ~ ¢¤‡		*Architect (1814–83), Haresfield Court, Gloucester; for some reason the 1846/9 membership lists have a 'Niblett, T' and a 'Niblett, Rev. Francis' both of Haresfield Court; F.N, who was a significant local architect, is not thought to have taken holy orders ; no T. N. is known as an architect; T:N. disappeared by the 1856 membership list, F.N. is still (no doubt wrongly) given the title 'Rev.' as late as the 1863 membership list*
Nicholls, Henry George	Late 40	Trinity	*PC Holy Trinity, Forest of Dean, Glos 1847–67*
Nicholson, Rev. *Henry Joseph Boone, D.D.* Late 40 ~ ¢¤‡		Magdalene, Oxford	*D 1820, P 1821, R S. Albans 1835–66, RD S. Albans 1846, hon. can. Rochester 1862–6, chapl. to Duke of Clarence, FSA, F.R.A.S., author of a history of S. Albans Abbey*
Noel, *Charles George, Viscount Campden*	28.11.44 ~	Trinity	*M.P. for Rutland 1840–1, High Sheriff 1848, on ES committee from 1850, succeeded as Earl of Gainsborough 1866, Lord Lieutenant 1867–81*
Norman, Rev. George Bethune	1846 ~	Trinity	*C Prescot, Lancs 1842–3, asst minister S. Mary de Crypt, Gloucester 1846, minister S. Mary Magdalene chapel 1846 w. S. Margaret chapel, Gloucester 1847–50, disappears from CL 1868*
Northampton, *2nd Marquess of, see Compton*			

421

name	date elected	Cambridge college or other	Addresses/location given in *The Ecclesiologist*/ career details
#Norton, John	23.2.54¢¤		*Architect (1823–1904), 24 Old Bond St, pupil of B. Ferrey from 1846, ARIBA 1850, FRIBA 1857, partner of P. E. Masey*
*Nugée, George, B.A.	13.2.43 ~ ¢¤	Trinity	*C S. Paul, Knightsbridge, London 1847–55, R Widley w. Wymering, Hants 1858–72, formed a nursing sisterhood at Wymering, 1st Warden of Lambeth Dio. Penitentiary, founder & Provost of S. Austin's Priory 1872–92*
Oakes, Henry James	21.2.42	Emmanuel	*Of Bury S. Edmund's, banker, various public offices, + 1875*
Oakes, James Henry Porteus	22.11.41 ~ ¢¤‡	Emmanuel	*Son of H. J. Oakes, adm. Inner Temple 1845, succeeded father as a banker, + 1901*
O'Brien, Stafford Augustus, M.P., M.A.	21.2.42	Trinity	*Blatherwycke Park, Wansford, Northants, M.P. for Northants 1841–7, assumed additional name of Stafford, 1847, + 1857*
#O'Connor, Arthur	23.11.52¢¤		*Stained glass artist (1826–73), 4 Berners St, became a partner of his father, Michael c.1851*
Ogle, J. W., M.D.	11.7.64¤		*Upper Brook Street, London*
Okes, John, M. B.	Late 40 ~ ¢	Sidney Sussex	*Of Cherry Hinton Hall, Cambs, medical career, + 1870*
Okes, Rev. Richard, M.A.	14.11.43 ~	F 1820–6 King's	*Career at Eton 1821–48, D 1822, P 1827, chairman of Cambridge Waterworks Corp. 1858–87, J.P., + 1888*
Oldham, George Alfred	6.12.41 ~	Trinity	*Eccl wrongly states initials as 'J. A.', C Hove w. Preston, Suss 1846–9, C Godshill, I.O.W 1851–3, C Dorking, Surr, 1854–9, disappears from CL 1865*
Oliver, John	6.12.41	Queens'	*V Warmington, Northants 1844–73, chapl. King's College Hospital, London 1855–62, Warden London Dio. Penitentiary, Highgate 1856–83*
Oliver, Rev. William Hutchinson, B.A.	Founder	Trinity	*Kenwyn, Truro, Corn, C Tonwell & Waterford, Herts, C Brington, Bythorn & Old Weston, Hunts 1844–6, C Normacot, Staffs 1848–51, listed in CL 1855 but no appointment stated, C Bengeo, Herts 1856–62, R Stapleford 1863–73, disappears from Crockford 1874, the Kenwyn address has not been traced in CL*
Osborne, Francis, M.A., Lord Godolphin	10.11.42 ~	Trinity	*M.A. 1811, Gogmagog House, Cambs, M.P. for Helston 1799–1802, for Leues 1802–6, for Cambs 1810–11, High Steward of Cambs 1836–50, created Baron of Farnham Royal, Bucks 1832*
Otty, William	28.11.44 ~	Queens'	*Matriculated 1844, no other details available*
Overton, H. B.	10.11.42		*Grimstone, Norfolk, White's Directory (1845) lists a Robert B. Overton, surgeon, at Grimstone*
Packe, James, M.A.	13.2.43	F 1824–48 King's	*Vice-Provost King's, career at King's, + 1873*
+Page, Rev. Cyril William, M.A	13.2.45 ~ ¢	Christ Church, Oxford	*Christ Church, Oxford Cloisters, Westminster, B.A. 1827, PC Christ Church, Westminster 1843–73, ES auditor 1854–5*

Name	College	Date	Notes
Page, Rev. Luke Flood	Corpus Christi	1.5.41 ~ ¢	R Woolpit, Suffolk 1837–63
Paine, Cornelius, junior		1845–6 ~	Islington, in 1843–7 POLD has a Cornelius Paine as a broker in Paine & Young of Kensington
+Paley, Frederick Apthorp, M.A.	S. John's	< mid-40 ~	On CCS committee 1840–1, a secretary 1841–5, resident at college 1838–46 but required to give up his rooms on being suspected of encouraging a pupil to become a RC, became RC himself 1846, private T. to various families 1847–56, returned to Cambridge 1860, T till 1874, Professor of Classical Literature at Catholic University of Kensington 1874–7, prominent ecclesiologist, wrote first prefatory address in Eccl (according to Boyce's Memorial), +1888
§Palmer, Charles John		Late 40	Solicitor, Great Yarmouth, FSA (14.1.30)
Palmer, Mr Jonathon		10.11.42 ~	Cambridge
Parker, Rev. John, M.A.	Oriel, Oxford	18.4.42 ~	Sweeny, Oswestry, Salop, R Llanemarwic, Montgom 1827–44, V Llan-y-Blodwell, Salop 1844–6
•Parker, John Henry		3.40 ~ ¢¤‡	Writer and publisher (1806–84), Oxford, election date from BWD (23.3.40), listed as the Oxford publisher of Eccl, succeeded his uncle Joseph as a booksellerand publisher, published for leaders of the Oxford Movement, edited the 1848 ed. of Rickman's Attempt to Discriminate…, wrote the popular Introduction to the Study of Gothic Architecture (1st ed. 1849), FSA 1849, first keeper of Ashmolean Museum 1870–84
•Parkins, William Trevor, S.C.L.	Merton, Oxford	1845 ~ ¢	Secretary OAS in 1845, Barrister-at-law, Inner Temple 1851
Parkinson, John Allen.	Corpus Christi	22.11.41 ~	C Foulsham, Norfolk 1846–52, R Hazeleigh, Ess 1852–69
Parnell, Hon. & Rev. Geo. Damer	Downing	11.5.43	C Ash nr Wrotham, Kent 1850–4, C Elson, Hants 1857–9, C Ash-next-Sandwich, Kent 1859–61, V Long Cross, Surr 1861–75, +1882
+Parnell, Hugh, M.A.	St John's	Late 40 ~ ¢¤‡	Adm. Lincoln's Inn 1842, called to the Bar 1845, ES auditor 1849–50, at Lincoln's Inn in 1864, +1906
Parnell, John	S. Peter's	5.3.44	Adm. Lincoln's Inn 1847, called to the Bar 1850, +1900
Paroissien, Rev. Challis, M.A.	Trinity	Late 40	V Everton w. Tetworth, Beds 1833–6, R Hardingham, Norfolk 1839–74
+§§Parry, Thomas Gambier	Trinity	< mid-40 ~ ¢¤‡	Artist (1816–88), FSA (19.2.35), B.A. 1837, purchased estate at Highnam, Glos 1838, built Highnam church 1849–51 under H. Woodyer and decorated it himself in 'spirit fresco' 1850–71, on ES committee 1856–probably 1868, J.P., High Sheriff 1850, letter to Eccl 28 (1867), 335–41

name	date elected	Cambridge college or other	Addresses/location given in *The Ecclesiologist*/ career details
Parry, Rev. William Henry, M.A.	Late 40	Late F 1811-29 S. John's	Shipwash, Northumb, C Swavesey, Cambs, 1808, R Holt, Norf 1828-37, R Bothal, Northumb 1837-45, Select Preacher at Cambridge 1827
Parsons, Rev. John, M.A.	7.2.42	Oriel, Oxford	V Marden, Devizes, Wilts 1816-44, wrongly given initials of 'D. A.' in Eccl and 1842-3 membership lists
*Patterson, Rev. James Laird, B.A.	1845 ~	Trinity, Oxford	Treasurer OAS in 1845, C S. Thomas, Oxford 1847-50, seceded to Rome 1850, President S. Edmund's College 1870-80, Bp of Emmaus
Pattinson, William Henry	6.12.41	Caius	Melberley, nr Carisbrook, I.O.W, major in I.O.W. Artillery Militia 1875
+Pearson, Frederick Burnet, M.A.	Late 40 ~ ¢¤‡	Trinity	Eccl wrongly gives initials as 'F. H.', B.A. 1823, military career, ES auditor 1862-3, +1870
Pearson, Henry Hugh	<mid-40 ~	Trinity	Professor of Music at Edinburgh University 1844, composer, +1886
Pearson, John, B.A.	<mid-40	Caius	Adm. Lincoln's Inn 1841, called to the Bar 1844, knighted 1882, +1886
#Pearson, John Loughborough	21.6.59¤		Architect (1817-97), 22 Harley St, in office of I. Bonomi, Durham 1831-41, with Salvin (q.v.) in 1842, then P. Hardwick, began own practice 1843, FRIBA 1860, succeeded Scott as surveyor to Westminster Abbey, Royal Gold Medal 1880, FSA 1853, R.A. 1880, joined by his son Frank 1881
Pearson, Rev. William	13.3.43 ~ ¢	Exeter, Oxford	Challock, nr Charing, Kent, C Kingsdown, Kent 1843, C Great Chart, Kent 1844-8, PC Thanington 1848-62
*Pearson, Rev. William Henley, M.A.	1848¢	Christ Church, Oxford	Preb. Heytesbury 1838, R S. Nicholas, Guildford 1837-56, chapl. to Viscount S. Vincent till 1867, took name of Jervis 1865, author of The Gallican Church ... (1872), +1883
Peile, Rev. Thomas William, M.A.	10.11.42	F 1829-31 Trinity	Asst master Shrewsbury School 1828-9, Head Liverpool Collegiate School 1829-33, PC S. Catharine, Liverpool 1831-4, T. at Durham 1834-41, PC Croxdale, Durham 1836-41, Head Repton School 1841-54, V Luton, Beds 1857-60, V S. Paul, South Hampstead 1860-73, +1882
Pennington, Philip	14.11.43 ~	Christ's	C S. John, Longton, Stoke-on-Trent 1848-51, C Calbourne w. Newtown, I.O.W., 1851, C Brightwell, Berks 1852-3, C S. Paul, Cheltenham 1854, civil chapl. Mabébourg, Mauritius 1855-63
#Penrose, Francis Cranmer	8.11.41	Magdalene	Architect (1817-1903), pupil of E. Blore 1835-9, ARIBA 1846, FRIBA 1848, surveyor of S. Paul's Cathedral 1852, Gold Medal 1883, president RIBA 1894-6, also archaeologist and astronomer, FRS. 1894, FSA 1898
#Penson, Richard Kyrke	6.3.45 ~ ¢¤		Architect (1815 or '16-86), Oswestry, Salop, studied in London 1843-8, pupil of father T. Penson, ARIBA 1849, FRIBA 1861, retired 1864, Eccl wrongly gives his name as 'J. Penton'

Name	College	Date	Notes
Percival, Captain E. A.		11.5.42 ~ ¢	Langford, Somerset, in 1849-65 of Chapel Cleeve, Taunton
Perram, George Jubb	Clare Hall	22.11.41 ~	C Nettlestead, Kent 1843-9, C Clymping, Suss 1849-57, British chapl. at Düsseldorf 1857-9, at Tours 1859-60, C S. Peter, Walworth, Surr 1865-8, C S. George the Martyr, Queen's Sq. 1869-70, chapl. Central London Asylum, Highgate 1870-5, +1904
Perry, Rev. Charles, M.A.	F 1829-41 & T 1832-40 Trinity	1.5.41	Not a member by mid-1842, 'a stout Evangelical'; V S. Paul, Cambridge 1842-7, 1st Bishop of Melbourne 1847-76
Perry, James Gideon Frederick, B.A.	Trinity	1.5.41 ~ ¢	C Clitheroe, Lancs 1842-6, C Holy Trinity, Lambeth 1846-9, V Tottington, Lancs 1849-81
*Perry, Thomas Walter	Chichester Theological in 1843	21.2.42 ~	20 Steward Street, Spitalfields, London, D 1845, P 1846, C S. Peter the Great, Chichester in 1846-50, C All Saints, Margaret St 1850-5, C S. Mary, Addington, Bucks 1857-62, C Sub-deanery church, Chichester 1857-62, C S. Michael, Brighton 1862-72, on Royal Commission on Ritual 1867-70, V Ardleigh, Ess 1872-91, hon. can. S. Albans 1883, author on ritual legalities, e.g. Lawful Church Ornaments (1857)
Petty, Thomas Edmund	Trinity	13.2.45	PC Bardsea, Lancs 1852-4, disappears from CL 1855
+Phelps, Rev. Robert, M.A.	F 1838-43 Sidney Sussex	<mid-40	CCS auditor 1841-2, Master Sydney Suss 1843-90, Vice-Chancellor 1844-5 & 1847-8, R Willingham, Cambs 1848-90, President CAS 1847-8
Phillips, Rev. Charles, B.A	Trinity	Founder~	C S. James, Gloucester, 1841-3, C S. Mary, Somers Town, Midx 1844-5, C S. Luke, Kings Cross 1847-9, evening lecturer S. Swithin, London 1847-56, V S. Matthew, Oakley Sq., S. Pancras, London 1849-88
Phillips, Rev. George, B.D.	F 1831-46 & T Queens'	10.11.42	D 1831, P 1832, R Sandon, Ess 1846-57, Vice-Chancellor 1861-2, President of Queens' 1857-92
Phillips, Henry Walter	Corpus Christi	11.5.44 ~ ¢	C S. Levan & Sennan, Corn 1847, PC Chacewater 1847-8
§•Phillips, Sir Thomas		11.39 ~	Apparently joined again 1845 or '46 when address given as Temple, hon. member, Middle Hill, Warks, FSA FRS, Neale's diary (21.11.39) records 'Sir Thomas Philips, the greatest bibliomaniac of the day' as joining
Phillipps, Robert Biddulph	Longworth, Hereford	30.4.44 ~	
Philpott, Rev. Henry, B.D.	F1829-45 & T S. Catharine's	10.11.42	D 1831, P 1833, Whitehall Preacher 1837-8, Master S. Catharine's 1845-60, Vice-Chancellor 1846-7 & 1856-8. chapl. to Prince Consort 1854-60, Clerk of the Closet to Queen, Bp of Worcester 1861-90, +1892
Philpott, Rev. Richard Stamper	S. Catharine's Hall	7.11.65	C Christ Church, Epsom, Surr 1850-8, chapl. to Duke of Hamilton & Brandon from 1851, V Farrington Gurney w. Stone Easton, Som (patron R. P. Philpott) 1858-62, V Chewton Mendip w. Emborrow, Som 1858-86, preb. Wells 1879-84, +1894

name	date elected	Cambridge college or other	Addresses/location given in *The Ecclesiologist*/ career details
Philpotts, Henry, Bp of Exeter	6.12.41	Corpus Christi, F 1795–1804 Magdalen, Oxford	Adm. patron, V Kilmersden, Som 1804, V Bishop Middleham, 1805, V Stanton-le-Street, Co. Durham 1806, R Gateshead 1808, preb. Durham 1810–20, R Stanhope-in-Weardale 1820, Dean of Chester 1828, Visitor Exeter College 1831, Bp of Exeter 1831–69
#Phipps, Charles John	1.3.60		Architect (1835–97), 5 Paragon Buildings, Bath, articled to J. Wilson and T. Fuller in Bath and stayed with them till 1857, began practice 1858, ARIBA 1860, FRIBA 1866, moved to London 1866, partner and successor was son-in-law Arthur Blomfield Jackson
Picton, John Owen	7.2.42 ~ ¢	Queens'	I Smithill's Chapel, Deane, Lancs 1848–50, C Chippenham, Wilts 1852–3, C Rowde 1854–7, C All Saints, Leicester 1858, C S. George, Leicester 1859–60, R Desford 1861–82
Pilling, *Charles Richard*	5.12.42	Caius	C Shaw, Lancs 1846–9, C Bolton 1851–3, master Rochdale G.S. 1853–60, C S. James, Rochdale 1853–60
#Place, George Gordon	5.3.44 ~ ¢		Architect (fl. 1844–59), Nottingham, worked in Notts, Lincs and Derbys, specialising in churches, magistrate in 1844
Plater, Herbert	1848¢¢	Merton, Oxford	Asst master Marlborough College 1852–4, Head Newark G.S. 1854–93, R Kirton, Notts 1893–1900
§Platt, *Thomas Pell*, M.A.	Late 40 ~	F 1820 Trinity	Bramshot Place, Liphook, Hants, Librarian of British & Foreign Bible Soc, a distinguished Orientalist, +1852
Podmore, Rev. *Richard Hillman*	<mid-40 ~ ¢¤‡	Trinity	C Yarnscombe, Dev 1846–9, chapl. & P Ottery S. Mary 1849–52, asst minister to 1st Bp of Fredericton 1852–6, C S. Columb Major, Corn 1857–64, V Rockbeare, Dev 1864–1902
Pollen, Rev. *George Pollen Boileau*, M.A.	1846 ~	Corpus Christi, Oxford	R Little Bookham, Leatherhead, 1823–47 (patrons 'Pollen's representatives")
Poole, Rev. –	29.7.52	Probably S. Edward Hall, Oxford	Probably Alfred Poole, C S. Barnabas, Pimlico, joined ES at same time as J. Skinner, senior C at S. Paul's
Poole, John Copeland	14.11.43 ~ ¢	S. Peter's	C S. Martin-at-Oak, Norwich 1847–9, C Stockton, Warks 1850, C Helidon, Northants 1850–2, R Clay Coton 1852–99, +1915
*Pope, *Thomas Alder*	11.5.43 ~	Jesus	C & lecturer Stoke Newington 1847–9, PC Stoke Newington 1849–53, became RC 1853 or '54
*Portal, Rev. *George Raymond*	22.6.52¢¤	Christ Church, Oxford	C Wilton, Wilts 1850–2, C S. Barnabas, Pimlico 1852–7, R Albury, Surr 1858–71, R Burghclere 1871–89, hon. can. Winchester 1882, author e.g. of Sermons on Some of the Prevalent Objections to Ritual Observances
Porter, Rev. *Charles*, M.A.	10.11.42 ~	F 1820 & T Caius	Not mentioned as a T. in AC, V Stamford Baron, Northants 1833–41, R Aughnamullen, Ballibay, Ireland 1842–50, V Ganton, Yorks 1850–5, V Raunds, Northants 1855–77

Name	College	Date	Notes
Powell, Rev. Edward Armett, M.A.	Christ's	14.11.43 ~	C Ampthill, Beds in 1841-3, R Toft w. Caldecote, Cambs 1843-92, built new rectory at Toft
+Powell, Francis Sharpe, M.P.	S. John's, Oxford	By mid-64□	Adm. Inner Temple 1853, M.P. Wigan 1857-9, 1881, 1885-1910, Cambridge 1863-8, ES auditor 1863-4, joined ES committee 17.3.66, M.P. W. Riding (N. Div.) 1872-4, + 1911
Powell, N.		15.7.62	
Power, John, B.A.	F 1841 Pembroke	5.12.42	T 1852-70, career within Pembroke College, +1890
Powis, 8th Earl, see E. J. Herbert			
Powles, Rev. Richard Cowley, M.A	F 1842-50 & T 1846 Exeter, Oxford	13.2.45 ~ ¢	Held a school at Blackheath 1850-69, then at Eversley, Hants
§Pownall, Rev. Charles Colyear Beaty, M.A.	Clare Hall	7.2.42 ~ ¢□‡	C South Carlton, Lincs 1831-4, chapl. to Earl of Portmore 1831, C Milton Ernest, Bedford 1834-5, V there 1835-80 (church restored 1864-5 by Butterfield (q.v.) whose brother-in-law lived at the Hall), RD Clapham, J.P. from 1844
Pownall, George Purves	Trinity	13.2.44 ~ ¢□	C Dursley, Glos 1846-8, C S. Anne, Soho 1848-9, C S. Giles, Cripplegate, 1849-52, chapl. Western Australia 1852-63, Dean of Perth 1858-63, C Isleworth, Middx 1863-4, V S. John, Hoxton 1864-98, RD Shoreditch 1879-90, +1900
Poynder, Rev. Leopold, B.A	Trinity	<mid-40 ~	Chapl. H.E.I. Co., Bengal 1848-66, C Blyborough, Lincs 1867-9, C Tuxworth, Hants 1869-71, C-in-charge Weeting, Norf 1873-5, +1904
Pratt, George Charles, Earl of Brecknock	Trinity	<mid-40	Succeeded also as 2nd Marquis & Earl Camden 8.10.40, seat at Bayham Abbey, Suss, +1866
Pratt, Rev. Jermyn, M.A.	Trinity	11.5.42 ~	R Bintry & Themelthorpe, Norf 1823-6, C Fordham 1823-30, R Great Bircham & of Harpley 1831-2, R Campsey Ashe, Woodbridge, Suffolk 1836-67
#Preedy, Frederick		23.11.52¢□	Architect and stained glass artist (1820-98), Worcester, trained perhaps under Harvey Eginton, Worcester, began practice c 1850, moved to London 1859
#Prichard, John		13.6.61□	Architect (1817-86), Cardiff, pupil of T. L. Walker and A. W. N. Pugin, ARIBA 1839, partner of J. P. Seddon 1852-63, diocesan architect for Llandaff 1847-86
Prichard, Roger	S. Peter's	1.5.41	Matriculated 1840, 'died early'
Probert, Charles Kentish		10.11.42 ~ ¢	Newport, Ess
Proctor, Rev. Dr George	S. Edmund Hall/Worcester, Oxford	1845-6 ~	Kemptown, Brighton, M.A. 1820, R S. Michael, Lewes, Suss 1826-41, R Monken Hadleigh, Herts 1846-60, chapl. to Fishmonger Almshouses, Maidenhead, Berks 1860-80, his niece married G. E. Street (q.v.), +1881

name	date elected	Cambridge college or other	Addresses/location given in The Ecclesiologist/ career details
Prower, Rev. John Mervin	8.11.41 ~ ¢¤‡	Wadham, Oxford	B.A. 1806, V Purton, Cricklade, Wilts 1827-69, hon can.Bristol, M.P. for Cambridge, possibly an Evangelical since he attended the Rev. Charles Simeon's services in Cambridge (H. E. Hughes, Charles Simeon of Cambridge (1977), 201)
Pryme, Prof. George	?	Trinity	Present at meeting 8.5.45, Professor of Political Economy 1828-63
#Pullan, Richard Popplewell	6.56¤		Architect (1825-88), FRIBA 1861, married Mary, sister of W. Burges (q.v.)
Pulling, Frederick William	13.2.44	Corpus Christi	C Revelstoke, Dev 1847-9, C Tywardreath, Corn 1850-1, C Modbury, Dev 1851-61, C Shebbear-cum-Sheepwash 1861-3, V Pinboe 1863-1902
Pulling, Rev. James, M.A.	1.5.41 ~	F 1838-50 Corpus Christi	C Grantchester, Cambs 1842-4, career in Corpus Christi, V Belchamp S. Paul, Ess 1863-79, brother of above
Radali, Prince, see Wilding			
#Railton, William	14.11.43 ~		Architect (c.1801-77), 12 Regent Street, London, pupil of W. Inwood, FIBA 1835, architect to the Ecclesiastical Commissioners 1838-48, retired 1859
Raine, Rev. John, M.A.	10.11.42	F 1830 Trinity	V Blyth Rectory, Bawtry, Notts 1834-74
Ramus, Charles Meade	14.11.43	Trinity	C Boldre, Hants, 1848-51, PC South Baddesley, 1851-65, R Palyden w. East Guldeford, Suss 1865-95
Randall, Alexander	11.5.42 ~		Gentleman, Maidstone, lived in King St in 1846
*Randolph, Edmund	6.12.41 ~ ¢¤‡	Jesus	V S. Clement's, Cambridge 1846-9, C Little Hadham, Herts 1855-6, C Kimpton, Hants 1865-70, +1892
Randolph, Francis, B.A.	<mid-40~	S. John's	C Spetisbury w. Charlton Marshall, Dors 1843-55, C All Saints, Worcester 1846-7, C Dolton, Dev 1851-5, C Little Hadham, Herts 1856-75, C Winwick, Northants 1875-6, V Brent Pelham w. Furneaux Pelham, Herts 1876-98
Randolph, Rev. Herbert	11.5.44 ~	Balliol, Oxford	V Abbotsley, Hunts 1839-49, chapl. to Marquis Downshire 1850-87, I Holy Trinity, Melrose, Roxburgh 1849-55, C-in-charge Pulham, Dors 1867-70, C Ringmore, Dev 1872-4
Randolph, Rev. John Honywood, M.A.	28.11.44	Christ Church, Oxford	R Burton Coggles, Lincs 1816, chapl. to the British factory at S. Petersburg 1818, preb. S.Paul's 1821, R Fobbing, Ess 1822, R Northolt, Middx 1822-35, R S. Leonards-on-Sea 1835, R Mistley-cum-Bradfield & Manningtree, Ess 1839-45, RD, R Sanderstead, Surr 1845-68
Randolph, Rev. Thos	13.2.43	Christ Church, Oxford	R Much Hadham w. Little Hadham, Herts, 1812-75, chapl-in-ordinary to the King 1825
Randolph, Rev. William, B.A	<mid-40 ~ ¢¤‡	S. John's	C Cheriton w. Navington, Kent 1840-50, C Sutton Waldron, Dors 1852-4, PC Alderbolt 1854-7, thereafter no clerical appointment, not in Crockford 1865

Name	Date	College	Notes
Raven, Rev. Vincent, M.A.	28.11.44 ~	F 1837 Magdalene	Dean 1844-6, T 1846-53, C S. Paul, Hammersmith, London 1840-1, C S. Pancras 1841-3, C West Hackney 1843-4, R Great Fransham, Norf 1853-87
Rawle, Rev. Richard, M.A.	7.2.42 ~ ¢	F 1836 Trinity	R Cheadle, Staffs 1839-47, Principal Codrington College, Barbados 1847-64, V Felmersham, Beds 1867-9, V Tamworth, Staffs 1869-72, Bp of Trinidad 1872-88, Principal (again) & Professor of Divinity, Codrington College 1888-9
Rawlins, Rev. Charles, M.A.	5.3.44 ~	Trinity	C Creeting, Suff 1841-51, V Chaddexden, Derbys 1851-72, +1894
Rawsthorne, Thomas Cragg	5.3.44	Trinity	Adm. Inner Temple, +1851
Ray, Rev. George, M.A.	10.11.42 ~ ¢¤‡	F 1834 S. Peter's	V Little S. Mary's, Cambridge 1835-44, R Statbern, Leics 1844-66, R Rexford, Som 1866-7, C All Saints, Leicester 1867-74, V there 1874-81, +1887
Read, Rev. C.	7.11.44		Ticehurst, Suss, not traced in AC, AO or CL
Read, David	1845 ~ ¢		32 Lincoln's Inn Fields, not traced in POLD
Read, William	6.12.41¢	S. John's	C South Mimms, Herts 1850-1, chapl. of the chapel of ease, Worthing, Suss 1852-82, +1884
Redfern, J.	?		Present at 1862 anniversary meeting
Redhead, Rev. T. S.	10.11.42 ~	Trinity, Dublin	Rock Ferry, Liverpool, no doubt Thomas Fisher Redhead, minister Higher Bebington, Ches (includes Rock Ferry) 1842-82
Reichensperger, August	3.12.56¤		(1808-95), hon. member, profoundly influential promoter of the Gothic Revival in Germany, architectural theorist, worked for the completion of Cologne Cathedral, author and politician
Reid, Rev. C. W., M.A.	<mid-49	S. John's	Possibly Charles Burton Reid, P 1338, C Wadhurst, Suss 1844-7, C Deeping Fen, Lincs 1849-50, Army Chapl. Hounslow Barracks, at Kneller Hall military school of music, Whitton Middx 1853-67, C Hanworth 1871-3, C Cowtenhall, Northants 1873-4, V S. Gregory, Norwich 1874-7, disappears from Crockford 1878
Reyner, Rev. George Fearns, M.A.	8.11.41 ~ ¢¤‡	F 1840-76 S. John's	Various University offices, including Sadlerian Professor of Mathematics 1847-57, chapl. Horningsea, Cambs 1845-8, V Maaingley 1852-5, R Stapleburst, Kent 1876-92
Rhodes, Quintin	<mid-40	Trinity Hall	Adm. Middle Temple, +1844
Richards, John	Late 40 ~	Trinity	C Matson, Glos 1844-5, chapl. Trinity College 1846-8, C S. Andrew the Great, Cambridge 1847-8, chapl. H.E.I. Co 1848-65, = Madras University, H.M. inspector of schools for India 1855-8, V Asb-next-Sandwich, Kent 1869-84, R Tansor, Northants 1884-98

name	date elected	Cambridge college or other	Addresses/location given in *The Ecclesiologist*/ career details
+*Richards, Rev. William Upton, M.A.	1845–6 ~	Exeter, Oxford	B.A. 1833, D 1836, P 1837, asst in MSS Dept at British Museum and continued there for a while after taking holy orders (CL seems to indicate till 1853), C Margaret Chapel, London 1841–5, minister there 1845–9, V All Saints, Margaret St 1849–73, ES auditor 1848–9
Richardson, E. G.	13.3.43 ~		6 Hales Place, South Lambeth, London
Richardson, H. B.	14.11.43 ~ ₵¤		3 Regent's Park Terrace, London
#Rickman, Thomas	Late 40 ~ 12.39	Downing	Adm. Downing 1839, no details known

Architect and writer (1776–1841), hon. member, Neale's diary (5.12.1839) records the intended offer of hon. membership, sometime partner of H. Hutchinson and R. C. Hussey, author of Attempt to Discriminate the Styles of Architecture in England from the Conquest to the Reformation (first ed. 1817) which coined the terms 'Early English', 'Decorated' etc to describe English medieval architecture; |
Riddale, Rev. Robert	8.11.41 ~ ₵¤‡	Clare Hall	C Hertingfordbury, Herts 1815–18, C S. Andrew, Hertford 1819–26, V Kirdford, Suss 1826–31, R Knockin, Salop 1826, R North Chapel, Suss 1831–4, R Tillington, Suss 1834–76
Rivington, John	22.5.43 ~ ₵¤‡		Sydenham, Kent, probably of 'Rivingtons, London' who are listed as the London publishers of Eccl
Roberts, John Arthur Jeafferson	1841–2 ~ ₵	Christ's	C Potterspury, Northants 1846–7, C Calne, Wilts 1847–8, C Tickenham 1848–52, R Hamilton, Bermuda 1852–7, C Old Weston, Hunts 1857–8, C Manea, Cambs 1858–67, C Bothal, Northumb 1867–81, C Chillingham 1881–8, R Byrnes 1888–1901
Roberts, John Harris	6.12.41 ~ ₵	Clare Hall	C Brierley Hill, Staffs 1843–5, C Thornton, Suff 1847–57, thereafter no cure or benefice, +1897
Robinson, Rev. Arthur Dalgarno	2.5.60¤	Trinity	13 Richmond New Rd, Shepherd's Walk, C Holy Trinity, Westminster 1857–9, , C S. Saviour, Paddington 1859–60, V S. Clement, Kensington 1860–7, V S. Helen, Kensington 1867–98, chapl. to Marquess Townshend 1870–98
Robinson, Rev. Hastings, D.D.	1.5.41 ~	F 1816–28 S. John's	Whitehead Preacher 1821, R Great Warley, Ess 1827–66, bon. can. Rochester 1862–6, J.P., FSA
Robinson, J.	10.11.42		11 Hart Street, Bloomsbury, London, POLD notes a George J. Robinson, 'surveyor &c', at no. 11A in 1844
Robinson, John Matthews, M.A.	1.5.41 ~	Trinity	V Barrington, Cambs 1837–52 (restored the church c.1840 (*Eccl* 1 (1842), 62)
Robinson, Rev. Philip Vyvyan, M.A.	7.11.44 ~ ₵¤	S. John's	R Ruan Major and of Landewednack, Corn 1844–88
Robinson, Rev. Thomas	<mid-40	Trinity	Professor of Arabic 1837–54, chapl. to Archbp of York, chapl. to Bp Heber, transferred with him to Bengal and remained his constant companion, Archd. Madras 1828–35,

bencher of Middle Temple 1845, Master of the Temple 1845-69, R Therfield, Herts 1853-60, preb. S. Paul's 1847-54, can. Rochester 1854-73, translated Old Testament into Persian, author of other books and pamphlets

Name	College	Date	Details
Robinson, T., B.A.	Trinity	1.5.41	Probably Thomas Robinson, Island C of the United Churches of Snowden & Providence, Midds, Jamaica 1848-64, chapl. to Bp of Jamaica 1852-66. Head Potsdam School 1864-6, V Chart Sutton, Kent 1868-94, +1895
#Robson, Edward Robert	Trinity	21.7.59a	Architect (1835-1917), Durham, pupil of J. Dobson 1853-6, improver in Scott's office 1857-60, began practice c.1858, ARIBA 1860, FRIBA 1864, in partnership with W. Walton-Wilson, architect to Dean & Chapter of Durham 1858-64, partner of J. J. Stevenson 1871-6, specialist on schools
*Rodmell, Rev. John, M.A.	Trinity	1847	17 Claremont Crescent, Edinburgh, C Burford (3rd portion), Salop in 1841-3, subsequently without cure or benefice, disappears from CL 1867
Rogers, F. H.		7.11.44 ~ ¢a	Truro, Corn, address Lemon Street, Truro in 1846, of Rosewarne House, Camborne in 1857-64
Rogers, F. S.	Corpus Christi	10.11.42	Possibly Frederick John Rogers +1874
Rogers, H. E.	Queens'	<mid-40 ~	Not traced in AC, probably Alfred Edward Rogers, C Stogumber, Som 1841-50, disappears from CL 1851
Röhrs, John Henry, B.A.	Jesus	30.4.44 ~ ¢	B.A. 1843, M.A. 1846, no other details available
Rolfe, see Neville-Rolfe			
Romanis, William	Emmanuel	13.2.43	Asst master, Cheltenham College 1848-56, C Axminster, Dev 1856-8, C S. Mary Reading 1858-63, V Wigston Magna, Leics 1863-88, V Twyford, Hants 1888-95, +1899
Rooper, Rev. William Henry	University, Oxford	8.11.41 ~ ¢	C Abbots Ripton, Hunts, 1846-50, PC S. Andrew's Chapel, Brighton, Suss 1856-62
#Roos, Alessandro		5-12.45 ~ ¢	Architect, Rome, also of Half Moon Street, Piccadilly in 1846-9, not traced in the Biografico Italiano (1993)
Roscow, Thomas Tattersall	Downing	5.12.42	B.A. 1846, M.D. 1854, medical career
•Routh, Rev. Dr Martin Joseph, D.D	F 1775-91 Magdalene, Oxford	11.5.42 ~	President of Magdalene, Oxford (1791-1854), first President of the Oxford Architectural Society, elected hon. member, R Tilehurst-cum-Theale, Suss 1810-54, an early champion of the catholic understanding of the Anglican Church
Rowe, James Boone	S. John's	5.12.43	Matriculated 1843, no other details available
Rudge, Edward	S. Catharine's Hall	11.5.42 ~	C S. Peter, Stepney 1843-4, C S. Luke, Chelsea 1844-50, chapl. North Surr District Schools at Anerley 1850-6, C S. Matthew, Westminster 1857-9, chapl. Saddlers' Company 1859,

name	Cambridge college or other	date elected	Addresses/location given in *The Ecclesiologist*/ career details
			chapl. & superintendent *King Edward's Schools, S. George-in-the-Fields, and Witley, Surr 1856-86, R Bramdean, Hants 1886-7, V Withycombe Raleigh, Dev. 1887-90, V Matching, Ess 1890-6*
Rumsey, Lacey Henry	*S. John's*	8-9.50□	Re-elected 2.5.60, migrated to Brasenose, Oxford, B.A. from New Inn Hall 1850, T Trinity College, Glenalmond 1851-3, vice-principal Bishop College, Jamaica & I S. John & S. Mark in parish of S. Andrew, Jamaica 1853-5, C Netheravon, Wilts 1855, C Sunderland, Durham 1855-6, C Hurworth 1856, I Newcastle, N.S.W. 1857-8, I Ipswich, Queensland 1858-66, second master Guildford G.S. in 1867, C Brent Pelham w. Furneaux-Pelham, Herts 1867-72, C S. Saviour, Highbury 1872-3, V Llanstadwell, Pembs 1873-82, disappears from Crockford 1883
+*Russell, Rev. John Fuller, B.C.L.	S. Peter's	<mid-40 ~ ¢□‡	C S. Peter, Walworth, Surr 1838-9, C S. Mary, Newington Butts 1839-41, PC S. James, Enfield 1841-54, CCS/ES auditor 1844-5, 1850-1, his election to ES committee 26.7.66 is the last recorded such election, Greenhithe, Kent 1856-84, Vice-President Royal Archaeological Institute, FSA 1853, author of numerous religious and archaeological works, general editor of Hierurgia Anglicana (published 1843-8), contributor to Eccl (e.g. 20 (1859), 1-9, 100-8, 345-8, 21 (1860), 7-11)
Rutley, J. Lewis		16.12.62□‡	5 Great Newport St, London W.C., POLD notes a Thomas Rutley, picture dealer, at this address in 1865, election date 16.12.62, not 16.12.63 as stated in Eccl
#St Aubyn, Jas Piers		22.5.43 ~ ¢□	Architect (1815-95), Furnivals Inn, pupil of T. Fulljames, Gloucester 1831, began practice in London 1842, ARIBA 1837, FRIBA 1856, in partnership with his former pupil H. J. Wadling and retired from active work 1885
St Aubyn, Rev. Richard John, M.A.	Trinity	10.11.42 ~	B.A. 1833, in holy orders but held no benefice or cure, of Lime Grove, Putney, +1849
Salt, Thomas		7.11.44 ~ ¢□‡	Banker, Stafford
§Salt, William		30.4.44 ~ ¢	Banker, Lombard Street, London, FSA (20.1.42)
#Salviati, Dr Antonio		24.6.62□	Proprietor of Venetian glassworks (1816-90), hon. member, gave up law to join Lorenzo Radi, a glass maker and mosaicist, founding Salviati & Company in Venice 1859; a branch of the firm was registered in London; it was bought by H. Layard and others and was then known as The Venice & Murano Glass & Mosaic Company, Salviati then set up his own company in Venice in 1868
#§Salvin, Anthony		<mid-1840 ~ ¢□	Architect (1799-1881), Somerset St, Portman Sq., London, hon. member, pupil of J. Paterson (+1832), in office of John Nash, began practice 1828, FIBA 1836, FSA (26.1.24)
Sandford, George	Magdalene	Founder	C Acton, Ches 1840-7, Vice-President Sheffield Collegiate School 1843-6, V S. Jude, Sheffield 1846-80, V Ecclesall, Yorks 1880-98

Name	Date	College	Notes
Sandford, W. A.	<mid-40	Trinity	Not traced in AC
Sandham, *Charles Freeman*	10.11.42 ~	Caius	+ 1846
Sandys, H. B.	18.4.42 ~	Trinity	Not traced in AC
Saunders, Barrett	8.11.41 ~	Queens'	First name given as Barrett in Eccl, + 1843
Saunders, Harry, C.	1847		
Savile, Hon. *Arthur*, M.A.	<mid-40	Trinity	Methley Park, Leeds, C S. Clement Danes, London 1843, C S. Nicholas, Warwick 1844–6, C Monk's Kirby w. Withybrooke, Warks 1847, V Ashby Magna, Leics 1847–50, R Fowlmere, Cambs 1850–70
Savile, *Frederick Alexander*	<mid-40 ~ ¢¤‡	Trinity	C Holy Rood, Southampton, Hants 1843–5, R Kings Nympton, Dev 1845–54, R North Huish 1854–60, C S. Thomas, Exeter 1860–6, R S. Mark w. S. Matthias, Torwood 1868–79, J.P., assumed name of Stewart 1874
Savile, Hon. and Rev. *Philip Yorke*	7.2.42 ~ ¢¤	Trinity	R Methley, Leeds 1842–97
Say, Rev. *Francis Henry Stoddart*, M.A.	7.11.44 ~ ¢	S. John's	C Braughing, Ware, Herts 1827–46, V there 1846–77
Scarth, Rev. *Harry Mengden*, M.A.	13.2.43	Christ's	C Eaton Constantine, Salop 1837–41, R Kenley 1841, R Bathwick w. Woolley, Som 1841–71, preb Wells 1848–90, R Wrington 1871–90, RD Fortishead 1880
Scot, Rev. R. T.	23.11.52		Brasted, Sevenoaks, not traced in CL, a Robert F. Scot was C Houghton-le-Spring, Co. Durham in 1852
Scott, Sir Francis, Bart	6 or 7.50¢		Joined committee 15.5.1861
Scott, Rev. *Frederick Thomas*, M.A.	1846 ~ ¢¤‡	Worcester, Oxford	C & V Hythe, Kent 1853–76, V Silverswold 1853–76, V Hartlip 1876–91, + unknown
#•Scott, *George Gilbert*	7.2.42 ~ ¢¤		Architect (1811–78), 20 Spring Gardens, articled to J. Edmeston 1827, worked for builders Peto & Grissell in 1831, entered Henry Roberts' office 1832, and began practice 1834 and in partnership with W. Moffatt until 1844, FRIBA 1849, knighted 1872
+•Scott, Rev. *William*, M.A.	13.3.43 ~ ¢¤	Queen's, Oxford	PC Christ Church, Hoxton, London 1839–63, on ES committee 1848–59, Chairman from 1859, President Sion College 1858, V S. Olave Jewry 1863–72
Scougal, *Henry Boydick*	13.2.44 ~	Corpus Christi	C S. Margaret, Durham 1847–9, C Baswich, Staffs 1851–7, C Ilfracombe, Dev 1857–65, disappears from Crockford 1868
*Scudamore, Rev. *William Edward*	6.12.41 ~ ¢¤‡	F 1837–40 S. John's	R Ditchingham, Bungay, Norf. 1839–81, warden of sisterhood of All Hallows, Ditchingham

name	date elected	Cambridge college or other	Addresses/location given in *The Ecclesiologist*/ career details
#Seddon, John Pollard	25.11.57¤		*Architect (1827–1906), Llandaff, articled to T. L. Donaldson 1847–51, ARIBA 1852, FRIBA 1860, partner of John Prichard 1853–69, partner of J. C. Carter 1884–94, Dio. & Cathedral Architect to Llandaff 1886*
+Sedgwick, Prof. Adam	1–5.41	Senior F 1810 Trinity	*D 1817, P 1818, Woodwardian Professor of Geology 1818–73, president of British Association 1833, can. Norwich 1834–73, CCS auditor 1842–3, distinguished scientific career, F.G.S.*
Sedgwick, Leonard	5.12.43 ~	Trinity	*In holy orders but availed himself of the Clerical Disabilities Relief Act (1870), +1879*
Sellers, Samuel Bamford	5.12.42 ~	Corpus Christi	*B.A. 1848, no other details available*
Selwyn, Rev. William	6.12.41 ~ ¢¤‡	S. John's	*R Branstone, Lincs 1831–46, can. residentiary Ely 1833–75, V Melbourne, Cambs 1846–53, Ramsden Preacher 1857, preb. Ely 1857, chapl.-in-ordinary to the Queen 1859, hon. joint curator Lambeth Palace Library 1872, +1875*
Sendall, Edward	5.12.42 ~	Trinity	*C Great Glembam, Suff 1846–9, R Vange, Ess 1849–64, R Litton, Som 1864–83, +1884*
Seymour, Rev. Sir John Hobart Culme, 2nd Bart.	13.2.44 ~	Exeter, Oxford	*R Horley & Hornton, Oxon 1824–53, preb. Lincoln 1827, chapl.-in-ordinary to the Queen 1827, can. Gloucester 1829, R Northchurch, Herts 1830–80*
*Sharp, Rev. John, M.A.	Late 40 ~ ¢¤‡	Magdalene	*Surname spelled probably wrongly with 'e' in Eccl, PC Horbury, Wakefield, Yorks 1834–99, hon. can. Ripon 1885–8, hon. can. Wakefield 1888–1903*
#Sharpe, Edmund	8.11.41 ~ ¢¤	Caius	*Architect (1809–77), Lancaster, began practice 1835, joined by E. G. Paley (his partner from 1845), married sister of J. Fletcher (q.v.), active in civic affairs in Lancaster, mayor 1848–9, retired from architecture, concentrating on railway building and other business activities, prolific writer on architecture which earned him the RIBA Gold Medal in 1875*
Sharpe, J. C.	1847¢		*19 Fleet Street, London, of Gosling & Sharpe, bankers (see also F. S. Gosling and M. J. Lomax)*
Sharpe, Martin R.	1848¢‡		*12 Wellington Street, Strand, London, in 1864 of Gloucester House, Highgate, not traced in POLD*
Shaw, Rev. George, B.A.	Founder	S. John's	*C Fen Drayton, Cambs 1843–5*
#Shaw, George	11.5.44 ~		*Architect (fl. 1845–70), S. Chad's, Uppermill, Saddleworth, Yorks*
Shaw, R. J.	1845–6 ~		*5 Chancery Lane*
*Shaw, Rev. Morton, M.A.	1847	Brasenose, Oxford	*C Hawkhurst, Kent 1843–4, C Marden 1845, C Barcheston, Warks 1846, minister of Arley Chapel, Great Budworth, Ches 1847–52, minister S. Peter's Chapel, Charlotte St, London 1853, C Bulmer w. Belchampton, Suff 1854, R Rougham in 1854–72, RD*

Name	Date	College	Notes
Shaw-Lefevre, Rt Hon. Charles	6.12.41 ~ ¢	Trinity	Adm. Lincoln's Inn 1815, Speaker of the House of Commons 1839-57, other political and public service offices, created Viscount Eversley 1857, +1888
Shaw-Lefevre, John George	6.12.41 ~ ¢¤‡	Auditor & F 1819 Trinity	Adm. Inner Temple 1822, younger brother of the above, political and public service career, +1879
#Shearburn, William	14.11.43 ~ ¢¤		Architect (1799-1860), Dorking, began as a carpenter or joiner, became a successful builder, undertook some design work, notably Dorking workhouse 1839-41 on which he did the carpentry himself
Shears, J. W.	<mid-40	S. John's	Probably James Henry Shears +1842
Sheffield, Rev. Charles	Late 40 ~ ¢¤‡	Christ Church, Oxford	Brigg, Lincs, R Flixborough w. Burton-on-Stather (patron Sir R. Sheffield) 1822-82, RD 1848-82
Shepherd, Malin	1845-6 ~ ¢¤‡		Sheffield
Sherwood, Rev. Thomas Moulden	6.12.41 ~ ¢¤‡	Downing	Newent, Glos, adm. Inner Temple 1824, called to the Bar 1833, D & P 1839, PC Oxenhall, Glos 1839-48, V Pauntley 1841-8, PC Hucclecote 1851-8, +1870
Shilleto, Rev. Richard	8.11.41 ~ ¢¤‡	Trinity	Educational career, F Peterhouse 1867, asst master Harrow 1843-5, a great Greek scholar, +1876
Shipton, Rev. Dr John Noble	1845 ~ ¢	Balliol, Oxford	R Hinton Blewitt, Som from 1830, V Othery, Som 1832-64
+Short, Col. Charles	1845 ~		14 Queen's Square, Westminster, described as 'Lieut. Colonel' in POLD (1844); Eccl notes a Lieut-Col. Short of Albert Terrace, Knightsbridge joining 1850-1 but it seems likely this is the same person rejoining after lapsed membership, ES auditor 1851-2
#Shoubridge, William	<mid-40 ~	Caius	Studied architecture and art in England and Italy, became an accomplished artist, +1891
Shuttleworth, Charles Ughtred	5.12.43 ~	Trinity	Matriculated 1843, no other details available
Shuttleworth, Rev. Edward, B.A.	13.2.43	S. John's	C Brindle, Lancs 1829-33, C S. Kenwyn, Corn 1833-40, PC S. Mary's, Penzance, Corn 1840-9, V Egloshayle 1849-83, hon. can. Truro 1878-83
Simpson, Rev. James Dalziel	10.11.42	F 1841-50 & T Sidney Sussex	PC Stoulton, Worcs 1851-60, +1864
Simpson, James Harvey, B.A.	10.11.42	Trinity	C Kemsing, Kent 1848-50, C Springfield, Ess 1850-2, C Bexhill, Suss 1852-7, R S. Mark, Bexhill 1857-1905, preb. Chichester 1892-1915
Simpson, Joseph	14.11.43	Trinity	B.A. 1847, no other details available
Simpson, Rev. R.	6.12.41	Trinity	Not traced in AC

name	date elected	Cambridge college or other	Addresses/location given in The Ecclesiologist/ career details
Simpson, Rev. William Hirst, M.A.	13.2.45 ~	S. John's	Louth, D 1835, P 1836, C Keddington & Stewton, Lincs 1842–9, C Folkingham 1849–55, PC Thornton-le-Fen & Langreville 1855–62, R Lyndon, Rutl 1862–4, R Stretton 1864–71, disappears from Crockford 1872
#Skidmore, Francis Albert	?		Metalworker (1816–96), Coventry, at 1856 anniversary meeting, joined his father 1845, established own business 1850
*Skinner, Rev. James, M.A.	29.7.52¢a	F 1844–9 Durham University	B.A. 1837, D 1841, P 1842, Vice, chapl. to the Forces, 1844–50, warden of the Beauchamp Charity, senior C St Barnabas, Pimlico 1851–7, V Newland, Worcs 1861–77, seems to have retired, not in Crockford 1884
Slade, Henry G.	16.12.63a	S. John's	Stockbroker (of Irving & Slade), 5 Eldon Rd, Kensington
*Slade, James	6.12.41 ~		C Wootton, Northants 1843, V Little Lever, Lancs 1843–93
#Slater, William	6.4.54¢a		Architect (1819–72), 12 John St, Adelphi, London, articled to R. C. Carpenter (q.v.), ARIBA 1855, FRIBA 1859, took over Carpenter's practice on the latter's death in 1855, partner of R. H. Carpenter (q.v.) 1863–73, architect to Chichester Cathedral
Sloane-Evans, W. S., see Evans, W.S.			
+*Smith, Rev. Barnard, M.A.	Founder	F 1840–61 S. Peter's	CCS auditor, 1839–40, P 1841, P 1843, Dean of S. Paul's 1842–4, PC S. Mary-the-Less, Cambridge in 1844–6, R Glaston, Rutl 1861–76, RD Rutland 1876
Smith, Benjamin Frederick, B.A.	22.5.43 ~	Scholar of Trinity	C Holy Trinity, Tunbridge Wells 1845–50, C Rushall, Kent 1850–64, V there 1864–74, hon. can. Canterbury 1867–87, R Crayford 1874–87, RD Dartford 1874–87, chapl. to Archbp of Canterbury 1883, Archd. Maidstone, can. Canterbury 1887–1900
Smith, Charles Francis	14.11.43 ~	Trinity	C S. John, Westminster 1847–9, C Bishopthorpe, Yorks 1849–54 and V there 1854–65, R Breeford w. Lissett & Dunnington 1865–72, disappears from Crockford 1874
Smith, George Edmund	30.4.44	S. Peter's	+1845
Smith, George Percival	<mid-40 ~	Trinity	Adm. Lincoln's Inn 1843, called to the Bar 1849
+Smith, Rev. John James, M.A.	Founder	F 1828–49 & T. Caius	D 1830, P 1831, V Loddon, Norf 1849–83, minister Laura Chapel, Bath 1875–9, a founder of the CAS; although an Evangelical, a CCS vice-president 1840–2 but resigned 1843 accusing it of Romanising tendencies
Smith, Lorenzo	14.11.43	Emmanuel	C Pendleton, Lancs 1848–9, C S. Peter, Manchester 1850–5
+Smith, Robert	1.5.55¢		9 Welbeck Street, London in 1857, ES auditor 1860–1
Smith, Samuel R., D.D.	<mid-40	Christ Church, Oxford	PC Daventry, Northants 1795, preb. Southwell 1800, preb. York 1801, chapl. House of Commons 1802, can. Westminster 1807–24, Sub-Dean 1809, Treasurer 1813, Dean 1824–31, R Dry Drayton, Cambs (own patron) 1808–29 & 1831–41, RD Dry Drayton from 1808

Name	Date	College	Notes
#Smith, Thomas	8.11.41		Architect (1798–1875), Hertford, FRIBA 1842, County Surveyor for Herts 1837–75 and Beds 1847–54
Smith, William, B.A	13.2.45	Lincoln, Oxford	C S. John, Uxbridge Moor 1847–5, PC there 1849–53, sub-warden S. Peter's College, Radley 1851–3, Principal Fishponds Training College 1853–71, V Newland w. Redbrook Glos 1871–88, RD Dean Forest 1884–8, possibly retired 1888, disappears from Crockford 1907
#Smith, William	21.6.64¤		Architect (1830–1901), 12 John St, Adelphi, pupil of R. C. Carpenter (q.v.), asst of W. Slater (q.v.), ARIBA 1866, assumed name Bassett-Smith c.1882, in partnership with his son C. A. Bassett-Smith
Smith, Rev. Dr	<mid-40		Left CCS by mid-41, R Dry Drayton & preb. Durham
Smyth, Rev. George Watson, M.A.	5.12.42 ~	Trinity	C West Tisted & Tichborne, Hants 1835–7, R Fyfield, Hants, 1837–51, asst master Cheltenham College 1851–70, + 1878
Smyth, William Henry	7.11.44 ~¢	Caius	Surname given, apparently wrongly, a final 'e' in Eccl, Adm. Inner Temple 1846, called to the Bar 1849, of Elkington Hall, Lircs, J.P., High Sheriff of Lincs 1882, +1912
Smythe, Hugh Blagge, B.A.	5–12.45 ~ ¢	Jesus	Initials given, apparently wrongly as 'H. H.' in Eccl, PC Thorne, Yorks 1847–56, V Houghton Regis, Beds 1856–79, J.P.
Snow, John Pennell	6.12.41 ~	Trinity	Adm. Lincoln's Inn 1842, called to the Bar 1848, C Edwinstowe, Notts 1852–6, C Sydenham, Kent 1857–62, PC Perlethorpe, Notts 1862–75, V Melton Ross w. New Barnetby, Lincs 1875–89
Soames, Rev. William Aldwin, M.A.	10.11.42	F 1830 Trinity	V Greenwich 1833–65, preb. S. Paul's 1847, +1866
Somers, John, 2nd Earl Somers	7.11.44 ~		Eastnor Castle, succeeded 1841, Lord-Lieutenant of Herefordshire, 1852
Sommerard, M. du	24.6.62¤		Hon. member, director of the Hotel de Cluny, not traced in the Index biographique français (1998)
Southwell, Rev. George, M.A.	5.6.52	Trinity	C S. George, Brandon Hill, Bristol 1837–8, C Compton Martin, Som 1838–41, C Boyton, Wilts 1842–9, V Yetminster w. Chetnole, Dors 1849–83
Southwood, Thomas Allen	Founder	S. Peter's	Asst master Cheltenham College 1845–79, treasurer 1868–75, + 1885
Sparke, John	10.11.42 ~		Bury S. Edmund's
Sparke, Rev. John, M.A.	22.5.43	F Clare Hall	C Wrawby-cum-Brigg, Lincs 1840–4, then no clerical appointment, disappears from Crockford 1860
Spence, Rev. George	8.11.41 ~	Jesus	V St Clement, Cambridge 1837–46

437

name	date elected	Cambridge college or other	Addresses/location given in *The Ecclesiologist*/ career details
+ *Sperling, Rev. *John Hanson*, M.A	6.5.59¤	*Trinity*	C *Kensington* 1849-56, R *Wicken Bonhunt, Ess*, 1856-62 (*restored the church there 'without professional aid' but to the praise of Eccl* 20 (1859), 212-4), on ES committee 1861–probably 1868, *R & V Westbourne, Suss* 1862-71, author of *Church Walks in Middlesex, article on bells* (*Eccl* 26 (1865), 255-71), *became RC* 1871, +1894
Spinks, Frederick Lowten	<8.11.41	Magdalene	*Adm. Inner Temple* 1839, *called to the Bar* 1843, *legal career, M.P. for Oldham* 1874-80, +1899
Spurrell, Frederick	14.11.43	Corpus Christi	C *Newhaven, Suss* 1847-8, *chapl. at Stockholm* 1849-50, C *Barcombe, Suss* 1850-3, R *Faulkbourne, Ess* 1853-98, *author of various local history works*, +1902
Staley, *Thomas Nettleship*, B.A.	5.3.44 ~ ¢	F *1847-50* Queen's	T & Principal S. *Mark's College, Chelsea* 1844-50, Principal *Collegiate School, Wandsworth* 1850-61, *Ramsden Preacher* 1862, *Bp of Honolulu* 1861-70, *chapl. Most Noble Order of Kamehameha* 1862-70, R *Oakley w. Croxall, Derbys* 1872-96, +1898
Stanley, Hon. *Edward Henry*	28.11.44	Trinity	*Political career*, 1893
#*Statz, Vicenz*	21.6.59¤		*Architect* (1818-98), *Cologne, hon. member, trained as a carpenter and mason, worked under E. F. Zwirner at Cologne Cathedral from* 1841, *began practice* 1847
Steabler, *Mr W. A.*	13.2.45 ~ ¢¤‡		*High Street, Sunderland, in* 1853-64 *he is the Rev. W. A. Steabler, Cape Town, not in CL 1863-5 in Cape Town Dio.*
Stephen, *Alfred Hamilton Hewlett*	1845-6 ~ ¢¤	Trinity	C *Christ Church, Sydney, N.S.W.* 1849-53, *chapl. of immigrants, Sydney* 1854-5, V S. *Paul, Sydney* 1855-84, *can. Sydney Cathedral* 1869-84
Stephens, Prof. *George*	12.6.51¢¤		*A contributor to Eccl, Professor of Anglo-Saxon in University of Copenhagen, hon. member*
Stevenson, *Mr T.*	<mid-40		*Cambridge, publisher of Eccl.*
Steuart, *Andrew*	22.5.43 ~ ¢	Scholar of Trinity	*Adm. Inner Temple* 1844, *M.P. for Cambridge* 1857-63, +1905
Stock, *John Russell*	<mid-40	S. John's	PC S. *John, Finchingfield, Ess* 1842-9, V *All Saints, Islington, London* 1849-53, V *Finchingfield in succession to his father* 1853-60, *secretary to the Clergy Orphan Corporation* 1861-83, R *All Hallows-the-Great w. All Hallows-the-Less, London* 1860-87, *preb. S. Paul's* 1884-7
Stokes, H. G.	13.2.45		*Trull, Taunton, Som*
+Stokes, *Scott Nasmyth*, B.A.	Late 40	Scholar of Trinity	*On CCS committee* 1843-4, *a secretary* 1844-5, *BWD* (22.5.45) *says he resigned, adm. Inner Temple* 1849, *called to the Bar* 1852, *school inspector*, +1891
+Stooks, *Thomas Fraser*, B.A.	Founder	Trinity	*Joined CCS committee* 21.7.39 *but resigned from it* 19.10.39 (*BWD*), C S. *Martin-in-the-Fields, London* 1845-8, PC S. *Luke, Berwick St, Oxford St* 1848-52, PC S. *Ann, Highgate*

Name	College	Date	Notes
Stothert, G.	Trinity	Founder	Rise 1853–68, V Holy Trinity, Brompton 1870–2, preb. S. Paul's 1863, chapl. to Bp of London 1869–74
Stracey, William James	Magdalene	13.2.43 ~ ¢¤‡	Perhaps James Stothert; however, he was at Trinity but migrated to Sidney Sussex Oct.1838 C Skeyton, Norf 1846–7, R there 1855–72, R Oxnead w. Buxton 1855–89, +1912; curiously Eccl and the membership lists give his first name as 'Edward' until 1849; no Edward Stracey can be traced in AC; the fact that they are the same person receives support from the fact that the 1846 membership list says he is of 'Sprowst, Norwich' - surely an error for Sprowston; the 1849 list also gives W. J. Stracey as of 'Sprowst, Norwich'
#Street, George Edmund		24.4.45 ~ ¢¤	Architect (1824–81), Cornwall Terrace, Lee, Kent, articled to O. B. Carter of Winchester from 1841, in G. G. Scott's office 1844–9, commenced practice Wantage 1848, FSA 1853, architect to the dioceses of Oxford, Ripon, Winchester and York, moved to London 1856, FRIBA 1859, married a niece of George Procter (q.v.)
#Street, Thomas Henry		24.4.45 ~ ¢¤	Cornwall Terrace, Lee, Kent, elder brother of the above, took over his father's solicitor's business 1839 but in 1849 & 1853 membership lists described as 'architect' when his address of North End, Hampstead is also that of his brother
+Strickland, Charles William, B.A.	Trinity	10.11.42 ~ ¢¤‡	Appears to rejoin 1846 when address is 113 Jermyn Street, adm. Lincoln's Inn 1841, at Middle Temple 1849, called to the Bar 1847, legal career, on ES committee 1848–probably mid-1850s, succeeded as 8th baronet 1874, supposed to have been 'Martin' in Tom Brown's Schooldays, +1909
Strong, Sidney G. R.		11.6.60	108 Westbourne Terrace, Hyde Park, London
+*Stuart, Rev. Edward	New Inn Hall, Oxford	1846–7¢¤‡	9 Upper Harley Street, B.A. 1842, PC S. Mary Magdalene, Munster Sq. (his own patron) 1852–77, ES auditor 1853–4
Sturgis, Rev. Frederick George		1849¢	C Bodiam, Suss 1841, no appointment stated in CL 1842–3, 1848, 1854–8, 1880, C Holbeck, Leeds 1844–6, C Ridgmont & Husbourne Crawley, Beds 1847, C S. James, Enfield Highway in 1849–53, chapl. to the Union & C Easthampstead, Berks 1859–76, without appointment in 1877–81
Suckling, Alfred Inigo	Pembroke	1–5.41	Hon. member, R Barsham, Suff 1839–56, various papers to CCS (e.g. Eccl 1 (1842), 165–6, 188–90, 2 (1843), 90)
Suckling, Rev. Maurice Shelton	Trinity	<mid-46	Chapl. Wangford Union, Suff 1850, R Shipmeadow 1850–95
*Suckling, Robert Alfred	Caius	8.11.41 ~ ¤‡	Initials wrongly given as 'R. J.' in Eccl, C Kemerton, Glos 1843–6, PC Bussage 1846–51

name	date elected	Cambridge college or other	Addresses/location given in *The Ecclesiologist*/ career details
Sutton, *Sir John*	1–5.41 ~	Jesus	*Generous benefactor of Jesus Chapel (gave organ, established choir school and taught choristers for ten years), succeeded as 3rd baronet 1855, + 1873 at Bruges*
Swainson, *Charles Anthony, B.A.*	5.12.42	F 1841–52 Christ's	*Various posts in Cambridge University including professorships of Divinity 1864–87, Cambridge Preacher at Chapel Royal, Whitehall 1849, Whitehall Preacher 1849–51, C.S. George, Hanover Sq. 1851–2, C Mortlake, Surr 1853–4, Principal Chichester Theological College 1854–70, preb. Chichester 1861–4, V S. Martin, Chichester 1861–4, can. residentiary Chichester 1863–82, Warden S. Mary's Hospital, Chichester*
Swan, Henry	11.5.44 ~	S. John's	*Morpeth, C Bredon, Worcs in 1849, missionary at Newcastle, N.S.W. 1850–1*
Swinny, *Rev. Henry Hutchinson, M.A.*	1–5.41 ~ ¢	F 1836–40 Magdalene	*Impington, Cambs, V S. Giles & S. Peter, Cambridge 1840–4, C Mortlake, Surr 1847–9, PC there 1850–5, V Wargrave, Berks 1855–9, Principal Cuddesdon Theological College & V Cuddesdon 1859–62*
+Sykes, Christopher	21.6.64		*1 Seamore Place, London, on ES committee 1864–probably 1868, possibly 2nd son of Sir Tatton Sykes, 4th baronet*
Tabor, *Robert Stammers*	6.12.41 ~ ¢	Trinity	*C. S. George, Bloomsbury 1842–4, PC Christ Church, Enfield, Middx 1844–55, Head Cheam School 1855–90, licenced preacher dio. Canterbury 1902, +1909*
+Talbot, J. G.	2.5.60‡		*Falconhurst, Edenbridge, Kent, on ES committee from 1860*
Tanquery, *Truman*	1–5.41 ~ ¢¤‡	Pembroke	*R Tingrith, Beds 1847–99 in succession to his father*
Tate, *Rev. Alexander*	6.12.41	F 1838 Emmanuel	*C Chalk & Ifield, Kent 1838–40, C S. Michael, Cambridge 1843–7, V Brompton Regis, Som 1847–85, disappears from Crockford 1894*
Tayler, *Archdale Wilson*	5.6.52	*Christ Church, Oxford*	*B.A. 1806, chapl. Dacca 1815–25, R Stoke Newington, Middx 1830–52*
#Tayler, A. W. L.	<mid-53		*Architect (location not stated)*
Taylor, James	8.11.41		*Moseley Hall, Birmingham*
Teale, *Edward John*	11.5.43 ~		*Leeds, attorney and clerk to the magistrates, of 20 Trinity St in 1848*
Tennant, *Rev. William, M.A*	10.53¢	Trinity	*C S. John, Westminster 1840–7, V S. Stephen, Westminster 1847–9, member of the Motett Society in 1853*
#Teulon, *Samuel Sanders*	c.1854¢¤		*Architect (1812–73), elder brother of W. M. Teulon, (q.v.), AIBA 1835, began practice 1838, FRIBA 1842, Trans. RIBA 24 (1873–4), 216 says his work at S. Michael on the Mount and S. Peter at Arches, Lincoln (1854) 'is said to have been the means of procuring him the honour of membership of the Ecclesiological Society'*
#Teulon, *William Milford*	1847¢¤		*Architect (1823–1900), 5 Harpur Street, Red Lion Square, younger brother of S. S. Teulon, ARIBA 1854, FRIBA 1860*

Thacker, Arthur	1–5.41 F 1839–57 Trinity	*In holy orders but no clerical appointments, +1857*
+Thackeray, Dr Frederick, M.D.	8.11.41 ~ Emmanuel	*CCS auditor 1843–4, S. Andrew's St, Cambridge, medical career, +1852*
Thackeray, Rev. Joseph, M.A.	13.2.43 F 1827–46 King's	*Dean King's 1833–48, R Horstead & of Coltishall, Norf 1846–80*
Theed, Edward Reed, M.A	13.2.43 F 1834–59 King's	*R Sampford Courtenay w. Sticklepath, Dev 1859–93, R Honeychurch 1875–93*
Thomas, Henry	13.2.44 ~ ¢ S. John's	*B.A. 1830, legal career*
Thomas, John Harries	6.12.41 ~ ¢¤‡ S. Peter's	*Migrated to Trinity 5.1.42, C Muswell Hill, London 1844–5, C S. James, Westminster 1846–51, P-in-ordinary to the Queen 1851–63, minister Archbp Tenison's chapel 1852–7, R Milbrook, Beds 1857–63, Archd. Cape Town 1863–8, V Hillingdon, Middx 1869–95, R Uxbridge 1882–95, +1903*
+Thomas, Mesac	Founder ~ ¢ Trinity	*CCS committee member 1839–40, C Bp Ryder's Church, Birmingham 1840–1, C S. Mary, Birmingham 1841–3, V Tuddenham S. Martin, Suff 1843–6, PC Attleborough, Warks 1846–51, Secretary Colonial Church School Society 1846–63, Bp of Goulburn, N.S.W. 1863–92, Dean of Cathedral 1884–92, some of the CCS church schemes in Lambeth Palace Library were completed by him*
Thompson, G. D.	22.6.52¢	*Brixton, London*
#Thompson, James	14.11.43	*Architect (1800–83), 57 Devonshire Street, Portland Place, London, pupil of J. B. Papworth 1814–21 and later his asst, worked extensively for J. Neeld (q.v.); his only churches were two for Neeld*
Thompson, P. P.	<mid-49¢	*1 Osnaburgh Place, Regent's Park, London*
Thompson, Rev. William Hepworth, M.A.	1–5.41 F 1834 Trinity	*Asst T 1837–44, T 1844–53, Master 1866–86, Regius Professor of Greek 1853–67, Vice-Chancellor 1867–8, can. Ely 1853, +1886*
Thomson, R.	Late 40	*Librarian of the London Institute*
Thornton, Henry Sykes	6.12.41 ~ ¢¤‡ Trinity	*B.A. 1822, banker, partner in William, Deacon & Co., London 1826–81*
Thornton, Rev. Watson Joseph	6.12.41 ~ Trinity	*R Llanwarne, Ross, Heref's 1833–55, preb Hereford 1833–55, can. Hereford 1842*
Thorp, Disney Launder, M.D.	6.12.41 ~ ¢¤‡ Caius	*M.B. 1830, early medical career in Leeds before moving to Cheltenham, +1888, Eccl wrongly spells his surname with a 'e'*
+*Thorp, Archd. Thomas	Founder ~ ¢ F 1820 Trinity	*President of Union 1818, asst T. Trinity 1822–34, adm. Middle Temple 1824, 1824, D & P 1829, junior dean 1829–32, senior dean 1832–6, T. 1833–44, vice-master 1843–4, President CCS/ES S 1839–59, a trustee from 1845, vice-master Trinity 1843–4, Archd. & Chancellor Bristol 1836–73, R Kemerton, Glos (now Worcs) 1839–77 (restored chancel there 1843, rebuilt church under R. C. Carpenter (q.v.) 1847, except for tower), ES patron from 1859*

441

name	date elected	Cambridge college or other	Addresses/location given in *The Ecclesiologist*/ career details
Thring, *Edward*, M.A.	13.2.43 ~	F 1844–53 King's	*C S. James, Gloucester 1847–8, Private T. Marlow, Bucks 1848–50, C Cookham Dean, Berks 1850–2, C Skipsea, Yorks 1852–3, Head Uppingham School 1853–87. Wrote many theoretical works on education and translations of Classical poetry*
Thring, Rev. *John Gale Dalton*, LL.B	10.11.42	S. John's	*Alford House, Castle Cary, Somerset; R Alford, Som. 1808–58, R Bishopstow, Wilts 1831–45, RD Cary, + 1874*
Thurlow, Rev. *Thomas*	8.11.41	S. John's	*Baynard's Park, Guildford, C Wolverton, Bucks 1812–16, R Boxford, Suff 1816–39, succeeded to judicial sinecures 1829 (abolished 1831 but granted a £11,734 annuity in lieu), + 1874*
Thurlow, *Thomas Lyon*	8.11.41	Trinity	*Baynard's Park, Guildford, adm Inner Temple 1835, + 1894*
Tindal, Sir *Nicholas Conyngham* M.A.	3.40	F 1801 Trinity	*B.A. 1799, adm. Lincoln's Inn 1802, called to the Bar 1809, CCS election date from BWD (23.3.40), legal & political career, Lord Chief Justice of Common Pleas 1829–46*
Todd, Rev. *James Hentborn*, D.D.	21.6.64□	Trinity, Dublin	*Hon. member, B.A. 1825, F 1831, B.D. 1837, D.D. 1840, Treasurer S. Patrick's Cathedral, Dublin 1859–65, Regius Professor of Hebrew, Trinity College, Dublin & Precentor S. Patrick's 1866–9, disappears from CL 1870*
Tompkins, *Richard Francis*	22.11.41 ~ ¢	S. John's	*C Bignor, Suss 1846–54, V Tortington 1854–97, + 1898*
Tovell, *Mr W. S.*	10.11.42 ~		*Ipswich*
Townsend, Rev. *George*, M.A	Late 40 ~	Trinity	*C Litleport, Cambs 1813–14, C Hackney 1814–15, professor Sandhurst 1816–22, C Farnborough, Hants 1816–22, chapl. to Bp of Durham 1822–57, preb. Durham 1825–57, V Northallerton, Yorks 1826–39, PC S. Margaret, Durham 1839–42*
Townsend, *Henry, see Baynard*			
Tozer, *J. H.*	23.11.52		*Teignmouth, Devon, a John Chappell Tozer was a solicitor there in 1875*
Tozer, Rev. *William George*	16.12.62	*S. John's, Oxford*	*Hon. member, V Burgh-le-Marsh, Lincs 1857–63, Bp of Central Africa (or Zanzibar) 1863–73, of Jamaica 1879–80, of Honduras 1880–1*
+Travis, *William John*	<mid-40	Chapl. 1833–44 Trinity	*On CCS committee 1840–1, R Lydgate, Suff 1840–4, disappears from CL 1845*
Trench, Rev. *Richard Chenevix*, M.A.	13.2.43	Trinity	*C Curdridge, Hants 1835–40, C Alverston 1840–5, R Itchenstoke 1845–56, chapl. to Bp Wilberforce 1847–64, Professor of Divinity King's College London 1847–58, Dean of Westminster 1856–64, Archbp of Dublin 1864–84, + 1886*
*Trevelyan, Rev. *Edward Otto*, M.A.	18.4.42 ~	Corpus Christi, Oxford	*C Stogumber, Taunton, Som 1841–80*
Trevor, Rev. *George Alexander*	<mid-56	*Corpus Christi*	*C Chieveley, Berks 1846–50, C Withyham, Tunbridge Wells, Kent 1850–7, C Rokeby, Yorks 1858–61, subsequently of 48 Queen's Gdns, Lancaster Gate, London, +1907*
+Tritton, *Henry*	<mid-46 ~ ¢□		*Beddington, Croydon, ES auditor 1863–4, of 32 Portland Place in 1864*

Name	Date	College	Notes
Triton, Robert	1846		London
#Truefitt, George	1848¢¤‡		Architect (1824–1902), 6 Bloomsbury Square, *pupil of L. N. Cottingham at age of 15 for 5 years, then in offices of S. Wood and H. Eginton of Worcester, FRIBA 1860, retired 1890*
Turnbull, Rev. Thomas Smith, M.A.	<mid-40 ~ ¢¤‡	F 1817–48 Caius	Adm. Lincoln's Inn 1814, called to the Bar 1819, D & P 1822, FRS 1831, R Blofield, Norf 1847–56, +1876
Turnbull, Charles	21.7.59¢‡		Four Posts Hill, Southampton
Turner, John	5.12.44		43 Lower Belgrave Place, London
Turner, John Bowman	6.12.41 ~ ¢¤‡	Caius	C Wartling, Suss 1847–8, C Barford, Norf 1848–59, R there 1859–92, +1892
Turner, John Richard	5.3.44	S. Peter's	C S. Andrew, Ancoats, Lancs 1848–50, C Foxearth, Ess 1850–4, C Whaplode Drove, Lincs 1854–9, C Spalding 1859–63, C Woston-under-Edge, Glos 1863–9, V Coaley 1869–75, V Wroughton, Wilts 1875–1908
Turner, Rev. Michael	22.11.41 ~ ¢¤‡	Emmanuel	S. Matthew, Ipswich, D 1841, P 1842, C S. Luke, Berwick St, London 1844, C Cotton, Suff 1845–7, R & patron there 1847–90, +1903
*Tute, John Stanley	5.12.43 ~ ¢	S. John's	C Cleckheaton, Yorks 1846–8, C Morpeth, Northumb 1848–9, V Markington, Yorks 1849–97
Twining, James, B.A.	<mid-40 ~	Trinity	C Battersea, Surr 1851, PC Holy Trinity, Twickenham, Middx 1851–62, R Little Casterton, Rutl 1862–74
•Twopeny, William, F.S.A	Late 40		4 Lamb Building, Temple, London (still there in 1861), hon. member
Tylden, Rev. William	1845 ~ ¢¤‡	Balliol, Oxford	M.A. 1844, C Paddlesworth, Kent 1848–50, C Stanford, 1851–2, V & patron Stanford 1853–75
§Tyssen, John Robert Daniel	10.11.42 ~ ¢¤		Hackney, London, name wrongly 'Tyssen' in Eccl but corrected in 1846 membership list, FSA (21.6.38), conceived project to rub every bell inscription in England, this work continued by his son who published first county bell book (or. Sussex) 1864.
Underwood, Thomas	2.4.57		Dentist, 16 Bedford Place, London
Vansittart, Augustus Arthur	14.11.43	Trinity	Adm. Lincoln's Inn 1849, called to the Bar 1852, benefactor of the Fitzwilliam Museum and Museum of Geology, +1882
Vansittart, George Nicholas, M.A	28.11.44 ~ ¢¤	Trinity	Adm. Inner Temple 1843, of Florence in 1846–64, +1889
*Vaughan, Rev. Charles Lyndhurst	7.57¤	Oriel, Oxford	C S. Neot's, Hunts 1854–65, RD 1860–5, C Christ Church w. S. John, S. Leonard's-on-Sea 1864–95, disappears from Crockford 1896
+Vaux, William Sandys Wright, M.A.	1850-1¢	Balliol, Oxford	B.A. 1840, asst in Dept of Antiquities at British Museum, ES auditor 1851-2 +1885

name	date elected	Cambridge college or other	Addresses/location given in The Ecclesiologist/ career details
+Venables, Edmund, B.A.	Founder ~ ¢¤‡	Pembroke Hall	CCS committee member 1842-4, C Hurstmonceaux, Suss 1844-53, C Bonchurch, I.O.W 1853-5, can. and Precentor at Lincoln 1867-95, Ramsden Preacher 1879, gave paper to CCS (Eccl 1 (1843), 89-90)
Venables, F. E.	Late 1846¢		Wooburn Mills, Beaconsfield, Bucks, member of the Oxford Architectural Society from June 1847
Ventris, Rev. Edward, M.A.	22.5.43	S. Peter's	C Stow-cum-Quy, Cambs 1825-86, sometime chapl. to Lord S. Leonard's and to county gaol, Cambridge
Vickers, Archdeacon William, M.A.	5.12.42	Trinity	R Chetton w. Deuxhill Glazeley, Salop 1813-51, Archd. Salop 1830-51
Vincent, Thomas, B.A.	10.11.42 ~ ¢¤	Trinity	C Long Sutton, Hants 1842-4, C Bolney, Suss 1845-6, C Wantage, Berks 1847-68, R Pusey, Oxon 1868-89, + 1908
#Viollet-le-Duc, Eugene-Emmanuel	1849-50¢¤		Architect and theorist (1814-79), Rue Verneuil, Paris, hon. member, worked for Jean-Jacques-Marie Huvé, then Achille Leclère, various educational posts, prolific writer, notably Dictionnaire raisonné de l'architecture française du XIe au XVIe siècle (10 vols, 1854-68), and Entretiens sur l'architecture (1863-72)
Vogüé, Count Jean Melchior de	13.6.65		Archaeologist and diplomat (1829-at least 1902), hon. member, specialised in the arts and history of the Middle East, explored Syria and Palestine, wrote Les églises de la Terre-Sainte (1859) and other, later works, ambassador in Constantinople 1871-5 and in Vienna 1875-9, a reference to him in Eccl 25 (1864), 175
*Wade, Rev. Nugent, M.A.	1850-1	Trinity, Dublin	Chapl. at Elsinore 1833-9, I S. Paul, Finsbury 1839-46, R S. Anne, Soho, London 1846-91, can. Bristol 1872, Proctor for Dean & Chapter of Bristol 1886, not in Crockford 1895
*Wagner, Arthur Douglas	10.11.42 ~	Trinity	C S. Paul, Brighton 1848-50, PC there 1850-1902, Chancellor Chichester Dio. 1871-7, a great patron of church-building in Brighton
Wakeling, -	?		Present at 1856 anniversary meeting
Walford, John Berry	7.11.44	S. John's	Solicitor, practised in Abergavenny
Walford, Rev. Oliver, M.A.	21.2.42 ~	Trinity	Asst master Charterhouse School, London 1836-55, D 1838, P 1839
Walker, J.	5.3.44	S. John's	Probably John Walker (1822-1887), V S. Paul, Bury, Lancs 1848-64, V S. Saviour, Pimlico, London 1864-87; less likely John Walker (1821-1904), C Slingsby, Yorks 1844-5, C Burslem, Staffs 1845-6, PC Knottingley, Yorks 1846-8, C S. Botolph, Knottingley 1848-52, C Malton 1855-64, R Bradwell, Suff 1864-1904
#Walker, J. S.	1848¢¤		Architect, Stephenson Terrace, Worcester, probably John Severn Walker. Educated as a chemist and druggist under Lea & Perrins but retired and devoted himself to architectural

*Walker, Rev. Samuel Edmund — Trinity — 8.11.41 ~ ¢‡

and archaeological pursuits; no known architectural works but the leading figure in the Worcs Dio. Archit. Soc., and contributed many papers to it, + 1975

Walker, Rev. William Henry, M.A. — F 1826–44 Queens' — 10.11.42 ~ ¢

D 1834, P 1834, C Friern Barnet, Middx & Totteridge, Herts until 1841, R S. Columb Major, Corn (patron E. Walker, his father) 1841–69, restored the church there 1845, practically rebuilt the rectory under William White (q.v.) 1849, chapl. to Viscount Valentia in 1846–65, engaged in building speculation at Gravesena and Notting Hill and went bankrupt owing £90,000, built All Saints, Notting Hill under White

R St Botolph, Cambridge 1840–3, R Hickling, Notts 1843–57, chapl. to S. George's Hospital, London

---

#Waller, Frederick Sandham — 7.57□

Architect (1822–1905), Gloucester, partner of T. Fulljames, FRIBA 1856, architect to Gloucester Cathedral, in partnership with son, F. W. Waller 1873–1901, Eccl has second initial as 'T.' but there can be little doubt this is an error

---

Waller, Henry — 1847 ~

3 Stone Buildings, Lincoln's Inn (POLD (1847) does not list him at this address which was occupied by 3 QCs and 10 Barristers but by 1853 he appears as a barrister at 8 New Square, Lincoln's Inn)

Waller, Thomas George — 13.2.43

Essex Court, Temple

Walpole, Hon. Henry — 25.5.64□

17 Half Moon Street, London, 2nd son of 3rd Earl of Orford

Walsh, Francis Clarke — University College, Oxford — 13.2.43

C Hallow, Grimley, Worcs in 1850, CL lists no benefice in 1854, master at Kenilworth G.S. in 1865 a master at a preparatory school in 1890

Walsh, Rev. William Horatio — 14.11.43 ~ ¢□

C Marychurch, Dev., C-in-charge Whittington, Derby, S. Lawrence Parsonage, Sydney, N.S.W. in 1849–51 or '52, I Christ Church, Sydney w. Chippendale & Redfern 1852–68, can. S. Andrew, Sydney, chapl. to Bp of Lichfield 1868–70, preb. Lichfield 1868, V Alrewas, Staffs 1869–75, V Penn 1875–83

#Walter, Mr James — 6.12.41 ~ ¢

Architect, Cambridge, of 4 Trumpington St in 1851

Walters, John Thomas — 8.5.45 ~

6 King's Parade, Cambridge, publisher of Eccl vol. 4 (1845) with F. & J. Rivington of London

---

Walters, Rev. Nicholas, M.A. — Trinity — 13.3.43

C All Saints, Stamford, Lincs, R S. Peter, Stamford & V All Saints, Stamford 1836–74; RD Beltisloe, disappears from Crockford 1876

Walton, Rev. Jonathan, D.D. — Trinity — 1–5.41

C Gosforth, Northumb 1800–1, R Birdbrook, Ess 1801–46, RD

#Walton, John Wilson — 24.4.62□

Architect (1822 or '23–1910), 18 Adam St, Adelphi, London, articled to Henry Roberts, asst to Sir Charles Barry 1847–9, began practice 1853, moved to Durham 1859, partner of

445

name	date elected	Cambridge college or other	Addresses/location given in *The Ecclesiologist*/ career details
Walton, William, M.A.	<mid-40 ~ ¢¤‡		E. R. Robson for two years, ARIBA 1860, FRIBA 1862, retired 1892, latterly changed name to John Wilson Walton-Wilson
	F 1868–85 & asst T 1868–85	Trinity	BWD (24.5.39) notes he was at what was probably the CCS foundation meeting but Boye's Memorial does not record him as founder, career at Trinity, +1901
+•Warburton, Rowland (Eyles) Egerton., M.A. 7.2.42 ~ ¢¤‡		Corpus Christi, Oxford	Arley Park, Northwich, Cheshire, built chapel at Arley Hall, 1842–5 to Salvin's design; showed design at CCS meeting 11.5.42, J.P., High Sheriff 1833, on ES committee from 1858
#Ward, Henry	7.11.44 ~ ¢¤		Architect, Stafford, probably later borough surveyor for Stafford, active till at least 1883
Ward, Rev. John	1–5.41 ~ ¢	Christ's	C Froxfield, Wilts and of S. Mary, Marlborough 1824–6, V Great Bedwyn, Wilts (patron Marquis of Ailesbury) whose chapl. he was 1826–61) 1826–50, RD and surrogate, V Wath-on-Dearne (patron Marquis of Ailesbury) 1850–61, RD East Div. of Catterick in 1860
Wardroper, Rev. Cutfield, M.A	7.11.44	Trinity	Upleadon, C Slaithwaite, Yorks 1843–8, PC Farnley Tyas 1848–99, +1905
Warren, Rev. Charles, M.A.	<mid-40	Trinity	C Burton Latimer, Northants 1832–4, C Edmonton, Middx 1834–5, PC Enfield Highway 1835–40, V Over, Cambs 1840–73, author of various works on church organisation, + 1883
#Warrington, William	14.11.43¤		Stained glass artist (1796–1869), 42 Upper Berkeley Street, London, restored old stained glass from 1833, made windows for Pugin 1838, retired 1866 but the business was carried on by his son; a W. Warrington was also elected as an ordinary member 15.7.62 (perhaps re-admitted after lapsed membership)
Watford, A.	10.11.42 ~	Cambridge	
Watson, Rev. Alexander, M.A.	14.11.43 ~ ¢	Corpus Christi	C S. Andrew, Manchester 1839–40, asst minister S. John Cheltenham 1841–50, V S. Marychurch w. Coffinswell, Dev 1851–5, R Bridestowe w. Sourton 1856–8, V Bedford Chapel, Bloomsbury, London 1859–61, involved in a Chancery suit regarding the Bedford Chapel and became insolvent, C S. Mary, Soho 1863–4, +1865
Watson, Rev. John David, M.A.	1–5.41 ~ ¢¤‡	Trinity	C Guilsborough, Northants 1830–5, V there 1835–64, +1869
Watson, Joshua	1–5.41		Clapton, Hackney, leader of the High Church group known as the Hackney Phalanx, first treasurer of the National Society in 1811, treasurer of the S.P.C.K. 1817, treasurer also of the Additional Curates's Assistance Society, on committee of the SPG, one of the founders of the ICBS, one of the Commissioners for Building Churches, played an active part in founding King's College, London, + 1855
Watson, Thomas, M.D.	7.11.44	F 1816–26 S. John's	16 Henrietta Street, London, medical career including professorships at University and King's Colleges, London, created a baronet 1866, +1882

Name	College	Date	Notes
Watts, Rev. John, M.A.	University College, Oxford	10.11.42 ~	Whitehall Preacher 1824; preb. Salisbury 1846, R Tarrant Gunville, Dors (patron – University College) 1828–72
+ Waud, Rev. Samuel Wilkes, M.A.	F 1825 & T Magdalene; Trinity	<mid-40 ~ ¢¤‡	V Madingley, Cambs 1837–43, a CCS auditor 1842–3, R Rettendon, Ess 1844–87; RD
§•Way, Albert, M. A. 1-5.41	Adm. Inner Temple 1833, FSA (7.3.39), Director Society of Antiquaries 1842–6, a founder of the Royal Archaeol. Institute 1845 and its Secretary 1851, +1874		
Weale, W. H. James	?		Bruges, present at 1862 anniversary meeting
+*Webb, Benjamin	Trinity	Founder ~ ¢¤‡	(1819–85), son of Benjamin Webb of Webb & Sons, wheelwrights, Doctors' Commons, London, entered Trinity 1838, with Neale (q.v.) the driving force behind the formation of the CCS, a Society secretary 1839–68, Chairman 1845, B.A. & D 1842, P 1843, M.A. 1845, C Kemerton, Glos 1843–7, married the daughter of W. H. Mill (q.v.) 1847, C Christ Church, S. Pancras, London 1847–9, C Brasted, Kent 1849–51, PC Sheen, Staffs (presented by A. J. B. Hope (q.v.)1851–62, V S Andrew, Wells St, London 1862–85, preb. S. Paul's 1881, editor of Eccl and Church Quarterly Review, composer of hymns and anthems, great ecclesiological writer
Webb, Henry		6.12.41 ~ ¢¤‡	Doctor's Commons, London; younger brother of the above, BWD 17.8.54 notes 'Henricus frater nat. (1821)'
Webb, Rev. John Blurton, B.A.	Corpus Christi	<mid-40	C Garveston, Norf 1845–6, lived at Barton-under-Needwood, Staffs 1847–9, R North Cleobury, Salop 1849–59, PC Marcnington w. Woodlands, Staffs 1860–5, R Old Cleeve, Som 1865–73, R Hawksworth, Notts 1873–8, latterly lived at Windermere, Westm, +1883
Webb, Theodore Vincent	Trinity	Late 40	Lived at Great Gransden, Hunts 1858–85, J.P.
Webster, Samuel King	Emmanuel	6.12.41 ~ ¢¤‡	C Barnack, Northants 1842–9, V Ingham, Lincs 1852–87
Wegg-Prosser, F. R., see Haggitt			
*Weguelin, Rev. William Andrews, M.A.	Emmanuel	14.11.43 ~	R South Stoke, Arundel 1832–56, became RC 1856, +1892
Welldon, Rev. James Ind, M.A.	S. John's	30.4.44	C S. Giles, Shrewsbury & second master Shrewsbury School 1838–43, Head Tunbridge School 1843–75, V Kennington, Kent 1875–96, bon. can. Canterbury 1875–96
Wellesley, Hon. & Rev. Gerald		<mid-64	Dean of Windsor, ES vice-president 1864
Wells, Frederick Fortescue	Trinity	7.11.44	Matriculated 1844, no other details available
West, Charles Atkinson	S. John's	1845 ~	C Grasby, Lincs 1853, C Wickenby 1854–5
West, George John Sackville, 5th Earl de la Warr 10.11.42~ŧ⊡	Trinity		Succeeded 1795, took Sackville as additional name 1843, Neale's patron at Sackville College, various offices at Court, +1869

447

name	date elected	Cambridge college or other	Addresses/location given in *The Ecclesiologist*/ career details
+ West, Hon. & Rev. Reginald Wyndsor Sackville, M.A.	1845 ~ ¢¤‡	*Balliol, Oxford*	*R Withyham*, Suss 1840–65, chapl.-in-ordinary to the Queen 1846, assumed the additional name of *Sackville* 1843 and dropped that of *West* 1873, ES committee member 1848–at least 1851
Weston, George Frederick	6.12.41 ~ ¢¤‡	Christ's	C *Kendal*, Westm 1847, V *Crosby Ravensworth* 1848–87, hon. can. Carlisle 1879
Weston, J. E.	13.2.44 ~		Longdon Hall, Knowle, Birmingham
Whateley, Edward, M.A.	10.11.42 ~	Trinity	Adm. *Lincoln's Inn* 1832, migrated to *Inner Temple Court* 1835, D 1843, P 1846, C *Badgeworth and Shurdington*, Glos 1843–7, took name of *Pyddoke* in lieu of *Whateley* 1847, C *Bisley* 1847–55 and 1857–75, SPG chapl. to forces in the Crimea 1855–6, +1894
Wheatley, Edward Balme	<mid-40 ~	Downing	Of *Cote Wall, Hopton & High Close, Loughrigg*, Westm, assumed additional surname of *Balme* 1857, J.P., High Sheriff 1866, +1896
Wheeler, Rev. William, B.D.	13.2.44 ~	F 1836–43 Magdalen, Oxford	V *Shoreham*, Suss, R *Old & New Shoreham* 1843–55 (patron – *Magdalene College*), ordained RCP 1855 or '57
+•Whewell, Rev. Prof. William	Founder	F 1847 Trinity	Asst T 1818–23, T. 1823–39, a CCS vice-president 1840–2 (resigned Apr. 1842 (BWD 16.4.42), Master of Trinity 1841–66, Vice-Chancellor 1824–3 & 1855–6, Professor of Mineralogy 1828–32, Knightsbridge Professor of Moral Philosophy 1838–55, F.R.S., author of *Architectural Notes on German Churches...* (1830), and *Notes during an Architectural Tour in Picardy and Normandy*
Whitcomb, J. H.	<mid-64‡		*Gloucester*, possibly the same person as the following and that there was some confusion over the spelling and initials
Whitcombe, J. A.	<mid-46 ~ ¢		*Gloucester*, see the above
*White, George Crosby	28.11.44 ~ ¢	Trinity	C *Wantage*, Berks 1848–9, Provost of Cumbrae 1851–3, C S. *Barnabas, Pimlico* 1856–66, V there 1866–76, V *Malvern Link*, Worcs 1876–7, V *Newland*, Worcs 1877–97, hon. can. *Cumbrae* 1900, +1918
•White, Rev. Henry Master	11.7.64¤	F & T New, Oxford	Present at 1862 anniversary meeting, *Principal Dio. Collegiate School, Cape Town* 1849–57, C *Andover*, Hants 1857–61, C *Masborough*, Yorks 1861–5, V there 1865–70, Archd. *Grahamstown, S. Africa* 1871–92
#White, William	1848¢‡		Architect (1825–1900), Truro, pupil of *D. G. Squirhill* 1840–5, asst to *G. G. Scott* 1845–7, began practice in Truro 1847, moved to *London* 1852, FRIBA 1859, President Architectural Association 1868–9, FSA
Whitelock, Benjamin	Founder	S. John's	C *Barnes*, Surr 1842–7, C *Egham* 1847–8, C *Groombridge*, Kent 1848–93, +1896
Whytehead, Rev. Thomas, M.A.	Late 40	F S. John's	C *Freshwater, I.O.W.* 1839, chapl. to Bp of New Zealand 1841, *arrived in Sydney 1842*, +1843

Wilding, Prince George *William Augustus*, of Radali	5.12.43 ~ ¢	S. John's	Born Hanover 1827, matriculated 1843
Wilkins, The Ven. George	11.5.42	Caius	C Great Plumstead, Norf 1808, C Hadleigh, Suff 1808–15, V Lexington, Notts 1813–15, V Lowdham 1815–17, V S. Mary, Nottingham 1817–41, vicar-general of Southwell 1823–65, V Wing, Rutl 1827–39, Archd. Nottingham 1832-65, R Beelsby, Lincs 1843–65
Wilkins, *Thomas* Hodsall	22.5.43 ~ ¢	Emmanuel	C Slipton, Northants 1849–53, chapl. Thrapston Union 1852–60, chapl. at Darmstadt 1861–7, latterly at Ipplepen, Dev, disappears from Crockford 1881
Wilkinson, Rev. Henry James, M.A.	1846 ~ ¢¤		C Alverthorpe, Wakefield in 1846, C Camberwell, Surr and chapl to Earl Ashburnam in 1849–68, PC Troutbeck, Westm and C Windermere in 1855, V Hooton Pagnell, Yorks 1855–68
#§•Willement, *Thomas*, FSA	Late 40 ~ ¢¤		Stained glass artist (1786–1871), hon. member, 25 Green St, Grosvenor Sq., London, made first window 1812, FSA (17.5.32), writer on heraldry
+•Williams, Rev. George, M.A.	1846–7¢¤	F 1835–70 King's	Hon. member, PC Great Bricet w. Wattisham, Suff, 1838–40, chapl. to Bp of Jerusalem 1841–3, chapl. S. Petersburg 1844–5, warden S. Columba's College, Rathfarnham, Dublin 1850–2, Vice-President CAS in 1858–9, on ES committee from 1859, V Ringwood w. Harbridge & Bisterne, Hants 1869–78, Lady Margaret Preacher 1870, hon. can. Winchester 1874, had a great knowledge of the Eastern Church and a notable antiquarian, read papers to ES (Eccl 20 (1859), 81–91, 304–15)
Williams, Rev. Henry	6.4.54¢¤	Christ's	C Kirkham, Lancs 1848–51, C Middleton 1851–2, V Croxton, Norfolk, 1852–91, R Rockland All Saints 1891–1902, +1906
Williams, Henry Griffin	6.12.41 ~ ¢¤‡	F 1842–54 Emmanuel	Sir Thomas Adams's Professor of Arabic 1854–70, R Preston, Suff 1854–70
Williams, Rev. R.	?		Present at 8.5.45 meeting
•Williams, Robert, jun.	10.11.42 ~	Oriel, Oxford	Bridehead, Dorset, M.P. for Dorchester 1835–41, High Sheriff 1855
Williams, Rev. R. H.	6.3.45 ~ ¢¤‡		Master Asaph G.S. in 1846, not in CL 1848, not traced in AC or AO, of Byford Court, Hereford in 1856
Williams, T. S.	5.12.42	Trinity	The initial 'S' seems an error and this is likely to be *Thomas Lockyer Williams*, asst master Cheltenham College 1847–9, C Tetbury, Glos 1849–51, V Porthleven, Corn 1851–89, +1919
Willis, *Blankley Perrins*	Early 49¢		Draper, 14 Temple Row House, Birmingham
•Willis, Prof. Robert Founder		Caius	D & P 1827, Jacksonian Professor of Natural Experimental Philosophy 1837–75, a vice-president of CCS in 1840–2 resigned 4.42 (BWD 16.4.42), founder member of British Archaeological Association, President of its architectural section, President CAS 1845–6, 1851–2,

name	date elected	Cambridge college or other	Addresses/location given in *The Ecclesiologist*/ career details
			architectural scholar and writer, author of the Architectural History of the University of Cambridge (3 vols, published posthumously, 1886)
Willis, Rev. William Downes, M.A	11.5.43 ~ ¢¤	Sidney Sussex	*V Kirkby-in-Cleveland, N Yorks, 1816-41, R Elsted w. Treyford & Didling, Hants 1841-71*
#Wills, Frank	1848		Architect (+1856), New York, went from Exeter to Fredericton, Canada 1845 as architect to Bp John Medley (also from Exeter) there, migrated to New York by May 1848, in sole practice until 1852-3 when he was joined by Henry Dudley (also from Exeter), helped found the New York Ecclesiological Society in 1848 and worked as its official architect
Wilmot, R. E. E.	2.5.60		Chaddesden Hall, Derby, added to committee on election
Wilson, A., jun.	28.11.44 ~	Queens'	*Probably Archibald Wilson, matriculated 1843, no other details available*
Wilson, *Charles Henry*	<8.11.41	Trinity	*C Beetham, Westm 1841-3, C Heysham, Lancs 1843-52, C S. James, Cheltenham 1852-4, C Upton Warren, Worcs 1855-7, C Shurdington, Glos 1859-65, R Coberley 1866-1912, R Colesborne 1871-1912*
Wilson, Capt. F. J.	1848		52nd Light Infantry; Dallam Tower, Milnthorpe, *Westm*
Wilson, *Stephen Lea*	Founder ~	S. Peter's	Eccl and membership lists incorrectly give initials as 'J. L.', *C Bovingdon, Herts 1842-4, C Berkhamsted 1844-51, C Bocking, Ess 1852-4, C Prestbury, Ches 1855-8, V there 1858-9, bon. can. Chester 1873-99, latterly resided in London*
Winchester, Rev. W.	15.12.53¢		East India United Service Club, *chapl. to Hon. East Co. Dacca 1840-60, not in CL 1861*
Windsor, Rev. *Samuel B.*	1846-7¤		Tasmania, *chapl. to Bp of Tasmania in 1850, at Bishopsbourne in 1851-2, warden Christ's College 1851-4, surrogate by 1854, no appointment recorded in 1857*
Winter, -	?		Present at 11th anniversary meeting 16.5.50
#Withers, Robert Jewell	5.3.44 ~ ¢¤		*Architect (1823 or '24-94), Ryde, Isle of Wight, articled to T. Hellyer (q.v.), I.O.W., began practice Sherborne, Dors 1848, ARIBA 1849, moved to London 1851, FRIBA 1864*
+Witts, William Frederick, B.A.	18.4.42 ~ ¢¤	F 1840-63 King's	On CCS committee 1844-5, ES Treasurer 1845-6, *C.S. Giles w. S. Peter, Cambridge 1844-61, chapl. & asst master Uppingham School 1861-73, C-in-charge S. John the Evangelist, North Woolwich 1874-8, R Ringwood w. Harbridge, Hants 1878-84*
Wolfe, Arthur, B.A.	1-5.41 ~	S. John's	*F Clare 1844-63, T 1856-63, Lady Margaret Preacher 1860, Select Preacher 1863-4, asst master Tonbridge School 1843-7, R Fornham All Saints w. Westley, Suffolk 1862-96, +1892*
Wolley, Rev. John, M.A.	13.3.43 ~ ¤	Trinity	*Adm. Middle Temple 1846, S. John's Vicarage, Beeston, Notts, +1859*
Wood, Charles L.	11.7.64¤		

Wood, Peter Almeric Lebup B.A.	11.5.43 ~	Magdalene	Middleton, Lynn, C Littleton, Middx 1843–53, can. Middleham, Yorks 1844–97, R Devizes 1853–61, R Copford, Ess 1861–78, R Newent, Glos :878–97
Wood, William Page, M.A.	Late 40 ~ ¢¤‡	F 1824–9 Trinity	Dean's Yard, Westminster, adm. Lincoln's Inn 1824, called to the Bar 1827, Q.C. 1845, M.P. for Oxford 1847–57, political, legal and public service career, Lord Chancellor 1868–72, +1891
Wood, William Spicer	8.11.41	F 1840–6 S. John's	D 1844, P 1845, Head Oakham School 1846–75, C Brooke, Rutl 1853–65, V Higham, Kent 1875–97, +1902
Woodard, Rev. Nathaniel, B.A.	13.2.43 ~ ¢¤	Magdalen Hall, Oxford	B.A. 1840, V S. Bartholomew, Bethnal Green, London 1841–6, C S. James, Clapton, London, C Old & New Shoreham 1848–50 (patron – Magdalen Hall), Provost Lancing College from 1848, can. Manchester 1870, sub-dean there 1881, R S. Philip, Salford, Lancs from 1888, founder of the Woodard schools, +1891
Woodcock, Henry	30.4.44 ~		Gentleman, Bank House, Wigan, Lancs
Woodford, James Russell, B.A.	< mid-40 ~ ¢¤‡	Pembroke	Bishop's College, Bristol, C S. John, Bristol 1843–5, secretary of the Bristol Architectural Society from 1842, V Coalpit Heath, Glos 1845–7, V Easton 1847–55, V Kempsford 1855–68, chapl. to Bp of Oxford 1863–9, hon. can. Christ Church, Oxford 1866–73, Select Preacher, Cambridge 1864, 1867, 1873, Ramsden Preacher 1871, V Leeds 1868–73, chapl. to Bp of Winchester 1869–73, chapl. to the Queen 1872, Bp of Ely 1873–85
Woollaston, Thomas Samuel	22.11.41 ~ ¢¤‡	F 1841–67 S. Peter's	C East Tuddenham w. Honingham, Norf 1843–7, C Porlock, Som 1867, R Exford 1867–9
Woolley, Rev. Joseph, B.A.	< mid-40	S. John's	R Crostwight, Norf 1847–8, Principal School of Naval Construction, Portsmouth 1848–53 and subsequent educational in naval architecture and marine engineering, relinquished holy orders 1873, +1889
Wordsworth, Rev. Charles, M.A.	10.11.42 ~	Christ Church, Oxford	Master Winchester College 1835–45, Warden of Trinity College, Glenalmond 1847–54, Bp of S. Andrews, Dunkeld & Dunblane 1852–92
Wordsworth, William	5.12.42	S. John's	Poet (1770–1850), Rydal Mount, Cumberland, hon. member, poet laureate 1843, attended Society meeting 7.11.44
Worlledge, Edmund	22.11.41 ~ ¢¤‡	Clare Hall	C Leigh, Ess 1842–4, PC Cowling, Yorks 1844–50, C Enfield, Middx 1850–6, chapl. Anerley District Schools, Surr 1856–7, lecturer Whitelands Training College, Chelsea 1857–74, C Thurnham, Kent 1874–8, V Wood Dalling, Norf 1879–83, then lived at Kew, +1888
Wratislaw, Albert Henry, B.A.	8.11.41 ~ ¢‡	Trinity, F 1844–53 Christ's	Head Felsted School 1850–5, Head Bury S. Edmund's School 1855–79, V Manorbier, Pembs 1879–89, +1892
*Wray, Rev. Cecil, M.A.	1846 ~ ¢¤‡	Brasenose, Oxford	I S. Martin's, Liverpool 1836–75, +1878

451

name	date elected	Cambridge college or other	Addresses/location given in *The Ecclesiologist*/ career details
Wrench, Rev. Frederick, M.A.	1845 ~	*Trinity, Oxford*	R Stowting, Kent 1840–70, V Newington-next-Hythe 1875–80
*§Wrench, Rev. Jacob George, LL.D	10.11.42 ~	Trinity Hall	R Stowting, Kent 1814–35, chapl. to Duke of Sussex 1815–17, chapl. to Embassy of Constantinople 1817–22, V Blakeney, Glos 1826–34, V Salehurst, Suss 1827–60
Wright, Rev. William, M.A.	1845 ~ ¢	Pembroke	D 1830, P 1831, no other details known
#Wyatt, Matthew Digby	?		Architect (1822–77), present at 1862 anniversary meeting, in office of brother T. H. Wyatt from 1836, R.A. Schools 1837, ARIBA 1849, FRIBA 1854, surveyor to the East India Company from 1855, first Slade Professor of Fine Art, Cambridge 1869–72, Royal Gold Medal 1866, knighted 1869, numerous architectural publications
*Wyatt, Robert Edward, B.A.	5.6.52¢	Exeter, Oxford	C Sheen, Staffs 1852–5, C Haywards Heath 1855–66, V S. Wilfrid, Haywards Heath 1866 until at least 1888, not in Crockford 1892
•Wynne, William Watkin Edward, M.P.	21.6.59□	*Jesus, Oxford*	Added to Committee on election, M.P. 1852–65, +1880
Yates, Rev. Edmund Telfer, M.A.	13.2.43	Oriel, Oxford	C Birchington, Kent 1835, C Bekesbourne (n.d.), V Aylsham, Norf 1839–67, RD Ingworth, V Holy Trinity w. S. Faith, Maidstone, Kent from 1867
Yonge, Rev. John Eyre, B.A.	14.11.43 ~ ¢	F 1839–44 King's	Asst master Eton 1840–75, C Neumarket, Suff 1875–6, C Loders, Dors 1875–6, chapl. to Lord de Lisle, R Hempstead w. Lessingham, Norf 1876–90, +1890
+*Young, Rev. James Gavin, B.A.	Founder ~ ¢□‡	Trinity	Joined CCS committee 11.39 (BWD 9.11.39), a secretary 1840–2, auditor 1861-2, C Boxwell w. Leighterton, Glos 1842–8, R Dunkirk, Glos, C Ilfracombe, Dev 1848–9, C Brigstock, Northants 1849–54, I Kilmarton, Argylls 1854–9, V Ettington, Warks 1860–6, V Hursley, Hants 1866–1906 (after Keble (q.v.)
Young, John, LL.B.	13.3.43	Trinity Hall	Thrapston, Northants, LL.B 1841, no other details available, probably a son of the Rev. B. C. Young of Thrapston
Young, Rev. Walter	10.11.42 ~ ¢□		C Lisbellaw, Clogher, Enniskillen, Ireland till 1867, R Templecarn (Clogher), Pettigo 1868–81
Zwilchenbart, Rodolph, junior	5.12.61□		Merchant, of Rodolph Zwilchenbart & Son, Queens Insurance Buildings, Liverpool

Patrons of the Society (admissions by year)

By/in 1840 reported at the general meeting on 28.3.40, all except the first two listed here are called vice-patrons at this stage of the Society's history: Archbishop of Canterbury, Lord Lyndhurst (High Steward of the University), Bishops of Gloucester & Bristol, Ely, Hereford, London *(the latter withdrew 11.41 (BWD 30.11.41)* (all the foregoing bishops were Trinity men), Nova Scotia, Dean of Peterborough (Regius Professor of Divinity), the Masters of Clare, Downing and Magdalene, Rev. the Provost of King's College, D.D., Chancellor of Cambridge University (the Duke of Northumberland, *withdrew 1.45 (BWD 30.1.45)*)

1841: Archbishop of Armagh, Bishops of Bath & Wells, Chester, Edinburgh, Exeter (withdrew 12.44), Lincoln *(withdrew 1.45 (BWD 30.1.45))*, Winchester, Worcester

1842: Bishops of Down, Connor & Dromore (resigned 28.2.43), New Jersey (U.S.A.), New Zealand, Ross & Argyll

1843: Bishops of Aberdeen (adm. 14.11.43), Bangor *(withdrew 1.45 says BWD (9.1.45), yet he appears in membership lists 1846–56 so must have changed his mind)*, Glasgow (adm. 14.11.43), Norwich, S. David's (adm. 13.2.43), Tasmania (adm. 13.2.43), Dean of Westminster, D.D.

1845: Bishops of Colombo, Fredericton, New Brunswick (adm. 13.2.45), Newfoundland (adm. 13.2.45)

1846: Bishop of Jamaica

By mid-1846 all English bishops had withdrawn and the list of patrons consisted of the Bishops of Aberdeen, Bangor, Colombo, Fredericton, Glasgow, Jamaica, Moray, Ross & Argyll, New Jersey, New Zealand, Nova Scotia, Tasmania, Lord Lyndhurst (High Steward of Cambridge University)

1847: Bishops of Australia, Cape Town

1847–8: Bishop of Brechin

By 1849: Bishop of Sydney (+ 1852 or '53)

1853–4: Bishop of Natal

1854: Bishops of Graham's Town, Moray & Ross (both adm. 6.4.54)

1855: Bishop of Argyll (ad. 1.5.55)

By 1856: Bishops of Oxford, S. Andrew's

1857: Bishop of Montreal (adm. 25.11.57)

1858: Bishop of Kilmore (adm. 26.1.58)

1859: Bishops of Brisbane (adm. 21.7.59), Perth (adm. 21.7.59), S. Helena, Wellington (J. C. Abraham, a member since 1847), Western New York, Archd. T. Thorp

1860: Bishop of Labuan (adm. 2.5.60)

1862: Bishops of Central Africa (adm.16.12.62), Down, Connor & Dromore (adm. 1.7.62), Honolulu (T. N. Staley, a member since 1844), Nova Scotia (adm. 24.4.62)

1863: Bishops of the Goulburn, Mauritius, Orange River State

By mid-1864: Archbishop of Armagh, Bishop of Salisbury (adm. 21.6.64), Bishop Chapman, Bishop Nixon

1865: Archbishop of Canterbury

1866: Bishop of Dunedin (present at 3.12.66 meeting)

'A CHURCH AS IT SHOULD BE'

Wood Engraver to the Society: 1841–3, O. Jewitt

Modeller to the Society: 1841–3, J. Flack

Acknowledgements

I am grateful to the following for kindly supplying information: Ken Brand, Alan Brooks, Chris Brooks, Thomas Cocke, Ed Diestelkamp, Paul Joyce, Michael Kerney, David Meara, Chris Miele, Aart Oxenaar, David Parsons, Chris Pickford, Teresa Sladen, Alan Teulon, Shaun Tyas, Adam Waterton, Alexandra Wedgwood and Sarah Whittingham. Also I am grateful to the staff of Lambeth Palace Library and Birmingham Reference Libraries for their friendliness and patience.

INDEX

The index is divided into three: places, 'general' and people. It aims to be reasonably comprehensive but does not cover material in the footnotes or the large appendix.

Index of Places

General Index

Index of Names

1 (Webster). St Stephen, Robin Hood's Bay, North Yorkshire, 1821.
(RCHME © Crown Copyright)

2 (Webster) *right*.
All Saints, Margaret Street, London.
(Photo by the author)

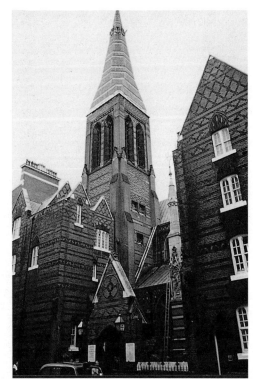

3 (Webster) *below*
St Mary, Whitby. The building was begun
*c.*1100 and was subsequently extended at
various dates. This illustration shows the
interior as it has existed since 1819. Note
the patron's pew of *c.*1620 built across the
chancel arch. (Courtesy of the Rector and
Churchwardens of St Mary, Whitby)

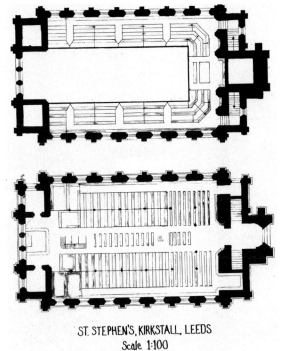

ST. STEPHEN'S, KIRKSTALL, LEEDS
Scale 1:100

0   10   20   30   40   50
FEET

4 (Webster) *left*.
R. D. Chantrell, St Stephen,
Kirkstall, Leeds, 1827–9.
(Drawing by Christopher Webster)

5 (Webster) *below*.
R. D. Chantrell, St Stephen,
Kirkstall, Leeds, 1827–9. (Detail of
a watercolour by W. R. Robinson,
1849. Courtesy of Leeds City
Libraries)

6 (Webster). L. G. Hales, Christ Church, Cobridge, Stoke on Trent, 1838–40.

7 (Webster). John Nash, St Mary, Haggerston, London, 1826–7.
(Engraved after a drawing by T. H. Shepherd)

8 (Webster). Francis Bedford, St John the Evangelist, Waterloo Road, London, 1823–4.
It may well have been churches like this that Neale and Webb had in mind when
writing the introduction to *The Symbolism of Churches and Church Ornament*.
(Engraved after a drawing by T. H. Shepherd)

9 (Webster). William Hogarth, Plate 5 of *The Rake's Progress*, 1735.

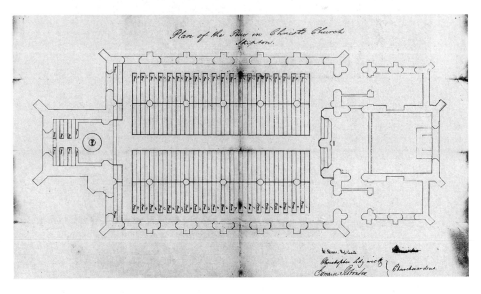

10 (Webster). R. D. Chantrell, Christ Church, Skipton, 1836–9. The plan has no author's signature and is probably not by Chantrell himself.

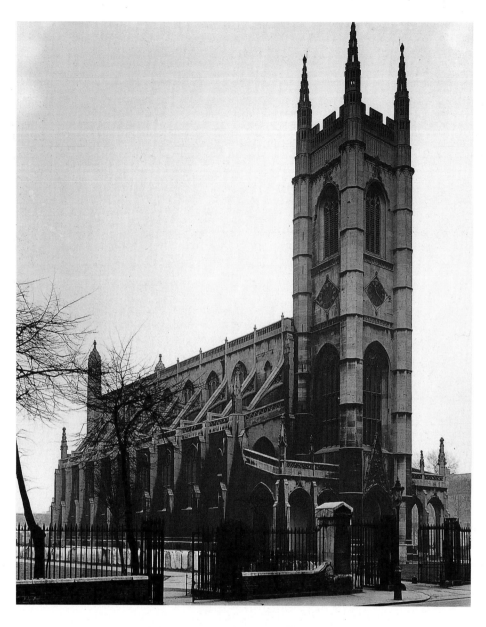

11 (Bradley). St Luke, Cheslsea, London, by James Savage, 1820–4.
(RCHME © Crown Copyright)

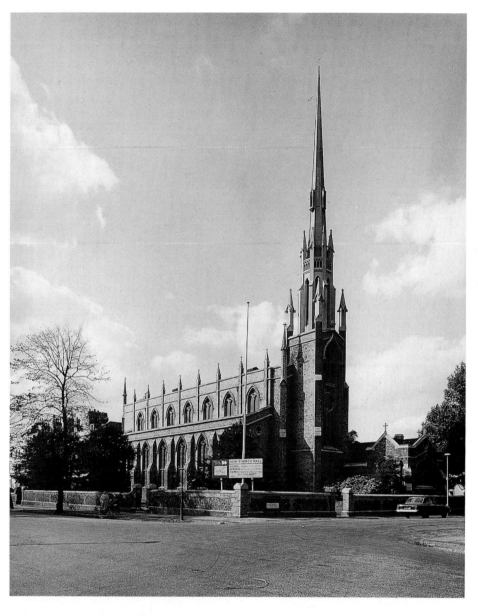

12 (Bradley). St Michael and All Angels, Blackheath, London, by George Smith, 1828–30.
(RCHME © Crown Copyright)

13 (Bradley). Methodist Chapel, Newbury, Berkshire, 1836–7.
(RCHME © Crown Copyright)

14 (Bradley). Churchwardens' 'improvements' satirized,
from the anonymous *Hints to Churchwardens* (1825), plate xii.
(Courtesy of the British Architectural Library, RIBA, London)

15 (Bradley). St Sepulchre, Cambridge, interior.
(From John Britton (ed.), *The Architectural Antiquities of Great Britain*, vol. 1, 1807)

16 (Bradley). Mickleham Church, Surrey, interior. From P. F. Robinson, *An Attempt
to Ascertain the Age of Mickleham Church in Surrey*, 1824, plate viii.
(Courtesy of the British Architectural Library, RIBA, London)

Master Punch. "PLEASE, Mr. BISHOP, WHICH IS POPERY, and WHICH IS PUSEYISM?"
Bishop. "WHICHEVER YOU LIKE, MY LITTLE DEAR."

16 (Bradley). Mickleham Church, Surrey, interior. From P. F. Robinson, *An Attempt to Ascertain the Age of Mickleham Church in Surrey*, 1824, plate viii. (Courtesy of the British Architectural Library, RIBA, London)

18 (Brandwood), *above.*
'Plain, simple and impressive'. A rare example of a pre-ecclesiological interior in use without any visual sarcasm. Taken from a memorial to the Duke of Wellington, it shows the Duke in his well-attended parish church of Walmer, Kent. Like the rest of the congregation he is reverential and attentive. Despite box-pews and curtains, and all the messages to the contrary, it was possible to conduct seemly worship in a pre-ecclesiological church. (*Illustrated London News*, 25 September 1852)

17 (Brandwood), *opposite.*
'Idleness and apathy'. Two Victorian caricatures of the unrestored and unrevitalised church. Above, the family turn to the largely empty building to be greeted by the pew opener. Two clergy and the clerk occupy the three-decker pulpit. Below, desecration of the sanctuary. (Courtesy of the Bedfordshire Record Office)

Master Punch. "PLEASE, Mr. BISHOP, WHICH IS POPERY, and WHICH IS PUSEYISM?"

Bishop. "WHICHEVER YOU LIKE, MY LITTLE DEAR."

THE HOT POKER.

21 (Brandwood), *above.*
Another of the 1850-1 cartoons from *Punch*. Watched by a Marian martyr, the bishops of London, Oxford and Exeter experience the consequences of Puseyism. Henry Philpotts of Exeter had already felt the temperature of feelings over 'innovation' in worship during the mid-1840s. (*Punch*, 20 (1851), 15)

19 (Brandwood), *opposite, above.*
'Papal Aggression' – the re-establishment of the Roman heirarchy – led to many *Punch* cartoons in 1850–1. A few years before Mr Punch might well have substituted 'ecclesiology' as the last word in his question, and received the same answer. (*Punch*, 19 (1850), 237)

20 (Brandwood), *opposite, below.*
St Sidwell, Exeter, the scene of surplice riots in 1845. (*Illustrated London News*, 22 February, 1845)

22 (O'Donnell), *right.*
St Mary's, Uttoxeter as published in July 1839,
redrawn by Peter F. Anson, *Fashions in Church
Furnishing* ... (London, 1960), p. 27.

23 (O'Donnell), *below.*
Camden Society seal, designed by A. W. N.
Pugin and first published in September 1844.

24 (O'Donnell), *opposite, above.*
A. W. N. Pugin 'Design for the new Catholic
Church of St Andrew Cambridge', engraved by
T. T. Bury, March 1842 (*courtesy of Cambridge
Central Reference Library*).

25 (O'Donnell), *opposite, below.*
The St Andrew crucifix: 'the gift of A. Welby
Pugin AD 1843 St Andrew Pray for us', church
of Our Lady and the English Martyrs,
Cambridge (RCHME © Crown Copyright).

Design for the New Catholic Church of St. Andrew, Cambridge.

26 (Brooks). St Augustine's College, Canterbury.

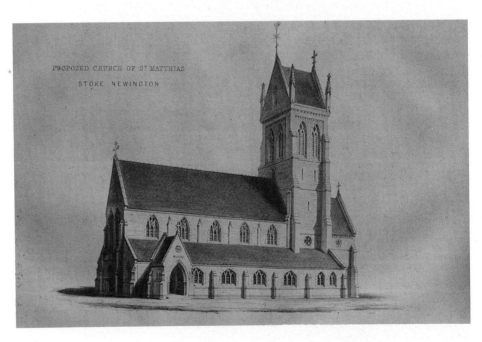

27 (Brooks). Perspective view of St Matthias, Stoke Newington (*Ecclesiologist*, 1850).

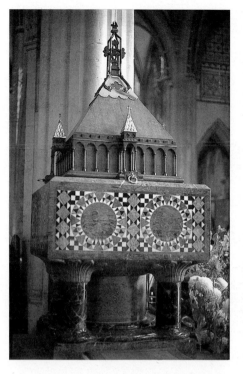

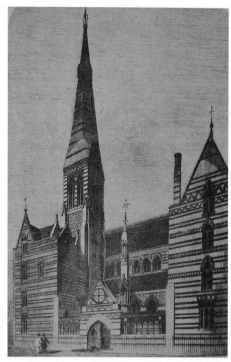

28 (Brooks), *above, left.*
Font of Ottery St Mary, Devon.

29 (Brooks), *above, right.*
Exterior of All Saints, Margaret Street,
London.

30 (Brooks), *left.*
Interior of All Saints, Margaret Street,
London.

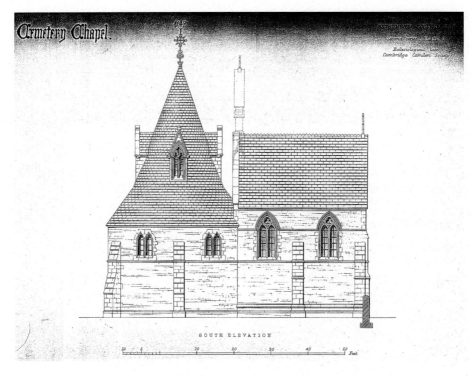

31 (Brooks). Design for a Cemetery Chapel by Butterfield
(*Instrumenta Ecclesiastica*, 2nd series, 1856, plate 3).

32 (Elliott). St Mary Magdalene, Munster Square, London. Exterior.

33 (Elliott), *above, left*.
St Mary Magdalene, Munster Square, London.
Interior.

34 (Elliott), *above, right*.
St Mary Magdalene, Munster Square, London,
Carpenter's original design.

35 (Elliott), *left*.
St Paul's, West Street, Brighton (1845–8).
Carpenter's original design, from *Ecclesiologist*
(1846), p. 156.

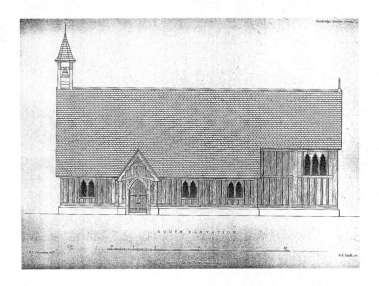

SOUTH ELEVATION

39 (Stamp), *above.*
The Martyrs' Memorial, Oxford, view from the north. (Lithograph by Louise Haghe, 1840)

36 (Elliott), *opposite, top.*
St John the Baptist, Cookham Dean, Maidenhead (1844–5). Exterior.
37 (Elliott), *opposite, middle.*
The Wooden Church. (*Instrumenta Ecclesiastica* (1856), pl. xx).
38 (Elliott), *opposite, below.* Holy Innocents, Prosser's Plain, Tasmania (1846–8). Lithograph, *c.*1850.

Plate 18.

40 (Stamp). St Giles Church, Camberwell, London. View of the exterior from the north. (from A. Capes and the Rev. J. M. Capes, *The Old and New Churches of London*, 18880)

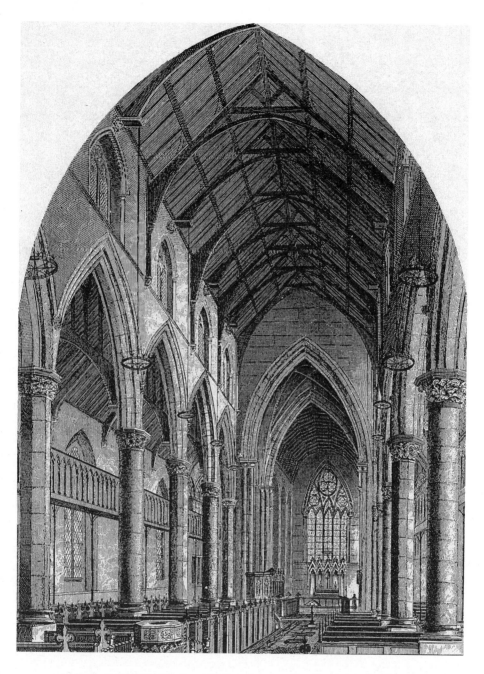

41 (Stamp). St Giles, Camberwell. Interior view showing original galleries.
(From *Cassell's Old and New London*, n.d.)

42 (Stamp). St Nikolai-Kirche, Hamburg. Interior view.
(*Builder*, 26 June 1858)

43 (Stamp). All Souls, Haley Hill, Halifax.
(*Ecclesiologist* (1860), p. 84)

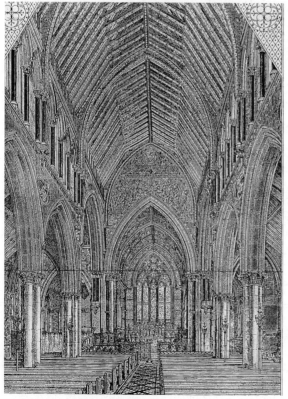

44 (Stamp). All Souls, Haley Hill, Halifax.
(*Ecclesiologist* (1860), p. 145)

45 (Dishon). Street's impression of Italian brickwork.
(G. E. Street, *Brick and Marble in the Middle Ages*, 1874, p. 122)

46 (Dishon). Street's design for St James-the-Less, Westminster, 1859.
(*Ecclesiologist*, 1859)

47 (Dishon). St James-the-Less, Westminster: north-east view of the tower.

50 (Dishon). St James-the-Less, Westminster. Chancel floor, marble and encaustic tiles.

49 (Dishon). Interior of St James-the-Less, Westminster. (*Builder*, 15 March 1862, p. 187)

48 (Dishon). St James-the-Less, Westminster. Tower arches looking towards the north-west door.

53 (Grainger). St James, Weybridge. View of spire, completed in 1856.

52 (Grainger). St James, Weybridge. View of sedilia and inlaid marble sanctuary floor, 1883.

51 (Grainger). St James, Weybridge, designed 1845, built 1846–8, with later alterations and additions in 1858, 1865 and 1883–5. View from the east.

56 (Grainger). St George, Cullercoates.
View from the south-east.

55 (Grainger). St George, Cullercoats.
View of interior from the west.

54 (Grainger). St George, Cullercoats, Tyne & Wear.
Designed 1878–81, built 1882–4. View from the west.

57 (Reid), *above*. Church of St Michael and All Angels, Bude.

59 (Reid), *opposite, top*. Chapel of St John, Treslothan: roof trusses and lancet windows.

60 (Reid), *opposite, below*. Christ Church, North Brentnor (previously known as Brent Tor).

58 (Reid), *below*. Chapel of St John, Treslothan.

61 (Miele). James Essex's 1781 reconstruction of the Church of the Holy Sepulchre in Cambridge, from *Archaeologia*, vol. 6 (1782) (*courtesy of English Heritage*).

62(a) (Miele). Samuel Prout's sketch which John Britton issued in 1805 and later reprinted in *Architectural Antiquities of Great Britain and Ireland*.

62(b) (Miele). The church today (© Crown copyright, RCHME).

64 (Miele), *above*. Engraving of Pugin's new chancel at Peper Harrow, from Brayley's *History of Surrey*.

63 (Miele), *opposite*. Lithograph of Salvin's perspective view of the restored church, issued by the Cambridge Camden Society in 1846 as a record of the interior as furnished and decorated before the Rev. Faulkner removed the altar. (Reproduced with the kind permission of the Society of Antiquaries)

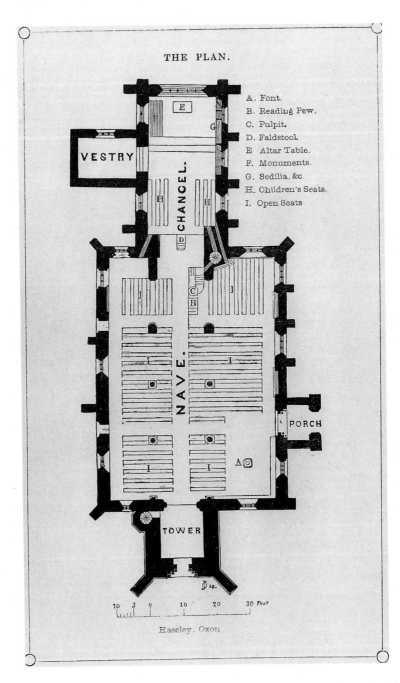

THE PLAN.

A. Font.
B. Reading Pew.
C. Pulpit.
D. Faldstool.
E Altar Table.
F. Monuments.
G. Sedilia, &c.
H. Children's Seats.
I. Open Seats

VESTRY

CHANCEL.

NAVE.

PORCH

TOWER

10 5 0   10   20   30 Feet

Haseley. Oxon

65 (Miele). Seating plan of the furnishings installed at Great Haseley church, Oxfordshire, as part of the OAS's restoration conducted by John Derrick in 1841–2, and published in James Barr's *Anglican Church Architecture* (Oxford, 1843).

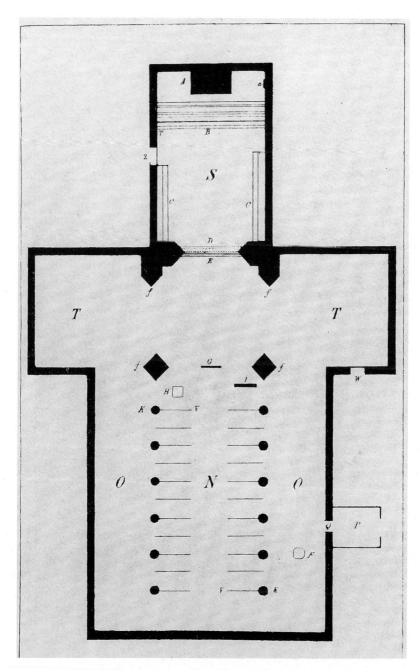

66 (Miele). An illustration of the proper 'Catholick' arrangement of a church, based on the ground plan of an unnamed 'village church in Sussex'. Published in the Society's 1841 *A Few Words to Church Builders*. Most of the elements are self-explanatory, but extracts from the accompanying text description are illuminating: (A) stone altar; (CC) miseres, a double row each side; (D) a roodscreen; (G) faldstool facing east; (H) pulpit; (I) eagle desk facing west.

67 (Miele). View looking east of the furnishings designed by Derrick for the OAS restoration of Great Haseley Church, and published in James Barr's *Anglican Church Architecture* (1843).

68 (Miele). Engraving of St Dunstan's, Stepney, 1815. (RCHME © Crown Copyright)

IV. *Nave.*

1. Nave Arch. *Wooden rafter, in Tudor (?), from Corbel Angels to Shields. On N Shield*
2. Rood Screen. *"Fear God!" on S. "Honour the King"*
3. Rood Loft ~~and Staircase.~~ *Door remaining on N.*
4. Piers, { N. 5 O. 5 } *Those last towards W concealed. NS 2 orders, roll M.*
   { S. 5 O. 5 } *The N. A. I. on N. differs in having*
5. Clerestory. *5 & 5 Db 2 L. 3f. a continuous rebate M round (?)*
6. Triforia. *and down P, which is more mysore*
7. Belfry Arch. *2 orders, 1st continuous*
8. Windows, { N. roll M. 2nd shafted
   { S.

V. *N. Aisle.*

1. Windows, { N. 4 P. 3 L.
   { E.
   { W. 1 P. 3 L. 5f. *(Doorway between W and N. buttress.) 3 Dormers to Gallery*

VI. *S. Aisle.*

1. Windows, { S. 4 P. 3 L.
   { E.
   { W. 1 P. 4 L. 5f. cut short below
2. Sedilia. *{ Nave Wds. Low Tudor (?)*
3. Piscinæ. *{ Chancel Wds. E (?) good P. }*

VII. *" Ornaments."*

1. Niches.
2. Aumbryes.
3. Corbels. *To N (?) vid. sup. 2 to last rafter of S & 2 to the only rafter in*
4. Brackets. *the N. Angels &c. On N. shield an Agnus Dei to flag of cross.*
5. Mouldings. *Round C. a billet 42. On S a Dove descending.*
6. Arcades.
7. Benatura. *At E of S Door and W of N Door a plain Benatura partially bloc...*
8. Eagle Desk or Lettern.
9. Misereres.
10. Poppy Heads.
11. Pulpit.
12. Roofs and Groinings. *N. flat ceiling, pannelled. S to C flat to a mod. Dormer.*

VIII. *Font.* (*Position and Description.*)
Compr. mod. P. 8... 4 ft. with closes. Shaft 8 ... buttress at ea corner above each buttress a Cherub. Sg. headed pannels between buttresses. Formerly there was a very old Font. not now in church.

69 (Miele). Church scheme for St Dunstan's, Stepney, filled out by John Mason Neale in 1839.
(Reproduced with the kind permission of His Grace the Archbishop of Canterbury,
from the Archives of his library at Lambeth Palace)

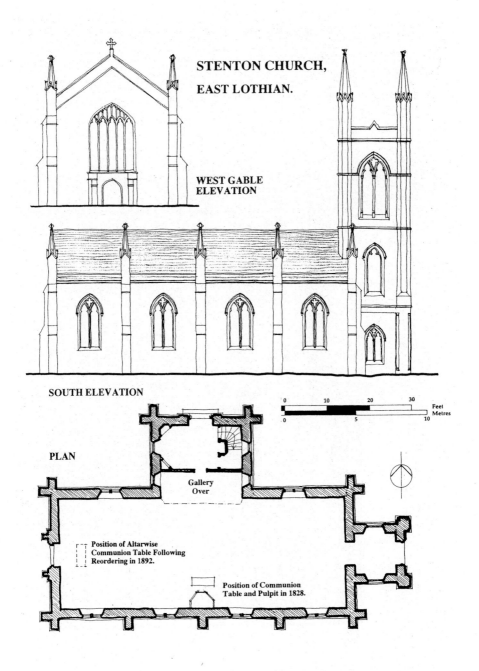

STENTON CHURCH, EAST LOTHIAN.

WEST GABLE
ELEVATION

SOUTH ELEVATION

PLAN

Gallery
Over

0   10   20   30   Feet
0   5   10   Metres

Position of Altarwise
Communion Table Following
Reordering in 1892.

Position of Communion
Table and Pulpit in 1828.

70 (Sanders). Stenton Church by William Burn, 1828, showing the position of the communion table in 1828 and after the reordering of 1892.

71 (Sanders). St John's Episcopal Church, Jedburgh, by John Hayward, 1844.

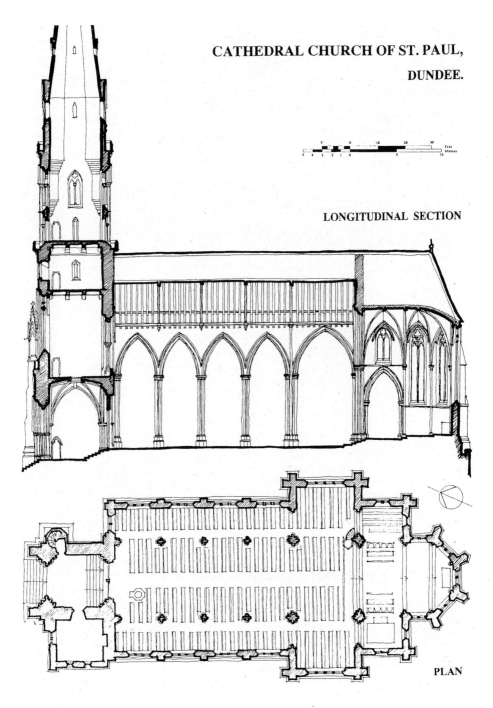

CATHEDRAL CHURCH OF ST. PAUL, DUNDEE.

LONGITUDINAL SECTION

PLAN

72 (Sanders). St Paul's Episcopal Church (now Cathedral), Dundee, by Sir George Gilbert Scott, 1852. The drawings are traced from Gilbert Scott's 1852 design drawings and show his original intentions for the position of furnishings. The design was revised in execution. Gilbert Scott's drawings are in the National Monuments Record for Scotland.

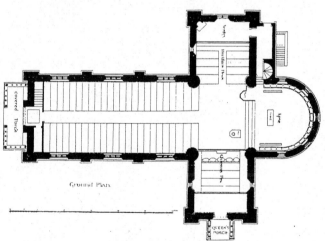

NEW CHURCH AT CRATHIE.

73 (Sanders). Crathie Church, by A. Marshall Mackenzie, 1893.
(From A. Marshall Mackenzie, 'The New Church at Crathie',
Transactions of the Aberdeen Ecclesiological Society (1897), facing p. 257).

74 (Sanders). King's College Chapel, Aberdeen, following the restoration by R. Rowand Anderson, 1891. (From *Transactions of the Aberdeen Ecclesiological Society* (1892), facing p. 64)

75 (Sanders), *opposite*. St Giles High Church, Edinburgh. Interior looking west. Photograph taken *c*.1890 following William Hay's restoration of 1881–3, which removed the partitions that had divided the former cathedral into three or more churches since 1639. (National Monuments Record for Scotland)

76 (Stell). Pugin's comment on a false Gothic front concealing 'a very meeting-house', from *The True Principles of Pointed or Christian Architecture* (1895 edn, facing p. 38).

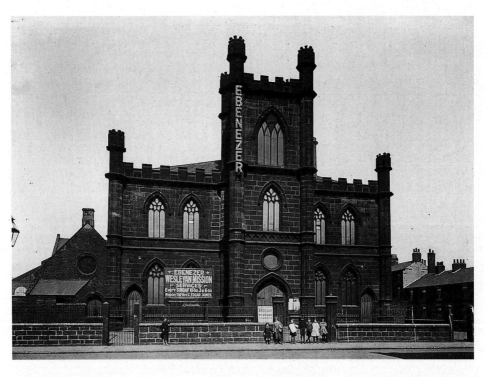

77 (Stell). 'Ebenezer' Wesleyan Chapel, Acorn Street, Sheffield, 1823 by Joseph Botham (RCHME © Crown Copyright).

78 (Stell). Cavendish Street Baptist Chapel, Ramsgate, 1840, by James Wilson.

79 (Stell). Former Baptist Chapel, Bourton, Berks, 1851, by W. F. Ordish. (RCHME © Crown Copyright).

80 (Stell). Hyde Chapel, Gee Cross, 1846–8, by Bowman and Crowther.

81 (Stell). Catholic Apostolic Church, Liverpool. Commenced 1840. Lithograph of 1851 showing original design. (RCHME © Crown Copyright)

82 (Stell). Friends Meeting-house at Scholes, Cleckheaton, Yorkshire, 1883, by W. H. Thorp.

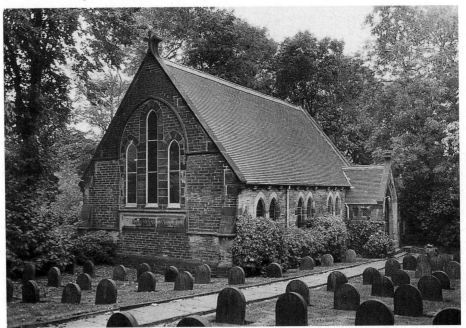

83 (Stell). Fontlet: Methodist chapel, Hawkshead, model of Winchester font, made 1840. Height 8¼ inches.

84 (Stell). Fontlet: Park Lane Chapel, Aston-in-Makerfield mid 19th century, by Copeland. Height 6½ inches.

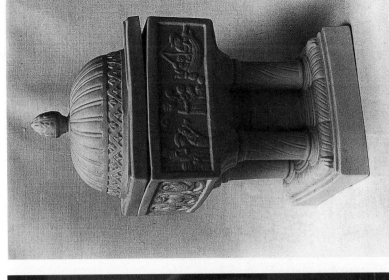

87 (Stell). Fontlet: Mary Street Chapel, Taunton. After font in Church of St Mary, Nottingham. Height to finial 12 inches.

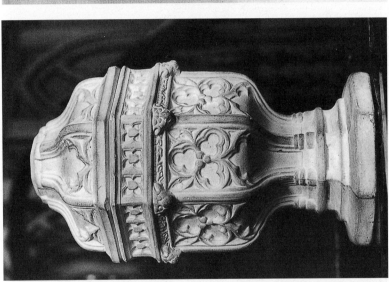

86 (Stell). Fontlet: King Edward Street Chapel, Macclesfield. After font in church of St Mary Magdalene, Oxford. Dated 1842. Height to top of cover 8⅞ inches.

85 (Stell). Fontlet: Methodist Chapel, South Milford, Yorkshire. Mid 19th century, by Shaw & Son, Congleton. Height to rim 7⅞ inches, to finial 11¾ inches